D1478572

Patriarch and Patriot

Publication has been assisted by a generous grant
from the Utah Foundation.

Patriarch and Patriot

WILLIAM GRANT BROUGHTON 1788–1853

Colonial Statesman and Ecclesiastic

G. P. SHAW

MELBOURNE UNIVERSITY PRESS

1978

First published 1978
Printed in Australia by
Academy Press Pty. Ltd. Brisbane
for Melbourne University Press, Carlton, Victoria 3053
U.S.A. and Canada: International Scholarly Book Services, Inc.,
Box 555, Forest Grove, Oregon 97116
Great Britain, Europe, the Middle East, Africa and the Caribbean:
66 Wood Lane End, Hemel Hempstead,
Hertfordshire HP2 4RG, England

National Library of Australia Cataloguing in Publication data
Shaw, George Peter, 1934– .
Patriarch and patriot.
Index.
Bibliography.
ISBN 0 522 84122 8.
1. Broughton, William Grant, 1788–1853. 2. Church of
England—Biography. I. Title.
283.0924

To Jan

Contents

Illustrations

Permission for the reproduction of these paintings and photographs has been granted by the holders

Acknowledgements

My good fortune was to meet Manning Clark. He suggested this study, and with magnanimity backed it through a decade of research and writing. He may, however, be excused accepting its conclusions. My other good fortune was meeting Gavin Vance. In his library I, as a schoolboy, discovered riches such as Keats found in Chapman's Homer. I salute both as mentors and acknowledge that this is, in part, their book also.

My other debts are many. Charles Grimshaw, Paul Crook and Chris Penders of the University of Queensland gave me good advice, as did Bede Nairn, Don Baker, C. M. Williams and John Eddy at the A.N.U. Damodar Singhal gave me sound direction at a critical point when research funds were not forthcoming. I thank the governors of the many institutions whose manuscripts I read: the Mitchell Library; National Library of Australia; University of Tasmania; St David's College, Hobart; the archives of the Dioceses of Sydney and Melbourne, St James, King Street, and Christ Church, St Lawrence, Sydney; St Mary's Cathedral, Sydney; the King's School, Parramatta; the British Museum; the Public Records Office; the House of Lords; Lambeth Palace; the Overseas Bishopric Fund, Westminster; the Society for the Propagation of the Gospel, London; the Church Missionary Society, London; Pusey House, Oxford; Pembroke College, Cambridge; the Department of Palaeography and Diplomatic, University of Durham. I am particularly grateful to P. Millward for unstinted access to the files of the Joint Copying Project, London; to G. Moase, Hobart, and the Duke of Wellington for permission to quote from private collections; to Peter Yeend for access to papers at the King's School, Parramatta; and to Peter Hockey for a year's valuable assistance.

In Australia Peter Bennie of St Paul's College, University of Sydney, and David Saunders and Eve Buscombe of the Power Institute of Fine Arts, University of Sydney, assisted in the search for illustrations. In England I had similar assistance from Patrick Strong of Eton College, and Anthony Camps and A. V. Grimstone of Pembroke College, Cambridge.

This project was made possible by generous support from the Australian National University, the University of Queensland, the Australian Research Grants Commission for research in Australia, and from the Myer Foundation, the Australian Academy of the Humanities, and the Nuffield Foundation for research abroad.

Conversion Factors

(to three decimal places)

1 guinea	A$2·10
£1	A$2
1 shilling (1s)	10¢
1 penny (1d)	0·833¢

(This is a conversion of Australian currency adopted in 1966)

1 acre	0·405	hectare
1 sq. mile	2·59	sq. kilometres
1 mile	1·609	kilometres
1 foot	0·305	metre
1 horsepower	0·746	kilowatt

Fahrenheit to Celsius $°C = 5/9 \, (°F - 32)$

Before New South Wales

> How very much I often think, of one's character and principles
> is made up of these odd out of the way impressions picked
> up one hardly knows when or how, and remembered one
> cannot tell wherefore. No boys in New South Wales have
> any such reminiscences or regards. It would be well for
> them if they had.
>
> Broughton to Coleridge 15 August 1844

Dusk had fallen. Across the precincts a door opened. From a lighted
hall a small group of boys filed on to dew damp lawns which crossed
imperceptibly under the cover of darkness to the solid, immovable,
perpendicular monument that had towered upwards almost a thousand
years, an unrepentant memorial to England's Christian conversion.
The clatter of eager steps soon mingled with others more weighty, more
strident, more measured, to announce that the boys had met the masters
in the cloisters and were moving towards a side entrance to the cathedral.
Hush clothed the group. It formed itself into a tiny procession and
moved two steps up past stone-still Archbishop Pecham who had stood
sentinel at the north door for five centuries; and then down past wily
old William Warham with his gaze fixed on the spot where Becket fell.
Three stairs more and the group had passed from the organ encrusted
chancel into an aisle which led down behind dusty clusters of elaborately
carved choir stalls to the transept where the candle-lit chapel of St John
awaited them.

The boys knelt. Some prayed. Then the Reverend Christopher Naylor,
whose keen mind and flexible wrist had helped bring them to this moment
of glory, rose up; and calling each boy forward by name uttered the
venerable bidding: *introitum tuum et exitum tuum custodiat Dominus*!
At this sign, as if by some sacramental rite, the prim gown and purple
tasselled cap, which outwardly decked each boy, was intended to move
inward and fix in his heart a will to become part of the great enlivening
purpose whose memory lay all around in tombs, effigies, plaques and
shrines; Canterbury's unique possession. The boys' replies echoed up
into vaulted ceilings that covered a thousand years of history.

For the moment the boys were tired and their minds fatigued by long
hours of examination. They were also very young. Ample time remained

to teach them the meaning of their initiation; that as young scholars of the King's School, Canterbury, the cradle of Britain's Christian education, they had been singled out for moulding as custodians of a tradition at once sacred and national.[1]

The headmaster did not prolong the service. Its formal requirements completed, he extinguished all but one candle and guided the boys out into the cold December air. In the precincts the boys divided, some with the headmaster, the others with the second master the Reverend John Francis. In Francis's group walked young William Grant Broughton.[2]

It was the Advent of 1797. Young Broughton, now in his tenth year, had been born on 22 May 1788 in the heart of London's Westminster district, at Bridge Street, one year and one week after the First Fleet weighed anchor in Portsmouth's harbour. He belonged to an inbetween generation; born too late to be comfortably at home in Regency laxity, and too early to be schooled exclusively in the ethical puritanism Wilberforce laboured to make fashionable. Paley's rational theology was still considered a virtuous means to an orthodox faith; and the Proclamation against Vice and Immorality, which George III foisted on the indulgent society of 1787, had begun to breed that distinctive style of propriety which subordinated intellectual to moral excellence at all times.

Part of the old, part of the new, broke in on those who acquired their stock of learning at the turn of the century. Some boldly embraced uncharted futures while others stood firm by the excellences of the past. At Eton, Shelley learned a little science and unlearned the doctrine of Original Sin, cursed kings, priests and statesmen as the source of all human misery, and dedicated his life to uncreating the gods which human pride had built out of its ignorance. Canterbury, pre-eminent symbol of the old and for many the very best, was less disturbed by the newer fashions. Its school remained strictly and narrowly classical, boasting no lessons in science and few in the modern languages and mathematics. A fond ambition caused Broughton's parents to remove their son from the Grammar School at Barnet, just north of London, to the King's School. The Broughtons were minor residents of their district and genteel beyond their means. Mrs Broughton offered every caller a glass of wine and complained of her modest home.[3] So the award of a King's Scholarship to their son William was as gratifying for its pecuniary relief as cherished for its honour.[4]

Eight exceedingly happy years in and around the privileged quiet of the Cathedral precincts left a lasting impression on Broughton's mind. He came young, impressionable, and unformed, to a place where the *genius loci* was a strong one, and he yielded unreservedly to its memories. 'From Canterbury he had derived all that he prized in life', he later wrote. In the schoolroom transformed from the ancient chapel of the pilgrims, Broughton pondered the classical authors who, enshrined in a remote and impenetrable glory, appeared before the young as masters of an immutable knowledge. Outside, the Green Court playing-field lined with lime bushes attracted him indifferently. He preferred to wander through the age stained Gothic gateway into the old ecclesiastical

city, and round by the ruins of Ethelbert's tower to the bowling-green
where all the boys gathered for fireworks on national occasions.[5]

Broughton was a bright pupil. The senior monitor Henry Hutchisson
singled him out for extra lessons; and John Francis's concern to polish
his Latin led, in senior years, to many a warm drink in the housemaster's
sitting-room and the chance to chat to a girl 'with *very* black hair and a
very white frock'. In his final year the headmaster chose him to deliver
the Latin oration before old scholars at the annual Feast Day. He tried,
too, for Cambridge and in December 1804 won an exhibition to Pembroke
College.[6]

In the first fortnight of that Advent man and nature cursed Europe;
Napoleon turned emperor, Vesuvius erupted, Spain declared war on
Britain, and the unrepentant Bourbon prelate M. de Conzies, once
the brightest star in France's ecclesiastical firmament, expired, exiled
in poverty and broken by the news of 'the scandalous journey of Pius
VII and the sacreligious coronation of Napoleon I'. He could bear all
but the sight of one lawful authority, the church, expediently divorcing
another, such as a legitimate monarch, for the benefit of a favourable
settlement that had the appearance of peace. He was not the last to bear
that sight, or to be broken by it. The English establishment had so far
been spared the spectacle of such expediency at work in its own finely
balanced fabric of religious and political rights. But the day could come
when the spirit of the age would force England's leaders to declare for
the maintenance of principle or the expediency of change. If the present
generation escaped that ordeal the coming one could scarcely hope to.
Broughton belonged to the coming generation. He farewelled his school
and Canterbury the day the Bourbon prelate de Conzies died, and if
he succeeded well in his higher studies he would have the honour of
jostling for place and authority in a society which had escaped the fury
but gathered the force of the change that had swept France.

Broughton did not arrive at Cambridge. The exhibition paid too
poorly. Instead he spent two years in obscure employment. Then in
April 1807 a hefty push from the Marquis of Salisbury, a Barnet neighbour, put him into the East India Company. By then Broughton's father
was dead and his income essential for the family. He was secure in his
future but disappointed in his hopes.[7]

The move to London took Broughton into the midst of a war-time
society preoccupied religiously and intellectually, as well as economically
and politically, with the spectre of an 'ambitious and violent Bonaparte'.
Tories turned reactionary, Whigs conservative and radicals cautious.
England's doctrinaire Jacobins passed through the vale of disenchant-
ment: Southey turned Tory in the *Quarterly Review* while Coleridge's
The Friend became counsellor and confessor to a society dangerously
adrift from fixed principles. 'The spirit of innovation is generally the
result of a selfish temper and confined views', added Burke; and men
everywhere discovered a new fondness for England and things English.
Few fostered this cause more than the rampaging Bonaparte.

The British government had barracked its French prisoners around
Canterbury. Broughton saw their camp, but the hatreds and excesses

spawned by the Revolution belonged to a past that Broughton and his companions were too young to remember. They learned of the pagan voluptuousness which auctioned the cathedral of Metz at the third hour of the morning, that toppled church steeples which towered indecently above village roofs and sewed altar linen into men's shirts, from a pulpit oratory set to declaim against the age as evil, adulterous, ignorant, apostate, and foppish. Then to temper the rhetoric of the preacher a new literature urging a more profound assessment of the Revolution began to pour on to the market. Broughton with an ear to the pulpit and an eye for the publishers' lists was admirably positioned in London to build up a point of view, partly intellectual, partly emotional, of this most momentous event of modern times. Even more fruitful was the opportunity London afforded him to hear firsthand the public debate on Bonaparte, a debate never far removed from arguments about irreligion, immorality and mobs. The mob, violent because it was irreligious; the mob, easily manipulated because it had no fixed principles; the mob, always master of its teacher; the mob, ignorant and fit only to destroy the good and the orderly in established society. The House of Commons rehearsed this creed, and it found its way into the peroration of sermons and the conclusion of tracts. Its frequency witnessed to its acceptance if not its truth. When Sir Francis Burdett castigated it as the 'old bugbear' he was galled more by its effectiveness than its fiction.[8]

The Westminster Broughton knew in his twenty-second year buttressed such fears and theories. At night on 19 February 1810 the British Forum Club met in a coffee shop in Covent Garden to debate whether parliament's exclusion of strangers from its gallery was a greater outrage on Englishmen's rights than the recent attacks on the freedom of the press. The House of Commons recompensed the British Forum's manager with accommodation at Newgate; and when Burdett asked the House to repent of such unconstitutional behaviour he found himself put down for a room at the Tower.

Both moves were designed to forestall expressions of a popular will against the supreme authority of parliament. Together they succeeded only in demonstrating the unpredictable strength of the mob. Burdett barricaded himself away from the bailiff and a mob thronged the streets of Piccadilly for four days shouting, throwing stones, and 'obliging everyone that passed to take off his hat and cry "Burdett forever"'. Burdett finally reached the Tower escorted by infantry and cavalry. The day parliament rose the mob returned to carry Burdett off in a hero's chariot. Three thousand came mounted, three thousand walked; they carried banners, played music and wore the blue cockade reminiscent of another mob.

London seemed in the grip of a fourth power. In the same disturbed times fourtune deflected a blow meant to decapitate the Duke of Cumberland in his bed. It moved less adroitly on the steps of parliament and the Prime Minister Spencer Percival fell dead before an assassin's bullet. St Paul's Cathedral lost seventeen hundred ounces of silver gilt, and Daniel Eton went to prison for publishing a 'blasphemous and profane libel on the Holy Scriptures, the works of Thomas Paine'. As men racked their minds for explanations, Lord Sidemouth in parliament called for numerous reports framed to show that irreligion and unconstitutional behaviour went hand in hand with a drift from the Established Church to dissenting meeting houses. And so the nineteenth century was supplied with another of its leading ideas.

Broughton lived these years to the full. He rushed with 'youthful enthusiasm' into the streets to celebrate Nelson's victories, fell on every word Coleridge wrote, and signed petitions on end in support of the established order. On weekends and holidays he played the 'ardent lover' dashing on horseback to Canterbury to court Sarah Francis the girl with very black hair. But his heart was not in the East India Company.[9]

In 1813 'the years of hope deferred and disappointment' ended.[10] On 2 February Broughton's uncle in the employ of the East India Company died unexpectedly at the Tavistock Hotel, London.[11] He was fifty-three and being without heirs left Broughton £1000. It reopened the way to Cambridge. Broughton went straight to Canterbury to be tutored by his former school monitor, Henry Hutchisson, now a handsome but jilted lover who sighed as he expounded Euclid.[12] On 7 May the following year, 1814, Broughton went to Cambridge, to Pembroke College his former housemaster's old college.[13]

Pembroke was a small but ancient element in an unreformed Cambridge. The eighteenth century had brought it few distinctions. Other times had been different. Nicholas Ridley hymned it on the road to execution as 'studious, well learned, and a great setter forth of Christ's Gospel'. Elizabeth I took from it her 'black husband' Archbishop Whitgift, and Edmund Spenser found the muse within its walls. Under Lancelot Andrewes the college conspired in the cause of James I and remained a royalist, Laudian and a high church stronghold. For this the eighteenth century penalized it with obscurity. Masters with scant hope of preferment served long tenures; Broughton entered in Joseph Turner's thirtieth year. But the college remained sound in scholarship. The Elder Pitt singled it out for his son, and in turn the Younger Pitt lent it a bright moment of patronage at the end of the century. Broughton entered in this glow and found to his liking a community tory in politics, gentle in the arts, firm in scholarship, and a quiet champion of the alliance between church and crown.

Students at Pembroke belonged also to a wider university fraternity. Cambridge, though poised for reform, remained in the grasp of old traditions. Broughton came to receive well tested knowledge by time honoured methods. The old scholastic curriculum lingered, radically rearranged rather than decisively altered; and Broughton's task was to prepare for the ordeal of disputing with his examiners, in Latin if he vied for honours, a number of mathematical and ethical propositions. Religious tests and celibacy underpinned the established order. University authorities demanded due submission from all undergraduates in an intolerably wide field of activities. They might, for instance, support but not organize a local branch of the British and Foreign Bible Society. They could form a debating society but not polish their wit on political matters; and when the Cambridge Union dared do so in 1817, Broughton saw the vice-chancellor disband it. He saw progress falter too. The splendid unfinished doric porticos of Downing College stood across from his room. Their construction in 1800 heralded a brash assault of the sciences on the traditional curriculum, but no stone was added for a half century after 1810. The College founders meant it as a monument to encourage reform: to Broughton and his contemporaries it served as a warning against it. Those who loved the old institutions and the traditional studies were strengthened in their belief that they were the best ways.

A triumvirate of outstanding personalities awaited Broughton at the university to help turn the romantic impressions of his school days at Canterbury into fixed theological principles and give him a theory of ecclesiastical polity. Each expounded a different tradition: Herbert Marsh was a scholarly high churchman; Isaac Milner an equally scholarly evangelical; and Charles Simeon the brilliant exponent of a new and fashionable pietism. Broughton rejected Simeon and his evangelical puritanism, and Marsh became his mentor.[14]

Marsh restored the popularity of theology at Cambridge. With characteristic audacity he disregarded the provision of his Lady Margaret Chair, that divinity lectures were to be delivered in Latin, and delivered them in English regularly before crowded undergraduate audiences. He ended an era. His predecessors had adhered faithfully to the Latin tongue and had been relieved of the necessity of delivering lectures for want of an audience. Marsh also taught theology differently from his evangelical contemporaries. He studied at German universities and infused English theological studies with the fruit of the German enlightenment. Without calling in doubt the divine inspiration of scripture he invited students to consider its books as documents written by human hands; and with a keen eye sharpened by a critical mind to discover the literal meaning and intention of the individual authors. This alone could yield the true meaning of the text. Marsh instructed his students to regard scholarship as the foundation of true piety and sound preaching, and he invoked Dryden's ridicule on the generation of undergraduates who looked to the Spirit for the doctor's degree:

> Study and pains were no more their care,
> Texts were explained by fasting and prayer.
> This was the fruit the private spirit brought,
> Occasioned by great zeal and little thought.[15]

This profoundly influenced Broughton. He resolved to eschew emotion in his sermons, to acquire the sophisticated tools of textual criticism, and to master the scholarly commentaries on the scriptures. He chose a text, not for the opportunity it afforded his imagination to take flight, but for its aptness as a point of entry into an explanation of God's historic dealing with the old and the new Israel. Subscribing as he did to the ancient poet's belief that there was nothing new under the sun, and in faith holding the history of Israel to be a paradigm of the history of all nations, he unfolded his explanation to convince his hearers that, though in a later age and on a different soil, they stood in the same posture before God as did the ancient Israelites. Furthermore, they were judged under the same laws, guilty of the same offences, and deserving of the same judgement. Broughton found in the story of God's historic dealing with Israel the substance of a lifelong study, and to the end of his days he compiled his own biblical commentaries to discipline his scholarship and record his enquiries for use in preaching and prayer. 'Ours ought to be an enquiring profession', he insisted.[16] Marsh had scarcely a more devoted pupil.

Broughton's Cambridge abounded in controversy. One centred on the education of the children of the poor. It began at St Paul's Cathedral on 13 June 1811 when Marsh preached in support of the London charity schools and accused churchmen who contributed to the Royal Lancasterian Society, which had banned the Church Catechism from its curriculum in order to attract non-conformists into its schools, of fostering 'a principle of self-destruction' in the Established Church. 'Children educated in such seminaries would acquire an indifference to the Establishment', Marsh argued. 'And not only indifference, but secession from the Established Church will be the final result'. He warned against misguided philanthropies that would contribute to the withering away of the traditional order, and called on the National Society to redress the danger. Broughton pledged the National Society and its Church Catechism schools his exclusive loyalty and wrote in support of them.[17]

Marsh suspected the British and Foreign Bible Society of introducing among adults the same careless concern for the Church of England that the Royal Lancasterian Society planted in the young. By its constitution the Bible Society forbade the distribution of confessional material along with its bibles. As such, it functioned in opposition to the Society for the Promotion of Christian Knowledge (SPCK) which dispensed copies of the Book of Common Prayer with all scriptures. The SPCK believed that the bible without explanation left the poor at the mercy of ignorant village teachers and a mass of delusions. Marsh tolerated the activities of the Bible Society until it began recruiting in earnest among the future ordinands at Cambridge. He then condemned it for being in Cambridge. He attacked churchmen who took a lead in the matter, and argued that dissenters surrendered nothing in distributing the bible alone whereas churchmen who suppressed the Book of Common Prayer deliberately hid away part of their Reformation heritage. Without the liturgy the bible inspired only 'a general protestantism', and once churchmen lost their affection for the liturgy they soon relaxed their vigilance against dissent. Repeal of the Test Act was the dissenters' aim, Marsh warned; and the walls of the Established Church once breached might fail to keep out other more dangerous enemies of true religion. Broughton made Marsh's arguments his own.[18]

Isaac Milner, third in the Cambridge triumvirate, was professor of mathematics, and Broughton took the mathematics tripos. They faced each other early in 1818 and Broughton acquitted himself sixth wrangler at the top of the Pembroke list.[19] He did not test his luck for a fellowship—Attwood who trailed him as seventh wrangler did and succeeded—but

immediately limped off to Canterbury to marry Sarah Francis. Broughton's lameness was the legacy of a prank by an unruly Merchant Taylors'
scholar Michael Prendagast who had tumbled him down a college staircase
in 1816.[20] Finally the Bishop of Salisbury ordained him deacon on
letters dimissory for the Bishop of Winchester, and on 16 February
1818 he was licenced in Hartley Wespall.[21] There he served in succession
two pluralists: an aristocrat, the Honourable and Reverend Alfred
Harris, and the redoubtable Dr Keate of Eton College.

Hartley Wespall, in the rural quiet of Hants and a little off the main
road, midway between London and Winchester, was an agreeable place
to make a beginning. A large vicarge with three sitting-rooms, seven
bedchambers, servant quarters, and a farmyard, gave him space and an
ample supply of poultry and bacon. He kept a horse, brewed his own
beer, and turned the space into a profitable school. So from the inception
of his ministry he planted together the dual interests which dominated
his life, education and the ministry of the Gospel. As the school prospered
and amplified his income, he took in servants and contemplated the
purchase of a farm in the neighbourhood. He knew domestic sorrow
and joy: a son died, but two daughters survived.[22]

Broughton worked hard in both parish and school. Keate praised his
energy but thought him tainted with Cambridge enthusiasm. Broughton
once asked permission to turn Passion Week into a Lenten teaching
crusade. Keate demurred: might not it reflect on the older clergy? Why
toll the bell daily for evensong and keep the church door shut? Broughton
replied. That Lent he preached all Passion Week.[23] Despite an occasional
difference, a happy respect united curate and incumbent. Broughton
looked forward to Keate's end of term visits; and Mrs Keate, with a
slap on the back and tale on the tongue, sent Sarah, now called Sally,
into peals of mirth.[24] Keate hoped Broughton would stay indefinitely,
and promised to abandon the vicarage to his use should he ever retire
from Eton. Broughton thanked Keate and confessed a deep love for the
place and its countryside, but he needed more than Hartley Wespall
could give. He wanted his own incumbency to keep from his family the
insecurity that had cursed his youth.[25]

Broughton was already turned thirty before his ordination to the
priesthood and needed to move quickly. He had no family connections
to exploit for patronage and, in eschewing a university fellowship for
marriage, he had bypassed the normal means which fed talent its opportunity. It remained for him to attract attention by advertising his wit in
print. A sermon in praise of foreign missions was acclaimed and printed
by his own Rural Deanery in 1823.[26] Broughton advocated exclusive
support for the Society for the Propagation of the Gospel (SPG), established himself in the district as a staunch high churchman, and got
the offer of a fashionable curacy at Margate. The offer, though more
lucrative than Hartley Wespall, could not accommodate the school that
had become an indispensable part of his income and Broughton declined
it.[27]

In the same year he bid for patronage and dedicated a work on the
Elzevir text of the Greek New Testament to his diocesan bishop, George

Tomline, the formidable Tory prelate and a former Fellow of Pembroke. It was a purely academic flourish designed to illustrate that the Elzevir text owed more to Latin than Greek sources. It taught Tomline that he had a parson in obscure Hartley Wespall possessed of 'no small share of learning and knowledge', and Marsh that at least one student had taken the tools of critical scholarship from Cambridge into the country-side.[28]

In 1826 Broughton entered a more fashionable controversy over the authorship of the *EIKON BASILIKA*, a seventeenth century tract that blamed the execution of Charles I on religious rivalries. Tory churchmen believed Charles I himself wrote it, and that it proved him to be a martyr-king. Whigs believed that a Bishop Gauden wrote it on fee from Lord Clarendon, and the martyr-king a myth. The Tories had the better of the argument until 1821 when fresh evidence for Gauden's authorship turned up in Lambeth Library. So ended, wrote the *Edinburgh Review*, another 'Tory attempt to falsify English history'.[29] That inspired Christopher Wordsworth at Cambridge to pen two massive volumes in defence of the traditional royal authorship. They fell on an excited reading public and Joshua Watson pronounced the evidence conclusive.[30]

Broughton believed in the royal-martyr and accepted the royal author-ship until he read Wordsworth's apology. 'Voluminous evidence commented on with a refinement often bordering upon that of the special pleader', he winced, and turned to settle the question for himself. Using the latest techniques of German textual criticism Broughton compared the style and language of the *EIKON BASILIKA* with Gauden's proven correspondence and found his scholarship at odds with his politics. 'Whatever my earlier presupposition and wishes', he concluded, 'I am compelled, after examining the case to admit Bishop Gauden was the author.' He published and defended his findings.[31]

The martyr-king did not suffer in Broughton's findings. 'The martyr is there without reproach', he wrote, 'and faithful to those principles of probity and truth which when banished from the world find their resting place in the heart of kings.' The king had fulfilled his role as defender of the church, but Broughton accused Bishop Gauden of abandoning his by succumbing to the 'maxim, even now scarcely exploded from the world, that in politics and in private life two different standards of morality were to be used'. The bishop's fraud in issuing an apology for episcopacy in the condemned king's name, pious though its intention, had cast a reproach on those who laboured honestly in support of the monarchy and the church. Good causes, Broughton insisted, never needed dishonest aid.[32]

Broughton's lucid and scholarly pamphlet with a moral peroration won him the patronage he courted. 'I strongly incline to your side of the question', Bishop Tomline of Winchester wrote to him, thus ending nine years of obscurity and setting in motion events which left him a prelate at the end of another nine. On 17 February 1827 Tomline licensed Broughton as an assistant at Farnham. On 1 March 1827, he added from his own plurality a further licence as master of the Farnham free grammar school, allowing Broughton to sustain his interest in education.[33] The move flattered Broughton more than appeared. The grammar school was a large one, and Broughton took over most of the active parish duty preaching three times a Sunday.[34] Moreover, the advowson of the Farnham parish church belonged to the bishop's private wealth, and he maintained at Farnham (to Cobbett's annoyance) a magnificent estate in readiness for his retirement. The great prelate would send to Farnham only one with whom he could maintain a pleasurable association. At the same time Tomline intended Broughton should have his own incumbency when one fell vacant. In November 1827 Tomline died in office without acting on his promise and his successor Charles Richard Sumner was not bound to fulfil his predecessor's intentions.[35]

Tomline's death did not shut off Broughton's hope for patronage. By Hartley Wespall stood Stratfield Saye, the Duke of Wellington's country estate, and the Duke's domestic chaplain Mr Briscall had introduced Broughton to the Duchess. He took an interest in the education of her sons and she in time confided in him. The friendship, Broughton once said, was an amalgam of business and pleasure: the Duchess asked for his prayers and he asked the Duchess for patronage.[36] In 1826 he told her of his preference for a librarianship being created at the British Museum to care for a bequest of books from the late King: 'One great step towards success I believe is to have timely knowledge of what is intended to be done and to whom the application ought to be made'.[37] No appointment came his way. But when the Duke's hour came in January 1828 the Duchess whispered to her husband, and the former curate of Hartley Wespall became a chaplain to the Tower of London. That gave him a room in London with very little idea of comfort and sad dinners of gibbet pie that tasted of dish clouts, a pension, and a better footing in the church establishment.[38] Between Farnham, the grammar school and the Tower he calculated his income above £1000 a year, and with a certainty of preferment in the years ahead he confessed himself 'amply satisfied'.[39]

Other wheels turned. Around September 1828 the Colonial Office accepted the resignation of T. H. Scott as archdeacon of New South Wales. Governor Darling's despatches as well as the letters of the archdeacon himself described a colony in the grip of unbridled factiousness; and one of its more malicious parties had tabbed Scott 'old priestcraft and tyranny' and buried him in ridicule. Scott confessed he was not the man for the job. Darling agreed. The Duke of Wellington decided Broughton had the qualities Scott lacked. 'I know of nobody else that I will recommend', he wrote to the Secretary of State for Colonies; and on 27 October 1828 sent his domestic chaplain off in the dark to Farnham to offer Broughton the archdeaconry.[40] The curate who once praised foreign missions believed he was asked to exchange elegant Farnham for log huts.[41]

Broughton wrote for information to his brother at the Admiralty,[42] and the Duke sent over a fair picture of colonial life from the *Quarterly Review* of January 1828 which contradicted all Scott said. Sydney had apparently grown into a place of industry and opportunity where the best inhabitants dressed in London fashion and the native-born showed a superiority in spirit, courage and morality. The earlier rebellious spirit was spent and the feud between immigrant and emancipist all but settled. Strangers were cheated less there than in London, enjoyed comfortable accommodation, and Bathurst cheese equalled any from Cheshire. Apart from a few natives prowling naked in search of tobacco and spirits, and 'abusing in language more gross than the grossest Billingsgate' when refused, a visitor might imagine himself in an English rural town.[43]

Henry Dumaresq, the governor's brother-in-law, was on leave and met Broughton in London to confirm the picture.[44] The Duke made it even rosier. Broughton would double his present income to £2000 in cash and enjoy such extras as, 'local advantages', a five year tour of duty, and after that a pension or further government preferment. 'A most noble offer', he wrote to his mother, '. . . and such as I could never have raised my thought to'.[45] For the price of a brief separation from his homeland he could turn the terror of insecurity from his door for ever and relieve his mother's impecunious widowhood. 'Everyone ought while they are young and able to make provision for their children; that in their old age they may not be troubled with anxiety what is to become of them', he reasoned with his wife; '. . . my appointment will quite protect *us* against this and enable us to provide for our dear children such a moderate competency as will secure them from difficulty during their lives.'[46] The material terms emerged as decisive. Broughton accepted the appointment.

But the Duke had erred. He overstated the perquisites.[47] The appointment was a one-way ticket to the colony for an indefinite period and was without pension or compensation in the event of death or retirement abroad, or any guarantee of government patronage on retirement.[48] Moreover, Scott had warned his ecclesiastical superiors in London to caution his successor against expecting profit from his appointment. Scott had repaired to the colony for gain and failed as miserably in that as in everything else. Nine-tenths of his income went in the costs of office, and he was a bachelor.[49] Wellington found Broughton hesitant after learning of this and offered him an opportunity to withdraw. The Bishop of Winchester called at Farnham, and as the two men knelt before the parish altar Broughton decided he would ever reproach himself as 'backward and fearful' in his Master's service if he declined.[50] His substantial £2000 salary allowed him to offset some insecurity by purchasing insurance policies; and the fate of his family in the event of his untimely death abroad he left in the hands of the Duchess of Wellington.[51] It was preferment no man could congratulate himself on obtaining, he commented; and accepted.[52]

On 28 December 1828 Broughton preached on the resurrection of the dead. 'Take away the expectation that the body shall hereafter be raised', he said, 'and many shall be reduced to sorrow without hope.'[53] The parish of Farnham thanked him with a silver dinner service and he left for Canterbury. For the next three months he was in and out of London dining with prelates, consulting at the Colonial Office, and arranging passage and outfit. 'It requires all the patience in the world not to be put out of humour', he wrote to his wife after a visit to the Admiralty. The Admiralty had allocated the family and its two servants berths to sail with the Dumaresqs on the *Waterloo*, but the ship left early. It then offered him comfortable alternative accommodation on the female convict ship the *Sovereign*, but Mrs Broughton feared for the indelicacies to which she and her daughters might be exposed. Broughton reassured her that the female prisoners 'will be quite separated from your sight and hearing', and accepted the passages.[54] The *Sovereign*, however, was not due to sail from Woolwich until April 1829.[55]

Meanwhile in March 1829 the Duke of Wellington shook the English establishment with plans for Catholic emancipation. Broughton had signed a dozen petitions opposing it in the past, and told the Duchess her highly exalted spouse was plainly wrong.[56] She agreed, and Broughton sent a memo through Mr Briscall to the Duke recommending that the bill of emancipation require every Roman Catholic office-holder to solemnly recognize the Church of England as an independent church not subject to any outside ecclesiastical jurisdiction. The Duke refused. 'No doubt he spoke very honestly: but where was his foresight?' Broughton commented. 'The Church of Rome would have thundered its denunciation but I think the *laity* would have felt the proposal reasonable.'[57]

In mid-April the whole family came to London to board the *Sovereign*. Then one of the girls fell ill and the *Sovereign* sailed without them. The Admiralty found alternative passages on another convict ship, the *John*, set to sail on 9 May.[58] On 23 May it still rode at anchor. Broughton could ill afford these delays. His outfit had cost £1000;[59] his allowance was £150; and his salary did not begin till he arrived in the colony.[60] Twice he begged relief from the Colonial Office, only once with success.[61] Finally a message came to board the *John* at Sheerness. The family went, and then spent two days in an hotel waiting for a gale to blow over. Broughton whiled away the time compiling the Duchess a prayer for her husband's better protection of the 'church and true religion'.[62] It was his final act for England. Around 5 p.m. on Tuesday 26 May he stepped with his family into an open boat to be rowed to the *John* at anchor off Little Nore. It was a short formidable journey through the rolling seas left behind by the gale—Broughton's first taste of the sea, and not to his liking.[63]

Once safely on board Broughton found himself more relieved that the waiting had ended than excited by his prospects. He had been born and bred to the English countryside. He admired England's traditions and was a model of Coleridge's parson: 'a neighbour and a family man whose education and rank admit him to the mansions of the rich landowners while his duties make him the frequent visitor of the farmhouse and the cottage'.[64] From this congenial milieu Broughton had been called away. None of the expectancy that had fired a Paul, a Xavier, or a Wesley about to cross from one continent to another, entered his soul. Like Isaiah, Jeremiah, and many others called to tasks for which they had never trained, he accepted this call as a burden laid upon him by his Lord. At the beginning of the missionary venture destined to take him around half the globe, he sought his first night's rest, not with joy flooding into his soul but, he coolly confessed, 'dispirited and uncomfortable'.[65] He prayed, however, to be spared a watery grave. That the sea would give up her dead he did not doubt, but he preferred to await the resurrection in a simple grave at Hartley Wespall beside the remains of his infant son[66]

Next morning Broughton joined the convicts who had come on deck to take a last look at the land that had stolen their liberty. He thought the armed guards a little nonchalant for good security, and a whisper from the first mate, amid peals of tawdry oaths, that the crew had too many novices, sent Broughton to the Psalms.[67] He adopted for the voyage the motto: 'My trust is in the tender mercy of God'.[68] Later, when he discovered that convicts readily betrayed each other for a favour he relaxed more. Not commendable, he admitted, but 'a great source of security to the passengers'.[69]

Broughton found no romance in a ship. 'A dirty, noisy, crowded machine of boards', he called it, but soon adapted to its ways.[70] Each day, under an umbrella when necessary, he took a calculated two hundred and twenty turns on the poop and washed down the plain coarse food with a hearty measure of wine.[71] Apart from leaking water-buckets he had little to complain of, and was surprised at his own contentedness.[72]

On fine Sundays he preached to the crew on the quarterdeck and to the convicts penned up on the poop. He quoted old sermons and missed familiar faces—old farmer Everard, for instance, erect on two legs and straining forward to catch every word. Still, his present congregation appeared surprisingly attentive and this encouraged him in a hope of permanently impressing a few. He called them to repentance with a threat of worse things to come, but that passed their imagining.[73]

Broughton classed convicts as either first offenders who had erred from 'bad counsel, bad example, or through very powerful temptation', or those of 'settled and inveterate malignity'.[74] The latter baffled him. Early in the voyage Broughton saved one of them from thirty-six lashes hoping 'to acquire an influence to turn him to better purposes', but the man proved to be a complete rogue.[75] Among the first offenders, however, he found John Bridges, a baker who later became his assigned servant.[76] But convict boys utterly defeated him. Mr Finn, an accomplished forger and teacher whose life was a shadowy dream passed back to him at the foot of the gallows, taught the boys in daily classes to recite parts of St Matthew's Gospel and the Psalms with 'creditable correctness'. All the same, Broughton was neither pleased nor impressed for while the classroom echoed the chorus 'Hallelujah, Praise the Lord' the whole ship rang with shocking tales of wicked boyish behaviour. 'I am greatly in doubt whether to offer any encouragement, knowing how great a deficiency of religious principle there is among them', he said. Broughton's own son lay dead in the innocent grave of childhood, and for the boys on the *John*, who possessed no innocence of life, he could arouse 'neither sympathy nor tenderness'.[77]

Broughton read a good deal. Bishop Heber's *Indian Journeys* was the saga of a missionary poet who rode himself to death in three years, and reviewers praised him extravagantly as a 'saint in lawn' who might even have won Scotsmen back to episcopacy.[78] Broughton dissented: 'I do not find my idea of an apostolical bishop realised'. Heber had combined the zeal of the missionary with the inquisitiveness of a tourist. What could a Hindu conclude from a Christian leader who gazed interestedly at pagan temples but that heathenism was not so objectionable after all? And all that heroic travel—was it apostolic? The great missionary apostle said, 'Into whatsoever city ye enter there *abide*'. So Broughton counselled himself against rambling visitations:

> Let him [the bishop] be at all events permanently settled somewhere during the greater portion of every year ... distant points must I admit upon this system be deprived for some years at least of their bishop's presence ... for this the blame must fall not upon the bishop but upon those who appoint a single man to fill a position too wide for any one human being ... it is better to do *real good* within a contracted sphere than to aim at the reputation of appearing to do it upon a much more extended theatre.[79]

Broughton read Elisha Cole's work to test his opposition to Calvinism. It survived.[80] He re-read Hoadley's writings and the treatises of other eighteenth century sceptics who had accepted high ecclesiastical office while denying many of the traditional interpretations of the Thirty-nine Articles. Had such men deliberately deceived the church? Broughton withheld final judgement but their subtleties offended him: 'Surely a Christian and above all a minister of the Gospel professing his assent to the doctrines of his church, may speak the truth from his heart without all these refinements, reservations and subtle distinctions'.[81] He read, too, Harris's life of Charles I to understand the cause of bloody revolutions. 'All Englishmen ought to have their minds well made up about this period', he noted. Broughton decided Puritanism had inspired the first revolution and he wondered whether Catholic emancipation might not inspire a second. Under such conditions everyone should seek to understand when to compromise, when to resist, and whether ever to resist unto bloodshed. Broughton concluded:

> Where a violent outcry and opposition is raised against a government both as to theory and practice, they must not strive by rigor and severity to withstand every demand for change, but take an enlarged view of the real condition of affairs; examine impartially what is really wrong in their system, and right in that of their opponents; and so timely and prudently amend the one and adopt the other, whilst the voice of reason and moderation can be attended to.[82]

Broughton read more and thought more clearly in the first half of his journey. Once the *John* entered tropical waters he felt the strain of a long journey into unfamiliar conditions—a beating heat, a breathless air, and a smooth sea that rocked the ship in a see-saw motion without pushing it onwards. He shortened Sunday services and still found them more exhausting than a full sabbath's duty at Farnham. Finally he succumbed to boredom: 'We have neither heard, seen or done anything worthy of record' was the fruit of a week's observation.[83]

When the *John* cleared the tropics it ran into a gale and winds buffeted it for a month. Sarah Broughton took ill. Then Broughton fell, was badly bruised, felt bitterly cold, and chilblaines covered his fingers. Water flooded his cabin and his clothes seemed constantly damp. At night the roar of the seas robbed him of sleep. Even the consoling glass of wine disappeared while the ship rolled and pitched. Nature possessed no charm in the 40th Parallel and when Broughton spotted an albatross, the poet's 'flying swan', he noticed only its inelegantly short neck.[84]

On 6 September the southern tip of Van Diemen's Land broke the early morning horizon and Broughton caught the first glimpse of his archdeaconry. Nothing stirred in him: 'Where we are going there are none of those whom we desire to see'. The strangeness of the lower latitudes overawed him with its awful sunsets, elongated shadows falling in unfamiliar directions, and long deserted coastlines. Still, six days later he stood on deck for hours peering through the night at the beacon by Port Jackson. He suddenly felt welcome. The beam from the lighthouse told him the perils were over and on shore he would meet a people 'capable of making great attempts and succeeding in them'. He slept well that night.[85]

Next morning as the pilot guided the *John* into the harbour Broughton preached on St Matthew 7.13. From good will come good fruit, and from evil, bad fruit in the new land as much as the old, he told his hearers. The law was immutable, only their opportunities were new. At half past one the *John* dropped anchor opposite Sydney Cove. It had all ended. By then Broughton had a new spirit. He saw light and shade in the rocks and trees around him, noticed the movement of small things, and felt the gentleness of breezes.[86] The curate who tried to retire from the rural quiet of Surrey to the solitude of the British Museum had arrived to meet Betsey Bandicoot and bold Jack Donahoe.

The Reception

It is the counsel and pleasure of God I repeat to raise up
here a Christian nation.

Broughton preaching in St James church 1829

When the *John* dropped anchor Archdeacon Scott and the respectable
citizens of Sydney who had kept the sabbath were at dinner. Colonel
Dumaresq came out alone to meet the ship. He boarded with the governor's greetings and a large basket of fresh fruit for the traveller he had
met earlier that year in London. Dumaresq's arrival and departure
exhausted Broughton's list of colonial acquaintances. None but strangers
awaited him on shore and he arranged to meet them on Wednesday.
Meanwhile on Monday 14 September Broughton landed unofficially
for discussions with the retiring archdeacon at Woolloomooloo. After
two days Scott emerged satisfied. 'I do think they have made a most
admirable selection', he told Colonel Arthur, his one remaining confidant.
'He appears active and methodical and *Liberal*, and very amiable but
I think firm.' All the virtues were commendable but the last especially
so. Scott insisted he had been 'far too easy' and his successor had the
unenviable task of measuring out strong discipline to an increasingly
refractory clergy.[1]

When Broughton took leave of Scott early on Wednesday morning
and returned to the ship to prepare for the official landing, he arrived at
the moment for which everything in his past life had been but a preparation. In heart and head he was well prepared; his affections were
firmly fixed on things above and his mind as well schooled in the principles
of reformed Christianity as the best of England's places of learning
could provide. But in the most indulgent moments of self-gratification
that so rapid a rise to high office might induce, Broughton could not but
have realized that the first forty-one years of his life had left him untried
and untutored in the skills of public office, its administration and its
politics. He would need wit as well as prayer to survive and prosper.
His conversations with Scott must have put light and shade into the
whimsical portrait of colonial life in the *Quarterly Review*. But Scott's
point of view could have been as misleading as it was enlightening.
Darling knew Scott well yet wilted before the difficulty of disentangling
opposition to Scott's ecclesiastical policy from plain opposition to Scott

as a person. Broughton could not hope to come to any settled opinions after two days of discussion with such a man. What Broughton needed on that cold crisp September morning, as he gazed from the ship across to the houses, streets, and buildings, where civilization seemed to have but a toe's hold on a vast land still jealously guarding her mysteries, was a few months of peaceful retirement in which to come to know this 'young city of a deserted wilderness'.[2]

Fortunately in the latter half of 1829 the colony enjoyed a rare but well deserved rest from the bitter political joustings that had left so many scars on the previous two years. The frenzied agitation whipped up in a desperate effort to win some liberal concessions in a new Constitution Act in 1828 had spent its force. Wentworth, bitterly disappointed with the Act, led a few of the hardy malcontents in a bitter reaction. They made a *cause célèbre* of the Sudds and Thompson affair, and spread it abroad as far as the halls of Westminster that this was the style of tyranny which flourished in at least one of His Majesty's colonies. By September 1829 even this matter had reached its limit in the colony; and all parties, the maligners and the maligned, were settling down to await news of the reaction at Westminster.[3]

For the most part the population of New South Wales was more preoccupied with the tyranny of the heavens than the illiberality of the governor. The heavens had become as brass and the earth as iron, and for want of rain the pastures themselves looked like beaten highways. But the voice of the optimist could not be silenced. In forty years Sydney had grown into the largest town south of the Tropic of Capricorn: in forty more, it was confidently proclaimed, she would be Queen of the South and rival anything this side of the equator, Lima and Rio de Janeiro included.[4]

To this land, to these people, and into such hopes, Broughton moved at the middle hour of Wednesday 16 September 1829 as the governor's bargemen rowed him to the landing-stage in Sydney Cove where 'all the first people of the colony' had gathered to welcome him. The scarlet of the law and the black of the church mingled with the red and decorated uniforms of the colonels of the regiment; there stood Mr McLeay, Mr John Macarthur and the members of the Legislative Council; there, too, stood the black gaitered figure of Archdeacon Scott, erect and defiant, with the ageing Reverend Samuel Marsden of Parramatta on one side and the benevolent Reverend Richard Hill from St James church on the other, waiting to assist Broughton and his family ashore the moment they arrived. Just on twelve noon a battery of cannon, kept a little to the west at Dawes Point on the far side of the Cove, peppered the air with a bit of military pomp Broughton 'would much rather have dispensed with', and it was known that the new archdeacon had landed. The colony knew nothing of him except that he had been to Cambridge, and even that came from an Indian newspaper. Once on colonial soil Broughton met the senior officials and quickly filed off on foot to government house where Darling waited. Darling saw at the head of the procession a man of modest stature, broad in the shoulders but not tall, and afflicted with a distinct limp. Something stirred in the

governor at the sight of the new archdeacon; he broke protocol, left the
verandah where he had been standing with his aide, and walked down
the path to greet a new friend and fellow worker. Together they walked
back to the great red and brown stone building, which looked more like
an ancient overgrown cottage than the residence of a governor, and into
its large reception hall. There, as the *Monitor* put it, 'the ceremony of
swearing in Mr B. took place in the usual manner'.[5]

Once Broughton had taken the oaths and made the requisite declara-
tions, he and his family left with Scott for Woolloomooloo, where they
were to remain until a suitable residence could be fixed up for them. In
the meantime, Darling intended that they should return to government
house for a dinner party to meet their fellow workers under less formal
circumstances.[6]

Broughton wasted little time choosing a residence. He loved space.
In Sydney the market was scarce and he found his choice narrowed to a
single house at the western end of Bridge Street. It had a sufficient supply
of rooms but he complained that they were all badly arranged; and the
front garden was little more than a sand pit. By way of compensation
the property afforded its occupants a magnificent view of the harbour;
a grand sheet of water, he told his mother, much like the picture he left
behind with her in England. The one real drawback was the locality;
the house sat uncomfortably close to the Rocks area, a place so notoriously
wild and unruly that the government had considered making every
publican there an ordinary magistrate and charging each with responsibility for keeping his own premises in order. Broughton took a lease
for one year.[7]

The archdeacon found the colonists kind and attentive, and the press
as respectful as he could have dared hope. E. S. Hall, the editor of the
Monitor who had gingered Scott's life, had no use for bishops, archdeacons, or any ecclesiastical dignitary (though heaps of time for the Christian
gospel) but was prepared to welcome Broughton as a fellow Christian and
for the moment keep his peace. Indeed Hall almost claimed Broughton
was his gift to the colony. In 1828 Scott had unceremoniously locked
Hall out of his pew at St James church and Hall protested to the Archbishop of Canterbury. He calculated that, after allowing time for travel
and a little consideration, Scott's resignation coincided with the arrival
and reception of his protest. By forcing Scott's resignation in favour of
an archdeacon properly and regularly bred to his profession the *Monitor*
claimed it had restored preaching to the colony's pulpits.[8] The *Australian*, however, did not try and compete for laurels, and was content
to introduce the new archdeacon to its readers with a bit of that corn it
occasionally sprinkled over its pages:

> Archdeacon Broughton, we hear, has expressed his intention to pro-
> mote public harmony in more ways than one, and among others by
> patronising, with his presence, Mr Levy's next concert. We give the
> Venerable Gentleman every praise for his friendly intentions.[9]

From an office in George Street another newspaper the *Gazette* extended Broughton the truly friendly hand. Its editor pledged the archdeacon

genuine support in all his Christian endeavour and warned him against the polite embrace of his competitors the *Monitor* and *Australian*. Both those papers had built their circulation on a policy of spirited opposition to constitutional authorities, lay and ecclesiastical; and the *Gazette* warned that 'when the invidious motive for the present civility shall have passed away be he eloquent as Apollos, zealous as Paul, and mild as Barnabas—[he, Broughton] will not escape the calumny of the press'. E. S. Hall didn't care to have his motives impugned, and told his rival at the *Gazette* to stop pulling at the archdeacon's cassock like a little baby trying to attract his countenance. And in this manner Broughton was introduced to the colonial way of doing things.[10]

Broughton stood in no need of the *Gazette's* timely reminders. His own two eyes were sufficient. He read the attacks on Scott as they continued to the bitter end, and was present on the landing-stage by the water's edge when an attorney delivered Scott a parting gift from E. S. Hall—a summons to the retiring archdeacon to appear the following week in a libel action to be heard in one of His Majesty's courts, Sydney. Scott preferred to board H.M.S. *Success*, and left the dead to bury their dead. Nor did Broughton have long to wait before witnessing the spectacle of having one of his senior priests posted in the *Australian*, for 'apparent nonchalance' at Mrs Pittman's funeral.[11]

But the press offered Broughton a truce. Don't complain too soon, the *Australian* counselled the laity: 'It will be better that the venerable gentleman should have a proper leisure time allowed him, in order that he may form something like an accurate judgement of certain past transactions, as well as the people by whom he is now surrounded'.[12] Nevertheless the press kept him under scrutiny. It knew where he preached, whom he married, when he was ill, where he dined, and how he fell out of his carriage.[13] Then a chance, but false, rumour that the archdeacon did not intend to take his seat on the Legislative Council flushed them into the open; and Broughton read a touching plea that the colony needed him very much in its politics:

An honest man is not one to be readily dispensed from a Colonial Council constituted as this is; and we trust that so long as the Colony is condemned to have a body of men, over whose election the Colonists have no choice or controul, the present Archdeacon may continue to hold a seat with advantage to the community and therefore with credit to himself.[14]

On 12 October the heavens relented and poured rains on the just and the unjust. Water flowed everywhere, through the streets and over drains: it filled up ditches and swept away the anxieties of the parched colony. The people rejoiced to see the end of three years of heart-breaks and uncertainties; and the governor, mindful of duty and decorum, proclaimed 12 November a public holiday so that the inhabitants of the colony, on their way to market, could call at a church and thank Almighty God for ending the severe drought and averting from the colony his threatened judgement. Even the *Australian*, calculating that there were 'solid benefits' in store for all from the Almighty's change of heart, commended the governor's gesture and urged its patrons to join in the spirit of the occasion. Rarely before had the wolf and the lamb agreed to feed together in the House of the Lord; and Broughton, who was to preach the principal sermon of the day before the chief officers of government assembled in the church of St James, could count on an unusually receptive congregation. It might not remain so for long; soon the soft earth would yield harvests, and the cattle grow fat by running creeks, the merchants gather the wool, and man would again consume his days in vanity. Before that day returned, Broughton poured forth his vision of the wondrous ways of God.[15]

Just after midday on Thursday 12 November when Broughton mounted the pulpit in St James church and, in the lucid and balanced phrases characteristic of a scholar, announced as his text Isaiah 46.10: 'My counsel shall stand, and I will do all my pleasure'. He spoke of the 'inseparable connection between obedience and prosperity' as God's way of making his pleasure prevail over man. This theme was the marrow of Israel's history. And the melancholy records of peoples, nations, and whole empires given up to punishment and decay as soon as they had proved themselves unqualified to fulfill the purposes of God proved, he said, that Israel's history was a paradigm of world history. No kingdom of the past had been excepted from this judgement, nor would any to come. So it behoved all people in every age to enquire into their elected destiny, fearful lest, ignoring their calling, they forfeit their prosperity eternally. Then Broughton exploded with an exhilarating message:

> If there be any here present . . . who have witnessed the exaltation of the English nation, and its gradual extension of power to the limits of the habitable world without ever considering this but as effected in the natural course of things, and not, as it assuredly is, by the particular and evident providence of the Lord, for the fulfilment of His own purposes; if such there be among us, let them, I say, awake and take a new view of passing events.[16]

He told them of the greatest of all passing events; the astonishing extension of the English name to the east and to the west, to the north and to the south. He told them of the great event passing that very hour before their eyes; the extension of the English name to the shores of New South Wales as the resistless word of God incorporated yet another land into His grand design for redeeming the world. Why should a great continent left in darkness for so long be suddenly peopled by a new race, if it were not for some purpose? Why were vast tracts of land, desolate since the beginning of time, suddenly made to blossom like Eden, unless the Lord had commanded it? 'We are therefore to consider ourselves not as placed here accidentally, nor even for the fulfilment of a temporary or unimportant purpose,' he told them all, for the design was too grand, 'but as conducted by the providence of God to bear our part in the execution of that eternal purpose which was laid in Christ Jesus before the world began.'[17]

So much for the colony's beginnings. What could be said of its response? Here the preacher had a less felicitous tale to recount; a tale of vice and lewdness, of drunkenness and unchastity, in almost every quarter of the

WILLIAM GRANT BROUGHTON,
Metropolitan of Australasia.

PEMBROKE COLLEGE, Cambridge,
with Wren Chapel.

settlement, so that the colony's predicament could be justly described as chosen of God but unfit. As with Israel of old, there was only one solution to this; first the Lord would visit the land with one of his four sore judgements, the sword, the noisome beast, the pestilence, or the famine, and allow a time for repentance. Should that fail to work a correction, He would then withdraw His favour, and allow the land to be given over to decay after whatever means it cared to fashion for itself. The rains, Broughton encouraged his congregation to understand, were more than water; they were the sign that the Lord had suspended His judgement and still wanted the colony to play a role in His great plan to have His glory cover the whole world:

> I discern, with the plainness of demonstrative evidence, the final end of all that calamity which the sovereign Lord of all so lately threatened us. Well was it qualified to awaken among us those Christian disposi-tions in which we are all too manifestly wanting ... It is the counsel and pleasure of God, I repeat, to raise up here a Christian nation.[18]

The sermon lasted full fifty minutes. Broughton drained each to the limit to save the infant colony falling short of its destiny. Darling, who had invited men to hear it, had himself departed Sydney for a tour of the country before the day of fasting had arrived. But he later read the sermon. For some time he had watched an evil principle take root in the colony and mature, corrupting one by one the press, the courts, the army, and almost every branch of civil life. He had tried to curb its extravagances only to meet with vexatious frustrations and outright humiliations. One judge opposed his purifying censorship of the press; another agreed that it was improper even for a governor to impute un-worthy motives to Mr Wentworth; and, as for putting irons on poor Sudds and Thompson, almost everyone seemed to agree that that was no way to go about restoring discipline in the ranks of the militia. Was all this protesting just a healthy dose of liberty, such as every Englishman had a right to express, making its long delayed appearance, or, was it an evil principle at work?[19] If Darling had any misgivings, the great news of 12 November was that God felt the same way as the governor: there was an evil spirit in the land. Darling wanted the whole colony to know this, and to know that God was on his side in doing battle against it; so he ordered that Broughton's sermon be published for sale throughout the colony. Within three months Darling wrote flatteringly of Broughton. 'The Public is indebted to you', he told the Secretary of State for Colonies, 'for placing a person of his worth and qualifications in the eminent and important station he holds.'[20]

Broughton's was not the only vision of the divine invasion of the Pacific. The Reverend J. D. Lang had seen it before him and accepted the challenge on behalf of Scotland and the Presbyterian Church.[21] Progress was slow, and when Broughton seized the challenge for England and its reformed Christianity he believed the work was about to begin. And yet, those who heard him preach of his prophetic vision mistook his purpose if they received his words as national flattery. He had taken his stand in the pulpit to stir their watchfulness, not to titillate their pride: to awaken them not to glory but to a grave responsibility and to a knowledge of the fearful consequences of neglecting it. And for those who could read between the lines the sermon foreshadowed the principles by which the colony could expect to find the archdeacon disposing of the powers of his office, in the church, in 'the parliament of the country, and in . . . the Governor's privy council'.[22] He would support nothing calculated to hinder the sanctification of the colony, but, like the prophets of Israel, denounce and oppose it with every fibre in his person. On 12 November 1829 before a public gathering in the colony Broughton stated his belief: the colony belonged to God. There were others, some present, who had been there longer than he had, and they were in the habit of regularly publishing a different conviction: vox populi, . . . vox dei, they said.[23]

Three weeks later Broughton had the chaplains riding into Sydney for his Primary Visitation. It, too, was held in St James church and attended by all the first people in the colony, including this time the nonconformist clergy who nodded their approval as the new archdeacon charged his brother clergy in measured tone to abide close by the 'spirit of the Apostles and the views of the Reformers'. Set aside, he said, the modern trend to deliver *general* discourses from the pulpit, and utter unceasingly this truth—that since Jesus Christ the Redeemer has paid an inestimable ransom for man's release no man, in or out of the colony, is at liberty any longer to live otherwise than in subjection to God's will. 'We hear it sometimes maintained . . . that the preacher who thus frames his discourses with constant reference to one leading truth, must acquire a contracted style of thinking', he continued. 'Such apprehension I must consider as founded either in prejudice or mistake.' He then charged them as pastors to strive for the honour of being chosen the family adviser; and to win this honour they must be among their flocks during the week as habitually as they were over them on the sabbath. While their own districts were their first concern, he reminded them of the remoter settlements where piety had decayed and the sabbath passed unobserved for want of a ministry; 'Much practical good, I am satisfied, may be done by periodical visits to such districts as lie beyond the reach of your regular and ordinary ministry'. He reminded them, too, that as priests they had been ordained for the guidance and instruction of other men, and could expect their conduct to be narrowly and jealously observed. He welcomed that scrutiny and prayed that from every quarter he would hear 'of the diligence, the uncorruptness, the habitual piety, and of the edifying example of the clergy of the Established Church'.[24]

Broughton further charged the clergy to bestow their assiduous care and encouragement on the colony's parochial schools, the real source of Australia's future greatness so long as they diffused religious impressions and virtuous habits along with the rudiments of ordinary learning. The school system Scott had zealously established, virtually single-handed and in the face of many difficulties, Broughton hoped to maintain and expand with an equal zeal. With that mention of Scott's name Broughton felt compelled to add a little more: Scott, like everyone else was liable to err, but after enquiry into his plans and achievements Broughton felt constrained to make a personal testimony in his favour: 'I do not hesitate to express my persuasion that a man of purer intention, stricter principle and less under the bias of self-interest, never trod these shores'.[25]

Finally Broughton charged his clergy to have a special regard for convicts and the colony's original people. He asked for a keen ministry among the convicts so that as many as were victims of ignorance, or some momentary weakness rather than a settled malignity, might amend their unprofitable pasts and be restored to the community, not simply as servants but as beloved brothers.[26] As for the Aboriginal people, Broughton admitted their condition had shocked him: at best they remained in their original benighted state; all too often they had been reduced to a state of barbarian wildness by a fondness for intoxicating liquor, a habit they had imbibed from the Englishman's example. It was an appalling legacy for a half century of contact with a Christian people. It did even less credit to a Christian nation, he said, that it should have abandoned, under the weight of failure and despair, all attempts at converting these natural occupants of the country. If the Christian religion had overcome the obstinate superstition of the Jews and the philosophic arrogance of the Gentiles, it could subdue the erratic habits of the Australian native. Despair was not a fitting sentiment for any Christian; and on this note he drew his charge to a close:

> Every advancement of the Christian religion, from its first origins to this day, has been effected in opposition to difficulties which, in a natural sense might be termed insuperable. Its excellency and its derivation from a heavenly source has been best demonstrated by surmounting such opposition.[27]

By and large Broughton had revealed himself content to follow the policies of his predecessor. He promised nothing new, nothing different, and seemed mainly concerned to encourage his brother clergy in a more diligent pursuit of their pastoral ministry, an emphasis Scott might well have encouraged him to adopt. By avoiding rash comment on the colony at large Broughton had avoided Scott's initial error; and if there was little sign of any enthusiasm for what he had said, there was none of that adverse criticism which had come close to driving Scott from the colony in 1825.[28] It was, too, a less anxious and a more homely Broughton who spoke out on 3 December: a zeal for good works had replaced the earnestness of the prophet with its overtones of threatened judgement. The difference did not pass unnoticed: he appeared amiable, pious, benevolent, and to have 'the happiness of the people sincerely at heart', the *Gazette* remarked.[29] Nevertheless, behind that amiability Broughton had managed to deliver a firm rebuke to Scott's critics and possibly to have offended them. The opposition press snubbed the occasion. The *Australian* acknowledged that the archdeacon had held his Visitation; but after devoting lavish space to the St Andrew's Day dinner where Lord Brougham was toasted as champion of the people's education, the editor regretted he had no space to report what the archdeacon had said.[30]

In his charge the archdeacon had touched on one matter currently exciting renewed interest in the colony—the state of its education system. If, as in Broughton's most sanguine estimate, Scott had managed to bring near to perfection a system of primary schools, neither Scott nor anyone else had been so fortunate as to secure the permanent foundation of one school of higher learning. In the original plans Scott sent down from Whitfield to London in 1824 before coming to the colony, he proposed the erection of one central establishment for higher learning in each county.[31] The Colonial Office approved the idea, the governor gave it his enthusiastic support, Scott even had teachers lined up for the first schools at Parramatta and Windsor, and textbooks in store at Sydney; but the project collapsed.[32] It was denied funds. Yet, bitter though Scott was over that, he had frankly admitted the presence of another factor: 'the strange perverseness of character of the population of this Colony, who seem generally to prefer persons of their own class to educate their children than more respectable and capable persons'.[33]

Scott's failure to put his resources to work was the more regrettable because the Sydney Free Public Grammar School, set up by a group of public spirited colonists in November 1825, had collapsed at the end of 1826 for the want of a satisfactory teacher. Had the two groups combined, one good grammar school may have come into being before 1830; but neither group seemed prepared to abandon its ideal (the one standing for ecclesiastical control and the other for the more Whiggish ideal of management vested in public sponsors) so long as it was possible each might succeed at a future date. If their differences impoverished the provision for higher education in the colony, they had the comfort of knowing that the desire for it was insipid. In the meantime anything above primary education had to be bought at a number of academies, like Timothy Cape's Classical Seminary in King Street, or Captain Beveridge's Merchant and Naval Academy.

In February 1829 many of the masters of these private schools came under fire publicly for 'intellectual murder'. 'Latin, Greek, mathematics and other elements of a refined education', ran an editorial in the *Gazette*, 'are pompously professed to be taught by individuals in no degree qualified for an adequate execution of the task.' These remarks released a suppressed sense of outrage in the colony. Letters soon poured into the newspaper's office: some abused, by name, many of the colony's teachers and suggested that the newspaper itself perform a public duty and expose their chicanery for the benefit of all colonists; others wanted teachers to be licenced; still others advocated the formation of citizens' inspection committees; finally the editor returned to the scene suggesting that the 'criminal negligence of parents is . . . the real gangrene in the vitals of the community'. It urged parents to enquire carefully before enrolling a child in a school, and thereafter to study its progress, and pending the establishment of better schools, to attend without failure the public examination at the end of the year.[34]

This episode focused attention on the inadequacies of the colony's higher education facilities and stimulated enquiry into how other colonies had met their needs. Lang had received the prospectus of an impressive venture undertaken by the Dutch Reform Church in the Cape Colony just before Broughton delivered his Primary Visitation charge, and persuaded a newspaper to publish it. Whether Lang intended it or not, the editor took the liberty of putting the scheme on Broughton's doorstep: 'It would not be unreasonable to indulge the hope that with so enlightened and so liberal a director as the Venerable Archdeacon Broughton, the Clergy and School Corporation of this Colony would appropriate a portion of their funds towards the salaries'.[35] When two days later Broughton delivered his charge without even a passing reference to higher education in any form the *Gazette* quietly took him to task. It agreed with Broughton that the colony certainly was not deficient in the lower branches of education but reminded him of how lamentably poor it was in all means of developing the full enjoyments of the intellect. As things stood, the editor summed up the situation, the young had no prospect of growing up any different from 'the backwoodsmen of America, dead to all that is worthy of immortal man, and engrossed by the one isolated sense of mere animal existence'.[36]

It was no comfort to Lang or to the editor of the *Gazette* to learn, about the same time, that the trustees of the Sydney Free Public Grammar School planned to revive their foundation. They had failed in two attempts in the last two years. Moreover, the absence of any religious principle in its organization reduced its value to Christian gentlemen: 'highly as we prize intellectual cultivation, we should be sorry to see it imparted after the model of ancient Greece or Rome, whose academic institutions . . . left the minds of their pupils to roam unchecked among the endless mazes of philosophy and atheism'.[37] These anxieties relaxed a little on 19 December when news leaked out that the civil and ecclesiastical authorities were about to do something about higher education. Little information was available; but rumour had it that any school set up would admit 'all ranks in the community, and all denominations within the wide pale of Christianity'.[38] Lang immediately waited on Broughton for more particulars, and left pleased with what he learned.[39] Broughton, too, was pleased to have the interest and co-operation of Lang. But few were more pleased with this turn in events than the editor of the *Gazette* who had given the archdeacon such unstinting encouragement since the day of his arrival.

This editor was the Reverend Ralph Mansfield, a resolute and resourceful young man just thirty-one years of age, whom sorrow had managed to bow but not break; in less than ten years he had carried to the grave five of his six children. Mansfield, a Wesleyan preacher at odds with his superiors as well as a journalist, was driven by a mixed and often antithetical set of ideas. Though he had earned the wrath of his superiors for disregarding Wesleyan etiquette by preaching in opposition to the parish church in his district, he publicly advocated the extension of religious establishments and the proliferation of colonial bishoprics as the only efficient means of Christianizing new settlements. Though an unrepentant Wesleyan, he believed the Church of England was rooted in 'the immovable basis of Scriptural Christianity' and fully able to stand 'the keenest investigations of reason and philosophy'. He believed, too, that England's bishops were the divinely inspired leaders

of the age in the struggle against infidelity. He defended the Church
of England's right to receive tithes, and thundered against all reforms
that weakened the Church Establishment. 'Let the ark be demolished—
let the Established Church be broken up', he preached to his readers,
'and of England it might truly be recorded, "Her Glory is departed".'
A dissenter, yet he despised radicals as 'seven times heated Whigs'. He
hailed Wellington as the saviour of the age and an aristocracy as the
only secure basis for a society. What gave him greatest strength of all
in 1829 was a firm conviction that in England, under the guidance of
men like Bishop Blomfield, churchmen and dissenters had mended
their differences and acknowledged only one common enemy—infidelity.
Broughton, 'our present worthy and universally beloved Archdeacon'
as he called him, was in this tradition; and Mansfield put his paper at
the archdeacon's disposal, a favour the archdeacon accepted.[40]

While Broughton discussed his plans and his friends congratulated
him on his initiative, the trustees of the former Sydney Free Public
Grammar School acted quickly. They met on 14 January and renamed
their venture the Sydney College; then with a covetous eye on the patriotic
sentiment only 26 January could provide and a wise eye on the spirit
of optimism that the rains had put into the commercial world, they
arranged to set the foundation stone of the new college in less than two
weeks, on the coming anniversary of the founding of the colony. Nothing
which happened that anniversary day could have convinced Broughton
that he and the Sydney College trustees should work together. The day's
celebrations began in the saloon of the Royal Hotel two hours in advance
of the ceremony. At about 11.45 a.m., when the gathering was about
eighty strong, the chief justice arrived and led them off in a procession
which 'resembled one associated for similarly patriotic purposes in the
purest days of Greek and Roman virtue'. Then on an acre and a half by
the Domain, in a straight line between the Catholic chapel and the
racecourse, the chief justice set the foundation stone of Sydney College
to a salute of twelve rifles. He told the three hundred spectators that
this college 'would be the means ... of forming dutiful subjects to the
Mother Country; subjects who would imitate her loyalty, her literature,
her justice, and her glory'. The people then stood, far too long for a hot
sunny day according to the *Monitor*, while Dr Lang, who had decided
against co-operation with Broughton, blessed the venture with fervency
and pathos. He reminded those present that, if the Lord was its builder,
the college would be one means of delivering the heathen in these
uttermost parts of the earth into God's hands. Few present cared for
the heathen, and none but Lang looked upon the college as a mission
outpost in the heart of the Pacific; but to them all it was a sound educational venture long overdue, a gift from this generation to the next,
and 'the best and grandest work this Colony has been engaged in since
the Public Meeting to Petition Parliament for Trial by Jury'.[41]

Broughton stayed away from the ceremony to attend a conveniently
arranged meeting of the Executive Council.[42] He did not disapprove of
people with ideas differing from his own being active in the cause of
education. This he made clear. 'I would wish distinctly to disclaim the

assumption of any right to call individuals to account for the opinions they may entertain', he wrote to Lang, 'or to interfere in any way with the exposition of the principles on which they believe education may be best conducted'. He stayed away from the ceremony on the 26 January because he wished to avoid any appearance of giving public approval or commendation to a venture whose consequences he feared. Education, like that to be offered at the Sydney College, which fell only a little short of totally excluding religion from among its business, worked, in Broughton's estimate, an evil effect upon the community. The school, by giving an appearance of laxity in religious teaching, certified to its pupils that revealed truths were not of supreme value and worthy of close study; and, as a consequence, turned out young men defective in moral knowledge and satisfied to remain so. Then, year by year as the colony received into its adult population a fresh group of young men caring little for moral excellence, the community would be confirmed in the corruption of its ways.[43]

Defenders of the Sydney College argued that each boy received a bible and time to read it; and that was sufficient to reinforce the grand principle of protestant Christianity that 'God is his own interpreter, and he will make it plain'. This allayed none of Broughton's fears. He viewed man in a strictly pessimistic light as a creature who loved vice better than virtue, and would seek where possible to excuse the delinquencies of the one rather than enforce the discipline of the other. The past was not without examples of how scripture itself, abounding as it did with ambiguities and obscurities, could be artfully construed to yield just those excuses man desired to cover his baseness. Broughton believed this practice would persist wherever the bible was put into the hands of the young without accompanying instruction from elders schooled in the understanding of the highest notions of virtue. Ignorance of scripture was to be deplored; but the exploitation of it in support of an evil cause was to be abhorred above all else. For reasons such as these Broughton confessed that he had opposed liberal trends in education in England, though he admitted they were winning fashionable approval in many quarters. He felt himself bound to oppose them even more strongly in New South Wales; for, whereas England possessed many well established institutions to counteract the ill effects of the new style of ideas, the young colony possessed none. 'If they', Broughton wrote of Sydney College and such schools, 'should ever obtain general acceptance in this colony, [they] will render it, I venture to predict, the most frightful moral spectacle that has ever been exhibited upon earth.'[44]

The day before Judge Forbes laid the foundation stone of Sydney College the Committee of the Trustees of the Clergy and School Lands forwarded to Darling detailed copies of plans for two other schools of higher education; the first, it hoped, in a system of establishments to be spread over the whole colony. The committee pointed out that the schools would be under the direction and control of the Established Church, as provided for in section XXVIII of the Church and Schools Corporation's Charter. And lest any should doubt the wisdom of that provision, the committee, five of whose members were laymen, testified that in their opinion it was still to be reckoned as the most effective means for securing good order in the colony.[45]

The idea that Broughton should, so soon after his arrival, busy himself in setting up grammar schools belonged to the Colonial Office rather than to Broughton. The suggestion was put to him on his appointment, and he probably arrived with well formed plans.[46] In New South Wales his principal task was to gauge the support for such schools, and on 8 December 1829 he asked the clergy to estimate the number of likely candidates from among the 'good families' in their areas. Broughton stressed 'good families' because he read in Scott's melancholy reflections on the failure of his plans for a grammar school, a suggestion that the fee-paying upper classes in the colony had objected to their children mixing with the sons of humble or immoral parents brought to the school by scholarships for fear of being contaminated by the association. Within a month the chaplains' figures encouraged Broughton to believe 'very few Parents would hesitate to avail themselves on their Children's behalf of the means of good instruction, if the same were made of easy attainment both as to locality and Expense'. Scott's enquiries and experiences had told a strangely different story. But Broughton was confident that with goodwill at the Colonial Office and the support of a local committee of the trustees, six of whose nine members were members also of the Legislative Council, a vigorous new beginning could be made.[47]

Then for a moment on 26 January his optimism faltered. Would the economically minded men at the Colonial Office relax their concern for higher education in New South Wales now that the foundation stone of the Sydney College had been laid? Before retiring that evening, Broughton wrote Darling a long letter; a supplement to the plans recently submitted by the Church and Schools Corporation, in which he armed Darling with good reasons why he should 'induce His Majesty's Government at home to lend the sanction and support which are requisite for carrying into effect and consolidating such a system' as he proposed.[48]

The syllabus of Sydney College, with its provision for a museum and a department of natural philosophy, was set to follow the modern theorists who advocated enlarging education with a liberal study of the sciences.[49] A widespread schoolboy interest in science was in evidence at Shelley's Eton as early as 1809; and by 1830 the itinerant science teacher moving from school to school with his travelling laboratory, and delivering a series of lectures to pupils at a guinea a head, was an accepted part of the school scene. The man of science, however, was not without a flaw in his reputation: if he looked to have a head of gold, stored with the pure knowledge of a wonderful world around and above him, he appeared all too often to possess the clay feet of a radical. His stock in trade was too often mere cleverness; sometimes applied with mephistophelean grandeur as in Shelley's 'Queen Mab'. This prophetic epic, which in the 1820s became the bible of the Owenites, professed, in all sincerity, to foretell from a study of tropical fossils and the slope of the earth's axis, the approach of another age in which men would live free from priest, king, and the 'icy chains of custom'. When the itinerant science teacher turned up at Rugby and Arnold sent him packing, it was a sign that, in some quarters, it had been decided that a premature acquaintance with science seriously threatened the proper development of a boy's intellect. Broughton was in the vanguard of this revolt.

It was the archdeacon's opinion that schools should do two things well: exercise a boy's reasoning powers and instill in him habits of patient investigation. The study of science did neither; it aimed simply at stocking a boy's mind with a great variety of facts, and as a result the lad left school with a well trained memory but a poor sense of judgement. That was a disaster both intellectually and morally, Broughton said,

> The learner, being thus enabled to make a display of information, is elevated in his opinion of his own powers, and experience proves that persons so educated, having their memories cultivated at the expense of judgment, are prone to contravene all established opinions, to despise the authority of all former times, and to decide without any hesitation upon points which have exercised for Ages the minds of the most reflective men.[50]

Broughton feared that a 'disposition to dogmatise upon questions relative to Government and Religion'—the spirit of the Shelleys, the Godwins, and the Owens—was already in embryo in the colony and needed to be checked. Broughton advised Darling that the system of classical studies long established in the public schools of England, perhaps with a little more mathematics (for Broughton was a good product of Cambridge), would provide some measure of restraint. At the very least, it would ensure that before the young took off in imaginative flights of their own they would have spent a considerable time contemplating the wisdom of their fathers and perhaps have learned to respect it.[51]

By such arguments Broughton explained why, so long as men treasured the spirit of English institutions, the presence of Sydney College reinforced rather than disposed of the need for the Church and Schools Corporation to establish colleges in opposition to it. He proposed building one school for 100 day-scholars in Sydney, and a mixed day and boarding school at Parramatta to foster the growth of a class of landed gentry.[52] In his tour of the county of Cumberland, early in January 1830, Broughton would have learned of the levelling effect of life in the interior where the uncertainties of distance and isolation made each man's closest neighbour his most needed friend, whether a property owner, a hired labourer, or an assigned convict servant. This constant mixing of the classes augured ill for the future of the colony: 'In too many instances', he wrote of that class which would inherit the large properties and in future exercise influence, 'I have heard of their sacrificing all their respectability and influence by associating habitually with their own Convict Servants. Such a forgetfulness of what is due to themselves and Society, I need scarcely remark, could not occur, if their minds were duly cultivated'.[53]

Broughton saw the future of New South Wales through English eyes: he had none other through which to see it. The peace and sobriety of England rested on the willingness of the gentry, small and great, to serve on juries, act as Justices of the Peace and magistrates, and to sit in the House of Commons. The present generation of property owners

in New South Wales had few of these responsibilities; but with a bill
providing for trial by jury in civil cases almost through the Legislative
Council, and further agitation for some form of elected Assembly constantly in the air, their sons could hardly escape some measure of it. To
prepare them Broughton had first to get them away from their home
environment, a proposal Scott had strongly advocated; and then by
filling their minds with sound learning awaken a yearning for excellence
that would flow into good government. The establishment at Parramatta
was to do this.[54]

Since Broughton saw his schools as of decisive importance for the
general welfare of the colony, he tried to attract boys irrespective of
their religious backgrounds. A willingness to abide by the school regulations was the only qualification for enrolment. The regulations included:
attendance at daily morning prayer, attendance at a place of worship on
Sundays, and participation in classes of *general* religious instruction.
There would be no religious tests, no subscriptions, and no compulsory
classes in *confessional* religious teaching. 'Every individual, maintaining
a good character and a correct behaviour', Broughton promised, 'shall
be at liberty to avail himself of the means of instruction ... for any
period of time.'[55]

Instruction, nevertheless, was decidedly Christian: Tomline's *Introduction to the Bible*, but not his *Elements of Christian Theology* which
only churchmen could accept; Archbishop Leighton's *Short Catechism*
written to attract the Scottish covenanters as well as Scottish episcopalians; Paley's *Natural Theology*, which argued for God's existence from
the marvel of design in creation.[56] None were distinctly Church of
England books though all were by Church of England writers. Masters
must be clerics of the Church of England, but Broughton promised to
choose men as little exclusive as possible.[57] This had proved possible
in England and won dissenter co-operation.[58] Broughton sought no
special advantage for the Church of England but 'considered it the
soundest policy to trust the extension of the Established Church to the
influence of a general persuasion of her desire to promote the good of
all'.[59] Special catechetical instruction for the Church of England pupils
came at a separate hour and from a purer stream—Lancelot Andrewes
and Bishop Ken; but parents could exempt their children provided
they did so at enrolment.[60]

Broughton proposed a more liberal system than Scott, who had insisted
on the National System with its strong catechetical bias; and a cheaper
one: £28 for boarders (Scott suggested £30 rising to £100 in the upper
forms) and £8 for day-scholars (Scott proposed £14 rising to £30).
'Education in New South Wales bids fair to be as easy of attainment ...
as in Scotland', commented the *Gazette*. In a colony where a man's
labour returned 3s 10d a day—a week's wages in Lancashire—and bread
and meat cost half what an Englishman paid, who could not afford 3s
a week to send a son to a good school? Broughton's fees were about
half the £50–£60 charged by the colony's private educationalists.[61]

Broughton asked Darling to press for royal patronage of the proposed
system of schools. One day, he said, New South Wales could be studded

with grammar schools honouring the House of Hanover much as Edward VI and the House of Tudor were honoured in England as the founders of its modern grammar schools: 'a design ... calculated ... to have a powerful effect in preserving this Colony for a long series of Years in cheerful dependence upon the Crown of Great Britain'. Moreover, it permitted Broughton the use of the title 'The King's Schools'; attractive partly for its sentimental recollection of Canterbury but more because it signified that the monarchy had extended to the dominions its patronage of the cause which sustained in unity churchmen and secular learning.[62]

Darling approved the plans and Broughton expected ready Colonial Office acceptance.[63] He proposed nothing more exclusive than what had appeared in Lord Brougham's Education Bill of the 1820s, which allowed the Established Church to supervise schools but by law removed all religious sectarian material from the syllabus. Now Brougham was a Whig, and darling of the rowdy colonial patriots who ate and drank to a future without governors.[64] Could Broughton have offered more?

The reverend dissenter who edited the *Gazette* thought not. The grammar schools were solidly Christian but without signs of bigotry or exclusiveness, and Presbyterians and dissenters could attend them without sacrifice of conscience, he wrote; 'Further than this they could not expect an Episcopalian body to go'. Shareholders of the Sydney College, however, attacked the scheme, fearing Sydney could not sustain two grammar schools. 'Worthy Mr Broughton's High Church college is better for such old fashioned folk who are a century behind the rest of the world in religious and political light', jibed one. Another raised an alarm: 'It is not said indeed that the whole course of education will necessarily be Episcopalian; but it is too evidently implied and understood, to be doubted for a moment'.[65] Broughton genuinely disappointed some shareholders of the Sydney College. They believed he would have joined them but for the intervention of a remnant of 'colonial priestcraft' from the Scott era. In the face of domestic clerical opposition the meek archdeacon had dissolved into timidity, but that was soon forgiven him:

> This gentleman's character for 'true and undefiled religion' stands so high, that, as charity covers a multitude of sins, so his sterling worth as a real man of God, converts his very weakness into amiabilities. Thus it was with Macquarie—thus it was with Brisbane—thus it is with Mr Broughton.[66]

Broughton never entertained the liberal sentiments towards Sydney College that E. S. Hall imagined; though the trustees of the old Sydney Free Public Grammar School may have hoped he would supply the backing Scott had denied them. Yet Broughton suffered his own disappointments in the matter. He had wanted Lang, the colony's Presbyterian chaplain, on the board of management of the King's Schools. The two men, in an exchange of opinion about Christian education, found themselves in total agreement. They shared, too, a vision of the colony's destiny, under divine Providence, to give law, language and a Christian civilization to the East. But Broughton behaved too secretively.

Lang was eleven years his junior and without experience as a school-master. Broughton neither divulged the details of his scheme nor confided to Lang that his name was actually on the list of a prospective board of management. Lang professed goodwill towards the venture at first; but without firsthand knowledge of its workings or certainty of a place in its government, he found himself easily persuaded by other Presby-terians, so he alleged, that the scheme lacked sound liberal safeguards. Broughton might be of a liberal mind, but would his successor? Presby-terians might share in the management of the schools, but would this amount to a genuine influence over their affairs? Presbyterians feared they would be unequal partners of the Established Church, and 'mere puppets in her train'.[67]

So in early January 1830, while Broughton was up country, Lang quit his connection with the archdeacon. He turned to Darling for land to found a Presbyterian college, but was refused. He next courted the trustees of the Sydney College; and finding them receptive to a suggestion for adding bible reading and prayer to the classroom threw in his lot with them. Here were men who listened to Lang; indeed, he soon boasted of having plucked higher education single-handed from the grip of 'the exclusives and the incapables': the Established Church and the bunch of indolent trustees who had ruined the first Sydney Free Public Grammar School and were on the way to confounding the second. Moreover, Lang found riding between the chief justice and Sir John Jamison at the head of the procession on 26 January a more dignified pastime than loitering in the antechamber to Broughton's study.[68]

Unfortunately Lang's co-operation was exchanged for his enmity. The Presbyterian predilection for finding a Laud in every set of gaiters convinced Lang that Broughton, if personally liberal, was not part of a liberal system; and must be watched. So Broughton acquired his first colonial adversary.

On 10 February 1830 Darling despatched the plans for the King's Schools to the Colonial Office, and Broughton boarded H.M.S. *Crocodile* for Hobart where he was welcomed quietly and soberly on 19 February. 'He declined any of those noisy demonstrations, which would have so delighted his predecessor', commented the *Australian* still chained to its hate for Scott. But Hobart was not sore against Scott, and merely expressed relief that the vacancy had been 'so ably and in so superior a manner supplied'.[69]

The small southern community took seriously Broughton's earlier comments to the Sydney clergy that Christianity could subdue the barbarism of the Aboriginals, and invited him to proceed. The settlers had tried friendship and firearms, and failed: no white settler felt safe and no Aboriginal was safe. But, curiously, in repeating his charge to the southern clergy Broughton omitted all reference to the ameliorating power of Christianity. The *Hobart Town Courier* promptly published the full text of the Sydney charge.[70] So Broughton gave Lieutenant-Governor George Arthur a report on the Aboriginals for his Executive Council: stay away from tribal waterholes; avoid hunting-grounds; shoot only if attacked; and bring over some of the more peaceful mainland

Aboriginals as pacifiers. Arthur liked that; but Darling vetoed the plan:
'In opening a communication between the natives of the two colonies,
the hostile spirit of the one could scarcely fail of being communicated
to the other'.[71] Arthur asked for a special prayer instead. Broughton
denied it him: 'Are we entitled to think that God will vouchsafe to us extraordinary means when those which he placed within our reach have not
been diligently employed?' So Arthur decided to form a bushman's
army and round up the Aboriginals. 'My God, subdue their rancour,'
cried Broughton, and gave Arthur his prayer.[72]

One event marred the archdeacon's visit. On Monday 19 April Mary
McLauchlan, mother of two children, was hanged for the infant murder
of her third child while in detention at the Female Factory. She was
the first woman executed in Van Diemen's Land, and her case agitated
the whole colony. The Executive Council hesitated to confirm the
sentence, with Arthur and two of the other three members of Council,
influenced by a letter from the jury, disposed towards leniency. That
was Friday 16 April. Overnight everything changed. When the Executive
Council reassembled at 2 p.m. on Saturday Mary McLauchlan had
only a minor councillor to plead for her. What changed Arthur's attitude?
In the Executive Council on Friday 16 April Arthur stated his desire
to take as precedent the practice of the Executive Council of New South
Wales in the handling of female prisoners capitally convicted. Who
better to ask than his house-guest, Broughton, fresh back from a country
visit? Broughton probably declined to discuss Mary McLauchlan's fate
as he refused to attend the Executive Council in Sydney for the review
of capital convictions. However, he could tell Arthur, from a report
to the Executive Council in Sydney last December, that infant exposure
at the Parramatta Female Factory had increased alarmingly; and the
popular plea to spare Mary McLauchlan because her crime was a rare
one was unhappily false. Whatever event turned mercy from Mary
McLauchlan on the night of 16 April, she went to the gallows while
Broughton resided in the town, and under circumstances which suggest
that a firm plea for mercy could have saved her.[73]

Broughton repaid Arthur's hospitality with a load of plants and grafts
from Sydney; but he had found the lieutenant-governor somewhat
humourless, a little self-righteous and puritanical. Arthur's conversations
tended to become complaints. He groaned unendingly of vile convict
behaviour. 'But are *we* so pure?' Broughton asked him.[74] He apologized
for the spirited behaviour of the young at the archdeacon's farewell
party; but Broughton chided him with envy at the loss of his own youthful
gaiety. He complained that official duties too often forced him to preside
at festivities that warred against a proper cultivation of the spirit. Broughton warned him against being over scrupulous: 'Many persons I have
known to exercise themselves with scruples which to the best of my
judgment were unnecessary; nor indeed have I found the ascetic disposition favourable to the growth of any of the virtues except temperance'.[75]

This was the temperate man of mild character and modest appearance
whom the colonists welcomed in 1829 and 1830. His origins were obscure

and he seemed only a little above the ordinary; and that pleased them. His accomplishments, as far as could be learned in so short a time, lay in things purely ecclesiastical. He preached well, and they liked that. He had an enthusiasm, but it seemed to be for the things above; and they liked that too. They could look after the things below. Some thought him a little dated in his ideas, but he was such a welcome relief after Scott that men wanted to get along with him. However, he must understand, they said, that where his ways were not their ways there would be ample room for both. This was a new land. Broughton noted this and kept his peace.

3

The Darling Years:
Prospects Better than Progress

A clergyman has an opportunity here of rendering himself
the instrument of great good to a great number of souls.

Broughton September 1831

Broughton's return from Van Diemen's Land ended a round of tours
designed to acquaint him with the general conditions of his immense
archdeaconry. At the beginning of June 1830 he settled down amidst
general goodwill to deal with the problems of the church and to fulfil
the broader obligations of his office.

His role on the Executive Council troubled him. Sharing in the management of colonial affairs meant tightening the rope around the necks
of the more wretched victims of colonial life; for at more meetings than
not, capital cases were put under review along with the other business.
Broughton did not like this and had once condemned Archbishop Laud
for participating in the administration of rigorous justice when his
office did not strictly require it. Since four others sat on the Executive
Council Broughton declined after 7 October to attend meetings reviewing
capital cases.[1]

In doing this Broughton cut his attendance by half and considerably
sacrificed his political influence, for the Executive Council, by virtue
of the secrecy imposed on its meetings and its right of prior consultation
with the governor, exercised a significant sway over local administrative
decisions and legislative proposals. It was also inconvenient, and Broughton found himself submitting his own urgent ecclesiastical business
before the Council in writing, as happened on 1 February when a chaplain
undertaking relief work in Sydney fell into desperate need of assistance
with house rent.[2] Darling, who once opposed Scott's successor sitting
on either Council, so welcomed the assistance Broughton gave that he
decided to readjust procedure to accommodate Broughton's susceptibili-
ties. The Council either reviewed capital cases at special sittings or
placed them first on the agenda, and Broughton entered the chamber
after they had been dealt with. From mid-1830 Broughton shared fully
in the general business of the Executive Council which, so long as Darling
governed, handled more of the colony's affairs than the Legislative
Council.[3]

35

Legislative Council business was more routine, and Broughton diligently attended interminable debates on insolvent debtors, stray dogs,
how best to collect custom dues or slaughter cattle, and occasionally
a matter, such as the control of liquor sales, for which he felt a deeper
concern. He served on a variety of subcommittees. One on immigration
interested him, but the obligation to accept a fair share of the mundane
matters found him enquiring into the problems of financing new roads
into Woolloomooloo and taking sheaves of evidence on the need for
breakwaters and quays. He became knowledgeable on roads and was
dubbed Botany Bay's Macadam.[4]

Occasionally more lively issues arose. One, a Newspaper Restriction
Bill, was passed in January 1830 to banish persons twice convicted of
publishing material bringing into contempt the governor or his government, or who excited colonists to alter by unlawful means the established
order in church and state. The measure, more severe than its counterpart
in Castlereagh's infamous Six Acts, originated in outraged tempers
following an attempted assassination of Darling in December 1829.
The would-be assassin, J. D. Shelly, was alleged to have kept company
with Hall the editor and to have fallen a victim to the unrestrained passion
of that publisher's attacks on the governor. Broughton saw every reason
for banishing a menace like Hall should he persist in his inflammatory
activities. If he had stirred one man to attempt murder, might not he
exite a mob to riot? Broughton voted for the bill, as did Forbes the
guardian of press liberties; but he opposed, unsuccessfully, a provision
that required proprietors of newspapers to lodge a bond with the government to be forfeited upon conviction of a libel. The provision was directed
at the impecunious Hall. Hall could not meet the required sum and no
creditor in Sydney was foolhardy enough to loan it to him. Hall had
either to retire from business or flout the law. He flouted the law. Darling,
after waiting years to get Hall, swooped in the Executive Council to
have Hall prosecuted to the utmost extent of the new Act. If Darling
could not put Hall out of business, he would have him out of the way.
To Broughton the Act, designed to punish libels, was misused if applied
to drive the unconvicted from business. But Darling won; and Broughton
recorded in the minutes of the Council that he objected to the provision
in general and to the enforcement of the penalty against Hall.[5]

Another lively matter concerned trial by jury and aroused more
interest. When Broughton arrived in September 1829 he found the
Legislative Council debating what qualifications to require of the jurors
to be empanelled under section 8 of 9 Geo. IV, c. 83, the Act passed at
Westminster in July 1828 for the administration of justice in New South
Wales. This Act provided for a civil jury in civil actions before the
Supreme Court where a plaintiff or a defendant requested it and the
presiding judge could discern nothing in it likely to prejudice an impartial decision. It was a small concession written into the Act as an
afterthought, and the Colonial Office meant it as a pledge that more
would follow as soon as colonists showed their fitness to receive it. Colonial
radicals received it as a disappointing moiety; and colonial conservatives
looked upon it as an unsettling concession which left colonists to decide

A VIEW taken at EATON. by F. Dighton

DR KEATE,
Incumbent of Hartley Wespall
and
Headmaster of Eton.

REVEREND EDWARD COLERIDGE,
Housemaster at Eton.

the equally prickly question of who should sit on the juries, an issue which divided them as deeply as the wisdom of the civil juries themselves.[6]

When the matter first came before the Legislative Council on 2 September 1829 opposing parties divided behind Forbes and the retiring Archdeacon Scott. Forbes, dissenting from an earlier opinion, advised the colony to adhere strictly to British practice and open jury lists to all with the stipulated property qualification unless they were serving a sentence or had been convicted of an infamous crime. The Colonial Office did not require this conformity, and Scott proposed to disqualify for life all persons brought to the colony under sentence of transportation. Scott put this motion to the Council on 15 September 1829 and Forbes moved to have it debated the following day. It was Scott's swan-song. The following day Broughton sat in Scott's council seat.[7]

John Macarthur carried on Scott's fight while Scott, describing himself simply as a member of the Light Company, sustained his opposition from outside and risking, in his opinion, assassination. On 16 September, immediately following Broughton's swearing in, Macarthur moved an adjournment of debate on the Jury Bill for a month, possibly hoping, with Broughton a guest in Scott's house, to win the new archdeacon's co-operation. He failed. Broughton was fresh to the colony and did not understand it, Scott later commented. When debate resumed Forbes spoke for two hours on a modified motion admitting emancipists as jurymen but excluding those convicted of a felony in the colony after transportation. Broughton seconded and 'decidedly supported' the motion, and the *Gazette* burst into praise: Mr Broughton had 'espoused the liberal side'.[8]

Forbes agreed to a second compromise. He proposed a £200 property qualification, his opponents £500, and both settled for £300. The compromise indicated that neither Forbes nor Macarthur commanded a clear majority and Broughton possibly helped to reconcile their opposition as the details of the bill were thrashed out between 16 and 24 September outside the Council. That Broughton should have been nominated to second Forbes's motion and, after only two weeks in the colony, elected to a seat on the subcommittee to draw up the final draft of the bill suggests he played more than a nominal role. Moreover, he brought McLeay over with him, and for one bright moment colonists glimpsed the colonial secretary posing as the friend of emancipists. For Broughton the bill involved no compromise of principle. He believed one criminal conviction could easily arise from a temporary weakness and ought to be forgotten in time, but a second conviction pointed to a deeper perversity and could not easily be overlooked.[9]

The compromise united the Council but stirred 'the people outside' to demand further constitutional concessions. Darling revealed that it was within his power to authorize the extension of civil juries to criminal cases and invited a written opinion from each member of the Legislative Council on the subject. Broughton submitted one of ten opinions opposed to any further immediate concessions, but for reasons quite different from all others. Most queried the propriety of trying alleged criminals before an ex-criminal. Broughton did not. He admitted emancipists

had leaned towards the convict class in many public matters, but where
life and property were at stake Broughton was confident self-interest
would keep them on the side of justice:

> ... knowing how necessary it is for the security of their own persons
> and properties that the guilty should not escape punishment, I do not
> think that the emancipists would suffer their verdict to be influenced
> by consideration of the class to which the accused belonged, nor
> that they should feel any due reluctance to condemn, when the evidence
> plainly required it.[10]

What troubled Broughton was a category of criminal activity peculiar
to the age—public disturbance and riot. Here the self-interest of the
emancipists might put them on side against the government. Broughton
invited Darling to consider a crisis in New South Wales similar to that
at Manchester in 1819, where, in an effort to maintain its own authority,
the government was forced to prosecute those who disturbed the peace.
Could the mixed population of emancipists, native born and free settlers
be expected to furnish civil juries who would bring an impartial mind
to the trial of such cases? Broughton doubted it:

> I am persuaded that the sentiment of obedience is so imperfect here
> that all restraint, beyond what is necessary for the repression of personal
> violence, finds little support in public opinion. There is a predisposition
> to believe that every man, who sets himself in opposition to such
> restraints, is morally innocent, though he may be legally guilty. Such
> persons are sure to have a perverted popular feeling on their side;
> and, if, under the influence of general excitement, juries should be found
> resolutely predetermined not to convict, the Government may be
> braved with impunity, and must be exposed to embarrassments.[11]

Reluctantly, Broughton advised Darling that, being wise to the antinomian spirit evident to some extent in all classes in the colony and having
regard to the jeopardy in which that could place general security, the
colony would benefit from the retention of military juries for a time.
He agreed with Forbes that military juries had served the ends of justice
well, but disagreed that their verdicts, however correct, were often held
suspect by the people. 'I cannot but think', Broughton reassured Darling,
'that upon questions accompanied with party-feeling, the verdicts of
the military are most likely to recommend themselves to the approbation
of impartial men.' Broughton's opinion had the support of people's
feet if not their words: of the 420 civil actions brought into courts in
1830 after the passage of the Jury Bill only 19 chose to go before the new
civil juries.[12]

Broughton dismissed the fear that as the number of colonial born
overtook the English born, a new race unappreciative of the blessing of
trial by jury would take over the colony and British institutions be lost
to it for ever. Broughton had dedicated his administration to the opposite
end. His King's Schools were to cultivate an affection for British institutions, and he recommended the retention of military juries as a 'temporary
expedient' to maintain the stability necessary for those institutions to
take root. 'I should without hesitation advise the immediate discontinu-

ance of military juries', Broughton added by way of a rider to his opinion, 'if I could be persuaded that through their partial adoption there was any danger of the Colony being ultimately deprived of Trial by Jury according to the regular constitutional form.'[13]

The need for such temporary expedients would vanish as education was more widely diffused, McLeay said. It would disappear as immigration closed the gap between free and freed, John Macarthur and Richard Jones added. To Broughton it was neither a question of free against freed nor simply of education, but of an overall moral improvement in the colony. To hasten that happy day Broughton had much to busy him around Sydney where free and freed were drawn into degradations which rendered them unfit to exercise the general responsibilities of free citizens under English institutions.[14]

The seamy side of Sydney's life greeted newcomers. More likely than not they took their first lodgings in one of the large boarding-houses close by the wharves in the older parts of the town. Those who could afford it went to one of the better inns, but even there the effects of hot, fiery, East India rum on the colonial thirst soon became evident. What they did not hear or see for themselves, idle gossip, the bane of a colony deprived of a theatre according to a former colonial surgeon, added and inflated. The press made its own sorry contribution; the filth and abominations that the English got rid of in underground sewers, Lang once said, was spread on Sydney dinner-tables in the guise of police reports.[15]

By June 1830 Broughton had confirmed the very worst rumours about the Rocks area he had come to know in journeying to and from his residence. Travellers knew it as the St Giles of Sydney Town, a place for the poorest and the lowest. Broughton knew it as a retreat for the perpetrators of almost every violation of the law; prostitution and theft were rife among its inhabitants, adultery and drunkenness its habitual occupation. The people there, if not ignorant of all religion, lived in total disregard of it. 'The only difference which I have found to exist between the Sabbath and other days', Broughton told Darling, 'is that, the people being then all at home and unemployed, there is a greater prevalence than ordinary of all sorts of disorder and wickedness.'[16]

Though he had never before contacted this class of people, Broughton decided to take the lead in evangelizing its worst areas. He found an unoccupied stone building to turn into a chapel at the northern end of Prince Street, where life was roughest, and planned to preach there morning and afternoon every Sunday he was in Sydney. The most useful of these sermons he would publish and distribute to aid the clergy in their own work among the more reprobate classes up bush. Broughton also asked Darling for a block of land for a school in Cumberland Street in the heart of the Rocks area. He hoped by the end of 1830 that this depressed and hitherto neglected area would have received the first material benefits of his taking control of the affairs of religion and education.[17]

Darling was enthusiastic and promised to hire the building in Prince Street for three years, outfit it for worship, and provide a chaplain to assist Broughton in the work. That was June 1830. Within two months the plan lay in ruins. In September Darling received a chilling reminder that the Colonial Office would sanction no deviation from the rules governing ecclesiastical expenditure as set down by Sir George Murray on 25 May 1829; that meant Broughton must first raise public subscriptions covering half the cost of the venture before any grant could be made from the colonial treasury. This was beyond the resources at Broughton's disposal, and Darling could do nothing more than refer the matter to the Colonial Office for special consideration. Within a year of his arrival Broughton tasted the bitter colonial reality of London's doctrinaire approach to the problems of the colonial church, and the frustration of trying to resolve urgent problems by the long sea route that separated them.[18]

In theory the British government had arranged for the ecclesiastical establishment to reign self-sufficient on the funds of the Church and Schools Corporation; and, as Scott soon learned, the inability of the Corporation to make good its position was pitilessly disregarded at the Colonial Office. During the declining months of his administration Scott concentrated on securing land for the Corporation so that he might retire consoled by the knowledge that his successor had inherited a situation materially better than he had ever enjoyed. He succeeded. In 1829 the Corporation received 419 199 acres of land. When Broughton first met the trustees of the Corporation on 1 December 1829 he witnessed the adoption of grandiose plans for the development of a whole village, to be named Hebersham in memory of Bishop Heber, on the Corporation's property at Rooty Hill. The Corporation seemed on the verge of prosperity.[19]

Not, however, for the first time did the right hand of the colony not know what the left hand of the Colonial Office was doing. While Scott badgered Darling to speed up the survey and transfer of the land, the Colonial Office studied the history of a similar venture in Canada where, under a scheme established in 1791, the protestant clergy were entitled to one seventh of all land grants for the support of their work. By 1828 the Canadian clergy derived an income of £930 yearly from 488 594 acres, and spent most of it collecting the rent. The experiment was deemed a failure, and in July 1828 a committee of the House of Commons recommended 'in the strongest manner the propriety of securing for the future any provision which may be deemed necessary for the religious community . . . by *other* means than by a reservation of one seventh of the land.' This recommendation bore fruit on 3 December 1829 when Broughton learned that the king had revoked the letters patent setting up the Corporation in New South Wales. Scott by this time was shipwrecked at the Swan River and blissfully unaware that his successor's financial plight was as uncertain and as restricted as his had been.[20]

Broughton required only a modest sum to launch the Rocks chapel; unfortunately he had less than a modest sum at his disposal. Nominal rents on land already leased by the Corporation amounted to £834 11s 5d annually, but poor seasonal conditions had halved the Corporation's actual receipts. In 1829 the Corporation had managed to raise a further £2401 17s 3d for urgent works, by the sale of small blocks of glebe land

and pastures attached to the orphanages. The opportunity of raising similar sums by the sale of remaining glebes, which in Sydney brought a good price, was frustrated by Darling's rigid interpretation of Murray's despatch as placing an embargo on all the Corporation's transactions including land sales pending fresh instructions. In mid-1830 Broughton's one hope for additional funds arose from the recent rains and the opportunity this gave the Corporation to press for the payment of arrears, amounting to £3911 17s 3d. That would take time.[21]

Meanwhile Broughton found other causes to occupy his attention. The Australian Aboriginals' wanton existence around Sydney upset him. Natives seemed either to wander aimlessly around the town's streets or to drink with undivided purpose and lie down stupid where their powers deserted them. Such was the white settlers' malevolent influence; and his fitful attempts at benevolence were hardly less degrading. The 'annual conference' between the governor and the natives at Parramatta was the principal occasion when white men distributed their bounty to the older black inhabitants. In 1830 this fell on 6 January and Broughton joined the governor's party as a spectator. From midday onwards he watched as 269 natives feasted on roast beef, pudding, and 'a reasonable quantum of grog', performed a corroboree by way of thanksgiving, and were then dismissed with a benediction of blankets. It was the Feast of the Epiphany, a day Christians celebrated the joyful surrender of old world superstitions to the light that shone in Jesus Christ. In New South Wales, the white settler, heir to centuries of that light, had abandoned the native to eating and drinking because he believed that in him he had found the darkness that had overcome the light.[22]

Churchmen had a hand in this. 'Mr Marsden considers them uncivilizable', one Christian gentleman bluntly told the Church Missionary Society (CMS) in a desperate attempt to forestall an Aboriginal mission likely to detract funds from the Maori mission. Marsden promised to keep a look out for projects likely to benefit the Aboriginals but never found one after 1820. Scott came, determined to do better. In characteristic fashion he commissioned a searching five-month survey of country areas only to conclude that the colonists were clearly united against any attempt to civilize the natives as too difficult, too expensive, too slow and of trivial benefit only. Only the Reverend Richard Hill did not succumb to pessimism having read in Christ's own teachings that in Heaven there would be representatives of every kindred, tongue, people and nation. He encouraged Scott to employ a man competent to lay down the rudiments of the Aboriginal language. 'Till this is done', Hill said, 'nothing I believe effectual can be done.'[23]

Judged by such criterion the Reverend Lancelot Threlkeld's work was of decisive value. Threlkeld, a Independent minister, had turned to working among the Aboriginals after failing to find any contentment on the protestant missions in the Pacific region. By 1827 he had published his initial attempt at reducing an Aboriginal dialect to written form. He attributed this success to the unique arrangement of his mission farm by Lake Macquarie where, with steady gratuitous handouts of grain, he had settled wandering natives for periods sufficiently long to be useful for linguistic investigations. By this same means he had spent £1800 in two years and greatly displeased his sponsor the London Missionary Society. The Society ordered him to cut expenses; but Threlkeld, full of the imperious certainty of one on a divine mission, defiantly drew bills as lavish as ever. The Society finally dishonoured these, threw Threlkeld into the Supreme Court as a debtor, and forced him, around August 1827, to temporarily abandon his mission.[24]

The Reverend C. P. Wilton, the chaplain at the Field of Mars and a Fellow of the Cambridge Philosophical Society, a scholar of talent with a weakness for debts, understood the value of Threlkeld's work and the harrowing annoyance of impatient creditors. He stood by Threlkeld, and called on the government to exercise a magnanimous spirit and provide the missionary with sufficient means to continue his linguistic investigations, if not his mission. No one listened. Meanwhile the London Missionary Society withdrew all support from Threlkeld and collapsed the mission at Lake Macquarie. When Broughton arrived in Sydney in 1829 he found all organized missionary effort at a standstill. Instead, the discomforting challenge to preach the Gospel of Jesus Christ had been supplanted by a goodwill vote in the colonial estimates of about £400 annually for blankets, provisions and clothing.[25]

It soon became evident to Marsden that the new archdeacon contemplated the re-establishment of a mission, and he tried hard to dissuade him from it. This was the counsel of despair Broughton repudiated in his Primary Visitation charge. But before the faintest glimmer of a new mission appeared Darling called in Broughton to sort out Threlkeld's future. The London Missionary Society had decided to hand over the assets at Lake Macquarie to the support of anybody willing to carry on Threlkeld's work. In January 1830 Darling asked Broughton to decide if Threlkeld's work was sound, and whether the government could support him without incurring the heavy costs that broke the spirit of the London Missionary Society.[26]

In the meantime Threlkeld approached the archdeacon independently to show off his linguistic achievements. Broughton's interest caught fire. He carefully examined the missionary's system of orthography, and pronounced it sound. Threlkeld's progress in translating the Gospels quite delighted him, and he suggested translating a few pages of the Book of Common Prayer into a native dialect. 'Our Church and Nation are under an obligation to make an effort for the moral and religious Improvement of the people whose Country we have occupied', Broughton wrote to Darling. The finest beginning he could suggest was for the government to grant Threlkeld an annual stipend of £150 for five years to put the Word of God into the native tongue. He recommended backdating Threlkeld's salary to the time his own London Missionary Society cut him off to help him out of debt, and that the contentious farm, which Threlkeld insisted was an essential part of his scheme, should be continued and tilled by four convict labourers.[27]

Marsden gritted his teeth to see Threlkeld so gloriously raised up. 'Archdeacon Broughton is an excellent man, and is anxious to do good to the Aborigines', the ageing chaplain wrote home to his friends. 'And from his wish to benefit them, will countenance Mr Threlkeld or any other person who may be likely in his opinion to promote this object.' Broughton more than countenanced Threlkeld. In the missionary's hour of need, after the London Missionary Society had abandoned him and before the government had adopted him, the archdeacon, though burdened with a £500 personal debt to the colonial treasury, dipped into his pocket and gave generously to the relief of the beleaguered pastor and his family. It saved the mission from immediate collapse and Threlkeld never forgot the gesture.[28]

While Broughton strove to excite a new compassion in the colonial government the Colonial Office in London underwent a change of heart. The mean mood of 1827, which had bluntly shelved all Aboriginal work until after the colonists' needs had been fully satisfied, gave way to new vision. No undertaking to civilize the Aboriginals with 'a fair prospect of success' would be permitted in future to languish for want of pecuniary aid. The man behind the change was no idle babbler, James Stephen told a friend. Sir George Murray the Secretary of State for the Colonies was the man, and in November 1829 he offered £500 from the colonial treasury to any missionary organization willing to place two or more teachers along the primitive fringe of the colony's settlement. James Stephen, who worked at the Colonial Office and was a zealous advocate of the Church Missionary Society (CMS), secured first option for that organization and a guarantee that it would be free to write its own terms for the control and conduct of the mission.[29]

The CMS accepted and found itself treading the rough and shoddy path to Australia. Murray fell into a dispute with the Bishop of London over the type of missionaries to be sent out: Murray favoured laymen of humble circumstances without a regular profession to retreat to in the face of difficulties; the Bishop of London insisted that without a priest in Holy Orders the mission could not offer full apostolic rites to the Aboriginals. They compromised, and selected a priest and a layman. Before either departed, the Whigs took office and had second thoughts about the project. They stalled it; abandoned it; then restored it. But it became a CMS venture with an annual government subsidy limited to £500, rather than an official undertaking in which the Society acted as the government's agents and the work was capable, in Murray's terms, of 'indefinite expansion'.[30]

Broughton knew nothing of this and prepared independently for the colony's renewed missionary endeavour. He subscribed to the CMS locally to assist its New Zealand mission but, being an SPG man, declined to join the Society's local corresponding committee. In February 1830 under pressure from McLeay he relented, and the gratifying news sped to New Zealand and London. Broughton realized there was room in New South Wales for a united effort between high churchmen and evangelicals; and he foresaw a day when the CMS, the SPG, and the colonial government would all unite under *his* direction in recruiting men and money for the advancement of the religious and material condition of the Aboriginal people.[31]

By mid-1831 Broughton was ready to begin. After two journeys inland to assay the countryside he asked for a disbanded convict settlement at Wellington Valley, 100 miles from Sydney, as the first mission station. Darling agreed. By a happy coincidence Johann Handt, the first of the new missionaries, landed in Sydney. Handt, a layman and Lutheran by confession, found Broughton attentive and in good spirits. Broughton took charge of Handt's arrangements and insisted he await the second missionary's arrival; then, as Handt recalled, the archdeacon said 'he himself would, if circumstances permit, proceed with us to the place [Wellington Valley] and arrange things properly'.[32]

According to letters Handt carried Broughton was not to take control. Handt had directions to report to Hill, chaplain of St James church and local secretary to the CMS, and to take instructions only from the Society's local committee. All difficulties were to be referred directly to the Society's London headquarters. Hill revealed these instructions and Broughton dismissed them as the zealous scribblings of a badly informed officer of the Society. They conflicted with the governor's official instructions to consult the archdeacon in all matters affecting the Aboriginals, and stood at variance with ancient apostolic order where, from the church's beginning, it had been the custom to have all missionary effort in a single area radiate from a bishop at its centre. Broughton had anticipated an arrangement whereby the CMS would choose men for a work on which the government would spend £500, but that the missionaries would be placed under the archdeacon as chaplains on their arrival. A letter to London would set matters right.[33]

Hill stood firm. The ways of the CMS were not the ways of the SPG. 'The Church Missionary Society is a pure and holy institution, administered only by those who know and practise truth'; and it had never automatically submitted to the governing authority of bishops, archdeacons, or of any church dignitary. The colonial corresponding committee believed that as firmly as the Society's London directors.[34] Hill quarrelled with the archdeacon but remained firm. 'It does not appear to me the duty of the corresponding committee to give up the Missionaries to the Archdeacon', Hill wrote home to London after cross words with Broughton; and he called a meeting for 8 November 1831 to plan Handt's future.[35]

Broughton's wrath broke. As a member of the committee he was astounded to find himself invited to join with his ecclesiastical subordinates and begin deliberations on matters he had already settled. 'Entertaining a persuasion that the superintendence and direction of a mission for the conversion of heathens cannot, without a breach of the order of the church, be committed to any other than the Bishop of the Diocese within which it is undertaken,' he wrote back to the committee on receipt of his invitation, '. . . I beg to decline attending the meeting of the Committee of the Church Missionary Society at which you propose to take this subject into consideration.' The corresponding committee was disappointed, and Broughton terminated his association with the Society.[36]

Broughton faced a bitter moment. Whether Handt's letter reflected an error, or conveyed in accurate terms the arrangements the Church Missionary Society had agreed to in London, the same result followed: another of Broughton's ventures ground to a halt. Already primary education had ceased to expand with the suspension of the Church and Schools Corporation. Religious growth had withered under the same curse, and the Rocks chapel had been swept into oblivion the moment it was to be opened. Now, after eighteen months of planning and investigation, Broughton had to put aside his scheme for Aboriginal advancement and await the outcome of a tedious exchange of letters with London.

Then another blow fell. Lang had left for England in August 1830 disgusted at the slow progress of the Sydney College; 'It is no part of the colonial system to act merely after having resolved to do so', he lamented. Lang feared that, for all his deft footwork, episcopacy would have the first school and still 'realise her fond prediction, uttered in the dark days of Archdeacon Scott and the Corporation, "I shall sit as a Queen, and see no sorrow"'.[37] To kill the ennui of his long journey Lang drafted the prospectus of another college where Latin and Greek gave way to useful colonial knowledge, and on 28 December 1830 forwarded the prospectus to the Colonial Office with a request for a £10 000 loan. Within a fortnight the Colonial Office promised £3500 and an assurance of more should the project prosper. Lang thanked the Lord; but the essence of his success was largely in his timing. Goderich had just assumed the seals of the Colonial Office and, as he had soon to confess, was imperfectly acquainted with the backlog of business. He knew nothing of the plans for the King's Schools or of the Sydney College which Murray had recommended for a government grant. To Lord Howick, the parliamentary under-secretary with whom Lang had most to do, the scheme embodied every virtue of nascent Whig colonial policy: It combined progress in the colony with the emigration of redundant English artisans without cost to Britain, or, finally, to the colonial treasury; for Lang's policy was to employ the £10 000 in bringing out artisans who would build the school to repay their passages. The plan Lang presented on 28 December 1830 was approved without enquiry or investigation; and on 12 January 1831 a letter left the Colonial Office instructing Darling to advance Lang the sum agreed upon.[38]

Lang's success became Broughton's despair. News of the *coup* preceded Lang's return to the colony, and Broughton learned of it before hearing of the fate of his own schools. This ruffled him. But two other despatches upset him more. In one the Secretary of State forbade the allocation of one penny to the Rocks chapel prior to a public subscription being raised; in the other he instructed Darling to place £1500 at Lang's disposal immediately he returned so that Lang could begin to build his college while launching a public appeal. 'Experience has proved that Men are prone to undervalue that which is too easily obtained', Goderich wrote to console Broughton in his disappointment; and left the archdeacon to ponder what, in recent years, had been more easily obtained than Lang's first £1500.[39]

But it was on 13 October 1831, when Lang sailed into the harbour

on board the ship *Stirling Castle* with its store of Scottish immigrants,
that Broughton realized how radically the position had changed. Lang
not only unloaded the artisans who would put up the walls of the college
but produced its masters; and he sent them out to deliver public lectures,
advertise their talent, and recruit the cream of the pupils awaiting higher
instruction. Being first in the colony was important, Broughton said.
He had investigated the demand for education and knew the situation
better than most. 'There is not room for two such undertakings at once',
he reported to London, and predicted the failure of one venture. 'By the
time the Masters of the King's Schools can arrive, Dr Lang will have
been able to obtain assurances of support for all or nearly all who have
children to be educated.'[40]

The *Gazette* sympathized with Broughton's disappointment, and
called on churchmen to 'rally around the Archdeacon' and await the
arrival of other masters. But Broughton was the first to understand
that this asked too much of parents. No one could reasonably be expected
to await the arrival of unknown instructors at some undetermined date
when a school, amply endowed and patronized by the government,
was open and ready to receive them. At the same time he washed his hands
of all responsibility for the prosperity of the King's Schools, and refused
to accept any liability for the loss in income which the masters would
suffer from depleted enrolments. He bluntly accused the Colonial
Office of gross discourtesy, and of handing the lead to a man whose
'tortuous course' in the whole matter of higher education would bring
him no credit and less respect.[41]

Broughton might complain but had no grounds on which to oppose
the grant, and on 8 November 1831 when the matter came before the
Legislative Council he attended and cast his vote for it.[42] It was the
gloomiest moment. Shortly afterwards the Reverend George Innes, an
Oxford graduate, stepped quietly ashore at Sydney. He had been chosen
master of one of the King's Schools. Once the Colonial Office had realized
its blunder in overlooking the King's Schools it went doubly quickly
about the business of appointing masters and had Innes in Sydney
before Lang dug the foundations of his college. Broughton rejoiced; and
realized in a twink that he might yet beat Lang to the start. He had
planned to renovate the crypt at St James church and put the first King's
School there, but abandoned this idea as too lengthy. Instead, he hired
rooms in the old subscription library in Pitt Street, and announced that
pupils would be enrolled from 2 January 1832. Lang fought back. He
assembled his friends in a council on 23 December, proclaimed the
existence of the Australian College, and announced that it would open
on 2 January 1832 in temporary premises at Mr Underhill's building
at Church Hill.[43]

To the colonists at large this holy competition could only do good.
Three colleges were better than two; it afforded parents a wider choice,
bestowed a more civilized image on the colony, and alerted the muse:

> Where'er I turn my gladdened eye,
> Prosperity extends her sway;

Her academic domes arise,
To spread the intellectual ray.[44]

Those who supported the Sydney College project were disappointed that their institution, first in the field and the only one with a permanent building under construction, should be the last to open. The *Australian*, however, did not anticipate much competition: 'We like the King's Schools ... but we anticipate little general good from their establishment.' The *Monitor* ran its eye over the curriculum and chuckled at the sight of Paley and Ovid side by side: 'We cannot understand how a College can teach religion and lewdness at one and the same time'. But for the supporters of the Sydney College the burning question was whether or not Lang had misled the Colonial Office into believing that his college was the same as the Sydney College. If so, had he scooped up for himself the bounty due to the other? As for Lang's title, the 'Australian College', the *Monitor* would not have a bar of it: 'We can allow *such* a title only to the *people's* College. The true Australian Catholic-like undeceptive College, is the Sydney College'.[45]

Amidst this banter Broughton announced the opening of a second King's School at Parramatta, and not a murmur was raised. Instead, there was a general feeling of relief that the Windsor, Richmond, Penrith, and Liverpool areas now had a school. Those principles of education from which so little good could be derived in Sydney were, apparently, expected to abound to the advantage of those who lived further inland.[46]

The unexpected opening of the King's Schools marked the high point in Broughton's achievement for 1831. The key to wider progress lay with the Church and Schools Corporation, and in 1831 its future was in doubt. The Tory government which created the Corporation in 1825 and suspended it in 1829 had promised the church an alternative source of funds. It found none. Instead, it confirmed the land grants already made to the church and put them under the management of a body of commissioners presided over by the archdeacon. The commissioners, however, could raise money but not spend it; they simply recommended how the governor might spend it. This arrangement banished the original Corporation's autonomy and opened the way for official interference.[47]

Broughton accepted the change without a murmur. By March 1831 he was eager to accommodate any reasonable arrangement which could dispel the general inactivity in ecclesiastical development. Darling co-operated better than ever; he promised the commissioners the remaining acres of Cumberland county and agreed to put surveyors to work carving out some good land in Bathurst, Durham and Northumberland counties. In June 1831 the reorganized Corporation seemed within grasp of prosperity. In July its fair prospects collapsed. Before any title-deeds had been handed over Darling received instructions to suspend all land grants, dismiss the commissioners, dissolve the Corporation, and return its lands to the Crown in as full and ample a manner as if they had never been granted. Churches and schools would live henceforth off annual treasury grants.[48]

In this manner Whig succession to power made its impact on the

colony and, in predictable fashion, carried off the property of the church
as its first victim. For years Whigs had displayed an open hostility to
ecclesiastical wealth, and delighted in counselling bishops that a church
which pursued purity in preference to property could afford to trust to
the affections of the people for its support. Goderich pushed the colonial
church half way to the Whig ideal and recommended Broughton trust
the treasury. In England Robert Southey, radical turned Tory, lampooned
such Whig sentimentality: 'Good principles enable men to suffer rather
than to act', he wrote. Broughton stood with him. The spirit of the age
was not with the church; and the archdeacon believed that any arrangement which saddled on the public purse an annually increasing expenditure for religion and education was destined to create a 'permanent
dissatisfaction'. The church which accepted this may do well in the
beginning, Broughton told Darling in his report of 1831, but eventually
it would find itself abandoned by a government forced to make peace
with its people.[49]

Broughton fought the change. When Darling put letters patent dissolving the Corporation before the Executive Council, Broughton
stalled their execution on the technical ground that letters patent could
alter the Corporation's constitution but only an Instrument of the King's
Privy Council could abolish it. Furthermore the lands of the Corporation
could never be resumed as if they had never been granted. Sections 36
and 37 of the Corporation's charter provided that, upon the termination
of the trust, lands resumed by the Crown must be disposed of as 'shall
appear most conducive to the maintenance and promotion of religion
and education of Youth in the Colony'. The judges of the Supreme
Court upheld Broughton's objections and the matter went back to
London.[50]

'Everything is unsettled', a bewildered clergyman William Cowper
wrote to his son at Oxford. 'The chaplains, I understand, are to be considered as the civil officers of Government.' Darling put the remaining
acres in Cumberland county up for sale, and Broughton composed the
plea which he hoped would reprieve the Corporation. He argued that
in an age of growing scepticism it would be impolitic to throw the church
on a government whose policies changed with the sentiments of the
people; he drew attention to the extraordinary situation of a colony
where the greater number of settlers came from the classes notorious
for their irreligion in England; and he questioned whether a secure,
alternative arrangement could be fashioned. He dared not suggest, as
those to whom he wrote dared not admit, that the government no longer
intended to secure the church its finance.[51]

Such arguments availed little: the sacred text for current colonial
policy was a report from the House of Commons in 1831 on colonial
finances.[52] Broughton studied its findings with dismay. The Corporation
had sinned greatly, in the eyes of its English masters, because its five
years of existence had brought the colonial treasury no relief. How
could it? Broughton asked. It spent its first two years waiting for land
and the last two under official suspension. In the one intervening year
with less than one-fiftieth of the colonial lands, and not the fabled one-

seventh, it could hardly be expected to produce instantly the large sums required to release the treasury from the cost of religion and education. Since such circumstances had prevented the king's instructions being punctually complied with in the colony, Broughton condemned as unjust any 'charge against the Trustees that they did not realise such an income as might enable them to dispense with pecuniary advances from the Government'. Moreover, there was 'no foundation in fact or in justice' for the complaint that the Corporation, by witholding its land in anticipation of future higher prices, had forced settlement into the bush. In the year 1828, which the report relied on for its facts and figures, the Corporation had been virtually landless. Yet, were it true, the government had only to require that the Corporation release its land on the same terms as the Crown. There were other means of regulating settlement short of dissolving the Corporation, Broughton argued.[53]

Broughton fought prejudice not reason; and prejudice had been the Corporation's foe from the beginning. The press had trumpeted the myth of the Corporation's land wealth till men everywhere believed it. 'All the reflections to which the Trustees have been subjected in this Country, have proceeded on the assumption that while they were applying for those advances [i.e. from the treasury], they had actually in possession a seventh of the territory', Broughton observed. 'The continual repetition of which assertion occasioned it to be very generally credited here, as it may also very probably have been by the Parliamentary Commissioners.'[54]

A brazen example of that prejudice had just appeared in a pamphlet by Lang. In London, in 1831, Lang had advised the Colonial Office that vast tracts of prime quality land, much of it belonging to the Corporation, lay unoccupied in the most accessible and eligible sections in and around Sydney. If sold it could finance artisan emigration and build many ventures like the Australian College. To overcome any reluctance by the Whigs to interfere with the Corporation's lands Lang passed on the information, which he said was not likely to have reached London, that the episcopal clergy were a mob of business men, who passed their time trading in land while their spiritual flocks languished for want of attention. Consequently colonial morals had reached an all-time low and religious observance was fast fading away. Worse still, the colonial youth murmured that the king had taken away their inheritance in the land their fathers had settled.[55]

Broughton exploded: 'He has preferred charges against the Corporation ... with the blind animosity of a political partisan'.[56] The *Gazette* concurred: Lang has injured the character of our youth, distorted the truth about the Corporation's running expenses, and in a most unseemly manner attacked his brother clergy behind their back before persons of high office 'whose displeasure might be the ruin of themselves and their families'.[57] The editor set the record straight:

It would be inferred from Dr Lang's putting, that they were perpetually immersed in business, like the managers of some large joint-stock company; that their pastoral duties were constantly interrupted by the drudgery of buying and selling; that they were more in the

counting house than in the pulpit ... Yet the simple fact is this—tha
the 'secularising' duty of the clerical Trustees consisted in *attendin,
a meeting once a quarter!* On one day in every three months ... fo
some two, three, or perhaps four hours, at the official board—t
hear reports, pass votes, and then quietly return to their pastora
labours.[58]

Since the Colonial Office had positively encouraged Lang's projec
subsequent to his laying these accusations, Broughton feared that the
had been accepted as fair and just comment. He therefore wanted th
matter set right where it began—at the Colonial Office. 'If there be an
foundation for the charge it must admit proof', he told Goderich; an
named the three clergymen who assisted him in such 'secular' affairs a
the superintendence of schools for the religious education of youth
providing for the maintenance and instruction of orphans and for settlin
them advantageously and honestly in life, the care of public charitie
and of devising facilities for public worship. They were Marsden, Cowpe
and Hill. 'I trust in justice to those gentlemen', Broughton continue
'your Lordship will have the goodness to call on Dr Lang to state 1
you, whether he knows or believes them to be, in the estimation of th
whole Colony, identified with secular pursuits.'[59] Indeed, only a ye
ago Broughton had intervened to prevent the clergy taking person
possession of land grants due to them for long service. He insisted c
all such lands being placed in the hands of lay trustees and develope
to provide an income payable to clergy in sickness or old age, or, mo
finally to their widows. By this means he took away not only the conce
for managing them, but the enticement to exploit them for addition
benefit during the period of their healthy ministry.[60]

Broughton also defended the Corporation, and his anger wax
stronger because his task was more desperate. As long as a faint hope
saving the Corporation remained, Broughton threw every talent in
'unmasking the artifice by which representations, true in appearance .
are palmed upon the world for the purpose of conveying an impressi
altogether erroneous'. Though Lang correctly pointed out that t
Corporation had drawn large sums annually from the treasury Brought
again asked what alternative it had so long as it was landless, or its la
valueless? The Corporation possessed not so much as a block in Sydn
or within seven miles of the main settlement, save one 'on the barr
sands and inaccessible shores of Botany Bay'. Would Lang have t
archdeacon suspend religious ministrations and abandon educati
until lands became available and profitable? Lang also accused t
Corporation of soaring its administrative costs to £2000 a year. B
Broughton showed that that had occurred only once, in 1828, whe
in anticipation of large land grants, the Corporation had employed ext
surveyors and clerks. Since 1828 administrative costs had dropped
£900 a year. Moreover, by 1831 the Corporation's £18 000 annual gra
supported more chaplains, many more orphans, and double the numb
of schools than in 1825. Lang's accusation of extravagance could not
supported by an unprejudiced examination, Broughton countercharge
rather, the Corporation's present management had relieved rather th

burdened the treasury. 'Dr Lang asserts that the whole scheme has utterly failed of its intended object,' Broughton noted. 'We venture to assure His Lordship that the capacity of the Institution to accomplish its object has never been fairly tried.'[61]

There was a pause in colonial affairs at the end of 1831. Darling's term of office expired, and he departed fearing something in the times would not be set right easily. Broughton read him a tribute from the Executive Council which extolled his labours: 'We have seen you devote yourself to the duties of your station with an indefatigable perseverence which left you scarcely those intervals for rest and opportunities of relaxation which are essential for health'. Yet, in uttering each word Broughton may have wondered to what lasting end Darling had applied this energy.[62]

Darling had given Broughton little energetic assistance. Though he rarely failed to approve the archdeacon's plans he never sent them off with the compelling or enthusiastic recommendation needed to soften the almost predictable official opposition to the expansion of ecclesiastical expenditure. Darling could be secretive, inefficient, and indecisive, especially where money was involved.[63] Once when Broughton, on medical advice, refused to admit extra children into the overcrowded dormitories of the female orphanage, Darling overruled his decision. When Broughton retaliated and threatened to turn the master's residence into a dormitory, Darling approved; and left Broughton the problem of engaging a supervisor who did not require separate accommodation.[64] During the same years, parsonages fell apart for want of timely repairs. 'A person standing in the lower rooms, can in many places see the sky through the chasms in the shingles', he reported after a visit to the Bathurst parsonage; and begged for immediate repairs. The rains poured in next winter.[65] A few shillings worth of forage for a catechist's horse could involve Broughton in more letters than the provisioning of an orphanage for a year. Darling, as the unclouded mind of the chief justice acknowledged, was solely responsible for the depressed financial state of the Corporation.[66] Darling alone made the decision not to transfer lands to it between 1826 and 1828.[67] In 1829 and 1830 he alone made the decision not to include valuable Cumberland county lands among the belated transfers. So when Broughton claimed that the Corporation had been condemned without fair trial, he might well have reflected that Darling had done more than any other to deny it that trial. No governor had been so advantageously placed for building up a materially strong church, yet he left the archdeacon a suppliant at the treasury door whether his need was to build a church or repair a window.[68] In 1831 Broughton shielded Darling from blame.[69]

Few other matters went smoothly. Broughton failed to arrange extra clerical duties to supplement the stipends of chaplains with large families. He succeeded better in a scheme where, in exchange for duties performed at jails and hospitals, chaplains received the services of two convicts to till their glebes. Yet his solicitude only added to his work. Chaplains complained of being sent the 'refuse of the prison people'. The Reverend Mr Reddall got one man so ill he had immediately to put him into hospital

while the other absconded within a week. Broughton was left to explain
that the proper performance of duties at hospitals and jails would depend
on the clergy being assigned convicts of 'a somewhat better class than
at present'.[70]
     Among the clergy there was a persistently troublesome element.
The Reverend Mr Vincent quarrelled with Captain Logan at Moreton
Bay, and Broughton removed him to restore unity in the settlement.
Thereafter Vincent complained of the inadequacy of his parsonage till
Broughton admonished him that 'the chief thing wanting to make it
commodious is a willing and content disposition'. The Reverend Mr
Wilkinson, irritated by an unconfirmed suspension imposed by Scott
for political behaviour ill-fitting to his calling, wrote Broughton insulting
letters and threatened to publish remarks 'derogatory' to his station.
The Reverend Mr Wilton's English creditors finally caught up with him
and Broughton had the unenviable duty of prying open the chaplain's
purse.[71] Caution must be exercised in the selection of future chaplains,
the archdeacon told the Colonial Office. He wanted university men and
insisted that colonists would be satisfied with nothing less. It was a
curious preference, for the two most regularly trained clergy in the colony
were the troublesome graduates Wilkinson and Wilton, while Cowper,
the only chaplain for whom Broughton expressed unqualified respect,
had no university training.[72]
     Under such pressure Broughton became irascible. When the steamer
Sophia Jane put on a public demonstration on the sabbath and towed
the ship *Lady Harewood* out of the harbour to an accompaniment of
booming cannon, Broughton urged Darling to avenge the 'insult to
Government and Religion' by a public prosecution.[73] Yet for all his
disappointments and frustrations Broughton resisted the despair that
overtook Scott in his first two years. Broughton still hoped the Corporation might be saved; the Aboriginal mission made fully his; the King's
Schools expanded; and the government brought to realize that the
outward exercise of religion was its best hope for peace and security.
To foster religious observance the people must have religious establishments 'supported *for* them in the first instance', Broughton insisted.
Only then could they be taught to value the church for its own sake and
finally support it from their own wealth.[74] Reason was on his side, and
he believed it would prevail.
     Broughton admitted to colonial life having a pace of its own and
abandoned all ideas of spectacular progress. He was prepared, he advised
the Colonial Office, to live out the next few years without many changes
in his staff. People attended church more regularly than pessimists
allowed, and his journeys through the archdeaconry had convinced him
of a turn for the better among all but the lowest and poorest classes.
Life centred on material gain, and without proper education he thought
nothing better could be expected. There was a great deal of debauchery
too, but the imbalance of the sexes had much to do with that. 'The
Almighty never has engaged to bestow upon the Ministry of His Church
such an efficacy as should enable it to prevail against the habitual violation
of his own declared appointment that it is not good for man to be alone'.[75]

Within himself there were signs of change. Though he discarded none of the dignity or the civil appurtenances of his office, he was beginning to understand what an apostolic ministry in the colony meant:

A clergyman has an opportunity here of rendering himself the instrument of great good to a great number of souls; but he ought to come prepared to carry on his ministerial labours in comparative obscurity; amidst a thousand discouragements, in thinly peopled districts; at a distance from cultivated society; and with abridged opportunities of study and improvement.[76]

Should his hopes be dispersed in disappointment and should he determine to live by the counsel he delivered to others, there seemed to be nothing in the past or future that could prevent the Tory-minded curate of Hartley Wespall staying in the colony till higher office, or death, called him away. His prospects were brighter than his accomplishments, but he had weathered the first storm of disappointment better than his predecessor.

4

Bourke and the Year 1832

I would request permission to remark upon the very anomalous, and personally irksome, situation in which I have been
placed.

Broughton to Bourke 24 September 1832

In April 1831 England's Whig government appointed Richard Bourke,
an Irish gentleman-soldier turned rhododendron-grower, governor of
New South Wales. Darling was bitter. His abrupt removal looked like
dismissal, and Broughton found him inconsolable. Men of unwarped
judgement will receive the news with sincere regret, commented the
Gazette; but a 'shrivelled remnant of a once noisy cabal' was expected
to rejoice.[1]

Rejoice it did. The tale was told around the colony that as the general
departed so too would 'tyranny's dire scourge'; and only then would
the way be made straight for settlers to rediscover the peace and beauty
of their adopted land. Hall celebrated by his flag-pole at Cockle Bay
ladling punch to *Monitor* subscribers who had supported him in the
darkest days of his incarceration under the tyrant's rule. Wentworth
indulged more extravagantly. He scored handsome fees defending the
tyrant's victims and ploughed back his gain into a festival at Vaucluse.
He invited as many as wished to drop by. He put an ox on the spit and
passed around colonial gin and beer by the tubful. There was a band
and entertainment to taste; dancing and blind-man's buff for the tender-
spirited; hurling, wrestling, and boxing for the young and lusty.[2]

When the day passed into evening without any interruption to the
gaiety, McLeay failed to discern the difference between Wentworth's
house and a common grog shop; except one was regularly licensed. He
recommended that the attorney-general prosecute the owner of Vaucluse
for distributing liquor to the public without a licence. But a search of
the statutes proved every Englishman could dispense unlimited hospitality on the lawns of his own home. McLeay's suggestion was a token
of the deep resentment aroused among the governor's friends by the
event. They were offended, not so much at the sight of Hall or Wentworth
or of any of the governor's declared opponents rejoicing at the governor's
departure, as by the knowledge that so many of the ordinary, well-
dressed citizens had joined with them. The 'shrivelled remnant' on
parade had turned out to be a multitude 4000 strong, willing and ready to

54

sport a tricolour, or toss high a hat before the harangue of the 'patriot of Australia', Wentworth, the antipodean Burdett.[3]

Broughton had seen it all in London in 1812. The *Gazette*, dipping its pen in ridicule, dismissed the event as a people turned rabble on the 'ginerous' hospitality of a rogue.[4] Broughton could not dismiss the rabble. He feared it. He believed it had a dangerous tendency to persist and find its fulfilment in destruction. The boisterous revels at Vaucluse confirmed Broughton in his opinion, and exonerated his view, that a widespread antinomian spirit had taken its grip on all classes in the land. Darling's firm hand had held it in check. Now that it had reared its head more daringly than ever before it was all the more necessary for his successor to reassert that firm hand.

At midday on Saturday 3 December 1831 Broughton stood in the dockyard waiting to greet that successor, the colony's eighth governor. With him were the usual people. When the governor landed the usual ceremony took place, interrupted once by an unceremonious cheer from a crowd gathered outside the dockyard. A procession followed. Bourke, like a conquering hero, mounted a charger and took the lead. His 'lively, affable and intelligent countenance', passing along through the ranks of citizens lining George Street, seemed to promise that benevolent change the colony needed. To some observers it was therefore a strange thing that the people lining his route should have cheered so timidly. But six years' tyranny, they reflected, was not to be overcome or forgotten in a day.[5] For most people, however, the procession was not so very different after all. Immediately behind the governor came the chief justice and the archdeacon in their sedate carriages. The lean and gaunt face of the one a grim reminder that with or without the dashing Bourke theirs was a convict colony and crime was its chief business. The short rigid figure of the other, with its fixed, aloof stare, proclaimed that, whether Bourke arrived or Darling went, the unalterable law of God remained ruling kings and governing peoples.

There was little joy or reassurance in the procession for Broughton. The band of the 39th Regiment might rap out its familiar airs, and the militia that lined the streets snap smartly to attention in its finest military tradition; but this was so much dressing in an age when fundamentals were being shaken. Recent news from England had not been good. The malicious mumblings against the church, her bishops, her rituals and her revenue, once confined to the gutter press and a few hardy agitators, were now reported as issuing with rhetorical splendour from within the chambers of the mother of parliaments herself. Men stooped to invoke the privilege of one ancient institution as a means for hurling degrading and insulting remarks at another, more ancient and more venerable. Such was the odour of the new Whig rule.[6] Riding before him, erect and dignified, was a man chosen for office by those very same Whig rulers.

Broughton wondered for what purpose Bourke had been sent. Goderich had given little satisfaction in the matter of Darling's removal. He passed it off as a routine application of the new six year rule. Why then, the thought remained, should Arthur be allowed to enter his

eighth year without any hint of his recall? Moreover, if it was merely
routine, why had Arthur been passed over as a successor? His record
was impeccable and his reputation at a peak at the Colonial Office. He
had himself been led to expect some such promotion. Instead, a stranger
had been sent. Had he been hand-picked? If so, for what? Clearly, for
what the Colonial Office wanted most of all in New South Wales. Broughton shuddered. The innuendo in Goderich's communication to Darling
suddenly took on a menacing shape: 'I consider you to be free from
the blame imputed to you', the Secretary of State had written; '[but]
I cannot but feel at the same time that the misunderstandings and dissen-
sions, which have occurred in New South Wales, render it advisable . . .
[that] a new Governor should take charge of the colony'.[7] If a governor's
first duty was to keep the peace, how could he succeed against men who
preached that 'the best form of government is that which the people
approve'?[8] He must either trade concessions from the government for
co-operation from the people, or go the way of his predecessor. Confronted by men like Hall, who had shown themselves willing to suffer
imprisonment for their beliefs, the end result of such a policy was frigh-
tening. For a moment, it could have seemed to Broughton that Bourke
had come to open the doors of the colony to the gales of change blowing
through England.

When the procession finally halted by government house, Broughton
went inside for the official ceremony to swear in the new governor as
a member of the Executive Council. That done, the governor read his
Instructions. Broughton cocked a keen ear anxious to detect any change
in his responsibility for addressing the governor on matters concerning
the Aboriginals. He was stunned. In the presence of his fellow officials
and before a great number of invited civil and military guests, the archdeacon was reduced in status from third to fourth in the land. The
change was small, but significant. As the colony's third citizen he
enjoyed being the senior member of the Executive Council and,
because the chief justice was regularly absent on court business, the
most senior member present at the Legislative Council. Under the
new Instructions the chief justice remained undisturbed as the colony's
second citizen, while the archdeacon became inferior to the colony's
senior military officer. When governor and chief justice were absent
senior authority passed to the army. Henceforth, Broughton's status
was indistinguishable from that of officials such as the colonial secretary
and the colonial treasurer. The original order of governor, chief justice,
and archdeacon, had mirrored the traditional order of precedence in
England, of king, lord chancellor and archbishop. Broughton thought
the change capricious, unholy and mischievous.[9]

Broughton took his new place and protested. No ecclesiastic could
idly witness the elevation of the army above the church; and he condemned
the shuffle as ill-advised and illegal. The archdeacon's original status
was bestowed by a Writ of Privy Seal, a legal document of the highest
rank issued by the King's Privy Council itself; and this, Broughton
pointed out, had been set aside by a Commission under the Sign Manual,
a document of inferior status. Was such a move possible? Broughton

hazarded the suggestion that his reduced status originated not in the highest councils of the realm, but among some lesser body of officials set upon eclipsing the king in his ecclesiastical capacity.[10]

Bourke despatched the complaint to London along with a report detailing the archdeacon's moves to frustrate the dissolution of the Church and Schools Corporation with legal technicalities. Viewing both together Bourke decided that Broughton, rather than Forbes the chief justice, about whom he had been warned, would be his most 'prickly' adviser. He returned fire immediately. He read the Executive Council a hastily prepared minute announcing his intention to proceed promptly with a bill extending trial by jury to criminal cases. Bourke had read over the earlier objections of Broughton and other councillors, and rejected them in favour of more 'correct information' from 'persons most likely from their official situation and professional employments to be competent advisers'. Broughton, commended by Wellington and praised by Darling for his sound counsel, was pronounced incompetent by Bourke.[11]

Broughton overlooked Bourke's incivility. He could afford to. The roar of the lion echoed faintly with the neigh of an ass. The submissions of Bourke's 'competent advisers' turned out to be embarrassingly thin; an opinion Forbes wrote Darling sixteen months earlier, and a fresh one from Roger Therry, Commissioner of the Court of Requests. Bourke had consulted one person: it was not clear he had consulted more. Moreover, his talk about 'the people generally' desiring common juries rang hollow in a man of one month's colonial residence. Campbell Riddell, the Colonial Treasurer, said as much and accused Bourke of not consulting the records let alone the people. The records showed that the people had avoided the existing common juries because they felt jurors were not to be trusted on their oaths. How then could they desire new ones? Bourke nevertheless insisted he heard from small-scale immigrant settlers and the colonial born a loud cry for the abolition of military juries; and that was the noise he would attend to.[12] Moreover, in a dazzling display of the scarlet and gold of his office he swept aside the whole Executive Council insisting that one thing only was required for the implementation of new juries: 'that I should deem it advantageous to the colony'.[13] However, within a week Bourke had had the matter deferred for twelve months. Another voice had spoken above the clamour of the people. Bourke's strong sympathy for popular change had beguiled his good judgement, and he showed he would as likely rush and stumble over an issue as pursue it with calculated caution.[14] Against such a man there was hope.

Broughton and Bourke were alike in temperament: proud and inflexible. In doctrines they were to one another as Pharisee and Sadducee. The headstrong devotion to beliefs that each demanded of his integrity fixed a gulf between them. Broughton proudly submitted to the Church of England and became its inflexible servant. Bourke followed Christianity but was too proud to submit to any church. Spiritually Bourke dwelt with the liberal divines of the eighteenth century. Like them he found the doctrines of the Holy Trinity and the divinity of Christ a stumbling-block, and dealt with it after the manner of the tacit reformers. He would subscribe to it with his lips to secure a commission, but deny it in his heart as the remnant of an obscurantist past that parliament had no business enshrining in its law. Like them too, he regarded bishops more as ecclesiastical officials, appointed by the crown for the superintendence and restraint of the clergy rather than as modern-day apostles. Once, earlier in his career, he threatened to disband a school on his Limerick estate rather than consent to the diocesan bishop nominating its master. It counted for nothing that the gentry elsewhere accepted the practice. For Bourke it was a sufficient objection that he found it inconvenient: 'It would be exceedingly unpleasant to Mrs Bourke and me to have a master or mistress put in of whom perhaps we might not approve'. Bourke was captain of his own soul and master of his own vessel; one of that breed who accepted private judgement as the fundamental source of authority in matters of religion, and leaned to utility and expediency in politics. In Broughton's opinion Bourke was a man of 'Galileo's temper'; so indulgent towards the spirit of independence as to be careless of the authority of the church. Broughton abhorred the eighteenth-century apologists who, with support from the Hanoverian kings, had established a precedent which permitted men of quite unorthodox religious opinions to remain within the ruling caste of the church establishment. In the day of their eighteenth-century ascendency these men, some tacit reformers and all sceptics, had put the Church of England on trial. Their ascendency had passed, but their disciples remained. Fate, in 1832, deposited one of them in office, above Broughton, in New South Wales.[15]

Life had taught Broughton and Bourke different lessons. Like all men born in the latter half of the eighteenth century, they shared the experience of having seen the mob grow wild and dangerous. The mob best known to Broughton was the London rabble. He attributed its madness to ignorance and irreligion, and to the persistence in man of his original possession, a 'nature inclined to evil'. Bourke, after living among Irish peasants, understood this madness as springing from a thwarted dignity; from men cast low by poverty and lower still by the rights other men had rifled from them.[16] From religion, bishop and governor drew a different inspiration. Broughton lived in anticipation of the day God's glory filled the earth as the waters covered the sea. Bourke looked forward to a better world, made in the image of a profound change anticipated in Christ, a world rid of Jew and Gentile, bond and free, and peopled simply by men, equal and free.

Broughton and Bourke were soon at odds in another matter. From what seemed a bottomless bag of private instructions from London Bourke produced a new money bill. In future the salaries of the governor and Supreme Court judges were to be paid direct from custom revenues on warrants signed only by the governor. It was expedient, Bourke said in explaining the move, 'to make some certain provision' for these salaries. Expedient indeed! Bourke had just announced that future estimates for colonial expenditure would be printed and turned over to the Legislative Council for debate. 'I shall feel great satisfaction in diminishing any expenditure that may be shown to be unnecessary', Bourke added; but in the new bill he denied the Legislative Council the right to debate the high cost of governors or judges. With cries of 'no bishoprick above £1,000—no rectory above £400—no working curacy under £150 per annum' already in the colonial air, Broughton thought it expedient that the archdeacon's salary be granted a similar safe passage.[17]

Broughton demanded equal security. The terms of his appointment set out that 'in whatever manner the payment of the governor's salary might be fixed, the payment of the archdeacon's should be secured in the same manner'. Broughton pressed Bourke in private to acknowledge this. The governor refused; his Instructions did not allow it. Broughton decided to make issue of the matter in the Legislative Council, then reconsidered: 'I . . . [am] unwilling to urge any measure, which could embarrass Your Excellency's proceedings by giving rise to debate', he told Bourke. But the day after the bill was approved the archdeacon sent the governor a sharp note: 'I have now most respectfully to request your recommendation to the Secretary of State that the payment of my Salary may be provided for out of some permanent fund at the disposal of His Majesty'. If it had been improper for the governor to exceed his Instructions and provide for the archdeacon's salary in the right manner, it was not improper for the governor to request that the Colonial Office amend and correct these Instructions.[18]

Bourke marvelled at the fuss. But Broughton saw the measure as another attempt to downgrade his office and with it the church. Moreover, its ill effect would be heightened should the Church and Schools Corporation finally be disbanded. Every clergyman would then become a stipendary officer of the state forced to live off the annual vote of a parliament. 'I cannot but entertain most serious doubts how far the functions which appertain to an Established Church can be discharged by one which is merely stipendary', Broughton said. 'It is a question of great extent upon which past experience throws very little light.'[19]

Broughton regarded the Established Church as the nation's insurance against impiety and insurrection, and it needed a sufficient ministry and pure doctrine.[20] The suppliant status of a stipendary church threatened both. To Broughton a sufficient ministry meant one covering the entire population, confirming believers in their faith and converting the rest from error. Broughton asked: Could it be expected that non-believers would vote a slice of the public purse for the maintenance of a ministry they did not desire? Would not a colony like New South Wales, where 'the greater number arrive in total ignorance and disregard of religion', be left a grim and uncertain future. 'I cannot but fear', Broughton wrote, 'that unless new settlements have in the first instance at the *public* expense zealous and efficient ministers, by whom they may be gradually won over, the next and more numerous generation will grow up in infidel habits of thought, and in consequent addiction to immoral practices.' No worthy government would deliberately open the door to such a prospect.[21] Yet Broughton feared that Bourke's bill, by putting the church establishment to a vote in the Legislative Council, had done just that. Moreover, religion pure and undefiled was a stiff dose for frail humanity.

Once the laity voted their clerical teachers their stipends the archdeacon feared they would be emboldened to demand rites and doctrines to their taste.[22] Hall the editor reinforced Broughton's worst fears. Hall once considered entering the ministry and he still fancied himself a theologian. He was a conscientious pew holder at St James church and a model in word and deed, of the Christian gentleman Broughton feared might circumscribe his support with unwholesome conditions. In January 1832 Hall told Goderich how he would use a vote on religious matters:

> Provided a National Religion can be established among us on a cheap foundation, divested of all civil authority, a great majority of the colonists would concur in such a state of religion being maintained out of the Revenue of the Colony ... but they would require its mainte-nance to be on the same independent footing, as the army of the United Kingdom is, whose substance is voted annually by the people through their representatives in Parliament. And as the services of the Church of England and her Communion, are Catholic and Scriptural, very broad and liberal in their nature, I think the colonists generally would have no objection to her ceremonies and rites ... being used in the cheap National Church of New South Wales, thus paid for by them-selves.[23]

In London Goderich thought Broughton too anxious. He told the archdeacon his fears were groundless and the changes he sought pointless. Goderich considered the Church of England firmly established in the colonies and likely to remain so.[24] Men like Hall would never have a say in its affairs. Goderich's bland calm merely aggravated Broughton's anxiety and he would not let the matter rest. In adversity Broughton seemed to develop a resilience which, if it did not permit him to enjoy a contest, afforded him the determination to conduct one. The Duke of Wellington indeed knew his man.

Broughton meanwhile attended to other matters. The *Gazette* praised religious toleration: 'In no part of the globe is the *odium theologicum* less visible than in New South Wales'. McLeay, a leading churchman, had just donated £25 towards an Independent chapel in Sydney, and another churchman, J. E. Manning, gave £20 towards a Roman Catholic chapel. The disposition to go beyond a mere toleration of another man's conscience into helping him maintain his beliefs in outward dignity was considered a pleasing feature of colonial life. Protestants aided Protestants and Roman Catholics too. It was meagre but welcome relief for the large and impoverished Roman Catholic community which struggled for clergy, churches, teachers and schools. What excited public sympathy most was its struggle to complete the floorless and roofless chapel in Hyde Park. The colony measured its stature in buildings, and this 'immense gothic edifice' caught the imagination of many not Roman Catholic. 'I shall always feel pleasure in promoting whether by my pen, or by any other means at my command, that great and laudable undertaking—the Roman Catholic chapel', Mansfield the Wesleyan told the Reverend J. J. Therry whose dream it was.[25]

Roger Therry capitalized on this goodwill. Therry was an Irish lawyer and biographer of George Canning, the leader of a factious Tory group that Broughton dismissed as 'contemptible for their duplicity'.[26] He was, too, the first fruit in New South Wales of Wellington's one folly, Catholic Emancipation; and had landed within weeks of Broughton. Soon after this arrival in November 1829 Therry organized an appeal by Roman Catholics to the governor and Protestant community to help save the half-completed but partly exposed chapel at Hyde Park. John Macarthur presided over a Protestant Committee to Aid Catholic Brethren; Sir John Jamison, a Protestant with more property than most, rallied to the occasion; and Mansfield came good with his pen: 'Its object is most meritorious', he instructed the colony.[27] The appeal succeeded with the public but not the governor. Therry had unabashedly addressed the governor-in-council suggesting the chapel be completed as a memorial to that great measure of political equalization recently accomplished in England. In Broughton's recollection that great measure—Catholic Emancipation—had passed through parliament coupled with a declaration against further indulgences to Roman Catholics. Had not Peel told the House of Commons in 1829 that the great measure was for the strengthening of Protestantism? In 1830 Darling, with Broughton in his Executive Council, was determined to see it do just that, and turned down Therry's appeal.[28]

When Bourke arrived Therry revived his appeal. Bourke was not one of Peel's men. 'Peace and tranquility depend on a good gentry, good clergy, and good magistrates', Bourke said; and for the Irish Catholics of New South Wales 'good clergy' were Roman Catholic clergy. Bourke freed Roman Catholics from the patronage of Protestants and encouraged them to apply for substantial aid. 'A government is bound in my opinion', he wrote to a Sydney priest, 'to extend equal freedom of conscience, equal protection, and equal proportionate assistance to all classes of its subjects provided they teach nothing inconsistent with plain morality.'[29] Ironically the treasury had money to spare in 1832 because Broughton scaled down his demands. Provided two priests replaced two catechists and chaplains were appointed to penal stations, Broughton thought his establishment adequate until settlement expanded in the upper branches of Hunter's river. Bourke supported the archdeacon's request for the extra chaplains, and trusted to new land regulations to slow down expansion in the upper Hunter region.[30] That left him free to aid the neglected Irish Catholics in the established counties. The Legislative Council co-operated and voted £500 towards the Hyde Park chapel. It remained for Bourke to persuade the Colonial Office to approve. Roger Therry suggested that Protestants sign a Memorial expressing support for the grant and further government aid towards Roman Catholic chaplains, churches and schools.[31]

Therry wanted the best signatures and pursued them into the countryside. So in April 1832 Sir Edward Parry, manager of the Australian Agricultural Company, received Therry's letters and a request for his signature on the Memorial. Parry was a devout churchman likely to attend worship three times on Sunday. He had a zealous concern for the souls of others, and within two years turned the congregation at the company's settlement at Carrington from a handful of thirty (mostly convicts bound to attend) into a regular congregation of two hundred. He thought the colony 'an absolute moral wilderness' and was among those who had donated to the Roman Catholics in 1830. 'I did it', he recalled, 'in the sincere belief that to build a Roman Catholic Chapel where there was none . . . was rather the least of two very serious evils.' The same spirit moved him to distribute bibles and prayer-books to destitute Roman Catholics at Port Stephen. From such a man Therry anticipated automatic support.[32]

It so happened, over the week-end of 28 April to 1 May 1832 that Wilton, the high church chaplain from Newcastle, came to Table House where Parry lived, with news of Sir Edward's mother's death in London. From that devout woman Parry had learned all the great truths of evangelical religion. He had been her youngest and favoured son; a child, he admitted, 'of never ceasing prayer'. Therry's letter, arriving the same week-end, received unexpected treatment. 'I do from my heart most solemnly protest against the Church of Rome, as being, in my opinion, a system of idolatry and superstition', Parry wrote back to Therry. It was his mother's opinion; and Parry was paying his last respects to her evangelical fervour. The next day on the way to church Parry's horse stumbled and fell, tossing Parry on to the hard earth.[33]

Therry got nothing from Parry, but 2000 other Protestants put their signatures where he asked them. Roman Catholics then met on 29 July, and Therry announced the time ripe for delivering the Memorial to the governor with copies for such good statesmen as Lord Howick and Daniel O'Connell who might be induced to further their cause. Therry was profoundly thankful for Protestant support, but not content with it. Though Irish and Catholic to the core, he was anxious to appear as English as St George and slay the dragon of prejudice which remained in the colony. He took up Parry's letter and read it to the assembly of Roman Catholics as a typical example of the mischief circulating in their midst. 'Whence . . . did the worthy Knight derive his mission to be a denouncing and destroying Angel?' Therry asked. Catholics loved liberty, he added; and it was only Protestant blindness which refused to acknowledge that England's constitutional liberties were laid in Catholic England of the thirteenth century, by Catholic bishops and barons centuries before Protestantism was dreamed up.[34]

A Presbyterian penman leaped first to Parry's defence. He wanted it put right that English liberties arrived with Hampden, and that the rest of Therry's argument was 'as lame on the one hand, as it was uncharitable on the other'. The Reverend Henry Fulton, a chaplain as Irish as Therry, but Protestant, drew up a pamphlet supporting Parry's charge that Roman Catholicism was imbued with idolatry. Fulton had trouble disciplining his pen, and ended up with a discursive survey of papal aberrations from the Arianism of Pope Liberius to the unscriptural use of oil, salt, and tapers at baptism. The controversy expanded; debate became ham; and invective replaced argument.[35] Then suddenly Broughton contributed a pamphlet on a somewhat different plane.

For two years Broughton had watched the peculiar colonial system of Protestants aiding Roman Catholics with maturing alarm, but kept silent. Only when Therry attacked Parry in public and assailed the Reformation for good measure, did Broughton break silence and caution Protestants against further 'submission to the insidious paralysing influence which has been lately exerted to persuade them that they are justified in encouraging the Roman Catholic religion, as being another equally acceptable mode of worshipping God'. Protestantism and Roman Catholicism 'must *ever* remain distinct and adverse', he maintained; and spelled out what he hoped every Protestant already knew. Protestants derived their faith from scripture alone whereas Roman Catholics concocted their beliefs from an amalgam of scripture and an unwritten tradition. That unwritten tradition had opened the door to many unholy doctrines including those which had sent the English martyrs to their death. Protestants could not justify supporting the extension of such a system. Those who did had a misguided notion of charity. Charity 'rejoiceth in truth'. Protestant 'charity' to Roman Catholics amounted to a subsidy on error. So Broughton ruled: in future no Protestant may contribute to the establishment of colonial Catholicism 'without guilt'.[36]

Some Protestants responded by donating immediately to the Hyde Park chapel. Others accepted Broughton's reasoning and, like Parry, declined to repeat earlier liberality.[37] Therry read Broughton's pamphlet and shuddered: 'It breathes the spirit of retracting former relaxations and re-enacting former disabilities', he warned.[38] Yet Hall the editor, a fierce apostle of liberty, read and liked it. 'Forcible, logical and to us convincing', he wrote in the *Monitor*. 'We believe him [Broughton] to be an enemy to persecutions and intolerance of all kinds, whenever he can distinctly detect their probable presence.'[39] Men made what they liked of the pamphlet; and the many copies sold (a second edition being printed in just over a month) showed it touched upon a timely subject.[40]

Broughton had no objection to the presence of Roman Catholics in the colony or to the open practice of their religion. 'So long as men are earnest and sincere, even in erroneous views with respect to Christ, there may be in them a feeling of real piety', he maintained, and provided local Roman Catholics with a room in St James schoolhouse to practise their own mistaken piety.[41] He even defended their right to jingle bells during worship when the Presbyterians in an adjoining room complained of excessive noise on the sabbath.[42] It was a spirit of usurpation, which like so many of his countrymen he believed inherent in Catholicism, that worried him. Yet so long as Roman Catholics were restricted to expanding by their own means they posed no threat. The pittances Protestants gave, as well as the Legislative Council's £500, made little material difference, and, for that reason Broughton had suffered them in silence. But Therry's Memorial altered that. Every Protestant who urged the government to aid Catholic expansion risked importing the monster of Catholic usurpation into the colony. Worse still, however, was the liberal jargon in which Therry clothed his appeal. The Gospel, Broughton maintained, 'requires us to have in all our doings, a single eye to the advancement of truth'. The world at large eschewed such earnestness. It preferred a so-called spirit of toleration, which Broughton was wont to describe as a 'phlegmatic and listless unconcern respecting matters of faith and principle'. When Roman Catholics appealed for Protestant support what spirit did they hope to find in them? A single eye for truth or a listless unconcern for the principles of their faith? When they praised Protestant generosity they lauded not Protestant conviction but Protestant indifference. And when the time came for Roman Catholics to depart with their gain, they would leave behind a colonial Protestantism so conceitedly tolerant that it no longer bothered, or even considered it important, to search out the difference between truth and falsehood.[43] 'The system of giving countenance and support to religious opinions which are diametrically opposed ... may for a time promote the apparent interests of your Church', he warned Roman Catholic leaders,

> but I warn you of the injury which religion must sustain from the example of such an alliance. You will do no good, even according to your own understanding of the term, to those with whom you are united; and they will do you much harm. You will not bring them over to your Church: but what if they should carry into its bosom the spirit of their own indifference! In availing yourself of their assistance, you recognise a principle which, carried to its full extent, would authorise all men to encourage all sorts of opinions, without consideration of their truth or falsehood. I do not perceive where the limit is to be fixed; for if any of us may in one instance support that which we do not believe, why not in all?[44]

Against such notions Broughton pitted his wits; and to the discerning reader of his pamphlet it was plain that despite the dust of sectarianism, the archdeacon's chief foe was liberalism not Roman Catholicism.

Nothing went well between Broughton and Bourke in 1832. Broughton found Bourke unsympathetic and obstructive: Bourke found Broughton heartless; an impression he formed after clashing with the archdeacon in January 1832 over new land regulations. Broughton played the leading role in framing the land regulations of 1831, one of which required settlers to pay off quit rents owing on crown lands occupied in the 1830s and to surrender land not purchased outright by August 1832. Land-holders protested their ruin, but Broughton was unmoved.[45] He told Bourke the old Executive Council realized 'it could not be complied with', and that was its purpose; 'It would have the effect of procuring the surrender of considerable portions of land which it might be convenient to have on hand to disperse to newcomers'.[46]

Broughton was determined to rip land off the great landholders in a bid to save the Church and Schools Corporation. Lang blamed the shortage of surveyed land on the Corporation, and declaimed before clapping audiences that Lord Goderich was about to turn over the Corporation's acres to a hungry public.[47] To save the Corporation's lands Broughton wanted to unlock the massive holdings of the McLeays, the Dumaresq brothers, the Riddells, the Joneses and their like, men with an acquisitiveness bordering on unprincipled greed, who had taken up fresh acres before paying rents and instalments owing on their old ones. They had done this with both crown and Corporation lands; and their default in rents and instalments to the Corporation had helped increase its dependence on the local treasury, and cultivated that hostility Lang so cunningly exploited in his campaign to destroy the Corporation.[48] The landholders looked to Bourke for relief and got it. They met at Parramatta on 30 November 1831 and asked for five years credit. Bourke allowed them three. Broughton opposed the concession in the Executive Council: he said it was impolitic to leave in the hands of a few all the lands available to attract immigrants, and immoral to sell wealthy residents land on easier terms than the one month credit allowed on new sales. Bourke shrugged off such criticism: 'This appears to me to savour of injustice to one's old friends'.[49]

Broughton appeared heartless in another matter. Lang's Australian College was in difficulties within a year. Local shareholders had not matched the government grant and Lang, foreseeing difficulties, asked the Colonial Office to allocate the government's remaining £2000 on more liberal terms. In March 1832 he could not afford to await a reply, and turned to Bourke. Bourke was willing. He liked Lang's venture. Possibly he admired Lang's energy. He certainly approved of the way Lang poured his own funds into the project. But if Bourke was willing the Executive Council was not. Broughton referred the Executive Council to the minutes of 31 October 1831 and its own explicit recommendation that no additional money be paid to the Australian College until £1000 of private funds had been spent on it. Bourke in a fury retaliated by taking the matter to the Legislative Council where three of the College trustees sat. He asked that the Legislative Council vote the College's remaining £2000 into the governor's care for distribution 'upon the terms set forth in the despatch of the Right Honourable the Secretary of State, dated 12 January 1831'. It agreed. Lang received nothing immediately but Bourke had snubbed the Executive Council. In future he could deal directly with the College trustees as they fulfilled the conditions on private contributors. To succeed in this snub Bourke suppressed a second despatch of 29 March 1831 superseding the earlier one of 12 January, and which forbade the governor to even *approach* the Executive Council for the remaining £2000 until Lang had raised and spent £1500 of public subscriptions on the buildings. But in the war brewing between archdeacon and governor a dash of deceit was within the rules—as was a dash of cunning. To win Legislative Council approval for the £2000 subsidy Bourke sandwiched it between a vote of £600 to St James church and £500 to the Hyde Park chapel, challenging Broughton to object at the risk of losing his own grant.[50]

Broughton could also spice his moves with political cunning. Lang's claim that the Corporation's vast tracts of land were sufficient to satisfy all immediate immigrant land needs had touched off another newspaper witch-hunt, and aggravated Broughton's fears for the Corporation's future.[51] He was angry with Lang. So were the trustees of the Sydney College, and in January 1832 they accused him of deliberately misleading Goderich into believing the Australian College was the Sydney College.[52] Some of those trustees sat on the Legislative Council, and Broughton exploited their indignation. He proposed a censure which questioned

Lang's frankness and condemned his attack on the Protestant episcopal clergy (for being preoccupied with Corporation lands to the neglect of their flocks) as unwarranted, and their publication as highly improper. The Legislative Council approved the censure and instructed Bourke to transmit it to the Colonial Office. Bourke dismissed the move as vindictive, but complied; and Broughton had the satisfaction of seeing the governor, who made much of preferring the Legislative Council's judgement to the Executive Council's, reporting unfavourably on the man he wanted most to patronize. Bourke learned he faced a resourceful opponent.[53]

Broughton was too vulnerable for victory. In 1832 he asked that Bourke return him control over the Aboriginal mission. He argued: that the king's Instructions required plainly that Bourke, like Darling, consult the archdeacon on all matters concerning Aborigines; that the governor had no more right to choose when and when not to obey his Instructions than colonists to pick and choose between laws; that it contravened apostolic practice to have churchmen working in a district but free of regular jurisdiction; that it was personally embarrassing to have people wondering why the governor deemed him unfit in the matter.[54] But Bourke simply closed his ears: 'I shall have great pleasure in promoting the object, but have no reason to desire that the direction should be placed in other hands'.[55]

Broughton next asked Bourke to reinstate the Reverend Frederick Wilkinson to a colonial chaplaincy. Wilkinson had been suspended by Scott for 'unbecoming political activities' and by Broughton for gross discourtesy, and the Colonial Office referred the penalty to the Bishop of Calcutta for confirmation. At Calcutta three bishops died in five years and Broughton felt this had turned a once just sentence into a cruel and oppressive uncertainty. As archdeacon of New South Wales Broughton was also Commissary of the Bishop of Calcutta with authority to take disciplinary action when the bishop was prevented from doing so. Broughton believed the bishops being dead gave him authority to act. 'The two year suspension he [Wilkinson] had undergone may be regarded as sufficient punishment', Broughton advised Bourke. Bourke rejected the plea. Wilkinson could await the appointment of another bishop at Calcutta. Bourke denied Broughton's right to exercise disciplinary authority over his clergy, even to being merciful.[56]

Then fell the blow which most hurt. On 5 September 1832 the Reverend George Innes, Master of the Sydney King's School, died from a brain disease after a term of eccentricity that shrank the school to eight pupils. 'I hope all from Oxford will not be like him', Cowper commented; and Hill had refused all Innes's offers of assistance at St James.[57] Broughton wrote immediately to the Bishop of London for a replacement. The King's School Parramatta had pupils queueing for entry and Broughton believed a sound future awaited the Sydney school under better management.[58] Bourke differed. Nothing the Corporation patronized flourished, he said; and recommended the Colonial Office ignore the Parramatta success, withdraw its promise of three years aid, and suppress the Sydney school. 'The Australian College in the promotion of which Dr Lang the Presbyterian Minister has taken so active a part, promises more favourably', he reported. Bourke threw his full influence behind the Australian College impressed by Lang's sacrifice of personal property to keep the venture going after the Executive Council proved so hard-hearted. He confirmed Broughton's forecast that three colleges in Sydney were two too many, and to protect Lang's investment Bourke refused four times to discuss Sydney College finances in the Legislative Council and took advantage of Innes's death to remove the other competitor.[59]

The matter brought to a close a bad year for Broughton. He had accepted his appointment on the distinct understanding that his office carried such privileges as enabled him to preside effectively over the Established Church in the colony.[60] Within a year of Bourke's arrival he was reduced in status, ignored as a councillor, removed from the Civil List of guaranteed salaried officers, denied a permanent fund for the maintenance of clergy, bereft of means to erect churches, robbed of schools already established, deprived of the Aboriginal mission, and denied disciplinary authority over his own clergy. Moreover, a season for complaint had set in. They complained in Maitland because they had no parson or church. Up the Hunter River they complained because they saw the archdeacon to no good effect; he came, he went, and left neither parson nor trustworthy schoolmaster. On the Goulburn plains they complained that their children were deprived of the religious attention they were accustomed to in England. In the Illawarra they simply complained: 'I trust the Archdeacon is able to give some good reason for this apparent neglect of interests of the church'. Some accused him of inattention: some, however, commended him for doing the best under trying circumstances.[61] Whatever the right judgement, it worried Broughton that the church should appear inactive. So in September 1832 Broughton sought leave to report personally to the Secretary of State for Colonies on developments in colonial religion. 'As the object of His Majesty in appointing me to the Office I hold, was to provide for the welfare of the Church', he told Bourke, 'I conceive that ... I should be allowed to go where that object can be most efficiently promoted, rather than remain here while it is everyday in consequence receiving fresh injury.'[62]

Bourke said, No. He pleaded Broughton's need to be on hand should fresh instructions on the Corporation arrive.[63] Abroad, however, it was not the governor's finest hour. Goderich had just rebuked Bourke's bad taste in accepting an address of welcome reflecting offensively on his predecessor. Lang also had fallen into disfavour for his pamphlet attacking the clergy and the Corporation, and Goderich threatened to withdraw aid from the Australian College. On the other hand, Broughton's reputation rode high; and Goderich appeared eager, by some favour, to affirm his confidence in the colonial clergy.[64] Bourke wanted to keep Broughton and Goderich apart until this wave of contrition passed. He suggested the archdeacon visit Hobart again.[65]

Bourke denied the archdeacon assistance in the colony and refused him an opportunity to rally it abroad. 'I would request permission to remark upon the very anomalous, and personally irksome, situation in which I have been placed', Broughton wrote to Bourke.[66] But Bourke was tough.

5

1833. The Assault

> What do we but remind and warn the generation who are
> entering as it were by the gates of the Lord into another land
> of Canaan, that if they would enjoy happiness, whether
> national or individual, if the abundance of prosperity which
> it seems probable they may reap, is to prove to them a blessing
> not a curse, their principal care and concern must be to
> scatter plentifully the seeds of religion, the fear of God and
> the faith of Christ crucified, in all the quarters of the land.
>
> Broughton preaching on the forty-sixth
> anniversary of the founding of the colony[1]

Bourke was popular among the people and could afford a rupture with
his chief councillors. This popularity sprang from his timely concession
to the landed interests, his promise of trial by jury, his more regular use
of the Legislative Council and some talk of opening its chamber to the
public, and the publication of the annual estimates of expenditure.
But in the matter of a popular assembly Bourke disappointed the colonists.
The British government would not risk debate in the Commons, where
an Irish Party gathered strength, on a bill bestowing on a distant colony
the self-government it withheld from Ireland. Popular government
in New South Wales must await a solution to England's Irish problems.
In the meantime, the Colonial Office placated the democratic longings
of the colonists with a number of sops.[2]

One sop misfired badly. The publication of annual estimates was
meant to invite confidence by candidly declaring well in advance how
the colony's money would be spent. The published estimates merely
informed colonists it would not be spent as they wished. So, estimate
times became agitated times when the people meditated on their constitutional shackles and proclaimed how differently a popular assembly
would arrange matters.

Few before 1832 had questioned the propriety of the government's
ecclesiastical expenditure though its unequal distribution among the
churches sometimes drew a comment such as: 'Were the rulers at home
and in the colony *just*, and were they also wise as well as just, they would
not permit one third of the population of any colony to be baptized,
married, preached to, and prayed with, by one single clergyman'.
Some believed that ecclesiastical expenditure should be expanded

and others that it should be rearranged. Among the rearrangements spoken of were the closing down of the futile Aboriginal missions and the handing of the savings to the Presbyterians, and the shutting up of the orphanages—a ruse whereby the local rich kept their illegitimate offspring at public expense—and giving that money to the Roman Catholics. Few also before 1832 condemned the Church of England for hogging the estimates or suggested slicing up its funds, but they did query Broughton's personal need of so handsome a slice. His £2000 salary took a sixth of the annual Church of England budget. 'The Venerable the Archdeacon's salary is excessive by £1250', cried the *Monitor*; and the idea took root.[4] The archdeacon cost as much as six chaplains, took double the salary of the Archbishop of Paris, or, as Bourke reckoned it (and he was on the bandwagon) five times the stipend paid the Cape's senior chaplain.[5] Unless Broughton renounced voluntarily the excess in his salary, crusading colonists would one day strip him of it:

> We wish Archdeacon Broughton and the clergy of New South Wales to understand ... the right ... to our money, is derived solely from the command of Lord Goderich ... His Lordship will not be allowed much longer to fiddle for us ... And then there will be a radical reformation in Church matters. The colonists will always be willing to pay a working Clergy ... Such men will be content with a salary double that allowed by our Archdeacon to the Roman Chaplains of the Colony.[6]

By 1833 the 'esteemed' Mr Broughton had become Mr Moneybags. Politics mediated this change as ecclesiastical expenditure became the stalking-horse for frustrated colonial democrats to shoot at their rulers. Broughton's pamphlet war with Roger Therry helped too. It made him a public controversialist. He had attacked, and could be attacked. The result was an undignified skirmish. What was an archdeacon? 'A sly rogue who fares sumptuously every day', read the *Australian*'s ecclesiastical dictionary. Why pay the archdeacon £2000? Because he is the wrong sort of archdeacon—a political one who sits on councils instead of travelling the countryside. Such comment multiplied.[7] Then the storm broke. After suffering the frustration of their democratic hopes for a year the colonists stirred. In time-honoured colonial fashion they decided to hold another meeting, air their grievances publicly, and raise a petition. Petitions would achieve nothing, Goderich had forewarned. But colonists were not so dense as to miss the lesson of the age that when many people did a little for a long time they achieved much. Had not O'Connell liberated Irish Catholics on the pennies of the peasants? Colonists of New South Wales must imitate them, pester the Colonial Office with petitions, and regularly contribute their pence for the support of a vigorous agent in London. Then one day they would be free citizens. So, on 26 January 1833 the public met at the old spot, the court-house in King's Street, and resolved what they had resolved many times before: 'that the people of this country are fitted for a participation in the constitutional rights enjoyed by their fellow subjects in Great Britain'.[8]

A spark of genius shone in Wentworth that anniversary day. He occupied a principal place at the meeting; and as he took his audience

along the tracks of familiar arguments he beguiled them into looking at
new scenery. He told them what he had told them before: that they had
not the rights of common Englishmen. But he told them not to dwell
on that. Rather, he said, consider the iniquitous effects of it. And waving
a copy of the recent estimates before their eyes he launched into an attack
on 'this most iniquitous budget'. And the greatest iniquity in it was the
ecclesiastical expenditure, and that iniquity must depart from the land.
With that purpose in mind Wentworth moved to reap with gusto where
others for months past had sown.[9]

With a little wit to warm them to laughter and a clever turn of phrase
to establish his ascendancy, Wentworth quickly made his audience his
shadow. They followed wherever he took them. Then, when the applause
was right he released the devil in him. In England, he recalled, bishops,
archdeacons, and the like, were rapidly sinking to their proper level
and all the venerable absurdities and nonsense attached to them were
being got rid of. Strange tides seemed to have cast the effluence up on
the shores of the colony, he said. Eight years ago an obsolescent creature,
an archdeacon, was foisted on them, and for eight years had fed lavishly
at the colonial treasury. Every man, woman and child contributed £3
a year towards his upkeep and all the humbug that went with him.
'Gentlemen', thundered Wentworth, 'it is difficult to decide which is
the greatest,—the absurdity or the wickedness of such a system.'[10]

Wentworth spared Broughton little that day. He called him, by implication, a rogue for being the head of the most iniquitous land grant in
the colony; a fool for hunting up the blacks at Wellington Valley when
the simplest of souls in the colony knew that it was contrary to their
nature to remain more than three days in any one place; and a thief for
taking his salary. He lampooned him. He accused him of self-aggrandize-
ment. He charged him with constantly wanting to add to 'his satellites
of chaplains and catechists, wanting which, of course, he would be a
sun without his system'.[11] The point scored a laugh. Derision was Wentworth's weapon but not the *raison d'etre* of his performance. The archdeacon was his target but the church establishment was his quarry:

> Gentlemen, do any of you know the use of an Archdeacon? [a laugh].
> I mean no personal allusion to the gentleman who holds that office;
> on the contrary, although I have no personal acquaintance with him,
> I respect his character, which is that of a very amiable man. But,
> gentlemen . . . [12]

And that lingering 'but' disclosed Wentworth's purpose. Agitators
for a better colonial society could no longer afford to defer to Broughton
out of respect for his amiable and virtuous character. If he was blameless
his institution was not. It propped up Toryism, as recent news of the
episcopal vote against reform in the House of Lords showed, and impeded
the growth of a liberal and happy colonial society. The mood of the
Scott era had returned to plague again the colonial church. Broughton,
however, was aboard the ship *Duckenfeld* that anniversary day and
breezing his way calmly to Hobart having already decided to surrender
part of his salary for the support of additional chaplains.[13]

Hobart did not welcome Broughton. The press left his arrival in the obscurity of its shipping column and devoted an editorial to the *Duckenfeld*'s cargo of horses. Wentworth's performance was the hot news, and gave local bards their cue:

> What do we want Bishop or Archdeacon,
> Is not good sense, salvation's safest beacon?[14]

Broughton, with his family for company, hired a private residence and shrank from sight. His visit became a retreat to recover from the frictions of the year past and to plan a visit to England once he had overturned Bourke's opposition.

Though chairman still of the Aborigines Committee Broughton did not call a meeting during his five month stay. He appointed a Mr Wilkinson catechist to the natives at Flinders Island but within a year Wilkinson turned island storeman. Aboriginals preferred flour. Broughton addressed Arthur against extending subsidies on Wesleyan Sunday schools, Wesleyanism being a worm in the fabric of the establishment. Arthur submitted while Broughton stayed and subsidized the Wesleyans when he left: 'There is a *slight* difference in our opinion as to the countenance which other communions should receive', Arthur later confessed. Broughton also persuaded Arthur to establish a King's School-type grammar school in the colony. This disappointed those who wanted a college to teach the technical arts which prevented men erecting crooked buildings, impassable roads, and misplaced lighthouses; but the grammar school being cheaper was more acceptable.[15]

One event lured Broughton before the public. At the end of April 1833 a load of shipwreck survivors landed. An incautious officer on the ship *Hibernia* had inspected a rum cask by candlelight and set the ship ablaze. One hundred and fifty perished, and eighty survivors told harrowing tales of seven days adrift eating raw pork and slaking their thirst on brandy mixed in swine's blood. All Hobart listened, but when asked to contribute to a relief fund the rumour spread that immigrants properly insured needed no relief and others didn't deserve it. Broughton thought that hard-hearted; and being Whitsuntide he called on Christians to minister comfort in imitation of the great Comforter.[16]

Broughton, however, deemed the moment ripe for more than charity. At divine service in St David's church with some survivors present he preached a timely sermon. They had heard much of the anguish of those who survived, but what of those who perished? What filled their final moments as they rushed from beam to beam escaping the fire only to be caught by the flood? Every immigrant present in the church that day had crossed two oceans to arrive safely in this continent and had escaped that flood, Broughton said. But had they been spared the eternal fire? So the *Hibernia* became a parable:

> The image of that stately ship consuming, with so many that it contained, in the devouring rage of that conflagration, cannot but awaken and stir up, even the least sensitive, I think, to a remembrance of that day, when a consuming fire shall go forth from the presence of the Lord.[17]

Broughton performed without mercy. He assembled the congregation to comfort the survivors and dismissed it with freshly bruised memories of a hideous past. He found himself among a stony-souled community and took refuge in the gospel of the beleaguered prophet—an exultation in the elemental grandeur of the Divine that no human will can stay. Whether or not colonists sang the Lord's song in their new land, fire and heat, lightning, storm and tempest, would praise and magnify His name forever.

The *Hibernia* fund was Broughton's parting gift to the colony. The colony's parting gift to him was less generous. The cost of the archdeacon's visitation exceeded its value, moaned one newspaper; 'Had [he] even been visible at some *known* place for one single hour per diem, we should not have begrudged all the expense'. All in all, colonists were to be congratulated on the archdeacon's departure, commented another paper; he was pious, learned and charitable but his mind so tinctured with prejudice that the 'march of intellect' was passing him by. Broughton departed assured the colony needed either a different archdeacon or none at all. His was a lonely journey back on the ship *Jupiter* to another colony where many said the same thing.[18]

When the *Jupiter* docked in Sydney on 8 July 1833 it was winter, and a season of disappointments for Broughton. Many matters referred earlier to London had been resolved. Goderich confirmed the Church Missionary Society in its control of the Wellington Valley mission. He admonished Bourke to listen to Broughton's advice but bound him to nothing. 'I rely upon your own discretion, as well as upon that of Mr Broughton, in any attention which it may belong to either of you to give to this matter', Goderich wrote. In June 1833 that asked too much. Discretion was a shrinking commodity in the relationship of the two men. Goderich's palaver merely softened his total rejection of Broughton's plea to be restored control of Aboriginal missions.[19] Goderich also confirmed Broughton's reduced status. Though he had no idea why it occurred he thought it appropriate; and noting that Broughton had no *personal* interest in the matter, thought it best not explained.[20] As for the archdeacon's salary, Goderich assured Broughton the British treasury would pay it should colonists refuse. The British treasury, of course, knew nothing of the pledge.[21]

Broughton found the same riddle in Goderich's treatment of strictly ecclesiastical matters. Goderich promised all future chaplains would have minds and tempers adapted to contend against the vitiated and unruly passions of the settlement, and immediately appointed the Reverend Henry Stiles who suffered temporary aberrations of the mind in extreme heat. James Stephen had engaged Stiles as a family tutor and engineered the appointment. 'I am sorry that the Secretary of State should have been recommended by Mr James Stephen, as I hear, to make this appointment,' Broughton reported. 'The occurrence of any fresh casualty at this moment would do us more injury than I can well describe.'[22] Goderich approved Broughton's request for clergymen in place of catechists provided stipends were not increased; then informed Broughton that no chaplains could be recruited at that price. Finally,

Goderich approved the appointment of two penal chaplains and then instructed Broughton to appoint the newly arrived masters for the King's Schools chaplains in their districts so as to free one chaplain from Parramatta and one from Sydney for the penal work. Innes was dead three months before Goderich hit on that idea, and no church at Parramatta or Sydney had an assistant as earlier reports sent to Goderich made clear.[23]

Goderich solved problems by not noticing them, and confounded the adage that no man can serve two masters. He was both Tory and Whig. To one whose ministerial career survived the radical switch of administrations in 1830 it may have seemed that beneath the shufflings of the time no fundamental changes were intended. He counselled Broughton to believe such was the case.[24] But the counsel rang hollow in 1833 with news of government interference to suppress Irish bishoprics and redistribute the income of the Church of Ireland. Irish agitators against ecclesiastical tithes had their victory, why not colonial agitators against the ecclesiastical estimates theirs? While Wentworth agitated the market place a King's School old boy, Blaxland, warmed up the Legislative Council with protests first against civil salaries then the ecclesiastical ones.[25]

If the news awaiting Broughton's return was not reassuring, events were no better. On 9 July, the day after he landed, Bourke welcomed him back into Sydney's society at one of those urbane parties where the tongues of leading citizens wagged on until three in the morning. The day following that Wentworth paid his compliments, and congratulated Broughton on his return. Wentworth was, of course, playing the lion at another of those 11 a.m. meetings at the court-house. The petition of the previous 26 January for a popular assembly had not gone well up country and its promoters feared this might be interpreted to mean settlers out of town wanted policy determined in London rather than by the boys in Sydney. To urge waverers to consider the cost of their indecision, Wentworth and a few hardy campaigners preached another round of sermons on the expense of Mr McLeay's pension, Mr Busby's New Zealand sinecure, and Mr Broughton and his satellites.[26]

From the manner in which Wentworth on this occasion savaged the chairman before the real business of the day had been broached, it was clear his jaws were set for the maul. Once he had congratulated Broughton on his return, he asked why the archdeacon spent half his year away from Sydney? Was not this a gross neglect of those who paid him? So Wentworth complained of spiritual neglect! Yet not long before Broughton had been taken to task for not moving away from Sydney! It was not, however, the cost of having Broughton in or out of Sydney that nagged at Wentworth, but the cost of simply having him. What had happened to the archdeacon's princely salary since their meeting in January? Wentworth asked. Had it shrunk towards a reasonable figure? No! On the contrary it had swelled in Van Diemen's Land to an outrageous £2750! That, of course, was fiction. The Hobart visit cost the government £87. But fiction and fact served Wentworth equally. He was not out to reduce Broughton's salary but to abolish it, and cocked his nose at moderates who pleaded for efficient functionaries at moderate salaries. Wentworth proposed a new deal for colonial religion: 'those who require ministers should support them'.[27]

E. S. Hall thought that too conservative. After all, Scott had thrown him out of his pew at St James for not paying his rent. Therefore, in Hall's reckoning, no man who accepted a penny for preaching the Gospel, whether freely offered or officially paid, preached with integrity. No man, retorted the Reverend Henry Fulton, preached so wearisomely as the editor of the *Monitor*, and took a fee for every edition.[28] By and large, colonists thought that clergymen thrown on their congregations would become poor parsons, and 'poverty, such is human nature, is despised and rejected'. Government aid seemed the best, if not the ideal, solution; and a petition was got up to offset Wentworth, Hall and Blaxland when the ecclesiastical estimates came up for discussion in the Legislative Council. 'Your petitioners', the document said, 'whilst they protest against the principle of being compelled to support the clergy out of the colonial revenue respectfully contend, so long as any portion of it is so applied, that all sects have a right to equal participation in it, according to their respective numbers'. To Broughton this was only a little more acceptable than the abolition of aid. It was an irony of Broughton's predicament that those who spoke out most strongly against reducing his clergy to beggars before their congregations were determined ministers of other denominations should not beg from theirs.[29]

Meanwhile, the time came for Bourke to return to his jury bill. Having raised expectations he had to satisify them, he said; but unfortunately, the Colonial Office had not been enthusiastic and Bourke was able to introduce only a mild measure providing for petty juries in the trial of lesser criminal offences. Nevertheless the anticipated number of new juries made the inclusion of emancipists essential. Men proved trustworthy in the trusting, Bourke said; and he looked to the measure to soften the cleavage between emancipist and free.[30]

The moment was not good for such a commendation. The *Gazette*, once friendly to the measure, now bitterly condemned any simple transfer of English jury practice to the colony as tantamount to placing the administration of justice in the hands of men unfit for English citizenship and so better 'calculated to subject trial by jury in this colony to the ridicule of sensible men' than to dispense justice. The *Monitor* reluctantly agreed. Both newspapers had already reacted adversely to an experiment in trust in the Hunter district. Bourke never believed severity subdued the temper of a violent man and in 1832 hindered the felicity with which enraged masters visited their wrath upon assigned servants. Instead of allowing one Justice of the Peace to consent to a master chastising a lazy, disobedient, or abusive servant, Bourke required the consent of two acting together at the same time and place. By interposing an element of inconvenience between wrath and its expiation, Bourke ensured that only desperate masters beset by refractory servants would resort to summary punishment. Bourke hoped, too, that the restraint imposed on masters would be matched by a respectful subordination in their servants. But the opposite happened. Assigned servants did not respect their masters more by fearing them less, and crime and insubordination increased in the Hunter district. 'The Prisoners thought a New South Wales millennium had arrived', commented the *Gazette*. 'They beheld the authority of the magistrate defined and they became what among them is colloquially termed "bouncible".'[31]

This tendency among certain classes to bounce authority had turned Broughton against common juries in Darling's time. The cohort of 4000 that hooted Darling out of the colony confirmed its presence in the colony and the Hunter district crime wave proved it dangerous. So Broughton opposed Bourke's new bill as politically and morally wrong, and found Arthur in agreement. He argued that in a colony careless of religious precepts the average man's oath, whether free or freed, was of doubtful or, at best, unknown value. To function honestly, trial by jury relied on men of good conscience; for conscience alone checked secret dishonesties and the frauds no human mind could detect. What sharpened conscience but the regular practice of religion? What restrained those undetectable perjuries but a recollection of that unseen but all-seeing God who vowed, 'I will repay'? Broughton knew the religious habits of those classes providing the juries, and judged it morally wrong, as churchman and councillor, to approve a measure which required truthful and honest behaviour from men who, in his estimate, possessed no motive for respecting it under all conditions. The bill passed by one vote because Robert Campbell muddled his appointments.[32]

The archdeacon's behaviour armed Bourke for an attack. Broughton belonged to a party pledged to keep emancipists 'in a state of entire disfranchisement', he reported to the Colonial Office. This of course, distorted the archdeacon's position which condemned the whole self-made, well-to-do class, whether emancipist or free, as unfit for jury service because of its religious neglect and fitful contempt for authority. Bourke also reported Broughton as *alone* in resisting all compromise. He made nothing of the other opposition or of Blaxland's switch from support in 1832 to opposition in 1833, or of the *Gazette* and *Monitor* doing the same; or of McLeay's protest that some official members had supported the bill contrary to conscience because Bourke denied they had a right to block official policy. Exaggeration and distortion helped Bourke discredit Broughton in advance of any return to England.[33]

The ecclesiastical scene was also distorted. In February 1833 William Ullathorne arrived as vicar-general of the Roman Catholic community. Broughton had already met him over dinner at government house when his ship docked at Hobart, but was unprepared for this prince of action. Within two days of landing Ullathorne put a 'ponderous tomb of oblivion' over the church's domestic discord; within two weeks he had begun a reconnaissance of the countryside; he scribbled a pamphlet puffing at the Reformation, dismissed Broughton as a petty theologian and predicted the collapse of the Church of England; and after two months addressed Bourke on his need for pastors in all principal settlements. He wanted priests, not teachers: 'They would produce all the good effects of a vigilant, zealous and disinterested police', he promised

Bourke who, at the time, considered increasing the police to cope with a rise in nuisance crime.[34] Between the lame, middle-aged Broughton and the vigorous, twenty-seven-year old Ullathorne there was no comparison. Bourke threw caution to the wind and raised the Roman Catholic chaplaincy establishment from two to eight, despite an official ceiling of three, and promised eventually to station a priest wherever a numerous settlement sprang up. This gave Ullathorne half the clerical establishment of the Church of England for one-fifth of the population. So Broughton could expect over the next few years to see a Roman Catholic opposition spread efficiently through the countryside, matching his establishment almost priest for priest, perhaps school for school, and at the expense of a protestant government. It was the beginning of a system, Broughton later told Arthur, 'of which I cannot venture to calculate the consequences'.[35]

In the face of this new combination of Ullathorne and Bourke, Broughton simply sweated. While Ullathorne recruited young men Broughton kept old men, and whatever extra Bourke granted the Church of England was gobbled up in perquisites adorning earlier appointments made under more lavish masters. By 1832 £500 went annually to compensate chaplains who had turned their glebes over to the Corporation in 1829; in 1833 £700 went to the Reverend Mr Vincent and the Reverend Mr Docker, and to the latter by the skin of his teeth, for having succumbed to the bottle he was about to be dismissed, in lieu of land grants for long service; close to £100 disappeared in upkeep for convicts tilling chaplains' glebes; and £500 went annually renting parsonages. Broughton had no room for manoeuvre. Bourke sympathized, and offered £4000 for parsonages over the next few years. But such an offer, which reflected Bourke's priorities not Broughton's, was formulated with an eye to future economy rather than religious needs, and revealed the anomaly in Broughton's situation. He had lost control of the financial management of the church and the power to direct its growth. The suspension of the charter of the Church and Schools Corporation had set aside the formal machinery requiring the archdeacon to report regularly on church affairs to the Colonial Office. Since nothing required Bourke to receive a report he did not request one. He treated Broughton's recommendations as suggestions and smothered them in Sydney. Nothing from Broughton had reached the Colonial Office since the report of September 1831. In desperation in 1833 Broughton appealed to the Bishop of London to interfere on behalf of the colonial church.[36]

Meanwhile the Church and Schools Corporation was finally and utterly abolished. In London the question had never been more than a formality, but James Stephen insisted that all Broughton's legal objections be met. The matter went to the king-in-council in May 1832; but in May 1832 the king and his council were more busy reviewing other things. The House of Lords was in committee hacking at the Reform Bill, turning the House of Commons, as young Boz put it, into a conglomeration of noise and confusion. So long as the Lords upset the Commons, and ministeries, like good order in the streets, hovered around vanishing point, the king's thoughts were not to be detracted to the problems of the barren acres of a distant corporation. The matter waited until 4 February 1833. Then, in a twinkle, Broughton's hopes vanished; the king did finally 'dissolve and put an end to the said Corporation'. James Stephen, however, warned Goderich of another vexed problem. The judges of the Supreme Court of New South Wales had ruled that land already granted the Corporation could not be resumed by the Crown in as full and ample a manner as if they had never been granted, but remained a trust of the Crown for education and religion. Goderich must decide who was entitled to benefit from the revenue of these lands. Goderich, however, preferred to leave that to a future day. He was happy simply to have the Corporation irrevocably dissolved.[37]

Broughton protested at the decision. The Corporation, he told a public gathering, was 'the most unjustly aspersed of any with which I am acquainted'. And when the Macarthurs crowned a five year struggle with the Colonial Office by snatching another 17 500 acres of land from the Crown, including 3000 acres once earmarked for the Corporation, Broughton's bitterness overflowed. He told Bourke to record in the minutes of the Executive Council for His Majesty's government to read that the greed of such men had undermined the Corporation from its beginning, and they now fed their families on the sustenance meant for churches and schools. Henceforth he prayed that the colony be delivered from the grip of its covetousness and 'too general a desire for the hasty accumulation of wealth'.[38]

Though Broughton had lost the struggle to save the Corporation, he believed he had won the battle to save the lands already granted to it. Without instructions to the contrary he concluded that the former Corporation's 300 000 odd acres were a perpetual crown trust for the maintenance and promotion of the religious and education programmes of the Church of England. 'It seemed to me improbable that the King of England in making provision for "the promotion of religion" should have had it in contemplation to make provision for the promotion of the Roman Catholic Religion', Broughton reasoned with an eye cast backward into history.[39] Fortified with such logic, Broughton ordered his carriage one early September morning, 1833, and drove to government house bearing a memorandum entitled, *Proposed System for the Future Management of the Church and Schools Estates in New South Wales*.[40] Broughton explained to the governor that the problem confronting them was one of management. Though the former Corporation land might never be increased, they may never be decreased, and were potentially highly profitable. If the governor would appoint him and twelve other Protestants trustees with responsibility for the management of the estates he would strive as quickly as possible to have the lands return sufficient revenue for the support of a system of primary schools adequate for the needs of Protestant children in the colony. It was as wild a hope as Broughton ever expressed; remarkable for its fantasy, but more remarkable for its tacit admission that henceforth the archdeacon would be concerned with Protestant education only.[41]

Bourke turned pale as he listened to Broughton's attempt to 'revive the Corporation but under another name'. He promptly informed the archdeacon that, in the absence of instructions to the contrary, he had come to a very different conclusion. He intended to apply the revenue of the former Corporation's estates to the maintenance of religion and education 'without any limitation whatever'. But he had more to say: the old style Corporation had gone for good and the old style archdeacon with it. The former Corporation's lands would be managed by an agent appointed by the governor and responsible to him alone. The former Corporation's orphanages would be placed under the management of committees appointed by the governor and the Legislative Council. The archdeacon may or may not remain chairman of that committee; he may not even be on the committee. He would continue as Visitor and inspect and report on the buildings, but not appoint or dismiss staff. Moreover, that applied to the schools. The archdeacon's right to appoint schoolmasters had expired with the charter of the Church and Schools Corporation. In future the governor would control the schools in every aspect; set the syllabus, appoint the staff, approve repairs, decide on new sites and pay the salaries. He hoped one day to appoint local committees as his agents in these matters. In the meantime he would be pleased to work directly through the local chaplains.[42] Indeed, Bourke had ready for distribution instructions directing chaplains to communicate with the colony's auditor-general on all matters concerning their salaries, school salaries, forage allowances, building repairs and incidental expenses. For chaplains it meant five separate returns a month in duplicate in place of the former quarterly claim for salary and half-yearly report on buildings lodged with the archdeacon. Since Broughton had less administrative responsibility Bourke instructed him to dismiss his clerical staff.[43]

Broughton left government house that spring September day sensing a new crisis in church affairs. The temporal powers of the colony, he told the Bishop of London, 'will deliver the church over bound hand and foot to the will of her enemies'. Broughton did not believe the King-in-Council had intended the dissolution of the Corporation to be the excuse for stripping him of two-thirds of his office. Yet it was legally possible. Eight years earlier in the case of Walker versus Scott the chief justice had ruled that the visitorial authority of the archdeacon resided solely in the letters patent creating the Corporation. To reason with Bourke was hopeless; 'His decision was so formed that it was not to be changed by any argument from me', Broughton commented. But reasoning with Bourke was not the only avenue open to him. Broughton appealed to the Bishop of London to stall all further decisions on ecclesiastical affairs and help bring him back to England.[44]

Bourke already worked at other plans. Being an administrator he could not afford to talk in terms of truth and error, he told Broughton but of what made for the overall happiness of the people. Since the colony invited settlers of all religious persuasions it must avoid a dominant or endowed church. To remove an endowed church without removing Christianity Bourke recommended aiding the Church of England, and the Roman Catholic and Presbyterian churches. In Bourke's opinion Christianity's many forms served equally well to secure 'to the state good subjects and to society good men', and those three churches accounted for most colonists. The recommendation merely made formal the *de facto* policy that had grown up since Murray repudiated the Corporation in 1829 without providing an alternative.[45]

A more radical plan emerged for education. As late as 8 July 1833 the governor had intended subsidizing the development of denominational schools.[46] Then news arrived of Stanley succeeding Goderich at the Colonial Office. Almost immediately, Bourke proposed that Stanley's brain-child for Ireland, a single system of schools uniting diverse religious groupings for general education and separating them for dogmatic instruction, would be admirably suited to New South Wales. Bourke grew so enamoured of the idea that he boldly proposed wiping out the past and beginning afresh, as if the colony had been settled yesterday. The thirty-five existing parochial schools were 'of no great importance or value', he admitted in a damning indictment of his own administration; and Broughton could have the lot, buildings, furniture and all. Bourke would build new and better schools; appoint only well-qualified teachers, importing them from Europe if necessary; and pay them salaries comparable to the chaplains—nothing below £100 to £150. In fact, Bourke promised everything Broughton had recommended over the last four years.[47]

Bourke warned that Broughton and the clergy would oppose the scheme on principle, and the older landowners object to its cost, but the more intelligent citizens were behind him. 'The inclination of these Colonists', he assured Stanley, '... keeps pace with the Spirit of the Age'.[48]

The Spirit of the Age! Broughton turned pale at the mention of it. Behind that phrase and its high-sounding companion, 'liberal', Broughton saw lurking a spirit of sordid self-interest. Liberals trimmed between one opinion and another, served one cause today and another tomorrow, not because they saw something of the truth in everything as many fondly imagined, but because they were exclusively dedicated to staying in power and therefore could not afford to acknowledge an absolute truth in anything. Beware when the liberals triumph, Broughton warned; 'truth itself becomes emasculated ... and self-interest will at bottom rule the world'.[49]

As Broughton brooded over the encircling gloom of infidelity the twenty-sixth day of January came around. In 1834 it fell on the Lord's day. So Broughton went up to St Philip's church and proclaimed that day the forty-sixth anniversary of the founding of 'another land of Canaan'. Shall they find peace as well as prosperity in their new Canaan? he asked. Was it not a remarkable thing that the increased determination of colonists to rest the well-being of their society on rules and regulations dreamed up by their own ingenuity had ended in a wave of crime? The congregation knew Broughton's meaning; Sydney streets were alarmingly unsafe, bushranging increasingly audacious, the Hunter Valley allegedly aflame with disorder, and Bourke reduced to lugubrious death pageants to strike terror into criminals. On the eve of this very anniversary the colony had been stirred by the last days of poor Hitchcock and Poole, two mutinous convicts sent up country to hang in the hot, fly-infested plains of the Hunter Valley as a reminder of the end that awaited law-lessness. Such crime, Broughton explained, began in the unpunishable offences of the heart, in the promptings of greed, anger and wrath. To subdue such impulses men needed meekness and forbearance, virtues only the church could teach. Should the state be severed from the church as some colonists urged, then, said Broughton, lurching over his pulpit, Flee the colony! 'A society made up of persons wholly devoid of religion, could not subsist', he continued. 'But allowing the wicked full scope to prosecute their abandoned purposes without check or hindrance from the example of any who fear the Lord . . . they will bring down vengeance upon themselves through that inseparable connection between wickedness and destruction, which sooner or later is found to prevail in all human affairs.'[50]

In all human affairs indeed! Drink had got the better of Docker, the chaplain at Windsor, and loosened his tongue after a fashion unbecoming to his profession. To avoid the scene of an archdeacon's court he resigned, then created another by refusing to vacate the parsonage. While the new chaplain ran the church from a room in the local hotel, Docker, Sunday by Sunday, marched his family to the church and presented himself at the altar rail. At first Broughton wanted to evict him but, realizing that Docker had squatted in the parsonage out of desperation for a roof for his family, left him alone. He remained five months then quietly moved on. Wilton, the chaplain at Newcastle, was in hot water for failing to link up with the Hitchcock and Poole death pageant on Patrick's Plains. Bourke demanded an explanation. Broughton explained that the execu-tion had taken place at short notice in an unusual spot while Wilton was quite properly occupied in an extended country visitation. Bourke thought the excuse weak. E. S. Hall got wind of the matter and declined to believe there could be an excuse and complained to the Archbishop of Canterbury: 'Your Grace, our clergy are few, and such as we have are not all attentive to their duty'. That went for Broughton too: 'Our Archdeacon', the *Monitor* informed its readers, 'is a never failing Visitor to the Board of Enquiry deciding whether the woman kept as a mistress at the house of a settler in the interior by a civil servant of the Government, was the prisoner of the Crown or a free woman'. The subject of the enquiry was a little more delicate. The Secretary of State for Colonies wanted to know whether Mr John Stephen, the civil servant in question, had made a mistress of an assigned servant knowing that she was the wife of another man. The case, touching as it did a sensitive area of public morals, interested Broughton, but he was involved in it by com-mand, not by choice, when the Executive Council was directed to review the evidence and file a report. When Broughton was not wasting time he was allegedly wasting money putting elegant porticos on St James church.[51]

Friends found good points to praise. Broughton raised several hundred pounds for *Hibernia* victims who settled around Sydney, and through the clergy and on his own touring turned job-spotter for the Emigrants' Friends Society. He rallied Sydney to receive the *Red Rover*'s cargo of female immigrants; and those many wolves in grandma's bonnet, so eagerly sought before being sighted, proved difficult to place. As they dallied in Sydney awaiting employment Broughton took responsibility for their shelter and welfare, never forgot the experience, and advised the Colonial Office against repeating the experiment.[52]

Amid all this Bourke's attitude to Broughton sobered. The governor had demoted the archdeacon too far and burdened the colonial secretary with unnecessary correspondence. Bourke lacked, as Broughton had warned, the local knowledge to process claims without costly inspection or frequent reference to the archdeacon's registry. It took three letters to substitute screws for nails in a church roof and weeks of negotiation to repair £12 worth of church windows.[53] When Broughton, on tour, spotted an inefficient schoolmaster it took months of correspondence to decide whether the archdeacon could dismiss him or whether Bourke should send out his own inspector.[54] But it took the horse's hay to create a crisis. To reduce forage allowances to a minimum Bourke found he required the archdeacon's approval of the chaplains' peregrinations. So all forage claims were forwarded for the archdeacon's approval. Repair claims soon followed. Finally, Bourke reinstructed the chaplains to communicate, in the first instance, with the archdeacon on all ecclesiastical matters.[55]

By this time 1833 was gone and Stanley had overturned Bourke's objections and granted Broughton permission to return to England for consultation at the Colonial Office.[56] Tattlers said it amounted to a resignation, but others thought 'a snug well-paid' £2000 a year not to be sneezed at; 'The Colony could well spare the benefice it is true, but could the Incumbent?' Broughton thought it his duty to return. 'Nevertheless I have no *wish* to come, but quite the reverse', he told Arthur, 'and therefore have no personal fear of consequences which may arise from insisting upon what I consider proper terms'.[57]

Before leaving Broughton called his clergy to a visitation in Sydney and encouraged them to battle on amongst 'an unreflecting people'. The destroying drought of 1829 and the later redeeming rains had altered nothing. 'Men are thrown so much upon their own resources they acquire a habit of ascribing all to their own policy and exertion', he said. As God's ambassadors the clergy must prevent a spirit of self-dependence becoming the sole national characteristic. Then with a swipe at Bourke, who was ill and absent, Broughton accused the government of neglecting the rules of convict worship and idly watching the sabbath drift into a drunken holiday.[58]

A few days later the archdeacon's household goods went under the hammer. He sold all that he could not carry, partly to defray the costs of his journey which, to his astonishment, the Colonial Office insisted he pay himself.[59] Officially he was holidaying abroad. So Broughton hired the most comfortable quarters he could find and on 15 March sailed away in the *Henry*. With him went a cargo of fine colonial wool and the echo of Ullathorne appealing for 'liberal and kind' Protestants to share the cost of an altar for St Mary's chapel.[60]

6

Waiting in Corridors

Must we quit the field at once, because opponents are prepared to enter it? Let us rather hold the Christian advantage
which prior occupation always gives.

British Critic 1836

The departure of the *Henry* did not cheer Bourke. Broughton, however
troublesome in the colony was a danger abroad, and Bourke's attempt to
calculate a safe period for Broughton's absence had misfired. By 1834
a coterie of malcontents were gathering in London. Parry, Broughton's
friend, had gone over to complain of Bourke's interference with the
lands of the Australian Agricultural Company. The Macarthur agents
had taken up the cause of the Hunter River magistracy who had threatened mass resignation over Bourke's interference in their duties. Newspapers and pamphlets underpinned their protest; and the formation of
a counter-committee to expose 'the political juggery now in existence
to obtain the removal of Governor Bourke' affirmed that the governor
was threatened where he was most vulnerable—in the garrulous chambers
of the Colonial Office accessible to all but a governor in office.[1] As Broughton sailed into this gathering storm Bourke feared he would add to its
fury. 'Though very correct in the discharge of his professional duties
he still finds time for politics', Bourke warned Thomas Spring Rice a
friend and parliamentary secretary to the treasury. 'As he will probably
mix with some of the Macarthur family and others of that faction, he is
likely to be influenced by their views and his own feelings, and to assert
in those general terms which hardly admit of refutation that the colony
is not better for my government.'[2]

Bourke had hoped his son Richard would beat Broughton to London
and set up a lobby on his behalf. Richard was to contact Spring Rice,
a Limerick neighbour and a highly-placed Whig politician closely
associated with Stanley's Irish education reforms. Richard was also to
urge his brother-in-law Mr Percival to exploit his friendship with James
Stephen, senior legal officer at the Colonial Office. Though Percival
and Bourke did not see eye to eye on the drift of political affairs, Bourke
had attempted to appoint him to McLeay's job and looked for a gesture
in repayment. When Broughton beat Richard Bourke off the mark the
governor sent Spring Rice a letter advising him to caution Stanley that

behind Broughton's pleasant manner stood a man illiberal to the core, vowed to keep Presbyterians and Roman Catholics in fetters, and dedicated to the exclusion of emancipists from government forever. By the time this letter arrived in London the odds had changed and Spring Rice was Secretary of State for Colonies.[3]

Broughton landed at Brighton on Saturday, 16 August. He rested there the Sunday, then took his family on a sentimental journey through the countryside they loved to London to meet his mother. Next it was on to Canterbury, where, in the shade of memories that were the starch of his soul, Broughton hired a house to await the outcome of the plans to which he tied his future. On the green downs of Kent and among the old grey stones of Canterbury, Broughton felt he belonged: 'If I thought myself quite free to consult my own inclination I should prefer a very humble station at home to the highest that could be offered me abroad'.[4]

Many good things happened in Canterbury, and a gathering of the King's School Feast Society on 18 September was among the best. By a stroke of luck the Duke of Wellington was the day's patron. He brought publicity and a bevy of local politicians. During the day's mixed ritual of worship, prize-giving, and feasting Broughton took counsel of the Duke and others on the men he must deal with. Their communications were not heartening but their mood was defiant; so defiant indeed that, with the aid of a little wine, the Feast's dinner at the Fountain Hotel turned itself into a Tory rally. Howley the Archbishop of Canterbury, possibly influenced by a meeting earlier with Broughton, spoke up in defence of traditional education. Reformers might change but they would never improve the training imparted in the classical syllabus of England's endowed schools, he said. In seminaries like the King's School, Canterbury, the young learned to unite the manliness of the ancients with the morality of Christianity, and that, the archbishop concluded, had given the English nation its fibre. At that sound those fibres rose up and cheered. Broughton stood up too: 'There is now a King's School in the antipodes', he shouted above the din. They cheered again and toasted the archdeacon's health. Broughton, finding them full of good cheer and warm to ancient institutions, craved liberty to add a few words explaining his presence. 'He had been placed at the head of Christianity in a land where education was unknown', he said, 'and it was part of his duty to attempt the removal of difficulties produced by the absence of an establishment for inculcating religious and general knowledge.' He had come to England to see to that. Someone present noted down the fact, and the *Times* reported it to the nation.[5]

Broughton met many people in those early months; some important, a few eminent, but mostly the wrong people. The Whigs ruled, not the Tories. As he moved among the staunch Tory community of Canterbury and East Kent he grew daily more familiar with the opinions of those with whom he agreed, while the men who would decide his fate remained strangers. Even the Archbishop of Canterbury, to whom he had ready access, carried less influence than the Bishop of London in circles where decisions were made. By October 1834 Broughton had got into the *Times* but not the Colonial Office.

Broughton reported his arrival to the Colonial Office and had requested an appointment in August. He received a cool acknowledgement. The under-secretary Sir George Grey insisted he first state his business in writing. Broughton thought no mystery surrounded that; but he had drafted a number of submissions on board ship and sent Grey these in the first week of September. They probably hindered his cause. Broughton hounded the Colonial Office on matters considered closed: his demotion in the Councils and the injustice of reducing him to half salary during his absence. The half salary regulation was for the benefit of officials who returned for relaxation or private business, the archdeacon noted; and he assured the Colonial Office that he had no private business to transact and sufficient public business to preclude any likelihood of relaxation. He also accused the Colonial Office of retreating into fiction when it maintained he came of his own free choice. That, he argued, implied he was equally free to choose not to come. The history of his appointment told another story. In 1829 he had departed for the colony with a clear set of instructions and in less than five years lost them. What the Colonial Office had not changed it had varied; and so often changed and varied, he emphasized, that 'the disorganised state of all matters connected with the church left me no choice but that of proceeding hither for fresh instructions'.[6]

Throughout September 1834 the postal service remained Broughton's one means of entry into the Colonial Office. Doors would not open. His appointments vanished as the hour struck. Spring Rice arranged and cancelled two interviews. Sir George Grey called him to London for an extensive working session and Broughton, laden with pamphlets, papers, and draft plans, stepped from the Canterbury coach only to learn that the meeting had been postponed. He waited in London a week for alternative arrangements. None were made.[7] He spoke to underlings, but discovered nothing of ministerial opinion on Bourke's proposals. Silence had sealed him off and he feared he faced an indefinite stay in England.[8]

While the latch was down on the Colonial Office Broughton busied himself at the Bow Street office of the Society for the Propagation of the Gospel. This venerable institution, he addressed its secretary, had through its timely intervention saved the name of sterling Protestantism from extinction in many of His Majesty's American colonies; and invited it to do the same for New South Wales.[9] To his dismay Broughton found two competitors on the same doorstep, a newly formed mission to Western Australia and the South Australian Church Society, and each asked that he lend his name to their appeals. He declined; the Society might assist one antipodean suppliant, but not three.[10]

In the past ten years the Society had twice attempted to adopt New South Wales as a mission. The more recent attempt in 1831 was made conditional upon government aid that did not materialize. Broughton therefore came where there was goodwill.[11] Unfortunately it was an unpropitious time to launch a third bid for adoption. In July 1832 the Society fell victim to a Whig budget reform which withdrew an annual £15 500 subsidy from the North American church. In one stroke the Society's missionaries lost half their salary, and to prevent further deterioration the Society terminated odd payments to works undertaken outside its principal areas of concern. Broughton arrived amid this overhaul and was unaware that New South Wales was to be excluded from the Society's coffers. Two letters crossed him in mid-ocean, one cancelling the Society's offer to provide Parry's chapel with a chaplain and the other terminating a thirty-year-old grant towards a teacher's salary at Parramatta. The saving was a negligible £60 a year, but the retrenchment severed the nominal link between colony and Society Broughton hoped to build on.[12] When Broughton approached the Society's secretary he knew he had to present an exceptional case.

His case was that the government and people of England were in dereliction of their Christian duty. They poured 4600 convicts a year into the Australian colonies without contributing one shilling towards their religious conversion. Since 1826 the local community had carried the burden alone; and Broughton commended the colonial government's gallant struggle to preserve some religious and educational facilities and praised those colonists who dipped into their pockets to assist. The task was obviously beyond them. But was the community which received those felons more obliged to care for them than the community which expelled them? Broughton believed not. Every Englishman who nightly rested more safely on his pillow because thousands of his felonious countrymen were removed half a world from his person and property, should consider how to retain within Christ's fold those banished in the interest of peace and safety. Broughton saw no evidence of any such concern: 'So far as the Government and people of this country are concerned those crowds of offenders are cast forth upon the shores of New South Wales without the slightest concern being displayed whether they and their posterity from want of religious ordinances degenerate into heathens and pagans'. Need this be more than stated to be amended?[13]

The Society capitulated. In January 1835 Broughton received the key to its nationwide organization. The London Committee relayed the tale as he told it to local committees throughout England, and invited the archdeacon to travel in the Society's name, as far and as wide as time allowed, driving home that appeal. By way of an immediate amendment the Society handed over £1000 and pledged itself ready to meet the archdeacon's claims 'with the largest possible measure of relief which the state of its finances may enable it to bestow'. Almost immediately the Society for the Propagation of Christian Knowledge followed up with another £3000. Broughton had justified his journey.[14]

The religious societies earmarked their gifts for building churches and schools. Finance for manpower remained a problem. James Stephen dissuaded Broughton from campaigning for the recovery of exclusive rights to the former Corporation lands, and referred him to the lessons in a current Canadian rumpus. The legislature of Upper Canada had been as little disposed as Broughton to acquiesce in the loss of clergy reserves and boldly threw out a bill drafted by the Colonial Office to resume them. Tremors of indignation shook the Colonial Office and a ruling went out that colonial legislatures might modify but may not reject the principles of bills presented to them by authority. Where the

Canadian legislature failed, Broughton, single-handed, could hardly expect to succeed.[15]

Being in England also disabused Broughton of his suspicion that New South Wales was a peculiar victim of the irreligious reformers. He found the mother church of the Empire as much besieged by invective and fraud as the church abroad. 'Everything valuable to us as Churchmen is at stake', one high church editor summed up his impression of 1834. 'We are still in a state of fearful expectation as to the future that awaits us.' And nothing was more at stake than the property of the church. Did it, or did it not, belong to the state? Lord Althorpe asked the question in 1833, and Lord John Russell suggested a simple majority vote in parliament could alienate it to other purposes. Property bestowed eight hundred years ago seemed no more sacred than property received eight years ago, and a rumour in 1834 that an Irish church property bill was being drafted set churchmen discussing the proper thing to do. Broughton sailed into this discussion. He found some churchmen were for bending with the wind, some were not. The *British Critic*, founded 'to fight under growing disadvantages the battle of a dispirited side', counselled its readers to mix high principles with circumspection. 'The wishes of the administration—at least, of its most able and estimable members— are not hostile to the church', it insisted, 'but we do exceedingly fear that ministers are not masters of their own purposes.' It counselled churchmen to surrender nothing essential, to ask for nothing impossible, and to remember the bargain moderate Whigs would strike, may be the best the age can offer.[16] Broughton, a *British Critic* reader, accepted that advice. If it was not an age in which to lay claim to the impossible or the time to ask for more, it was at least circumspect to preserve what one had. Broughton launched his negotiations on future church expenditure with an offer to freeze his demands at the level reached in 1832.[17]

In 1832 the Church of England cost the colonial government about £9200. Broughton offered to radically overhaul its distribution and free as much as possible of it for the supply of clergy alone. 'If this sum continue to be voted by the Council', Broughton informed the Secretary of State, 'any and every expense incurred beyond this will be defrayed from sources which the Archdeacon will point out.' Broughton fore-shadowed charging parsonage repairs to the clergy as was customary in England, and of introducing a pew-rent system to cope with church repairs. Standard stipends would drop by £50 to £200, with an annual £30 limit on horse and forage allowances. Broughton would cut his salary by £300 to £1700 and hoped to persuade the older chaplains to accept less compensation for their surrendered glebes. Gone were the days when Broughton had insisted that no man could fulfil his vocation on less than £350 a year. Gone, too, were all perquisites; affection alone would honour long service and goodwill reward the call of extra duties. This reorganization, Broughton said, could add eight new chaplains without increased expenditure.[18] He confidently believed the scheme a winner: 'So long as anything can be accomplished *without increase of expense*, I think they will comply'.[19]

The Colonial Office did not comply. It did not even discuss the matter.[20]

Broughton's offer came too late. A few years earlier when Goderich urged the Church of England to accept a modest priority in the colonies it would have been welcome.[21] Instead, Broughton had then fought for exclusive government patronage. By the time he accepted a modest priority the Colonial Office was considering Bourke's recommendation for equality among the colonial churches. Until the British government had decided on that (a policy opposed to its own domestic program of retracting government aid from church bodies) it had no ear for Broughton. His offer was delivered and acknowledged by post, and pigeon-holed.

Broughton failed to win a snap victory in purely church matters. The schools question was even slower. In 1833 Stanley promised to consult Broughton before reorganizing colonial education and had put Bourke's proposals aside.[22] He could see one great difference between the system he introduced into Ireland and Bourke's plan. In Ireland he had the backing of the Protestant Archbishop of Dublin, whereas Bourke acted in defiance of local ecclesiastical authority and, to all appearance, the Bishop of London.[23] His successor Spring Rice was less cautious, and in the opinion of the *Times* honoured with appointments above his abilities. Though Irish and proudly Protestant, Spring Rice was heir to one of the largest land fortunes in Ireland with much to gain from the sale of a little church property that placated Irish tempers. The church, as Spring Rice read history, had acquired its property by grant and bequest on behalf of the nation in an age which considered the church the natural and sole educator of the nation. Years of religious toleration had changed that till, by 1830, the Church of England was but one of the nation's tutors and no longer entitled exclusively to the revenues of property set apart for the education of the whole nation. Statesmen were obliged, however unpopular the move, to redistribute property in accordance with the needs of the nation and the intentions of its ancestors. So Spring Rice approved Bourke's attempt to do for the colony what he was pledged to do for Ireland. He approved even more Bourke's decision to abandon a sectarian system in favour of a system almost totally out of the hands of the clergy. Such an experiment accorded with a longstanding prejudice of his own.[24] So on 22 July 1834 Spring Rice took Bourke's scheme off the shelf and circulated it among the ministry.[25]

In October 1834 Broughton enquired after Bourke's recommendations on education and learned nothing. Young Richard Bourke, by then in England, had access where Broughton was barred and Spring Rice showed him the comments of the Ministry. 'They all agreed in praising the system', Richard assured his father, 'and the decision of Government on the point is therefore no longer doubtful.'[26] Six weeks later everything was doubtful. William IV dismissed Lord Melbourne's ministry. It was a Tory millennium and they turned as merry as grigs. They toasted their God and His Protestant cause, and decorated the king with addresses praising his 'glorious declaration of inviolable attachment to our constitution in church and state'. The *Times* remarked, however, that the difference between the outgoing and incoming ministers

would be one of style.[27] Church reform must proceed. Broughton benefited from that change in style. Lord Aberdeen the new Secretary of
State for Colonies opened doors Spring Rice kept shut, but told Broughton
the Irish system appeared to suit conditions in New South Wales.[28]
The high-minded Aberdeen had survived youthful doubt to anchor,
like Bourke, in a rational and serviceable Protestantism that fretted
over the fine lines theologians drew splitting churches and dividing
the state.[29] He demanded sound reasons before upsetting Bourke's
recommendations.

Broughton objected to the Irish system as an unequal bargain. It
weakened Protestant repugnance to Rome without increasing Rome's
toleration of Protestantism. Rome retained its principle that only those
parts of scripture may be read which priestly authority approved, while
Protestants, in the cause of harmony, suppressed the principle of 'the
whole Bible'. Six days a week Roman Catholic children read their book
of carefully selected Bible passages and acknowledged the authority
of the priest to put bounds to divine knowledge: six days a week Protestant
children joined them admitting their principle was not one to insist on.
Where was the 'principle of perfect impartiality' in that? Broughton
asked.[30] Aberdeen did not reply. He told Broughton to prove the system
had worked to Protestant disadvantage in practice. That suspended
dialogue. Broughton knew nothing of the system's day to day effects
and turned to an old Pembroke colleague, the Dean of Kildare, for
information.[31]

Aberdeen acted more decisively in another matter. In March 1835,
when a month of Whig threats looked like shaping into an assault that
could topple the Tory ministry, Aberdeen authorized the Archbishop
of Canterbury to offer Broughton the new bishopric in New South
Wales.[32] The offer put Broughton in a quandary. He had coveted the
appointment: 'Whether the appointment would be offered to me I cannot
decide; but I think it ought to be', he confided earlier to Arthur. Bourke
favoured it too.[33] Yet he had left the colony vowing not to return but
on proper terms; and in April 1835 the terms looked anything but proper.
Apart from the probable resurrection of a King's School in Sydney
none of his requests appeared likely to succeed.[34] Moreover, Broughton
was expected to return promptly once consecrated.[35] So Broughton
outlined his conditions. He would return and leave Howley to negotiate
an education settlement. Howley's opinions coincided with his and, to
young Richard Bourke's disgust, Aberdeen had made the archbishop
a permanent third party to all discussions. However, Broughton insisted
the British government free him of all obligation to support or participate
in any educational establishment modelled on the Irish system. Moreover,
he would require, he wrote to the archbishop, 'such arrangements made
as will leave me at full liberty, in the event of the colonial funds being
withdrawn form the Church of England schools, to use any means or
influence which I may possess to keep them in existence by voluntary
contributions'. He sought freedom for competition with Bourke's
scheme, not opposition to it. In case the thin line separating the two
disappeared, Broughton was anxious to remove beyond Bourke's grasp

that muzzle of official silence he had tried to strap on him in the jury debates of August 1833.[36]

Broughton accepted the bishopric as the Tory government fell. The Hon. Charles Grant succeeded Aberdeen and confirmed the appointment.[37] Grant, soon to be created Lord Glenelg, was reputedly intelligent and religious. He was also tight-lipped. Few men rode to higher office on fewer words. He could maintain a year's silence in parliament. His opinions were unknown. He had divulged no sentiment in the debates on church property. His attitude to Howley was untested. He was a Whig likely to prefer the more sanguine counsel of Blomfield the Bishop of London. Howley, suspicious of change, saw the evils of concession. Blomfield weighed the dangers of compromise against the disasters of intractability, and confessed England's church establishment was the only essential one in the empire. Many Englishmen rested the defence of the English church establishment on the 'peculiar nature of English circumstances', and in one short step concluded that in different societies abroad other arrangements might be equally beneficial. Broughton feared betrayal. He respected Blomfield but thought him subtle. The *Times* thought him subtle and sly.[38] Without Howley to rely on Broughton decided to stay and oversee his own interests.

Glenelg was disappointed and tempted Broughton to 'turn bishop' immediately with *carte blanche* approval to act as he wished over school policy in the colony. The offer impressed Broughton. He decided to press the Secretary of State to a further concession. Should Glenelg instruct Bourke to maintain the existing thirty-five parochial schools under the new bishop as visitor, as a pledge of the government's good faith not to exclude him from colonial education, he would return. His friends and the SPCK could negotiate the final settlement.[39]

Glenelg nibbled at the idea. The word at the treasury was economy and it made economic sense to put existing schools and church contributions to use extending education rather than beginning afresh with the government bearing the entire burden. Broughton rubbed home the point; and English churchmen used it against those itching to remould English schools on some new continental system. A compromise system did operate in the West Indies where subsidies were paid to all efficient schools using the British and Foreign system or the Irish system, whether run by churches or local committees. Glenelg promised to consider that system for New South Wales and in June 1835 again asked Broughton to return. Young Richard Bourke thought his father's system lost.[40]

Broughton was not confident he had won. He disliked the West Indies system in principle but thought the Church of England could profit under the scheme. Yet he doubted Glenelg would carry the cabinet with him. Glenelg was a moderate, and the Irish and radical members had the initiative.[41] So Broughton played for time. In mid-June he told Glenelg the University of Cambridge could not confer the Doctorate in Divinity indispensible for consecration until October, though one week remained to proceed by Royal Mandate. Glenelg told him to get the degree by whatever method he could, and to keep it whether he ultimately became bishop or not. The University felt less generous.

To proceed by royal mandate his appointment as bishop must be 'fixed and certain'. Glenelg said the government considered it fixed. Broughton added that he would too if, in the one remaining week, the government showed where it stood on colonial education. An impasse had arrived. Glenelg turned aside to deal with a fresh crisis in Canadian affairs.[42]

Broughton abandoned the corridors of power for a rest at Canterbury, then, after a brief pause, he stayed a week at Hartley Wespall with Dr Keate and three weeks in London with his mother. Late in July the family took a summer vacation around Dover and Hastings. Broughton relaxed. He ambled along cliffs, clambered over ruined castles, and took the children for donkey rides. Of a week-end he preached for the missionary societies at Margate, where in 1826 he had almost become curate, at Reading, Bath, or one of the London churches. On weekdays he sought out familiar faces in old places. There were dinners at Stratfield Saye, the wedding of Fanny Keate at Hartley Wespall, and many a pleasant evening at the homes of the local gentry, Lord Irvine, General Fellows and so on.[43]

Sarah Broughton found the confusion of politics a blessing. Every upheaval in the Commons that kept her husband in the antechambers of the Colonial Office, gave her those treasured extra days with her ailing mother. Once parted they would never meet again. Though she could enter with gusto into trips to Dover Castle, to London, Bath and Winchester, dine at Lambeth or at Stratfield Saye with the Duke, or take in a concert at Drury Lane, her delights were in the more simple things. She loved to drink tea with her mother, to dress her daughters for a party, and then of an afternoon, to stroll into the parks and on to the cathedral where, by the monuments raised to heroes of a greater past, she could hear the Evensong anthem. Out of quiet prayer and music came the strength to bend her life in perfect hamony with her husband's. She loved Canterbury, and she enjoyed the gift of the delay.[44]

Business of state gave way to pleasure but the affairs of the archdeaconry followed him; a fact Broughton duly emphasized in his struggle for full salary.[45] Arthur complained by every post of the archdeacon's 'troops' in the southern colony; and Dr Drought, chaplain of Green Ponds, was at the centre of the complaints. Drought behaved oddly, and Broughton once censured him for solemnizing marriages in inns and taking the fee in spirits. But there was more of the devil in Drought than entered from the bottle. In 1834 Arthur heard from snoopers around Green Ponds that the degree of affinity between Drought and his 'daughter-housekeeper' was one neither registered in the *Book of Common Prayer* nor hallowed by it. Luck had never blessed Drought. After an unceremonious exit from his parish at Shadwell by London, he settled in Iceland and from there engineered his way past the Ecclesiastical Board into a colonial chaplaincy. Drought travelled from the globe's far north to its far south, and still shunning crowded places moved along bush tracks to Green Ponds hoping for solitude to pass quietly his remaining days with his daughter. But the hound of heaven kept pace. It drove to the same shores and up the bush tracks to Green Ponds Shadwell's old tailor. To him Miss Drought looked remarkably like his former partner's wife. A stunned Drought confessed: his daughter was no tailor's wife but his own child, though, unhappily, not the offspring of his wife. Arthur paled. His vigilance against evil earned him the title 'the Just', and he intended carrying it into the Resurrection. This 'disgraceful member of your corps' must go, he informed Broughton; and electing himself the archdeacon's *alter ego* in his absence instituted proceedings to remove Drought.[46]

Broughton cut short the interference. 'As I am appointed to *correct* and *superintend* the clergy, I feel very *deeply* how incumbent it is upon me to be their *protector* also', he wrote back to Hobart and ordered Drought's reinstatement. The case against Drought rested on hearsay and must be confirmed at its source or dismissed. In mid-1835 Broughton was busy checking those sources. He found nothing, and Drought remained with his daughter.[47]

Broughton condemned Arthur's apparent willingness to receive whisperers. In 1835 those whisperers were also at work against Bedford the former senior chaplain. Bedford resented the elevation of an outsider, the Reverend William Palmer, as rural dean with authority over all chaplains, and refused to submit. Broughton had warned that the appointment, a legacy from Scott's day, could not succeed, as rural deans possessed no regular jurisdiction at law. Broughton tried to persuade Cowper or Cartwright to go south, trusting to a respect for their long service in the colony to compensate for the defect in regular jurisdiction.[48] He failed. In 1835 Broughton bargained with the Colonial Office to appoint a second archdeacon, and was busily sifting candidates. His eye had fallen on an old Pembroke friend, the Reverend William Hutchins of Kirk Ireton, Winksworth. Hutchins was more an evangelical, but Broughton believed that would enhance his chances of succeeding with Arthur.[49]

Meanwhile the feud between Bedford and Palmer reached a crisis. Palmer tried to discipline and humiliate Bedford before his church-wardens, and was rebuked by Broughton. Thereafter Palmer whispered to Arthur about Bedford's pecuniary affairs, a subject the colony at large discussed from time to time. Bedford in return whispered to Arthur about Palmer's methodistical habit of using lay preachers at the Hobart jail. Arthur was bewildered; but in the end he preferred Palmer's whispers to Bedford's, and wrote confidentially to Canterbury telling Broughton Bedford had outlived his usefulness in the colony.[50]

That infuriated Broughton. He saw Bedford's reputation being maliciously and systematically destroyed, and declined to respect the confidential tag Arthur tied to his communication. 'I cannot at pleasure assume a private character, and *in* that character receive communication upon points which it would be a *breach of public duty* in me to neglect', he wrote back to Arthur. Moreover, he found ruinous tales about Bedford planted all over the Colonial Office. Broughton demanded he stop, and that Bedford be either openly convicted or cleared. So Broughton blew the lid on Arthur's confidential letters. He wrote to Bedford for an explanation wrapping his letter in the hope that all 'charges have originated in misinformation'. He warned Arthur against being the rural dean's echo chamber: 'The private enemies of any of the clergy would have nothing to do but to convey unfavourable reports to the Rural Dean, who might communicate the same to you; and thus the character of an individual may be blasted and his prospects ruined without his being able to trace the influence through which all this has been accomplished'. He told Palmer straight that he was 'sitting in judgment on one of the most laborious and useful men who have been in the colony'. Nothing dragged up from Bedford's past would carry any weight. Broughton had investigated it and concluded that Bedford's labour and record in public charities 'should in equity be allowed its full weight as a counterbalance to any human frailties which may have been in the course of years discoverable in his conduct'.[51]

Arthur froze with mortification and struck back with two well placed letters at the Colonial Office. He asked James Stephen to block any arrangement affording Broughton a say in the selection of clergy for Van Diemen's Land, and accused the archdeacon fo meddling like a partisan in Bedford's favour on the Executive Council.[52] In the colony Arthur cultivated those with a grudge against Bedford, and collected evidence proving Palmer's whispers were not mere tattle. Arthur never forgave Broughton the indiscretion of making public his private letters. 'Circumstances have occurred between Mr Broughton and myself', he told Bourke a year later, 'which render it improbable that any *cordiality* will ever again exist between us.' That suited Bourke.[53]

In those same days Broughton's principles almost cost him Parry's friendship as well. Back in July 1833 Parry had appointed the Reverend Mr Price, an unemployed Independent minister in Sydney, to a temporary chaplaincy on the Australian Agricultural Company's estates. He promised to replace Price when Broughton appointed an official chaplain. Price in a gesture of goodwill promised to conduct all services according to the ceremonies of the *Book of Common Prayer* except Holy Baptism, where he, regrettably, found the notion of baptismal regeneration repugnant. 'The people here, as well as ourselves, have no objection', Parry said at the time. The archdeacon did, but refrained from interfering; and Parry instructed Wilton, the chaplain at Newcastle, to cease visiting the Company's estates. When in due time Lady Parry was delivered of a male child he was received into Christ's Church according to the rites of the Reverend Mr Price. Four of the Company's senior officers disdained the novelty and applied to Broughton for a chaplain to baptize their infants according to rites known in times past. Broughton ordered Wilton to Shroud on 29 December. Parry denounced the move as 'little, if anything, less than a trespass', and instructed Wilton 'to intimate to the authorities under whom you act that I cannot in future permit any arrangement to be made for the performance of Divine Service on this Estate without my previous consent'.[54] Parry thought that ended the matter until, arriving in London, he heard mumblings about a studied discourtesy around the Australian Agricultural Company's estates towards chaplains of the church establishment. Parry, fearing this might prejudice the Company's land claims, sought Broughton out in London and asked him to discredit the tale. Broughton dubbed the tale an exaggeration but not an untruth. He admonished Parry for having a hazy head at odds with a good heart, the one preparing for destruction what the other clasped in affection; and he thanked God the Australian Agricultural Company had employed a number of officers not satisfied to follow Parry's example.[55] The London directors of the Company abruptly terminated a five year quibble over their obligations to provide a full salary for a chaplain and, with studied discourtesy to Broughton (for they bothered neither to consult nor to inform him), appointed the Reverend William Macquarie Cowper, a 'Currency' lad polished up at Oxford and serving a curacy in Dartmouth. Broughton had already singled out Cowper for a chaplaincy at Goulburn; a rugged place where 'they dislike religion in every shape', warned Cowper's brother. Macquarie Cowper preferred the Company's offer.[56]

Early in August 1835 Broughton was asked to call on Mr Powell Buxton MP when he came next to London. Buxton planned a parliamentary enquiry into the condition of native peoples in the colonies and wanted Broughton's opinion on the Australian Aboriginals. The Australian Aboriginals were a quick and intelligent people for whom the Europeans had done no good, Broughton said. Moreover, he doubted whether they ever could. Their cultures were incompatible: 'Whenever Europeans meet with them they appear to wear out, and gradually to decay'. All efforts to reverse this had failed; and Broughton yielded before his enquiries that from a missionary point of view the natives of New South Wales were, with trifling exceptions, abandoned to their ignorance and degradation. Broughton saw no prospect of change. It was impossible to uncover a want for which the knowledge of Jesus Christ was a fair exchange, he said. Build them a house and they will live in the open; offer them a farm and they go hunting. He knew of no way to break in on the lives of these people and he doubted whether many would be there to break in on in years to come. 'Within a very limited period those who are very much in contact with Europeans will be utterly extinct', he told Buxton. 'I will not say exterminated, but they will be extinct.' And with those words he took leave of his hearers and set off by coach for Bath and the good company of old friends.[57]

On 5 September Broughton stopped touring and returned to Canterbury. Within days Glenelg wrote again suggesting he return to the colony. Broughton weighed his responsibilities. By returning he would double his salary and resume control of the church from a tired and ageing Marsden, never an able administrator and in 1835 pitifully decayed by grief at the loss of his wife. Against that Broughton reckoned an immediate return without any assurance on education as tantamount to spending close to £4000 in fares, sustenance and sacrifice of salary for no certain gain. Moreover, the Colonial Office had complicated the issue by allowing a Roman Catholic bishop into the colony. The future head of the colonial Church of England must now also be a bishop. Since bishops do not resign their sees in mid-office, and since he would neither go back an archdeacon and serve under another bishop nor return again later for consecration in England, Broughton told Glenelg he would need to know the full conditions he would return to work under. 'I had not

taken so long a voyage only to be placed in a worse situation than before',
he said; and threatened to resign if pressed to return immediately.[58]

That said, Broughton prepared for a distinguished engagement.
The King's School Feast Society had elected him its preacher for the
September festivities of 1835. During August Broughton studied a
manuscript by his old friend the Reverend H. H. Norris on the spread
of popery in England, and his mind was full of the subject. For years
Broughton imagined Rome to be edging its way into England, but not
until his eyes fell on Norris's manuscript, painstakingly researched in
the British Museum, did he realize Rome stood already four square in
the mainstream of English life.[59] Broughton's prejudice became a obses-
sion, and when his turn came to go into Canterbury's cathedral on
17 September and, amid monuments rich in praise of Cranmer, Latimer
and Ridley, to address the King's School Feast Society, he felt he could
leave England no finer legacy than a timely warning of what the enemies
of true religion were at.

Rome had conceived a gigantic design to replant her errors in every
land from which the Reformation had driven them, he warned his congregation. And with the accusing finger raised high he singled out those
statesmen of the hour who boasted of having outgrown 'the ancient
prejudice' as their chief abettors. This so called 'ancient prejudice', he
continued, was the once praised desire of wanting to impress religious
opinions on others. But statesmen objected that theirs was a new age
and a new spirit lived in man. By that they meant, Broughton continued,
that 'we shall be at liberty to think as we please provided only we admit
that all opinions are equally indifferent, and that there is no essential
distinction between truth and falsehood'. Having discarded the cloak
of prejudice and donned the mantle of 'bland conciliation' towards all
beliefs, those statesmen were confident that the old hostilities born of
former rivalries would never return to England. But their indifference
was no match for Rome's passions, the preacher warned; Rome disdained
all compromise, modified no opinion of her own, tolerated none belonging
to others, and 'will never permit us to enjoy repose upon any other terms
than of a complete surrender of that liberty of conscience which our
forefathers vindicated and won for us by their unbending firmness'.[60]

The congregation agreed and published the sermon. Broughton
reinforced his accusation in an historical appendix compiled from Norris's
notes and illustrating Rome's gains in England since the Reformation.
'It might be one means of awakening public attention to the subject'
he confided to Marsden. The *British Critic* found it delightfully different
and among a literature distinguished for its extravagances its reviewer
praised Broughton's discourse as 'the production of a man eminently
distinguished for sobriety of mind'.[61]

Broughton's antipathy was for Rome's system not for its servants
and he directed his anger against the Protestants who abetted it and no
the Roman Catholics who benefited from it. He made this clear when
the Colonial Office reopened the case on the Reverend J. J. Therry'
suspension with a view to reinstating him. Since Scott had engineered
Therry's removal for disrespect towards the colonial Church of England

the Colonial Office called for Broughton's recommendations in the light of his behaviour since 1829. Broughton reported that he had nothing to say against Therry, despite twice recommending his prosecution in the Executive Council, once for raiding a Protestant funeral and demanding the corpse of an executed prisoner on the point of burial, and once for playing tricks with the colony's marriage rules. The second incident had set tongues wagging. Around 1820 Marsden united in holy wedlock John Ready and Elizabeth Curtis. It was Ready's second marriage, his first wife having removed herself so completely from his life at the time of transportation that a decade of enquiry failed to establish her as living or dead. Broughton believed, as did Marsden, that according to every just view of the obligation of marriage Ready and Curtis had been solemnly united in the sight of God and man. Ready felt that way too; and for many years the colony saw the couple live as man and wife. Then suddenly Elizabeth Ready sported another husband united to her by rites and ceremonies performed by the Reverend J. J. Therry. Therry had John Ready justify the swap in a newspaper advertisement declaring his marriage to Elizabeth Curtis null and void by reason of news, recently received from England, that his first wife was hale and hearty this side of the vale. In Broughton's opinion Therry and the Readys made a mockery of the regulations drafted to stabilize the institution of matrimony among a population where many earlier marriages had been demolished by transportation. Yet in England in 1835 Broughton made nothing of either incident. 'I should be sorry to be supposed to feel any greater repugnance to his restoration than to the appointment of any other person', he advised the Colonial Office. Therry's faults were those of a fervid and strict papist. Broughton reckoned fervour in religion a virtue, and since the British government no longer objected to popery Therry's acrimonious outbursts against Protestantism were fair play within the framework of Colonial Office policy. Broughton would raise no finger against Therry's readmission to a chaplaincy; but 'to the lawfulness and expediency of a Protestant Government giving countenance and support to the Roman Catholic priesthood' he promised unbending opposition.[62]

By November 1835 Glenelg had used the parliamentary recess to resolve the education issue. He decided the colonial government should accept responsibility for education with the governor setting the limit to expenditure and the Legislative Council determining its distribution. The Council could support exclusively a national system or a denominational system, or mix the two. Glenelg intended supporting Bourke without deserting Broughton, and passed to the Legislative Council the decision he could not make for himself. However, if Glenelg took seriously Bourke's complaint that Broughton was a leader of the colonial Tories who dominated the Council he was handing Broughton a fair change of keeping up Church of England schools.[63]

Glenelg's proposal satisfied none. Neither Broughton nor Bourke would gamble on a political tussle in the colony. Bourke openly condemned the Legislative Council as unfit to decide the fate of his reforms, and asked that they be settled out of the colony and in the British parliament.

Broughton for his part feared Bourke had influence in the Council, as was shown by the governor winning the vote on jury reform in 1833. 'When the influence of the Governor over that body [Legislative Council], coupled with the express opinions of His Excellency upon the subject of education, is considered', Broughton told Glenelg, 'he [Broughton] would have but a slender prospect of obtaining such regulations with respect to religious instruction as would afford security to the Church of England.'[64] He begged Glenelg to send the Legislative Council firm instructions to support Church of England schools and chiselled his requirements to a minimum. He wanted the existing school houses placed under the bishop as Visitor with sole right to appoint and dismiss staff, and 'a sum *not exceeding* £1000 p.a. appropriated to support the schools ... upon condition that an equal sum be contributed from private sources towards the same object.' For the rest, Broughton would trust to the SPCK, his own energy, and local goodwill.[65] He failed to conceive of a more liberal offer: a less liberal one he declined to accept;

> I ask, it will be perceived, for no new establishments; but only that those which have existed from the beginning of the settlement ... should be preserved from destruction. I advocate no new principle; but one which was recognised and recommended by the House of Commons Committee on Education so long ago as 1818; and which was prominently dwelt upon by Lord Brougham in the House of Lords on the 21st of last May—if you will subscribe a certain sum, Government will grant you the rest.[66]

Glenelg's patience broke. The appeal to English, Irish and West Indian precedents was a red herring. 'In a case so new as that of the Australian Colonies, few analogies can be drawn from Institutions of the Parent state to our assistance', he told both archdeacon and governor; and in late November directed the Legislative Council of New South Wales to fashion a scheme answering local needs.[67] Glenelg restricted himself to simple guidelines: there should be *one* system, not separate Protestant and Catholic systems, and it must attract a majority of the Church of England as well as a majority of settlers; the Council should study both the British and Foreign and the Irish systems but slavishly follow neither and must use the full New Testament as a textbook; dissenting groups were to be assisted but Glenelg expected Bourke to see that they were few. [68] Bourke's indefatigable task was to unite the colonists in a common education without doing violence to the conscience of any. He would need a rare combination of diplomacy, conciliation and inventiveness to succeed.

On 1 December 1835 Glenelg forwarded Broughton these details together with Bourke's original education despatches hitherto kept secret from him. With them came a final offer of the bishopric and a plea to Broughton to lend his 'concurrence and co-operation' to the making of a new system of education.[69] Broughton refused co-operation. He would, however, accept the bishopric short of a guarantee of the Church of England schools (despite a promise a week earlier to insist on it) provided he was allowed to exercise the prerogative of a Protestant bishop and oppose the enemies of the Reformation whenever and in whatever guise they appeared. That could mean, he warned, speaking up against moves to subsidize Roman Catholic churches and exhorting Protestants to forsake schools which prohibited the use of the Bible.[70] Glenelg acquiesced. 'It was not my intention to impose any condition upon your acceptance of the Bishopric', he wrote back to the archdeacon, 'or to fetter the free exercise of your judgment, in the course which you may feel it incumbent upon you to pursue, either in your Episcopal or Legislative capacity'.[71] So on 10 December 1835, with an open ticket to return to the colony and raise hell against Bourke, Broughton formally accepted the bishopric of New South Wales.[72]

A week later the arrangement lay in ruins. In a fit of pique over salary arrangements Broughton withdrew from the See and asked instead for the pension customarily given public officials whose office is suppressed. Broughton had asked the Colonial Office either to meet the full costs of consecration or to restore him a full salary from the day of consecration. It offered £1000 with full salary when he stepped ashore in Sydney. Broughton calculated his costs at £2058 plus loss of half salary for two years, and sighed that he would quit England a bishop poorer than he had quit Hartley Wespall a curate. 'Justice to my family forbids me to involve myself in such formidable difficulties', he wrote to Glenelg, and resigned.[73]

Fresh bargaining began. Glenelg offered to meet the cost of Broughton's letters patent, his D.D., and whatever a quick trip back for consecration would have cost. Broughton could claim fares for himself and family but not his servants, and the cost of carting moderate baggage but not all his worldly possessions. Glenelg reckoned this at £1350. Moreover, the bishopric being an equivalent alternative to the archdeaconry cancelled all claim on a pension. Broughton thought the bishopric more an expensive substitute than an equivalent alternative and prattled on about his losses till the under-secretaries itched to demolish his quibbles in sarcasm.[74] But the thought of who might be sent in his place sobered Broughton. Might not the Whigs appoint a favourite from the Arnold and Hampden school who would delight to join with Bourke and link all Protestants in one big church without respect to the doctrines of the Church of England? After the sacrifices of the past why quibble in midstream at a few more?[75] So on Christmas Eve Broughton relented: 'I feel that though I cannot yield my conviction, I am bound to overcome my reluctance and to sacrifice my interest', he wrote to Glenelg, and withdrew his resignation.[76] But he demanded a domestic chaplain and promptly appointed one only to be told that domestic chaplains, like ornamental architecture, were not for Botany Bay.[77]

Glenelg prepared Broughton's letters patent with careless haste to return him speedily to the demesne of his apostolical labours. The See was called *Australia* rather than *New South Wales* though James Stephen crusaded for *Sydney* as more in keeping with the apostolic tradition of naming bishoprics after towns.[78] Broughton accepted *Australia* on the understanding its limits would not deviate from those of the existing archdeaconry. The Colonial Office assured him they would not and when the letters patent arrived they did.[79] Broughton found himself bishop of the Swan River as well, and that ruined his life assurance. His family was not protected once he ventured beyond the boundaries of his late archdeaconry. 'I shall be prepared to visit Western Australia . . . only upon condition that the charge, necessary to secure my Life Insurances under this contingency, should be supplied on the part of the public and not from my own private resources', he informed Glenelg. Glenelg, alarmed lest his arrangements disintegrate over a few shillings, agreed Broughton should neither hasten to the west nor be out of pocket.[80]

As 1835 gave way to 1836 Broughton balanced his gains against his losses. 'I am gratified by knowing that I have done *some* things by coming to England which I could not have done by continuing as you say "at my post"',[81] he wrote in self-consolation to Arthur. He had gained a bishopric, prevented the quick adoption of Bourke's education scheme with the outcome still uncertain, but lost government support for both King's Schools. The Colonial Office refused to revive the King's School in Sydney and jumped at a suggestion from Bourke that the Parramatta school be left to the support of the rich it served. So long as the government provided that privileged school with commodious buildings the parochial schools must remain hovels, and if the well-to-do were to be educated by expensively imported Oxford and Cambridge graduates the poor must be content with convict schoolmasters. Bourke recommended the government subsidize instead schools like those 'found in Yorkshire, where Boys of the middle classes are lodged, boarded, clothed and taught for a very moderate annual charge'.[82] Mr Squeers had his colonial protagonist.

Broughton's greatest disappointment, however, was to return in clerical loneliness. Many clergymen 'who would be a blessing to any community' had offered him their services, but without passage money [let alone a stipend] Broughton turned them away. Glenelg promised nine extra chaplains, subject to Legislative Council approval, after the new legislation on religious provisions had been passed. Broughton shuddered at the delay; in December 1835 he instructed Marsden to circulate petitions among the laity in nine areas needing chaplains, and to have them ready for presentation to the Legislative Council when he returned. 'The more quietly the affair can be carried on the better', he advised his deputy, 'and a great object will be to obtain as many signatures as possible.' He wrote by the same mail begging McLeay to be busy about his politics and prepare the Legislative Council to approve the petitions. With luck the clerical drought could break around the end of 1836.[83]

Ironically the one new chaplaincy created at Norfolk Island remained unfilled. Broughton found two suitable candidates, both rugged men of mature age, not in Holy Orders but ready for them, and equipped in his opinion to survive the ordeal of life in a receptacle of vice. The Bishop of London declined to ordain either. Broughton in turn refused to let Glenelg seek a substitute from the London Missionary Society.[84] Convict settlements ranked low on Broughton's list of priorities. He felt a certain futility in attempting to convert men who regressed from

assignment to the chain-gang, and on to Moreton Bay or Norfolk Island.
'I cannot venture to hope that the exertions of any individual, even if
an angel, could effect any very general reformation . . . in those receptacles
of the worst of Criminals', he told the Secretary of State.[85] He certainly
did not intend to direct chaplains away from other areas for their benefit.
And when, in a last minute change of heart, Glenelg offered Broughton
£800 for itinerant chaplains to the scattered chain-gangs, Broughton
accepted on the condition that they could minister to free and convict
alike in the districts they passed through. He saw a grave risk in turning
single men into the vast loneliness of the interior and did not believe a
ministry to convicts alone warranted it.[86]

In the chilly late winter of 14 February 1836 a small put polite gathering
found its way into the grey stone chapel of Lambeth Palace. Inside only
the scarlet and black of doctors' gowns relieved the drabness of the
heavy oak panelling. Howley of Canterbury, Blomfield of London,
Sumner of Winchester, and Monk of Gloucester, were there ready to
perform, in subdued tones and with staid formality, the ritual for con-
secrating Broughton a bishop in the church of God. Beside Broughton
sat the Reverend George Jehoshaphat Mountain; and he, the preacher
said, would soon depart for a land where episcopacy had been well
established. Broughton would not. He must return to a place peopled by
men who had borne the brand of Satan, and there attempt to plant and
preserve sound doctrine. He must go into a tractless wilderness and
raise up a refuge where the outcast, the adventurer in search of wealth
and the poor in search of hope, may find far from their earthly father's
home the true riches of their Heavenly Father's grace. And he must
never forget, the preacher added in a timely aside, that episcopacy could
vanish from England and men would then look to the colonies for its
revival. Had Broughton raised his eyes to where Howley sat he would
have seen the archbishop heavy in thought. Howley had just learned that
Lord Melbourne had dismissed all his nominations for the vacant Regius
Chair of Divinity at Oxford, and had appointed one considered dangerously unorthodox. With such a candidate occupying the chief chair of
divine studies in England there seemed no limit to the potential dangers
before the church. So the preacher charged Broughton with the double
responsibility of establishing sound doctrine in a new land and of keeping
episcopacy alive within the English nation.[87]

A week later on 22 February the barque *Camden* carried Broughton,
his family, two servants, and a brand new carriage out into the Atlantic.
He was content to depart. Too much had changed in church and state
not to leave him with the feeling that he was forsaking one strange and
uncertain land for another. He might sigh to himself 'O Sweet England',
but within he knew the sweetness lay in the memory of past times, a
few friendships, and places like Hartley Wespall, and these must ever
remain adjuncts to life's main work. He was exchanging one battleground
for another. But whereas in England he would remain a spectator, his
friend had convinced him that in the colony he had a unique role to
fulfil. 'It was the conviction', he recalled, 'that if I declined no one else
could take up the matter in an instant so as to be prepared to carry it

on as I might do, which decided me upon coming back.'[88] So Broughton sailed to build in the colony that *citadel*, which others would have to build in England, where the Christian faith would find its refuge when the unholy league between Rome's old superstition and modern liberalism let loose its full terror.[89]

7

Founding the Citadel. 1836

...they who are prepared with me to encounter the rage of
the adversaries, will lay the foundation here of a citadel,
within the walls of which the Christian faith will find a sure
refuge when all without is laid waste.

Broughton to Arthur 21 September 1836

Captain Valentine Ryan anchored the *Camden* in Sydney Cove on the
afternoon of Thursday, 2 June 1836. Broughton sighed relief. The
weather had been rough, the crew had mutinied and someone killed an
albatross; 'But we escaped the penalty', Broughton said. On land the
bell of St James church tolled. Richard Hill its pastor had 'died by the
visitation of God in a fit of apoplexy'.[1]

Broughton returned to a lively Sydney. Good seasons had brought
drink and merriment, and a promise of more tomorrow. Firkins of
Bristol butter appeared in the stores, and the palate grown stale on Coopers
could be revived on bottled beers from London. At night, for 5s in a
box or for 2s in the pit, the Theatre Royal played *The Merchant of Venice*
with a one act farce rounding off the evening and Mrs Taylor singing
the 'Daughter of Israel' between acts. There was value in that. But
there was better value at government house. From nine on the evening
of Monday 30 May till dawn on Tuesday it cost nothing to dance endless
quadrilles in the governor's ballrooms and to wander around brilliantly
lit foliage before turning back to 'long tables groaning under every
substantial good and delicacy of the season', including a fine range of
superior wines. That was 'not usual at routs' and a sign of true liberality,
commented one Sydney newspaper.[2]

Bourke had cause for liberality. A K.C.B. had fallen into his lap
unsolicited, and Darling thought it unmerited. Bourke considered the
award of little value in itself but found the sentiment touching. The
sentiment belonged to Spring Rice and few men, Bourke said, had such
a friend. But the people of Sydney were mighty proud of it. At public
functions over the weekend of the King's birthday they were as happy
to see that red collar dangling round Bourke's neck as Bourke delighted
in wearing it. The ball celebrated, too, the opening of the Legislative
Council with good prospects for many a lively sitting.[3]

Dissatisfied justices and rebellious councillors already peppered the

101

air. Judge Burton declined to acquiesce in the appointment of Judge
Dowling as acting chief justice during Forbes's leave of absence. Dowling's
elevation surprised many including young Richard Bourke who, believing
himself to be about his father's business, had notified the Colonial Office
that the governor wished Burton to succeed Forbes. Bourke did, and
argued that Dowling's being a temporary appointment left Burton's
claim to succession intact, but Bourke undoubtedly held Burton back
in 1835 to reduce Tory strength in a Legislative Council destined to
reconsider the near ill-fated Jury Act of 1833. Burton, caring not a twig
for the seat on the Council but desperately in need of an increased salary
fought to upset the appointment.[4]

Bourke also hit at other Tory officials. He expelled the colonial treasurer
Riddell, from the Executive Council, and declared war on the Hunter
River aristocracy. Riddell, the long-standing 'frondeur of the government
nominated for a public office that Bourke ruled him ineligible to hold
In a political tussle reeking with sectarian overtones and master-minded
by an anti-Catholic Hunter River faction, Riddell defeated Bourke's
nominee, Roger Therry.[5] Bourke blamed the campaign on a flowering
of sectarian prejudice planted earlier by Broughton and Parry, and
feared it would bedevil the area for years if allowed to pass unchecked.
So he struck down Riddell. This aroused the 'extreme hostility' of the
honourable Richard Jones, and in April 1836 he hit back with a petition
criticizing the governor's powers of control over legislation, expenditure
and the magistracy, and called him to account for an increase in crime and
the poor performance of civil juries. Petitions then became the thing, one
begetting the other. Some said convicts were more mischievous than ever
others that the Legislative Council was more mischievous than everyone
Another begged the admission of a few popularly elected members into the
Legislative Council; and another, an 'Anti-House of Assembly ultra con
servative Petition', went into circulation to keep them out. The les
ambitious got up an 'Open Door Petition' praying for the right to peep a
what went on inside the Council. With most petitions went a meeting, an
none more stirring than those at 12 o'clock where Jamison took the chai
and Wentworth the hide off every seeker of place and wealth who criticize
Bourke.[7]

Though the opening of the Legislative Council would heat up the
agitation, Bourke sailed into it with merry-making and a heart lightene
by the loss of a year of doubt and mistrust. Six months before he ha
believed Broughton the victor in the struggle over national school
'I am sorry to find that the prejudices of one Religionist should be allowe
to stand in the way of the general education of the People', he had writte
to his son on hearing of Glenelg's partiality to the West Indies system
'I must only do the best I can upon the system prescribed for me.' H
had talked then, crushed in spirit, of returning, like Archdeacon Sco
before him, to 'make an exposé' of the officials who had control of th
place.[8] Then came 18 May, and the *Henry Tanner* after a miserable on
hundred and fifty-two day voyage from London landed Glenelg
despatches. 'The Church and Schools matters have been settle
according to my wishes', Bourke wrote exultantly to his son Richar

on whom the doors of the Colonial Office had snapped shut.[9] He told few others, preferring to ponder how best to use the news.[10] He pondered, too, what else might follow. Should his recommendations on civil juries and an elected assembly have received equally favourable countenance at Westminster, then the McLeays, the Riddells, the Joneses and the Broughtons would soon be his footstool! So, on the evening of 30 May as Bourke's feet danced his heart leaped and the good wine flowed freely, but the best was to come. The only dark cloud on an otherwise bright horizon was Broughton's unexpectedly early return.

No news of Broughton's departure had preceded him and official notification of his appointment as bishop was still at sea on the *Stratfieldsaye* when the *Camden* anchored on 2 June 1836.[11] So Broughton announced his own arrival and created his own ceremonial landing. He requested a government boat to land him on the spot where His Majesty's officials were traditionally received. Bourke sent the boat and left for Parramatta, but a storm confined Broughton to quarters. By Saturday word had spread of the bishop's return and an impressive gathering braved cloud and wind to welcome him ashore and conduct him in a friendly procession to temporary quarters at the Pultney Hotel, York Street.[12]

Broughton began his public episcopal career next day, Sunday 5 June, when Marsden installed him in office in St James church, King Street. Bourke stayed away but the bishop's friends rallied. They had said in an address the day before, that the bishop was there by his 'Majesty's gracious resolution', and it behoved His Majesty's faithful servants to honour the event. So McLeay put on his official uniform, for he was still one of the king's men and in the king's service despite rumours that Bourke had edged him into retirement, and led a contingent of Supreme Court judges, Legislative Councillors, and the high sheriff, into the front pews where important people sat on special occasions. Behind them sat the respectable inhabitants who graced every occasion the press cared to report, and stayed four hours. It was a stodgy occasion with Broughton preaching 'at considerable length upon the leading doctrine of the Church of England'. Only towards the end did he warm to his congregation and pay tribute to its dead pastor, Richard Hill. Many an eye moistened, and convinced the *Australian* that the congregation had assembled to pay homage to the dead rather than to welcome the bishop![13]

The next day Broughton went to take his seat on the colony's councils. Bourke barred his way. No news of Glenelg's intention to admit the bishop to either council had arrived and the judges of the Supreme Court, Burton concurring, ruled that mention of it in the bishop's letters patent afforded no ground for his installation. A week later the slow-moving convict ship *Stratfieldsaye* landed a despatch confirming Broughton's right to the seats he claimed, but omitted a warrant for formally installing him. Bourke took refuge in the oversight. He declined the bishop a seat, and begged Glenelg, in the interest of colonial peace, to renounce the promises he had made and exclude the bishop permanently from both councils.[14] The colonial press supported that, alleging that the bishop had intrigued with James Macarthur in England to rewrite the New South Wales Act contrary to the interests of ordinary colonists. Broughton denied the accusation for the lie it was; but fearful lest sometime after his departure Glenelg had retracted his bargain (which was to leave Broughton in both councils until the New South Wales Act was revised and then to retire him from the Legislative Council) wrote reaffirming his need of both seats for the present.[15] Glenelg ultimately kept faith, but the bungling of 1836 kept Broughton out of the councils at a moment most convenient for his opponents and Judge Burton refused to believe it unintended. Broughton agreed to see it as 'a very singular but I believe unintentional omission'.[16]

Meanwhile a section of the local press took the community to task for all the mellifluous 'My Lords' turning up in welcoming addresses. The colony had survived satisfactorily for two years without an archdeacon (though Bourke thought the Church of England asleep on the eve of Broughton's return) and needed no bishop let alone a *Lord Bishop*. 'There will be no Lords in New South Wales, either spiritual or temporal', averred the *Monitor*. 'They have done enough mischief in England.' Unless such nonsense stopped, warned the *Gazette*, the colony will soon find itself financing cathedrals and an episcopal palace; and supporting a port-filled bishop too comfortable to go riding up bush, added the *Colonial Times*. Theirs must be a land of the 'Mister Bishop'. At the same time the religious press dissected the new bishop in search of his newly acquired apostolic character. It discovered none. Was there ever so unheroic a tale, commented the *Colonist*, as that of a man who, having come from a land in vital need of moral renovation, knocked on the door of the Colonial Office to ask for chaplains and took 'No' for an answer? Had he received the faintest infusion of apostolic zeal he would have led fifteen curates out of London itself 'on the simple assurance that they were coming to the land of plenty'. Broughton realized he had returned to New South Wales.[17]

Beneath these jaundiced eyes Broughton set to work free of the obligation to attend to Legislative Council business. Much had changed in his absence. Hill's death, Marsden's old age, and Cowper's failing sight highlighted the predicament of his clerical establishment which remained numerically unchanged since 1829 but diminished in vitality. Seven chaplains of the Church of England were older than the Reverend J. J. Therry, senior in age and service among the Roman Catholic clergy, and three were soon to follow Hill to the grave. Rome had fewer churches but they were more eye-catching, and Polding contemplated appointments in districts Broughton had tried unsuccessfully to fill for years. Broughton feared Rome matched him in stamina if not numbers, and gave his first energies to correcting this.[18]

On Monday 20 June Broughton attracted sixty men to St James vestry to hear a report on his work in England and his plans for a diocesan committee to raise local subscriptions for the erection of schools and churches. The men who came did not hesitate, and formed themselves into a committee to implement the bishop's plan. Marsden wept; he never expected to see the day when men so politically opposed as McLeay and Deas Thomson, Judge Dowling and Judge Burton, and many others, would unite to advance the church at their own expense. That night Broughton put down £215 5s. James Macarthur promised £500 for a church, school and chaplain of his own choice at Camden; Bowman gave £235, Colonel Dumaresq £152 2s, Robert Campbell £150, a Robert Scott £125, Philip King £108, Judge Burton £100, Edward Macarthur £85, Hannibal Macarthur and McQuoid £50 each, and McLeay £25. These were the gifts of the men Bourke called the 'notorious' Tory-minded enemies of the people. The advocates of voluntaryism did not match them or prove how much better affection prospered the church than land endowments. Judge Dowling headed their ranks with £31 10s; Deas Thomson followed with £10; and Bourke the architect of colonial voluntaryism had an empty purse then and thereafter at subscription time. The response of the colonial Whigs showed Broughton that, whether or not he wanted close ties with the landed Tory party he needed the financial support they willingly offered.[19]

Broughton also appealed to smaller settlers through a committee headed by Cowper and the new high sheriff McQuoid, who had accompanied him on the *Camden*. This committee worked on selected candidates by post, soliciting first permission to enrol them on a subscribers' list, then later asked for the size and object of their bounty, whether it was for the general fund, local use or some personally favoured project elsewhere. To bring this money in Broughton formed district committees and sent the chaplains riding days on end with willing laymen rounding up the pledges. When his own presence might extract a bigger donation he spared no effort. His industry, the Reverend Richard Taylor remarked after accompanying him on one day's duty, would be 'a lesson for our English bishops'.[20]

Broughton also toured the countryside encouraging local building committees. Scone raised £300, East Maitland £420, West Maitland £620, Paterson £350, and at Whittingham on Patrick's Plain near where Hitchock and Poole had been strung up to put fear in the air, they raised £430. Broughton discussed the plans of each local committee and left behind a gift from his privy purse of SPG and SPCK funds. In these first weeks Broughton wrung £3078 10s from 123 families and added £10 000 more before the first anniversary of his return. The church Bourke found asleep in May Broughton had humming by July.[21]

On 26 July 1836, while Broughton systematically exploited the diocese for funds, Bourke tabled a bill on church subsidies. It provided more liberal aid than Bourke's despatch of 30 September 1833 had foreshadowed and incorporated two of the concessions Broughton strove for in England. Broughton asked the colonial government to subsidize donations raised abroad and to relax the rules for subsidies in the outer districts. Bourke agreed to both and this surprised the Colonial Office.[22] In general Bourke required one hundred adults to pledge their support for a church before the government provided the first £100 towards a clerical stipend. In scattered districts where local settlers could provide a building for worship but not a congregation of one hundred the governor-in-council could still grant a £100 stipend, or, where the population was too un-settled to warrant the erection of a church building a small congregation that raised £50 towards a stipend could apply to the government to supply the rest. But to the annoyance of the *Colonist* and *Herald* Bourke agreed to convict servants signing up as part of the congregation. The *Colonist* wanted them excluded to restrain Roman Catholic subsidies while the *Herald* believed the British government should meet the full cost of evangelizing its exported criminals.[23]

The bill, however, was less generous to the poor. It restricted free sittings in government subsidized churches to one sixth. What 'bastard Christianity' had seized the rulers and clergy that they should condemn the poor to the aisles? asked the *Monitor*.[24] Broughton had earlier wanted half the sittings free, and in 1833 the same newspaper had ridiculed him for enlarging St James church to provide them.[25] But with Bourke insisting that pew-rents pay for the parish clerk and all repairs to church, belfry and graveyard, Broughton thought one-sixth the maximum the church could surrender. He even sought powers to sue pew holders in arrears to avoid debt. Bourke balked at that. The aisles were for the poor; free sittings, Bourke told the bishop, were for convicts, ticket-of-leave men and the armed forces.[26]

The Church bill passed the Legislative Council on 29 July 1836 without opposition. Bourke had released copies of all despatches on the subject in June to test public feeling and been told 'there appears to be no dissenting voice on this subject'.[27] Broughton of course objected to the principle underlying the bill and told Bourke so whenever the matter was raised between them, but did not campaign against it. In July 1836 Broughton seemed more to fear the arrangement would be too short-lived. 'The Government ... is going to involve itself in a labyrinth out of which it cannot be extricated except by removing, at no distant date, all concern about and connection with, the interests and affairs of religion; and obliging, I fear, all sincere Christian men to look upon the Government as less and less the friends of the cause of truth', he warned Bourke, and public comment certainly nourished such fears.[28] Praise for the measure was often coupled with a menacing insistence upon more thorough change in time. The *Colonist* rejoiced at the immediate ill done Church of England pretentions at playing the establishment and, hoping the bill would be but a brief pause in 'the Half-Way-House on the high road to the Voluntary Principle', looked forward to the journey's end. So did the *Gazette* which thought aid 'dubious' but temporarily justifiable where its sudden cessation would be too much of a 'wrench' for colonial religion to sustain without serious damages. The *Australian* thought more highly of the matter. 'An Established Church is absolutely necessary to our well being', its editor insisted and praised Bourke's novelty of a multi-denominational colonial church establishment. The *Herald* half supported that, but served Bourke notice of its intention to watch closely the progress of the matter. The provisions were 'ostensibly religious', it said, 'but we cannot shut our eye to their political tendency'. By this it meant it would withdraw its suppor should any section of the community reap a greater proportion of subsidies than its capital investment in the colony earned in taxes. This really meant the *Herald* would rock the boat the moment the poorer Roman Catholics benefited from the productivity of the richer Protestants.[29] Amid this Broughton was clear-sighted enough to realize the alternative to some aid was no aid. Moreover, in England in 1835 Broughton had based his negotiations with the missionary societies on the proposition that 'the great contrariety of religious sentiments' among the colonial population seriously limited the ability of the government, however willing, to exclusively favour the Church of England.[30] The financial settlements he had then urged upon the Colonial Office showed him to be preoccupied more with the idea of modest, long-term grants useful as a basis for planned development, rather than a relentless hankering after exclusive aid. Broughton knew New South Wales could not be isolated from the liberalism Newman denounced as the offence of the age. It must needs be that offences come, the bishop wrote to Bourke in an exchange of opinions on the Church bill, but woe to 'the Man by whom the Offence cometh'.[31]

That stuck in Bourke's throat, and led him to comment that Broughton had intended opposing the Church Bill publicly but lacked an audience.[32] It was a gratuitous remark made in the heat of another debate. When finally Broughton did comment publicly on the matter after his readmission to the Legislative Council Bourke had to admit to Broughton's restraint: 'He spoke well and with great moderation professing only to desire to record his opinions in the recollection of those who heard him'.[33] In 1836 the Church bill did put money into Broughton's hands for church expansion and provide him with six more clergy immediately.[34] It was his best deal with government since 1830. Broughton might moan over the principle of a government aiding conflicting religious bodies, but in practice he had accepted it.

Indeed, Broughton had gone further and rationalized his acceptance. He would not have cared to see the prevailing English church establishment transported to New South Wales. Statesmen in England were reshaping that church with a keen ear to the multitude and a careless eye on principle, and churchmen co-operated! 'Too many of her sons have forgotten what she really is', he complained to Keate, and thought even Howley something of a waverer. 'My own policy would never be to give up anything that I thought *right* in the hope of appeasing the tumult. I would rather clear off whatever I thought was corrupt or useless; but with what remained I must take my chance either to sink or swim.'[35]

To swim in New South Wales Broughton decided he must turn the church into a citadel, preserve the true faith, and await the nation's return to good sense. It had done so before in the age of the Stuarts after wandering in the wilderness of the Commonwealth. In that age the promise of liberals, like Cromwell, had come to naught, and the gimmicks of well-wishers, like Gauden, had served only to embarrass the cause of true religion. Truth and fidelity then, as ever, remained religion's sole and necessary ally; that lesson he drew a decade before from the *EIKON BASILIKA*. The pattern of the past would prevail to confound the present meddling of the temporizers. 'You . . . prefer to swim smoothly with the stream', he sniffed at Arthur, who had just spoken up in favour of a multi-church establishment. 'It only shows me how fatally the pursuit of political objects . . . can blind the most sagacious judgement.' For himself he had chosen a more excellent way: 'They who are prepared with me to encounter the rage of the adversaries, will lay the foundation here of a citadel, within the walls of which the Christian faith will find a sure refuge when all without is laid waste.'[36] The new Church bill demolished the Church of England as a privileged establishment but gave Broughton the money to build that citadel and furnish it with keepers.

For the very reason Broughton acquiesced in Bourke's religious settlement he withstood the educational arrangements coupled with it. The one strengthened his citadel with churches, the other undermined it by destroying his schools. To defend his citadel Broughton needed to train the young in fixed principles during their impressionable years. He saw no future in relying on youths brought up in a 'hesitating neutral system, which leaves their mind at liberty to halt, not between two opinions only, but between as many opinions as the will of man can conjure into existence'.[37] Others felt the same, and the first shots in a renewed battle for denominational schools had been fired on 19 January 1835, long before Broughton returned from England, and by churchmen of other denominations.

On that day Lang spotted Roger Therry and the Roman Catholic vicar-general Ullathorne enter the vestry of Scot's church, Sydney, and join a Protestant discussion on the education of poor colonial children. When the meeting moved to adopt the Bible as a textbook Therry and Ullathorne interjected. Roman Catholics wanted to join in a united school system and suggested adopting the principles of the colonial Presbyterian educationalist Henry Carmichael. Lang was immediately on his feet denouncing Carmichael as his sorriest recruit ever. Carmichael had disjoined religious and general education, put the Bible on the shelf as optional reading, confined prayer to the home and, in Lang's opinion, expected a child to imbibe a sense of divine awe through unravelling the mystery of an air pump. When the meeting rejected the visitors' offer Therry and Ullathorne behaved badly. Later at another meeting the Roman Catholic chaplain McEncroe behaved equally badly and when the Protestants silenced him Ullathorne flourished a pamphlet condeming the Bible as a school text. So Lang decided in April 1835 that the rumour of Bourke's wanting a single system of schools had driven Carmichael, Therry and Ullathorne into 'a regularly organised plan' to mislead Bourke into believing colonists would welcome the Irish system or some modification of it. 'We are inclined to be liberal, but determined not to be liberalised in the modern sense of the term', Lang said, and affirmed his preference for denominational schools. At that point in 1835 little separated the practical policies of Broughton and Lang.[38]

In May 1836, just before Broughton's return, Lang sensed a renewal of purpose among supporters of the Irish system and he reaffirmed the implacable opposition of dissenting Protestants to that system.[39]

He spoke for the Australian School Society, a group more vocal than organized, more determined than strong and exclusively nonconformist. To mend this Protestant dissenters asked Broughton on his return to bring the Church of England into a united Protestant opposition and take over its leadership. 'This was certainly a determined step to take', he reflected a month later; for Broughton despised the opportunism of English dissenters who had united with anyone willing to harm the English church establishment. But beside the peril from Rome all other squabbles paled. 'The danger being I think not less close and obvious that it was in the reign of James the Second', he continued, 'I took therefore the bold and perhaps hazardous resolution of setting myself at the head of the "Protestant Association", as it was termed.'[40]

This Association took formal existence on 26 June 1836. Protestant leaders met at the Pultney Hotel where Broughton lived and issued a manifesto of conscientious objection to any school system 'interdicting either wholly or in part the use of the Holy Scriptures according to the Authorised Version, and of prayer in which the doctrine of the Blessed Trinity may be unequivocally acknowledged or implied'.[41] That disposed of both the Irish system and Carmichael's deism. Then under Broughton's chairmanship, the Association forged its strategy. It enlisted twenty laymen willing to set up a fighting fund and used the *Colonist* newspaper to expose, what Broughton knew and Bourke concealed, that Glenelg neither required nor recommended the out-and-out adoption of the Irish system but had requested the governor 'to consult and respect the opinion of the public.'[42] It formed twenty-five subcommittees to gather 10s subscriptions and hawk around a petition in support of denominational schools, and appealed to the clergy to exhort their congregations 'to a hearty and prompt co-operation.'[43]

The preamble to the Protestant Association's petition leaned heavily on arguments Broughton had already tested in England. These queried the integrity of the government's claim that it could implement the Irish system without depriving each child of one full day's catechetical instruction a week. In towns where the clergy had access to the classrooms the Association saw no problem. But what of country schools? Did the government propose to recruit talented latitudinarians or virtuous imbeciles for these? Who else could instruct a variety of denominations each in its own catechism? The Irish system would quickly infest country districts with a type of teacher whose 'want of fixed principles would be a chief recommendation for his appointment'. By contrast denominational schools offered a predictable and properly supervised course of general and religious education.[44]

By mid-July the scale of the Protestant Association's opposition startled Bourke; and though the *Gazette* dismissed it as an 'uncalled for stir' Bourke was vigilantly 'writing minutes and circulars and endeavouring to remove prejudice by all possible means'.[45] Bourke marshalled the crown's officers against the clergy and, on 'an order issued from the Horse Guard' as the *Herald* put it, directed all police magistrates to denounce the Association's resolution charging the Irish system with interdicting the free use of the whole Bible as false. Such a direction complicated the life of a police magistrate like Major Lockyer who sat on the Association's Parramatta subcommittee, and embarrassed the colonial secretary McLeay who by day despatched Bourke's propaganda and in the evenings sent out the Association's correspondence.[46]

The Association's lively opposition compelled Bourke to reassess his strategy. He knew, from a canvas of opinion the previous December, that the Legislative Council did not support wholeheartedly the Irish system.[47] To put an education bill before a vacillating Legislative Council likely to be overawed by public petitions was to risk its extensive revision. Though that was exactly Glenelg's intention it was not yet Bourke's. He expected a fresh and part-elected Legislative Council by 1837 and preferred to have that body determine the issue. So in July 1836 he asked the Legislative Council for £3000 to build *one* or *two* experimental schools on the Irish system and allow colonists to decide from experience the merits of the rival schemes. Bourke was not over confident of obtaining the grant.[48]

Broughton sensed the direction of this manoeuvre and immediately engaged Bourke in a fresh duel of tactics. A vote of £3000 for *one* or *two* Irish system schools with £3150 for thirty Church of England schools suggested some heady experiment to give the Irish system an irresistible appeal, or, a concealed stratagem. By building a few experimental schools in one district one year, and a few elsewhere the next year, the Irish system could be established by stealth and without debate. 'If after a sufficient period of trial, the system should be proved to be attended with those pernicious effects which are anticipated ... it will be too late ... to abandon it', Broughton argued. To expose those pernicious effects and delay the Council's vote until the Association's petitions had revealed the force of Protestant opposition Broughton asked leave to address the Council in its chamber. The Council refused. Broughton then petitioned it warning that 'the direct tendency and necessary effect of that [Irish] system ... must be to consolidate a power, whose aim and object will be to dash the Bible out of the hands of the people, and to place it again under lock and key'.[49]

Such Orangeism had no pull in the Council. Bourke got his £3000 and Broughton made no apology for his sectarian outburst. 'If we have spoken strongly it is because we feel strongly', he said, and reminded his critics that in the contest over schools the losses were heavy and permanent.[50] Bourke also fought ruthlessly. He withheld the British and Foreign School reports Glenelg sent to the Legislative Council,[51] and prevented the Council setting up a committee to take evidence on the schools issue. Bourke revealed no syllabus; but preferred, he said, to leave that to be worked out by a board after the scheme had received approval. He alone would select the board. There would be three Anglicans, but none need be the bishop; two nonconformists, but that could be Carmichael and a friend; seven churchmen in all, but none need be a minister of religion.[52] 'Education is the business of the State', Bourke maintained, and asserted his dogma without compromise to create two camps—one for and one against him.[53]

By August 1836 the Protestant Association had deflected the Irish system, but many Protestants believed only a co-operative venture in education would defeat the appeal of the new experimental schools. The Association met on 3 August to test how far Broughton's newly demonstrated capacity for co-operation would stretch in this direction. Broughton took the floor first and pipped the move. 'Gentlemen', he said, 'Before we enter upon the immediate business of the day, I request permission to offer a few observations', and invited all Protestants to unite with and expand the Church of England parochial school network. The bishop professed never to have received a complaint from non-conformists who had used the schools in the past, and confirmed that non-Anglicans would be exempted from catechetical instruction and the other religious teaching made generally acceptable. Broughton believed survival was best ensured by reinforcing resistance at its strongest point. 'So long, therefore, as that Church [of England] stands and continues faithful to her principles', he said, 'you never can want a bulwark within which all Protestant communions may find shelter when their title to enjoy the free use of the Bible is directly or indirectly threatened.' If that was not acceptable to the other Protestants Broughton pledged to support their claim for a share of public funds towards non-Anglican Protestant schools provided they taught no doctrine adverse to the Church of England.[54]

It took a week for the Reverend John Saunders of the Baptists to recover and reply on behalf of outraged Protestants. Times had changed and dissenters would never gather like chickens under the wings of the Church of England, Saunders said. Though dissenters without Anglicans had little pull in affairs, Anglicans without dissenters had little more. The colony could have a Protestant future but never again an Anglican one. Saunders accused Broughton of an exaggerated respect for the Church catechism. 'It has been made the wicket to the school instead of the gate to the Church', he sneered; and called upon the Association to affirm the unity the bishop repudiated, and to appoint a subcommittee to plan Protestant schools tempting to the Church of England clergy if not the bishop.[55]

Broughton ceased to attend Association meetings and its secretary, the Methodist Mansfield, wondered why![56] The Association not only planned to drive a wedge between Broughton and his clergy but betrayed the understanding on which he had joined it. The *Colonist* clearly recollected the June arrangement:

> ... the Bishop did not go to the Dissenters, but the Dissenters to the Bishop; that the interview they sought with His Lordship had for its primary object a 'union' against the Irish system; and that to this 'union' his Lordship gave a cordial and unhesitating 'pledge.' As to the extension of this 'union' to a system of education common to the Protestant body at large, the Dissenters thought of it as a matter of secondary importance, nor did they at any time entertain a sanguine hope of its practicability.[57]

Bourke took heart at the determination of a party of Protestants to condemn Broughton for blocking a unity he vowed never to attempt.

With Broughton and the Association at odds, with Presbyterians allegedly showing interest in a general system, with petitioners reported to be withdrawing their signatures, and with a breach in the phalanx of Broughton's clergy when Wilkinson at Woollongong came out in support of the Irish system, Bourke hoped the Association would splinter and defeat itself before a crucial vote was taken in 1837.[58]

By August 1836, however, initiative had passed to the Association's subcommittees dominated by Broughton's clergy, and local pulpits were beginning to sting.[59] Moreover, after years of coolly disregarding Broughton as an expensive and expendable colonial functionary the *Herald* went volte-face and announced that wealthy and intelligent laymen of all Protestant denominations were turning to him 'not from blind obsequiousness, but from a conviction that his guidance is safe'.[60]

The *Herald* represented a class apt to believe the entire resources of the colony arose from the capital and intelligence of immigrant land-holders. Such men educated their children in schools of their own choice and believed workers received wages adequate for educating their children to an appropriate level. Children of dissolute parents might properly receive a charity schooling but nothing so fantastic as an education equal to that given a provident worker's son, which was Bourke's proposal. Who would pay? So the *Herald*, speaking for the immigrant landowning class, denounced general education as an 'iniquitous and impudent attempt to tax *them* ... for educating the children of all the profligate vagabonds, freed and fettered'. By a law as old as Moses the sins of the fathers were to be visited upon the children and the *Herald* would not exempt New South Wales from it. Moreover, after paying for the general education of a mass of young Irish Catholics the Protestant landowners would find their social supremacy challenged by them. So again the *Herald* warned that Bourke's general education would give an ascendency to the children of the present race of transported Irish papists, at the expense of the Protestant landholders of this country.[61]

By nimbly exchanging the term 'Protestant' for 'landowner', and 'papist' for Irish labourer, the *Herald* hid its concern for the economic and social interests of free-immigrant landholders under a verbiage of concern for the survival of Protestantism. Beside the Orangeism of the *Herald*'s outbursts Broughton's was mild, but because the newspaper identified itself with Broughton's cause Broughton found himself identified with the newspaper's rhetoric. The bishop could not lose by such tactics and did not attempt to disassociate himself from them.

Gradually the campaign swung even more in Broughton's favour. His close friend Richard Jones bought into the *Gazette* and combined with the *Herald* to expose the imprudence in Bourke's campaign.[62] Why had he excluded Broughton from the Legislative Council? Ignored the Association's petitions? Declined the Council all opportunity to discuss the scheme? What whimsical priorities moved him on the same day to dismiss a request for a committee to enquire into education yet approve one to investigate designs for a new official residence? Did the drains of the governor's mansion deserve more attention than the system proposed for the nurture of countless young for years to come? Had not Glenelg advised the governor to consult the Council? Did not he expect the system to have popular support? Why such indecent haste and so arbitrary and narrow an interpretation of Glenelg's despatch? Why did papists applaud? Was the governor secretly a papist? What of the reports from England of Irish national schools with altars in the classroom? Bourke had clearly failed to consult the people for fear of learning that they despised his scheme. Three thousand of these people had signed the Association's petition but only two townships had requested experimental schools, Woollongong in August at an allegedly picked meeting of childless couples, and Yass in September.[63] 'We gave this said "System" such a decisive blow', Broughton boasted, '... it was evident it could not be carried into effect.'[64] But the decisive blow came from Glenelg. He deferred reform of the New South Wales constitution and condemned Bourke to re-arguing his case in 1837 before the same Council with Broughton a likely addition to it.[65]

In his frustration Bourke turned on Glenelg. Had the Secretary of State acted irresponsibly in simultaneously approving a system of education and a bishop to upset it, or, had Broughton exceeded the limits of permissible dissent? The bishop's bigotry had torn the soul of the community and Bourke demanded his removal from all political office.[66] Others supported that. 'Bishop Broughton should not remain in New South Wales', the *Monitor* maintained. 'He is a good man; but he is too narrow in his views for *this* colony.' It asked instead for the appointment of another 'dumb dolly of a trader like Archdeacon Scott'.[67] But this campaign to pin extreme culpability on Broughton struck others as the pointless tactic of a low political faction. 'We think *we* have quite as much influence in this matter as the Right Reverend Prelate', claimed the *Herald*. 'Though he [Broughton] may be looked upon as the leader of the oppositionists, the latter would have deputed some other to that post, even had his lordship joined the ranks of the "liberals".'[68]

A medley of concerns for Bibles, acres and pounds converged to excite the opposition of 1836. Some of it was directed towards preserving Protestant education, some to forestalling new taxes, and some to securing the social ascendancy of the reigning landowners. Broughton represented only one stream of this but the prolonged campaigning took toll of his strength. He found the constant opposition, he told Keate, 'harassing and painful to me whose genius and inclination certainly do not point *that* way'.[69] An acute housing shortage had confined him to the Pultney Hotel for three months after his return and he chafed at the expense. He contemplated moving to Parramatta when a Sydney merchant in financial trouble offered him a near-finished house on the high rise between Wooloomoolloo and Rushcutter's Bay at £250 a year, the first two years' rent going into improvements. Broughton accepted, though the rent outraged him. The house, Tusculum, had doric pillars and all the builders' rubbish, but no pantry, cellar or water pump, and every chimney smoked. More a huge stone workhouse than a Fulham or Farnham, he said. From the front verandah the house had a fine view seaward, but when he dropped his gaze to the shoreline Broughton saw snug white villas in 'marvellous bad taste', monotonous bush, and the

Right Reverend J. B. Polding, Bishop of Hiero-Caesarea *in partibus infidelium*, holding court in Archdeacon Scott's old residence. Broughton had rested there seven years before at the end of his first journey from England; and he remembered it as spacious, comfortable, and a more fitting episcopal residence than Tusculum.[70]

8

Building the Citadel

In the present temper of the world I cannot hope to roll the stone uphill again so far as to recover possession of *all* that we were unjustly deprived of and therefore as an act of prudence I confined myself to petitioning for an equitable measure of support.

Broughton to Coleridge 25 February 1839

Protestant colonists saw the defeat of the Irish system as a check on papist advances and Broughton entered 1837 determined to prosper his advantage. From November 1836 to February 1837 he toured stirring up further support for brick and mortar. Since Bourke had decided to support parochial schools for a while longer Broughton concentrated on erecting churches aware that every building earned a subsidy and another government-paid minister. Later in a second round he hoped to give every priest a school. By mid-1837 forty churches, chapels and parsonages, and three new boarding-schools were going up. 'This colony . . . is not inferior to any British settlement in sincerity of attachment to the Church of England, or in active effort or liberal contribution, for its maintenance and extension', he reported proudly to the SPG.[1]

Broughton turned to the SPG for clergy. He qualified for fifteen and wanted university men 'sufficiently masters of the subject of controversy' to baffle the doubt sowed by papists.[2] They must remain obliging under criticism, withstand bodily fatigue and manage on £150 a year until the Chief Shepherd returned with the crowning reward. All would be novices, for Broughton did not expect beneficed clergy in England to surrender their security for what the colony offered. Simeon thought few at Cambridge ready for the sacrifice. Broughton pinned his hopes on Oxford where Mr Newman nurtured the art of controversy and expounded principles of ecclesiastical authority that repudiated the papal system without capitulating to those who would sink all differences between Protestants. 'It is among the young men brought up in their principles', he told the Reverend Edward Coleridge of Eton College, whose brother-in-law the Reverend J. Chapman was in the thick of it at Balliol College, 'that I should expect to find the temperate ardour which appears to me the first requisite for a man's doing his duty well and finding his *chief* support and reward in doing it.' Dr Pusey, Newman's collaborator, and a group of tutors and students from Balliol, Christ-

church, Exeter, Merton, Oriel, Trinity and other colleges had all chipped
in to an appeal for the new diocese. Surely Broughton could snare some
of their men.[3]

Oxford encouraged Broughton's expectation by contributing freely
to a private appeal Coleridge had launched. Coleridge was Dr Keate's
son-in-law. He had met Broughton in 1835 and at the bishop's consecration pledged not to see the new diocese in need. By March 1837 he had
£3000. Broughton was overwhelmed by the list of well-wishers but
£10 from Darling struck him as a mean recompense from the only
contributor personally indebted to him for years of disinterested support.[4]
At first Broughton planned to invest the money in the booming land
and cattle trade and create a miniature Queen Anne's Bounty 'to serve
as a foundation of a secure and independent provision for the clergy for
ever'. This bounty fund would release the diocese from the insecurity
of a voluntary system and the stultifying effect of the Church Act, both
of which condemned Broughton to staffing a diocese with low-paid
parochial clergy. 'A mere parochial clergy will not suffice,' he protested.
He wanted no priest anxious for his bread; he also wanted a means of
engendering zeal through the expectation of additional rewards; and
to attract a few men of exceptional talent he needed funds to create the
canonries that would provide the leisure profitable for scholarship
'I am not so worldly in my views as to assume that the cause of Christian
truth cannot be supported without endowments', he apologized lest his
enthusiasm for real estate should seem misplaced, 'but neither am I on
the other hand so visionary as to expect that if we neglect all measures
of worldly prudence and foresight, miracles will be wrought.'[5]

A colonial benefactor also appeared. Broughton had often rested
overnight on Moore-Bank, a lush 4000 acre property near Liverpool
with beautiful views of a river's serpentine windings in its meandering
towards the town. Thomas Moore the owner had a humble origin and
his wife a disreputable one, but Broughton counted them friends. '
never thought it necessary to go back into former histories', he explained
'not always a pleasant enquiry even in the best of places; and *here* peculiarly ticklish and dangerous.' In 1837 Moore turned seventy and spoke
to Broughton of his acres and the desire to render back to the Almighty
some of the manna that had enriched him. Being without heirs he willed
his property to the Diocese of Australia.[6]

Encouraged by what he had received and might expect, Broughton
decided to build a cathedral rivalling the architectural pretensions of
the papist structure by Hyde Park. 'Without such a stronghold of faith
we cannot keep our position', he told Coleridge. The edifice was to seat
1800, have a nave like St Mary's in Oxford and a tower like one of
Magdalen College. The SPG agreed to aid the project, colonists subscribed sufficient to attract a £1000 government subsidy, Broughton
offered £500 from the Coleridge funds, and £300 from his own salary
to shift to a better site the foundations Macquarie had laid earlier for
church in George Street. Bourke saved him that expense, and all was
set to lay the foundation-stone of St Andrews cathedral on 'the sixteenth
day of May in the year of human redemption 1837'.[7]

Broughton planned the day as a Protestant festival. Bourke at first agreed to meet the bishop on the George Street site and set the stone after Broughton had worshipped further up the hill at St James. He then switched plans and went to church to hear Broughton extol Macquarie as a builder of churches. Next came the Protestant parade. Bourke's carriage led off, Broughton's followed, behind him rode the officials of the land, then the gentry, and finally the others either riding or walking with six hundred parish schoolchildren carrying bright banners flapping against a threatening sky. When Bourke had set the foundation-stone Broughton ordered the children back to St James school room for roast beef and plum pudding. The governor looked in and smiled. Broughton did the same and received three gravy-filled cheers.[8]

Behind this outward display of Protestant strength Broughton concealed a growing preoccupation with Rome's political pretensions. He believed the dogmas of popery compelled it to seek domination. Conversations in England had convinced Broughton that 'inherently wicked and mischievous' Jesuits were at work recovering the English race and had put New South Wales 'in the forefront of the battle'. Popery had managed to re-enter British public life by exploiting mild concessions; and only in retrospect, Broughton maintained, could it be observed how inoffensive concessions had been piled one on the other to release a viper in England.[9] The same had happened in New South Wales. Bourke originally sought a Roman Catholic bishop to discipline the papist clergy and care for the convicts. No more laudable a task had befallen anyone and Polding prospered at it. Then came the Church Act and immediately Polding appeared to nudge his commission further. Polding reasoned that in approving the Church Act His Majesty had placed all religious denominations in New South Wales on a 'footing of perfect equality'. So on 29 May 1837 Polding donned a purple soutane and drove to a levee at government house to express his gratitude to the king, his church's 'protector and friend'.[10]

For Bourke the sight of a purple figure entering his drawing room was but one of the day's mishaps. Earlier in Hyde Park Major Baker had slid from his horse in full view of the public just as the 80th Regiment fired its salute, and at the Pultney Hotel decorations were going up for a protest dinner against the governor's failure to hold a birthday ball. Broughton had left the levee before Polding appeared, but soon heard of the purple escapade. For five years Bourke had chipped at the dignity of Broughton's office with impunity, and finally the chisel had slipped. Protocol for levees at Sydney would seem to have departed from that at Dublin and London, Broughton observed in a note to Bourke. Was that an authorized departure?[11]

Broughton believed Roman Catholic prelates had crept into the king's dominions by a fiction and should be bound by that fiction. Polding, for instance, was in New South Wales under the pretension of awaiting the liberation of his diocese of Hiero-Caesarea from the Turks. Officially he was an ordinary citizen, and ordinary citizens did not wear purple soutanes. Broughton had no doubt Polding was testing how far he might evade constitutional restrictions on foreign prelates thousands of

miles from London, and to ignore it was to encourage further challenge
So braving the ridicule of those who would see it as a mere quibble ov
clothes, Broughton told Bourke to nudge Polding back into his place or l
prepared to see Sir Robert Inglis raise the matter in the House of Con
mons. Broughton believed the Whigs would restrict Polding's publ
dress rather than have parliament debate whether removing the disabil
ties of Roman Catholics required pruning the Church of England of i
advantages in the colonies.[12]

Polding's dress had surprised Bourke and he undertook to enfor
the Dublin protocol. Polding returned Bourke a lecture on ecclesiastic
garments denying that a purple soutane was part of the distinctive dre
of a Catholic bishop. Distinctive episcopal vestments were worn insi
churches only. Bourke also rebuked Broughton's impertinence in thre
tening him with a debate in the House of Commons.[13] Broughton offer
no apology.[14] He had wearied of Bourke's touchiness. Had not Bourl
tried underhandedly to place the King's School Parramatta und
trustees independent of the bishop? Had he not walked out of a chur
when Broughton turned up as the preacher? Had he not invited t
bishop to stay overnight at Parramatta and then left him to pass t
whole evening with that unrepentant womanizer Sir John Jamison?
'His object has been to take opportunities of behaving to me in a w
which is certainly not usual towards a Bishop of any church', Broughtc
confided to Keate, '. . . [but] like all Whigs he is pertinacious and vengef
when thwarted.'[16]

Despite some upsets Broughton had reason to celebrate his first ye
in episcopal office and dined the Diocesan Committee at the Pultn
Hotel. There on 20 June 1837 toasts were raised to £13 000 in cash,
a crop of new churches, chapels, parsonages and the new cathedral,
the preservation of the parish school system, to the bishop's return
the Legislative Council, and to the recent procession which was t
largest outdoor gathering many could recall. Even the *Monitor* concede
with a bitter grudge that the 'Pultney Hotel conspiracy' had triumphed.

But Broughton rode the crest of success that evening. From Londc
came a chilling message that chaplains were not to be found for £150
year. Without them the affectionately toasted buildings remained shell
It appeared that English recruits had jibbed at the insecurity of the £1
stipend rather than its smallness. The Bishop of London could recru
men only if they were ordained to a *title* worth a minimum of £150, b
Glenelg ruled that out. The initiative in paying salaries must rema
exclusively with the local government. Few English clergymen famili
with the rhetoric of reform would entrust their future to a stipend depe
dent on a Whig government's goodwill. The first fruit of a drift towar
the voluntary principle was as Broughton had anticipated.[18]

Other troubles Broughton had not anticipated. In Hobart Arth
was still sore with Broughton for breaking confidence on Bedford, an
the two were soon squabbling over the southern grammar school. Broug
ton understood Arthur to have approved of a King's School back
1833, but the moment trustees advertised it Arthur repudiated its exclu
siveness. He instructed the trustees to free pupils for worship anywhe

in Hobart on Sundays or forfeit government aid. Bourke applauded.[19] Broughton promptly dumped Arthur and had the trustees go ahead on £500 from the SPCK.[20]

In Hobart there was no forgiving Bedford either. Palmer flourished his authority before bowing to a new archdeacon and accused Bedford of falsifying school returns to conceal neglect. Arthur cited Bedford to answer the charge before an Executive Council consisting of Palmer his accuser, the colonial secretary Montagu, who had earlier abused him in the street, and the chief police magistrate Forster, who was Arthur's nephew by marriage and had once stormed out of St David's church while Bedford preached. Bedford fled to Broughton for protection. Broughton instructed Bedford not to appear before any government tribunal. Glenelg, on an appeal from Arthur, condemned Broughton and Bedford for conspiring to establish a newfangled 'benefit of clergy' on Protestant soil and commanded the Executive Council to proceed, discipline and even dismiss Bedford.[21]

Benefit of clergy! Broughton was outraged. What was the trial of a clergyman before a council sworn to secrecy but a revival of the Star Chamber! To uphold ecclesiastical authority Broughton again held Bedford duty-bound to defy Glenelg; and risking his own dismissal Broughton told the Secretary of State his ruling was unconstitutional, partial and reeking with absurdities. Glenelg had not only swept aside the bishop's letters patent, in which he himself had explicitly reserved to the bishop full jurisdiction over his clergy in all matters connected with their 'offices and stations', but had pronounced the colonial Church of England subject to exceptional state interference while Bourke intoned the doctrine of colonial church equality. Consider, too, Broughton said, the predicament of the new archdeacon. Should the archdeacon take his seat on the Council he will learn of clerical misdemeanours his articles of office obliged him to communicate to the bishop but which the Council's bond of secrecy forbade him to communicate to anyone. Should he decline to sit, then the Council's secrecy would deny him the information necessary for exercising those disciplines his office was created to dispense.[22]

Behind Glenelg's lack of consistency and logic lay an unresolved problem. Who had authority over chaplains discharging state duties in prisons and schools? The office of King's Visitor had been created to remove such conflict, and the clash over Bedford derived from the government abolishing that office while sustaining its payment to church schools. It was the fruit of a half-altered system. Good sense alone made it workable. In New South Wales Bourke came to accept Broughton as his intermediary in school business though he believed he was not legally required to. In Van Diemen's Land Bedford was spared by Arthur's sudden recall late in 1836 and the arrival of William Hutchins as archdeacon early in 1837. That broke the chain of hate against Bedford. Nevertheless, Broughton was intent upon establishing the integrity of his ecclesiastical powers and called for a copy of the evidence taken against Bedford in the Executive Council. He was told to come and read it in Hobart.[23]

Meanwhile in Sydney Bourke trimmed a different corner from Broughton's letters patent. A young blade of a missionary, William Yate, had cut a dashing figure in and out of St James' pulpit leading the foray against the Irish school system and offering Broughton desperately needed assistance, when suddenly he was accused of immoral behaviour with a ship's captain.[24] Broughton thought the charge so extraordinary that he wanted the accusers to give evidence under oath in a duly constituted Consistorial Court. The crown solicitor Francis Fisher delighted Broughton by volunteering to administer the rules of evidence. Bourke ruled that 'inconvenient'. He wanted the government free of all ecclesiastical disciplinary proceedings. Broughton then pointed to where his letters patent directed governor and judges 'by all lawful ways and means' to assist the bishop in erecting his courts. 'No more than words', retorted the Roman Catholic attorney-general, Plunkett; and he showed Bourke how to escape responsibility in the clumsy wording of the patents. They were modelled on the Calcutta patents with one 'very important difference'; since the superior court heard ecclesiastical appeals in Calcutta the bishop had to transmit a copy of his proceedings to the government there, but appeals from New South Wales went to the Archbishop of Canterbury to whom alone Broughton was required to transmit copies of his proceedings. Plunkett thought this a clear indication of the Colonial Office desiring weaker links between church and state.[25] So Broughton examined Yate in the corner of a vestry listening to evidence in which falsehood was not perjury. He let Yate slip away free of the full penalty he suspected his guilt deserved. For attempting to preside over a court armed with the power of the state he was accused of aping an ancient feudal baron: for taking evidence quietly in a vestry he was charged with concealing crime in the colony.[26]

A spectre of Broughton the inquisitor also appeared. A Mr G. M. C. Bowen had retired from the 39th Regiment to a life of usefulness visiting the sick around Windsor and Broughton offered him ordination. Bowen promptly published a set of theological principles for 'renovating' the liturgy and 'saving' the church. 'I am fully prepared to meet with expressions of surprise', he said, but was shocked when Stiles bypassed him at the altar rail on Christmas Day 1836. Bowen had harmed his neighbour in deliberately publishing heresy, and Stiles considered him excommunicate. But eight years of ridicule in the army for temperance had steeled Bowen for a fight, and from an embattled Windsor parsonage Stiles turned to his neighbour Hassall for support. 'I am no Philosopher, Metaphysician or Astrologer', replied Hassall. Broughton intervened on a sharp note. 'My injunction to you is that you abstain altogether from Mr Bowen and leave to me the responsibility of dealing with the case', he wrote to Stiles; and withdrawing the Windsor interdict he examined the offending book himself somewhat bemused that Bowen had dined often at Tusculum without betraying error. Meanwhile a file of correspondence between the parties was slipped to the press and Broughton was publicly scolded for interference with a laudable venture in intellectual honesty. The bishop, wrote the Presbyterian *Colonist*, appeared more determined to be master of his own house than a servant in His Master's house! However, the open warfare within colonial Presbyterianism reassured Broughton and made plain the penalty of having many masters. Bowen was not ordained for want of letters test-imonial but continued to visit the sick; and finally, cornered by Stiles in the vestry at Windsor, he abjured all error to secure his dying wife's wish to see their son baptized.[27]

Many suspected Broughton of seeking formal ecclesiastical courts to evade the levelling effect of the Church Acts. If his church was backed by a hierarchy of courts reaching up to the House of Lords it would naturally have enhanced its stature within the colony. Yet without those courts Broughton queried not the stature of his church but the status of his authority. Would decisions from colonial ecclesiastical courts set up at variance with their British counterparts survive an appeal to the superior ecclesiastical courts in England? That had narrowly escaped a testing in 1836 and 1837. The charges against Bedford faded with Arthur's removal; Yate fled; and Broughton did not have to refuse Bowen ordination as the candidate failed to supply letters testimonial in his own favour. Yet, after lying low for a time Yate received preferment in England and when Broughton objected the Archbishop of Canterbury ruled the Sydney vestry enquiry deficient in law for inhibiting him. What would happen the day a convicted chaplain stood his ground and appealed in the colony? When Bourke resigned in 1837 he left the colonial Church of England without special privilege and Broughton with peculiar problems.[28]

Bourke gave only twelve days notice of his sailing off on 5 December 1837. Plans for a harbourside festivity in imitation of Darling's farewell fell through but many hounded him to the water's edge. Others burned incense where his shadow fell. Bourke farewelled the lot with a cold stare. Broughton accompanied Bourke to the wharf but snubbed the address presented him by the civil officers. No governor, he wrote after Bourke had embarked, had done him or his cause greater harm.[29] The *Herald* comforted Broughton with a reminder that the Church of England would enjoy a primacy of honour wherever the laws of Britain were established. The *Colonist* saw the situation more clearly: 'Her bishop is only the head pastor of his own voluntary flock'. Broughton would have been content if that were beyond doubt the case.[30]

In the isthmus of time between Bourke's departure and the advent of his successor the colony's fiftieth anniversary cropped up. Was it to be dismissed with the standard skyward discharge from Dawes Point or decently marked as a national jubilee? The question stirred men differently. Some saw nothing to celebrate. Others planned divine services, others a procession, or a picnic, or fireworks, or a day outdoors under the colony's Italian skies where every citizen would survey the gay metropolis and with a just boast say: 'These are the works of only fifty years'. The *Gazette* prophesied unbounded progress and hailed the fiftieth anniversary 'as the commencement of a new era in the annals of our progress'. To deflect progress in the right direction Broughton called the Diocesan Committee to St James church, and on that fiftieth anniversary exhorted them to an effort that would close the next half century in a Christian jubilee.[31]

Shortly after, the new governor Sir George Gipps slipped into the colony wearing civilian dress. The next day, 24 February 1838, he put on a dashing blue uniform to receive Broughton and other officials. No colonist knew then that Broughton and Gipps had been to school together, but the *Colonist*'s sharp eye picked out the governor's name among the donors to Coleridge's appeal and warned against any deals in aid of the Church of England. Broughton laughed: 'My old school fellow, but a Radical I fear for all that ... [but] I am prepared to try to walk in concert with him'.[32]

On 7 April 1838, while Gipps received many a caution and much advice, Broughton slipped off to the southern archdeaconry. His ship the *Conway* called at Port Phillip where in a wooden hut close to the centre of the settlement Broughton celebrated the settlement's first Eucharist. It was Easter. After worship the inhabitants addressed him on their loyalty to the Church of England and need of a clergyman. The bishop agreed to send one, convinced the area would become 'very speedily an opulent and important scene of business'. After seven days he sailed south.[33]

At Hobart he fell into the welcoming arms of Bedford, and Lady Franklin, the new governor's wife, squeezed him into an overcrowded government house. For seven weeks she delighted and taunted him with urbane chatter. A hostess who sat the Protestant Archdeacon Hutchins on her right and the Roman Catholic Ullathorne on her left, both opposite her husband Sir John, and then orchestrated an argument on education taking each side in turn, coped well with Broughton. She found the bishop interesting, intellectual and benign. She scolded him for sending the riff-raff among the clergy to Van Diemen's Land, and expressed a hope that Arnold of Rugby would come to the colony as bishop. If not, Arnold would leave another mark. Sir John Franklin had asked him to draft a charter and select a headmaster for a new school in Hobart. If that school conformed to Arnold's latest ideas it would not be officially connected with the Church of England, Broughton warned; for Arnold dreamed of building his classrooms around a row of chapels and letting each denomination supply a headmaster in turn.[34]

Broughton visited every establishment in the colony performing tasks with the rapidity he condemned in Bishop Heber's tours. He affirmed the exclusiveness of the Hobart grammar school and launched a similar venture in Launceston. He read the Executive Council evidence on Bedford's case and condemned it so scathingly that years later the House of Commons had to edit his report before publishing it. He founded a local committee of the SPG, and left the colony content that it was in good hands. Hutchins the new archdeacon was sound and Sir John a better churchman than Arthur.[35]

When Broughton returned to Sydney he declared himself ready for business. He entered the Legislative Council and demanded elevation in rank above the officer second-in-command of the forces. The attorney-general shrugged his shoulders. Someone had blundered. Gipps's commission returned Broughton to the status he enjoyed before Bourke's arrival![36] Broughton, however, was not in an obstructive mood. He threw his full support behind Gipps's proposal to double the Legislative Council and elect half on a high property franchise without respect to convict origins. Dowling, Burton, Deas Thomson and Plunkett all demurred fearing the high property qualification would aggravate emancipist frustration and the election of emancipists exacerbate conservative fears, and so satisfy none. So in 1838, on the eve of himself possibly having to step down from the Legislative Council, Broughton supported the admission of emancipists to government, and was more disposed to assist than to hinder the evolution of liberal government.[37]

Broughton also sprang to the colony's defence when a committee of enquiry in London mocked it as a sink of iniquity. 'There is a deep feeling of religion among the settlers of the colony, which only requires to be drawn forth, and it will form a fortress of good feeling, which in a few years will alter the face of the country', he told the Legislative Council and proposed a resolution rebuking the London enquiry. But when others added that the colony's glorious religious future made it a receptacle *par excellence* for reforming convicts, and invited the British government to use the facilities, Broughton objected. He would have the colony done with transportation as soon as possible.[38]

Broughton's performance impressed Gipps and the governor asked him to chair an enquiry into the likely effect an end to transportation would have on immigration. Landowners had already assessed the situation and recommended a drastic cut in family immigration with its host of wives and children who had to be fed but could return no labour. Only single men, too poor to set up on their own and too ignorant to be more than shepherds or labourers, could replace the convicts. Given such labour the landowner would turn the wilderness into the 'Wool Mart of the world' and build a virtuous nation possessing the language, religion, laws and customs of England.[39]

Broughton recommended the opposite. Single males might benefit the landed class but they did not necessarily suit the colony, and without an acre, sheep or ox to his name Broughton's only concern was the latter. He believed the excessive importation of unmarried males violated the Almighty's declared appointment 'that it is not good for man to be alone' and only added to the moral turpitude free immigration was designed to remove. He knew that previous shiploads of unmarried females had washed little of the stain away. So Broughton's committee set the colony's need at 3000 adult male workers, and advised the governor to issue 9500 extra bounties on women and children to secure them. The colony's future lay with family immigration. But it would be quite immoral, Broughton added, to uproot such families from village, church, and parson, without attempting to settle them amid the same comforts. There was a religious aspect of immigration not to be lost sight of.[40]

Broughton also presided over an enquiry into the 'Aboriginal question'. There was indeed a question. The committee sat in September 1838 under the shadow of a dark deed. On the Liverpool Plains, 350 miles north of Sydney where the Myall Creek joined the Big River, twenty-

eight Aboriginals, adults and children, had been butchered in a libation
to fear and revenge for fifteen white stockmen fatally speared in the
district in as many years. The *Gazette* screamed that it was a foul deed,
yet understandable given the government's consistent failure to protect
white settlers from increased black aggression. The witnesses before
Broughton's committee told a different tale. It was the Aboriginal who
needed the protection, especially of a legal officer who could investigate
and revenge at law the scores of isolated murders and multilations in-
flicted by white settlers.[41] By coincidence Glenelg had just ordered the
governor to employ five white wanderers to follow, befriend and protect
tribes, and hopefully induce them to settle, farm, and prepare for a future
Christian education. Lang had first proposed the idea in 1835. Broughton
thought the sentiment fine but futile.[42] But the governor had already
appointed George Robinson chief wanderer in New South Wales and
Broughton acquiesced with a caution against allowing Robinson any
of his so-called civilized aboriginals from Flinders Island as offsiders.
They were the descendants of countless generations of warriors, Broughton said, and only a fool would believe six or seven years residence at
Flinders Island had driven out that spirit. No such miracles had occurred
at Wellington Valley where the once optimistic missionaries had just
reported 'little hope of effecting any good amongst the aboriginal natives'.
Broughton learned nothing new from the enquiry in 1838, and reported
only that his committee would like to try again in 1839.[43] In the meantime
the melancholy tale of murder and mass cremations near Myall Creek
unfolded. In court the judge reminded the jury before it retired that
'the life of a blackman is as precious and valuable in the eyes of the law,
as the highest noble in the land'. In the jury room they were considered
'a set of monkeys', and in fifteen minutes a civil jury hailed the defendants
not guilty. After a retrial seven were hanged a week before Christmas.
As Broughton's committee went into recess this was the best known
solution to the Aboriginal question.[44]

Broughton clearly enjoyed being back in the Councils flexing his
talent with the freedom and prestige of Darling's day. Some thought
he enjoyed himself too much. The sight of him rolling along in his chariot
from meeting to meeting wearing the air of a prelate, some said, mocked
the principle of religious equality enshrined in Bourke's Church Act.
So the *Colonist* called for Broughton's removal from the Councils and
invited laymen of the Church of England to sack him and elect a leader
less addicted to 'the sublime and papistical nonsense of apostolical
succession'.[45] The *Colonist* was the voice of Presbyterianism in schism
and Lang's mouthpiece, and Lang had an imagined grievance against
Broughton. After the colonial Presbyterian church split the Executive
Council decided to subsidize only one faction, and Lang's missed out.
Lang blamed the decision on Broughton and thought it either the bishop's
pay-off for earlier attacks on the Church and Schools Corporation or a
cunning plot to ruin Presbyterians by feeding its corrupt ministers and
starving the pure.[46] Broughton, however, had not attended either Executive Council meeting at which the decision was hammered out. The
presence of Colonel Snodgrass and Riddell, two members of the rival

faction, sufficiently explained the ruling. But in July 1836 Broughton supported it when Lang appealed to the Legislative Council for relief. He feared the government would all too soon tire of supporting competing churches let alone rival factions within the same denomination.[47]

While Lang's faction begged for their bread Broughton turned up at the Pultney Hotel full of glee and heartiness to celebrate the second anniversary of the Diocesan Committee. He had wrung extra money for clerical stipends from the SPG and Diocesan Committee, and the first recruits had arrived. New buildings were in use. The SPCK had formed a permanent lobby to plead his needs in England, and letters from abroad hinted that a sizeable benefaction of around £1000 was to come. That morning, too, the Reverend Macquarie Cowper had preached in a style which proved that currency lads were safe custodians of the traditions and institutions of the Church of England. It was a ripe moment for a celebration. But some believed it improper to celebrate with wine and had condemned the previous year's dinner as an ungodly affair. So when Broughton stood up to respond to a toast on behalf of the church he prayed that the spirit of Puritanism would never get a footing in the colony. Now McLeay was a teetotaller and in the chair, but Broughton was not to be put down. When the gathering toasted the ladies present Broughton again leaped to his feet and raising his glass high encouraged the bachelors present to abandon their present state.[48] Newspapers reported these proceedings; and a few days later the drawn countenance of one settler blushed to read of another anti-Puritanical dinner disgracing the colony.[49]

While one blushed with shame another reddened with anger. Polding had no quarrel with Broughton's claret and turkey. He knew that a man was defiled by what came out of his mouth, and for that reason a fury gripped him when he read, in reports of the dinner, that out of the mouth of a newly arrived but rather cantankerous Mr Justice Willis had proceeded statements about the Mass of Roman Catholics being idolatrous. So on Saturday 28 July the community of Sydney awoke to find the town plastered with signs summoning Roman Catholics of all classes to meet their bishop on the sabbath, and to condemn the judge's wanton and unprovoked remarks as 'calculated to enkindle the flames of religious discord in the colony'. Polding tried hard to start the fire. He called not one but eight meetings, and was not put off when he learned from an interested press that Her Majesty Queen Victoria had dropped a similar remark at her recent coronation.[50]

Broughton resolved to waste no time on this, and left the defence of Judge Willis to an eager young Presbyterian William McIntyre.[51] He intended, however, taking issue with Polding in another matter. He detected a scoffing tone in the many Roman Catholic references to him as merely 'the Protestant bishop' in contrast to 'John Bede by the grace of God and the appointment of the Holy See, Bishop, and Vicar Apostolic of New Holland', and the undoubted servant of He whose kingdom is from everlasting to everlasting. And yet, as Broughton examined his letters patent the jibe seemed uncomfortably justified: William Grant Broughton was allowed by His Majesty's writ of 18 January 1836, 'full power and authority to confirm those that are baptised, and come to the years of discretion, and to perform all other functions peculiar and appropriate to the office of bishop within the limits of the said See of Australia, *but not elsewhere'*. Was he to move only at the behest of he whose kingdom began at Westminster? Could he, for instance, go to New Zealand? He no sooner thought he couldn't than his head rang with the indictment of the Oxford Tract writers who condemned Anglicans for resting their authority on too low a ground: a Commission under the Great Seal, for instance, rather than the Apostolical succession.[52]

This became an urgent matter late in 1838. By then Marsden was sealed in a tomb of colonial earth, and news flooded in of papal inroads into the New Zealand mission. Broughton studied his letters patent and decided that though they made him Bishop of Australia, they no more made him a bishop of the Church of God than a copy of the *Times*. They were a legal instrument only, defining the range within which he might exercise his spiritual powers for the sake of good order within the queen's dominions. Beyond those bounds, Broughton maintained to puzzled observers in England, 'I contend that every bishop has an inherent right, in virtue of his consecration, to officiate episcopally whenever the good of the church may be promoted by his so doing'. With that settled he planned to set off to New Zealand. There he would ordain, confirm, and consecrate churches and burial grounds in a land not mentioned in his letters patent; and so 'give a flat contradiction' to the false pretence of the papists that he served only at the bidding of an earthly monarch.[53]

The Church Missionary Society urged the bishop on. His friendship with Sir Robert Inglis, a vice-patron of the London parent committee, had helped soften his earlier estrangement from the Society, and in 1837 in a magnanimous gesture of reconciliation Broughton rejoined the Sydney Corresponding Committee. On 13 December 1838 he sailed for New Zealand with the Reverend Octavius Hadfield whom he had just ordained deacon in Sydney for the mission in defiance of the King's Writ restricting the Bishop of Australia to ordaining men 'for the cure of souls within the limit of the said Diocese of Australia only'.[54] He landed at the Bay of Islands on 21 December. The missionaries came and hailed him their protector in succession to their beloved founder Samuel Marsden. Broughton thanked them, and prayed for a measure of the unconquerable perseverance which had filled that 'justly venerated man'. He came only with the authority imparted him at his consecration, he added, and they were only bound to accept his direction as far as they recognized his Apostolic succession.[55]

Broughton tarried three weeks performing apostolic tasks and examining a translation of the liturgy into a native dialect. The natives disappointed him. He found them a joyous but rather dirty and indolent people and feared they had lost vitality from contact with the white settler. So the paradox began to form in Broughton's mind that some peoples thrived in barbarism and withered in peace. Puzzled and mystified he sailed off on 11 January 1839 to pay his first visit to Norfolk Island before returning to New South Wales.[56]

Back in Sydney Broughton was among the people with whom he increasingly identified his life's mission. By going to New Zealand contrary to the plainest interpretation of his letters patent he showed that the King's Commission had shrunk in significance for him, and his mind had filled with a deeper realization that his vocation was to serve a people, their land and its future, in direct response to the apostolic command to go into all lands. 'My own opportunities of observation have been very numerous and I do not hesitate to say,' he wrote to the SPG,

that, ... surrounded it cannot be dissembled by much that is base and disgusting, there is nevertheless an extensive, and in point of actual influence a preponderable proportion of integrity and worth; from which if suitably encouraged and supported now, there may hereafter spring forth a wise and understanding people to occupy this land. It is on behalf of these truly exemplary and deserving people that I am anxious to make every exertion.[57]

A Season of Black and White

He had talked with many of his Protestant fellow workmen
on the subject, and they always said, away with Dr Broughton
and his clique.

John Lynch at Catholic immigration
meeting, *Aust. Chron.* 16 Sep. 1841

The trip to New Zealand proved to Broughton that he had an apostolic
ministry. He had come to New South Wales to serve an establishment:
he remained now to serve a church. In 1829 he had seen the expanding
influence of the English nation as a sign that God had singled it out for
a great work in the Pacific. But over the last decade those principles
that had put a soul into the English nation had been progressively
abandoned, and it amazed Broughton that the young Tory politician,
W. E. Gladstone, should squander his time writing *The State in its
Relations with the Church* to reaffirm the old principle of an inseparable
church and state. Such principles could no longer bear 'the wear and
tear of active service'. After a decade in New South Wales Broughton
ceased to talk of the role of the English nation: he spoke only of the role
of the Church of England; 'We have a wonderful and mysterious scene
unfolding in this hemisphere; in which I am anxiously looking for the
Church of England to appear dispensing the elements of primitive
truth'.[1]

He had laid the foundation for this new mission in his citadel. In
1839 he needed time to expand it, yet felt he had at the most a decade
before the grudges and hostilities of those in power succeeded in cutting
off aid. So in 1839 Broughton prepared for a decade of 'reckless' expansion
planting churches and schools wherever settlements appeared, building
a colonial theological college, and establishing a circulating library
to save his isolated clergy succumbing to ignorance. At the same time
he vowed to exploit his remaining influence in government to win
maximum aid for the Church of England, and to take sharp action against
any move to rob him of gains already made.[2]

Broughton first took sharp action over education. A year before in
August 1838 Gipps had warned religious leaders that government
support for denominational schools had one year to run. 'There should
be comprehensive schools or none', Gipps had remarked; and Broughton

replied that 'he would rather see no schools than comprehensive ones'.[3] There in 1838 the matter rested. Gipps, like Bourke, worked alone at the problem. He did not consult either council or attempt a public enquiry. Instead, in the quiet of his own study he traced the events of 1836, read James Macarthur's testimony before the Committee on Transportation in London, analysed the report of the Protestant sub-committee of 1836, and discovered a decisive preference within the colony for the British and Foreign school system.[4]

While Gipps contemplated Broughton acted. On 4 June 1839 the bishop announced plans to set up four district committees, part clerical, part lay, part appointed, and part elected, to develop local education. These committees were to build primary schools wherever private contributions attracted government subsidies and were to charge pupils with the cost of instruction. A model school was to be set up in Sydney to guide them. Broughton suggested, too, that each committee raise debentures for the erection of an upper school, administer it like a business, and concentrate on commercial studies. And to the objection that fees would drive pupils into the cheaper government schools, which were only a matter of time away, Broughton replied that the quality of education he envisaged would outweigh the extra costs to parents. 'My conviction is' he confidently forecast, 'that by a little perseverance in requiring the very moderate rates which it will be sufficient to fix, they will come over to our terms, and give our schools the preference over all others.' Prior occupation was the essence of the venture's success.[5]

Gipps moved quickly to deny Broughton priority. He made a counter offer: rather than subsidize private donations towards primary schools the treasury would contribute $\frac{1}{2}$d a day towards the education of every child enrolled in a British and Foreign school; Roman Catholics would receive substantial relief to support a system of their own; other separatists could apply for a 50 per cent subsidy on fees if they averaged a daily attendance of thirty. So in New South Wales a Bible education became cheap; the Roman Catholic catechism added a little to the cost; the Protestant catechism added considerably more. Gipps made no apology for this discrimination; 'people who indulge in such exclusiveness must pay fot it'.[6]

Gipps's offer struck at the foundation of Broughton's plan. Without a £1 for £1 subsidy on private donations the district committees had to build every new classroom unaided and meet the full cost of tuition until enrolments reached the statutory minimum. Moreover, Gipps's plan threatened existing small country schools already dependent on handouts from the Diocesan Committee and the subsidy that attracted. Nine schools with low enrolments would be disqualified immediately and another five, with around forty pupils, faced a precarious future. It could cost Broughton £900 more to maintain existing arrangements. 'A more shameful and flagrant attempt to destroy our church was never made', Broughton alleged. Moreover, the bishop faced a personal challenge. The diocesan schools would only close if the people preferred comprehensive ones, Gipps said. Broughton had therefore to hold Anglicans to existing church schools and stop them, at the first pinch of sacrifice, from throwing their lot in with the governor's cheap British and Foreign schools.[7]

Broughton responded to Gipps's challenge with the resolve of a man who had much at stake. He had petitions gathered in areas with established parish schools praying that there be no diminution in their grants. He wanted to show that those who had sacrificed to establish and support a parish school would be more aggrieved than flattered by Gipps's offer to supplant their achievment with a new British and Foreign school. By August 1839 Broughton placed 3000 signatures before the Council, most from Anglicans but some from Roman Catholics and Presbyterians who supported his cause, and more were on the way. Even without them, the bishop reminded the governor, the Church of England single-handed had raised a greater protest than the combined Protestant churches in 1836.[8] At this point, and in an unguarded moment, Gipps let it slip that he feared his plan lost.[9]

Then at the eleventh hour Gipps rallied and adopted Bourke's tactic of 1836. Rather than risk the rejection of a detailed plan Gipps asked the Legislative Council to vote on four resolutions amounting to an approval of the principle that New South Wales should have a major system of unrepentantly Protestant schools and that Roman Catholics should receive some compensation for exclusion from it. Gipps appealed to Broughton to see that these resolutions favoured the Church of England. The bigger the system of schools the better it would be, and the strongest denomination within that system would naturally draw matters in its direction. It might be called British and Foreign but it could be largely Anglican. 'If no advantage is given to the Protestants, if no advantage is given to the Church of England', Gipps told the Council, '. . . then I say put an extinguisher on the whole plan.'[10]

Broughton leaped to his feet in the Council to do just that. He did not consider the four resolutions mere 'abstract propositions' as the governor suggested. Approve them, Broughton told the Council, and you write a bill of attainder against the Church of England; for those despised creeds and articles of religion, which it was the object of the British and Foreign system to put to one side, had been framed to save the church from ignorance and heresy. What advantage could the Church of England gain now from their prohibition? He would show them the advantage; and picking up a House of Commons Report the bishop read the Council tales of teachers in British and Foreign schools in England who admitted that the Society's principles had forced them to dismiss the great truth of the Atonement as a 'nice point' to be picked up after school years; and of others who defined their understanding of the Society's rule of impartiality as amounting to a constant 'guard to see that neither Master or boys introduced Trinitarianism or Calvinsim into the school'. So much then for the advantages of the system the governor promised would prosper the Church of England![11]

But the bishop had somewhat more to add. Men had sacrificed their lives to preserve the distinctive doctrines of the Church of England. Was not Cranmer one, and Ridley another? Would the governor who had been born and bred in the Church of England and nurtured and trained in a school founded by Cranmer and presided over by Ridley, snuff out the Church of England as a distinctive body? He sought no special advantage for that church, the bishop said; he pleaded only that it be accorded an equal right with the Roman Catholic church to maintain itself as a separate organization, distinctive in its doctrine and discipline. He asked this for himself and the 3000 others whose signatures lay before the Council. He had met a woman, the bishop concluded, who had learned her catechism in a parish school-hut by the banks of the Hawkesbury, and who could be found that day living in a region almost beyond the limits of civilization and rearing up her eleven children in the godly and orthodox truths of her faith. Dare anyone repeat that those parish schools had failed.[12]

The bishop sat down and Plunkett pronounced the performance worthy of His Holiness the Pope. Lady Franklin, holidaying in Sydney at the time, thought it marvellously eloquent and bought copies of the speech for her friends in England. In London Lord John Russell admitted some force in Broughton's charge that the scheme harboured an inequity against the Church of England, and in the colony Judge Dowling, after ranting against the Protestant Association in 1836, crossed to support Broughton in 1839. That shocked Gipps. But Dowling, pointing to the petitions, said 'we have opposers but no supporters'. Gipps differed. 'Those who are not against me are with me,' he said; for he knew his scripture if not his catechism. Yet his supporters were hardly with him. The Council chamber was a Laodicea, neither hot nor cold. The members of Council would have voted eight to six in favour of the resolutions, with two abstentions, but the best of that support was only lukewarm. Councillors frankly preferred the Irish system. Gipps did too. So when the governor saw that the odds were so weakly in his favour he withdrew the resolutions convinced that the still considerable energy necessary to establish the British and Foreign system would be better directed towards campaigning for the Irish system.[13]

Nevertheless, Broughton's speech had angered Gipps. 'Rome had become more tolerant than Lambeth', he snapped as the bishop sat down. 'The fact is', Broughton confided to Coleridge, 'he was in a desperate ill humour at the time and could not help showing it; his purpose being frustrated and that being attributed to me.'[14] Gipps also blamed the Wesleyans. He had anticipated their full co-operation, and when he learned from Mr Jones in the Council chamber that they would press instead for denominational subsidies he realized, as Mr Jones observed, that the scheme would not be very comprehensive.[15]

This victory gave Broughton only a respite. 'For the present we have repelled the attack [but] . . . I am sure no effort will be spared to deprive us of our schools', he told the SPG. It would be repeated, perhaps staved off again, but for how long he could not venture a guess. He must work as a man who would one day lose his battle and 'endeavour to get them [the schools] in the interim firmly established, so as to last as long as this country'. Broughton switched the Coleridge funds to education and applied to have them subsidized.[16]

Gipps refused. 'Private subscriptions only will be admitted', he ruled.

'And sums given by large incorporated societies cannot be included as private subscriptions.' To Broughton's astonishment Gipps named the Diocesan Committee an incorporated society and refused subsidies on the donations it raised in one district and sent to another. He would subsidize only 'private subscriptions from persons interested in each particular school'. When Broughton argued that the ruling contravened the Secretary of State's direction of 1836 Gipps further narrowed the subsidies. He excluded boarding-schools, then schools for the middling classes, and finally any school not 'actually attended by children of the poorest classes of society, and intended principally, if not exclusively for them'.[17] Gipps intended to starve the parish schools and 'to introduce a better system, when called for ... by the voice of the Public'. The government would never move ahead of the people: but without the government the people would never move ahead. That was Gipps's reply to his defeat by Broughton in 1839.[18]

Broughton appealed to the Colonial Office against Gipps's ruling and meanwhile withheld church funds from education.[19] Gipps did the same and returned colonial education to the stagnation of 1833. After two victories the bishop could make no headway: despite two defeats the governor retained the initiative but could not advance. Yet the episode, Broughton declared, had illustrated 'the attachment of the people of this Colony, I say *the people* in the strict and proper sense, to the Church of England'.[20] The bishop had triumphed personally.

The money Broughton kept from schools he put into churches. Thirty-two centres had requested a clergyman and the bishop rode through the Hunter River and southern districts from January to May 1840 determining priorities. Midway in this visitation the SPG sent some 'disastrous intelligence'. The Colonial Office refused to approve the appointment of additional Church of England chaplains. That meant the SPG must despatch them without either the government's passage allowance or its guarantee of a first year's stipend.[21] Broughton straightway ferreted out the origin of the ruling and found himself staring Gipps in the face. In 1838, after nine months in the colony and before quitting Sydney, Gipps had decided there was 'no want in the Colony of Clergymen of any denomination'. He recommended an embargo without notice on Church of England appointments and a caution to Wesleyans and Roman Catholics that they had till 31 December 1841 to land their appointees.[22]

Broughton inveighed against the decision as a misguided assessment of the colony's needs, partisan, and totally at odds with the spirit of the Church Act. Was it religious equality to remove the advantages the Church of England had once enjoyed in clerical appointments and then, by manipulating subsidiary arrangements (such as the passage allowances which were not part of the Church Act) disadvantage that church in bringing its legal quota of chaplains to the colony?[23] 'The Church Act', Broughton had only just told his clergy, '... is likely to have very ill effects upon the religious welfare of the community, but still, as it is the Law of the Land it must be treated with respect.'[24] The purpose of the Act was to free religious aid from whim and prejudice, and by a strange twist in affairs Broughton found himself invoking the Church Act for the protection of the Church of England.

Gipps yielded. He protested a misunderstanding. He had meant to suggest that no church needed *more* convict chaplains. The Colonial Office also turned tail and foreswore interference. Broughton would have whatever the Legislative Council in Sydney approved. But the wrangle delayed the arrival of many chaplains by two years. Moreover the few who came out at their own expense and took charge of districts with over 1200 Church of England families were denied any reimbursement. Gipps claimed to have no funds.[25] At the same time he scandalized Broughton in the Executive Council by approving a Presbyterian minister for Lower Portheadland on a petition of 140 signatures from a district a recent census showed had fifty-eight Presbyterians. Broughton demanded an investigation, but Gipps claimed authority under the Church Act to act as he had. An exasperated Broughton turned elsewhere for redress. 'I am aware of instances in which the public funds have been granted under the Church Act where there existed not the slightest grounds to justify such an application' he wrote to the *Sydney Herald*.[26] That shook Gipps. What would the Colonial Office make of a public attack by the head of the church on his 'honour and integrity' as governor? 'It exposed to hazard a friendship of which the foundations were laid forty years ago', he told Broughton, and for a time denied the bishop direct access to government house.[27]

This cranky relationship between Broughton and Gipps had more eccentric moments. Once at a public dinner the bishop had to toast the governor's achievements. 'There would be no doubt a sufficient supply of bread and water', he said, and bade the company drink to Gipps's memorial in roads, dams and grain stores.[28] In a more prickly exchange Gipps twice demanded that Broughton order the aged John Cross, chaplain at Port Macquarie, from his home. 'That clergyman has got possession of a house he has no right to, which never was a parsonage, but which he nevertheless refuses to give up', Gipps told Broughton. Several years earlier Cross had moved into the Commissary's residence, the Commissary into the surgeon's house, and the surgeon, taking over Cross's £60 parsonage allowance, found his own quarters. When a new Surgeon demanded back his official residence Cross found nothing to his taste for £60 in the inflated rent market of 1840 and stayed put. Broughton refused to eject him. He argued that Cross's terms of appointment entitled him to a residence and Gipps should build one. Gipps suggested Broughton shift Cross to a parish with a parsonage. Broughton said Cross was too old to shift. Gipps then threatened to rent the surgeon a house and debit it to Cross's salary. And so it went on. Gipps finally found Cross a house and deducted £1 5s 9½d from his salary for damages to the surgeon's residence.[29]

Though there was nothing Whiggish, radical or anti-church establishment in Gipps's tampering with denominational schools and the flow of chaplains, Broughton had reason to fear its consequences. Gipps had the misfortune to inherit Bourke's generous policies without his treasury surpluses. Expenditure on immigration, gaols and Aborigines

had considerably expanded by 1840 while the economy contracted. To
stabilize costs Gipps re-examined church and school policies. Under
regulations agreed to at the time of the Church Act the clergy received
passage money. But did they have to? Colonial Office rulings allowed
governors to subsidize denominational schools. But were they obliged
to? 'His Excellency desires me to remark to you', the Colonial Secretary
informed Broughton, 'that it is painful to him to be forced to view all
subjects connected with the payment of the clergy not as your Lordship
does, with reference solely to the want of the Church or the advancement
of religious instruction in the colony, but also to regard them in a
pecuniary point of view.'[30] Unlike Bourke who had a vision of where
he would take the colony Gipps was essentially an administrator who
watched his treasury like a hawk. Gipps made decisions on the spot,
and later in appealing to the Colonial Office for confirmation drew up
crisp financial statements that touched off other enquiries. Tables of
the mounting cost of the Church Act, which Gipps forwarded in support
of his decision to cut down passage money, set the Colonial Office questioning the liability of that Act. Was it a hasty extravagance? Similar financial
tables on the cost of denominational schools revealed the enormous
costs involved in retaining them along with national schools. Perhaps
Glenelg's policy of allowing both had been a hasty mistake? In this
way, though in the beginning his wish was simply to trim the budget,
the thorough administrative technique of Gipps touched off wider
reappraisals of the religious and educational policies of the 1830s that
gave Broughton grounds for concern. Perhaps he had less than a decade
to establish his citadel.

Other doubts consolidated. Was Rome about to spring a surprise?
'My mind is full of the subject', Broughton admitted in 1839. 'Indeed
it departs not from me day nor night.' Within a decade Rome had increased her clergy from three to twenty, bought a seminary, established
a branch of the Catholic Institute, and entered the 'business of agitation'
with its own newspaper the *Australasian Chronicle*. That newspaper's
intent was to explain and uphold the civil and religious principles of
Catholics but soon had Broughton between its talons. 'There is more
to this prelate's philosophy than men dream', it warned; and in its fancy
saw vast schemes to raise Broughton sole ruler over God's heritage in
the colony. 'We will endeavour to get behind the scenes', the editor
vowed and circulation soared. Meanwhile, with Bourke gone Polding
swaggered into the governor's levee in 1839 dressed to the inch as a
popish prelate. An impish gesture? Or a trial of Gipps's mettle before
bolder action? Broughton did not linger in speculation. He shot off
another protest with copies to Lord Lyndhurst in the House of Lords
and Sir Robert Inglis in the House of Commons. Were Her Majesty's
civil officers, duly sworn by the Oath of Supremacy, now permitted to
receive publicly on Her Majesty's behalf Roman Catholic bishops who
dressed unmistakably as the agents of that foreign ruler the pope?[31]

When Polding heard of this he put on still more popish garments
and in St Mary's cathedral inveighed against Protestant privilege and
Protestant intolerance. We came in peace, he said, and they have taken

away our tranquility; we asked their co-operation in renovating the face of this land and in encouraging the arts and sciences which improve and adorn social life, but we have been condemned as itching after superiority; we have been promised religious equality, yet we smart under the 'inquisitorial control' of the Bishop of Australia. The inquisitorial control of the Bishop of Australia! That was a sore point. Four times in the last twelve months the Executive Council, with Broughton present, had raised technical points to reject Catholic applications for subsidies. Polding had them one by one reversed, but it rankled that he had to plead his case in facts and figures that Broughton could examine. Broughton was privy to their affairs though they knew nothing of his, Polding exclaimed; and the congregation grew indignant. It sent agents into the countryside to gather a memorial praying Her Majesty to remove the Protestant bishop from all Councils.[32]

'I don't know what to say about being expelled by a posse of Romanists', Broughton reflected. Then for a year both parties nourished their fears. Broughton saw the Catholic press wax insolent while priests paraded openly in flowing robes. Broughton, too, gingered the uncertainty. When Judge Burton returned in 1841 he threw a dinner, and for two hours a hundred and fifty of the colony's judges, magistrates, merchants, landowners, army officers and Legislative Councillors raised glass upon glass in an evening redolent with Church and Queen. 'It was clear that God had joined the two together and he hoped that man would never put them asunder', said Broughton in a mischievous opening toast. Catholics cringed at the sight of the guest list. It revealed that when half the Legislative Council and all the Immigration Committee worshipped on Sunday it was simply Broughton's Diocesan Committee at prayer.[33] 'It ought to be known to the whole world', the Catholic press protested, 'that the immigration committee of the legislative council of this colony, who exercise a control over the crown land fund, consist of the identical individuals who compose the semi-clerical committee of the diocese of Australia.'[34]

That thought confirmed Catholic resolve to be rid of Broughton. Broughton's seat on the Councils was a glaring symbol of a religious inequity that had survived the Church Act. Another was his near control of immigration. And in immigration they found Broughton's Achilles Heel. To relieve the shortage of agricultural labourers Broughton had suggested sending ships in 1841 to England's eastern ports. That could be interpreted as a deliberate effort to steer them clear of Ireland and the *Australasian Chronicle* quickly laid the charge: 'We do insist and maintain that Dr Broughton year by year makes use of his situation as chairman of the immigration committee to protestantise this colony'. Catholics, it was said, were three steps from proscription: Broughton wanted to fill the colony with Protestants, enfranchise them, then repeal Catholic Emancipation. 'The question', as the convert Duncan saw it, 'was whether or not Catholics should submit to be overwhelmed by a system of sectarian immigration, carried on at the public expense, as a prelude, no doubt, to their being placed without the pale of our future colonial constitution.'[35]

Within weeks 500 Sydneysiders jumped the puddles of Castlereagh Street to be in the Old Court House by seven o'clock for a protest. Most were Catholic but the organizers, Murphy and Duncan, had got Dr Bland into the chair. Bland worshipped with the Church of England, but as Sydney's leading patron of constitutional reform he desired Broughton's retirement from government. Moreover his presence fended off accusations of the meeting being a Catholic gang-up. Murphy the vicar-general opened proceedings and suggested locking bigots like Broughton in a hospital for incurables. Then a draft petition was read. It asked for representative government, for the protection of the immigration fund from sectarian misuse, and for Broughton's immediate deposition from the councils. 'He had rendered himself truly obnoxious to the great majority of the colonists by his political career', the secretary read out to 500 cheering Shylocks after Broughton's flesh. That found Bland immediately on his feet speaking sweetly of Broughton. 'The bishop was a well educated and enlightened man . . . [and] the colony was indebted to him for many wise and salutary acts', he said. Bland declined to put to a vote any motion requesting Broughton's immediate removal in a way that reflected on his integrity. So that evening Murphy and Duncan trudged back through the rain carrying a petition gutted of all reference to Broughton, and did not bother the queen with it. 'We must eat our Christmas pudding with a motion of proscription hanging over our heads', lamented Duncan. Broughton had no peace either. Maynooth could flood the colony with priests at a wink and Jesuits were waiting only for a nod from Polding.[36]

While Catholics agitated for his removal Broughton matured in stature as an elder statesman. The years 1840 to 1841 were indifferent to progress. Though the governor greeted his Councils with an assurance that prospects were good, half the members had ridden in though drought afflicted areas. In 1840 land still sold, but more slowly with many settlers choosing instead to squat beyond the boundaries. Prices stayed high but had steadied. Government revenue grew but the bill for administration mushroomed. For relief Gipps turned to tap the land fund but met the bishop's stern gaze. Broughton calculated the fund inadequate for immigration and advised Gipps to try new taxes. Gipps suggested a £2 to £5 head tax on convicts in private service but masters threatened to return their servants before paying what amounted to a 'tax . . . for the liberty to employ the greatest ruffian on the earth'. Gipps then drafted legislation to set up town corporations empowered to levy rates for local development and a district police.[37]

Indignation split the air. What had the doubling of the upset price of land in 1839 been but a new tax? And it would have been a sufficient tax for all local needs had not the British government immediately devoured the proceeds by renouncing its half share of the bill for convict prisons. Colonists therefore viewed any additional tax, however disguised, as a tax in effect to relieve the British government of its obligation to pay for its overseas prisons. The Council preferred to see Sydney a lake in the wet than yield to further taxes without representative government, and rejected the legislation.[38]

Broughton regretted the Council's intransigence. He believed colonists must accept local government and pay for it or see their trade hampered by poor roads and bad bridges. Can there be a nation without trade? he asked. Broughton then took aside James Macarthur who led the opposition and persuaded him to agree at least to the appointment of a commissioner for highways with authority to levy rates and improve roads. Macarthur did, and Broughton earned the title 'member for roads and drains' so derisively bestowed by Lang a decade earlier.[39]

Broughton turned broker in a second dispute. The estimates for 1840 showed how, by a snap of the finger in London, the colony had been made to pay out an extra £30 000 a year for prisons. 'So monstrous a proposition', wrote the *Sydney Herald*, 'was never before recorded for the consideration of men of sense and integrity'. Gipps foolishly defended it. He claimed the colony derived more profit from its convicts than the prisons cost. James Macarthur withstood that. 'The direct pecuniary saving of the Parent State ... far outweighed any gain the Colony can derive', he said; and claimed to know no landowner who would not prefer free labourers. Macarthur was so irritated by Gipps's argument that he made a formal motion of his statement and challenged the Council to divide behind him or the governor. A slender margin stood with the governor. Broughton did not. He supported Macarthur. He saw little difference between Macarthur's complaint and his own in 1834 which accused the British government of cynically compelling settlers to pay up for the moral reformation of prisoners or live in fear of their vicious habits. Moreover, if the British government swallowed up every colonial surplus by repudiating one after another its obligations Broughton would never be free to apply to the land fund for grants towards the religious education of free immigrants.[40]

The folly of the Council's vote was soon apparent. 'Lord John Russell would see how fond Colonists are of being taxed', commented Berry a considerable landowner. Broughton then went into a huddle with the attorney-general who had supported Gipps. 'The case was not so desperate', he soon announced. 'The objection was to the wording not the spirit of the resolution.' Broughton took aside James Macarthur to work out a modified protest: England and Australia, it ran, have benefited equally from transportation and should share equally the cost of the system. Gipps agree to this modified protest and despatched it to London.[41]

More delicate for Broughton was a debate on New Zealand lands. For some time colonists had been doing brisk trade in lands with Maori chiefs, and there had been bargains. Wentworth got millions of acres for a few hundred guineas. In the Sydney rooms of Messers Hebblewhite and Vickery these bargains were auctioned off, and what an ingenious trader had earlier paid 6s an acre for fetched up to £400 in 1840. Around 1 p.m. on 6 January 1840 the clerk of the Legislative Council entered one auction with the news that the British government would not confirm any land transaction between Maori chiefs and white colonists. Broughton welcomed the news. He had seen Maori chiefs in 1839 'very sorrowful and indignant' over tricks played in land transactions and warned they could erupt into war. Nevertheless the decision affected the Church of England. All its New Zealand missions stood on land bought from Maori chiefs and every clergyman and schoolmaster of the future would depend on them for a living. Moreover, the bishop's plans for a New Zealand bishopric hinged on the development of 1500 square miles recently negotiated from Maori chiefs in the north island.[42] So when Gipps put before the Council a bill appointing commissioners to review all land dealings Broughton approved the measure in principle, but found himself attacking the bill's preamble which rested the government's right of interference on the assumption that natives could only lawfully dispose of land to natives. Natives had every right to yield up part of their heritage for churches and schools, the bishop said; and insisted the transfers stand except where they threatened domestic tranquility. For that very reason he wanted Wentworth's rape of the south island upset. Broughton voted to have Wentworth defend his purchase before the Council and prodded the caged lion with reminders that he drew his legal precedents from events in the American colonies during the English Civil War 'when there was no government in England'. Wentworth pleading before Broughton! What a reversal of roles. Broughton, however, found the performance tedious and when it rambled into a second day stayed away. When the final vote was taken Broughton voted with a minority against the preamble; then, cutting his losses, supported the bill as a whole to ensure the commissioners were appointed.[43]

Later still in 1840 colonists learned of the arrival of documents, sealed with the finality of the Sign Manual, ordering Gipps to carve up the colony. Lord John Russell had just ended transportation to the mainland. He believed New South Wales, with its high concentration of convicts, would remain a peculiar area for some time and decided to reduce its borders to the nineteen settled counties. All the territory beyond, much of it thick with squatters and their cattle, was to be split up into new colonies for development after the very different pattern of South Australia.[44]

This news engendered anger and abuse. 'This is an evident attempt on the part of the Whig Jobber, Colonel Torrens, to injure this colony', claimed the *Sydney Herald*. The new boundaries stigmatized New South Wales as the 'convict Colony' and added to the attraction of other colonies like South Australia. But anger and abuse could not upset the Sign Manual; a prompt and well argued debate in the Legislative Council might. It was decided the Council should take advantage of an extraordinary sitting, called for 8 December 1840 to amend legislation for a census, to debate the issue. Who in the colony could organize a knowledgeable debate within hours? James Macarthur declined. The finger pointed at Broughton. He had the mind for detail and the wit to master his facts; he had an unrivalled knowledge of the land regulations and a head packed with the findings of a recent survey of occupied and unoccupied lands; moreover, he had no personal interests in land ownership to compromise his motives. And Broughton, who had never before taken a lead in opposing the government in a matter not strictly ecclesiastical, agreed to this exception 'solely because no other member, on so short notice, appeared prepared to do so' and he feared its injurious consequences on the colony.[45]

Broughton argued that if New South Wales were reduced to the nineteen settled counties the unoccupied lands remaining in them would yield so trifling a revenue for immigration that New South Wales would be annihilated in a stroke. The good lands given over to other colonies and other treasuries would attract immigrants to other ports; 'and where the emigrants arrive', Broughton continued,

> there will be great demand for produce of all descriptions; there stores will be built and merchants reside: where ships arrive there will the wool be carried for shipment, and there will the supplies be purchased for the stations: there will the money circulate, and there will merchants congregate.

In short, Lord John Russell's reforming zeal augured the decay of Sydney as a commercial port. To prevent decay Broughton argued for New South Wales keeping the five well watered territories to the north around Port Macquarie and the Liverpool Plains, and in the south the Manero together with all the lands from the Murrumbidgee to the Murray. Settlers from Sydney had spent wealth and energy exploring those districts and, in the bishop's opinion, they should benefit from their development.[46]

The Council unanimously approved the bishop's case and made an address of it for presentation to the queen. A week later a public meeting of colonists cheered it on its way. 'The colonists', the *Sydney Herald* remarked, 'are highly indebted to the Bishop of Australia for the manner in which he laid the matter before the Council and the public.' Lord John Russell abandoned the changes, and years later when the Colonial Office formed new colonies it followed the bishop's boundaries.[47]

No one cheered the bishop six months later when he tried to clamp a strict sabbath observance on the colony he had helped save. It began over a craze in Sydney for stuffed parrots. This took many an enterprising gunman into the bush on a Sunday, and in blasting at his prey he often set the carriage horses of the gentry into an uncomfortable Sunday gallop. The Council agreed to ban the sport on Sundays. Broughton asked it to ban also boxing, cock-and dogfighting, boating, cricket and the sale of fresh meat. The butchers were delighted, but governor, council, police chief and most newspapers cried opposition. 'Such legislation treads on the very verge of constitutional freedom', warned the *Sydney Herald*; and two prize-fights were set down for the following sabbath. The proposal died, and Broughton muttered that something of the young colony's soul died with it.[48]

The matter of the colony's boundaries and the abortive sabbath legislation highlighted Broughton's predicament as a colonial official. His usefulness depended on steering clear of ecclesiastical matters. When he appeared seeking ecclesiastical advantage he met opposition. His friends in the Council, with the exception of Richard Jones who would 'most cordially adopt every word which fell from his Lordship', were haphazard allies. Broughton blamed this on himself and realized it could have been different had he learned to trim his principles. 'Some who are politically opposed to Sir George Gipps might be disposed to side with me if I would with them: but I am particularly careful *not* to give encouragement to such alliances', he told Coleridge. 'There is little sense or comprehension what it is to oppose a Government measure upon principle.'[49] His principle was that the moral law of Christianity was part of the law of the land while the majority in the Council made clear, during debate on the sabbath legislation, their principle that there was nothing in the precepts of the divine Author of Christianity to authorize the calling in of the civil law to support religion.[50] With that stated in parliament and approved in the press in 1841 it was clear Broughton and the Legislative Council had parted company. His expertise remained at the Council's disposal for use in mundane matters so long as he was a member. From time to time, too, he might spice its meetings with reminders of where a Christian duty should lead it, but such flourishes were more echoes of his conscience than serious proposals for debate and adoption. Denied an effective platform in Council Broughton had either to abandon the struggle to keep the Church of England in a prominent place or move the battle into the market-place. He chose the market-place. The archdeacon who had once instructed the clergy to go about their vocation silently and never to impede the measures of governments by captious objections or to exhibit themselves in opposition to its authority, was prepared now to call the clergy out into vigorous and outspoken opposition against government and others in the colony.[51]

By 1841, two years after his pledge to expand recklessly, Broughton was at a loss to assess his gains. 'I hardly know whether I am to send to you a favourable or unfavourable account of the state of things', he reported to Coleridge in 1841. His personal burdens had increased enormously. Cowper departed suddenly for England to save his sight and left Broughton the insoluble problem of providing Sunday services. He could either close the church or do duty himself—thanks to Gipps's gaffe about the adequate supply of clergy. 'It falls on me accordingly', he said, 'to read prayers, preach, administer the Holy Sacraments, and baptise children.' In the new and neighbouring parish of St Andrews matters were little better. A master from the King's School rode down every Sunday for services but left Broughton the weekday calls. Then the temporary St Andrews went up in flames just after lightning had toppled a new church tower at Kelso near Bathurst and damaged the parsonage. He wanted to visit the Manero but could not leave Sydney. Paperwork piled up and the Colonial Secretary's office called for overdue returns required under the Church Act. The SPG promised the help of a domestic chaplain but Broughton knew any extra clergy must be sent into the bushlands where the need was even more desperate.[52]

Nothing had come of the plans to launch a college for training a local ministry. By the end of 1841 the SPCK had put up £3000 for a building and promised a professor of theology, but Broughton lacked candidates. 'He had only met one instance of a native educated in the colony, on

which he thought himself justified in conferring Holy Orders', he admitted
in 1840. That was John Elder made deacon on Trinity Sunday 1840.
Sons of the rich he encouraged to go to England, find a good tutor, and
get into Oxford. Other local candidates could be trained more economically under superior chaplains like Allwood and Macquarie Cowper.[53]
A thoroughly professional theological preparation for Holy Orders—and
Broughton would entertain nothing less, abhorring the idea that the
colony should ever have a second-class clergy—must await the establishment of a grammar school capable of matching the classical schooling
of the English sixth form. So he loaned the SPCK's £3000 to the new
St James Grammar School arguing that by the time it was repaid there
would be candidates of the required standard to make a theological
faculty in a college worthwhile. In the meantime Tom Bodenham presented himself for ordination and was placed under Allwood's tuition.
Bodenham was Cape's pupil from the Sydney College. So much for that
godless institution! The King's School had proved a disappointment and
Broughton transferred his affection to St James Grammar School.[54]

The diocesan library, however, was a huge success. Coleridge tipped
off Pusey as to the bishop's needs, and books pulled from the shelves
of dons all over Oxford soon piled up in the corridors of Tusculum. 'I
think Origen is the only one of the *Great* Fathers that we have not',
Broughton boasted in 1841. Hundreds more arrived. The Evangelical
party got wind of this and sent their own contributions. Broughton felt
the clergy, graduates included, were intellectually 'light weight' and
needed to sharpen their wits for the controversial combats ahead. Of
course there were exceptions: Allwood, Clarke, Walsh, and the bright
young Etonian Sconce for whom the bishop felt a special attraction.
The laity needed gingering up too. Broughton was thrilled to find Charles
Kemp, an editor-proprietor of the *Sydney Herald*, keen to set up a
theological library for the laity. He brought the Church of England
Book Society into being on 26 August 1841 and the Society sponsored
a series of annual public theological lectures. After providing for the
clergy and laity Broughton looked to the rulers of the future and, over-
coming initial opposition, set up a library for the Legislative Council.[55]

If Broughton's clergy were not brilliant they were not troublesome.
'There appears to me never to have been a time when a stronger tendency
to agreement ... prevailed among the clergy', he reported. It had been
that way for some time. 'Poor heedless Dicker' was the only outright
casualty among the SPG recruits. He arrived drunk and Broughton
placed him under discipline: he stayed drunk and Broughton placed
him on a ship. The other casualties were misfits.[56]

The serious casualties were among the laity. William McQuoid was
colonial sheriff, lay secretary of the Diocesan Committee and a 'respected
friend' whom Broughton commended for his 'domestic worth, genuine
religion and gentlemanly qualities in private life'. Around 1841 he shot
himself. He had made a quick pound in the boom conditions of the late
1830s investing funds belonging to the sheriff's office and was exposed
when the colony's economy stuttered in 1840–1.[57] J. E. Manning, registrar
of the Supreme Court and another prominent layman who often hosted

Broughton on his inland tours, was caught by the same misfortune. Manning's son wanted to pay the debts amounting to £9400 but the *Sydney Herald* demanded a prosecution for embezzlement. Broughton, who was sheltering McQuoid's widow and daughter at Tusculum, pleaded leniency in the Executive Council to avoid driving another man into a desperate last act; and mercy prevailed.[58]

The economic reverse that claimed McQuoid and Manning tumbled also the wool merchant Sparke and forced the sale of Tusculum. A new landlord demanded an exorbitant £350 annual rent and Broughton felt he may have been forced to quit. 'It is the more tiresome', he moaned, 'as we are just now *beginning* to enjoy the fruit of the labour which I have been for five years bestowing upon my garden ... a source of enjoyment and amusement.' He thought of building; but the 10 per cent to 12 per cent interest charged in New South Wales deterred him. He approached the SPG for a loan and then decided it was an unjustifiable diversion of resources. In the end he kept Tusculum at £300 a year, but lost its ten acre park, horse-paddock and orchard. For a moment he dreamed the SPG might acquire the ten acres and some adjoining blocks as the beginnings of an endowment for the diocese. Within twenty years they would be most valuable building sites, he urged; and in a hasty move negotiated the purchase of one allotment for a church paying £400 for what others picked up for £300 a few weeks later at auction. The bishop's sense of the market did not inspire the SPG. The plan died and Broughton resigned himself to having Tusculum surrounded by tenements and 'the sound of squalling children'.[59]

Van Diemen's Land added other troubles. On 3 June 1841 Hutchins, the archdeacon, dined at Hobart's government house and left in a casual good humour. Next morning, peering into the sunrise he announced to his wife the coming of a glorious day and, stooping to tie a lace, tumbled from life. The event dismayed Broughton. He had hoped to hand Port Phillip over to Hutchins. Instead he re-inherited the southern arch-deaconry just when South Australia demanded attention and New Zealand bristled with the problems of approaching independence. And to aggravate the situation Franklin, without pausing for consultation, appointed the Reverend William Palmer archdeacon *pro tempore* and bishop's commissary 'during the Governor's pleasure'. The governor's pleasure! And Palmer an archdeacon! Broughton had spent six years removing authority from Palmer. 'I have many and serious objections to the course which has been adopted', Broughton commented, 'and certainly cannot recognise Mr Palmer either as Archdeacon ... or as my Commissary with jurisdiction over the rest of the clergy.' However, he let Palmer keep the titles on the condition that he did not exercise the authority inherent in them, and Palmer complied.[60]

The year 1841 ended where it began. Broughton advanced some of his projects, others regressed, most stood still. More clergy served in the countryside, fewer in Sydney; more churches were begun, few were finished; another grammar school opened but no new parish schools; the SPG increased its contribution but Coleridge warned his sources were drying up. 'We certainly have our portion both of the black and white', Broughton remarked, 'but neither so predominantly as to exclude the other.'[61] By the law of effort and reward progress ought to have predominated. Broughton had never worked harder, the Diocesan Committee and local committees also worked hard, the SPG worked hard, and Coleridge was working himself into a nervous collapse. Why, then, did progress lag? Broughton blamed Gipps. The governor had cut so many former subsidies that every increased effort was swallowed up keeping pace with the past.

How far to Retire?

The legislative career of the Right Reverend Prelate has
been marked on all occasions, by very eminent ability, by
great industry and moderation; and a testimonial to this
effect may well be got up without reference to political party.

Australian 8 March 1843

Late in 1841 colonists learned that Lord Melbourne's Whig government
had for the sixth time deferred their new constitution. 'This is positively
too bad. It is trifling, not only with our rights as a British province,
but with our allegiance to the British Crown', protested the *Sydney
Herald*, and challenged colonists to turn November 1841 into a month
of protest or endure an interminable enslavement. Little happened.
In November 1841 falling prices, dwindling incomes and an unprece-
dented rash of bankruptcies preoccupied colonists. Broughton sympathized with the disappointed *Sydney Herald*. 'The establishment of
representative government on a basis not extravagantly popular is
desirable', he said. '[But] I do from my heart hope that the Government
of England will never be led, in order to silence, for it would not satisfy,
a few factious persons, to yield anything like universal suffrage, or even
a very low scale of qualification for voters.' England must be aware
that concessions in the colony will eventually be demanded at home.[1]
  The signal to act came in February 1842. With news of a switch from
Whig to Tory rule James Macarthur, Charles Campbell and the 'gallant'
Captain O'Connell called a public meeting to prod Peel into sparing
an early thought for New South Wales.
  They set the meeting for 1 p.m. Wednesday 16 February in the lower
saloon of the new Royal Hotel, the squatters' city rendezvous. For
working men the hour was awkward and the location intimidating;
but the *Australasian Chronicle* urged workers to sacrifice their wages
and keep an eye on 'the would-be lords of the soil'. They did. Two
thousand sturdy Britons turned the meeting into the colony's largest
ever and shifted it into the Victoria Theatre, and almost on to the racecourse. James Macarthur opened the proceedings. He pleaded with all
factions to set aside the divisive issue of the franchise and to let England
simply witness them united in their determination to enjoy representative
institutions. His supporters—'the loyal party'—then produced a petition

whose 'dry facts' were that the colony's large population and considerable
wealth in property and commerce entitled it to dispose of its own internal
affairs. But some thought those facts not quite so dry. From the argument
that the colony's considerable wealth entitled it to representative institutions it was but one step to the conclusion that a colonist's considerable
personal wealth was his justification for a vote. So a 'liberal party' led by
the wine merchant Henry Macdermott and Robert Cooper (whose ale
Wentworth had freely dispensed at Darling's departure) proposed amending the petition to shift the claim for representative institutions from the
value of the colony's 'dirty acres' to the inalienable rights of its settlers as
British subjects. Upon such a suggestion the meeting foundered; and
that 'entirely confirms the opinion which I have held for many years',
Broughton commented, 'that representative government may be a very
proper boon to bestow on this community . . . but with regard to those
arrangements [of self-government] the people themselves are not qualified
to form any opinion whatever and the terms must therefore be fixed
for them by those who are better informed'.[2]

Broughton considered himself among the better informed and wrote
to Coleridge the day after the big meeting hoping the doors of Eton
might open on to the House of Commons. He wanted an old Etonian
in parliament to lobby for the colony's true interests—a high franchise
and a bicameral legislature. Broughton opposed a low franchise as
tantamount to handing over the colony to the republican sympathies
of the Irish and the colonial born. Irish immigrants had shown no more
affection for the monarchy abroad than at home and an influx of Maynooth
priests had kept it that way, he said. 'There is no such feeling, in the
minds of those who were *born* here as that of loyalty', he added; and
alleged that the colonial born looked on the queen as a remote name
much like the Hindu looked on the East India Company. Moreover, to
the colonial born the rule of government meant rule by a changing
succession of governors and councils, and this being more a republican
than a monarchical experience had turned their sympathy to American
rather than British institutions. Lower the franchise too far and these
classes will dictate the changes.[3]

Broughton thought a unicameral legislature equally dangerous and
likely to lead to rule by a city oligarchy. Because of long colonial distances
country representatives would need to set up a Sydney household for
the three to four months the legislature sat. But few could afford it,
or afford to be so long absent from their businesses without ruin. 'The
effect of all this would . . . throw the management of affairs and the
chief influence in Council into the hands of a few active men living in
or near to Sydney', he said. 'And thus in truth the *people* of the Colony
would be less *represented* than they are by the existing Council.' So
Broughton pleaded the colony's need of an upper house of crown nominees
with power to reject legislation not in the interest of the whole colony,
and dared prophesy that the unfranchised would soon hold it in higher
esteem than the elected house.[4]

To this Broughton added a quite personal hope that English statesmen
would one day adopt a constitution that made every colony a county

of England where the great aristocratic families might set up branch houses. Then will Britain have 'a Colonial empire more extended and powerful than any the world has ever yet witnessed'. It was a misty but thoughtful vision never far removed from the reflection that monarchy and aristocracy promised the church a better deal than democracy. Broughton also believed the aristocratic principle with its gradations of greater and lesser ranks gave colonists something to aspire to beyond money, and they needed that badly. Moreover, when men could not turn to the queen as the fount of honours they pandered to the people. And finally, to entice the reluctant aristocracy abroad Broughton argued that colonial markets would one day be vital to the maintenance of those protective tariffs that guaranteed the aristocracy its income and status.

> To the aristocracy I think it may fairly be urged, that without a continually extending foreign trade giving employment to the manufacturer, it will be impossible to uphold that system of protection upon which the fortunes of the landed interests depend; and where, when foreign nations are ceasing to be our customers and rather becoming rivals, is that outlet for our manufacturers to be found except in our own Colonies? Where else can an outlet be sought for to dispose of that accumulation of numbers which is confirmed at home, *must* be liable to distress; and distress will engender dissatisfaction; and the whole frame of society will be torn asunder by their struggles. In fact therefore whatever is done to promote the advancement of the Colonies, and to preserve them in close and willing dependence on the parent state, must collaterally be for the benefit and security of the aristocracy in England.[5]

Coleridge, with Peel's two sons in his house at Eton, was well placed to serve Broughton. Peel was prime minister by the time Broughton's letter arrived and Lord Stanley soon had it on his desk at the Colonial Office. 'An honour I hardly expected for them', the bishop remarked. The reply he did. The English aristocracy did not need their colonial saviour, and Stanley dismissed the matter with an observation that there could be no hereditary rank in the colony because of legal impediments to the maintenance of hereditary property. Broughton awoke from his dream. The notion that a mixture of aristocracy and monarchy might restore the church to its traditional place had been a lapse in Broughton's realism. Whatever the interests of the aristocracy the church was not one of them. Whatever the so called 'Conservative party' planned to conserve it was not the church. After all, the Tory Aberdeen had been no more helpful in 1835 than the Whiggish Glenelg in 1836. Why should Broughton expect more of Stanley than Russell? 'We are in the hands of those who, as a *Conservative* party, are wholly ineffective', he lamented. 'The present Government is in truth but carrying out the destructive policy of the last.'[6]

In 1842 no one could guess what fate awaited the colonial churches under a new constitution. Lang took advantage of this indecision, and hired the School of Arts in Sydney to denounce Bourke's Church Act as 'a tyranny of the worst kind'. It taxed Protestants to support Catholic idolatry and Catholics to support Protestant heresy, he said; and in April 1842 announced the struggle for civil and religious freedom had begun and would continue till 'the present monstrous politico-ecclesiastical system has been upset'. Lang believed the colony's economic distress would decrease government revenue to a level where new taxes must be imposed to meet the expense of the Church Act. A nominated council might agree to that but Lang dared any popularly elected assembly to tax Englishmen for the relief of religion.[7] He foretold an early victory for the voluntary principle, and thoughtful clergy spoke of an insecurity in their future. Broughton was adamant that the Colonial Office must not surrender control of ecclesiastical expenditure, whether on education or churches, to an elected assembly. Archbishop Howley thought it unlikely they would, but could give Broughton no assurance.[8] Stanley kept his counsel and the clergy sweated.

There was much to help Broughton pass these months of anxious waiting. He sat regularly in the Legislative Council and took a leading stand against the revival of transportation. A petition already in circulation begged fresh supplies of convicts for road and bridge building in remote areas, and unofficially there was mention of importing 3000 annually. But the publicity surrounding the petition festered with evidence that more would be sought in time. Some older settlers condemned the abolition of transportation as economic folly from the start and many younger ones spoke frankly of being misled into emigrating on the expectation of enjoying the use of free convict labour. Such men would press for the return of assigned servants, and the *Australian* supported their cause forecasting economic collapse without it. The *Sydney Herald* led the opposition arguing that transportation would retard the cause of self-government. Up country, however, settlers preferred to abandon their franchise before their flocks and the petition was reported 'fully and respectfully' signed, and ready for despatch to England where a surfeit of convicts augured a warm welcome.[9]

Broughton attempted to arrest that support. He understood the colony's economic difficulties and, ten years before the *Australian*, had lauded the power of open space to reform the convict temperament.[10] But he thought many beguiled into supporting the petition on the misunderstanding that in dismissing convicts to remote areas the colony could enjoy the benefits of transportation without its concomitant evils. It was a great risk, the bishop said; and though he declined to attribute moral havoc to transportation he thought the colony mightily improved by its cessation. 'Although transportation had only been discontinued about two years', the bishop told the Legislative Council, 'the improvement in the moral and general disposition of the people had been so great, that none who had not cause to observe the change so much as himself would be able to credit it.'[11] No temporary economic gain should be allowed to arrest that trend. So the bishop made transportation a moral rather than an economic or constitutional issue. 'And what honest man—what virtuous woman—what affectionate husband—what faithful wife—what father ambitious for the honour of his sons—what mother jealous for the purity of her daughters, would not join with the BISHOP of AUSTRALIA?', wrote the *Sydney Herald*.[12] The *Australian* retorted that Broughton was about as competent to decide on the colony's economic needs as the Archbishop of Canterbury to fix the path of England's railways; but the moral issue stuck and all future transportationists had to answer it.[13]

In the same session Broughton charged Russell, Stanley's predecessor as Secretary of State for Colonies, with unbecoming behaviour towards Governor Gipps. The colony had set its labour requirement from June 1840 to June 1842 at 24 000 and Gipps, guided by statistics showing two out of three bounty orders had lapsed in the past, issued 71 315 new orders. He expected 23 000 to be filled. When after only fourteen months bounty agents had embarked 20 000 settlers and signed up 10 000 others the colony was in strife. It had an immigration bill for half a million pounds and less than £100 000 towards it. On Broughton's advice the government issued debentures, secured against future land sales, to escape financial embarrassment. That offended fiscal orthodoxy at the Colonial Office and Gipps took a towelling: 'I shall endeavour however to the best of my power to counteract the mischievous effects of your improvidence, for which you alone are responsible', Russell wrote.[14] Gipps *alone* responsible! The *Australasian Chronicle* would have none of that: 'We should like to see a due share of the onus removed to the shoulders of the Bishop and committee'.[15] Broughton accepted a share of responsibility. He admitted an error in calculation, but defended large-scale immigration as basically sound. As for Russell's further suggestion that the colony's irresponsible immigration programme had contributed to its financial depression that was, the bishop said 'humbly', utterly false. Broughton pulled from his pocket, in full view of the Legislative Council, a letter he wrote in 1836 forecasting that distress must follow the current excessive speculation in land and cattle. The colony suffered from irresponsible trading not irresponsible immigration; and it suffered, too, from Russell's irresponsible language. How could Russell expect colonists to respect a governor admonished as mischievous and imprudent? The very language was 'destructive of all authority', Broughton said and urged Gipps not to resign over the issue. 'If censure were at all deserved there were means more dignified, more becoming, more fit, in which to convey it.' Personal rudeness within the ranks was unacceptable to Broughton. A cleric who spoke disrespectfully to his bishop soon found his presence unwanted in the diocese; that was Wilkinson's fate in 1830. The standard Broughton applied to the church he extended to the state, and gave Russell a lecture to 'cause him to blush'.[16]

The year 1842 had its more pleasant moments. A note slipped to Broughton in the Executive Council in mid-April sent him hurrying from the chamber. The Bishop of New Zealand waited in the annexe. It was the most gratifying moment in ten years. 'In all the difficulties I have had to encounter here', Broughton said, 'the greatest of all has been that I have *never* had an associate in my own profession with whom I could hold unreserved communication on points of difficulty.' Now at last he had a brother in purpose and spirit stranded on his door step. Selwyn's ship had been holed entering the Heads and his departure delayed. Delighted by the misfortune, Broughton installed the Selwyns in the rooms just vacated by McQuoid's widow in Tusculum, and got Robert Campbell's town house for the rest of the missionary party. For the next few weeks Darlinghurst buzzed with comings and goings more characteristic of Polding's residence than Tusculum, and 'whether in the estimation of R. Catholics or Dissenters, the effect has been most felicitous for the Church in witnessing the spectacle of the Bishops acting in truly fraternal and affectionate accordance'.[17]

Broughton considered it essential for the two bishops to agree on common policies. Only a united Church of England would smite the ungodliness of native paganism and Roman error in the Pacific. Now, while there were only two bishops, was the time to lay the foundations of united action. There would be three or four in time and the task more complicated. So the bishops mulled over the problems of the Oxford Tracts, of education, finance, clerical training and ecclesiastical discipline, and found agreement. All Selwyn needed was a 'few lessons in colonial episcopacy' and the handling of ultra-liberal governors, and Broughton provided these.[18]

The evenings at Tusculum became great family gatherings where Mrs Selwyn's 'lively' chatter set the pace of gaiety. Broughton had first met her in London in 1835 at dinner with Joshua Watson. Watching her now across the dinner table he marvelled how little the prospect of missionary privation diminished her zest. Indeed among women Broughton admired none so much as the gay-hearted clerical wife. Women like Mrs Selwyn, Mrs Sconce, indeed his own wife who trekked off to balls and parties unescorted but for her daughters, proved that a wife was no barrier to sacrifice and sacrifice no bar to joy, and so vindicated the wisdom of the Church of England in abandoning celibacy. There were outings, too, into the near countryside inspecting new churches; 'little bits of Coleridge', Broughton called them. Broughton also arranged for Selwyn to preach from Marsden's pulpit at Parramatta on Sunday 8 May.[19]

At Parramatta Selwyn heard fresh from Marsden's son-in-law the saga of the missionary's first landing in New Zealand and how Marsden had slept there in safety with the spears of the savages stuck around the stone on which, like Jacob, he had laid his head for a pillow. That fired Selwyn to be immediately on his way. Broughton protested: Selwyn had promised to address a special gathering of the Diocesan Committee at a dinner for which tickets had been sold. Moreover, Broughton was planning a most apostolic farewell for Selwyn, a great public meeting, the presentation of an address covered with signatures from all over the diocese, a commendation from the Church of Australia culminating in a procession to the water's edge—the sort of farewell Paul got at Antioch and Polding more recently. But Selwyn dismissed it all. His one fault Broughton commented, was 'a little impetuous self-will'. Nevertheless, Broughton scurried around gathering what signatures he could and presented them at a hastily arranged public matins, where, in a voice so much affected that he could scarcely speak, Broughton paid tribute after the service to his friend:[20]

> We have indeed taken sweet counsel together and walked in the house of God as friends; united in hearing his word; in offering the daily sacrifice of our prayers and praises; and in receiving the solemn pledge of our common Redeemer's love to our great and endless comfort. In thus cementing our fraternity, and hallowing the ties of personal fellowship, and association by sanction which bind together in one, the many members of that body of which the Head is Christ, we have renewed, I sensibly feel, the example of episcopal union which attracted the reverential notice of the yet untainted church when Anicetus and Polycarp, bishops like ourselves, worshipped at the same altar.[21]

As Broughton's voice faded some wept. But for all that there had been a dash of episcopal arrogance in Broughton's performance. He had monopolized Selwyn's stay and the Reverend W. B. Clarke bitterly resented it. Clarke had more than episcopal isolation to contend with. He came to New South Wales seeking new health and a refuge from debts. As a fine classical scholar, scientist and poet Broughton welcomed him as a candidate above the ordinary, but cooled when Clarke failed to settle down at the King's School. Clarke went to Castle Hill 'a really underserving area humanly speaking', failed to raise a congregation, lost the government subsidy and lived off donations from the SPG. Illness drove his wife back to England. Ironically, Clarke found health and lost everything else. He heard of Selwyn's noble character and hoped for a meeting. No invitation arrived. Selwyn passed in an orbit which avoided the clergy. 'In Australia, Bishops and curates seldom meet', Clarke told Coleridge after Selwyn's departure.[22]

Once Selwyn departed Broughton turned to drafting the report on immigration for 1842. His appointment as committee chairman had been routine but his report could ill afford to be. The colony's immigration programme was £78 000 in debt and land sales so depressed as unlikely to yield £16 000 in 1842 compared with £316 000 in 1840. This prompted the Colonial Office to place an eleven month embargo on emigration, and its extension seemed inevitable. The 12s an acre minimum upset price imposed on the sale of crown lands in 1839 was reckoned as 7s to 9s an acre above the current market value of much of it and likely to remain so for three more years. With land sales postponed indefinitely the colony had no finance for immigration and faced a bleak labour shortage likely to lead to rising wages amid depressed market conditions. The remedy most commonly spoken of was for the government to abandon its dogma of a minimum upset price or at least shrink it to 5s an acre. Then, in turn, land sales would revive immigration, restore productivity and increase the general revenue. This appeared so obviously the solution that colonists expected Gipps would move towards it in May 1842. Instead, Lord Stanley had him put a £1 an acre upset price on land in new districts and reserved to the British parliament the sole right to alter it. 'Good God! how grievous and cruel a thing it is', exclaimed the *Australian*, and appealed to the Committee on

Immigration to put some reason into Stanley, that 'ass greater than Dogberry'.[23]

Broughton set to work with the colony listing its choices as cheap land worked by free immigrants, or expensive land worked by convicts or coolies, or ruination. Broughton rejected the lot. He opposed convict labour for moral reasons and coolies as likely to deprave the colony's constitution, and in 1842 favoured a high upset price on land as the only way to direct capital away from speculation to more productive ends. He believed the fall in land sales that coincided with the 12s upset price to be a case of *post hoc ergo propter hoc* as private land at 6s an acre had remained unsold during 1839. Broughton also believed the colony had overlooked another choice, and though it had been rejected twice before he pushed it to the fore again. Broughton wanted immigration financed on capital borrowed in England, and he blamed the severity of the existing depression partly on the rejection of such a proposal in 1839. What colonists lacked was not the opportunity of buying land but finance to develop the land they already owned. No one had much cash. Farmers had goods but no buyers. Barter trade sufficed for simple transactions but more complex deals were stranded. Church building, for instance, had ceased because quite prosperous settlers could not convert their property and goods into money to meet subscriptions. It was the novelty of bankruptcy amid good seasons rather than a fall in land sales that demanded explanation, and Broughton found it in the excessive shipments of specie to London to pay passage money for immigrants. Under normal trading conditions much of it would have returned as payment for exports, but when wool prices fell sharply in England the specie stayed abroad. That deprived the colony of capital and halted development. The Committee on Immigration had a duty, Broughton said, to revive immigration without exporting specie; reducing land to 12s an acre would not assist in that whereas debentures raised in England would.[24]

At first the Legislative Council took only tentative hold on the idea. It asked Broughton for a detailed report without any commitment as to its adoption.[25] Gipps, blaming the colony's ills on a 'mania of speculation', made a policy of having no policy but to await the future; and this puzzled observers until Stanley unwittingly betrayed that the governor believed the colony exaggerated its need for labour.[26] Most who sat in the Council clung resolutely to the lower land price as the salve for all sores, while a few spied in the loan the beginnings of a 'national debt' with its permanent interest bills and new taxes.[27] But the *Australian*, the staunch advocate of everything Broughton opposed on convicts, coolies and cheap land, was quite enthusiastic; and 'believing that the sentiments of the Bishop are not so clearly and precisely understood, by the public at large, as it is desirable they should be', gave the loan proposal generous publicity.[28] Dr Bland did the same. He rarely agreed with Broughton, but at a public meeting called in June 1842 on quite another matter took time off to congratulate the bishop for 'candidly and with much magnanimity' admitting the blunder in over-exporting specie and backed the loan proposal.[29] To such friends Broughton had only to explain how an empty and mortgaged Land Fund might attract investors. Indeed the cheap land party saw this as the most exciting aspect of the proposal believing the government, in resorting to a loan, must drop land prices in order to rejuvenate the Land Fund and attract investors by offering a respectable security.[30]

Broughton had a more wily plan. New settlers should be encouraged to squat on crown land and contract to buy it over fourteen years. By that time their labour would have made the land worth £1 an acre or more. The settlers' squatting fees would pay the interest on the debentures and their later annual instalments, together with the revenues derived from the naturally increased productivity of the land, would more than redeem the loan. To encourage squatting Broughton recommended leasing settlers ten or more acres at a nominal rent for every one acre they contracted to buy. This would add to the colony a most desirable class of modest but independent land-owners who, in turn, would attract a better class of immigrant. By paying passage money from English loans the colony kept its capital for local expansion while the new settlers were being absorbed. That capital would also relieve pressure on bank loans, reduce interest rates, and so assist the new settler in buying his land at the new high upset price.[31] Indeed, Broughton saw so glowing an advantage in his scheme that 'if the government could sell as much land as would be required for immigration he would still say borrow, and keep the money received from land to improve the resources of the colony'.[32]

Debate on Broughton's scheme had scarcely begun when the *Australian*, snipping through English newspapers in search of fill, came upon a speech in which Stanley dissented in 'very explicit language' from the principle of land mortgages for immigration. Stanley also directed Gipps to split the proceeds of future land sales between immigration and a cluster of public projects including Aboriginal welfare and road building. 'British Emigration to New South Wales bids fair to be at a stand still for a considerable period of time to come', commented the *Australian*, and dismissing further debate on Broughton's proposals as empty ritual turned attention to the colony's last resort, coolie labour. 'If we could have British Emigration, we would say, no Coolies', declared the editor. 'If we could immediately revert to the Transportation and Assignment System, we would say, no Coolies. But in the absence of both of these expedients, the force of circumstances compel us to say, it is better to introduce Indian labour than to encounter national ruin.' Land and stock owners stood firmly behind that. Opposite them the *Australasian Chronicle* marshalled the working classes of Sydney for the defence of the British worker and his wages.[33]

This confrontation enhanced the wisdom of Broughton's recommended loan as an alternative to the forecasts of economic ruin without coloured labour and a wage depression with it. The colonial secretary was the first to announce his conversion to the bishop's scheme in September 1842, and in a Legislative Council debate that followed only Gipps sustained a serious resistance. As the sworn adviser of Her Majesty's government Gipps said 'he should not recommend a loan, or a guarantee, until the colonists had gone hand in hand with him in reducing the expense of the government, and in endeavouring to raise a revenue for immigration themselves'. But the Legislative Council voted so overwhelmingly for the loan that Gipps reported his opposition with a brevity that allowed Stanley to go volte-face and approve colonial debentures for 4000 adult passages annually. That broke through the impasse on immigration by July 1843, the deadline Broughton had earlier laid down for avoiding the ill effects of a labour shortage.³⁴

Broughton's contribution to the settlement was ungrudgingly acknowledged. 'The speeches of the Bishop of Australia are eminently characterised by that clearness and precision which is only possessed in perfection by minds of a superior order', commented the *Australian*.³⁵ Though that newspaper intended to fight on for a reduction in the upset price of land (a recommendation forced into the final draft of the report on immigration and disowned by Broughton in debate) it was generously conceded that Broughton's well chosen language and lucid arrangement of topics early in the discussion had enabled colonists to better grapple with a more than difficult subject.³⁶ The *Sydney Morning Herald* wholeheartedly agreed and forecast that Broughton's report would dispel the 'darkness and delusion' prevalent in Westminster's discussions of Australian affairs. Indeed the *Sydney Morning Herald* handsomely honoured the bishop's 'inestimable state papers' on immigration: 'A stranger desirous of understanding the peculiarities of this colony, as the theatre of capital and industry, may find in these Reports a richer collection of facts, and a surer guide to accurate conclusions, than in any other publications that ever came under our notice'.³⁷

In a second matter Broughton fared less well. The colony had used two different modes of immigration, a government and a bounty system. Under the government system the government hired ships and employed agents to recruit suitable immigrants. These ships landed their cargoes in manageable numbers at regular intervals. The system's disadvantage was that, as departure dates approached, agents filled vacancies with all willing immigrants whether the colony needed their skills or not. The bounty system avoided this. It left shipping as well as recruiting to agents, and only reimbursed them the passage money of immigrants who measured up to requirements. As a result bounty agents hired ships only when they had a satisfactory cargo and landed them in the colony in unpredictable numbers at irregular intervals.³⁸ On Broughton's recommendation in 1839 the colony swung exclusively to the bounty system as more economical. He considered the inconvenience of that system preferable to the wastefulness of the government system, and he and his family were ever involved in the scramble that followed the arrival of an unexpected ship.³⁹ But in February 1842 1000 immigrants had arrived in two days and colonists scurried for tents in what Gipps must have considered the crowning imposition of an experiment that had scorched his reputation for good management and edged the colony into debt. When the tents came down Gipps vowed an end to the existing bounty system. Good colonial administration required a more predictable system and the search for it sparked off a new wave of opposition by the bounty system's long-standing opponents.[40]

Many of the major employers had wanted change for some time. They believed the system was controlled by a coterie of mercantile schemers who veered to the edge of the regulations and packed their ships with Irishmen too depressed to quibble at discomfort, and though skilled enough for a bounty proved restless and indolent to the point of incompetence. Unfortunately this group's formula for change added to costs. The other opponents of the bounty system were the Irish settlers themselves. They wanted government ships back on the run before Protestants tightened bounty regulations to stem the flow of Irishmen.[41]

Broughton at first ignored these criticisms.[42] Even in 1841 'the plain arithmetical fact, that within the last eighteen months the Protestants have received above $36\frac{1}{2}$ per cent. LESS, and the Roman Catholics nearly $41\frac{3}{4}$ per cent. MORE, than their respective quotas of immigrants' stirred other Protestants more. Broughton stuck by the bounty system for its economy and merely recommended four of England's more eastern ports to the attention of the bounty agents.[43] The Irish still flooded in, and claimed 16 892 of the 25 330 bounties paid between January 1841 and June 1842.[44] 'Observe this scandalous disproportion, colonists, this cruel use of your Protestant Emigration Fund', thundered the *Australian*; and with frenetic anxiety demanded why 'neither the Lord Bishop of Australia nor Mr James Macarthur have chosen to use, in this cause, those weapons of station, influence, and talents, which they might have wielded'.[45]

Despite this Broughton again championed the bounty system in 1842. He extolled its better-than-ever economy (down 2s 4d a head on 1841) and denied any inferiority in its cargoes. 'We have no right to expect immaculate persons', he told the Legislative Council, and believed tighter regulations could eliminate the extravagantly publicized frauds and immoralities in the system.[46] But the party bent on change was strong. Deas Thomson the colonial secretary and Mr Merewether, the colonial immigration agent joined it, and the Colonial Office made no secret of its hurt at the abandonment of government ships as implying incompetence in its management of them.[47] So Broughton, anticipating some interference, warned against any change that returned initiative in the selection of immigrants to the Colonial Office or its agents. 'They were not sufficiently independent of the government', he maintained. 'He could not forget the tendency to select from the Poor Law Union on the one hand, and the Crown witness from Ireland on the other.' Free passages to New South Wales for criminals willing to turn queen's evidence! That had irked Broughton from the moment he uncovered it in 1841, and confirmed his conviction that the colony receiving immigrants must select them.[48]

But did that selection extend to choosing between Englishmen and Irishmen? Broughton thought not, until mid-1842 when he suddenly confessed to seeing a possible 'future inconvenience' for religious liberty in the unrestricted flow of Irish Catholics. 'He could not find any single instance where the Church of Rome did not show a desire, where it had the power, to interfere with those who were not of her faith', he told an embarrassed Legislative Council; and bluntly charged that if this were a predominantly Roman Catholic colony under a Roman Catholic governor with a Roman Catholic bishop controlling immigration a similar Protestant influx would have been smartly cut off. Yet Broughton found it a tricky business acquitting his religious conscience without betraying 'the public interest so much involved in having a cheap and efficient system of immigration'. He finally took refuge in a formula that condemned the concentration of bounty operations around Great Britain's western ports as being in violation of the Land Fund's obligation to 'introduce emigrants from the various divisions of the United Kingdom without any undue difference or distinction.' The system erred not in excessively importing Irishmen but by inadvertently excluding the non-Irish, and Broughton proposed interference with the latter only. Roger Therry thought that a bit of sophistry in the light of the bishop's allusion to 'future inconvenience' in an excessive Irish presence. So as a 'peace offering' Broughton withdrew that offending allusion. That satisfied Therry and dismayed others. 'To offer battle', wrote the *Australian*, 'and then, through voluntary pusillanimity, to suffer defeat, is, in the eyes of the Protestant Churches of the Colony who are wont to look to their leaders at least for firmness of purpose, a painful spectacle.'[49]

But a more painful spectacle was the unabated flow of Irishmen. Bounty agents, prepared to extend their ferry operations beyond Plymouth, could still pour their Irish recruits into ships anchored at eastern ports. Broughton ever insisted he had done nothing to restrict physically the flow of Irishmen or Roman Catholics,[50] and Lang woefully agreed. 'To the Bishop's services in connection with immigration', he wrote, 'we are indebted for the immense disproportion of Irish Roman Catholic immigration, for the promotion of which, in preference to British protestant immigration so large a portion of the funds of the colony were recklessly expended.'[51]

Broughton endured these criticisms 'from a disinclination to mix up religion in any document of this sort, [the Immigration Report] except when he was absolutely compelled to do so'.[52] So long as he chaired the Immigration Committee his avowed object was to secure the right skills at the lowest cost.[53] In debate the Legislative Council swung behind Broughton's support for the bounty system only to be overruled by the British government. The Colonial Office assumed control over immigration quotas to guard against extravagance; and shipping, to ensure regular arrivals. Even so, Broughton had a partial victory, for the colony retained the right to refuse payment on unsatisfactory immigrants.[54]

None of this summed up Broughton's achievement in 1842. When he first consulted his committee the colony nourished itself on pessimism. Gipps was more eager than the Colonial Office to suspend immigration indefinitely; the Macarthurs saw only the depression, and futility in planning; the majority press, between cursing the upset price of land

and abusing Stanley, proffered the social distortions of convicts and coolies as a panacea for economic ruin; and the Colonial Office anticipated and prohibited every remedy.[55] The moment was not fashionable for the optimist, yet Broughton declared his unshaken confidence in the stability of his adopted country. 'Australia, like Rebecca, has nations in her womb, which, I trust, may be brought in safely . . . to the advantage of the whole world', he bade colonists remember when many thought her stuffed merely with perishing crops and unsold wool.[56] And those at the *Sydney Morning Herald*'s office who had sat through the bishop's admonitions in the peak of the gloom could still, six to nine months later, warm at the recollection of his rhetorical flourishes:

> While 'the sages of the land' around him were yielding to unmanly despair, and chanting their requiems over the ashes of departed and irrecoverable prosperity, the BISHOP alone maintained a serene confidence in the radical soundness of the colony, and, mildly censuring the wails of his lugubrious compeers, ventured to anticipate the return of brighter days.[57]

Selwyn's visit had helped reconcile Broughton and Gipps. The three families dined together regularly, and Lady Gipps turned nurse to Whytehead, a dying New Zealand missionary. Whytehead's was a timely decline; it had placed a sound high churchman of elevated character in government house at a most 'providential' moment, said Broughton. Providential because Whytehead lay in the Gipps's care when Broughton had cause to apply for government legal assistance in setting up an ecclesiastical court. Where previous requests foundered this succeeded. Gipps instructed the Roman Catholic Roger Therry, acting as attorney-general, to supply the bishop with all necessary legal advice. The decision took some nerve: it reversed Bourke's policy of severing all special links between the Church of England and the state just as the old Bourke forces, with Roger Therry well to the fore, rallied to hail the arrival of their former governor in bronze and at a great open air meeting proclaimed immutable his policy of religious equality.[58]

Broughton needed the ecclesiastical court to deal with the Reverend Mr Brigstocke at Yass. Brigstocke wrote anonymously to a newspaper accusing a local magistrate, Cornelius O'Brien, of sabbath breaking by 'hallooing in chorus with his dogs and in company with his assigned servants on a Sunday', and was convicted of libel. Brigstocke refused to defend his action. The whisperers said he had acted from malice, and the judge condemned him so harshly that Broughton felt the verdict left 'a very strong presumption of moral guilt against our brother'. Had Brigstocke broken that other law: Thou shalt not bear false witness? Moreover, there were rumours that Brigstocke was not zealous in his office and prone to bad debts. An ecclesiastical court must decide.[59]

Broughton appointed five clergymen to act as assessors. Therry presented the case against Brigstocke, proper legal counsel defended him, and all legal documents were handled by a commissioner of the Supreme Court. The assessors cleared Brigstocke, but called him a coward for writing anonymously in the first instance. Brigstocke returned to Yass where the public took up a collection to pay his fine; and O'Brien no more hallooed in chorus with his dogs on the sabbath. The due process of law had benefited Brigstocke. Broughton believed Brigstocke guilty of deliberate misrepresentation; and had he heard the charges in a vestry without proper legal advice, in the way Bourke and Plunkett forced him to deal with Yate in 1836, Broughton admitted he would have convicted Brigstocke and withdrawn his licence.[60]

August 1842 opened another era for the colony. The new constitution arrived. Although Broughton dismissed it as something the Tory's 'found in the pigeon holes of the Whigs',[61] the British government had not thrown the churches on the mercy of the Legislative Council. The new Constitution Act provided £30 000 for distribution under the Church Act. The colonial legislature might augment the amount but, to Broughton's relief, only the British government could lessen it. Nevertheless, religion's long-term prospects remained obscure. 'What may be the result of the deliberations respecting the church in the new Legislative Assembly, I can not surmise', commented the Rev. W. B. Clarke; but Broughton certainly thought the £20 elective franchise tantamount to a universal franchise that would 'fill our new House of Legislature with those who would devote us to instant destruction'.[62]

The constitution also opened a new era for Broughton. He had requested a seat on the new Legislative Council, and permission to resign it. 'I do not merit removal from them now in any such way as might imply disrespect, or such as would give a triumph to those who are always on the alert to rejoice in what they deem the *depression* of the Church of England', he said.[63] The Church of England must appear to abandon the government, not the government the Church of England. Stanley played along with this. He offered Broughton a nominated seat on the Legislative Council in recognition of his *personal* services in the outgoing Council, and not because he was bishop. Broughton 'voluntarily' rejected this 'handsome and unsolicited offer'.[64] The press praised his self-sacrifice and political good sense in accepting 'that under the approaching changes, he could not with propriety, have retained his seat'.[65] In the Legislative Council Roger Therry spoke warmly of the bishop's 'high talents'.[66] Never had the bishop appeared so fair as in fading. However, when a civic testimonial, organized by the mayor of Sydney, became entangled with the idea that he had 'vacated his seat in Council, for the love of peace and the good of the people', Broughton scattered the arrangements. Outwardly he pleaded his 'quiet and retiring habits' for not attending; but inwardly Broughton would not hear himself publicly congratulated for bowing to what he believed to be mistaken sentiments about the proper relationships between church and state. Indeed, he bowed out of the Council shaking his fist at those 'who would impute his retirement to his inward conviction of the impolity and impropriety of a Christian bishop being engaged in legislative affairs'. 'He did not yield an iota to the quantity of cant, as it must be termed, which had been uttered upon that subject', he said; and had Lord Stanley offered him a seat in an upper chamber he would still be there.[67] Nevertheless, he was glad to be done with a Council where the low £20 franchise would introduce a popular element from whose 'warmth and impetuosity of debate' Broughton said, 'he must witness and hear many things not suitable to the character he bore'.[68] That tickled Lang: 'It is essentially the vulgarity of a Colonial House of Commons that he objects to'.[69]

Lang more than laughed. He nominated to fill the place Broughton vacated, and that disgusted everyone. 'The Lord Bishop of Australia has twenty time the claim of Dr Lang in point of respectability, weight and talents', commented the *Australian*. But Lang believed Broughton had still to be watched. The bishop had left the Legislative Council but remained on the Executive Council which had the patronage over the £30 000 for religion. Removing the Church of England from public office was a slow business and Lang vowed to enter the new Council to see that it was properly done.[70]

By the time Broughton resigned his place on the Legislative Council electioneering for its twenty-four general seats was under way. Personalities and not policies were the issue. The primary aim of the elections was to return a firm but responsible opposition to the governor and win for the Legislative Council control over land policy and, by reducing the Civil List and police expenditure, control over the colonial treasury. Individuals might pledge themselves to be active in education, or banking, or in safeguarding emancipist rights, but only in the vaguest of terms. 'The intention of most', observed the *Sydney Morning Herald* early in the campaign, 'appears to be, by making general assertions, to pledge themselves to no decided course.' The one attempt to force Sydney candidates into a debate on specific measures for the recovery of the economy failed. When Wentworth saw such a meeting advertised he went along to protest that 'the causes of distress of the country, and the remedies for that distress, could only be enquired into and ascertained by the new Legislative Assembly'. Other candidates who attended, agreed; and so finally did the newspapers. Deep involvement in specific issues could only detract from the pressing need to elect *right* candidates. These would be the decently educated 'sons of the soil' with considerable property and relatively unspotted reputations, such as the Macarthurs, Wentworth, 'gallant' Captain O'Connell and Charles Cowper, a son of the cloth. Or, they could be men with a distinguished record of colonial service like Alexander McLeay or Dr Bland. Therry's literary talents also qualified him in the eyes of colonists, and exceptionally so in his own; 'but we must say he has given us rather too much of Mr Canning's speeches during his canvass', quipped the *Sydney Morning Herald*. It was, however, quite improper to have made a fortune from gin like Cooper; or to have resided less than a decade in the colony like Hustler, the sheriff, or Hosking, the ambitious new mayor of Sydney; or to be immoral. Lang's 'Austral-Scotch bastard education' and trailing history of failures made him unacceptable to New South Wales. His Australian College was heavily in debt, his second newspaper the *Colonial Observer* was rescued from bankruptcy only by a political bribe from Wentworth who wanted its support in the elections, and he himself had been cast out of the fraternity of Presbyterian ministers. Criticisms from such men in a council would more likely excite contempt than co-operation at the Colonial Office. So, as the elections proceeded, citizen committees and the newspapers united to thrust to the fore the good candidates, scorn the bad, and reduce the elections to a competition between acceptable equals.[71]

Whether religion would embitter the elections would depend on the handling of two issues. Many colonists demanded representatives 'independent alike of favour or of frowns' and opposed the candidature of government officials as likely to weaken the objective of raising a strong opposition to the governor. Would an officer of the police force, or the courts, rigorously oppose a governor upon whom he relied for promotion? Unfortunately Roger Therry, who fell under this ban, was the one Roman Catholic candidate likely to be elected. It became a delicate thing to oppose Therry without appearing to be either anti-Irish or anti-Catholic.[72]

Religious friction could also arise from the handling of that 'foul blot', the £81 000 Civil List with its £30 000 for public worship.[73] Any reduction of the total meant a corresponding reduction of the religious provision; and the Roman Catholic press argued that a Legislative Council dominated by members of the Church of England could reason that since it was too expensive to aid all churches and useless to divide a reduced sum between them all, the colony should return to the support of the most populous church. In short, an attack on the Civil List could open the way for an attack on the principle of equality in the Church Act. 'Another struggle is contemplated in behalf of ecclesiastical demo-cracy', warned the *Australasian Chronicle*.[74] Every candidate was obliged to declare his position on the Church Act. Wentworth pledged support. Lang promised no opposition for five years.[75] Indeed, observed the *Sydney Morning Herald*, 'We have within the last two months heard an avowed adulterer, a man whom we are confident has not entered a place of worship for years, have the impudence to avow himself a *friend* of religious liberty!!'.[76] The Church Act was to be maintained 'whole and entire' for the moment.[77] Broughton topped that with a declaration that 'if there were weakness or danger attending the cause of the Church they must be met and removed by the members of the Church acquiring a truer acquaintance with its principles, and by manifesting their earnest adherence to them, rather than by any support which could be afforded by him holding a seat in the Legislative Council'.[78] That appeared to put religion out of the elections.

Unfortunately religion made a third, and unsuspecting entrance. Broughton wanted a reliable spokesman for the Church of England in the new Council. Liberal and radical churchmen would be well re-presented but Broughton did not trust them to speak for his position. He wanted Charles Cowper the former secretary of the Church and Schools Corporation.[79] The Roman Catholics also desired a responsible spokesman. 'There are 40,000 Roman Catholics in this colony', said Therry in opening his campaign, 'and ... if I fail in this election there will not be a single member of that religious body returned as a representative.'[80] Unfortunately Cowper and Therry both nominated for the seat of Camden.

Because the Irish vote in the Illawarra district of Camden electorate was thought to give Therry the edge in the contest the *Australian* supported Cowper as part of its campaign to keep government officers out of the new Council. James Macarthur upset this. In December 1842 after he had decided Camden was unsafely Irish for himself, Macarthur first enquired of Cowper's intentions and, finding him undecided on whether to stand himself, urged Cowper to support Therry and 'show the Roman Catholics that moderate protestants had no desire to exclude them from the representation'. When Therry nominated, Macarthur exchanged him his support in Camden for Therry's support in Cumberland. Cowper immediately opposed Therry and put Macarthur in the embarrassing position of supporting a Roman Catholic candidate against a fellow member of the Diocesan Committee. Who persuaded Cowper to change his mind? Since Cowper nominated after Macarthur announced his 'Camden for the Catholics' campaign it appeared he had nominated in order to trounce it.[81]

Some suspicion fell on Broughton. The bishop certainly had an eye for the religious implication of every political move. At the precise moment Cowper entered the contest Broughton tried to break up a committee of Protestants and papists formed to support 'gallant' Captain O' Connell as a candidate for Sydney. Broughton had no quibble with O'Connell, a staunch churchman; but he took exception to members of his Diocesan Committee like McLeay, Richard Jones and Robert Campbell, joining with Roman Catholics like Therry and Duncan to promote a common candidate. Duncan's '*sole* occupation for years', Broughton said, 'had been to revile the Church of England and abuse me in every possible way'; whereas Therry's great political ambition was to establish 'the Irish-system Education scheme'. The sight of his closest lay associates linked up with the opponent of all he stood for in education filled him with foreboding as to what other deals might be done. 'Besides which it is disrespectful to me', Broughton said, and gave his Diocesan Committee the choice of consulting with him, or consulting with Therry and Duncan.[82] Most stayed with Therry; all remained on the Diocesan Committee; and there were no further deals.[83] But the incident annoyed Therry and led him to suspect that the bishop stood behind Cowper's candidacy. Someone also slipped Therry a copy of Broughton's letter to his Diocesan Committee accusing Therry of being an unacceptable associate for Diocesan Committee members by reason of his being the 'foremost advocate' for the national schools. 'No doubt the Right Reverend Prelate meant this as a ground of objection rather than of merit and praise', Therry told a public meeting, 'but a higher compliment he did not covet'. And that April, at Berrima, Therry donned the mantle of Sir Richard Bourke and made the Camden election an issue of civil and religious liberty. He proclaimed himself guardian of Sir Richard's religious peace and champion of Sir Richard's education vision. He condemned Cowper as a bigot with a ready hand and a willing heart to re-enact the civil disabilities of Catholics.[84] He challenged Protestants to repudiate Cowper as a pledge of their commitment to religious liberty.[85]

Cowper dismissed religious liberty as a red herring. 'The House would have very little to do with religion', he maintained. 'Sir R Bourke's Church Act is passed, and £30,000 is secured for the support of religion.'[86] Nevertheless Cowper believed Macarthur had miscalculated the Irish vote and that he could win if all Protestants voted for him. So he urged a Protestant loyalty on voting day.[87] In reply the Catholic press sought to split the Protestant vote by asking whether Cowper was a desirable Protestant. 'Mr Cowper stands on the well known high church principle of ascendancy', charged the *Australasian Chronicle*. And so by some colonial magic the poll in Camden became a battleground between the forces of religious ascendancy and religious liberty.[88]

Therry won. 'Well done, honest men of Camden', said the Roman Catholic press. 'You will never have cause to regret the manly stand you have taken.' James Macarthur did. When Cowper lost Camden he turned up to challenge Macarthur in Cumberland. The clergy came with him. Eight 'black coats' stood at the hustings and two removed their hats as Cowper spoke. The parish clerk from Parramatta distributed handbills saying 'Take care of Popery', or, 'Do not vote for Macarthur'. Then up went a poster hailing Macarthur 'Patron of White Feathers' and people called him the Prince of Renegades. Macarthur stormed the local printery and discovered that the Reverend W. B. Clarke from Dural had placed the order for the handbills. He demanded the original and recognized the writing of the secretary of the Diocesan Committee. So the bishop's office was involved! commented the *Australian*.[89]

Next Charles Campbell, Broughton's close friend, resigned from Macarthur's committee accusing him of being Protestant north of the Nepean River and Roman Catholic south of it. That began such a run that the *Australian* tried to frighten support back to Macarthur with a reminder that a split Church of England vote would put Brennan the Roman Catholic candidate in. 'Do you suppose that the enemies of the Church of England do not laugh at your most silly squabbles, at your short-sighted piques?' They did not laugh. Cowper won, William Lawson came second and Macarthur third.[90]

'Talk of Jesuits', exclaimed Macarthur. He blamed a black band of political parsons for his defeat. He indicted eight, and one only denied the charge. The clergy had canvassed with 'marvellous enthusiasm' for Cowper; and in some pulpits Macarthur had been all but denounced by name for his 'Camden for the Catholics' policy. Nevertheless, at a public dinner to crown him 'martyr' to the cause of civil and religious liberty Macarthur good-humouredly toasted the clergy of the colony, and he stayed on Broughton's Diocesan Committee.[91]

Religion died quickly as an issue once Wentworth had declared for Cowper. 'It is absurd, therefore, to keep up the cry of civil and religious liberty, unless for some sinister purpose', commented the *Sydney Morning Herald*.[92] Macarthur was simply the victim of a political deal which misfired. His cry 'Camden for the Catholics' was but the response in a

litany which began 'Cumberland for Marcarthur'. As a religious liberal
Macarthur's pedigree was suspect. Duncan had pointed that out early
in the campaign, and for denouncing Therry's deal with Macarthur
was sacked as editor of the *Australasian Chronicle*.[93] The collective
wisdom of the Catholic board of management was on the side of political
expediency, not truth. The editorial board of the *Australian* was no
better. It supported Cowper in Camden to prevent the election of a
government officer, it opposed Cowper in Cumberland as 'the avowed
enemy of Sir Richard Bourke's Church Act pledged to overturn it if
he can'; and then announced him victorious as 'a gentleman of respectability'.[94] All that in two weeks! Most colonists seemed to have tumbled
into arguments about religion to fill a vacuum in an election fixed on
personalities not policies. Had candidates fearlessly discussed the issue
of land, immigration and transportation, coolie labour, prices and civic
corporations, which were to occupy the new Legislative Council and
divide the colony, the Church Act may never have been mentioned.
What Roman Catholics sought in the election of Therry was not the
preservation of the Church Act but an assurance that their religion
was no longer a social or political impediment. Broughton and the clergy
of the Church of England did not expect Cowper to overturn the Church
Act, but to represent the Diocesan Committee faithfully in those matters
where religion still touched politics, especially in education.[95] Had
Therry and Cowper contested different seats the elections might have
been exceedingly dull. Broughton's retirement from the Legislative
Council and his determination to push Cowper's candidacy had gingered
them.

Abroad Polding had also gingered events. After months of secret
plotting at the Vatican he crossed the Channel to England and recruited
twenty priests. Then, brazen as ever, he donned 'full state robes canonical
of the Catholic Church' and called on the Secretary of State for Colonies
to announce his appointment as Archbishop of Sydney. Polding dressed
up again! Lord Stanley receiving him 'most graciously'! If Polding
returned to New South Wales as Archbishop of Sydney without letters
patent, as rumour had he would, the Pope would have done in a stroke
what Queen, Lords and Commons could not do without repealing all
the Acts of the Reformation. 'Tell Lord Stanley', said the bishop, '. . . that
the Church of England cannot trust *him* as the guardian of her interests.'[96]
But Lord Stanley had acquitted his obligation to the colonial Church
of England by offering Broughton a seat in the new Legislative Council.
The rest was politics. Stanley had no doubt that Polding's elevation
was part of a new wave of papal propaganda, but he was helpless in
opposing it. Sir Robert Peel had a chest of documents tabulating the
Catholic Bishop of London's schemes to return the Whigs to power
in exchange for concessions to the Catholic hierarchy. If the Tories
could snatch back the initiative by a grant to Maynooth, or a glass of
port in the afternoon with Polding however he was dressed, that was
politics.[97]

Broughton understood none of this, and it would not have moved
him if he had. To him the overriding consideration was that his diocese

had been singled out by the Pope to test British reaction to the possible reintroduction of a papal hierarchy into the British Empire. Sydney was the first town assigned by the Pope to a Catholic bishop since the Reformation. If the queen did not feel her jurisdiction impaired Broughton considered the Archbishop of Canterbury's was; and who would speak up for the archbishop, if he did not? But what was he to say? Declare the whole proceeding unconstitutional? Repeat again that unless crown and mitre stood together both would go 'down, down, down, down continually towards a fatal gulf'? Threaten again that concessions made in the colony would be ultimately demanded in England? Why, the British cabinet already appealed openly to concessions made in the colonies as justification for changes in Ireland. All the old arguments were limp. The age of Queen Victoria was rewriting the English constitution, sometimes by altering a law but most often by forgetting one. Broughton recognized the mood; 'So little reliance have I on temporal aids, or those who administer them, that it is not my intention to appeal to them'.[98]

The Oxford Tracts had convinced Broughton of a higher ground of appeal than the Acts of the Reformation settlement. From ancient Christian times there had never been more than *one* bishop in *one* place. So Polding's *late* claim to Sydney was, by the canons of the ancient church, either schismatical or a denial of Broughton's apostolical character. Broughton could not be a silent party to a schism and would not quietly suffer a denigration of his apostolical character. But alone, and separated from competent advisers, could he claim to act on behalf of the Church of England? What if the Archbishop of Canterbury disowned his actions? Broughton had misgivings. He asked Coleridge to get him advice; and yet he knew that before his letter rounded the Cape he must act.[99]

Broughton found the courage to act on his own initiative in a parcel from Coleridge containing the first volumes of a new *Anglo-Catholic Library* and the Parker Society reprints of English theologians. The publication of both series stemmed from an interest the Oxford Tracts had created in the catholic foundations of the Church of England. Lancelot Andrewes's treatises launched one series Nicholas Ridley's tracts the other. Both Pembroke men! Both had been called in their day to take a lead in the opposition to Rome and other errors; and the Church of England had recalled them to do their work again. Was not he, Broughton, a Pembroke man? Whatever the cost he must stand up to Polding's invasion and carry forward the crusade that had so distinguished his College.[1] But, he said, 'I shall take the matter up upon *church* principles only'.[2]

Then, the moment Broughton resolved to act the papists turned friendly, and confused him. After calling him 'Bishop Broughton' for five years in a way that implied he was not Bishop of Australia, he found himself addressed as 'the Bishop of Australia' and even 'the *Lord* Bishop'! 'This would not merit attention were it not that they do *nothing* without a motive', Broughton reflected. What did it mean? Perhaps they hoped that by giving Broughton the title he liked he would return Polding the new one he had acquired? On the other hand, Broughton wondered whether Polding might bring a real offer: on the historic occasion of a reintroduction of the papal hierarchy into British dominions Polding may return with instructions 'implying on the part of Rome a disposition (if that be possible) to recognise an episcopal character in our Church'. On the eve of Polding's return Broughton seemed to have resolved that he would accept the spirit of Rome's eirenical gestures and live in peace with Polding provided, in proclaiming his new office, Polding did not deny the apostolic authority of the Church of England.[3]

Polding returned on 9 March 1843. The cannon roared, Catholics crowded the wharf, and a procession went up to St Mary's tramping to the tune of 'See the Conquering Hero Come'. 'Our feelings as pro-testants are outraged', commented the *Colonial Observer* demanding an end to outdoor religious processions.[4] But the event Broughton dreaded took place inside the cathedral. Polding proclaimed himself Augustine of the south, sent by Pope Gregory XVI to erect a truly apostolical order in the new colony just as the original and Great Gregory had sent Augustine to England.[5] That was enough. Broughton had his clergy in the vestry of St James by 16 March. Some advised action, some restraint. Broughton hesitated for a week then recalled them to St James church on Saturday 25 March at 10.30 a.m. sharp.[6] 'It is not without a full sense of the risk of great annoyance, and the possibility even of destruction to myself that I have taken this step', he explained.[7] The party processed into the church where, in the middle of Divine Service and surrounded by six clergy, Broughton read 'a solemn and imperishable' edict. Since Rome and Canterbury both acknowledged the ancient canon that 'there can neither be two Metropolitans of one Province, nor two bishops in the same Diocese' the Pope's decision to send a bishop into Sydney, Broughton said, could only be construed as 'an act of direct and purposed hostility towards us ... to proclaim their persuasion that we have no canonical bishop, no Catholic Church, no such administration of the Holy Sacraments among us, as shall be effectual to everlasting salvation'. To preserve a belief in his own apostolic character Broughton protested that the Pope had given Polding title over Sydney 'contrary to the laws of God, and the Canonical order of the Church'. In short, the Pope had perpetrated a formal schism within the colony. Against that Broughton and his successors would for ever protest.[8]

The protest re-echoed from every parish pulpit. It showed, as his opponents admitted, that Broughton had moved away from his old styled church-state constitutional arguments.[9] He took his stand by apostolic authority, and it backfired. He had attacked Polding only to claim for himself 'an exclusive and divine right to be regarded as the cock of the ecclesiastical roost', charged the *Colonial Observer*.[10] But the Roman Catholic press retained an eirenical pose. It very pleasantly affirmed Broughton was no apostolic bishop, and asked the Church of England to carry on as if it were the only church in the colony leaving Roman Catholics to do the same.[11] But Duncan the ex-editor of the *Australasian Chronicle* thought that insipid. With time on his hand while Polding considered his appeal to be reinstated as editor of the Catholic newspaper, he published a telling criticism of Broughton's argument. Invoking those very canons of primitive Christianity to which the bishop fondly appealed, he showed that the jurisdiction of the Archbishop of Canterbury had never extended to New Holland and Broughton's appointment was irregular. Allwood fought back lecturing the public every Wednesday night through May and June. Broughton himself composed a spirited pamphlet vindicating the consecration of Matthew Parker, an Elizabethan prelate upon whose proper consecration the catholicity of the Church of England periodically rested. And to wrap it up young Sconce, that apple of Broughton's eye, published a compendium of arguments against desertion from the Church of England.[12]

Broughton's protest generated little steam. 'It is painful, my Lord, to witness with what degree of indifference, not to say levity, this solemn Protest of your Lordship appears to have been received', mocked Duncan.[13] Politically it was stillborn. Gipps flatly refused Broughton's extraordinary request to have it all printed in the *Government Gazette*.[14] Stanley refused to decide whether Broughton should continue to administer the Oath of Supremacy in the colony. Broughton thought he ought not. Why should the clergy deny all foreign prelates ecclesiastical and spiritual jurisdiction in the realm when the civil powers admitted them freely?[15] The Archbishop of Canterbury approved the protest, but very privately. He had just confused the issue by intruding a bishop into Jerusalem well outside his province.[16] A lot of Oxford dons wrote supporting him, but no one got a debate up in Oxford. The SPG gave it wide publicity yet no one raised a question in parliament. 'The case will be otherwise when the *same* pretension is set up (*as it will be in due time*) in the Diocese of Canterbury and London', Broughton said.[17] Nevertheless, some good had come of it all in the colony. Churchmen had been made aware of the situation and talked of the issues involved.[18] The real thunder at the end of March 1843 came not from the altar of St James but the boardroom of the Bank of Australia. The bank crashed and set off a run on savings accounts. 'Little else is talked about in Sydney at this moment', said the *Australian*; and the din helped drown Broughton's protest.[19]

The crash of the Bank of Australia affected Broughton in other ways. It was the colony's oldest bank with a pure merino clientele, the class backing many of his building projects. The drought of 1838–9 and the soaring prices due to the labour shortage of 1840–1 had already slowed down progress.[20] The monetary crisis now threatened to end it. 'Persons of the most extensive *property* cannot raise *money* even to a small amount', he said, 'and the consequence is that all or nearly all the Churches and parsonage-houses which were in the course of erection have been suspended from want of funds.'[21] The clergy had literally begged from door to door and still sixteen churches were incomplete.[22] Local trustees faced personal liability, and one fisherman at Wiseman's Crossing had his fishing boat seized to pay church building debts.[23] Clergy faced the loss of government stipends for failing to meet building obligations under the Church Act, and partly constructed buildings were exposed to the

deteriorating effect of the weather.²⁴ The Church of England seemed
to halt while Polding marched on with fresh supplies of clergy and
inexhaustible funds.

To Broughton it was inconceivable that Divine Providence intended
the lead given to the Church of England should now wither before
forces hostile to the Reformation. There must be money somewhere.
It was not in the colony: the SPG must have it. So Broughton decided
to inspect his diocese, assess its needs, and charge them to the SPG.
The Society could expect a bill for £1000 to £1500, he wrote admitting
the procedure was unorthodox. 'But my conviction of the necessity of
making good our position here, in opposition to that very formidable
confederacy by which we are assailed is *so decided*', he said, 'that I shall
not dread the disapproval of the Society.'²⁵

On 13 June 1843 Broughton, at fifty-six years of age, set out on horseback for a non-stop eight week visitation of the Hunter River and Bathurst
districts. He rode up to forty-seven miles a day through dry-creek
country, then heavy rain, and finally the snow, visiting twenty centres
and scores of homesteads. He sometimes rode alone and was apt to lose
his way, sometimes with the clergy, and occasionally (like old Heber)
with an armed escort through bush-ranger territory. He inspected
churches, parsonages and schools, and sites for future development.
He met local committees, discussed their debts, arranged small loans,
set out the conditions for a full-time schoolmaster and reflected on the
prospect of more clergy. He preached from pulpits, verandahs, doorways,
in stores and inns, and impromptu in the open to groups of shepherds.
At night he rested in homesteads. Some were so crude that he expected
to be drenched by rain in bed. Most were the comfortable residences
of the old guard, the Busbys, Coxes, Closes, Bowmans, and even Sir
John Jamison and Lady Forbes welcomed him; but all held tightly to
their purses. 'I am expecting a visit from the Bishop', Edward Hamilton
wrote ahead to James Macarthur. 'I hope he will not ask for contributions—I will give him a few sheep to boil down but nothing else.'²⁶

Broughton took time off to go over to Bryn Allyn and inspect the
progress young William Boydell had made on a church and cottage.
Miss Phoebe Broughton had been chosen to occupy the cottage and
chaffed at its slow progress. She reminded Mr Boydell that while her
sister received the constant attention of her suitor, the Reverend George
Vidal, she simply sat and waited. So the bishop did the fatherly thing
and called in to urge young Boydell along.²⁷

Despite pockets of infidelity Broughton was cheered by the numbers
of young people who turned out for baptism and confirmation. 'The
sight of these young people is most gratifying', he noted in his diary, 'as
it affords our best hope that there is a generation rising up, carefully
trained in an acquaintance with the truth of Christianity.' But the state
of the building programme distressed him more than he had anticipated.
Then in mid-journey at Singleton a letter reached him from the SPG
cautioning against extra expenditure. The SPG had not had a good
annual appeal. That dashed the prime purpose of his visitation. So at
Singleton he promised the congregation nothing. Instead, he called

for gifts of cattle, sheep and grain to help meet debts. Further on through
Fal Brook, Muswell Brook and Scone he viewed a melancholy trail of
incomplete buildings promising nothing but a review of the situation
in 1844. Even the finished sections distressed him, so little did they
resemble a traditional church.[28]

Broughton also closed down the Wellington Valley Aboriginal mission.
It succumbed to the want of local financial support. After Bourke removed it from the bishop's control Broughton refused it diocesan subsidies, and being beyond the bishop's jurisdiction it was also wracked by
feuds: 'The disagreement of the missionaries having become notorious,
many persons who had been favourably disposed towards the missions,
have given their support to other institutions'.[29] Bourke's arrangements
proved as bad as Broughton had warned. When the remaining missionary,
the Reverend John Gunther resigned and Broughton offered him a
chaplaincy, Gipps cut off aid. Polding inherited the challenge and immediately set up a Moreton Bay mission. 'Whenever we are compelled
to abandon a position, I see others prepared to fill it', Broughton remarked
ruefully;[30] but his defeat dated back to his sterile report as chairman
of the Committee on the Aborigines Question in 1838.[31] There had
been money then but no ideas. Docker the once drunken cleric, however,
had made consistent use of them in industry, and Broughton grasped
at a hope that, justly treated, Aboriginals would become useful shepherds.
But he warned: 'These people have sufficient sagacity to perceive the
footing upon which they are treated . . . and . . . can be made to acquire
the steady habits of Europeans, only by being gradually put upon the
same footing with them'.[32] The black shepherd was, nevertheless, to
remain among the lost sheep.

Back in Sydney the picture was brighter. The proposed cathedral
was beginning to show character and stood fair to be the 'noblest ornament
of the city'. Christ Church St Lawrence had raised £1200 and neared
completion. The temporary church of St Andrew, built to hold 250, was
filled twice a Sunday, and £1000 had been raised from private subscriptions and government subsidies to double its seating capacity. All seats
were free. Broughton was so encouraged by the attendance of these
poorer people that he contemplated shifting his episcopal throne into
the temporary church to be among them. Local parochial associations
had sprung up to concentrate on local needs and did well. St James
raised the entire stipend of a second minister. Yet, if local needs did well
diocesan needs suffered. After reviewing the findings of his visitation
and exhausting the coffers of the Diocesan Committee Broughton
decided he must draw on the SPG for aid to five projects despite its
warning. He spent £320, not the contemplated £1500. For the rest he
would look to the future.[33]

After a brief rest he was off again on a visit to Port Phillip. He spent
the shipboard journey arguing with the captain's wife who had 'turned
Presbyterian out of compliment to her husband'. The captain's wife
attacked Pusey, and Broughton defended him.[34] At Port Phillip Broughton
found a township thriving commercially but listless in religion, and
this disappointed him as reports led him to expect the opposite. The

only church, St James, had finally got a roof, some bare walls and a £900 debt. The fruit of six year's effort! Broughton blamed this partly on the government's withdrawal of a £500 subsidy and partly on the chaplains. Grylls, the original chaplain, stammered his way through every service inside the church and displayed bad temper outside it. Thompson, who followed him, was in debt, and to forestall court action Broughton put up a personal £500 bond during his visit. Had he allowed the court action to proceed, Broughton said, Thompson would have been convicted, suspended, and Port Phillip left without a single clergyman. At Portland Bay another chaplain, Wilson, was also 'scandalously' in debt. Amid this the bishop stayed two months. He walked door to door to collect money and raised £400. He sat for a portrait to be sold to raise more. He dashed into the interior where he met much goodwill and empty pockets. He departed once more pinning his hopes on the young who again came with 'attentive and becoming deportment' to be baptized and confirmed. Short of buildings, short of clergy, short of money, Broughton returned to Sydney determined to focus the attention of the SPG on the settlement and to persuade the Society to make it an area of special endeavour. It was too primitive yet for a bishop.[35]

In the districts beyond the boundaries Broughton reported unexpected progress. The SPG had already supplied them funds, and three unforeseen recruits arrived. The Reverend John Gregor 'one of the best qualified among the Scots ministers in literary and scientific acquirements' swapped his Presbyterian calling for an Anglican one, and to escape Lang's withering tongue Broughton sent him to Moreton Bay. The Reverend James Allan did the same and Broughton gave him asylum at Braidwood. The Reverend John McConnell just turned up. He had always been a churchman. He had originally left London for Nova Scotia and found it too cold, changed to Jamaica and found it too warm. Sydney was just right. He impressed Broughton and found himself pioneering on the River Clarence.[36]

As 1843 gave way to 1844 Broughton hoped by a judicious management of his lean resources to preserve the accomplishments of the past. Progress must wait: 'Looking to the future I am, although at times depressed, yet not in despair.'[37] His tours revealed too much goodwill for despair.[38] But he could not expect the church to receive automatically its due share of wealth as prosperity returned to the colony. The building campaign would need to be deliberately revived. It was that which depressed him. The clergy suggested he go again to England and stir up enthusiasm there as a spring-board for another colonial effort. Broughton refused. The SPG would give to its maximum, he said 'and having that, we must rely on God's support and our own effort'.[39] Colonists must build their own future. Yet at fifty-five he lacked the stamina to roam a diocese the size of England doing again what he had done in 1836–9. 'I have carried things perhaps to the point which my qualifications were best suited for', he confided to Coleridge, 'and there *may* be a fresh impulse necessary which a successor would communicate with more effect.'[40]

A retirement had other attractions. A change to a cooler climate would benefit Mrs Broughton's health. She had never thrived in the warmth of New South Wales, and the summer of 1842 had exhausted her. For the past two years she had struggled on, never seriously ill but rarely well. She could not accompany the bishop on visitations and his extended absences left both feeling anxious. Miss Emily Broughton had also a reason to leave. Her fiance, the Reverend George Vidal, lost his life's savings when the Bank of Australia crashed and was to return to England. Miss Emily wanted to follow. Broughton felt deeply for her. Miss Phoebe Broughton, however, complicated matters. She planned to marry William Boydell in April 1844 and stay in the colony. A final separation from either of his children to whose company, together with his wife's, he looked for relaxation, was too painful a thought. Equally painful was the thought of Phoebe living up bush in a tiny cottage remote from civilization, church and pastor, and on a farm for which he saw little future. He thought of persuading his prospective son-in-law to return with them, should he retire, and take a position in London, keeping the colonial farm as an investment. The bishop wanted his family around him.[41] For himself, personally, Broughton would regret leaving Sydney. He found the place honest, the people frank and unencumbered, and the bush a tonic. Where else did birds sing the whole year round, trees blossom in mid-winter, and the day bow out in sunsets 'of such gorgeous splendour'? 'Were I only five and twenty', he said, 'I should like exceedingly to sit myself down in "the bush" with an agreeable partner for life.'[42]

Who would replace Broughton? Coleridge? Selwyn had the news that Coleridge might go to Adelaide. Broughton scotched that: 'There is no opening there worthy of you'. Coleridge could have Sydney for the asking. If necessary Broughton would go to England to clinch the arrangement. He would even return to work under him. 'Here you would have a hard battle to fight, but upon a stage where you may prove your qualities to the full', he wrote. 'Indeed I know no grander destiny.' Broughton put the suggestion to the Archbishop of Canterbury. In 1843 and 1844 it seemed proper to Broughton to retire.[43]

II

Eminence grise

> We have been shown by the experiences of the last session,
> that there exists within this Colony a power at the disposal
> of a single man far greater than is consistent with the efficient
> working of the representative system.
>
> *Atlas* attacking Broughton 17 May 1845

Broughton had a year to wait for an answer. Meanwhile the colony's
education deteriorated. A Diocesan Committee appeal for school funds
in 1843 was piously approved and postponed. The *Australian* invited
letters on the state of colonial education and got one in two months.
Lang failed to make education an issue before the elections of 1843 and
the Legislative Council refused a debate fearing it would reopen the
question of town corporations and the levying of local rates for education.[1] Meanwhile, Gipps spent his affection for education inventing
ways of redistributing the subsidy he was determined not to increase.
He met Broughton's appeal for extra funds at the peak of the immigration
influx by halving the subsidy allowed on poor Protestant pupils. 'It is
not without difficulty that I am able to prevail on them [teachers] to
carry on the schools', Broughton reported.[2] Then in a search for economies Broughton demanded back classrooms in the old Church and
Schools Corporation building in Castlereagh Street loaned earlier to
Roman Catholics. 'The claim of the Church of England has been postponed for several years from mere unwillingness to urge it although
considerable extra expenses have been incurred in hiring school rooms',
Broughton explained. Gipps considered the claim just, but thought it
impolitic to evict the Roman Catholics and asked for time. As a concession Gipps restored the full subsidy on poor Protestant pupils but
withdrew a subsidy on school books.[3] Broughton then appealed directly
to the Legislative Council for funds to educate immigrant children
cast into the outer districts. How much better is a man than a sheep?
he asked. But the Council could not decide, and the *Sydney Morning
Herald* thought 1844 early enough to debate an issue unlikely to admit
of a solution.[4]

By 1844 the issue demanded an unexpected solution. Lang had contrived his election to the Legislative Council on promises of 'education
and separation' for Port Phillip and was pressing the Council to grant

170

extraordinary funds for southern schools. The few schools Port Phillip had were all denominational, and to forestall the growth in a new district of the denominational system he wanted uprooted elsewhere Gipps needed a mandate for steering the special grant away from the churches. Closer home, too, at Parramatta a district council was formed and had voted to set up its own school system. Should future councils follow suit the colony could sport an absurd medley of school systems.[5] Gipps, therefore, decided on a general enquiry to test what changes the public would stand. He chose Robert Lowe as chairman, passing over Edward Hamilton formerly a Cambridge Fellow and highly respected by all parties within the Legislative Council. Lowe being an outsider of unknown prejudices appeared to give the enquiry an impartiality; but secretly Lowe had pledged Gipps his support.[6]

Broughton would trust no committee of the Legislative Council. 'I do not think there are two men in it earnest for the Church', he quibbled and thought of withholding his co-operation.[7] However, on 15 July 1844 he turned up to tell Lowe that by English standards colonial education had progressed fairly, given the government's parsimony and a parental disposition to consider a colonial education complete at ten. He admitted much remained to be done, but was not convinced any education was better than none. There were triple offenders at Norfolk Island with a good average education. Had *mere* knowledge saved them? Moreover, Broughton believed there would be little wasteful duplication in a denominational system if all schools were requested to have a minimum enrolment of twenty. Parents had co-operated more than critics allowed. Most Presbyterians and many Roman Catholics had no objection to the first part of the Church Catechism, which was the limit reached in a primary education; and Broughton pledged to tolerate the eccentric whims of parents who withdrew their children from religious activities including prayers. It was better, he said, for denominational schools to concede to individual whims than to abandon the denominational principle.[8]

That said, Broughton left the enquiry with a distinct impression of having sat out a 'judicial visitation' determined to convict the Church of England of a failure to educate colonial youth. Deas Thomson, the Colonial Secretary and a member of the committee had arrived with statistics so hastily assembled for a destructive end that he inadvertently classed as uneducated all infants from one to three years. Lowe betrayed his prior commitment to the Irish system; Lang, a hostility to things English; and Therry, a disposition for 'promoting charitable feelings as neighbours' among children by separating them from the clergy for as much of the week as possible.[9] Finally Lowe reported soundly in support of the Irish system and scandalized Windeyer, a fellow lawyer and committee member, who alleged that Lowe had presented his report for adoption before half the committee had arrived. Moreover, since only five of the twenty-one witnesses favoured national schools uniformly tied to the Irish system, Windeyer accused Lowe of reporting in violation of the evidence and contrary to instructions 'to find out what the different denominations would be content with'.[10] That heartened Broughton. He considered Windeyer a wrong-headed radical churchman who would never support him out of sentiment.[11] If Windeyer opposed Lowe's report others, surely, would listen.

Broughton launched a campaign against Lowe's report on 2 September 1844. He spoke for two hours in St James classroom while, further down the street at the City Theatre, McEncroe and 'a mob of illiterate persons, principally Irish' collapsed a meeting of the friends of the Irish system. 'I have no wish to mulch myself and you of advantages attending on the support of government', Broughton told his audience, '. . . (but) practice had rendered it [Irish system] one great denominational system'. Presbyterians controlled northern Irish education, Catholics the southern, and neither respected the rights of minorities. For proof Broughton took a letter from his pocket and read an appeal in April that year from an Irish school inspector calling for an investigation into such discrepancies. After that it remained for Broughton to circulate petitions.[12]

Friday 4 October 1844 was 'an anxious day with us all', Broughton recalled. The Legislative Council debated Lowe's report. By then Bland, Wentworth and Windeyer all admitted some force in Broughton's arguments and were prepared to keep and even expand denominational schools provided the churches agreed to apply to a central board for their subsidies. When, however, 25 000 Catholics, Jews and Protestants petitioned against the Irish system and only 5000 for it, Bland and Windeyer bowed to the popular will. 'No influence could have got up such petitions unless the feelings of the people had gone with them' Windeyer admitted and with Bland's support proposed a compromise dual system. Where local inhabitants sent fifty pupils (not the twenty Broughton suggested) to a denominational school the government should respect their choice and grant aid. Elsewhere it should plant national schools. Since few districts outside the larger towns could enrol fifty pupils the national schools would quickly dominate the countryside, Windeyer argued; and he predicted the towns would follow. Wentworth would have none of that. 'We are the people', he told his fellow councillors, and pushing the petitions aside insisted on the concept of a central education board administering the whole government vote for education. Wentworth gave Broughton a personal guarantee that a schools board would subsidize efficiently-run Church of England schools without interfering in their instruction; but Broughton knew Wentworth could give no such guarantee. Wentworth then proposed amending legislation to guarantee freedom of denominational instruction and grants *in perpetuity* to church schools whose property was handed over to local trustees of which the bishop could remain one *ex officio*. Broughton sniffed at that too. Behind Wentworth's determination to lure all church schools into one system with promises of independence Broughton saw the motive of the old heathen tyrant who wished 'that the Church had only one neck that he might despatch it in one blow'.[13]

Had the Legislative Council voted on 4 October Windeyer's dual system would probably have won on the Speaker's casting vote. But after Lang spoke into the night for three hours Cowper sought an adjournment to put Broughton's case to fresh minds. Over the intervening week-end Wentworth wooed Bland to his side; and the Council, with nine members absent, adopted Lowe's report by one vote.[14]

Broughton had expected defeat. But his opponent's slender victory encouraged him to renew the offensive. 'The people were unanimous; the clergy were unanimous; but the Council was divided', he told yet another public meeting; and the laity vowed never to hand over Church of England schools to local trustees. Without such buildings the national system must everywhere begin from scratch and that was not possible so long as the Legislative Council rejected legislation erecting district councils with authority to levy local rates. So in December 1844 the Legislative Council went volte-face and by fourteen to eleven voted to sustain the denominational schools it had decided by thirteen to twelve to extinguish in October. National schools had to await a solution to the Council's differences over district councils and local rates.[15]

This contest left a mark on Broughton. 'Who is sufficient for these things?', he wrote to Coleridge in the midst of it all. He had slipped out of the Legislative Council to avoid the cut and thrust of popular debate only to be thrown into the public arena with its 'constant imputations of bigotry, obstinancy, and the rest'. This fight was the more irksome because his policy led the church schools into a voluntary decline. Broughton saw his choice as either to relinquish a grip on education or to compromise the truth. The latter was 'treason to a holy cause', so he risked the schools, conscious that even a partial acquiescence in the plans of his opponents would be rewarded by some share of their favour and protection. 'Who can support it without misgiving?', he asked.[16]

While education stirred the colony, a debate on the crown lands convulsed it. Broughton's involvement in the first was natural and in the second compulsive. 'From my first arrival here in 1829', he said, 'there has been no one subject, excepting such as directly and properly appertain to my office, on which I have bestowed so much care and attention as upon the mode of disposing of the vacant Crown Lands'. In 1844 Gipps steeply increased squatting fees and gave notice that after five years occupancy squatters must begin the purchase of their runs or move on. Many squatters, however, were depression-hit landowners who had turned squatter to redeem their property debts. Without sufficient money to purchase their runs they faced a second trimming of their fortunes and formed a Pastoral Association to defeat the regulations. When twenty-two members of the Legislative Council joined the Association a political storm broke over the colony and Broughton soon found himself 'siding with Sir George Gipps in opposition to the general feeling of colonists'.[17]

Broughton sided with Gipps because the regulations were his before they were Gipps's.[18] Every idea in them had appeared in the immigration reports of 1840 and 1842. Despite its religious and educational disadvantages Broughton saw in squatting the one means of turning the industrious poor into small independent property owners. It allowed a man to occupy for £20 land worth £9600 at auction, put all his capital into stock, and so begin to accumulate the wealth with which he would eventually buy the land.[19] Gipps had hedged on the idea at first, and by 1844 opportunists and mal-practitioners had tied up the readily available lands to the disadvantage of new settlers. Some of these held a thousand square miles at 2s a thousand acres while others sublet for a third of the annual increase in flocks, or sometimes for hundreds of pounds, runs they held for an annual £10 licence fee. Broughton supported any move Gipps proposed to break up such holdings for new settlers but lamented its lateness. 'The Governor *I* think would have done better to have taken my advice two and a half years ago, before this celebrated Legislative Council of ours came into existence', he reflected as a bitter political struggle unfolded.[20]

The Legislative Council launched a counter-campaign for control of the crown lands arguing that it was a constitutional mockery to deny the people's representatives control of the colony's greatest financial asset. In theory the claim seemed just. But with sixteen or more members of the Council members also of the Pastoral Association pledged to defeat the squatting regulations, local legislative control would predictably lead to a lowering of land prices, an extended period for squatter purchases, the cancellation of all arrears in rents, and an end of opportunity to new settlers. 'If the Council govern the lands with the revenue arising from them, and these gentlemen govern the Council, a monstrous pretty oligarchy they will have established', he warned. Broughton still recoiled at the unprincipled land-greed of the colony's leading settlers in and out of government. '[They] do not think of the public good, but how to get themselves out of debt, and claw and clasp all the lands of the Crown for their own private advantage', he charged.[21]

Broughton argued the case for the regulations in the Executive Council when no one else would. He drafted a point for point refutation of the Legislative Council's attack on them in its report on land grievances, and Gipps sent it unedited to the Colonial Office. He defended the regulations in the *Times* when agents of the Pastoral Association attacked them overseas. He had the Archbishop of Canterbury, the SPG and Coleridge rally Christian statesmen for their defence in the British parliament, and one day hoped to receive a slice of the new squatting fees for religious education beyond the boundaries.[22] 'But as to this religious part, nobody takes it up with earnestness', Broughton wrote to his English connections. 'Lord Stanley I fear will not have the courage to do anything effectual and I much fear Sir George Gipps is not the man to prompt him to attempt it.' To Broughton in 1844 it seemed one-way support for Gipps.[23]

Gipps's squatting regulations and his veto on national schools continued to tear him apart from his Legislative Council. Gipps appeared to use his exclusive initiative in financial management to make a mockery of the notion of representative government. The Legislative Council retaliated and Broughton feared for good order. The Council defeated Gipps 'sometimes upon five and six divisions in one evening', the bishop reported, amid talk of resistance, rebellion and a republic within fifty years. It was the first showing of that 'shocking spirit of democracy' he forecast would have its day in the colony.[24] Others shared his fears.

James Macarthur condemned the Council as unfit for moderate men and the *Australian* called for the foundation of a Conservative Club to oppose its sentiments. But when Gipps sought Broughton's advice on suspending Legislative Council sittings or even calling fresh elections Broughton advised restraint. 'Let them go on until they have shown sufficiently what their animus is', he counselled, 'and then the home government will know better how to deal with the question.' Broughton hoped the Legislative Council would betray itself with some 'fantastic trick' and compel Colonial Office intervention. He wanted a new constitution not merely a new Council.[25]

Broughton might hope for an improved constitutional arrangement. His relationship with Romanists could only deteriorate. Polding's return in 1843 marked the outbreak of a campaign to seek converts among the poorer classes of Protestants. Hospital wards echoed with tales of purgatory; anti-reformation pamphlets turned up in prison cells; and at a gala round of afternoon tea-parties for impecunious Anglicans the biscuits were passed around with 'doubt as to the possibility of salvation in the Church of England'. As many as seven or eight guests an afternoon swallowed it. Broughton watched this for months 'determined to have recourse to a public exposure'.[26]

His opportunity came in late May 1844. Polding rebaptized four Anglican inmates of the Female Factory at Parramatta, and had another seven ready for June. That violated a long-standing arrangement not to proselytize in prisons and orphanages. Broughton went post-haste to the Parramatta Factory, assembled its Anglican congregation and said: 'Take Heed ... I hear there have been among you agents of the Church of Rome, tampering with your belief', and so on. The sermon sold two editions in two months and annoyed Polding who genuinely believed he had baptized pagans not Protestants. Moreover, Polding took exception to being called a 'liar and hypocrite' (which was a liberal gloss on Broughton's words) by a Protestant bishop inside a public institution, and with much ceremony and publicity, called upon Gipps to institute a board of enquiry into the incident.[27]

So the bishops went to war. Where once they had fired shots into the air they now aimed at each other. Rome's strength came not from 'mere quietness and confidence, but aggressive effort', Broughton observed; and he no longer saw the Church of England, shorn of its constitutional advantage, as obliged to keep the domestic peace. Broughton followed up his Parramatta sermon with an attack on Rome's idolatry at a general church meeting in Sydney. He raised a fresh army of laymen, the Lay Association, which recruited 200 in two weeks and exhorted each to act 'as if all depended on his own exertion'. The *Southern Queen* appeared as an unofficial church newspaper. 'The "drum ecclesiastic" has never been beaten with such force in this colony as it is at this moment', remarked the *Colonial Observer*.[28]

While the drums beat Judge Burton left for Madras. 'I have none remaining like him on whom I can rely', Broughton lamented. Worse still, Burton's departure opened the way for the promotion of Plunkett or Therry, both Irish Catholic, to what had been a Protestant bench.

The prospect troubled Broughton. He raised the matter with Burton
but after prayer acquiesced in the judge's conviction that the offer to
be chief justice of Madras was 'the work of Him who is the disposer of
human events'. Yet never had He worked so mysteriously. Within
three months the chief justice of the local Supreme Court, Dowling,
was dead leaving vacant the office Burton repeatedly said would crown
his wordly amibitions. With Burton and Dowling gone Plunkett had a
strong claim not only to the bench but, on English precedent, for being
promoted from attorney-general to chief justice. Should Therry replace
Plunkett as attorney-general and become his heir apparent the colony
would have two Irish Catholic chief justices in a row! That prospect
aroused Broughton's political guile.[29]

Broughton undermined Plunkett's promotion in the Executive Council.
He argued that a first-rate English barrister would not accept colonial
service as attorney-general whereas he might as chief justice, so that to
promote the attorney-general to chief justice in slavish imitation of
English precedent would be to appoint a lesser man where a better
were available. He also questioned Plunkett's capacity in civil law where
much of the work of the chief justice fell.[30] This, and Gipps's own feeling
that Plunkett was too slow and ponderous to be an effective chief justice,
deprived Plunkett of immediate promotion.[31] The Executive Council
nominated Judge Stephen and left it to the Colonial Office to confirm
or upset as it saw fit. When the disappointed Plunkett applied for redress
to London, Broughton matched his energies urging Coleridge to interest
some good London barristers in applying directly for the job. An outside
appointment would plug all gaps on the bench, keep it Protestant, and
assure the colony on one institution of undoubted loyalty to the crown.
'Give us an Etonian if it can be done', Broughton told Coleridge. But
no Etonian came. Stephen stayed chief justice and Plunkett declined
a lesser promotion.[32]

To some the Plunkett affair revealed that Broughton ruled the roost
in the Executive Council. In the same year 1844 Gipps, prodded by
Broughton, had defied the giant pastoralist industry and overturned
the Legislative Council's vote on education. It appeared that unless
Gipps and Broughton were driven apart they would frustrate indefinitely
the wealth and intelligence of the colony. 'We have been shown by the
experiences of the last session, that there exists within this Colony a
power at the disposal of a single man far greater than is consistent with
the efficient working of the representative system', wrote the *Atlas*,
a new newspaper in search of a cause to give it an audience. The *Atlas*
preached that if colonists could break the source of Broughton's power
Gipps would be isolated and powerless, the Legislative Council restored
to its sovereignty, and the pastoralists freed at last to spread where there
was grass and generate wealth untold for the colony. In 1845 the *Atlas*
made a cause of the separation of Gipps 'the vassal forsooth of a gown
or a rochet' from Broughton, and set about harassing the bishop.[33]

The *Atlas* had first to create an evil image of Broughton. It paraded
him as a haughty prelate giddy with past success and prepared to sacrifice
further progress in the colony in his grasping after temporal aggrandize-

ment. He had made squatting expensive to restrict population because dispersion made priestly domination difficult. 'Dispersion may be a condition of pastoral greatness', continued the *Atlas*, 'but masses are essential to clerical domination.' The bishop opposed popular education because it enabled the young to read the scripture and despise priestly authority. One source of the bishop's power was a clergy 'entirely subject to his absolute will and pleasure' for its appointments and stipends, the *Atlas* alleged. Another was the marshalling of the laity into a Lay Association: 'He has shown his contempt for the representatives of the people; he now aims at having a popular assembly of his own'. For what end? Not even the *Atlas* knew, but that was the measure of the bishop they opposed.[34]

The remedy the *Atlas* proposed was for the laity to disassociate itself from the Lay Association and for the Legislative Council to pay government stipend subsidies to church trustees, not the bishop, and offer the colonial clergy the same security of tenure enjoyed by English incumbents. The *Atlas* assumed that between bishop and clergy there was a natural enmity, and liberated from the wrath of the bishop the clergy would automatically check episcopal pretentions.[35]

The *Atlas* had too crooked a view of Broughton and too brief an acquaintance with colonial history to win credence, and the *Southern Queen* on 31 May 1845 went to work correcting the record. The bishop had not opposed squatting. Indeed, after 1840 he had encouraged it, deeply regretting that the church's ministry could not keep pace with it. Only raw recruits to the local scene, ignorant of the debates of the 1830s, could be misled into believing Broughton an enemy of widespread education. To brand the parish school system, which Broughton favoured, a weapon of priestly domination was to wonder how, after 200 years of it, England came by a policy of religious toleration. Moreover, Broughton did not enjoy any unfettered control over his clergy. The government paid clerical stipends on the petition of the people; and 'when they have assigned a Stipend it remains a perpetual benefice', Broughton explained. Only the governor or the Executive Council could withdraw it. Moreover the bishop had not shown a high-handed authority. The Brigstocke case revealed him anxious to exercise his disciplinary powers only through legal procedures in an open court. The bishop did not avenge dissent. Wilkinson had opposed Broughton's education campaign in 1836 while chaplain at Woollongong but by 1845 Broughton had promoted him with liberal SPG assistance to Balmain. There were backsliding clergy during the 1844 education campaign but no chaplain lost his stipend or was removed to an inferior parish. For all its trumpetings in 1845 the *Atlas* could not name one victimized clergyman. Moreover, no clergyman could believe the *Atlas*'s boast that if Broughton did not support him the laity would.[36] There was no enmity between bishop and clergy to exploit. Broughton and his chaplains were of the one mould; all were SPG men and all believed in apostolic authority. 'A more studiously obedient body of men, generally speaking, is not in the Church', Broughton said.[37] The *Atlas* misfired in attempting to drive a wedge between Broughton and his clergy.

The *Atlas* scored little better in driving a wedge between Broughton and his laity by attacking the Lay Association. Charles Lowe, a Sydney lawyer, had formed the Association to raise funds for Broughton's diocesan projects. Unfortunately Charles Lowe's enthusiasm outstripped his discretion as he travelled the diocese proclaiming obedience to the church, trust in the bishop, and a readiness 'to promote and extend the influence of the church as a branch of the National Establishment'. The *Southern Queen*, owned partly by Charles Lowe, drove home the creed and after three months with several country branches in the making announced 'that the National Church *is* recovering its claim to rank somewhat higher than on a mere equality with surrounding sects'. Such indiscriminate references to the colonial Church of England as a 'National Establishment' worried Broughton.[38] 'You will pardon my observing that the expression scarcely seems accurate', he commented, and warned that the Lay Association misled itself and confused the colony if it pretended the Diocese of Australia was more than a colonial 'branch of the national establishment' without temporal advantages and privileges. But Charles Lowe crusaded on, heedlessly interchanging 'national establishment' with 'National Establishment' and 'National Church'. Thus it was a simple matter for the *Atlas* to excite suspicion of the Lay Association as the militant arm of a fresh drive to elevate the Church of England and its leader in the colony. Moreover, the Association's exalted language about church and episcopate betrayed the source of its inspiration—Tractarian Oxford. So the *Atlas* warned that what paraded as a Lay Association was a Puseyite Clerical Association and a front for the subversion of the diocese to the principles of the Tracts for the Times.[39]

Over many months in 1845 bewildered readers learned how to identify a Puseyite. He was a churchman with 'a protestant cloak over a popish heart, and the pride of Lucifer to match'. He allegedly held the three doctrines of clerical ascendency, sacramental sufficiency, and patristical authority. By the last he denied the sufficiency of Holy Writ, by the second he denigrated the ministry of the non-sacramental churches, and by the first he threatened to subvert the political order of the colony. The *Atlas* also fashioned the argument that through the doctrine of apostolical succession the bishop became the source of an exclusive authority which commanded obedience from the clergy who, in return for their sharing in that authority, lorded it over a laity dependent on priestly ministrations for salvation. In the *Atlas's* reckoning the doctrine of apostolic succession was the first step in the creation of a new 'clerico-politico' force which would destroy the religious egalitarianism of the Church Acts and turn New South Wales over to a Spanish or Italian style ecclesiastical despotism. In short, the colonial Puseyite was a political subverter.[40] And the *Atlas* spared nothing in proving that Broughton had adopted Puseyite principles because they ministered to his worldly political ambitions, and the clergy supported him because his success elevated them in society. Since only the laity were uncorrupted it fell to them to strike at Puseyism and guarantee the future liberty of New South Wales 'by stopping the supplies'. When the clergy found

the bishop had no money they would turn to the people and leave Broughton in isolation and humiliation. So the *Atlas* invoked economic sanctions
against Broughton.[41]

The *Atlas's* campaign was partly frustrated by the *Sentinel*, another
newspaper with a cause. The *Sentinel's* mission was to oppose any papal
takeover of the colony. 'Popery is gaining an ascendancy and sharpening
the papal blades to cut every Protestant's throat', it warned; and added
tales of Protestant Odd Fellows at the Lighthouse Hotel barely escaping
massacre by papal conspirators one night late in March 1846. Exaggeration was impossible. Only a militant union of Episcopalians, Presbyterians and dissenters could offer an effective opposition. Since other
Protestants were as loath to associate with Puseyites as Puseyites were
to identify themselves as Protestants, Puseyism undermined Protestant
unity and indirectly assisted the papal cause. So the *Sentinel* anathema-
tized Puseyism but never once trampled Broughton underfoot as one
of its foes.[42] There was a hollow ring in the *Atlas* pointing at Broughton
and crying Puseyite while the genuinely anti-Puseyite *Sentinel* pointed
elsewhere. Moreover, while Broughton's *Take Heed* sermon sat on
bookseller's shelves it was nonsense for the *Atlas* to charge Broughton
with popery. 'These men raise the cry of Popery not because they believe
it but because they hope thereby to do us harm', counter-charged the
Southern Queen.[43] As for economic sanctions, they were applied at
Moreton Bay and by a churchwarden and one parishoner of St Matthew's
Windsor who both abandoned the Puseyite practice of weekly offertories
for the more Protestant custom of occasional gifts. Few followed. The
Atlas's Puseyite witch-hunt had little religious impact being recognized
for what it was, a programme designed to discredit and remove Broughton,
isolate Gipps politically, and break up the squatting regulations.[44]

Broughton passed off the criticism as 'natural' among liberal thinkers
opposed to the church having a positive role in society.[45] There was,
in fact, a scarcity of Tractarian material in the colony. 'We have never
been able to find a single copy of the *Tracts* in any Anglican family of
our acquaintance', wrote the *Australasian Chronicle*. Broughton himself
had to wait two years for a copy of *Tract XC*.[46] Every shipment of mail
from England poured 19 000 newspapers into the colony and their
tales of English Tractarian excesses showed how regular ecclesiastical
life was in New South Wales. The worst the colony had produced was
a stone altar at Appin, which disappeared quickly at Broughton's command, and a controversy over lay-baptism. Some zealous young clergy
taught that only clercial baptism was effective for salvation, a disturbing
doctrine in country areas which saw rarely a clergyman. Broughton
ordered that to stop. The rest were mischievous complaints about Walsh
wearing a surplice instead of a preaching gown; Sconce introducing
novelties into services; and Christ Church St Lawrence having a cross
on its exterior.[47] Broughton dismissed such complaints. He set the tone
of colonial Tractarianism and believed it was under control. 'I find a
general carefulness to avoid all extreme opinions or practices, and a
spirit of ready and conscientious conformity to my wishes and instructions', he reported to the SPG.[48]

Broughton believed the Tractarians had recalled the Church of England to the teachings of the Reformers. Tracts bristled with names from Hooker to Laud and showed the Reformation to have been a highwater mark in a Christian tradition dating back to apostolic days. With this assumption Broughton laid down guidelines for the clergy. They were to interpret the Tracts by the light of the Reformation. Where the Reformers abandoned a practice don't revive it, he said; or condemned a belief, don't teach it; and don't alter the liturgy of the Book of Common Prayer. There remained still wide scope for novel thought. Surprisingly, Broughton found himself defending *Tract LXXV* on the breviary because it showed how biblical were its contents.[49]

The great truth the Tractarians recovered for the Church of England 'at almost the last hour' was the doctrine of apostolic succession. 'The title itself, and the train of ideas which it suggests', Broughton said, 'would ere long have fallen into disetude and oblivion.' By apostolic succession Broughton meant a 'transmissive spiritual authority conferred by ordination'. It did not confer an exclusive ministry. Broughton saw its value more in the obligations and guarantees it gave the church. It obliged bishops and clergy to maintain the 'original model' of the Christian church. It furnished bishops with a new ground of authority as governments abandoned their obligation to uphold true doctrine by law, and it steeled the clergy to resist those compromises the laity could push them to under the voluntary system. It also shielded the laity from the whims of individual preachers. In effect the doctrine of apostolic succession obliged every churchman to examine his actions in the light of the 'common voice' of a church that reached back to the apostles. Thus was individualism tempered and schism avoided.[50]

Broughton was nevertheless a 'wary and cautious' follower of the Tracts. 'It is not my wish', he said, 'to preach up indiscriminately the opinion of the Tracts, or as indiscriminately to join in a crusade against them.'[51] The Tracts needed sifting for error. Broughton rejected Newman's subtle reinterpretation of the Articles so as to have them avoid a conflict with the Council of Trent. The true meaning of the Articles was their plain and obvious one. Purgatory Broughton dismissed as fiction, and he feared some Tractarians came close to teaching a doctrine of transubstantiation. But what he most disliked was a vague, yet pervasive, softness towards Rome which could draw young and inexperienced readers to investigate Rome's position sympathetically.[52] So while one part of Broughton said 'it is good to be here' the other cried out 'there is a lion in the way'. And the lion roared with *Tract XC*, Froude's *Remains*, and when Pusey knelt before the host at a convent mass. Nevertheless, Broughton regarded these as aberrations. 'Really I hope never to forget', he quickly added, 'the great benefit which my own perception of many important truths has derived from familiarity with these writings.'[53]

Of the Tractarian writers Broughton liked Pusey best. 'I cannot conscientiously say he has shown "a right judgment in *all* things", Broughton admitted, 'yet no one holds him in more sincere estimation and respect than I.' Broughton believed Pusey firmly within the Reformation tradition. The two exchanged sermons. Broughton, however, thought it might appear cheeky of him to send Pusey a copy of his charge for 1844 with its strictures on Tractarian excesses. Instead, he suggested Coleridge slip him one quietly.[54] Thus Broughton helped calm Oxford in 1844. He thought Newman, whom he admired in 1836, bewitched by tradition. 'I fear, I fear. I fear he is gone', he said. But providence had found a 'perfect antidote' to Mr Newman's doubts in Mr Manning's certainty. The awe, mystery, reverence and devotion Newman sought in Roman writings Broughton found in 'abundance and profusion' in Manning's sermons. They, too, exchanged sermons.[55] A hint from Coleridge in late 1843 that the Tractarians might retire under pressure from the University of Oxford and the English bishops aroused Broughton's disapproval. 'Cranmer did not retire', he remonstrated. *'Peace* will gain nothing and *truth* will lose much by such a course.'[56]

Although in his apology on apostolic succession Broughton was careful not to denigrate the ministeries of non-episcopal churches he clearly irked the Presbyterians. The *Colonial Observer* challenged the bishop to erect a husting in Hyde Park and defend his apostolic claims.[57] Instead, the bishop stood up Gregor and Allan, two Presbyterian ministers recently ordained into the Church of England, to testify that it was the calm and unity of the Church of England in contrast to the turbulence and divisions of Presbyterians that had attracted them to episcopal government and belief in the doctrine of apostolic succession on which it rested. That put lustre into Broughton's arguments and venom into the *Colonial Observer*. Lang was angered at the deference Gregor and Allan paid their new bishop and offended that a mere human should accept it. So Lang called Broughton a pope.[58] It was a petty matter, but combined with the malice of the *Atlas* and the mischief of an *Australasian Chronicle* crying out 'Puseyites among the Anglican clergy of the colony? Success to them, say we' it amounted to an annoyance.[59]

Amidst this hubbub Broughton's domestic life changed. On 18 April 1844 Phoebe Broughton finally married William Boydell at a 'quite private' Thursday wedding. 'Really we all felt very much indisposed for company on the occasion', Broughton confessed. He gave the bride away, Allwood performed the ceremony, and Gipps loaned government house Parramatta for a week's honeymoon. Ten days later Broughton arranged a family matins, read the bride and groom the story of St Paul's shipwreck, and blessed them off on a steamer for Newcastle with a parcel of scales and account books. 'Rather a *strange* present, but a very useful one', he admitted. 'You will consult prudence and economy by weighing everything ... and you cannot manage your income properly or securely unless you set down carefully whatever you spend.' Phoebe delighted in her changed circumstances, was soon pregnant, and by the end of the year had her mother and sister Emily roughing it up bush with her. Once there, neither appeared anxious to return. Broughton coped alone with Tusculum, putting up a stream of visitors, sheltering missionaries in transit, and calling on Mrs Sconce to help out in the occasional crisis.[60]

Broughton missed Phoebe's company. He rarely looked beyond his family for relaxation and had found in her pious but gay spirit the

perfect foil for his own sombre temperament. She had the intelligence
to comprehend what he taught her and the submissiveness not to question
it; 'From the hour of her birth until now she never gave me occasion
to be dissatisfied with anything she ever said or did'. His wife and other
daughter Emily continued to join the 'secular people' at parties and balls.
The bishop never did; 'I am much better pleased to be left at home by
myself to take care of the fire and amuse myself with writing'.[61] He
sustained an enormous correspondence. He personally acknowledged
every gift above £5. In July 1844 he sent off eighty-seven letters and
in December another eighty.[62] Books poured in and he acknowledged
these too. Friends in England had placed permanent orders with ecclesiastical publishers; Coleridge's brother bequeathed the diocese his collection; and an old clergyman whom Broughton had known as one of
Bishop Tomline's chaplains sent out his library. These books had to
be sorted, catalogued, and read. Broughton hungered for time to study.[63]
Yet the business of Sydney was rarely finished before the call came to
set out on another visitation. From January to April 1845 he spent in
the southern counties, from September to December in the Hunter
River and New England districts. Since retiring from the Legislative
Council he had been 'almost constantly a wanderer upon the face of
earth or sea'.[64]

The Season for Exertion

With great deference I would press earnestly upon them [trustees of Overseas Bishopric Fund] the policy of... making *this* the season for exertion.

Broughton to Mr Justice Coleridge, 27 January 1845

Broughton failed in his attempt to retire. The Archbishop of Canterbury insisted that plans for the creation of extra Australian bishoprics had advanced to a point which made his continued presence in the colony crucial.[1] Yet no one considered Broughton's advice crucial and his opinion on the siting of the bishoprics was never sought. Back in 1842 he had simply been advised by a committee in London that four new bishoprics were planned for Hobart, South Australia, Port Phillip, and the Swan River. Broughton welcomed the news but disliked the locations. He wanted a bishopric at Hobart with the oversight of South Australia, another at Maitland taking in the Hunter River district, and one somewhere in the Manero. Since a sea voyage to Port Phillip was less fatiguing than a journey on horseback into the Manero Broughton suggested attaching Port Phillip to Sydney until it became an independent colony. When later, for financial reasons, the Australian quota of new bishoprics was halved the London committee's decision to give Adelaide first priority completely baffled Broughton. The arrangement totally ignored population densities and those geographical considerations which made for the convenient administration of one area from another, he said. By way of protest Broughton sent the Archbishop of Canterbury a map covered with relative information for future divisions as 'standing proof of my having been alive to the imperfections of our present system and having done my best to remedy it'. However, Broughton expected little change in the arrangements, and to relieve his own administrative burden divided his diocese into five rural deaneries centred on Sydney, Maitland, Bathurst, Goulburn and Port Phillip. The younger bishops would have the tidy new dioceses and he his 'six hundred Nottinghamshires' stretched from Moreton Bay to Portland Bay.[2]

Then on 8 September 1844 came the splendid consecration in Sydney of the Reverend Francis Murphy as the first Roman Catholic bishop of Adelaide. 'How beautiful upon the mountain are the feet of him that bringeth good tidings', said the popish preacher. How beautiful indeed! The romance in it touched even Broughton's imagination. Murphy left to establish his diocese with £235 in his pocket and 'no expectation of obtaining more than the stipend of an ordinary chaplain with no certainty even of that'.[3] By contrast the Church of England shuffled. Its radiant vision of new dioceses encircling the the globe began fading when it was announced. Why? Because the Church of England paid only lip-service to heroic apostolic virtues. Though the Bishop of London warned new overseas bishoprics to expect 'a very moderate provision' Lord Stanley insisted on such 'decent temporalities' as a permanently secured stipend of £1000 to £1200 a year or endowments of around £30 000.[4] 'Because we cannot do without large temporal means while another episcopacy *can* it may be urged against us that ours cannot be the *true* episcopate', commented Broughton. When the British government declined a contribution Broughton pointed to the scores of well educated conscientious country vicars with private incomes of £600 a year. Let the church consecrate them. 'Because Lord Stanley is immovable on the score of expense ... the possession of independent means appears almost to constitute a call', he said and found two month's comfort in the thought.[5]

A bishopric at £600 did not reach Stanley's expectation. 'But better to have a bishop with *merely* that income and a house to live in than *no* bishop', Broughton insisted; and blushed at his own £2000. To cut a more apostolic image he thought of separating his costs of office from the gross figure and publishing only the remainder as personal income. Even so it was £1300, and a grander sum than even Lord Stanley required. Broughton admitted he could live on less with one daughter married and his household well established. By paring his personal spending and adding to these savings money normally spent on official entertaining and charity he would have a sufficient sum of money to establish a bishopric where he wanted it. Might not that be an apostolic deed? He thought about it for a few months; then, by Blackheath in the Blue Mountains, he excitedly offered to help the Overseas Bishopric Fund set up two bishoprics straight away by surrendering £800 of his salary immediately and £200 more when his lease on Tusculum expired in 1850. He wanted the first, upon reconsideration, at Port Phillip and offered it £600. The other was to be at Morpeth, to begin immediately as an archdeaconry by adding £200 from his own stipend to the existing chaplain's stipend, and another £200 in 1850 to bring it up to a bishopric. 'We must have speedily an increase of bishops, or we perish', he said. 'Can any of us rest until we have done all that in us lies to carry into positive effect that which is not a mere theory but a sacred principle founded upon the Word of God?'[6]

Stanley's insistence on large endowments frustrated the efforts of the Overseas Bishopric Fund but gave Broughton's plan time to reach London. The Archbishop of Canterbury agreed to Broughton's priorities and the Overseas Bishopric Fund offered to assist. Then the miracle happened. Three months after Broughton's plans arrived Stanley resigned and the Overseas Bishopric Fund's own treasurer, Gladstone, became Secretary of State for Colonies. Within another three months

Gladstone had the queen assent to sees at Port Phillip and Morpeth.[7]

An immediate bishopric at Morpeth surpassed even Broughton's expectations. It was also beyond the budget of the Overseas Bishopric Fund and it fell to Gladstone to arrange the finance. He took legal opinion on the limits of favour the Church of England might receive under the Church Act and consulted James Stephen on how best to handle colonial authorities. Gladstone ignored Gipps, who, contrary to Broughton's belief, gave the scheme no support. Gladstone took £250 from Broughton's salary for each new bishopric, added £250 from Schedule C and £333 6s 8d from the Overseas Bishopric Fund, to give each an income of £833 6s 8d annually. He added a residence to the value of £2000 to be built from the unappropriated funds in Schedule C for 1844 and 1845. Though Gladstone made the new bishops poor bishops he would not let Broughton join them. Broughton was to receive a stipend of £1500 and a residence to the value of £1700 if he wanted it. The £1500 was made up of the rent from the forty acre endowment Broughton had earlier requested and the balance in cash from Schedule C. To inject stability into the calculation of these amounts Gladstone wanted the rent for the forty acres fixed at the average of its anticipated return between 1846 and 1850. Any surplus rents were to be a bonus for the bishop. This, together with the reductions in visitation expenses that followed the subdivision of the diocese, meant that if Gladstone's plan succeeded Broughton's sacrifice would be more apparent than real.[8]

Broughton found that a relief. His had been an impetuous sacrifice. It left him with less than £600 a year after rent, visitation and other expenses of office, and £200 in life assurance premiums to cover himself at sea. 'With an income so reduced it might not be in my power to make such provision as would be reasonable for my wife and children, and therefore perhaps I did wrong', he said. He had carried his family into 'wandering and exile' cutting them off from the advantages of English society and then, in a moment of enthusiasm, sacrificed the little monetary compensation he could offer them.[9] Remorse gripped him; and before his noble sacrifice had reached England the bishop was bargaining his way back into comforts. He asked Gipps for a land endowment to offset episcopal rent and £1500 from unspent funds in Schedule C to be invested for his life assurance premiums which he claimed were made excessively expensive by the occasional sea journey his office obliged him to undertake. Gipps agreed to the land but thought the £1500 a questionable 'bargain'. 'I fancied he really *meant* to say *job*', Broughton recalled, and dropped the suggestion.[10] Gladstone's decision to offer him a modest rent-free residence and trim £300 from his sacrifice was most welcome. 'I have really not a single wish upon the subject unfulfilled', Broughton commented on the final arrangement.[11]

Gladstone's conduct throughout delighted Broughton. Gladstone did not quibble at favour the Church of England or pander to democracy by referring the matter to the Legislative Council, and had plainly ordered the governor into 'cordial co-operation with the efforts of the Bishop' in erecting the sees. Broughton liked that firmness.[12] It reassured him, too, that Gladstone was not a temporizer. Earlier in 1844 Gladstone had failed to vote against Peel's Charitable Benefits Act which by increasing government aid to the Irish seminary at Maynooth had strengthened the papist assault on New South Wales. 'For him I hope yet fear', Broughton had then commented.[13] But Gladstone had walked resolutely in fixing the new bishoprics. When Peel's government fell in 1846 Broughton wrote immediately thanking Gladstone for 'that increase of the number of episcopal Sees of which we acknowledge you the author'. A friendship began and the two exchanged views on church and state. 'By constantly rubbing one against the other "as iron sharpeneth iron"', the bishop told Gladstone, 'we may come to an agreement which for practical purposes will be perfect enough.'[14]

Broughton sought more of Gladstone. For some time Polding had wanted the Church Act amended and its subsidies to reflect the religious distribution in the colonial census. He complained that the richer Protestant congregations had qualified for stipends more quickly than poorer Roman Catholic congregations and the imposition without warning of a £30 000 limit meant the fund was exhausted before Roman Catholics had caught up. Around 1844 Roman Catholics calculated that they received 2s 9½d a head from government while Wesleyans received 7s 8¼d and Anglicans 3s 9¼d. A re-allocation on Polding's terms would net Roman Catholics an extra £3000 at Presbyterian and Wesleyan expense, and the Church of England would gain about the same.[15] But Broughton argued that Polding, who already flouted the Church Act by pooling stipends and stretching them to support extra priests, could recruit more celibate priests with his £3000 than any Protestant church could married clergy for the same amount. Polding in effect stole an advantage in manpower and could with added strength attack neglected Protestant areas in the hope of claiming even greater subsidies. One day Polding could begin slicing into Church of England subsidies.[16] So Broughton asked the Colonial Office to reject the arrangement before someone interested the Legislative Council in it. The Church of England could ill afford a debate on the Church Act in a Legislative Council hostile to the very existence of Schedule C. The Colonial Office, however, not only refused to interfere but made a debate on the Church Act inevitable by insisting that the Legislative Council correct some other minor discrepancy between the Act and the new constitution.[17] When Plunkett decided he could handle the Colonial Office alterations without involving the Legislative Council provided the churches settled their differences, Broughton cooled his opposition. He accepted the distribution of religious subsidies on a ratio drawn from the 1841 census, but insisted that no stipend be withdrawn from Presbyterians and Wesleyans until their recipients vacated office.[18] Broughton also sought to restrain further revisions by having them made subject to confirmation by the Privy Council. James Stephen warned Gladstone against that. 'I have learnt, by long and constant observation', Stephen wrote Gladstone in a memo, '... [that] criticism is exercised unsparingly to detect incongruities or difficulties in such Instructions. The result almost invariably is that they are defeated and become ineffectual.' Gladstone did not involve the Privy Council but put a revision of the ratio beyond Legislative

Council jurisdiction for seven years. After that Broughton must take his chances.[19] In a Legislative Council with a 'sufficient liberality of feeling' to slice £1150 off the subsidies for Christian worship for a synagogue Broughton feared for the whole scheme. The Church Act did not preclude aid to the Jews, Robert Lowe had argued. If Jews, why not Turks, Infidels and Heretics? If them, why any?[20]

By assisting in the foundation of new bishoprics the SPG ran itself short of money and looked to New South Wales for economies. The Society offered to recruit more chaplains but not subsidize them.[21] Broughton, however, preferred the society's subsidies to its recruits. There were too many misfits unable to persevere under 'the tedium and frequent disappointments of their service'.[22] The SPG recruits were often young men looking for a break or older men in search of a fresh start. If the young men arrived wearing the airs of their university colonists took umbrage at their pretence. When older men betrayed the suspicion of having fled ill success elsewhere colonists waxed indignant at their parishes being turned into a refuge. Broughton admitted there were few gross misfits, but cumulatively the minor ones had a slackening effect. He instanced the case of Watson. The SPG had selected him for work in Sydney on his excellent qualifications as a schoolmaster. Broughton found him impersonal, indifferent to pastoral work, and a slovenly preacher with an impediment. 'I am *compelled*', he wrote, 'wanting *any* other better or worse, to put him in charge of a parish containing 4,000 professed members of the Church of England, generally ignorant, all careless, many profane.'[23] The colonial churches needed a distinctively trained ministry.[24]

England's bishops did not much care for the idea. As early as 1840 Coleridge had canvassed the idea of a missionary training college and within two years had 400 supporters. He planned an establishment at Oxford which, without being part of the university, would be staffed by volunteer Fellows such as Pusey and the Oxford liturgist, Palmer.[25] The English bishops vetoed the project. The Bishop of Oxford sensed opposition from the heads of colleges to a non-university college in the town; the Bishop of London objected to a non-university trained colonial clergy; and the Archbishop of Canterbury, though sympathetic, thought it unwise to mix a handful of missionary candidates with the highly intelligent and fairly affluent university community. Coleridge then considered occupying the old archiepiscopal palace at Southwell but, separated from the goodwill of Oxford dons, the venture ran into staffing problems. Oxford was the only workable site, and the more determined Coleridge was to enter it the more the Bishop of London opposed it. Without a site there could be no appeal for money; so the haggle over Oxford postponed indefinitely the project.[26]

In the meantime Broughton decided to proceed with his own college. He saw no reason why 'the ripe and good scholars' from England's lesser grammar schools, whom Coleridge had hoped to attract to the Oxford college, should not be shipped out and trained locally. Any loss in 'fine scholarship' would be 'more than corrected by the experience of living and learning in the environment in which they would have to work'. Selwyn agreed; and the idea of an Australasian theological college was born. Broughton rashly bought a site adjoining Tusculum and planned a building for sixteen residents, to be called either Corpus Christi or Pembroke Hall with Ridley and Andrewes gazing down from the gables.[27] He hoped land in the Moore bequest would pay off the building and applied for a 360 acre glebe at Campbell Town to meet its running costs. The scheme, however, foundered on the persistent land depression. By 1845 Broughton had no money and a block of land worth a quarter the price he paid. 'I shall lie upon my oars', he told Coleridge.[28]

Broughton could not lie there too long. No new clergyman had arrived in 1845, yet he had the new bishoprics to staff and twelve new chapels licensed in 1845 to fill as well as other vacancies. Among the chaplains the Vidal brothers had left without replacements, and illness hung like a pall over Sydney. 'The clergyman of the parish next to this is gone both in body and mind', he reported. 'One of my right-hand men, poor Walsh, has fallen into a state of dejection and debility. Dr Cowper fails fast. Allwood was never strong, and in another of the Sydney parishes I have a man of delicate constitution who may at any time get too unwell to work.' By contrast a dozen seminarians trailed Polding to mass each Sunday.[29]

Allwood persuaded Broughton to forego the grandeur of Pembroke Hall, Sydney, and begin lectures in a vestry. When that succeeded the diocese could rent a large house for a college. In March 1846 eight students applied for training. Broughton taught them doctrine and Allwood literature. 'Our design is narrow and opens under all the disadvantages of poverty', the bishop told his first class. By June ten students attended and the hunt was on for a residence. Broughton calculated costs at £400 a year; and, refusing a local appeal for fear of the colony's anti-Tractarians demanding a say in the organization of the college, he turned to England for half the sum.[30] He could ask no more of Coleridge. On Joshua Watson's advice he truned to Benjamin Harrison, Archdeacon of Maidstone in the Diocese of Canterbury, whom he knew slightly as Howley's secretary. He also approached Miss Burdett-Coutts, a young heiress who had once proposed to the ageing Duke of Wellington. Miss Burdett-Coutts had endowed bishoprics in Adelaide and Cape Town, and Broughton reasoned that a woman with so much would have more.[31]

By September 1846 Broughton was ready to move from the St James vestry and rented Lyndhurst, an old house three miles from Tusculum, for a college. By December he expected to have twenty students. There was talk, too, of admitting locally educated candidates to the Sydney bar, and Broughton imagined expanding Lyndhurst to prepare them in Latin and English literature. In the bishop's mind Lyndhurst grew into a university college, and he began a fresh search for land and to dream again of an £8000 building. Broughton was even prepared to alter his planned visitations up country and remain a whole year in Sydney if that helped ensure the college's survival.[32]

The grandeur of Broughton's vision altered Allwood's future. Allwood's practical approach had made a college possible in 1846. Broughton styled himself principal but Allwood was resident tutor and took 'the labouring oar'.[33] Earlier, however, Broughton had marked Allwood for the bishopric at Port Phillip. Then, to avoid sending Allwood abroad for consecration Broughton decided to fill Port Phillip from England and have the new bishop visit Swan River on his way out. He pressed Allwood to accept instead the archdeaconry of Morpeth and the eventual bishopric.[34] Allwood declined, professing himself unqualified for the exercise of authority and more interested in the college. Broughton did not intend accepting the rejection as final. He hoped to attract a London Tractarian scholar, the Reverend Mr Formby, to the college and free Allwood for Morpeth.[35] When in August 1846 Broughton learned he had to fill Morpeth immediately, Formby had just declined the college and Allwood could not be spared. Morpeth would remain a minor bishopric for years while the college would be the life-blood of all dioceses, Broughton said. So he clasped at Allwood's earlier rejection of the archdeaconry and made no further mention of the bishopric. 'I may have some selfish feeling in not having been more urgent in trying to prevail', Broughton confessed. 'To lose Allwood is nothing short to me, of parting with my right hand ... but in the College above all his removal will create a vacancy which almost threatens ruin.'[36]

Broughton required no sacrifice of Allwood greater than he demanded of himself. Coleridge had just warned Broughton to expect translation to the see of Calcutta. It meant promotion in status and wealth, but that appealed little to a bishop offering away half his salary. However, if good health constituted a vocation Broughton realized he must go. Three Sunday services in Sydney's midsummer fatigued him no more than the same duties seventeen years ago in Farnham, and he undertook country visitations indifferent to the seasons. He had ridden a thousand miles in the September to the mid-December period just past without the slightest exhaustion. Yet, his wife ailed and could never follow him to a scorching Calcutta. 'It would be a hard trial to have to quit wife and children', he admitted. 'But still if it must be for His sake and the Gospel's I am well aware that I must not hesitate.' He asked to be spared but was prepared to go if those 'qualified to decide' asked it. 'Depend upon it', Broughton averred, 'if life and strength remain you would not find me backward in obeying.' Broughton thought it a sham to hold the Archbishop of Canterbury responsible for his province and deny him obedience. Similarly, in New South Wales where he had the responsibility for good order he had had to decide that Allwood should stay in Sydney to ensure a supply of ordinands.[37]

Meanwhile in England Coleridge had made fresh headway with his college. He abandoned Oxford for a site opposite Canterbury cathedral. A missionary college at Canterbury! Broughton relished the thought of returning as foundation principal and linking the King's School, Canterbury, to it in some special way! 'I had no sleep last night from thinking of this and I dream of it by day', he confessed.[38] But the Bishop of Barbados, Coleridge's uncle, became principal. To turn the site into a college Coleridge had to raise £25 000 privately before the Archbishop of Canterbury would endorse a public appeal. Broughton decided the colony's turn had come to help Coleridge. He gave £50 himself, squeezed £100 from Gipps, placed two newspaper advertisements advertising the foundation, and planned to have the Diocesan Committee back a general appeal in 1846.[39] Then came trouble. 'My worthy friend Dr Cowper', Broughton reported, 'began to break forth into vehement denunciations of Puseyism, of which he knows less, God save the mark, than I of Arabic.' Cowper took his cue from a rumour that the missionary college was originally part of Newman's establishment at Littlemore and had removed to Canterbury to escape the tarnish of his defection without renouncing its aim of turning the colonies Puseyite. Broughton contradicted the tale but colonists found it cheaper to cry Puseyite than subscribe. So the colonial appeal lapsed. Instead, Broughton sent Coleridge a sweet solemn air from Haydn adapted by his daughters to fit the hymn 'Deprecamur te Domine' sung by Augustine's missionaries at Canterbury. At evensong Broughton hoped the students would sing it and think of Australia.[40]

The extra bishoprics and new colleges allayed Broughton's anxiety over manpower and created another in finance. During 1846 Broughton had struggled to mark time. For three years he had kept the diocese afloat on gifts—£2100 from Coleridge, a share of unspent money in Schedule C, and a £1000 overdraft from the SPG. Local subscriptions had fallen to a point in 1844 where Broughton cancelled the Diocesan Committee's annual dinner for want of an achievement to celebrate.[41] They totalled £392 in 1845 and £381 in 1846. Where could the bishop turn? Coleridge had pledged New Zealand £3500 and Gladstone froze remaining unspent funds in Schedule C for episcopal residences. The SPG gave its priority to new dioceses. It had just refused to extend any chaplain's subsidy beyond five years and that meant twelve of Broughton's clergy lost a fifth of their income.[42] The Society also cut out building subsidies. 'How great a chill is cast upon undertakings when the hoped-for contribution is announced to be unobtainable', Broughton reported. Moreover, to cease building was tantamount to handing the colony to popery and dissent. So despite the strictest injunction to economize the bishop pledged £800 of the Society's money to new buildings in 1846. If that ruined the SPG, he said, 'I must pay the debt and in my present circumstances as to income that will be no easy matter'.[43] The tactic worked. The SPG found the money but instructed Broughton to be self-supporting by 1848.

Meeting such a deadline taxed Broughton's ingenuity. Special committees were not the answer. Broughton had established these with abandon—the Lay Association, a parochial committee wherever two or three gathered together, school committees, choir committees, a cathedral committee, a committee to raise relief for New Zealand—until the efforts became self-defeating as every committee appealed to the same willing laymen.[44] An attempt to reach a wider public in May 1846 failed. Broughton drafted a minute on the religiously destitute areas beyond the boundaries, to be read from all pulpits, but admitted defeat in the opening paragraph. 'It is my duty to make known such wants although it be not in my power to propose any plan for an immediate removal of them', he confessed. None other had a plan. Many clergy declined to read the appeal or the laity to hear it. Broughton scrutinized the 1846 subscription lists and saw scarcely 'one name of a member of of Council, very few professional men, or those who have the entrée at Government House, or any of the tokens of Colonial rank or distinction'.[45] The old familiar names of Blaxland, Bowman, Jones, Lithgow, Macarthur, McLeay, Nicholson and Deas Thomson were absent. Many had succumbed to the economic recession. Richard Jones was bankrupt. Others had left town to live frugally on their properties where with returning prosperity they had failed to revive the old habits of giving. They offered varied excuses. Some mumbled about it being a Puseyite diocese; some begrudged supporting a bishop to whom the *Atlas* attributed the land regulations; others with longer memories may have recalled the bishop's heartless attack on land greed in 1844 when many of their members were humbled by poverty; and one colonial wag brushed off his indignation in cartoons (to be seen by tipping the doorman of a city building) depicting Broughton as 'Loyola advising Gipps; as Julius II leading the armed forces against the Squatters; as Cromwell giving thanks for routing his opponents'.[46] Broughton, however, believed most were too proud to advertise their straitened means by giving less than before, and took 'refuge behind that earnest of all pretences, an imputation of Puseyism, as an excuse for refusing to assist'. Time would mend that. Meanwhile, he turned elsewhere for help: 'But the very distinguishable and gratifying spirit of attachment to the Church ... which has sprung up among the middle classes of this community, and (in some degree) which is still extending among the humbler ranks, afford us all possible encouragement to persevere'.[47] To collect small regular donations from this class Broughton introduced a system of weekly voluntary offerings at the church door.

Broughton saw the potential in a weekly offering a year before the *Times* made a controversy of it in 1841. At the time it seemed to him a natural consequence of insisting on free sittings in the new churches, and in May 1842 he introduced the practice into St Andrews temporary church where all seats were free. Thereafter Broughton tirelessly peddled the idea on visitations, and the custom took root.[48] Christ Church in Sydney collected £25 at some services; St James raised enough to sustain an assistant curate; and an alarmed voice warned that bishop and clergy had a new power in their grasp. In reply Broughton argued that the insecurity of the Church Act, the ceiling placed on church subsidies by Schedule C, and the economic recession made it essential for the church to look to the voluntary system as a major source of future income.[49]

Through the lean years of 1845–6 there were pockets of progress. Sturdy merchant donors kept projects alive in Sydney. One customs agent offered £3000 towards the completion of Christ Church, and an ironmonger, auctioneer, draper and brewer added £100 each. One hundred and fifty traders and artisans put up £10 each to revive construction on the cathedral, and Broughton hoped to persuade them to repeat their gift four times over to finish the cathedral as a mid-century offering. The impoverished artist Conrad Martyns donated a painting which the bishop asked Coleridge to sell to Peel who had once scoffed at the

culture of Botany Bay. Martyns also melted down the only two pieces
of plate he owned for the cathedral's chalice. 'Truly noble', Broughton
commented. Congregations expanded too. Twelve Sunday services in
Sydney were too few. Builders had part of the roof off St James adding
accommodation for three hundred more. Balmain got another two
hundred seats. St Philips was to be completely rebuilt. Visitors and
missionaries did not find the town as wild as rumour primed them to
expect. They could choose between matins and Holy Communion,
said or sung services in morning or afternoon and seven different preachers within a mile of their hotel. None was a Luther, commented a
visitor, but Sydney pulpits echoed more good sense than most English
towns of the size. Broughton prided himself on the quality of Sydney's
ecclesiastical life.[50]

In June 1846 Broughton celebrated the tenth anniversary of his
enthronement as bishop in a much changed Sydney. Tenements closed
in on Tusculum, and the bishop was busy landscaping 'to shut out Mr
Riddells ugly red house'. Broughton also lost his orchard, but from his
upper-storey bedroom verandah he still saw water from the harbour's
entrance to Circular Wharf where seventy masts often stood in a cobweb
of ropes.[51] Fifteen ships a week sailed out, one a day to England and
the rest into the Pacific. They took off wool and horses, and brought
back variety and sophistication; fine French wines, Staffordshire beer
for the Homebush races, foreign spirits properly distilled of their rage,
and Broadwood grand pianos. Ladies could dress in the cloth of five
nations and, like the Misses Broughton, attend concerts every week.
Mrs Bushell somehow sang above the band of the 99th Regiment; the
Australian Harmonic Club sang for charity; and the Sydney Choral
Society sang for Broughton's insurance on the Castlereagh Street school
rooms. There was heavy and light theatre, and the inevitable weekly
lecture on phrenology where charlatans turned a coin dispelling the
anxieties of the future in a colony without a past. In the courtroom
insolvency seemed interminable. In the boardroom men planned a
railway age. Gipps was recalled. All Sydney had a bowel complaint.[52]

Much had changed, yet much hadn't. The fang and gall farewell given
Darling in 1831 was repeated for Gipps, and the day he left the militia
stood armed and six feet apart from government house to the wharf.
The new governor Sir Charles Fitzroy arrived at night like his predecessor,
but unlike Gipps he waited for sunshine and entered on a white horse.
His aristocratic demeanor pleased the crowd. Broughton did not go to
the wharf but waited on the verandah of government house content to
reflect on the fate of governors and how the colony changed them.[53]
Take Gipps for example. He had arrived with everything in his favour;
by reputation a Whig with a radical edge (how the people loved that!)
and by inclination disposed to promote national education, reduce
ecclesiastical expenditure, and elbow the bishop from government.
Yet he stayed to praise the bishop's 'firm and unflinching' role in government and opposed any reduction in the bishop's salary as likely to reduce
his status and influence in the colony.[54] Broughton's mind also shot
back to the day Gipps had turned angrily in Council to denounce him

as more intransigent than Rome. Yet Gipps ended up recommending
that a fifth of the Land Fund be given, over and above Schedule C, to
the support of clergy among the squatters, and himself gave £100 to the
Canterbury missionary college almost as a penance for once advising
the Colonial Office that the colony had sufficient clergy. How men
changed! 'He left us cured of many of his radical impressions "a sadder
and a wiser man"', Broughton reflected.[55] Broughton had seen three
governors leave broken or dispirited after six-year terms. Now after
sixteen years bearing burdens of church and state Broughton waited
to greet his fourth governor. How would the colony change him?

Fitzroy appeared at government house around noon on 3 August
1846 and Broughton administered the oath requiring him to uphold
the doctrines of the Church of England. A few days later he asked the
governor to become patron of the Diocesan Committee. Fitzroy did.
Broughton then invited Fitzroy to visit the newly established St James
College at Lyndhurst. Fitzroy went; and over dinner that night offered
the college more land.[56] Fitzroy also offered the Jews a £1000, blamed
the colony's discord on Gipps, appeared warm to a re-introduction of
transportation, and wiped off all quit rents more than twenty years in
arrears. '"King Charles", as they call him seems to lay himself out to
please everybody', Broughton commented.[57] Everybody locally, that
was. Within twelve months the Colonial Office had twice censured him
for indulging the wishes of the Legislative Council to the derogation
of the rights of Crown and Commons, and threatened him once with
recall.[58] To the colonists Fitzroy appeared to have his heart in the right
hemisphere, and the invitation to mischief was irresistible.

Be wary of the Executive Council on land matters, the *Sydney Morning
Herald* advised Fitzroy. Be wary! The Bishop of Australia *is* the Executive Council, the *Atlas* further warned: 'The Bishop of Australia is the
most dangerous counsellor that can be imagined ... and has been and
will be the source of incalculable evils to this colony'.[59] The advice
was stillborn. Broughton had already resigned from the Executive
Council and awaited only formal approval from the Colonial Office
to retire. The bitter, unsettled state of land politics prompted the decision.
Broughton discovered his critics using the *Times*, many of whose readers
subscribed to the SPG, to accuse him of meddling in land policy to
the neglect of his diocese. As a confidential adviser to the governor
Broughton could not publicly refute the charge, yet, left unrefuted,
it could hinder SPG appeals for his diocese. So Broughton decided to
be quit of politics. 'The consideration which really influences me',
he explained to the governor, 'is the disadvantageousness of the position
assigned me, in having to advise confidentially upon measures of government, without possessing any opportunity of stating publicly the reason
for such advice, in case the measure should be met by opposition.' Moreover, the changed circumstances of the Church Act facilitated his
departure. Once religious subsidies were distributed in a fixed ratio
there was no advantage in his sitting on the body that processed the
applications.[60]

Robert Lowe was a more determined mischief-maker. He had been

out to get Broughton for a year. Throughout 1845 he had expected
the clergy to petition him for deliverance from the Church Temporalities
Act which he claimed put their stipends and parsonages at the whim
of the bishop. Lowe promised to win the clergy freehold of benefice
for the asking. Without it they were subservient to the bishop to 'a
degree dangerous to public liberty', he said. When the clergy preferred
to 'hunt with the bishop' Lowe hoped the laity would demand freehold
for their clergy. But the laity were diffident in demanding control of
endowments they had declined to raise. So Lowe acted alone, and in
March 1846 foreshadowed legislation to force freehold of benefice on
the clergy. He alleged that Broughton and his enslaved clergy were stocking the minds of the young, left vacant by the failure of the general education bill, with Puseyite notions of priestly authority. 'He is engaged in the
attempt to raise a spiritual despotism in this land', the *Atlas* warned.
'If the clergy are not liberated for their own sakes they ought to be for
that of the public.' Then, in prose, rhyme and very blank verse the
Atlas raised a litany against the 'Australian Pope, Patriarch and Pontiff',
lover of stone altars and carved wood, emulator of Gregory VII, imitator
of Laud, disciple of Newman, friend of Walsh and Sconce, black cockatoo.
It was an act designed to condition the colony for legislative interference
in the Church of England.[61]

Broughton thought it bluff at first. No draft bill appeared. No victim
of episcopal aggression stood forward and the clergy unanimously
petitioned their confidence in the bishop's use of his disciplinary powers.
Broughton insisted his letters patent did not permit tyranny nor his
temperament allow it. In ten years he had deposed one clergyman
(who smartly departed), cleared another of alleged drunkenness, and
exonerated Brigstocke from charges of misconduct despite a personal
conviction of his guilt. 'This does not breathe that arbitrary and brash
spirit which some have been pleased to discover', the bishop said. But
Lowe had a fixed purpose. Whether the bishop actually abused his powers
was not as important as the fact that he had powers to abuse, Lowe
said; and he asked leave to present a Church of England Clergyman's
Benefices bill in September 1846. Broughton immediately sought permission to address the Council, and appeared at 7 p.m. on 22 September.
He arrived nervous: 'Should I break down, why then *actum est*'.
Broughton had little certain information and no time for consultation.
Neither Lowe nor Nicholson the Speaker had shown him the bill. He
had sighted only a manuscript draft at Cowper's the night before. 'We
were entitled to fair play', he told the Council from the bar as the clerk
handed him a copy.[62]

In its opening flourish Lowe's bill offered the clergy increased dividends
from their non-existent endowments and hedged with safeguards their
imagined benefices. The bill's chief aim, however, was to constitute
the Supreme Court a court of ecclesiastical appeal in all disputes over
ecclesiastical temporalities, and to restrict initiative in such actions to
lay trustees. 'The Bill was an atrocious attempt to oust the Bishop of
all control', Broughton claimed. 'It was generated out of hatred to the
Church universally, and partly to me personally.' It meant the bishop

could deprive a clergyman who turned Arian, deist or Monophysite of his licence but not of his living unless the lay trustees agreed to institute action in the Supreme Court. It meant, too, that a clergyman could turn drunkard, thief, or adulterer and retain his living if the lay trustees condoned the matter. No bishop in England was so powerless and no bishop in Christendom so humiliated, Broughton said. Moreover, for a clergyman, for instance, to be tried for drunkenness in his own home by a layman who could be drunk at home with impunity denied the principle of trial by one's peers. Just as the soldier who deserted was court-martialled so the clergyman who drank and swore to excess should be judged by men bound to the same discipline, and only an ecclesiastical court preserved that tradition. Finally, Broughton condemned the bill as partial. It left Polding and other church leaders lords over their clergy. 'If there is to be a deliverance from subjection let it be general deliverance', Broughton demanded. The Legislative Council had shrunk the Church of England to equality with the other churches yet behaved as if it were different. 'It is not competent for this Council', he concluded, 'seeing that it does not recognise the Church of England as the established church of the colony—that it does not confer on it any peculiar advantages or distinctions, to interfere in the temporal concerns of that Church.'[63]

Broughton finished at 9 p.m. and left the lamp-laden atmosphere of the chamber for a balmy night's drive to Tusculum. Inside, the chamber was silent except for the murmurs of an exchange between Lowe and Darvall, the bill's seconder. They decided to proceed. The prospect of an occasional inebriate or reverend heretic ought not to obscure the lift in morale a security of tenure would give the clergy, Lowe said. After all, what was heresy in the nineteenth century? 'An incumbent in Surrey not only turned Roman Catholic but became chaplain to the Archbishop of Cologne, and yet retained possession of his living', Lowe instanced. Should New South Wales boast any less a liberty! To keep the bill alive Lowe agreed to accept amendments in Committee that did not tamper with the principle of security of tenure. Darvall expressed great relief at Lowe's concession. The bishop's plea had touched him; and in seconding the bill Darvall foreshadowed an amendment replacing the Supreme Court with an ecclesiastical tribunal comprising bishop and beneficed clerical assessors. The bishop was a just man, Darvall said; and he believed tenure of benefice sufficient to guarantee an independent judgement by the clerical assessors.

Lowe was horrified. Darvall's amendment turned a bill designed to destroy episcopal authority into one that gave the bishop an ecclesiastical court of undoubted legality. For ten years Plunkett had outwitted the bishop's efforts to erect such a court under his letters patent and now Lowe's amended bill was about to hand him one! Rather than risk that Lowe cast his bill to 'the bats and the moles' and forgot about the clergy.[64]

The bill was ill fated from the start. Firm voluntarists like Robertson from Port Phillip and Lang believed the Council's only interference in ecclesiastical matters should be to repeal the Church Act. Cowper thought the bill hasty and possibly in conflict with the English Church

Discipline Act of 1840. Windeyer, who supported Lowe, admitted no
one had thought of that. Wentworth simply sat mute. Lowe itched
for the leadership of the Council and Wentworth left him to count his
followers. A newspaper rumour that the bishop had once refused Lowe
ordination called in question his motive, and the *Atlas*'s portrait of
Broughton lacked authenticity. Would a despot retire from the power
of the Councils? Would a lover of stone altars order their removal from
colonial churches? What the clergy *might* need, the *Sydney Morning
Herald* suggested, 'was protection against a successor who might not
be so judicious and considerate as the present Bishop of Australia'.[65]

Throughout this challenge the clergy stood firmly by Broughton.
He fought for their stipends, never demanded extra work without added
remuneration, never gave building priority over stipends, regularly
petitioned the Executive Council to increase their allowances under
the Church Act, and in better days badgered the SPG into extending
the subsidies on their stipends.[66] In 1844 the clergy had approved his
management by requesting he return on their behalf to England and
negotiate improved diocesan conditions.[67] Not one of them turned to
the Legislative Council for relief. After a decade of Council interference
to shrink the privileges of the Church of England, who expected a golden
handshake from it in 1846?

The troublesome clergy, from whom Lowe might have expected
support, owed Broughton most. Seven were debt ridden in 1846; some
fled English creditors, others had speculated in land and sheep, some
simply overspent, and one dodged repaying passage money borrowed
for a holiday to England. Their behaviour scandalized Broughton. 'But
the notoriety of a clergyman's pecuniary embarrassment does produce
such serious and lasting effects that I would decline no possible effort
to hide it from the world', he said. Broughton interceded with creditors,
put up personal bonds, offered advances against future stipends, expanded
stipends from building funds, and paid small debts from his own pocket.
Between 1844 and 1846 he risked £1000 staving off 'importunate clai-
mants', and only one clergyman failed to reimburse him.[68] All of them
for good reason stood by him in 1846.

Even those he disciplined stood by him. Wilkinson, whom he suspended for negligence and disrespect in 1830, personally petitioned
against Lowe's bill as 'unnecessary and dangerous'. Indeed Wilkinson's
career witnessed to the justice of Broughton's methods. In ten years
he moved from suspension to Ashfield with church, parsonage and the
maximum stipend.[69] Wilkinson had qualified by Broughton's strict
rules for promotion and received his due. Broughton's basic rule was
pertinacity; the clergyman who remained at his station ultimately improved his position. Naylor's was a typical case. He had few gifts but
after seven years caring for orphans and five for prisoners Broughton
appointed him to Carcor at £200 a year with £50 added by the SPG
for 'faithful service'.[70] When in a misunderstanding the SPG appointed
a London clergyman direct to Geelong at £250 a year Broughton complained that some colonial clergyman 'who had laboured very faithfully
in an inconvenient and undesirable parish' had been deprived of pro-

motion.[71] Broughton awarded talent more speedily. Stiles went quickly to Windsor on an above average stipend and Broughton engineered him a Lambeth M.A. He found Cowper a D.D. He brought the talented young Sconce into a tough Sydney district after the briefest country trial. As a general rule Broughton tested new recruits in an established district then sent them to tackle a deprived area. Colonial conditions did not allow him to nurture vocations; it was trial by ordeal. Those who complained he shifted; and those, like Edmondston, who walked out he shunned.[72]

Edmondston's walk-out in 1846 came too late for Lowe to profit by. After seven years in the colony Edmondston requested sick leave and indiscreetly vowed to stay abroad. Broughton heard of this and to force Edmondston's return refused to countersign the letters of testimony essential for employment in England. Imagine the injurious effect on the diocese, Broughton explained, if all the clergy wandered off in search of employment, naval, military or ecclesiastical, whenever they found conditions disagreeable. Clergy came voluntarily to the colony at considerable expense to the SPG, and the bishop worked hard to provide them with stipend, church and parsonage. He expected ten years service. He allowed any clergyman two years off for medical treatment abroad or eighteen months leave on half pay to visit England after ten years. By this rule Edmondston had three years to serve. Once abroad, however, Edmondston petitioned archbishops and bishops against Broughton's unreasonable demand, and finding them rigid published an appeal to the Church of England at large. That embarrassed the SPG into asking Broughton to relent. He refused. Then, when after two more years of wrangling the SPG finally prevailed on Edmondston to return, the ten years had almost elapsed and Broughton signed Edmondston's letters of testimony to keep him out.[73]

Three chaplains, however, used the occasion of Lowe's bill to query the wisdom of Broughton's exclusive control of patronage. They did not question the justice of Broughton's administration, but sought to have the Church Temporalities Act amended to provide for lay trustees to fill vacancies by direct negotiation with chaplains. The Reverend W. B. Clarke led the three. His slow progress in the colony surprised the SPG, but by Broughton's standards he began poorly. He rejected Campbell Town in favour of the King's School in 1839, then petulantly resigned within twelve months and contrived an invitation to a proposed new parish in Parramatta. Broughton suspected Clarke would take private pupils in competition with the ailing King's School and sent him instead to Dural, an area the bishop admitted was literally 'undeserving of attention'. Feeling desperate by 1844 Clarke accepted Broughton's offer of the new parish of St Thomas on the north shore knowing he could not occupy it for two years. Within months the parishoners of Campbell Town petitioned for Clarke to come there but Broughton ruled him obliged to go to St Thomas's. 'My wish is to consult the wishes and interests of the clergy unless there be a question between private inclination and public service, when of course the latter must have the preference', he explained.[74] Broughton twice sacrificed Clarke to the general good of the diocese. So Clarke asked that the Legislative Council adopt 'such a measure as would secure the temporal interest of the clergy without interfering with the discipline of the Church'.[75]

Broughton did not doubt that as a bishop he had an exceptional authority. 'I know myself to be herein declaring the true sentiments of the Church whose representative I am', he once pronounced quite unblushingly at the laying of the foundation stone of a new church.[76] Broughton did not speak with certainty because he was consecrated; rather he was consecrated because he had already learned to speak with certainty and had shown himself to the church to be informed in the study of the apostolic tradition and both willing to preserve and teach it. Episcopal consecration simply gave Broughton grace to fulfil the brief to preserve within the Church of England the religious truths founded in scripture, expounded in the early church, and confirmed by the Reformers. Broughton based his certainty on the triple authority of scripture, reason, and antiquity. Religious truth must have its origin in scripture alone without appeal to unwritten tradition. The writing of Christian antiquity to about 400 AD could help establish the meaning of scripture. Beyond that date Broughton found nothing reliable: 'The more I look into the Fathers of the fourth and succeeding century (Augustine and so forth) the more . . . I think you may pick out of them almost all the beginnings of Popery'. By reason Broughton meant an argument presented as a series of extracts from scripture, the early Fathers (Origen where possible), and the Reformers, linked together to demonstrate that Christendom had a long-established opinion on a matter. Despite his preference for the era before 400 AD Broughton sought the approval of the Reformers because he believed their scholarly sifting of the early Christian tradition the best guide to the early church's writings. A glimpse at Broughton's own doctrinal pamphlets on baptism and Anglican orders showed them to be a flood of quotations between mountains of references, and at times truth looked close to being numbers. Where possible an analogy added force to an argument, and Broughton himself had argued for the efficacy of lay-baptism by pointing to the efficacy of lay preaching in the New Testament. Where scripture, the early Fathers, the Reformers, and an analogy harmonized, Broughton believed the truth clear and conformity a reasonable demand.[77] 'A bishop should act decidedly in expressing his opinion and in enforcing compliance', he said; and he banned stone altars, prohibited the administration of provisional baptism, and discouraged chaplains from placing on the altar at the offertory the voluntary offerings of those who departed the church between matins and Holy Communion to avoid suggesting the absent could buy the benefit of the sacrament. Broughton always elaborated his reasons, replied to contrary opinion, then demanded conformity.[78] Even the clergy who disagreed appreciated a 'tight rein' in such matters, Broughton maintained. Most were SPG recruits; and beneath the 'variety of shades of opinion' natural to an educated clergy they shared the Tractarian belief in apostolic authority.[79]

The concord among his clergy gratified Broughton, though he admitted to welcoming some added bother if it meant receiving extra clergy.

The church in Sydney, which he had carefully groomed, pleased him most. 'Indeed there are three or four or even more of those around me who in every estimable property, moral or professional, may be set on a level with any in the whole Church', he boasted.[80] Allwood at St James was the rock; a godly scholar, a personable but Christian pastor of sober judgement and unquestionable integrity. Walsh at Christ Church had brushed by the cloak of Demosthenes. In 1838 he had preached in Sydney *en route* to Hobart and got no further. Sconce at St Andrews was Christ's cavalier on a Tractarian mount. He had the style, enthusiasm, and innocent abandon to grapple with Sydney's more squalid districts. Cowper at St Philips had the opposite appeal; he held men's confidence, Broughton noted. Among younger recruits Broughton singled out the Reverend F. T. C. Russell as a 'very superior man', and under his own eye set him to work among the tenements by Tusculum.[81] To secure even better talent for Sydney Broughton spoke of funding chorister scholarships at St James Grammar School for the future cathedral and three residentiary canonries to attract scholars and preachers to the colony. Gladstone had already suggested Sydney become a metropolitical city, and though Broughton blushed at the thought of becoming archbishop he believed Sydney deserved the dignity.[82] Indeed, in 1846 Broughton congratulated all the clergy for their achievement in founding the church in a new land. Their apparent error, he said, was to have done it peacefully. 'Why should we be charged with subserviency because we practise those precepts which we ought to teach?', Broughton asked those who advocated legislative interference. 'Why is the fact that they [the clergy] live in harmony to be perverted into an argument that they dare not differ?'[83]

While the Church of England Clergyman's Benefices bill disappeared, Lowe remained. 'The man's malice is quite inexpungible', Broughton said; and he saw the *Atlas* welcome-in 1847 with page-one broadsides against him. Four times in eight weeks it abused his land policy and infelicitous Latin prose as twin colonial tragedies, claiming the one had bankrupted squatters while the other corrupted the students at Lyndhurst.[84] As that wore thin late in February 1847 Broughton clashed with the *Atlas* over transportation. While the newspaper advocated the revival of convict road-builders Broughton petitioned the queen against them. His daughter Phoebe was again pregnant, and the first generation of Australian-born Broughtons was on its way to inheriting a portion of this new land. He was jealous for their future and told the queen there was no difference between distributing convicts around New South Wales and parcelling them out to the farmers of Kent. Broughton also encouraged chaplains to be active in local anti-transportation rallies. In Sydney the sight of Broughton's protégé Charles Cowper in the chair and the clergy in the audience at anti-transportation rallies excited the *Atlas* to denounce the whole anti-transportation movement as a front for a Puseyite attack on colonial liberties. The plot was subtle but plain to the *Atlas*. A clique of Puseyites led by the pious prig Cowper, Campbell of the wharf, Kemp of the press, Dillon of the law, and 'that good soul Martha, the old nurse of the paralytic ward in the benevolent

asylum', were exploiting anti-transportation sentiments to promote
Cowper's political image around Sydney as a prelude to standing him
against Wentworth at the next election. What motive could a Puseyite
Cowper have in defeating Wentworth other than a desire to see a sacer-
dotal despotism replace the present liberties of the colony?[85]

With the charge that anti-transportation was a Puseyite inspired
takeover of the colony the *Atlas* began its journey into the never-never.
When it began as a newspaper in 1844 the *Atlas* filled a gap left in the
radical press as old champions like the *Sydney Gazette, Monitor* and
Australian grew conservative or fell silent. They were harassed days,
and the paper sold well by filling page one with new plans for trade,
credit, insolvency and the constitution, with a chuckle at Broughton
on page three. By 1847 the paper scorned Broughton on page one and
reported intercolonial news on page three, and amid a returning prosperity trundled out the doctrine that the colony's future depended on
Broughton's disappearance and perhaps the clergy's too. 'The despotism
of Bishop Broughton is the firebrand which shall enkindle revolution',
the *Atlas* declared and began to vanish. Yet it ranted to the end, left
a scar on Broughton and the church, and burdened the colony with
irrelevant political comment.[86]

End of an Era

I candidly acknowledge that *all* the great interests in an attachment to which I was brought up, and which have so contracted sacredness in my regard, *have* sunk and *are* sinking.

Broughton to Coleridge 4 July 1848

In 1847 London was more the centre of the bishop's anxieties than Sydney. A Whig take over of government in June 1846 had driven Gladstone from office with the new bishoprics unfilled, and Broughton grew apprehensive as silence on the subject extended into March 1847. Before leaving office Gladstone had approached eight candidates for Morpeth, including the Reverend Henry Wilberforce, but none considered a colonial bishopric a prize.[1] Then Lord Grey took over. He had little confidence in Archbishop Howley and rejected any suggestion that Her Majesty's government should acknowledge Broughton's generosity in founding the sees by appointing men of a similar churchmanship able to work cordially with him. 'The Secretary of State must exercise his own judgment', Grey told Howley. 'No right on the part of the Archbishop of Canterbury to recommend the appointment could be recognised.'[2]

Grey favoured the evangelical party and complained to his wife of Howley's poor recommendations. One, the Reverend Henry Eley vicar of Beaconsfield, actually turned out to be paralysed. Lady Grey mentioned this over dinner to the Bishop of Bath and Wells who promised to draw it to the attention of Mr Thornton the banker, 'a great authority in ecclesiastical matters' with pull at Church Missionary Society headquarters. Thornton supplied three names and Grey selected two for Melbourne and Morpeth.[3] Howley considered two CMS candidates an unattractive proposition. Apart from their obvious lack of sympathy with Broughton, CMS appointees had given Selwyn trouble. Howley decided to co-operate in the appointment of one of Grey's evangelicals and to hope Grey would acquiesce in the nomination of one high churchman. Howley suggested sending a Cambridge Fellow, Charles Perry, to the more remote see of Melbourne, and installing an Oxford Fellow, J. Ley, closer to Broughton at Morpeth. A Cambridge evangelical and an Oxford high churchman—who could take exception to that? Grey didn't.[4] Perry accepted, but Ley withdrew for reasons of health. The Oxford Fellows rallied with the name of the Reverend George Hunting-ford, a Fellow of New College and a protegé of the Tractarian writer Moberly. Grey rejected him as a Puseyite. Howley angrily demanded to know on whose recommendation. He could deal with a difficult Colonial Office and a reluctant clergy, Howley said, but not a Secretary of State in league with 'an undisclosed confidant'.[5] Grey remained mute. Howley's secret antagonist was Lady Grey's dinner guest the Bishop of Bath and Wells to whom Grey passed on everything for scrutiny.[6] After that Howley abandoned Oxford and suggested a country vicar William Tyrrell, lost in the quiet of the Duke of Buccleuch's estates in Hampshire. Tyrrell lived too close to Moberly to be above suspicion Grey's spies reported, but the appearance of his name on a CMS subscription list redeemed that. Tyrrell was quite unknown, not remarkable but not peculiar, reported the local archdeacon. Grey nominated him.[7]

When the nine-month hunt for two episcopal candidates ended their letters patent had still to be drafted. Diocesan boundaries remained undecided and their names disputed. Should it be Port Phillip or Melbourne? The Colonial Office thought Port Phillip but Judge Coleridge insisted Broughton wanted Melbourne. Should it be Morpeth, Maitland or Newcastle? 'None were likely to be important enough to carry the rank of an episcopal See', Broughton predicted, but he nominated Maitland. The Colonial Office chose Newcastle.[8] There was, too, the question of episcopal jurisdiction. The issue of new letters patent provided an excellent opportunity for mending disciplinary arrangements. Broughton had sent the Archbishop of Canterbury a list of disciplinary matters requiring redefinition in any new issue of letters patent, and Gladstone raised others. Should Broughton be given only a titular seniority or seniority with appellate jurisdiction? Should a college of colonial bishops or the Archbishop of Canterbury be the ultimate court of appeal? Could the colonial bishops be given legal power to consecrate their own succes-sors?[9] Howley and Blomfield wanted maximum autonomy for the colonial churches. The Archbishop set up a committee with Archdeacon Harrison as his personal representative, Archdeacon Hale of the Overseas Bishopric Fund, Bishop Coleridge formerly of Barbados, and the jurist Sir Hubert Fust, to recommend changes. The committee met, discovered its ignorance of Australian affairs, and adjourned to await Nixon's arrival in December 1846.[10]

Broughton ideally wanted to be in London himself. 'If any of my friends had even casually expressed an opinion that any good was to be done by my coming I might not have hesitated', he told the SPG. Instead he briefed Nixon *en route* to England. Nixon had made the worst of a bad set of letters patents and Broughton feared the Colonial Office might skirt the defects in the letters patent by blaming the impasse in Hobart on Nixon's impetuous temperament. By the time Nixon arrived Grey had disbanded the Archbishop's committee and instructed James Stephen to consult with Harrison, the Archbishop's secretary, and resolve the issues quickly.[11] Stephen had drafted the original letters patent and pronounced them adequate except for a provision subordinating the new bishop to Broughton as metropolitan. He thought colonial bishops men of questionable judgement and unfit for an extended authority. 'The choice made by the Bishops of their Archdeacons in the West Indies, and in Australia, has not usually been well made', he instanced and explained to Grey that 'a Bishop going to such a place ... with such a disproportionate rank, is sorely tempted ... to attach to his person some dependents on whose deference he can count, and whose society will relieve the tedium of Colonial life.' Harrison argued for change but relented before the prospect of delaying indefinitely the new bishops' departure. As Broughton feared both Stephen and Harrison blamed Nixon's problems on his rash temperament and cited Broughton's own forbearance in avoiding conflict as testimony to the letters patent being workable. The new letters patent were imitations of the old drafted by a bureaucrat familiar with the road from Weymouth to London but untouched by the pleas of distant bishops assailed by governors and councils. Stephen believed his judgement impeccable in ecclesiastical matters and said so. 'I do not doubt that my answers are the right answers', he told Grey on a memorandum dismissing a colonial bishop's disquiet at his new letters patent.[12]

The letters patent were completed and the date of the consecration fixed only to reveal another crisis. 'The whole subject of these Australian bishoprics appears to be involved in difficulties so little foreseen by Mr Gladstone', James Stephen complained on learning that the surplus funds in Schedule C which Gladstone earmarked for the new bishoprics did not exist. Broughton had long since persuaded the Executive Council to distribute them to local projects; Perry's residence disappeared in twenty-one small donations to local church buildings and £500 reserved for Tyrrell's stipend had gone to the missionaries beyond the boundaries. Moreover, Gladstone miscalculated badly in believing that £10 000 invested in colonial lands would provide the £333 6s 8d promised to each stipend by the Overseas Bishopric Fund. The best land Broughton could invest in would not yield half that for years.[13] In short, Perry and Tyrrell could find themselves in Australia without a residence and £270 each from Broughton's salary as a stipend. Broughton urged the Colonial Office to reconsider Gladstone's financial arrangement. In April 1847 Grey called the bishops-designate to the Colonial Office and urged them to reconsider their appointments.[14]

The Archbishop of Canterbury postponed the consecration while the SPG scampered for money. A month lapsed. Then, on 29 June 1847 Westminster Abbey was handed over to the SPG and the bishops consecrated in a blaze of publicity. 'There has not been such a Communion [Service] seen in this our day, nor, as we believe, for ages in the Church of England', one journalist reported. Perry and Tyrrell sang their way through three hours of Tallis, received an apostolic commission, and left by the great west door for the highways of England to raise their sustenance for the next few years.[15] By the time they departed in September 1847 Broughton had reports of their doings; Tyrrell will be 'a co-adjuator after my own heart' he predicted, but Perry worried him. On the eve of his consecration Perry had embraced the dissenters too warmly, saying: 'If any man will assist me in the distribution of Bibles, I will not ask him what are his opinions'. Broughton disagreed, and had just sacked McLeay as chairman of the Diocesan Committee for expressing a similar sentiment in accepting concurrently the chairmanship of both the Diocesan Committee and the local Bible Society. 'Such sentiments will mar both his [Perry's] comfort and his usefulness', Broughton warned. 'I hope he *will* come by Sydney, that he may have the opportunity at least of benefiting by warnings which my experience will *justify* me in communicating.'[16]

Tyrrell's appointment both pleased and embarrassed Broughton. Back in mid-1846 when he had suppressed Allwood's candidacy for a bishopric to free him for the theological college Broughton was unaware that the Archbishop of Canterbury had already authorized the preparation of letters patent for Allwood's consecration in Sydney as bishop of Newcastle. Broughton learned of this in November 1846, congratulated Allwood, and lamented his loss. 'It is due to the church that he *should* go where his talents and virtues will make him useful to many', Broughton commented, and immediately handed the administration of the northern districts to Allwood. Around Sydney they called Allwood 'the bishop elect'.[17] However, while Allwood's letters patent were still only part prepared Nixon left for London and deprived the colony of the three bishops essential for a local act of consecration. Before the Archbishop of Canterbury could make alternative arrangements Broughton's letter of July 1846 arrived indicating Allwood's disinclination for high office, and the appointment was withdrawn.[18] This news reached the colony in July 1847 and dismayed Allwood. When Broughton enquired whether he would like to be bishop Allwood had felt bound to protest his unfitness, but had he known the Archbishop of Canterbury wanted him a bishop he would have accepted. 'God can work with humble instruments', Allwood reminded Broughton, and was the more embarrassed that it might appear he had been hastily appointed, investigated, and judged unfit. To allay rumour Broughton made known his part in the matter, and arranged for the clergy and leading laymen to present Allwood with 'a very pleasing address on the occasion of his not being appointed to the bishopric of Newcastle'.[19]

Broughton soon detected a streak of timidity in Allwood to cut short his misgivings. In December 1847 Allwood entreated Broughton to mark the opening of St James theological college at Lyndhurst with a Latin oration and promised to reply in kind. Being a public occasion Broughton demurred but complied, then sat open-mouthed as Allwood replied in elegant English. The press ridiculed Broughton's pomposity and congratulated Allwood for a down-to-earth attitude. When Broughton solicited an explanation Allwood admitted to an attack of nerves on the podium. The incident stuck in Broughton's throat. Perhaps Allwood lacked the pluck for a pioneer bishopric and performed better in a lesser command. Pluck or not 'he has escaped an arduous, and really in this colony, an unthankful duty', commented a fellow chaplain who had watched sympathetically Broughton's progress through insult and raillery.[20]

Broughton's own letters patent were redrafted creating him Metropolitan of Australasia and Bishop of *Sydney* rather than *Australia*. James Stephen had long wanted to be rid of the 'barbarous innovation' of naming sees after places not cities, and Broughton approved provided it didn't cost him money. 'Having already paid some three or four hundred pounds for the Letters Patent which were given me in 1836 ... I should not be willing to incur such expense over again,' he said.[21] Being Metropolitan bewildered Broughton briefly. 'It is more agreeable to me, and always was, to obey than to command', he confided to Coleridge, but quickly realized the more agreeable consequences of a wider command. He had long felt that without 'uniformity of views upon all the great points' the Church of England would not match the force of Rome's tight organization or the beguiling freedoms of nonconformity and liberality. Twice Broughton had attempted to confer with Nixon and Selwyn in Sydney. Once Nixon arrived but Selwyn didn't even acknowledge the correspondence. As Metropolitan Broughton finally had the authority to summon the bishops to a conference; so he pronounced the new rank 'proper'.[22]

Indeed, Joshua Watson's wilder suggestion of an autonomous patriarchate of Australasia was not far wide of Broughton's thought on the future. He favoured increasing local independence. He thought recent reports showed English bishops lacked resolution in their opposition to government and he did not care to be bound by their decisions. He thought their acquiescence in the suppression of Welsh bishoprics most melancholy. Even Samuel Wilberforce, whom he singled out as the coming leader of the bench, went 'about it and about it' never firmly tackling the government.[23] Even worse was the full story of Grey's veto on Huntingford's appointment to Morpeth. In effect a clergyman judged fit for episcopal office by the highest ecclesiastical authority was pronounced doctrinally unsound by a layman and, in a 'perfectly irresponsible' exercise of power, barred from office without appeal. Broughton vowed never to suffer its repetition in Australasia and said 'it will be most desirable to propose the question to the Primate whether, if a Metropolitan be created here, he ... should not have authority to consecrate such additional bishops as the exigencies of the Church may require, without the fomality of applying to the Crown for Letters Patent'.[24] The queen's letters patent, he puffed, were 'nothing more than waste parchment'.[25]

The Reverend John Duffus helped Broughton prove them waste parchment. Broughton had once rescued Duffus from debt with a personal loan and after that Duffus did well. Indeed, Broughton counted him one of the colony's more successful chaplains. He packed 250 people a week into his church at Liverpool and it came as no surprise to Broughton that Duffus's health should suffer. After seven years service Broughton granted him three months leave in January 1846. Duffus rested at Botany Bay and often rode over to relax at Jones' Chippendale tavern when, one day, George Armytage Esq., a Pitt Street evangelical, spied him smoking and behaving as if he had been drinking liquor in the taproom or was about to. That contravened the seventy-fifth canon of 1604 which forbade the clergy to enter a tavern except for 'honest necessity'. Armytage compelled Broughton to investigate. The bishop appointed five clerical assessors and cited Duffus to appear before them, with counsel, and answer the charge. Duffus came with Robert Lowe who minced the evidence and produced 106 witnesses, including a Miss Forbes who frequented Jones' tavern, willing to testify that Duffus's behaviour was orderly at the tavern and exemplary at home. Broughton dismissed the case with relief.[26]

But Duffus had no peace. He had gone to Botany Bay in January 1846 to recover from the shock of getting Miss Forbes pregnant. He contemplated his future and decided to baptize the child, place it in an orphanage, and after marrying Miss Forbes off to another parishioner, Mr Bull, to continue the liaison. The strain of unloved wedlock loosened the tongue of the new Mrs Bull and she sang the praises of her true love to her husband. Mr Bull summoned the church wardens to his house where Mrs Bull again sang her song, and on 14 August 1847 the wardens charged Duffus with incontinence and adultery. Broughton, usually sceptical of charges laid by laymen against the clergy, found this affadavit a catalogue of scandal precise in place, date and deed, and not to be dismissed. He appointed another five clerical assessors and cited Duffus to appear before them with counsel. This time Broughton offered to pay Duffus's legal costs. But Duffus declared himself above the need of counsel. 'My own consciousness of my innocence shall be my only advocate', he replied to Broughton. Later he engaged a solicitor. The clerical assessors sat for twelve days and recommended that Duffus stand trial before the bishop. The rest was a formality. Duffus took a fit, boycotted the trial, and did not challenge the evidence. Broughton withdrew his licence and closed the case to spare Duffus and his wife embarrassment.[27]

During the trial Duffus had tried to dodge judgement. He argued in a letter, quoting Blackstone, that England's ecclesiastical law, unlike its common law, did not extend automatically to the colonies. It required to be specifically enacted in every case and this had not been done for New South Wales. In effect Duffus maintained that due to legislative oversight a colonial clergyman's personal conduct was exempt from episcopal visitation. The argument was quite 'indecent', Broughton said, and more scandalous than the original misdemeanour. It was also possibly true. Robert Lowe had already raised the argument during debate on the Church of England Clergymen's Benefices bill and Broughton feared someone might make it the basis for a Supreme Court challenge to his disciplinary authority. In delivering judgement against Duffus Broughton propped up his authority with a variety of other arguments.[28]

Broughton asked himself a series of questions. Firstly, did the Christian constitution, as distinct from the ecclesiastical enactments of any state, require a bishop to be vigilant over his presbyters' behaviour? Broughton found I Timothy 5.19 did. Secondly, had the Church of England adopted the practice of I Timothy 5.19? It had. Both in Article Twenty-Six and the Ordinal of the Book of Common Prayer it enjoined on bishops the responsibility of correcting and punishing clerical offences against

God's word. Thirdly, had common law judgements acquiesced in the right of bishops to discipline clergy for deeds not considered offences in common law courts? Broughton found the evidence abundant, and he stressed the point as no one denied the full application of English common law in the colony. That left one hurdle. Broughton feared the hair-splitting lawyers might argue that since Broughton's appointment rested on letters patent derived from an ecclesiastical constitution that possibly did not extend to the colonies, the common law courts of New South Wales were not bound to recognize that he had within the colony the same jurisdiction as English bishops within England. Against this Broughton argued that an act of the parliament at Westminster, 6 and 7 Victoria C. 35, which clearly applied to the colony and could be the subject of action in its common law courts, referred to and clearly recognized the existence of the Diocese of Australia and *ipso facto* the Bishop of Australia. Put together Broughton's argument was, firstly, that the common law recognized him as a bishop in the Church of England; and secondly, that the Thirty-nine Articles, the Ordinal of the Book of Common Prayer, and the common law courts of England all recognize the Church of England as having adopted the Christian constitution of the New Testament era, and that constitution required a bishop to investigate accusations against the conduct of presbyters.[29]

'An able defence', Charles Kemp noted in his diary. He instructed his editor to cover the matter in the *Sydney Morning Herald* and stress the bishop's forbearance in the face of a crime 'revolting in the extreme'. No legal challenge followed and the Duffus case closed quietly with the *Atlas* underscoring the bishop's leniency in judgement as a tacit admission that he was obviously unsure of his authority.[30] Instead of pursuing the Duffus case the *Atlas* took up the cause of the Reverend Charles Woodward whom Broughton had refused to re-employ after resigning as chaplain at Port Macquarie on 30 September 1847. Broughton's refusal was a routine application of rule applied to clergy who forsook their charge, but secretly he was pleased to be done with Woodward. 'He has not behaved well', Broughton reported earlier to the SPG. Woodward had arrived in 1839, achieved little in his first appointment, lost government subsidies by failing to raise public subscriptions, and asked for the move to Port Macquarie where he expected to succeed the aged Cross. Unfortunately Cross did not resign and treated Woodward as a curate. Broughton asked Woodward to persevere and was negotiating the purchase of a government residence for him when he resigned. Broughton counted it Woodward's second failure, and dropped him.[31]

Woodward appeared wronged. 'More Broughtonic Despotism', bellowed the *Atlas* and called for a schism. It invited the able, eloquent, educated, and liberal Woodward to take over a vacant chapel in Macquarie Street and raise the beginnings of a Free Church of England. 'This is the first step towards an eruption in the Episcopalian church in this colony, and we shall not be at all surprised to see an extensive secession from her ranks', the *Atlas* forecast. One reader sent along

£10 but there was no rush. Woodward gave the matter no encouragement. He was content to turn schoolmaster and preach occasional sermons for the masonic brotherhood, an innocuous though superfluous organization in Broughton's opinion.[32]

Broughton eventually emerged the stronger from both incidents. The Duffus affair dramatized his need for disciplinary authority while Woodward's indifference to his self-appointed guardians exposed the *Atlas* as meddlesome. The legal challenge Broughton had anticipated prompted him into a better understanding of the foundations of colonial episcopacy, and Grey's intervention to prevent Huntingford's appointment as bishop set him in pursuit of greater autonomy for colonial churches. By 1848 Broughton saw his goals more clearly and was freer to achieve them. On 31 December 1847 he lopped South Australia from his diocese, on 31 January 1848 the Hunter River District, on 13 February 1848 Port Phillip. He created Cowper Archdeacon of Cumberland to escape much routine administration, and on the sixtieth anniversary of the founding of the colony shifted his episcopal throne from St James church to St Andrews to inaugurate the Diocese of Sydney and his rule as Metropolitan of Australasia.[33]

For Broughton the highlight of these changes had occurred on 18 January 1848. Late that morning he rode into Liverpool after two harrowing weeks on horseback in the flooded Illawarra district. At sixty this summer journey, coming on top of a nine-hundred-mile visitation the previous November, had exhausted the bishop. At Liverpool Broughton caught sight of Tyrrell and revived. Within twenty-four hours he had the new bishop installed in Tusculum where beneath portraits of several Coleridges, Joshua Watson and old Dr Keate, and surrounded by wills, insurance policies, accounts, and sundry instructions neatly displayed should he not return, Broughton fed Tyrrell his impression of colonial affairs. He talked for two weeks.[34]

Broughton told Tyrrell he was to govern a scattered diocese from a detached office and a six-roomed parsonage at Morpeth. He would inherit few sound parishes and an unequal share of the vast districts beyond the boundaries, for Broughton had ridded himself of all but one. Finance would be Tyrrell's most pressing problem. Broughton said there was nothing in Schedule C for new parishes; perhaps something in future land funds for outlying districts if the recommendation survived Legislative Council hostility; perhaps something, too, in the old Church and Schools Corporation land trust, worth £4000 a year, if they could agree to revive the legal battle for its control.[35] Where, then, should Tyrrell turn for regular aid? Certainly not the Colonial Office, Broughton advised. After eleven years it hadn't even got the Church Act straight. The local governing class was practically atheist in its unconcern, and the pastoralists, beguiled by 'unbounded acres and uncountable flocks', unreliable. Concentrate on the middle classes, Broughton advised. Their contribution and SPG aid would be Tyrrell's only reliable support.[36]

Broughton told Tyrrell the annual religious returns to government showed a steady improvement in church attendance, but warned that colonial churchgoers had sounder habits than principles. They were natural latitudinarians. 'They are so taught to hate *exclusiveness* that they are startled at *Truth* because it requires them to embrace one view in preference to others', Broughton lamented. Consequently, being busy folk and without established insititutions to reinforce tradition, they all too willingly co-operated with others, especially the Wesleyans. Bishops and clergy had therefore to stand inflexibly by church principles to offset that latitudinarianism and brush off all jibes of bigotry. Broughton instanced the case of the 'earnest' Mrs Chisholm who once sought his patronage for female immigration. Though quite above scheming herself she was a well known Roman Catholic and Broughton feared support for her in this instance could be misconstrued as a general approval for co-operation with papists in other ventures. Broughton refused her use of his name, gave her £5, and raised no objection to Mrs Broughton working closely with her. Broughton behaved the same towards the Reverend Dr Gregory, Polding's amiable offsider who had just called to welcome Tyrrell. Broughton refused to sign a public testimonial when Gregory departed in ill-health but called privately to express his regrets. The occasional clash with his own Diocesan Committee, as when he opposed lay leaders supporting O'Connell in the 1843 elections or told McLeay to resign the chair of either the Diocesan Committee or Bible Society, stemmed from the same sentiment. 'It must be their study to keep their own faith pure', he told the Diocesan Committee again in Tyrrell's presence in January 1848. Nixon followed this policy and Broughton hoped Tyrrell would.[37]

Broughton had other tips for Tyrrell. Ignore the press. Play down church party spirit. Stress the Reformers and forget about Oxford principles. That movement had spent itself. Its early doctrines strengthened the church, its late ones were a liability. 'So far am I from desiring an influx of what are commonly known under the name of Oxford principles, that in my opinion the less that such a man possess of them the better', Broughton said.[38] Be vigilant against popery. Once it invited proselytes to afternoon tea-parties, now it delivered roast beef dinners to sick-bed converts. Polding had just returned with fresh instructions from Rome and £10 000 from the Queen of France for untold mischief. Who could guess what mischief that meant. Where, for instance, would the priests hired with French money stand when Britain and France clashed in the Pacific? The need for vigilance could not be overstressed. Nixon had sounded the tocsin in Tasmania, where a new Roman Catholic prelate had usurped the title of Bishop of Hobart, and Broughton hoped Tyrrell would be as vigilant.[39]

Tyrrell departed Tusculum with few illusions but thankful for the experience. In the past two weeks he had compassionately searched the eyes of the ageing bishop and realized an added responsibility. 'One thought cheered and encouraged me', he wrote to Broughton on arriving in Maitland, 'namely that I was bearing a portion of your late burdens, and that you, after so much incessant labour, and noble self denial, were enjoying the comparative ease and peace, which you so justly deserved.'[40]

The peace Tyrrell offered Sconce took away. Sconce, Broughton's protegé at St Andrews, had talked freely among the clergy of late about the Church of England being a 'fragment of St Peter's See', albeit a firm one. Broughton knew for certain only what he picked up indirectly, and maintained his confidence in Sconce. Allwood, however, flashed the bishop a warning in January 1848 by cancelling an invitation for Sconce to preach at St James. Broughton immediately quizzed Sconce's orthodoxy and on 16 January 1848 gave him three days to produce satisfactory written answers to some questions. Sconce avoided the deadline. Instead he wangled an invitation to dine with Broughton and Tyrrell, and overpowered both bishops with protestations of loyalty to the Church of England. Sconce did not deny having had doubts, but they had fled. Broughton saw nothing extraordinary in that. It was an age of doubt. Even Coleridge appeared to falter in the wake of Newman's conversion. Tyrrell advised Sconce to lay aside reading for a time and abandon his energies to pastoral work. Sconce agreed, but in taking his departure slipped Broughton some questions on St Cyprian. The curate had decided to test the bishop's orthodoxy. Sconce found Broughton's answers deficient, and on 8 February poured out his doubt and anxiety to the bishop for the first time. Broughton remained calm. Years back, Broughton had noted in Sconce a tendency to slip from shaky premises to wild conclusions more dramatically than he needed. All Sconce required was an intellectual straightening-up. Broughton did what he could on the spot and offered Sconce books carefully marked in chapter and verse for further reading. Sconce scanned these passages and when he left the books behind Broughton assumed him satisfied. On the way home Sconce called on Walsh at Christ Church 'with a light heart and fully satisfied on the Bishop's assurances that he was not yet in such a plight, but that he might still continue to retain his cure'. At a four-hour meeting a week later Sconce grew argumentative and Broughton lost patience. He told the curate to take a holiday abroad or a written test of his orthodoxy. Sconce refused to risk his unregenerate Anglican soul on the high seas and opted for the test. That was Thursday 17 February 1848. Over the following weekend he found himself continually rowing against the Thirty-nine Articles, and decided to resign first thing Monday morning. On the Sunday he drove up to Newtown to warn the Reverend Thomas Makinson that he had accidentally betrayed Makinson's theological ideas during a debate with the bishop and he could expect a call to test his orthodoxy the next week. So on Monday 21 February Makinson resigned too.[41]

'The common-weal of the Church was rent', Broughton lamented. But it was the very promptness of this final step which scandalized Broughton. That two priests could plan their defection in concert without a decent period of withdrawal like Newman's at Littlemore, or worse, could without falter one week administer a sacrament they would deny valid the next, displayed a want of candour. 'I will not speak of it with the severity which it merits lest I should be thought to speak under the influence of anger', Broughton told his clergy. He considered neither man an honest man.[42] Makinson struck him as rather cool. He had interviewed him only three days before without detecting the slightest inkling of a defection. Worse still, it turned out Walsh and Stiles had been privy to Makinson's intentions and had for a month hidden it from their bishop.[43] But Makinson's defection paled besides Sconce's. Sconce had been to Broughton as a son. They walked together, ate together, shared the same church, divided lectures at Lyndhurst, and stood side by side at public meetings. Yet Sconce had not spoken frankly to him. Never had the reserve in the bishop's nature, which Broughton admitted barred him from familiarity with others, extracted so heavy a price. 'The blow I will not effect to deny', he said, 'has made a greater breach in my happiness than any occurrence during many years have done.' Had Sconce spoken up earlier Broughton believed it could have ended differently. Rome appealed to the imagination not the intellect, and given time Broughton might have set Sconce straight.[44]

It was a gratuitous wish. Sconce had a 'morbid enthusiasm' for Mr Newman's person and opinions, and Tyrrell admitted to having a little too; but Broughton had none and he probably failed Sconce when he repudiated Hurrell Froude and post-1839 Tractarianism. Had Mrs Makinson not held out to the last the converts would have departed without warning to Broughton on 18 January 1844.[45]

Sections of the press bragged of having foretold it all. And so they had if apostolical authority, a weekly offertory, and white surplices led inevitably to Rome. Rumour had Walsh of Christ Church, Bobart of Parramatta and Stiles of Windsor lined up to follow, and possibly nine other clergy in time.[46] Everybody's fidelity was suspect, Broughton reported. Sconce attempted to carry over some of his congregation including Charles Lowe, secretary of the Lay Association. None followed him in February 1848, but Broughton had no assurance none would. Indeed, he expected the worst believing the age attracted to strong central authority. Broughton thought the circumstances of the present age, where church and state were in conflict and the church divided sharply into parties when it most needed unity to meet the combined assault of liberalism, deism, and atheism, not unlike circumstances of the age which saw the birth of papal monarchy. Ambrose, whom Broughton believed had perfected the papal system, was better trained to politics than divinity and his system enthralled those who preferred political to theological solutions for the church's problems.[47] It was possible some in New South Wales would feel the attraction. Sections of the press aggravated Broughton's uncertainty by blaming the whole fiasco on his ineptitude. This 'Abbot of Misrule', scoffed the *Atlas*, was either blind to the trend of Sconce's Puseyism and therefore incompetent, or he was rotten with the same disease. Either way he should be dropped, and since the clergy could not be trusted the laity must act directly and purge their own churches. At Parramatta they acted, hired the court-house and called a public protest against weekly collections and Puseyite surplices.[48] After that 'the art of agitation' expired. The clergy and laity closed ranks around Broughton and the twenty chaplains in and around Sydney presented him with a public pledge of their loyalty to the Church of England. That assured the bishop

there were no hidden clerical defectors in and around Sydney, but he
remained apprehensive. 'The church requires support and I need comfort', he told them. The message spread and congregations throughout
the Diocese repeated the pledge. At the St Andrews meeting parishioners
clung to the window sills to hear the proceedings; at the Lay Association
they found more pledges than they ever did pounds; and at Penrith
the congregation spoke so bluntly on the matter that the Roman Catholic
chaplain complained officially of a want of Protestant discretion in
the area.[49] Meanwhile with unyielding severity Broughton stripped
Sconce and Makinson of both licence and orders and pronounced that
they had ceased to be deacons and priests in the Church of God as completely as if they had never been admitted to those orders. 'Too much
leniency and forbearance has been shown towards those who have
abandoned their holy calling', he said, 'and an act of firmness here may
be attended with good effects even in England.' He allowed the defectors
fifteen days for appeal. Broughton took charge of Sconce's old congregation at St Andrews and gave them seventy sermons straight. Not one
defected. 'We rallied all that was good and sound', the bishop boasted,
'and the fidelity of the Church of England to their own tenets has struck
deep disappointment into the expectant party.'[50]

Broughton overplayed his hand, questioning Sconce's integrity
from pulpit, platform and press till the convert could endure it no longer.
Sconce retaliated setting out the reasons for his conversion in a pamphlet
and appealed to his former friends to think better of him than the bishop.
Broughton interpreted this as the opening of a second drive for converts
sparked off by a disappointment that Sconce came over with his wife
and children only: 'But where is your flock, Mr Sconce?' Polding was
reported to have asked.[51] Broughton decided after fifteen minutes
scanning the pamphlet that it was of no substance, but he took exception
to Sconce's accusation that he had often, in conversation, rested his
defence of the Church of England on the nauseous and blasphemous
divine Dr Jortin. Tell the clergy, Broughton wrote to Archdeacon
Cowper, 'That this assertion of Mr Sconce is so utterly disingenuous
and incorrect as to convey a falsehood'. Broughton insisted he had
referred to Dr Jortin only once on a minor matter. Sconce unluckily
found a letter proving Broughton had referred to Dr Jortin twice, and
published it.[52] 'The Bishop of Sydney is particularly unfortunate as
a controversialist and still more as a tactician', commented the extremely
Protestant *Sentinel*. A scolding match ensued with Broughton doubting
Sconce's veracity and Sconce Broughton's. Sconce expanded his tale
into three pamphlets and the Catholic press supported him. Broughton
replied point by point with the aid of the *Sydney Guardian*, a new church
newspaper. Finally in June Protestants called a halt. 'The Bishop knows
little and apparently cares little for the Christian laity of the Church
of England, which are painfully lacerated by this unbecoming and
sickening strife', wrote the *Sentinel*'s editor. Broughton had lost a sense
of proportion. In pounding Sconce he was pounding a fantasy that
Polding had hired some Italian Jesuits and tucked them away in his
monastery to master-mind a mass drive for converts.[53]

Sconce was bitter. He blamed Broughton for the loss of all his former friends. Walsh, once his go-between with the bishop, dismissed him completely with the observation that converts retained old friendships only to win converts. Charles Lowe shrank from him in the streets as from something loathsome.[54] Only Stiles, twice godfather to his children, remained friendly and Sconce turned to him for his wife's sake. Mrs Sconce pined for her old companions. In the street her friends turned away and at home she had only Polding and Dr Gregory to gaze at. 'If you could see her poor thin pale face, you would feel for the suffering *she* too has endured', Sconce wrote begging Mrs Stiles to shelter his wife at Windsor. Mrs Stiles consented and her husband took a rapping. 'I think it little short of madness', Broughton told him. 'If you were to yield to this appeal to your feelings it would prove your total ruin.' Mrs Sconce did not visit Windsor. Broughton demanded complete ostracism. Some converts would have accepted that as inevitable and many would have borne it better; but Sconce admitted to an 'almost effeminate sensibility in some matters', and to lose all his friends at the bishop's behest was more than he could suffer silently.[55] Broughton maintained no other converts followed. Sconce put the tally at seventy, claiming Polding had suppressed the figure.[56] But there were casualties of another kind. Walsh took such a whipping in the press that he had eventually to retire abroad to recuperate. Stiles lost an appointment to St Andrews. Broughton offered him the parish until 'the magnifying medium of Mr Cowper's alarms' persuaded him that Stile's close association with Sconce rendered him a liability in Sydney. Stiles fell out with Cowper and behaved coolly to Broughton for a time, offended that the bishop could doubt his loyalty. He refused to preach in Sydney for a year and declined a second offer of St Andrews in calmer times. Young Peter Beamish was a more innocent victim. He left Newcastle diocese early in 1848 and being at a loose end when Sconce walked out Broughton appointed him to assist temporarily at St Andrews. Tyrrell took alarm and warned that Beamish had some extreme Protestant opinions likely to drive Sconce's friends after him. So Broughton muzzled Beamish at St Andrews and the young curate stored up resentment.[57]

Yet there were gains. Reformation principles withstood a challenge from popery. Sydney church attendances increased. The *Sydney Guardian* emerged to fight Broughton's cause. Better still, the laity won their spurs. Their unfaltering fidelity to church and bishop so impressed Broughton that he pledged to assign them definite functions in any future scheme of synodical government.[58] Best of all it jolted the other bishops from their diocesan preoccupations. Broughton made much of his isolation. 'It has been a heavy trial to me to be compelled to pass sentence of such severity upon my own unassisted fallible judgment', he wrote to Selwyn. By return mail Selwyn announced himself ready, indeed anxious, to meet the other bishops in Sydney. In Adelaide Short thought Broughton's judgement in the affair all too fallible and in need of advice. By July Broughton had plans for an episcopal conference later in the year around October 1848.[59]

Barely had Broughton foiled Sconce when Polding scored again.

On 1 June 1848 Grey demoted Broughton below Polding at official functions.[60] It was a Roman Catholic jubilee. Twelve years ago Roman Catholics had consecrated the Church Act into the Magna Carta of colonial religious equality and ever since kept vigil by it. Little by little Church of England privilege wasted: the governor accepted Polding's episcopal dress at official functions; at civic functions the traditional toast to the bishop and clergy of the Church of England was remodelled into a toast to the clergy of New South Wales; Allwood's appointment as chaplain to the Sydney Municipal Council lasted one night; Charles Cowper's attempt to open the Legislative Council with prayer died with the suggestion; Polding visited England on full salary, whereas Broughton had had to go on half, and was received in full pontificals by the Secretary of State for Colonies. Broughton carefully tallied the changes but found few to share his anxiety as to their likely upshot. 'Politicians say "you may follow *your* course and they *theirs*"', he observed wryly, 'but I am unable to reconcile such acquiescence with my notions of what a watchman's duty is.'[61] Realizing that he enjoyed senior status by virtue of his being a member of the Executive Council Broughton made his resignation conditional upon his retaining that status. The Colonial Office, overjoyed by the offer, volunteered to enhance his rank and, subject to Legislative Council approval, to exalt him to his former station above the chief justice. James Stephen even offered to smooth the way with his relative, the colony's chief justice. Broughton rejected that as unnecessary. Grey's assurance that his present status remained wholly unaltered by his retirement from the Executive Council met his wish. It was a surprise two years later to be demoted below Polding.[62]

Grey did not intend Broughton a personal slight. He had reorganized colonial ecclesiastical precedence with his mind fixed on Irish politics. For political gains Russell, in whose ministry Grey served, wanted Irish Catholic archbishops elevated above the bishops (but not the archbishops) of the Church of Ireland, and to obscure the political origins of the manoeuvre requested Grey to disguise it as a general colonial reshuffle. Since the Archbishop of Canterbury and Gladstone had earlier decided against the creation of colonial archbishoprics, to avoid legal complications, Grey's move automatically demoted every Church of England bishop wherever the pope chose to create a Roman Catholic archbishopric.[63]

Broughton's first impulse was to acquit his honour and resign, but realized his departure would leave his successor and the Church of England in a permanently inferior place. He asked instead that the laity take up a petition of grievance, but found them lukewarm. He then appealed to the Archbishop of Canterbury to shatter the complacency of the House of Lords with the grim foreboding of a similar change ultimately being applied to England. There was a catalogue of precedent to show that change left unopposed in the colony eventually craved consideration in England, the bishop added. It had been so in education and in the indulgence shown to Roman Catholic priests who had revived the outdoor performance of religious rites and public processions, and would be so in territorial titles for already Rome had leaked the news of its intention to create a new English hierarchy. Who would take precedence when the pope created an Archbishop of London?[64]

Should all protest fail and Polding retain precedence Broughton threatened to sever all links with the government including state subsidies under the Church Act. A penniless bishopric he could abide, a degraded one never. He would never cross beneath the towering arched entrance to government house and trail a Roman Catholic prelate seventy-five paces around the great hall greeting the representative of a queen indifferent to her duties under the Act of Supremacy. Fitzroy had till the queen's birthday levee in May 1849 to prevent a public breach over the issue.[65]

While Broughton battled against Sconce, Makinson and the figment of Italian Jesuits, Fitzroy revived the education issue. Hot upon his arrival in 1846 he had pledged the colony a national school system but Broughton, confident of the colonists' affection for denominational schools, deterred him with threats of fresh agitation. 'I am sure', he wrote to Fitzroy, 'that the same feeling remaining seated in the public mind generally throughout the colony, the same manifestation of it would follow any appeal which might be made to churchmen upon the question.' The *Sydney Morning Herald* agreed.[66]

Fitzroy might have successfully challenged that assumption had the Legislative Council supported him better. To do away with denominational schools Fitzroy needed a sum of money that only a local government education levy could supply. The Legislative Council still opposed the establishment of municipal corporations and so frustrated the establishment of the national schools system it craved. However, by 1847 Broughton's schools were vulnerable with the SPG phasing out aid and colonists coolly indifferent to the general fund of the Diocesan Committee. Moreover, high churchmen elsewhere had abandoned some of the denominational exclusiveness Broughton clung to. In England the British government had adopted the British and Foreign school system in a drive to educate new urban populations and a strident Tractarian like the Reverend Walter Hook, Pusey's curate at Leeds, offered his co-operation. Hook recommended the government take over weekday classes in secular instruction and admit to them free of charge every child who produced a certificate of Sunday worship. The arrangement received publicity in the colony and alarmed Broughton sufficiently for him to call a conference to condemn it.[67] Fitzroy realized the vulnerability of Broughton's position; but unlike his predecessors Gipps and Bourke, who had acted secretively in preparing an attack on the denominational schools, Fitzroy negotiated with the bishop. He offered to incorporate the denominational schools without loss of identity into a national system. Broughton, despite earlier threats, returned his co-operation to the extent of conceding the government the right to frame the syllabus and inspect its progress, but insisted that the clergy retain control over text books, teaching methods, religious instruction and staff appointments. Fitzroy accepted this offer but could not woo representatives of the opposing school systems into co-operating on a single board. Supporters of the denominational schools were determined to oppose the allocation of money towards the erection of any national schools likely to upset the viability of an existing denominational school. So Fitzroy formed two boards, and guaranteed them equality by appointing a member of the Executive Council as chairman of each. Riddell, the colonial treasurer, went to the Denominational Schools Board, while Plunkett, the attorney-general, took over the National Schools Board.[68]

The appointment of Riddell to the Denominational Schools Board delighted Broughton. 'The appointment of a Board is looked upon by the [Diocesan] Committee in a favourable light', Broughton told a gathering of churchmen. Riddell and Broughton had often been companions-in-dissent on the old Executive Council and there was speculation that Broughton would speedily become *de facto* head of the Denominational School Board. Riddell, however, showed an independent mind. He freely accepted Broughton's advice on teacher salaries and in timing the switch to the new system but conceded the bishop little in the management of the schools. Riddell placed each school under three local trustees appointed initially by the bishop but thereafter to be approached only through the Board. That ended direct rule by bishop and Diocesan Committee. Riddell also disappointed Broughton in not submitting the new regulations to his scrutiny before publication. Still Broughton pledged Riddell 'zealous co-operation and a continued good understanding' in furthering the Board's objective.[69]

Fitzroy's new education regulations of 1848 came close to fulfilling Broughton's request to Gipps in 1839 that Church of England schools be kept distinct from other Protestant schools and assisted to compete with rival systems.[70] His compromise in 1848 was to abandon his policy of absolute non-cooperation with the government in the fashioning of any national system. Broughton's trust was soon betrayed. In May 1848 the Legislative Council varied the charter of the National Schools Board to allow it to subsidize 'plain substantial buildings' in addition to teacher salaries but restricted the Denominational Schools Board to teacher subsidies. When Charles Cowper protested that this preference, combined with the appropriation of the title of 'national' by one Board, implied a precedence or expectation of eventual ascendancy, he was loudly denounced. A month later in the estimates debate Wentworth denounced the denominational schools as a 'tolerated nuisance' and the Legislative Council backed him 13 to 7 by voting exclusive control of a fund for bush education to the National Schools Board. The fair trial announced in January and affirmed in May died in June.[71]

For consolation in mid-1848 Broughton contemplated the turmoil he had escaped. It was an election year and from April to June Legislative Council and press echoed with the vituperation a poll excited. On the eve of polling day in Sydney Polding appealed to Catholics 'to repress every symptom of violence and even of rudeness'. On the leading issues—transportation, municipal corporations, reform of the Legislative Council, the separation of Port Phillip—Broughton had adopted earlier opinions that turned out to be unfashionable. In 1848 anti-transportationists surrendered to a beguiling offer from the Colonial Office to transport a free immigrant for every new convict the colony accepted; municipal corporations were again rejected; provision for a bicameral legislature shelved; the separation of Port Phillip overwhelmingly approved. Apart from a slap for his 'grossly bigoted and selfish' attitude to Port Phillip's freedom (which he opposed in 1846 in the Executive Council fearing separation would require amending the Church Act and risking its entire review by the Legislative Council) Broughton's politics otherwise escaped comment.[72] He had ceased to be of political importance to New South Wales. At the hustings no one even accused Cowper of being the bishop's spokesman. An era had passed.

Yet that era ended with Broughton and colonial leaders both rowing against the Colonial Office. Broughton wanted a church like Cranmer's, colonists wanted a parliament like Westminster's, and the enemy of both was the dilettante reformers of the Colonial Office. In constitutional affairs the Colonial Office had proposed replacing the Legislative Council with a hierarchy of councils and restricting a popular franchise to the election of the lowest body, a type of local government corporation. That resembled nothing at Westminster and the elections of 1848 menaced the proposals. No colonist would nominate for such councils, no man vote for them and so no government would assemble. 'We will commit no violence ... and we will be loyal to the throne, but ...', warned the *Sydney Morning Herald*, 'when the new constitution comes to us ... colonists will have nothing to do but echo and re-echo the watchword, "To your tents, O Israel".' There was little difference between that mood and Broughton's threat to boycott government house, challenge the legality of requiring an Oath of Supremacy from colonial clergy, and shake the three hundred year ban on synodical government.[73]

A Consultation

A synod is...a premature assumption of powers which we
could not fully vindicate against all objections.

Broughton to Gladstone 19 November 1850

Broughton hoped to make 1849 a year of ecclesiastical consolidation.
He had never been better situated for consultation or had fewer dis-
tracting obligations, or been so free of nuisance. The *Sydney Chronicle*
expired late in 1848 and the *Atlas* early in 1849, while Broughton's
own *Sydney Guardian* appeared to thrive. For the first time ever Broughton had no opposing press. In England a *Colonial Church Chronicle*
appeared with a hundred pages of colonial news quarterly. A spate of
lectures, pamphlets and books from churchmen and statesmen burst
on to the market examining the value of the colonies to the empire and
the Colonial Office took a shaking for its failure to grasp the loyalty
latent in strong ecclesiastical ties. In 1848–9 Lord Lyttelton and Lord
John Manners echoed the sentiments Broughton had hurled against
the Colonial Office and every governor since 1833. The prospect of
an attentive English audience had never looked brighter.[1]

Broughton did not foresee unusual growth. Despite five years of
toil and frugality since the crash of 1843 few of the old flock masters
and traders recovered their fortunes. Low wool prices, followed by
a loss of commercial nerve during the European riots of 1848, combined
with high labour costs and 'unrelenting creditors' to dissolve the rewards
of effort. 'The state of affairs whether pastoral or mercantile is not such
as to enable our best friends to do *much*', Broughton told the SPG as
he approached his deadline for self-sufficiency.[2] Nevertheless the church
had its friends. In 1848 within a ten-mile radius of Sydney the laity
subscribed over £5200 to special projects and put another £2000 into
the voluntary offering plate. What Broughton lacked was flexibility
in a general fund. Colonists contributed only £116 to the Diocesan
Committee in 1848 so that in 1849 when the Reverend George King
arrived unannounced from South Australia looking for employment
Broughton could place him but not pay him. Later when Naylor at
St Andrews fell desperately ill Broughton could appoint King to a
temporary charge only by withdrawing Naylor's stipend and throwing
his nine children on to charity. 'I do not know that a more distressing

case has occurred', he confessed. Broughton raised a public subscription to send Naylor to England for medical care but left him thereafter on the mercy of the SPG. Under such stringent financial conditions the mass immigration of 1849 with three to four shiploads arriving at a time scuttled Broughton's best hopes for self-sufficiency. 'There at hand . . . in their thousands', wrote the *Sydney Morning Herald* pointing to confusion on the wharves, '[are] agricultural labourers, parish pensioners, urchins from ragged schools, orphans from Irish workhouses, ticket-of-leave holding convicts from British prisons and we know not what.' All Broughton saw was their universal poverty. 'I have no power to raise upon the spot the resources required', he wrote as two more vessels anchored within sight of Tusculum. 'Among the many thousands who have lately been added to our population . . . there have not been ten persons possessed of so much capital or worldly substance as will enable them to contribute *anything* towards providing Churches or clergymen.' Once more the bishop threw himself upon the resources of the SPG and wrote also to the Earl of Harrowby, Chairman of the Colonial Emigration Society, arguing that large-scale emigration was a 'national undertaking for national benefit' and justified national aid. He asked Fitzroy for £100 for an immigrants' chaplain. Fitzroy 'gladly' found £100, the Earl of Harrowby nothing, and the SPG launched an appeal for extra chaplains and teachers. 'Kind, generous-religious England', sighed old Dr Cowper.[3]

There were other signs of kindness. The SPCK gave the diocese a fillip by taking over £1000 of old building debts and enticing colonists to see expansion in every new contribution. Broughton's old school pal George Gilbert, a prebendary of Lincoln, opened a cathedral appeal in England, and Henry Hutchisson the first monitor to take him in hand at the King's School donated hundreds of pounds to a variety of diocesan appeals. Coleridge and Joshua Watson between them continued to find the occasional spinster with a small purse to spare. But Broughton ever insisted that the staff of diocesan progress was 'the continual contribution of small sums regularly collected from a great number of persons during a sufficient interval of time'.[4]

Nothing had come of the bishops' meeting Broughton planned for October 1848. A volcano erupted to keep Selwyn in New Zealand and Perry wouldn't budge from Port Phillip. Perry had left England expecting to find a neglected people and instead found them heathen. The masses never worshipped, he reported, and the other classes had low moral standards and little spiritual religion. He gave Broughton no credit for his pioneering visitations and commended little in the achievements of the existing chaplains. It appeared no Christian voice had preceded Perry's, and his labours would decide whether the materialism of the land hardened white settlers against Christianity as it had the Aboriginal. Amid such urgency Perry had no time to quibble over the Act of Uniformity in Sydney. Moreover, it would have been impolitic of Perry, whose bishopric symbolized Port Phillip's approaching equality with Sydney, to make a hasty pilgrimage north.[5]

Broughton considered the bishops' meeting postponed not cancelled, and on Friday 16 March 1849 he conferred with Tyrrell at Tusculum on a future agenda. Around 11 a.m. a solicitor's clerk interrupted the meeting to inform Broughton that as the sole solvent stockholder of the Bank of Australia he was to be sued for £219 182 5s. Proceedings were to commence within a few days. Broughton rushed immediately to the solicitor's office to discover how he became a partner in the bankrupt Bank of Australia. He owned no shares in his own name, and in 1841, foreseeing the Bank's instability, he had refused to accept a bequest to the diocese of £1760 of the Bank's shares in the Moore estate of which he was executor. The solicitor explained nothing except that Broughton's liability had been confirmed in a legal opinion from the solicitor-general's office. 'They will not let me see this opinion; nor can I by any means learn upon what it rests', he complained. 'I have with difficulty prevailed on them to allow me a few days for consultation.'⁶

Tyrrell advised him to consult Robert Lowe. Broughton could not, so Tyrrell did. Broughton took an independent opinion of another lawyer Mr Michie. Both explained how a clerical blunder in January 1842 had turned him into a shareholder of the Bank. At that time Broughton, as an executor of Moore's estate, applied for all dividend payments outstanding on Moore's Bank of Australia shares at the time of his death to be paid into his estate. In January 1842 the Bank inadvertently added an extra £123 16s as dividends for the six months after Moore's death. Broughton instructed his registrar to return the sum as he did not intend to allow the diocese to take over Moore's Bank shares. The Bank paid no further dividends into the Moore estate. However, instead of withdrawing the £123 16s the Bank let it stand as part of a larger payment due to the same account. The procedure was illegal and left a formal entry on the Bank's registers designating the account of the executors of Moore's estate as recipients of a dividend on Bank of Australia shares. In law the receipt of a dividend constituted a partnership and by a judgement of the Privy Council in 1848 this meant liability for all the Bank's debts. Moreover, the Bank of Australia had listed Broughton's name as a shareholder on behalf of the Moore estate in an annual declaration to the attorney-general's office in 1841, 1842 and 1843. Broughton's failure to object was construed as consent. That Broughton had no knowledge of the matter did not weigh with the lawyers. 'I must acknowledge my own unacquaintance with the law of partnerships', he said, '[but] I never suspected the possibility that anyone could by implication be made a member of a firm without his own consent.'⁷

In the opinion of the lawyers Broughton was hopelessly positioned. Lowe thought the registration of his name as a shareholder decisively against him; and Michie believed the receipt of a dividend did in law constitute ownership of shares. Tyrrell's 'penetrating and really legal mind' scrutinized both legal opinions and agreed. Broughton faced 'beggary'. His own assets apart from furniture and a carriage were two life assurance policies worth £4700 'effected with a view to make some little provision for my family at my death'. He had come to New South Wales to provide for his family, and the thought that he could by staying 'leave his children above want' sustained him through many a difficult episode. Now his wife and his unmarried daughter Emily faced utter destitution. To fight the writ would cost as much as surrendering to it. 'If I fail my ruin is complete: and hardly short of it if I succeed', he said. He decided against a fight in April 1849 and instructed his solicitor to negotiate a settlement.[8]

Creditors of the Bank of Australia offered to settle for £1500 cash. Broughton would have paid immediately had he the means. While he pondered where to find it he reread the documents in the case. 'I was struck', he commented on completing the review, 'with what appeared to me a want of that careful exactness in them which were I a lawyer would not satisfy me in advising a client.' Why had neither counsel suggested arguing that a 'payment in error' was not a dividend? Why had neither counsel challenged the right of the Bank to enter his name as a shareholder while at the same time it withheld dividends? Why had not his counsel challenged the manner of the entry of his name in the register of shareholders? His name did not appear in substance but an entry 'Moore, Thomas (Representatives of Late)' had been scrawled across three columns that should have shown name, description and address. Did that conform to the law? What did the term 'Representative' mean? Executor or trustee? If executor his address would be Tusculum, if trustee it would have been the Diocesan Registry. Had the Bank entered Tusculum it would have meant the Bank regarded him as an executor and as such by law he could not be a proprietor and had no liability. To Broughton there seemed to be room for manoeuvre that might deter the creditors from pursuing the matter. Broughton put these questions to Lowe and Michie. Both lawyers revised their opinion and advised Broughton that he could resist the writ with 'a fair prospect of success'. Lowe who had often instructed Broughton in theology found Broughton instructing him in the law. In May 1849 Broughton challenged the writ.[9]

In the same May Broughton, succumbing perhaps to the strain of threatened financial ruin, cancelled the ordination of the young deacon Beamish and a new storm broke over the diocese. Bishop and curate had been at odds for two years. In London Beamish impressed the SPG with a spirit of self-sacrifice. In Sydney his self-confidence and vanity afflicted Broughton. Beamish had abandoned fair prospects in Ireland for excellent ones in New South Wales, and on arrival demanded immediate employment at maximum salary with optimum security—a colonial chaplaincy with a fixed income of £200 payable from Schedule C. The SPG had promised it and the bishop must honour it, Beamish said. He could, however, accept an appointment at £150 provided it was not clogged with the abominations of the voluntary system. Beamish was twenty-three years old. The township of Singleton fulfilled Beamish's criteria and Broughton, unwilling to take issue with the SPG, placed him there only to see him resign when Singleton was transferred to the Diocese of Newcastle. Beamish insisted he had volunteered to serve the Diocese of Sydney. Broughton put him on the staff of St Andrews Sydney until his inexperience, forgetfulness and inefficiency became a liability to the parish. The bishop then offered him Dapto with a guarantee of £200 for one year and no further preferential treatment. Beamish so croaked and sighed at the prospect of living off the 'caprice of a congregation' that Broughton mistook his acceptance for a refusal. 'I cannot help supposing that the same forgetfulness which characterised too often the discharge of the duties at St Andrew's Church must extend to your correspondence', chided the bishop. Beamish forgetful! The suggestion stung him. Had Broughton himself been more alert to his duties there never would have been a Sconce affair or Duffus scandal, retorted the young deacon. Broughton called Beamish impudent, issued him a licence for Dapto, and directed that all future correspondence be addressed to his secretary.[10]

Three months later the parish of Carcoar with the coveted £200 government stipend became vacant and Broughton offered it to Beamish. 'I suffered no dissatisfaction arising from his . . . offensive and insulting demeanour towards me on several occasions, to weigh against my disposition to do him justice even with rigorous exactness', the bishop explained. Beamish in the meantime had found a vocation at Dapto and requested permission to stay there rather than move to Carcoar. He calculated on the 'abominable' voluntary system yielding £50 a year by the beginning of his second year and trusted to the diocese, or government, or SPG for another £100. In April 1849, when that second year began, the Dapto voluntary system raised 15s a month and other sources nothing. Broughton had paid £125 of Beamish's previous year's salary from his own pocket and could afford it no longer.[11]

Broughton expected Beamish to throw himself on the mercy of the Dapto congregation for a short time while he arranged something better. Instead, Beamish moved in with his old college chum, the Reverend F. T. C. Russell, at St Marks Darlinghurst. About the same time Broughton reshuffled duties in Sydney to allow two underpaid curates to take advantage of temporary vacancies to augment their incomes. One vacancy had occurred at the Darlinghurst jail close by Russell's parish and Beamish fancied it for himself. When no offer arrived Beamish speculated on why the bishop had overlooked his claim? Was it his Protestantism? Between them Beamish and Russell fixed on the idea that only Tractarian sycophants had a future in the diocese. Beamish, ignorant of Broughton's preparations to appoint him to the parish of Balmain by Sydney, challenged the bishop to appoint him immediately to the Darlinghurst jail or risk the Legislative Council debating whether it was proper to appoint as sole Protestant chaplain to the Darlinghurst jail a Tractarian whose ministry Presbyterians, Wesleyans and others rejected. 'I have been treated with great injustice', he wrote to Broughton. 'And as I know no cause for this, except it be my attachment to *Protestant* principles, I shall, if my claims are overlooked, hold myself at liberty . . . to seek from the Colonial Legislature some determination of the matter.' It was for that incivility and insubordination that Broughton cancelled Beamish's ordination to the priesthood set for 3 June 1849, ten days time. 'May God protect the Church of England in this Colony', replied Beamish. 'May that despotic rule . . . treacherously and ever malignantly exercised ... which seeks to crush evangelical truth ... be in His own good time destroyed.'[12]

Beamish apologized. Broughton again dismissed all sense of personal hurt and, provided Beamish also apologized for calling the Sydney clergy sycophants, he could expect ordination three months later. In the meantime Broughton proceeded to finalize Beamish's appointment to the parish of Balmain.[13]

On Thursday 31 May 1849 Mr Mort, a Sydney layman, found himself on an omnibus in the company of the Reverend F. T. C. Russell and four others. Russell, who had persuaded Beamish to forsake Ireland for New South Wales, was sore in soul at his friend's exclusion from the coming ordinations. He held sway in conversation and stirred up the embers of old discord by contrasting the bishop's leniency towards Sconce with his stiffness towards Beamish. By the time the public conveyance turned into George Street Russell had convicted the bishop of being a 'romanist at heart', pronounced him a weak man and a tyrant, and counselled his hearers against contributing further to Whitsunday appeals for the Overseas Bishopric Fund until a new type of bishop emerged. Mort censured such unguarded candour in public and alighted from the omnibus. Russell pursued him on foot waxing more fulsome in his condemnation of bishop and clergy. 'You could select better men from Norfolk Island', he shouted as Mort disappeared into his office in Lloyd's Rooms. Mort, an auctioneer, later that morning called on his attorney Charles Lowe who was a member of the Diocesan Committee, and rehearsed for him Russell's behaviour on the omnibus. Lowe thought such gratuitous remarks from one still in the noviciate of the church's ministry disqualified him from the forthcoming ordination, and told the incumbent of St Andrews, the Reverend T. B. Naylor, so. Naylor considered the matter all Friday as Broughton had asked him to assist in the laying-on-of-hands at the ordination.[14]

At 11 a.m. on Saturday 2 June Russell and Beamish called at the Diocesan Registry. Russell took his oaths of ordination and pressed Broughton to interview Beamish who wished to offer an apology. Broughton declined, and at that point the deputy-registrar who was present for the oaths sensed an unpleasantness and left the bishop's office. A few minutes later Russell stormed out and called across the room to Beamish: '*All* must be published'. The two men returned to Darlinghurst where Naylor waited to challenge Russell on the remarks he had made in the omnibus. Russell assured Naylor he was misinformed. He admitted an anxiety over the bishop's treatment of Beamish but denied harbouring the slightest thought injurious to the bishop's character. Naylor left reassured of the propriety of his continuing to play a part in the ordination the next day.[15]

All that afternoon Russell brooded over Naylor's visit, and by evening had convinced himself of a Tractarian plot to debar his ordination. There had been many whisperers. Only last February the bishop had tackled him in his own vestry saying: 'Sir, many complaints have reached me as to the irregularities practised at St Marks'. The complaints were of the irregular celebration of the sacraments; of the administration of the chalice before the bread at Holy Communion; of the omission of morning service on Ash Wednesday and of collects on other days. Who complained? Russell put Walsh from Christ Church at the bottom of it all. He understood perfectly that a Tractarian like Walsh should wish to be rid of a pure Protestant like himself. But it disturbed Russell that a man of Naylor's stature should be so easily deceived into doubting his integrity. That night Russell wrote Naylor a letter and placed it in his prayer-book to take to the ordination next morning, and retired exceedingly late.[16]

At 11 a.m. on Sunday 3 June 1849 the congregation at St Andrews sat waiting for the bishop to enter. In the vestry the bishop sat waiting for Russell to arrive. Then a trifle late Russell rushed in clutching two letters. He gave Naylor one and Broughton the other. 'Mr. Russell', snapped the bishop, 'I have not time for reading Notes now.' He pushed the letter aside for later. Mr Naylor more knowingly read his and declined to take any further part in Russell's ordination. Russell then shouted something about Walsh being to blame, and a general hubbub ensued. Archdeacon Cowper begged the two men to shake hands while the Reverend George King pleaded with Russell to withdraw the letter. Broughton meanwhile opened his and after a quick glance dismissed the whole thing as 'frivolous'. He asked that they all compose themselves and move into the church. Naylor again refused to participate in Russell's laying-on-of-hands and Broughton postponed his ordination. Russell left for St James church.[17]

In the vestry after the service Broughton searched Russell's letter to discover the source of Naylor's agitation. 'Its being addressed to him [Mr Naylor] was a mere blind', Broughton later wrote to Russell. 'Your real intention was to offer an insult to the Bishop from whom you were professedly seeking ordination.' Russell's letter scoffed at Naylor's susceptibility to rumour, which he blamed on Naylor's long acquaintance with the lower tone of colonial life, but blamed Broughton for creating an atmosphere of mistrust in which rumour thrived. Quite frankly, said Russell, whether deserved or not the bishop had a reputation for equivocation. Had not Sconce once alleged that the vicarage drawing-rooms of Sydney echoed with the debate 'whether the falsehoods the Bishop was in the habit of uttering were to be accounted as deliberate violations of, or carelessness about the truth?' Why had not one Sydney clergyman denied it? That, and more, Russell handed the bishop at the moment of his ordination. When the sabbath had passed, for he would raise no pen on that day, Broughton banned Russell from Tusculum, vowed never to ordain him priest in the colony for it would take more years than Broughton had to live for Russell to reconstitute his character. While Russell remained deacon at St Marks Darlinghurst he must deal directly with Broughton's secretary, or find a clerical friend to intercede for him. He may never approach the bishop face to face.[18]

Russell, embarrassed at finding himself a deacon on Monday, bought a column in the *Sydney Morning Herald* to blame his humiliation on that coiner of base reports Walsh. 'No man can with truth affirm I ever maligned him', Russell insisted, and condemned his fellow clergy for fighting 'under the banner of Christ with the weapons of Hell'. He called the laity to a crusade against false doctrine and those who taught it, and Beamish chipped in with an advertisement in large print: 'The Bishop of Sydney thus identifies himself with that party whose AVOWED object is to UNPROTESTANTIZE our Church'. Within days they had Thos. Whistler Smith Esq. at the head of a volunteer corps of laymen organizing public meetings and buying column upon column of the *Sydney Morning Herald* where the most junior of the clergy could attack the most senior. 'I cannot subject myself to the degradation of undertaking to reply to them through the same channel', Broughton commented, and asked Archdeacon Cowper to bring them to their senses.[19]

Russell later apologized for the letter he handed Broughton in St Andrew's vestry, but stuck by his allegation that there was in the diocese a party of unprincipled romanizing clergy, knaves, caitiffs, and such assassins of mortal souls as the 'reverend perverts' Sconce and Makinson, the two clergy who witnessed Makinson's conditional re-baptism seven years ago, the clergyman who received a copy of *The Garden of the Soul* and kept it, the clergyman to whom Sconce had laid open his soul and who had raised no alarm, the students at the Lyndhurst college who attended Sconce's lectures without protest, and the proprietors, directors and editors of the *Southern Queen*, the *Australian* and the *Sydney Guardian*. 'If a distinct line be not drawn between "Tractarianism" and the *true principles* of the Church of England, the worst consequences may be expected to befall our communion in this diocese', concluded Russell.[20]

'Trifling anecdotes', commented Broughton as he tossed the document aside and decided to force Russell's submission or drive him from the diocese. Broughton had for years counselled the clergy to avoid party divisions like those wracking the church in England, and they had. Now a mere deacon called for a division—for a party of Presbyterianizers to match a party of romanizers. Who should rule bishop or deacon? Should the diocese have peace or strife? Silence would be a monument to weakness, Broughton said; and he warned that 'the zealots of a wild excess of private judgment and the advocates of a contumacious self-will . . . are now united in pointing the dagger to the throat of the Church of England'. The bishop cited Russell to appear in St James vestry by 10 a.m. on 25 July 1849.[21]

Russell came with a phalanx of seven laymen and a well prepared defence. It was, however, Broughton's day. He laid the charge, ruled out additional defence, summed up the evidence, allowed no cross-examination, ordered Russell to be quiet and to be seated, pronounced the verdict, suspended the deacon for three months, made his future employment dependent on an acknowledgment of fault, and entered in his *Act Book* that Russell had several times attempted to disrupt the proceedings. 'In claiming to be heard he was bent only upon offering me every kind of insult', the bishop noted.[22]

A few days later Russell met the parishioners of St Marks and renewed his call for a Protestant and evangelical struggle, rehearsed his condemnation of Romish teachings at the Lyndhurst college, and took counsel of

Robert Lowe on the legality of the bishop's proceedings. Robert Lowe was delighted. Someone had unfortunately dubbed the vestry proceedings at St James a consistorial court, and this opened the way for Lowe to take the matter into the Legislative Council. He argued, as he had in 1846, that ecclesiastical courts were illegal in the colonies and Her Majesty deceived as to the extent of her prerogative in issuing letters patent for their erection. But the repugnance of the court's illegality had been aggravated this time, Lowe stressed, by its being the scene of 'as much injustice and iniquity in a small compass as any recorded in History'. The court had denied the defendant prior knowledge of the charge, the right to cross-examine the evidence against him, to produce witnesses in his own defence, and finally the right to reply. 'If this Court is to be allowed to do again as it has done, it will be a great reproach to this assembly', Lowe said; and urged the Legislative Council to pass a Common Law Statute regulating the disciplinary powers of bishops over clergy. Then with a waltz of the tongue Lowe was suddenly reviling the bishop; arbitrary, wicked, iniquitous, more villainous in his proceedings than Judge Jeffreys and more corrupt as a judge than Pontius Pilate. 'I do not believe that after this exposure, the Bishop will dare to face the light', he concluded. Other members of the Legislative Council objected to the language, but vainly; for the Speaker Dr Nicholson was a parishioner at St Marks where the laity had published their own document in condemnation of the bishop's actions.[23]

Lowe failed. Plunkett persuaded the Legislative Council against interfering to the disadvantage of the Church of England after refusing for thirteen years to interfere to its advantage. Russell's remedy lay in an appeal to Canterbury. With that rebuff Lowe quit his challenge to the legality of ecclesiastical courts in the colony, though he had support for that aspect of his case. His quarry was Broughton, and when the bishop escaped Lowe cared little for the wider constitutional issue.[24]

The debate in the Legislative Council left Broughton to answer the charge that he had conducted an irregular court and dishonoured a promise to allow Russell to speak in his defence. It was uncharacteristic of Broughton to be careless of legal procedures. He had observed all due forms in the Brigstocke and Duffus cases, and in 1836 complained when the attorney-general precluded his following them in the Yate case. Why was he careless of procedure, as even Charles Cowper believed he was, in 1849?[25]

The foundation of this criticism was a gratuitous belief that the vestry proceedings of 25 July constituted a consistorial court. Whoever called them that blundered. The term appeared only in the *Sydney Morning Herald* report of the proceedings. Lowe, quoting hearsay, attributed the writing of this report to Broughton, but the archdeacon, the registrar, or Allwood, or anyone with access to Broughton's address could have composed it. Whoever did compose it added the term consistorial court after the proceedings. It did not occur in Broughton's address or in any of the bishop's correspondence with the archdeacon. Since Broughton had meticulously cited the legal pretext for his earlier consistorial courts his omission in this case indicated that he did not consider it a formal consistorial court in the same sense as the others. Moreover he did not need such a court to discipline a mere deacon. By the Canons of 1604 a deacon held office at the pleasure of the bishop and subject to good behaviour. When Broughton questioned Russell's behaviour he fulfilled all canonical requirements by conducting his enquiry through the archdeacon. When he delivered judgement Broughton was flanked by the Bishop of Newcastle, whom he considered a considerable lawyer, and Archdeacon Cowper whose praise, as Russell admitted, was in all the churches. They presumably concurred in the action. Lowe's attack on the legality of the court's proceedings was based on a false assumption.[26]

Equally false but more difficult to dispel was the allegation that Broughton had refused Russell a right to address the court after having promised it him. Lowe maintained that 'on the 23rd July he [Russell] received a letter informing him that on the 25th of that month, the bishop would deliver his judgment on that and two other charges, and stating that he would then be prepared to hear anything he had to say in explanation'. A committee of laymen supporting Russell alleged the same guarantee had been given and withdrawn by Broughton. Broughton, however, gave no such guarantee. Lowe misquoted the bishop's correspondence. Broughton had written through the archdeacon summoning Russell to be at the vestry of St James on 25 July at 10 a.m. and informing him that at 10 a.m. he would 'express his decision' on three matters, viz., Russell's behaviour in the vestry of St Andrews on the 3 June, his implication of Walsh in a plot to debar his ordination, and his public accusation that a romanizing party existed among the clergy and at the Lyndhurst college. On the first two of these three matters Broughton agreed to hear any fresh explanation Russell cared to offer *'before* he pronounced his decision', that is, before 10 a.m. Russell, however, arrived at 10 a.m. with seven laymen and immediately upon Broughton's formal entry demanded to address all present. Broughton thought Russell's tone insulting and his demeanour bent on disrupting the proceedings. Having given Russell till 10 a.m. to speak to him personally Broughton did not care to be upstaged by a deacon on the floor of the vestry before a gathering of laity and clergy.[27]

Had Russell spoken he would have apologized for accusing Walsh of attempting to wreck his ordination. That would have bettered Russell's character but subtracted nothing from Broughton's disciplinary action. The third was the serious charge. 'Knowing how the minds of our people are distressed and unsettled by constantly hearing that a Romanising party exists among us', the bishop said, 'I have considered this portion of Mr Russell's conduct as worthy of much graver consideration than any of the rest.' When asked earlier to retract this accusation Russell confirmed it repeatedly and publicly, and Broughton did not offer to reopen the matter before he delivered judgement. Russell's action subsequent to the disciplinary proceedings showed him quite unrepentant and claiming his suspension the ultimate achievement of the romanizers. Broughton published his correspondence with Russell and Beamish, and cleared his reputation. Russell fell mute, his lay support withered, and his three month's suspension aroused little sympathy. 'We believe the opinion of the great majority of those who have taken the trouble to make themselves acquainted with the facts is', commented the *Sydney Morning Herald*, 'that the sentence passed on him [Russell] is a most lenient one.'[28]

While Russell trumpeted about romanist teachings at the Lyndhurst college, Broughton only just avoided another Sconce-Makinson scandal. Indeed Russell's charges stemmed from the indiscriminate chatter of one of the first of the Lyndhurst students, the Reverend G. Gregory. Broughton ordained Gregory deacon in December 1848. In May 1849 he met his old teacher Sconce at the Benedictine monastery and they fell together on their knees before the altar to begin the pilgrim journey. Then Gregory stalled. He turned to Broughton and throwing himself at the bishop's feet made 'a noble and hearty confession'. He accepted discipline, part of which was to remain mute while Russell challenged him to confirm his earlier tale of romanism at Lyndhurst. Broughton suspended Gregory for twelve months and promised him re-employment in the bush districts if he reformed his ideas. In August 1849 he also suspended the licence of the newly appointed immigration chaplain the Reverend D. Cooper and promised him re-employment if he reformed his habits. Matron Fanny Capps had found Cooper wandering around the barracks drunk 'before midday'.[29]

The rebel laity were also active. Seven had formed a committee to defend Russell, and Broughton had barely won the battle against them when George Bowen re-entered Sydney with troublesome stride. Bowen, after questioning the restrictions of theology on scripture and forcing Broughton into a heresy trial in 1836, now questioned the restrictions of scripture on love. In 1846 Bowen had married his deceased wife's sister in London. He warned Broughton of his intention and challenged the bishop to prohibit his participation in the sacrament. Broughton did nothing. He found no obvious disciplinary rule on the matter, and believing Bowen's an isolated case left him to his dubious union west of Windsor. Then in July 1849 Bowen shifted to Sydney and canvassed the reform of the marriage laws. Broughton re-investigated the matter and united rubric and canon to inhibit Bowen receiving the sacrament at St Andrews. Bowen fled to Christ Church where Walsh took his side and accused Broughton of a want of charity in first accommodating then excluding Bowen from the sacrament. Broughton let Walsh follow his conscience, but at a price: 'It would create too serious a scandal if I were to pass over, and *you* were to admit, one and the same individual; and therefore I must abstain from attending such holy celebration'. This breach broke Walsh's spirit. He had been publicly taunted by Sconce, smeared by Russell, and flayed in the press with the *Atlas* ultimately demanding his expulsion as proof that Broughton had no Puseyite leanings. Within three months of Broughton refusing to unite in the celebration of the sacrament of eternal life at Christ Church Walsh sailed for a rest-cure in England.[30]

Outwardly Broughton bore his troubles. Casual callers at Tusculum found him cordial, simple, kind, and 'so truly episcopal'.[31] Inwardly,

RICHARD SADLEIR.
Organized lay opposition
against Broughton's plans for
synodical government.

REVEREND J. C. GRYLLS.
Organized *Southern Queen* and
Sydney (Church) Guardian to
to defend Broughton against the
Atlas.

CHARLES COWPER.
Dubbed Member for the
Church of England in
Legislative Council.

SIR ALFRED STEPHEN.
Spoke warmly of
Broughton's patriotism
in New South Wales.

distress had wearied him. Around mid-August he appeared to ail and on 23 August Dr Mitchell ordered him to bed. He suspected exhaustion, then took alarm as the bishop's pulse sank. He called in Dr Wallace. On 7 September both pronounced the condition mortal and Allwood brought the sacrament. 'Despise not thou the chastening of the Lord', Allwood exhorted, and as he delivered over the Host he watched Broughton, whose throat was too swollen to reply, wrestle for breath. 'Teach us in this and other like daily spectacles of mortality to see how frail and uncertain our condition is', Allwood added; and turning about left Broughton to the vigil of his wife and daughter Emily. The family called Phoebe to Sydney while Allwood prepared for the bishop's funeral. Then Broughton rallied on Tuesday 11 September. The same night Mrs Broughton, exhausted by the vigil, retired unwell. Next day haematic gout appeared on her right arm and the day after erysipelas spread its scorching butterfly-like wings across her face, and two maids carried her delirious from the bishop's bedroom. 'Be of good cheer, Sally', he whispered. They never again spoke. By Sunday she was dead. While one thousand stood by her grave the bishop lay feebly at Tusculum gathering to himself the memory of 'the little girl with *very* black hair and a *very* white frock' who once interrupted his Latin lesson to begin a half century of friendship. It all ended so abruptly.[32]

For a month Phoebe and Emily nursed the bishop then suddenly Phoebe's youngest child fell ill and died at Tusculum. Broughton turned comforter till the end of October when both Phoebe and Emily left for the Hunter River valley. Broughton returned to his office on 1 November and found a deputation of ten clergy and laymen awaiting him with a large box. Inside the bishop found a scale model of St Andrews cathedral wrapped in a scroll signed by three hundred heads of families pledged to work till the building stood complete.[33] Two weeks later Broughton set off prematurely on a seven hundred mile visitation southward and fell ill at the Middle River Inn a day's journey along the lonely west road out of Mulgoa. 'The symptoms of my recent illness returned upon me with such severity as to occasion me to apprehend that I might end my life in this remote spot', he later recalled. He recovered to proceed at a slower pace punctuating his journey with three and four day rests at the homes of such old friends as the Bowmans and the Icelys. He consecrated six churches and made a prolonged visit to the old Aboriginal mission areas at Wellington Valley where he was joyed to find black and white mixed at worship and very correctly singing the psalms. 'The native ear and voice, with moderate cultivation, are capable of attaining to a very satisfactory degree of musical proficiency', he reported to the SPG.[34] He returned on 19 December to an empty home, to loneliness and to a house that could be snatched from him by devouring creditors. The lively chatter of his Sally, and the family dinner that climaxed each journey was gone. He had loved them and deeply missed them. Was there a divine purpose in that? 'Was it quite good or safe to have such comforts in my own home as might make me less disposed to exchange them for the fatigues and hardships of distant "journeyings

often"?' Had he been freed from those comforts that once drew him
homeward to accomplish some final purpose?[35]

One sign into the future appeared among the newspapers piled up
in his absence. The Canadian bishops planned to confer in May 1850.
This, and the warning from his near death that time was short, spurred
Broughton's determination to arrange a similar Australian meeting.
'It is vain to hope by consulting individual consciences to bring all to
an agreement as to the time', he mused and fixed on Whitsuntide 1850.
Perry was the reluctant party. Knowing that Perry and his wife were
to visit the north of the new diocese in January 1850 he asked them
to come on to Albury. They agreed; and Broughton, still weak and
scarcely recovered from his visitation journey just completed, set off
to Albury.[36]

Broughton planned a four-day meeting. Perry spared him only two
and was less than frank in what he concealed of his intentions. He said
little, or perhaps nothing at all he freely admitted, of well-advanced
plans for a separate Church bill for Port Phillip which substantially
increased the power of lay trustees to appoint their own clergy, or that
he had already put his ideas to Grey for approval so that the bill would
be a *fait accompli* by the time Broughton learned of its content. Perry
did not share Broughton's belief that the subdivision of the Diocese
of Australia was a challenge to united action but embraced it as an opportunity for diversity. Before meeting Broughton he had already asked
Grey for the legislative freedom to make arrangements 'such as we feel
to be best suited to our own wants, without interfering with any arrangements, which may be adopted in the Dioceses of Sydney and Newcastle'. At Albury Perry agreed to attend an episcopal conference but
he was by temperament incapable of co-operative action and later confessed as much. 'It is a rule with me', he later told Broughton, 'never
to ask advice of a superior upon a question, the decision of which rests
with myself, unless I am prepared to act upon his advice.'[37]

Broughton understood the extent of Perry's independence only
after he returned to Sydney. In April Perry told him his registrar
Mr Moor, a member for Port Phillip, would introduce into the forthcoming session of the Legislative Council in Sydney two bills, one
reforming the Church Act for Port Phillip and one remodelling ecclesiastical discipline for all the dioceses. Broughton was aghast. Apart from
the presumption in legislating for other dioceses without the courtesy
of the slightest consultation, Broughton accused the new bishop of
pre-empting the work of the proposed episcopal conference. Worse
still, the move was politically stupid. Twice Broughton had fought
off the attempted interference of the Legislative Council in ecclesiastical
discipline and now Perry invited its intervention. Perry could find
his bill amended beyond recognition and his diocese saddled with courts
of less antiquity than his diocese. Perry was ready to risk that. 'Although
your remarks have led me to reconsider still more carefully the objections
and dangers ... of the proposed arrangement', he told Broughton,
'they have not shaken my belief in their expediency or even necessity

for the permanent well being of the church.' Perry restricted the application of the discipline bill to his own diocese and had Moor table the legislation in July 1850.[38] The *Sydney Morning Herald*, now part-owned by Charles Kemp a member of Broughton's Diocesan Committee, immediately appealed to the Legislative Council not to suffer a junior bishop fresh to the scene to disturb the policies of his Metropolitan 'a prelate of the station, character, and great experience of the Bishop of Sydney?'. Fortunately Lowe was gone and Windeyer dead, and while the lesser advocates of legislative interference in ecclesiastical discipline tarried, the clergy and laity of Port Phillip revolted. They took exception to the secrecy shrouding the preparation of the bills and accused Perry of seeking some untoward advantage in wanting them debated in remote Sydney on the eve of the district gaining its own council. Poor Perry! Within a month of dismissing Broughton's objections to the bills as the mumblings of a mind disposed to 'despotic government' Perry was himself assailed for meddling with the civil and religious liberties of colonists. Perry withdrew the bills to regain his flock and looked to the coming episcopal conference for a solution.[39]

Broughton and Perry seemed doomed to misunderstanding. The suspended curate Russell had approached Perry for employment in 1849. Perry believed Russell's suspension just but Broughton unduly severe in refusing approval for his employment elsewhere. This was to treat the sins of temper with the same gravity as immorality. Perry undertook to mediate between Broughton and Russell, and at Albury believed he won approval for Russell to transfer to Port Phillip provided he apologized and withdrew an appeal to Canterbury. Russell complied and Perry employed him without further correspondence with Broughton. But Russell had not apologized to Broughton's satisfaction. He withdrew none of the imputation of romanism against the Lyndhurst college (now St James Theological College) and Broughton informed Perry that Russell would be employed against his will as Metropolitan. This irritated Perry who believed Russell basically sound. 'I wish to avoid the appearance of placing myself in opposition to you', he wrote to Broughton, '[but] my dear Bishop of Sydney I have so far committed myself as to be unable, with propriety, to draw back.' To save face Perry asked Broughton to state that it had been necessary to revoke Russell's licence in Sydney but the ban did not extend to Melbourne. Broughton refused, and on 4 June 1850 Perry confirmed Russell's appointment.[40] Broughton, however, received more pleasant news from his solicitor. He had escaped bankruptcy. The creditors of the Bank of Australia dropped their suit provided Broughton did not sue for costs. Broughton was happy to quit for that small loss though Judge Coleridge believed he had the better case and the SPG was prepared to back him legally. Broughton immediately made over his insurance policies to his daughters and reduced his worldly possessions to the household furniture.[41] Even that was soon to be as much Emily's as his. Emily finally recovered from the Reverend George Vidal's flight to England and marriage there, and decided to marry George Crawley a Sydney businessman distantly related to Coleridge. Emily set the wedding for August 1850.[42]

Meanwhile in Sydney the queen's thirty-first birthday ended in a gunpowder haze. Only the usual happened but with a zest for the mid-century—more people came on to the streets, the troops paraded with precision, guns saluted louder, firecrackers went off longer. The people had a fine day and so had Broughton. He attended the governor's levée at 1 p.m. wedged between the Speaker of the Council and the Lord Mayor of Sydney, but one step ahead of Polding.[43]

Broughton had boycotted the previous year's levée leaving an unlicensed clergyman to represent the Church of England.[44] Since then Grey had restored his precedence, though reluctantly, at first hoping to hide his blunder behind the popular misconception that archbishops were always superior to bishops. His under-secretary Merivale weaned him from that. Merivale had kept a sharper watch than most on despatches from New South Wales and commented to Grey that he had unwittingly crowned 'a very general attempt in Australia to obtain for the Roman Catholic prelates a position in various ways superior to those of the Church of England'. Grey instantly decided to elevate Broughton and instructed the law officers to find a pretext without upsetting the new table of precedence. They suggested ranking archbishops above all bishops except those with metropolitical jurisdiction; and where both archbishop and bishop were metropolitans, as in New South Wales, the metropolitan deriving his jurisdiction from the 'Crown under the Royal Seal' should take precedence.[45]

That got Broughton to the levée in 1850. But he protested that his attendance did not imply satisfaction. 'The arrangement operates to my own relief', he told Fitzroy, 'yet it leaves the original *principle* still in force, and my Suffragans are still left in a position with relation to the Roman hierarchy which I would not be supposed even indirectly to countenance.' Grey had not removed the possibility of the senior Church of England prelate in every other Australasian colony being in time ranked below the senior Roman Catholic prelate. The pope had only to create the leading town of each colony an archbishopric to force Nixon, Selwyn, Perry and Short one pace to the rear. Broughton did not believe the British parliament understood this implication in Grey's regulations but supposed parliament to have assumed that the senior status preserved to the senior bishop of the Church of Ireland applied to the colonies in general. He wanted parliament to understand it did not, and to debate the propriety of the Colonial Office surrendering to the pope the final determination of precedence within Her Majesty's dominions. Should parliament approve Grey's regulation in full knowledge of its effect Broughton again threatened to stop the administration of the Oath of Supremacy to the colonial clergy. It was nonsense to require of the clergy an oath to protect the nation from popery while the queen smiled sweetly on it. Did the Colonial Office care to hear that tocsin sounded in the colonies?[46]

Fitzroy sat on Broughton's second protest for two months hoping vainly for its withdrawal. In England Merivale advised Grey to treat it seriously and rewrite the rules of colonial ecclesiastical precedence creating the senior Church of England bishop in every colony the first ecclesiastical dignitary. Grey decided parliament should settle the matter and put it aside for the appropriate moment.[47]

In July 1850 while Broughton worked hard at an agenda for the bishops' conference the Reverend Mr Abrahams arrived *en route* to New Zealand. He carried a letter from Gladstone calling the colonial church to its destiny. Earlier on 9 March 1850 while Broughton had moved in leisurely fashion from Braidwood to Bungendore the judicial committee of the Privy Council in London gave judgement in the Gorham case and sent clergymen scurrying in carriages all over London consulting on its implication. One of the busiest charioteers was Abrahams. In the few days left to him before his departure to join Selwyn he spoke with Wilberforce, Mozley, Keble, Pusey and Charles Marriott, and found among them as many views as voices on the matter. Wilberforce condemned the judgement; Mozley thought it not technically wrong; Keble said it merely proved the crown heretical not the church; while Pusey thought the intervention of the Privy Council so irregular as to deprive the judgement of any force. 'All have a theory to help them through—but who is acting?', Abrahams asked Gladstone. 'I shall try to persuade the Bishop of Sydney to call a Synod of the Bishops and Archdeacons of his Province, and if they can agree, to send here George Augustus New Zealand—and that would I feel save the Church of England.' Gladstone agreed and wrote the invitation himself. So in July 1850 Abrahams knocked on the door of Broughton's citadel church.[48]

Over the next few weeks Abrahams gave Broughton a firsthand account of the Gorham affair; of how the judicial committee of the Privy Council had directed a bishop to violate his consecration oath and licence a priest he believed unsound in doctrine; of how the same committee allowed the Church of England to teach that regeneration always does and sometimes does not take place at baptism; and how many had taken refuge in Rome, and more would. Broughton had expected bad news, and got worse. Yet the same fate would have been his had Lowe's schemes succeeded—only the Supreme Court of New South Wales and not the judicial committee of the Privy Council would have determined such questions. Broughton had averted that crisis by declaring from the bar of the Legislative Council that secular authorities had no business in such matters. It puzzled him that the English bishops had not protested earlier. 'Why did not somebody get up *before* the Court of Appeal sat', Broughton asked, 'and say I object to this tribunal ... it is not competent: and let its decision be what it may I protest against it?'.[49] It would be as wrong for churchmen to rejoice at a favourable decision from such a court as it was proper for them to bewail an adverse one. Broughton took Gladstone's cue. 'Let them look to the colonial churches', he wrote back to Gladstone. 'My colleagues would not shrink from an honest expression of what we hold to be the just interpretation of the formularies of the Church. Upon the turn these deliberations take will depend, I presume, the mission to England of one or more of our body.'[50] Unfortunately Perry pronounced the Gorham judgement 'admirable' before the bishops could meet and the mission to England collapsed.[51]

Early in September 1850 Tyrrell joined Broughton to put the finishing

touches to the conference agenda. Then on 20 September just as Broughton sat down to breakfast Selwyn walked in with four natives from
New Caledonia. That began 'a great bustle of taking down and putting
up beds' as Emily transformed Broughton's dressing-room into a bedroom for Selwyn and rearranged her own in preparation for the Perrys;
she exiled the maid to the storeroom and put up her old tent bed in the
maid's quarters to await the Shorts. Selwyn had prematurely aged
and was 'very bald' despite his hydrotherapeutic devotion to health.
He and Tyrrell relived their walking exploits that had made them a
legend among their fellow undergraduates. What virtue they once
had felt in an overnight non-stop walk from Cambridge to London!
Now, of course, Selwyn walked the distance from Edinburgh to London
in a single visitation. Nixon arrived next on 24 September looking the
eternal youth—handsome at forty-seven and still a bachelor. His Oxford
touch broke up the Cambridge reunion. But it was only after Perry
and Short arrived on 28 September with their wives that the dinner-table
at Tusculum sparkled with a conversation to lift Broughton's spirits.
'The women are so superior to us', he remarked.[52]

On Sunday 29 September Broughton put a bishop into every Sydney
pulpit. The following Tuesday he formally welcomed them to St Andrews
cathedral as his comprovincial bishops, not suffragans as stated in their
letters patent. Suffragan implied a subordination he did not desire.
They recited matins and shared the sacrament, then adjourned to the
conference centre in the bishop's study at Tusculum. The lot passed
unnoticed in the press but the clerical doubters spoke up. 'We are about
to have a synod', commented the Reverend Thomas Hassall, Marsden's
son-in-law. 'I fear it will do us little or no good but take up a vast deal
of useful time.'[53]

Business began at 10 a.m. on 2 October. Broughton posed the first
question: Could their meeting be a synod? In preparing for the conference Broughton had at first spoken freely of its being a synod then for
two reasons decided it 'must be in reality a consultation, and little more'.
The term synod implied a binding authority that Broughton thought
the bishops should not mislead themselves into believing they possessed.
They could do no more at this meeting than express 'a body of *opinions*
upon all the important subjects which have been proposed . . . without
the exertion of any coercive authority whatever'. The term synod also
had a legal connotation and Broughton feared some crusty colonial lay
lawyer might fly to his statute books and demand a royal licence of the
bishops for their assembly. Despite his contempt for such arguments
Broughton did not want his good work in bringing the bishops together
devoured in wranglings before they met. Indeed, he aimed for the opposite
effect. He wanted the colony to see the bishops of the Church of England
assemble, consult, and issue guidance acting on their spiritual authority
alone, and give the lie to the oft-repeated papist quip that the bishops
of the Church of England had no authority but that derived from the
crown. Broughton hoped the bishops would agree to a future synod,
and that Gladstone would in the meantime introduce legislation into
the House of Commons freeing colonial churches to fashion their own

forms of self-government. Such colonial synods would then be seen as originating in the will and authority of the local episcopate which first summoned them, and not in the crown.[54]

Perry thought Broughton had skirted the issue. Theirs could not be a synod simply because their letters patent outlawed such gatherings in the British Empire, he said. Broughton sniffed at the suggestion. The bishops would violate no enforceable law by assembling as a synod. Laws upholding the crown's ecclesiastical privilege had no force in the colony for want of competent courts. How could the crown execute a plea of praemunire against the Australian bishops? Ship out the Lord Chancellor and his court, or perhaps despatch a man-of-war and return them bound to Westminster? Theirs was not a legal conundrum of how to execute the royal prerogative in the colony, he continued, but a question of whether the bishops could conscientiously disregard their oath to uphold the declaration prefacing the Thirty-nine Articles which prohibited meetings to reform doctrine and discipline without royal assent. Broughton could. He understood the crown's prohibition on the church's free exercise of power to be conditional upon the crown sustaining the privileges of the Church of England, and when the crown lapsed in the one the church was freed from the other. 'The coercive authority of the Crown rests upon the King's religious *zeal* to conserve and maintain the Church committed to his charge', he said. '*Is* this condition fulfilled, or so much as attempted, with regard to *our* branch of the Church?' Broughton did not expect other bishops with scruples about the royal prerogative to adopt his argument in violation of their conscience but he wanted their procedure to leave no doubt that colonial synods originated in the apostolic authority of the episcopate.[55]

Short separated the sparring bishops. He suggested that those bishops whose conscience required a legal precedent for their meeting together to consider doctrine and discipline should consider the gathering a Metropolitical Visitation such as the letters patent allowed once in five years. That sent the bishops scurrying for books to establish precisely what was a Metropolitical Visitation. By nightfall they decided it was not synodical and not quite what they were engaged in. The bishops decided finally that they were simply meeting; and since they did not intend to legislate they could not offend the royal supremacy in whatever way it applied to the colony.[56]

Broughton made it abundantly clear that he looked forward to bishops meeting in the near future in a synod. To achieve this Broughton opposed any move that proceeded by way of a request to have clarified the meaning of the royal supremacy in the colonies. 'Asking questions touching the Supremacy would be made the grounds of *prohibitory restrictions*', he warned. The bishops would do better to list 'the embarrassments and injuriousness of the present doubtful force and extent of the Royal Supremacy' and ask the ecclesiastical and civil authorities in England for redress. Broughton did not so much want the royal supremacy clarified as cleared away to the extent it inhibited the life of the colonial churches.[57]

One of the bishops' complaints was that the present interpretation of the royal supremacy prevented them properly superintending their own dioceses. It denied them authority to subdivide their dioceses, expand the episcopate, and even to appoint new archdeacons without approval from crown and Canterbury and the risk of rejection. Yet crown and Canterbury indulged their whims without reference to the colonies. Selwyn denounced the arrogance of the new Archbishop of Canterbury, J.B. Sumner, who had only just subdivided the Diocese of New Zealand and appointed a second bishop without a word of consultation. Perry had also written recently to Grey demanding freedom in appointing his archdeacons. The bishops all agreed that initiative in expanding the superintendence of the Church of England in the colonies must rest exclusively with the colonial bishops. They disagreed, however, on what rights should be reserved crown and Canterbury. Nixon, Tyrrell and Short wanted local decisions referred to England for formal approval. Perry insisted the Archbishop of Canterbury retain a power of veto. Selwyn, however, favoured provincial autonomy and Broughton demanded it: 'The Provincial Church of England should be as free as the Wesleyan body'.[58] He would allow crown and Canterbury no initiative, veto, or formal approval, and he wanted the bishops to agree there and then to choose future colonial bishops from the colonial clergy. The other bishops demurred, protesting that Broughton could not expect for the Church of England in the colony a greater freedom than it enjoyed in England. Broughton did: 'If *we* ask more power than the Church of England as at present regulated enjoys, we ask no more than every other Denomination in the colony possesses'.[59] Three years earlier when Grey vetoed Huntingford's appointment Broughton vowed to secure the colonial episcopate its freedom. He believed it implicit it any letters patent creating him Metropolitan. He understood Archbishop Howley had intended the colonial church to enjoy that independence; but Howley was dead and neither Sumner, his successor, or Grey admitted his intention.[60] So Broughton argued from more ancient pretexts. The practice of the primitive church, he told the bishops on the evening of 3 October 1850, was clearly against any Metropolitan interfering in the function of another Metropolitan.[61] Since the Australasian colonies had been granted Metropolitical status Broughton insisted they should enjoy it.

On 4 October the bishops considered who might attend future synods. Broughton swiftly undercut any suggestion that the American Episcopal church had set them their precedent in admitting clergy and laity to a legislative role along with the bishops. 'The American church does not work satisfactorily', he pronounced; and urged the colonial church to look for more ancient precedents. Tyrrell and Nixon understood early English synods to have restricted legislative authority to the bishops. Short thought it a more ancient practice to consult the clergy. And so the discussion proceeded, each bishop invoking his cherished sample of antiquity until Perry called a halt. Ancient usage was one thing, Church of England practice another, and what was desirable a third, Perry said. He would have bishops and clergy unite in all functions, whether legislative, judicial, or administrative. Selwyn surprised Broughton by coming out strongly for the same idea. Broughton, however, stood firmly for a hierarchy of responsibility; provincial synods were for bishops, and for the government of the church in matters affecting doctrine, morality and discipline; diocesan synods were for bishops and clergy and for the discussion of matters affecting them mutually. In the end Broughton bowed to the other bishops: Australian synods would have both bishops and clergy.[62]

What of the laity? Selwyn proposed involving them extensively, and most bishops agreed. There was nothing new in the principle, Tyrrell said, for what was royal supremacy but an 'overstrained' instance of lay involvement in church government? Nixon, however, foresaw difficulties for his diocese where the many convict chaplains were paid servants of the crown. As bishop he had only recently, and with difficulty, won disciplinary rights over these chaplains and believed it futile to expect the government to concede further controls over them to a synod with a popularly elected lay element. In a surprise volte-face Broughton announced that 'the laity had no right to sit in a provincial or diocesan synod'. Two years earlier he held the opposite view, and in the wake of lay solidarity after Sconce and Makinson defected spoke of including the laity more definitely in church government. Since then a lay group had formed at Parramatta to oppose him on ritual matters and doctrine, and another at Darlinghurst had grouped around Russell to challenge his disciplinary powers. So Broughton changed his mind: 'Let them be employed to the full by voluntary associations of parishioners'. If the laity united to save the flagging Parochial Associations they would serve the church better than quibbling over doctrines and dividing a synod. If they saved the Parochial Associations he might then consider them more fit to share in synodical government.[63]

The bishops took two weeks to reach a compromise. They decided bishops and clergy would sit in synods and the laity sit apart but concurrently in a convention at both the provincial and diocesan level. Synods and conventions could debate what they wished but only the synod could legislate on matters of doctrine, discipline and ritual, but never alter the Thirty-nine Articles, Book of Common Prayer or the Authorized Version of Scriptures. Both synod and convention must concur in measures affecting the temporalities of the church and any subsequent change in the constitution.[64]

The bishops turned next to the problem of clerical discipline. Colonial dioceses appeared to attract delinquents. Tyrrell thought his diocese plagued by them, and so far in his brief episcopate he had dealt with a secession to Rome and other cases of immorality, drug addiction, slander, lying, rubrical irregularity, and the abandonment of a cure. Most delinquents left quietly once confronted by their misdeeds, he said; and the few who stood to fight should be tried before an archdeacon and a jury of presbyters with the bishop passing sentence. The bishops generally favoured that. Selwyn wanted the laity included, and he urged the bishops in passing sentence to attempt to redeem rather than simply remove offending clergy. For instance, downgrade them from a higher to a lower ministry or put them in an institution under close supervision,

but don't dismiss them to wander off and plague another diocese.
'Consume your own smoke', Selwyn said. Broughton thought that
'vague and novel'. 'Adulterers could not be employed in a lower office
or ministry', he retorted, and gave each bishop a copy of his translation
of Cyprian's *Epistle to Rogatian concerning a Deacon who had set himself
in opposition to his Diocesan* and urged them to be guided by Cyprian's
ancient practice. Unfortunately Cyprian had guided Broughton through
the Russell episode and excited a cry of episcopal arbitrariness. The
other bishops decided against Cyprian and Broughton, and designated
the synod as the court for the trial of delinquent bishops and clergy.
But the handling of appeals baffled them. Broughton insisted on ultimate
authority being invested in a court constituted under the Metropolitan
of Australasia while Perry insisted on appealing to Canterbury, and
so the matter lapsed.[65]

In more practical matters the bishops admonished the clergy against
shortening services or skipping saints' days, put a limit on extempore
prayer during prayer-book services, and ordered the proper keeping
of church registers.[66]

After tightening discipline on the clergy Tyrrell suggested tightening
it on the laity. He thought the ministrations of the church too easily
claimed by the ungodly: drunk men fell down dead and relatives claimed
Christian burial for them; women got up from the couch of an illegitimate
birth and asked to be churched; adulterers took communion; the unbaptized requested marriage; and notoriously lax people appeared
as sponsors at baptism. 'Timidity is the sin of the Church of England',
Broughton agreed; but like the other bishops he abhorred the introduction
of judicial procedures into a pastoral ministry. Moreover, there were
difficulties. The bishops abhorred concubinage but only encouraged
it by proscribing the marriage of the unbaptized. Apart from warning
'notorious ill-livers' to stay away from communion and cautioning
drunkards and concubines not to expect the full ministry of the church,
the bishops let the matters lapse. The colonial church must rely on a
fearless denunciation of evil and a zealous pastoral concern, and not
the rule of law.[67]

The bishops also decided to direct the laity through the confusion
raised by the Gorham judgement on Holy Baptism. 'When the minds
of pious and thoughful men are in perplexity', they recorded, 'we cannot
remain altogether silent.' The bishops spoke and produced the only
public division of the conference. Perry insisted that no infant was
known for certain to be regenerated through baptism since much depended
on the faith and repentence of the sponsors.[68] The other five bishops
maintained the opposite. Broughton insisted Perry's argument amounted
to a condemnation of the church for permitting the general baptism
of infants. Perry denied the implication. Broughton then retorted that
Perry's expression was not very lucid.[69] Nixon added a vow to drive
from his diocese any clergyman teaching Perry's view. Perry offered
to shelter them.[70] In the end Broughton ruled in accordance with a
procedure he laid down before the conference, that where an irreconci-
lable difference emerged over a matter on which it would be negligent

for the bishops to remain silent both opinions should be stated. They
were; and to Broughton's 'infinite regret' the episcopate was made to
appear as perplexed as the 'pious and thoughtful'. Yet it could have
been worse. Broughton had talked Selwyn out of recording a third
opinion.[71]

That justified a break. On 16 October the bishops reviewed their
progress and adopted their first formal resolutions. Next day Emily
Crawley, who had been busy arranging drives to the lighthouse and
strolls through the Domain and Botanical Gardens for the bishops'
wives, hosted a tea-party at Tusculum for the clergy wives to meet the
bishops' wives. The bishops meanwhile went to town where the clergy
and laity formally welcomed them and approved their meeting, and
the chief justice took up a subscription to record the event in stone.
He proposed erecting a column in the cathedral inscribed with the
names and armorial bearings of each bishop. Finally Archdeacon Cowper
announced the public would meet the bishops on 29 October.[72]

In the twelve days before that meeting the bishops had to decide
whether to launch a Pacific mission. Broughton had not put the matter
on the original agenda but still dreamed of a converted Pacific.[73] He had
urged Selwyn to rescue Tahiti from deist missions and had himself
volunteered to dash quixotically into the Orient to plant Christianity
at Hong Kong. But with his own mission bogged down around Cooma
it was fantasy more than policy to discuss the Pacific. '*My* mission is
not to convert heathens to Christianity', he told Selwyn, 'but by God's
help to prevent Christians from lapsing into heathenism.'[74] Selwyn
nevertheless insisted on discussing the Pacific. He had sailed north
of New Zealand and seen a ready harvest. The Overseas Bishoprics
Fund was exhausted and there would be no mission there if not an
Australasian one. So the bishops decided that while they could not
support a fullscale mission they might sponsor the formation of a
society to train Aboriginal and islander missionaries to work among
their own tribes in Australia and the Pacific. This was a novel idea,
and they advertised it for public discussion at the meeting on Tuesday
29 October.[75]

On 29 October 1850, the bishops arrived at the schoolroom in Castlereagh Street to find hundreds crowded outside the door. Inside only
the passage to the platform was vacant, and the Sydney choral society
greeted the bishops. Broughton, visibly older, thin, greyed and a little
bent from his illness, spoke first. He reminisced. At Reading in 1822
when he was invited for the first time to preach before his brother clergy
he chose to praise mission societies. Now he found himself called to
found another; and he perceived in the presence of so many gathered
ready to join him a marvellous unity in his ministry. The new mission
society also answered the first missionary prayer he uttered in the colony
when at his Primary Visitation in 1829 he prayed to do better than his
predecessors for the Aboriginals. 'Time has not passed without effort,
but it had passed without fruit', he admitted; yet he had never abandoned
hope. The goodwill of so many Christians in coming to support the
advertised purpose of training Aboriginal evangelists revived that hope.

Short and Perry ably supported this facet of the venture, and the mission to the Aboriginals was reborn.[76]

Selwyn shifted the scene to the Pacific and entertained the audience with tales of an adventure in a frail vessel among the islands of the north. But Nixon stole the night. He spoke with a painter's eye for colour, and with few Tasmanian Aboriginals left to convert followed Selwyn into the romance of the Pacific. What shall the Pacific Islander plead at the Judgement? he asked. That Christians came for gain and traffic, taught him drunkenness and sensuality, but spoke not of Jesus? And who spoke not? A people too poor and depressed to care? No! Sixty-two years ago only the cry of men encouraging one another in toil broke the solemn silence of the continent, but today whoever walked its streets passed churches, schools, hospital, library, and villa upon villa replete with the refinements of London society. Is this a people too depressed to care? Had they not themselves been blessed? In half a century the colony's religious life had passed from a weekly convict parade before a single chaplain to one where five bishops and a hundred clergy cast their watchful eye over every stage of the Christian pilgrimage. 'Up, Christian brethren, and gird yourselves', he cried. 'Up—and quit yourselves like men ... Up and be doing the Lord's bidding ... Up—with the determination to lift high the Gospel truth ...' And the people stood up. They sang the Hallelujah Chorus, approved a foundation committee, and pledged to find Selwyn £1000 for a seaworthy vessel so that no bishop was lost before a convert was gained. The Australian Board of Missions was founded.[77]

Three days later on Friday 1 November the bishops closed their conference with a public celebration of the Holy Communion at St Andrews. They then dismissed the two hundred lay worshippers and locked the doors to read the resolutions to the clergy.[78] Broughton allowed no discussion, though some bishops had suggested it. Everything would be published in time. Meanwhile, the world outside learned only that all resolutions were 'opinions ... not binding for the present', and that proper synods would meet in due time.[79]

Despite their month-long meeting the bishops broke up hastily without agreeing on a follow-up plan.[80] Perry left within twenty-four hours, Short a few days later. Tyrrell saw the resolutions to the printer then took Selwyn off to tour his diocese. Broughton went to Cabramatta to consecrate a church. Only after this did Broughton write seeking the co-operation of the Archbishop of Canterbury in a two stage plan to secure the church its constitution. First the Archbishop was to ask the queen-in-council to sanction an enquiry by either a convention of the clergy and laity of the Province of Australasia or a commission of royal appointees. Public discussion should accompany the enquiry so that popular opinion as well as specialist advice shaped any report on the constitutional requirements of the Province of Australasia. In the second stage Broughton hoped the queen-in-council would simply implement the convention's or commission's report. If not, the Archbishop encircled by the Lords spiritual should originate in the House of Lords a measure enabling the colonies to adopt an ecclesiastical

constitution. 'What we require', he stressed, 'is no more than an emancipation, by sufficient authority, from the obligation by which we conceive
ourselves bound *not* to assume the exercise of synodical powers, Provincial or Diocesan, without licence first obtained from the Crown.'[81]
Broughton, however, shrank before the spectacle of parliament even
appearing to debate and determine the constitution. The image was
as important as the substance: the constitution must be seen to originate
in the will of the local church to be governed by ancient practice not
the fad of a contemporary parliament. The charge of Erastianism must
fall dead. Broughton believed all this possible in 1850: 'The time is
good for *Recommendation* ... so that *when* State fetters drop off (as
they must ere long) we may be found *in possession* of a system of acting'.[82]
As a token of the post-conference spirit Broughton sent the Archbishop
of Canterbury a set of unsolicited letters dimissory authorizing him to
consecrate Jackson Bishop of Lyttelton in New Zealand on behalf of the
bishops of the Province of Australasia![83]

Perry knew Grey better and cautioned Broughton's optimism.[84]
Grey had just had the effrontery to force the SPG into endowing the
bishopric of Nova Scotia to avoid its suppression and then contrived
the appointment of his own candidate as bishop in preference to the
Society's. Grey told the SPG that the crown's ecclesiastical patronage
would not be eroded by allowing those who paid to have a say.[85] Perry
did not share Broughton's expectation of co-operation from such a
man. Tyrrell had other misgivings. Would a mere letter compel the
attention of the Archbishop? Tyrrell wanted the resolutions carried
to Lambeth and begged the bishops to unite in approaching Broughton
to go. All concurred in that but Perry. After the rebuke the clergy delivered
him in August 1849 Perry would not err again in committing his diocese
to ecclesiastical reform without open consultation. He also feared Broughton might push the case for provincial autonomy and cut off appeals
to Canterbury.[86] Broughton, however, could not go. With Walsh and
Grylls on leave, Allwood ill, King in poor health and W. B. Clarke
up-country on a government geological survey, Cowper needed Broughton
to assist in maintaining a ministry in Sydney.[87]

Moreover, Broughton had a vital obligation to stay and baffle any
attempt to procure converts locally from the Gorham shemozzle.
Shemozzle there was; and the colonial press recorded it. In England
the Bishop of Exeter, who began it all, defied the Privy Council's judgement and his secretary quit for Rome. In London churchmen held a
rally and asked Broughton to hawk its anti-Gorham petition around
the colony, but before he could circulate it Lord Fielding, who sponsored
the rally, gave himself and his parish church to Rome. Then, of course,
the colonial bishops themselves added to the shemozzle with their
divided opinion on baptism. Broughton dreaded that exposure. He
asked Perry to reconsider his dissent before the conference minutes
were published. He then preached two sermons on baptismal regeneration
to soften their impact. Nevertheless, Sydney's dissenting preachers
made a fury: Could the colony's solitary scriptural bishop lead the
whole Church of England into truth? Papists exulted: With its bishops

at variance and in bondage to the crown can anyone lead the Church of England? If one in six bishops could differ why not one in six of the clergy and the laity? Broughton trembled. 'I write under feelings of alarm and suffering, conscious how probable it is that before these lines can reach you, the seamless coat may have been irreparably rent', he told Gladstone. Yet Broughton fought back. What did a churchman gain who deserted a church disunited on some points of truth for one united upon almost every point of error?, he tirelessly asked. By May 1851 Broughton believed he had manacled the extended arms of popery. Gorham sent Rome no converts from his diocese.[88]

Uncompleted Mission

There is a spirit of greatness here after all: and if *self* could
be a little more driven out of their calculations I should
look with full confidence for a progeny worthy of the English
blood, and what is more, of the English *Church*.

Broughton to Coleridge 7 August 1851

In 1850 the laity of the Diocese of Sydney subscribed £1000 in one month
to buy the Bishop of New Zealand a new boat, and Broughton took
charge of the project. He inspected a local coastal trading vessel recently
put up for sale, tested that it had bunks fit for Mrs Selwyn, and after
a marine surveyor had examined it stamped the coat of arms of the
Diocese of Sydney on its stern, renamed it the *Southern Cross*, and
let Tyrrell take it to New Zealand. The ship sailed with a rotten rudder
through a violent storm and ran aground off Auckland. After that
Broughton ordered prayers for those on board whenever the litany was
recited.[1]

The laity's generosity to Selwyn both delighted and chafed Broughton.
'We have difficulty making any such effort for our own service', he
commented.[2] His own Diocesan Committee got only £168 that same
year for its special projects. Why could he not better inspire his diocese?
The question troubled Broughton. Was it his personality? He knew he
was stiff. Was he competent? He suspected the job had outgrown him.
Had he been indolent as a pastor? For months he stayed scarcely a week
in the same place, then lingered for months in Sydney. Had he cherished
home and family too much, and found a too ready consolation in his
library? He remained a bibliophile, and Sydney booksellers knew him
good for a sale. He taught himself Hebrew and wrote a commentary
on Job. Ought he instead to have been more in the countryside arguing,
like Job, the things that were right?[3] Did his churchmanship offend?
Many branded him a Puseyite. Yet whatever he published under the
pseudonym 'Churchman' earned him praise for moderation. 'This
writer is at least an open adversary', commented a reviewer, '... he
could hardly be a Puseyite, or even a high-and-dry churchman.'[4] Earlier
when English converts rushed from Canterbury to Rome he wanted
the name Tractarian and its party to vanish—but no longer. Still he
would force his opinions on none. He could work with any man who

243

owned the principles of the reformers and a co-operative temperament. Cowper, appointed archdeacon while sending broadsides into the Tractarians, proved that. On the Feast of Epiphany 1851 Broughton appealed for toleration, co-operation, and a united effort throughout the diocese: 'Work out then the principles of the Church ... in your own way; in any way ... But for God's sake let the work somehow be done'.[5]

Tusculum haunted Broughton. His daughter Emily kept house and her Eton-trained husband made interesting conversation. Phoebe stayed for the summer of 1850–1, but her children's prattle distressed the bishop. 'Their innocent voices bring back the memory of her who would *most* have rejoiced over them, so that like Joseph I am often obliged to seek where to weep', he confessed. Whenever he tried writing to the Keates his memory echoed with the hearty laugh of Mrs Keate as she characteristically threw her arms around the younger Mrs Broughton, and his letters lay unfinished. He could not yet write to her friends, and the friends of his own youth were gone. Norris was dead. Hutchisson was dead. Coleridge rarely wrote being more preoccupied with Selwyn's mission. 'This is all weakness', Broughton admitted; but the loneliness was stark. He absorbed his time in 'mere business', and longed to be back in the bush. He found solace in riding (mostly by carriage now as a concession to age) and had a 1200 mile visitation planned. But a deteriorating clerical situation detained him in Sydney in January 1851. Allwood was again unwell and Broughton took over the lectures at St James College. Alfred Stephen the curate at Christ Church in Walsh's absence collapsed; Bodenham the immigration chaplain who assisted Stephen on Sundays went down with consumption; and Carey, a new young clergyman who helped Broughton at Darlinghurst after Russell's dismissal, had a seizure and was useless.[6] Then gold was discovered.

Gold quite turned the mind of Sydney. Electioneering for a new Legislative Council stopped when news of the first diggings at Bathurst arrived in May 1851; and 'it was at one time feared by some that owing to the mania for gold the next election would be a failure'. The colonial government discussed gold at closed meetings and in confidential memoranda as if mutiny had occurred, while preachers pursued the topic with bell, book and candle. Then suddenly the colony awoke to the exhilarating realization that gold would turn it from a third-rate pastoral colony into a nation. 'No longer ... when only an Australian question was to come before the House of Commons, will no more than forty members be found on their seats, and the House counted out', boasted Mr Lamb chasing votes to represent the capital city of the new nation. His election opponents fell into line. Wentworth vowed to protect established colonists from the disorders that had afflicted California; Lang promised universal suffrage to make the new nation another United States; and Cowper pledged to improve Sydney's sanitation to cope with the influx. By August 1851 everyone braced themselves for a new era.[7]

Broughton expected a worse situation than California's. Gold would accelerate the already unmanageable bush. The diocese had no spare clergy, and building debts of £8300 precluded Broughton importing any till after 1852. No suitable ordinands had applied for training at

LYNDHURST,
where Broughton set up St James Theological College.

TUSCULUM
a little after Broughton's tenancy and enlarged by the addition of
partly enclosed side verandahs.

LYONS' TERRACE.

Broughton shifted into one of these fashionable terrace houses
in 1852. Sir Alfred Stephen occupied the fifth on the left.

ST ANDREWS CATHEDRAL 1849.

St James College in two years, and since the SPG had supplied only one of the several immigration chaplains already promised it was futile for the bishop to appeal there for help. So Broughton decided once again to 'leap into the yawning gulf' himself. 'If an example of self-denial for holy purposes be required who can be so peculiarly called as I to go before in the true and right way?', he asked, and offered to slice another £500 from his salary. If the diocese matched it three to one Broughton would have £2000 for eight extra clergymen. Earlier a similar gesture had produced two extra bishops when none seemed possible. Might not the magic work again? But Broughton had first to negotiate his way out of the high-priced lease on Tusculum and shift to modest quarters.[8] Meanwhile he visited the gold-fields.

Broughton arrived at Sofala by Bathurst five months after the diggings began, carrying prayer-book and pick. A congregation met him in the open air at 6 a.m. and together they recited matins under a warm sun. 'Now let us dig to the glory of God in ground undisturbed since creation', he announced as the service concluded, and swung his pick into the ground. By 8.30 a.m. the congregation had dug foundations for a church twenty-one feet by sixty-six feet. After breakfast timber arrived, then canvas for the walls and roof, and by midday a cart-load of ecclesiastical fittings. Four days later Broughton celebrated the first communion on the Australian gold-fields.[9] Before long Broughton was reining-in William Boydell's enthusiasm for the beguiling profits of the diggings. 'It is uncertain as to profit—very unsatisfactory as to morals—and very dangerous as to health', the bishop wrote to his son-in-law. 'My advice therefore to anyone would be and is *not to go*.'[10] Phoebe thanked her father for that. But hordes of others went deserting their wives and children—in four weeks five hundred were left in Sydney alone; and the call came for another public relief operation like that Broughton had organized at the height of the unemployment in 1839.[11] This time Broughton did not respond.

Broughton rarely now embroiled himself in public affairs. The age of the church citadel had arrived and he expended his energies within its walls. Even the imminent threat of renewed transportation in mid-1851 failed to lure him to the public podium. While Bishop Nixon led thirty-three of his Tasmanian clergy in a protest and McEncroe styled himself chaplain to the anti-transportation movement to bless its Sydney banquets, Broughton refused even to loan the anti-transportationists a meeting room. Only after a formal deputation by two leading laymen on behalf of the Anti-Transportation Committee did Broughton issue a statement: 'It is impossible to believe that any British statesman will be found, who, upon the ground of policy, and, still less, upon a principle of justice, will recommend the continuance of the practice'. Privately he believed Grey would create Moreton Bay another colony and dump the convicts there.[12] Others could fight that.

Broughton had barely contested the founding of a colonial university. Indeed the University of Sydney happened so suddenly that some thought it a 'job' hatched in the boardroom of the ailing Sydney College. That college needed money, and having a spare parcel of land its trustees suggested a university be built on it. Wentworth, a college trustee and shareholder, addressed the Legislative Council on the idea; and with disarming audacity proposed a select committee investigate it, nominated two Sydney College shareholders to the committee, and foreshadowed a report favouring a university 'kept entirely free from the teachers of any religion'. The Council connived at the request, and a month later Wentworth had a report 'without any evidence', £5000 promised by the governor, and a draft University bill which banned the clergy from the senate and all academic posts. In Wentworth's vision the institution was to be 'a fountain of knowledge at whose springs all may drink be they Christian, Mohammedan, Jew or Hindu'. Cowper objected to that. But an alliance of cynics and liberal Catholics and liberal Protestants swept him aside, and the bill was within a day of passing its second reading when Wentworth nominated Dr Bland to the foundation senate. Now, despite his colonial gentility and distinguished philanthropy, Dr Bland was an ex-convict. His nomination meant ex-criminals were more fitted to serve antipodean learning than the clergy. How Oxford would jeer! So ludicrous was the situation that members walked from the council chamber in self-respect, and the bill lapsed.[13] All that had occurred in the September and October of 1849 while Broughton flirted with death.

Broughton lived and lodged a protest, but in 1850 the Legislative Council merely fiddled with Wentworth's original University bill. It allowed clergy and ex-convicts to sit on the senate and admitted that its policy of religious liberty should not set out to disadvantage the existing churches.[14] Nevertheless, since the university was to crown the National Schools system and teach what offended none, its senate was to control both teaching and examining. 'It will be the great emporium of false and anti-church views in this hemisphere', Broughton puffed, and spurned Fitzroy's offer of a senate seat.[15] The price of Broughton's collaboration was a university restricted to examining candidates presented to it by self-governing colleges. Broughton and Tyrrell had already bought a grand old home, Roslyn Castle, in the rural quiet of Raymond Terrace away from Sydney for such a residential college, and if it could not be incorporated into the university Broughton intended to develop it independently. He was optimistic of its succeeding. He already operated the more successful grammar schools, had agents scouting Oxford for tutors and £1000 ready to hire them, and had decided to concentrate on professional training, especially in law, rather than the liberal studies planned for the university.[16] Fitzroy took the threatened competition seriously and had it leaked to Broughton that the office of foundation provost, which Wentworth coveted, could be his for returning the university his co-operation. Broughton was not to be flustered into a doubtful alliance by a dubious honour, and tossed the offer aside.[17] The matter of the university did not appear urgent. The grammar schools had first to produce acceptable matriculants, and in 1851 a stint on the gold-fields attracted the young more than a few terms in college.

In 1851 papal aggression didn't even fluster Broughton. 'Daring', he called it; but unexpected only to the heedless. Earlier in the year he thought the popish prelate, Nicholas Wiseman's use of the Sydney letters patent to impugn the spirituality of the English episcopate an overture to a grander act.[18] Wiseman found the letters patent printed in the *Parliamentary Papers* of 1850 and told a London congregation that Broughton's letters patent of 1836 left no doubt that the king had made him Bishop of Australia; and the letters patent of 1847 that the queen had later deposed him of his original see and sliced off most of it for others; and that Broughton had not objected because, together with the whole Church of England, he bowed to the monarchy as the fount of spiritual authority. So Wiseman asked: Was not this rampant Erastianism? The *Freeman's Journal* echoed the accusation around the colony and Broughton turned pamphleteer to deny it. The king had appointed him Bishop of *Australia* after the church made him a *bishop*: the church gave him *Holy Orders* and the king gave him *territory*. The queen had indeed sliced up his diocese, but at *his* request and only after the concurrence of the Archbishop of Canterbury as *Metropolitan bishop*. 'Not only was the proposal mine', Broughton told Wiseman, 'but so also were all the . . . minutest particulars of the scheme as it was afterwards carried out.' Broughton alleged that in order to traduce the Church of England Wiseman had debased his pulpit by misquoting half sentences from his letters patent. 'It is but the effect of the system under which you have been trained', Broughton sniffed. 'When you again address your congregation . . . come with your Bible in hand instead of *Parliamentary Papers*.'[19]

As a formal protest against papal aggression Broughton rehashed his declaration of 1843 against Polding's assumption of the title Archbishop of Sydney, but without ceremony or surpliced processions. Broughton saw the moment as a vindication without satisfaction. It had happened as foretold; and Broughton dug up letters written twelve years before warning of a coming day when Rome would cite its unchecked activity in New South Wales as 'precedent to justify encroachment elsewhere'.[20] Wiseman had conformed to the prediction, and craved public indulgence towards the new papal hierarchy in England by pointing to popular and official acquiescence in Polding's appointment to the see of Sydney.[21] Yet in mid-1851 Broughton feared more England's response than Rome's new initiative. He hoped the British government would not compel the papacy to title its English sees so as to claim a jurisdiction over Roman Catholics only. It had allowed colonial popery to adopt titles flattering to its claim of universal jurisdiction and left colonial Protestantism in isolation to baffle the effect as best it could. If a papist could be plainly the Archbishop of Sydney why not another plainly the Archbishop of Canterbury? Only the odium of some such claim would stir Englishmen to a more seasonable defence of Protestantism. Broughton feared the English church would lapse into its customary indifference once parliament shielded it with special legislation from the full impact of Rome's thrust for domination.[22] For Broughton the struggle against popery and infidelity had assumed proportions that only a global union of English, colonial, and American dioceses could effectively resist. He had already made plain his own commitment to matching Rome's universalism with such a global Protestantism by refusing to accept back for local use the £481 his diocese raised celebrating the tercentenary of the Book of Common Prayer in 1849. He insisted the Overseas Bishopric Fund devote it to some new diocese; and in 1851 he sent another £357 raised during the SPG jubilee.[23]

Meanwhile Broughton tackled a spot of local aggression. Polding adored music, and Mozart masses echoed from St Mary's cathedral. In 1850 the cathedral choir expanded into the St Mary's town choir for public concerts, and opened its ranks to all singers. 'It is part of a *system* meant to be the commencement of an intercourse through the medium of skilfully selected sacred music', Broughton warned and directed lovers of Protestant music to the St James singers.[24] Indeed colonial popery had an irrepressible audacity; it squeezed £2000 from the old Church and Schools estates to build Polding an episcopal palace, and sent Dr Gregory off to Rome under the guise of sick-leave (so Broughton believed) to talk the pope into creating a diocese at Moreton Bay.[25]

But in September 1851 the Legislative Council elections rather than the pope unsettled Broughton. Lang swept the Sydney poll under a reformed constitution which lowered the franchise to £10 and surrendered management of the £30 000 religious subsidy to the Legislative Council. Among Lang's 'claptrap radicalism' was a pledge to keep the vigil until the state withdrew its aid from religion. 'There are differences of opinion on this point', Lang admitted while campaigning, '[but] the question is a mere question of time.' Wentworth opposed him. He despised the ten-pounders and like Wellington gave them his back. He pledged instead to uphold 'all the time honoured institutions which instructed and governed us', and was barely re-elected. Those who overtly associated their campaign with the maintenance of religious subsidies did worse. One candidate, Longmore, allegedly lost because the priests openly supported him; and Cowper's churchly image made him the tail of the Sydney poll.[26] The 'democratic lion' had devoured those who did not stroke its mane, commented one newspaper; and Broughton feared no future candidate could afford to pledge support for religious subsidies:

> Admidst all the wild and intemperate expression of self-will, which prevails here on the part of men endowed with the sudden possession of political power, there is yet a feeling of rude generosity, almost of magnanimity, which may incline them to do more than one could at first look for from them ... But the desire of office and station, with power and emolument attached, may prove too strong for their integrity, and the Church may be made the sacrifice, or a stepping stone to ambition.[27]

On 23 September 1851, a week after Cowper's electoral defeat, Broughton took off on a four-month ride along a 3000 mile track. In the solitude of the bush he sifted the church's constitutional problems. Much had happened since the bishops met. Gladstone's attempted liberation of the colonial churches on the eve of the bishops' conference in 1850 had failed, and Broughton finally knew the details. 'There was no religious preference worth a straw from one end of the Australian colonies to the other', Gladstone had told the British parliament; yet the colonial churches were hindered by letters patent of dubious legality which no colonial government would enforce and no colonial church could wilfully violate. Gladstone explained how Blackstone argued that in ecclesiastical affairs letters patent had no force outside England yet the British government rested colonial ecclesiastical appointments on them; that those letters patent set up consistorial courts which Scottish Presbyterians believed violated the Act of Union; and that the colonial clergy had a right of appeal to Canterbury but its archbishop had no courts for hearing their appeals. 'The State had been playing pranks with the Church for a considerable time', Gladstone summed up; and he challenged parliament either to restore the colonial church the privileges of an establishment or to let it 'fall back upon original and natural freedom'. Gladstone wanted the Australian Colonies bill then under debate amended to free the bishops, clergy and laity of the Church of England in the colonies to assemble and by mutual consent draft rules for the internal government of their own dioceses, and to prohibit persons who had consented to those rules afterwards appealing against them to English courts. To colonial church supporters in England 'the remedy suggested was certainly as simple and inoffensive as possible'. But members of the House of Commons denounced such a licence as natural freedom anywhere in the Church of England, and a record 289 of them rushed in from the lobbies to dispute and finally overturn Gladstone's novelty.[28]

Broughton did not bemoan this failure. Gladstone had acted on outdated advice taken from earlier correspondence with Howley and Coleridge before the idea of an autonomous Province of Australasia took shape in Broughton's mind, and had the amendment succeeded it would have tied the Australian dioceses to Canterbury by vesting in the English archbishop a power to disallow local canons and to act as a final court of appeal.[29] Broughton quickly set Gladstone right on that point: 'If there be any appeal from a Metropolitan it must be, I believe, to his own Provincial Synod, and not to another Metropolitan'.[30] Yet the attempted reform in 1850 was not without its achievement. By persuading parliament to publish all official correspondence on ecclesiastical discipline in Australia Gladstone made it plain that the colonial church had a disciplinary problem. Gladstone had also prevailed on the Society for the Reform of Colonial Government, which met weekly while parliament sat and to which Lord Lyttelton and Mr Molesworth belonged, to add ecclesiastical reform to its causes.[31] No longer would the issue be dismissed as the concern of those with a quirk for religion.

Yet the episode perplexed Broughton. Why had the Archbishop of Canterbury sat mute through the debate? Did the Colonial Office and its Erastian secretary Grey approve or disapprove of colonial synods? Grey had opposed Gladstone's amendment as 'entirely false' *politically* but said little of it *ecclesiastically*. Grey simply thought it incongruous of Gladstone to interrupt a debate on a bill to extend the powers of a colonial legislature by inserting an amendment removing the colonial Church of England from the local legislature's jurisdiction. Moreover,

Grey feared special legislation for dealing with the problems of the Church of England, even if free of all hint of privilege, might rearouse the sectarian animosities Bourke's Church Act had lulled to sleep by treating all denominations indifferently. Grey nevertheless appeared to admit the colonial Church of England faced hitherto unsuspected problems worthy of investigation, and that the House of Commons might need to pass some future measure of general ecclesiastical relief for the Church of England throughout the empire. Whatever the content of that measure Grey warned 'he could not consent to place the Church in Australia on a different footing from that on which it stood in this country'. While that appeared to rule out synods Grey's parliamentary under-secretary and cousin, Sir George Grey, spoke in the House of Commons as though the Colonial Office would concede the colonial church any form of internal management mutually acceptable to its local membership and the colonial legislature; and the British attorney-general pledged no opposition from the crown to a colonial synod.[32] 'It is curious how the question is dealt with', wrote an English observer.[33]

The Colonial Office wished simply to be free of involvement. It appeared to invite Broughton to act as he saw fit, and then to rely on the local government to legislate him out of difficulties. One predictable difficulty would be a challenge from a cleric under discipline to the validity of local ecclesiastical courts. Broughton may then require the Legislative Council to enact a bill giving the locally fashioned ecclesiastical machinery its due force. He would naturally draft such a bill, but the presence in the Legislative Council of a party ready to meddle in the disciplinary arrangements of the Church of England would throw into doubt its passage unamended. Broughton could find himself bound to some hybrid scheme of ecclesiastical rule more destructive of church principles than the existing uncertainty. Fortunately a new lay-Catholic *Freeman's Journal* had already pledged its unremitting opposition to any local legislation which implied that the Church of England was so differently placed from other churches as to require special legislation.[34] In 1851, then, Broughton could still expect the matter to be resolved in England and beyond the meddlesome intervention of the local legislature.

Unfortunately in 1851 the Australian dioceses tendered the English authorities rather confused counsel. After Tyrrell returned from the bishops' conference in 1850 he read his clergy the bishops' resolutions from the altar and told them they would be consulted when the time came to draft legislation; and Newcastle diocese enjoyed 'uninterrupted peace'. In Hobart Nixon also told the clergy their opinions would not be required till later, and had endless strife. Short, too, had endless strife in Adelaide because he 'kindheartedly' asked the clergy for their opinions and found them too radical.[35] 'I fear our good brother Short has not shown all the wisdom of the serpent', Broughton commented.[36] But the worst happened in Melbourne. To avoid strife Perry agreed to discuss the future constitution with his clergy and laity immediately; and, to stave off a radical attempt to sever ties with Sydney and return Melbourne to the Province of Canterbury immediately Broughton retired, Perry agreed to the diocese having access to courts of the Arch-bishop of Canterbury and the Privy Council.[37] That eclipsed all hope of an autonomous Australasian Province, and Broughton turned bitterly on Perry. Had not the bishops agreed to defer local consultation until after the Archbishop of Canterbury replied? Perry could recall no such undertaking and Tyrrell confirmed there was none. Broughton never-theless accused Perry of wanting in 'canonical obedience' by calling an informal synod without consulting first with his Metropolitan. Perry affirmed that he (like the Bishop of Exeter) could call his diocese to conference on his own authority. But he soothed the ageing Metro-politan: 'While I am aware of there being a great difference of opinion between us upon many important matters, I both reverence your office and love your person'.[38] Broughton was to be respected, perhaps even loved, but he was not master; and to ensure he never was Perry com-municated to Lord Grey that he and his diocese were irrevocably committed to the overlordship of Canterbury in matters of ritual and doctrine.[39]

Broughton dismissed Perry's longing to snuggle down under Canter-bury's suzerainty as blind affection for the worn-out arrangements of a fading era of royal supremacy. Broughton wanted the Australian dioceses secured to a more stable principle. The royal supremacy had served England well, as earlier it had enabled Constantine to pull the church through the factious Donatist era; but Broughton insisted that 'in the colonial portion of the church the crown does not strive in support of the church ... and scarcely can think it equitable to retain over the colonial church a supremacy'. For New South Wales in mid-century the question was: After the royal supremacy, What? A papal supremacy? 'There is still too much substance of good sense and serious belief remain-ing in the Church of England to suffer this', Broughton boasted.[40] The colonial answer was autonomous colonial synods; and Broughton argued that in principle, though regrettably less so in practice, synods and the royal supremacy were not that far apart. The royal supremacy in its perfection never meant kingly rule over the church but rule by the crown in consultation with the whole church, its ecclesiastical order being represented by the lords spiritual and its laity by the lords temporal and the House of Commons. Supreme authority in ecclesiastical matters belonged to the whole church; and it was vested in the crown only so long as the crown represented the whole church. Once the crown by whim or expediency failed to prosper the church, as was the present case in New South Wales, then the church must govern itself by some other means. The synod was one alternative. It left undisturbed the principle of consultation between the ecclesiastical and lay orders, and could be arranged to ensure that neither order gained an absolute power. Broughton believed history stressed the need for a divided authority. The clergy must determine matters of faith but the laity must retain 'a corrective and protective' power remembering that ecclesiastical tribunals had erred in the past and even maliciously attacked the rights of individuals by treating as spiritual issues matters properly temporal. Such divided control reduced the possibility of injustice; though

Broughton admitted it doubled the opportunity for conflict. Even so, good could come from such an anomaly if it drew attention to the need for both clergy and laity to examine their principles. A single supreme authority might prevent anomalies but the removal of conflict often prevented the reform of error, as was clear from Rome's history. 'To express my opinion quite candidly', Broughton wrote,

> I think that for the general security it is necessary that ... a power of control should in some shape or other be exercised by the laity within the Church; and ... I can conceive no arrangement so just in principle or so easy and safe in practice, as that the Sovereign should be invested with this supreme authority on behalf of the laity of the Church as its representative. But ... the time may not be remote when the crown must be, if it be not even now, disqualified from the exercise of such a function in the colonies. Yet the lay element must not be excluded ...[41]

Even so, Broughton's wit expired before the challenge of resurrecting an equivalent to the royal supremacy from among the lawyers, merchants and farmers of New South Wales. 'It becomes an embarrassing question', he admitted; and took refuge in the lapse of time. 'It must be sufficient for me at the present time to have proposed the question. The determination of it will require most anxious consultation.'[42]

When during November 1851 and in mid-visitation up bush Broughton received Archbishop Sumner's reply to the bishops' conference memorandum his indecision fled. Sumner proved a dud. Apart from unreservedly denouncing synods as an infringement of the queen's unqualified supremacy he dodged all comment on the colony's quest for ecclesiastical independence. Tyrrell was dumbfounded, and at first suspected Broughton had mishandled the post-conference correspondence. But evasion was Sumner's tactic. Sumner, however, did offer to sponsor legislation reforming clergy discipline in the colonial churches, but he insisted that the bishops formulate their requirements clearly and leave the ultimate legislation to the Secretary of State for Colonies and the ecclesiastical law officers of the crown.[43]

'I will not assent to it', Broughton rebelled. 'To have our conclusions on church matters submitted to three official laymen for them to operate upon, is what I would not agree to.' For years Broughton had hoped a Protestant Hilderbrand would come and shake the Church of England free of praemunire and the other shackles which restrained its free exercise of apostolic authority. He resolved now on being his own Hilderbrand. Without consultation, but firm in the conviction that ancient custom was on his side, he decided to meet the clergy, then the laity, then both together, when he returned to Sydney in January 1852, and to have them plan together the diocese's future. 'Whether I shall *call* this a Diocesan Synod, I cannot quite determine, but it certainly will *be* one in effect', he told Tyrrell. 'But we must act ourselves.'[44]

Tyrrell gasped. He had only just weaned Broughton of his attachment to an autonomous Province of Australasia. Apart from Melbourne's 'wish for isolation' and Perry's refusal to allow another bishop to represent him in negotiations with the Colonial Office, Tyrrell persuaded Broughton the project had been visionary from the start given the diversity of their diocesan predicaments. No single constitution could suit New Zealand's native mission, Tasmania's extensive convict population, a colony of free settlers like South Australia, or two dioceses such as Sydney and Adelaide where one claimed and the other opposed state aid. Tyrrell had Broughton agree instead to unite the dioceses of Sydney and Newcastle. 'As regards any real Provincial union our two Dioceses and ours only must be expected to act together', Tyrrell wrote, and urged Broughton to secure the arrangements personally in England. When instead, and without consultation, Broughton decided on his January conferences Tyrrell thought him as precipitous as the other bishops. 'I should myself shrink from any such undertaking', Tyrrell returned Broughton notice. 'The laity were not ... in such a temper at Sydney, as would allow them to be consulted'. If Broughton was bent on consultation Tyrrell thought it better that he go to London and, with Grey, work out the terms on which a commission of enquiry could take evidence for a constitution from the colonial clergy and laity. But Tyrrell would never involve either clergy or laity directly in the drafting of such a constitution. Even Selwyn thought that a fruitless exercise. But Broughton was not prepared to go to England. He had the gold-field churches to nurture, a struggling school system, and he believed himself on the brink of victory in a six-year struggle to have bush parsons paid out of the pastoral licences. Moreover, there was not time enough to tie up local affairs and still reach England before others acted, Broughton said; and he counselled Tyrrell to remember with whom they dealt. Sumner and Grey were both attuned to a party of 'evangelical views and liberal principles' poised to recruit clergy and teachers to loosen the grip they imagined Tractarians had on the colonial churches. Sumner, too, had also shown himself in a recent pamphlet to approve experiments, like those being urged in Adelaide, Hobart, and Melbourne, of Presbyterianizing the episcopate by subordinating it to the control of a diocesan committee of clergy and laymen. 'Do you not fear lest our silence ... should be construed as an admission that the voice and feelings of the Church in all the Dioceses is in favour of such opinions', Broughton asked Tyrrell. 'My apprehension is that we shall hear of a Bill being presented for the ecclesiastical government of the churches in Australia, in the principle of which neither you nor I should be able to concur.' Yet the two bishops alone would protest in futility. Already the archbishops in the House of Lords had remarked on the commotion in Adelaide, Melbourne and Hobart as indicating that the bishops' conference was 'at variance with public sentiment'. To save their dioceses from unwanted interference Broughton believed he and Tyrrell must act promptly and show Sumner and Grey that their clergy and laity supported the request for an autonomous provincial synod in New South Wales. 'Even if, as with St Paul, no man stands with me, yet I shall make some effort', he told a still hesitant Tyrrell.[45]

Broughton delayed his tacit synod until Tyrrell met him in Sydney, then in February 1852 his conscience constrained him to abandon any synod-like assembly as at variance with the declaration affixed to the Thirty-nine Articles which his ordination oaths bound him to respect. He elected instead to have his clergy come to Sydney in April and petition the queen for a synodical constitution. But first he wanted the laity to confer on the idea in their parishes, and in mid-March circulated a draft petition and an explanatory declaration throughout the diocese. The draft petition requested the queen to remove all obstacles to the self-government of the diocese of Sydney by a *synod* of its bishop and clergy meeting concurrently with a *convention* of elected laymen; and in the declaration Broughton sought general approval of the resolutions of the Bishops' Conference of 1850 (which *inter alia* approved the idea of a provincial synod being the ultimate colonial court of appeal) 'as the basis of all subsequent proceedings' in the negotiations for a constitution. Broughton urged both documents on the laity as containing 'the best and most secure direction' he could offer them. 'But it is not my intention to imply that the course thus pointed out is absolutely the best', he added, 'nor do I desire that it should be followed, except so far as it may commend itself to the favourable judgment of the Church at large.' The bishop directed the clergy to report their laity's opinions to the April conference.[46]

At first it appeared a disaffected layman, Richard Sadleir from Liverpool, might give the parish debates a crabbed tone. He had earlier launched the Australian Church Society to salvage the diocese from Puseyism in the wake of Sconce's defection, and it flopped. Now he called on Sydney laymen to militantly support their Adelaide lay brethren's demands for equality with the clergy in ecclesiastical government. Sadleir branded the 'detached vestry meetings' a bit of episcopal chicanery for minimizing non-clerical influence and demanded the laity be heard in person at the clerical conference on 14 April. Sadleir circulated an alternative petition requesting the queen to approve a constitution 'wherein the clergy and laity may meet upon an equality', and offered her the power of a veto over all colonial deliberations. It was 'discourteous and unbecoming' of Broughton, Sadleir added, to suggest the queen should be content with a diminished ecclesiastical supremacy in the colony.[47]

Sadleir misfired. The diocese preferred Broughton's thought on the royal supremacy. 'What do we Churchmen get from our connexion with the State . . . ? I am not aware of anything', stated a little-known parishoner from St James. 'If these synods and conventions were necessary for the due government of the Church—they were certainly not required to approach the throne to obtain them', was the more authoritative opinion of Mr Justice Dickinson.[48] The Sydney laity ignored Sadleir's alternative petition, and at the Christ Church vestry meeting in early April 1852 the chief justice, Sir Alfred Stephen, lifted the debate to a more refreshing level. Stephen, like Sadleir, wanted a single convention of clergy and laity, but side-stepped the hubbub over episcopal tyranny and clerical despotism to rest his case on expediency. Any constitution which aimed at improving Sydney's diocesan life must arouse the laity from their apathy, and Stephen thought it fatal to begin by pronouncing the laity incompetent to discuss spiritual matters with their clergy. Stephen wanted the laity to meet the bishop and clergy in 'one compact and united deliberative and acting body, on every question, ecclesiastical or merely economical'. He did not oppose the convention dividing into clerical and lay factions to vote, though he preferred to see it remain united with laity casting one vote a congregation. 'And if it were supposed that the powers thus to be given, might even be exercised to control the Clergy, in matters where at present the Bishop alone had a voice', Stephen added, 'he would avow the opinion, with all respect . . . that occasions might exist, in which it would be good for the Church, that there should be such a controlling power'. Stephen challenged the clergy to stifle Sadleir's endemic distrust of their order by them-selves trusting the laity. Such trust, and a constitution similar to that Stephen outlined had, in less than seventy years, turned an American church, left near lifeless and without a bishop in the aftermath of the revolution, into one thriving with thirty-two bishops and two million members.[49]

Ironically the Christ Church vestry was among the few not to adopt Stephen's resolution. It perceived a distinction between religious and temporal affairs, and voted the clergy a pre-eminence in determining the former. But Charles Kemp thought as Stephen. He had spoken briefly of the American church constitution the day before at the St James vestry meeting, and learning of Stephen's full and able apology published it in his newspaper. Thereafter vestries endorsed the American model with lyrical fervour and distressed Broughton. 'But I am not . . . willing to admit the necessity of going to that distance for a model and a guide', he retorted. 'I am myself by conviction an English Churchman'.[50]

By the eve of the clergy conference the laity had approved Broughton's draft petition in principle but rebuffed the declaration. Twenty of the twenty-six vestries considered the Bishops' Minutes of 1850, and their distinction between clerical and lay functions, an unsatisfactory basis for constitutional negotiations. This surprised Broughton and befogged his plans. Since the Bishops' Minutes had circulated in Sydney for over a year with little adverse comment Broughton had prepared his conference strategy on the assumption of their being approved.[51] He scrutinized the April vestry resolutions and decided he had erred by failing to define satisfactorily the differences between religious and temporal affairs to justify the clergy meeting separately from the laity on purely religious matters. But that was unavoidable: 'We have this good reason for saying that it cannot be done, that it never has been done', he explained.[52] The laity suspected that what could not be defined did not exist, and amateur lay theologians pulled texts from scripture to show that the apostles even consulted women on spiritual matters. What then could the clergy properly withhold from men?[53] That sent Broughton thumbing through the conference proceedings of 1850 rethinking the bishops' individual arguments and re-examining all the authorities quoted. He concluded that the rejected Bishops' Minutes were true to apostolic precedent. By contrast he found the vestry resolutions oozed with a 'sort of "Rights of Man" argument', and to take the pretensions out of that decided to open the conference with a plea to the clergy to approve the Bishops' Minutes in opposition to their laity.[54]

On 14 April twenty-nine clergy turned up at St Andrews cathedral and forty uninvited laymen sat behind them. At 11 a.m. Broughton processed to his episcopal throne full of misgiving. Then the Seventy-first Psalm came up: 'For thou, O Lord God, art the thing that I long for: thou art my hope, even from my youth'. The bishop's mind darted to the morning of his consecration when he recited the same psalm. What more had he longed for since his youth but that the glory of the Lord should cover the earth as the waters covered the sea? That vision had driven him to the colony in 1829 and drawn him back again in 1836. He had not lived so long to forsake without a struggle the vision that had sustained him for half a century. Moreover, ought not he who assumed daily the care of *all* the churches expect a voice above those who cared for but *one*? Before the psalm had finished Broughton's doubt fled: 'Every verse went to my heart; and I there and then imbibed a resolution which may God grant me never to lose'. Broughton led his clergy to an adjoining schoolroom and after welcoming the uninvited laity lectured them for three hours on the defects in the vestry resolutions, corrected the biblical exegesis alleged in support of them, put afresh the claims of the Bishops' Minutes, and cautioned any clergyman against obliterating the distinction between clergy and people in order that men may speak well of him.[55]

Later, outside the cathedral, angry laymen mingled with disappointed clergy. Broughton had appealed to the laity for co-operation and reproached them for their zeal: 'Like the Witch of Endor, at whose incantations the dead Samuel appeared, he trembles at the spirit he has raised', scoffed a reporter. Even those better disposed towards the bishop must have felt he spoke with more conviction than persuasion. For instance, many vestries had hailed the election of Matthias to replace Judas as a lay appointment because one hundred and twenty Christians voted at a time when there were only eleven apostles, and from that had inferred the supremacy of lay over clerical power in the early church. Broughton replied by separating the one hundred and twenty voters into eleven apostles, seventy disciples, and only about twenty of the laity in the proper sense of the term; and then added that 'the actual election of Matthias was miraculous'. There was a fetch in such arguments. Moreover, Broughton's plea for the diocese to evolve its constitution from English traditions rather than American novelties merely expressed a preference. His own draft petition admitted Englishmen would find any form of an elected body of ecclesiastical lay governors a little novel. Why settle for a cautious but untried novelty when the bold American synods had succeeded?[56]

Allwood left the opening meeting of the conference unmoved, and Broughton realized the next day's debate was in difficulties. He knew Hassall had support for a motion to suspend the conference until elected lay representatives joined it, and at the other extreme young Napoleon Woodd and the stammerer Grylls had supporters to condemn the involvement of the laity in any form of synod as a 'step in a doubtful and dangerous direction'. 'As general Councils may err ... so may the unanimous opinion of six Bishops be of doubtful application', they argued openly in the press. Napoleon Woodd's party could not win, but Hassall's might. So in addressing the clergy Broughton stressed the political naivety of any move, like Hassall's, to convert proceedings at that stage from a clerical meeting to a clerical-lay conference. The Archbishop of Canterbury and Secretary of State for Colonies may well consider such a combined gathering a *de facto* synod, he warned; and since both statesmen had already told parliament that colonial synods were illegal they would be obliged to ignore the conference resolutions. Thus would the present gathering end in futility and vindicate the papist jibe that the queen's supremacy had left the Church of England fixed, bound, and near lifeless.[57] On the evening of 14 April Broughton, desperately needing a compromise motion to snatch all initiative from Hassall, invited Allwood to return with him to Tusculum and draft one. Broughton was more ready to compromise than his opening address suggested. He told Allwood he would accept any motion that upheld two principles:

> 1st. that the Bishop shall be a real separate estate, with a power of *veto* and not a mere chairman with a casting vote; and 2nd. that the essential distinction between clergy & laity should *not* be obliterated by requiring them invariably, on all occasions, to sit and debate unitedly.[58]

Allwood could not oblige the bishop on those terms. He did once express a similar viewpoint, but had since fallen under Stephen's influence and now favoured an American-style church constitution on the principle of united consultation but separate voting on *all* matters.[59] Broughton managed, however, to talk Allwood into a further compromise which conceded the second point without commitment either way on the first. The agreed resolution read,

> The clergy and the representatives of the laity should meet and debate together, reserving to each order the right of discussing any question that may come before them, and that the concurrence of both orders should be necessary to give validity to any act.[60]

Broughton assured Allwood the diocesan clergy would rarely, if ever, sit apart from the laity since diocesan synods were a mere fragment of the church and incapable of authoritative decisions on matters of faith and practice. However, Broughton wanted the right of the clergy to meet separately recognized so as to destroy the notion that because clergy and laity unitedly formed one church they must have identically the same office in the church.[61] The Tractarian in Broughton stood inflexibly for the apostolic character of the ministry.

On 15 April Allwood took charge of the clergy debate and, immediately Cowper concluded an incoherent plea for all to hold inviolate the Thirty-nine Articles, he condemned any constitution based on the Bishops' Minutes as pregnant with a disunity more destructive of ecclesiastical life than the prevailing perplexities. Allwood thanked the bishop for the letter he had attached to the original declaration giving the clergy licence to dissent from episcopal wisdom, and proposed the resolution agreed to the previous night. Allwood suppressed all mention of Broughton's connivance in the resolution, and promoted it as being more in harmony with the vestry resolutions than the principles outlined in the bishop's opening address. 'We cannot do better', Allwood concluded, 'than adopt the resolution which has been so unanimously agreed to by our parishioners at their respective meetings; and which comes recommended by the precedents and practices of our brethren in the faith in America'. Broughton looked the underdog. He stuttered a few studied objections and acquiesced. He nevertheless thought some of the clergy ungracious in the liberties they took in the discussion. George Macarthur, about the youngest member present, unkindly invited Broughton to make a gesture of *genuine* liberality and submit Allwood's resolution to a lay assembly for further endorsement; and the Reverend George King bobbed up and down with irritating reminders that the laity resented a powerful episcopate. 'I kept my temper pretty well', Broughton congratulated himself, 'and that being the case was able to keep up the dignity of the episcopal seat, and to carry weight.' As a result Hassall's motion to suspend the conference failed; Allwood's motion passed thirty to nineteen; and the bishop's draft petition to the queen was adopted with one vague and innocuous amendment (proposed by Broughton himself) that the laity would meet in 'connexion' with, rather than 'simultaneously' with the clergy. 'Allwood did me noble service', Broughton commented later in the week. 'Upon the whole I am satisfied thus far; and rather proud of our exhibition.'[62]

The satisfaction barely lasted two weeks. Recriminatory letters crept into the press accusing the clergy of deserting their vestries. Tyrrell, an observer at the conference, found the clergy in 'perplexity and doubt' on whether they were to express *their* opinions or their *vestry*'s. The Liverpool vestry sent its clergyman Mr Walker with *instructions* to oppose everything, and he did; and it lamented the failure of other vestries to bind their clergy. But were those vestry votes representative? Attendances ranged from 3 to 140 with most below 30. Grylls from Sydney's Holy Trinity parish quite bluntly questioned whether a vote of 7 to 5 from an attendance of 12 on a rainy night represented lay opinion in his parish, and he unblushingly supported the minority claiming they had more learning and less ostentatious piety than the majority. Indeed, many clergy believed the low vestry attendances showed the laity were willing to resign the decisions into their hands. They believed, too, that Allwood's resolution was a just compromise among expressed opinions. The bishop had been forced to concede to the laity the same rights as the clergy in initiating and deliberating on religious matters, and the provision allowing the clergy to debate apart from the laity on occasions was of little real consequence. Since *both* estates, clerical and lay, had to approve all resolutions, including those the clergy made binding only on themselves, the laity had what amounted to a veto provided the bishop did not vote as an estate in his own right. Just what value the bishop's vote was to have was raised but deliberately laid aside. Stephen's draft resolution, which most vestries copied, had excluded a separate episcopal estate by dividing the synod into *two* houses to vote, but Allwood's resolution simply spoke of 'both orders' needing to approve all decisions. Broughton threatened to 'lay down his life' in defence of a separate episcopal vote, but since he was committed to the constitution's details being written by a future clerical-lay conference, episcopal exclusiveness was in doubt. Indeed, Broughton's rhetorical choice of martyrdom rather than a merger with the clergy was a measure of his disappointment and defeat. 'The Bishop actually complained', wrote one observer, 'that the resolution (to say nothing of Mr Allwood's speech in moving it) uncourteously and unnecessarily censured or disclaimed the constitution recommended by the Bishops in their minutes.'[63]

Meanwhile, the approved form of Broughton's draft petition to the queen for synodical government went into circulation. Up country it was thought 'a desirable document ... procuring for the laity privileges they had not hitherto enjoyed'. Around Sydney dissent persisted but lacked leadership. Then a rumour spread that Broughton intended taking the petition to England to spike a fresh attempt being made by Gladstone to give the colonies a synod subject to the Archbishop of Canterbury's veto. Gladstone suddenly became the layman's hope, and gave Sadleir a cause to rally the disappointed laity.[64]

Lt Richard Sadleir RN (retired) was master of the Liverpool male orphanage. As a young man he had discharged his shot-gun at a tutor he suspected of romanism. He also dreamed of becoming 'a second Nelson', and though he never captained his own ship he was admiral of his own soul. Next to scripture he prized private judgement, and thought it no more outrageous to turn Mormon on the advice of Joseph Smith than to submit to theologians on the advice of some bishop. No one since the apostles could claim to have had a superior revelation, he said; and that meant every bishop, minister and layman must determine the truth for himself. Broughton thought Sadleir a latitudinarian, and some years earlier had denied him ordination believing he would not submit to church discipline. Sadleir thought Broughton something of a reformation pope, and pictured himself as another Huss burdened in 1852 with telling the conference of clergy that it, like councils of former eras, had erred.[65] In late April Sadleir called on Broughton with a warning that his petition would put a blight on lay activity; but finding the bishop adamant rode off on a tour of the Campbelltown and Penrith districts to decide if there was will enough for a fight.[66]

On 28 April, hostility emerged from another quarter. 'The jealousy and suspicion of the laity has been designedly aroused', Tyrrell charged;[67] and the *Empire* stood accused. Being a new publication in need of subscribers it feigned panic over the clergy conference, and denounced the bishop's very act in petitioning the queen for relief to assemble in synods as tantamount to an attempt to recreate a 'law made church' destructive of the colony's religious liberties. It forecast that one of the rival Presbyterian synods would follow suit and seek government protection, and that any application by the Roman Catholics for legislation enforcing their domestic discipline could find the colonial government patron of a new inquisition in the southern hemisphere. 'The question to be answered . . . is, Shall there be any sort of ecclesiastico-secular legislation permitted in reference to New South Wales?', the newspaper asked and it called on all, believers and the rest, to oppose the petition:

> For any man, therefore, to plead that because he is not of the Church of England the Bishop's movement does not affect him, is to plead his own ignorance that religious legislation involves the first breach of the universal right of man to be governed by conscience alone in all matters religious.[68]

The evil touch of the Lowe days had returned. For Broughton the *Empire* was the *Atlas* reincarnate, and the old taunts of tyrannical prelacy and ecclesiastical despotism reappeared. Whether Broughton meddled in land policy or delivered a lecture on St Cyprian there was someone, usually with a newspaper, ready to report him as up to mischief.[69]

Amid this renewed spirit of distrust Sadleir met forty laymen at the Royal Hotel in Sydney on 5 May. They boasted of having the numbers and means of bringing the bishop to his knees. 'Let it not be forgotten . . . that they had the power to stop the supplies', T. S. Mort the pioneer wool-broker reminded them. 'What fearful consequences to the whole Church would ensure if the clergy was left unpaid.'[70] Timothy Cape the schoolmaster feared more the scribbling reporters behind him. He had come to second a motion condemning Allwood's resolution at the clergy conference, but, realizing Allwood's motion closely resembled the motion he had voted for at the St James vestry meeting, feared he might appear inconstant. Cape turned to the reporters and asked that they record quite simply that he had changed his mind. Nevertheless the presence of the reporters surprised Cape as he understood the meeting was a private and preliminary one, and asked the chairman to explain its purpose. Mr Darvall MC, who had seconded every motion Lowe proposed to harass Broughton, was in the chair and rather confused: 'He, like many other gentlemen present, had been solicited by circular to attend, and this was all that he knew about the matter'. He thought it a public meeting to formally protest against the bishop's petition. A public meeting by invitation only! Even Sadleir could not accept that. Instead the meeting roughed out a counter-petition and appointed a committee to organize a public lay meeting where it would be adopted and signed, and then forwarded to Lowe for presentation to the British parliament.[71]

The lay counter-petition was ready within a week, the School of Arts booked for 19 May, and a search underway for sponsors known 'at home' as men of influence. 'A friend of the Bishops told me the names would be carefully scrutinised', Sadleir told the steering committee; and he fished boldly in Broughton territory for Charles Campbell's and Cowper's support. He thought he had Cowper's but got neither. James Macarthur offered support but wanted to redraft the petition. Sadleir snapped, 'No.' The Macarthurs always tried to bend matters their way, he said; but in desperation Sadleir put him on the list of sponsors. Apart from Darvall and Macarthur it was a committee of public obscurities like Sadleir, Cape, George King of the Sydney Fire Insurance Company,

George Pennington a law reporter for the *Empire*, T. Whistler Smith
auditor of the Bank of New South Wales and others even less known.
The search for a chairman was equally dismal. Macarthur refused to
attend the meeting and Darvall was needed to open proceedings with a
withering censure on Broughton's episcopate. Luckily, with a day to
go, Colonel Dumaresq MC agreed to preside and the gathering looked
to have tone. Then it rained.[72]

Still 150 'gentlemen of the highest respectability' turned up at 2 p.m.
after agreeing not to wait till 5 p.m. for the merchants and clerks. They
had four hours of devilish fun: they chastised the clergy for behaving
like schoolboys under the direction of their teacher rather than as responsible and thinking men; they heaped mock admiration on Broughton's
piety, zeal and learning while characterizing his episcopate as one of
unrelieved misjudgments; and they reviewed the ruins of the diocese.
'Behold one of the ruins', scoffed Sadleir fingering a report that showed
the Diocesan Committee had raised £3000 in 1838 and a mere £117 in
1851. 'Behold more of the ruins', Sadleir repeated liking the laughter;
and he listed the Lay Association, the denominational schools, Lyndhurst
College, and the journals the *Guardian* and the *Southern Queen*: 'Where
was the *Southern Queen* which rose in such grandeur to the public view?
Alas! no one was found to woo her?'[73]

Every ruin got its cheer but there was no debate. In a meticulously
managed sequence of addresses speakers alleged the bishop had an in-
ordinate love of power; that the diocese was near to schism; that because
the clergy conference had not decisively rejected the bishop's plea for
a separate episcopal vote they would ultimately confirm it; that the
Bishops' Minutes of 1850 had never been formally repudiated and the
way remained open for the establishment of a provincial synod. The
implication of that final point was pursued at length by Mr Piddington,
a young associate of Henry Parkes. He abused the bishops as a bunch
of 'Episcopal Napoleons' who, in an ecclesiastical *coup d'état*, had deposed
the royal supremacy to make way for their own supreme reign through
an exclusively clerical provincial synod with authority to overturn any
lay-inspired resolution of a diocesan synod it disliked. Piddington begged
the laity to recall how, at present, they could appeal against episcopal
rulings to a crown tribunal overwhelmingly composed of laymen, but
once the bishops won their way all churchmen must look thereafter to
a bench of provincial bishops for redress. Who then would enjoy a right
of private judgement? And without it where would Protestantism be?
The laity were on the verge of suffering all the fire and faggots of another
clerical ascendancy unless they reasserted their supremacy, and 'the
supremacy of the Crown is the supremacy of the laity', Piddington
concluded. So the laity counter-petitioned the queen to resist the establishment of an episcopal supremacy in the colony by erecting a single diocesan
convention where ecclesiastical and lay representatives never separated
for debating or voting, and by ever retaining all appellate courts under
her own royal jurisdiction.[74]

Broughton scarcely reacted. 'I have neither the right nor the disposition to question the privilege of any British subject to petition the

Crown', he replied on receiving notice of the meeting. Other observers accused the lay meeting of grossly distorting the truth by implying that Allwood's resolution affirmed the Bishops' Minutes of 1850 and that Broughton would never allow the laity a say or a vote in spiritual matters. Moreover, Darvall took so seriously the bishop's pledge 'to hold to his own power even to death' that he assumed the bishop, despite his undertaking to settle the constitution's details at a joint conference of clergy and laymen in Sydney, would sneak off to England and secure approval for an episcopal veto without the laity realizing it. 'The suspicion is not very complimentary to his lordship', commented an outsider in the lay audience.[75]

The suspicion was partly justified. Broughton had decided to go to England within days of Allwood forcing him to abandon the declaration of 8 March 1852 and with it the Bishops' Minutes as a basis for a synodical constitution. 'One portion of my business', he explained to the SPG, 'will be to try to have a . . . general Declaration drawn up, under authority, which it shall be required of all Colonial Churches to adopt, as the condition of being allowed that modification of Church constitution which so many are now applying for.'[76] By this strategy Broughton hoped to enlarge the debate out of its local context, and to have the more apostolic temper of the Canadian and South African dioceses modify both Sydney's near-Presbyterian laity and the fierce localism of Melbourne and Adelaide. He considered it a propitious moment for action abroad. The tercentenary celebrations of the Book of Common Prayer and more recently the jubilee of the SPG provided a foil for eulogizing the global aspect of English Protestantism, and for uttering his conviction that the future effectiveness of this global church lay not in each diocese being tied to Canterbury but in their being united to each other.[77]

Broughton was first booked to sail on 10 May 1852 with eighteen-months leave on full salary. He had few affairs to settle. He lived temporarily with friends on fashionable Lyons' Terrace having vacated Tusculum in February, and his personal belongings were still packed and stored awaiting the completion of the Crawley's house at Camperdown which he would share. He had no property to dispose of. His two insurance policies were 'all the inheritance which after nearly 40 years work I have to bequeath to my children', and he had smartly signed them over to his daughters the moment he escaped bankruptcy in 1850.[78] Even the diocese was better situated than a year ago to endure his absence. The SPG swept away some of his anxiety for the diggings by promising six gold-field chaplains and the governor offered each a full salary of £260. Coleridge gave other projects a fillip by turning Broughton's second threatened reduction in salary into a flurry of English donations. Broughton suspended his self-imposed programme of erecting a canvas church on every gold-field. The Sofala church was miserably attended and diggers around Orange dodged his call to put up a similar building. The site he had fixed for a church by the Louisa Creek diggings in 1851 was ill-situated to serve the diggers of 1852, and Broughton had to abandon quite advanced plans for a church at Wellington because of a

drop in population. 'It is difficult to make the best establishment permanently for the service of so fluctuating a population', he explained,
and deferred all country projects until populations stabilized. A brief
absence could save him bad decisions. In Sydney there was more money
than he could use. He had gifts of £4000 for a church and £1000 for
another grammar school conditional upon his raising matching subsidies.
If he stayed and raised the subsidies he would not spend them, or outlay
another pound on the cathedral, until labour costs, exorbitantly inflated
by the gold exodus, subsided. There was one exception. Broughton
wanted an official episcopal residence built at Camperdown as soon as
possible so as to free his successor of all rent burdens should the Legislative
Council slash church subsidies. Fitzroy gave the diocese land and
Broughton had the plans ready.[79]

Broughton handed Tyrrell direction of education. Tyrrell's optimism
fitted him better to deal with the government. The extent of lay co-
operation with the national schools since 1848 had outraged Broughton
and loosened his judgement on the subject. When Timothy Cape the
schoolmaster addressed the annual Diocesan Committee meeting in
1852 on the generous opportunities provided for religion within the
national schools Broughton accused him of placing another crown of
thorns upon the head of Christ. When a Unitarian chapel opened in
Sydney Broughton put round a circular warning that those who had
children at national schools would have their old age cursed by the sight
of their children filling that chapel.[80] Broughton found his Diocesan
Committee also 'drawn over to the adverse side' and in a mood to co-
operate with the University of Sydney. He had shut down the St James
theological college at Lyndhurst to concentrate on preparations for the
independent collegiate foundation at Raymond Terrace but could
generate no interest while the Legislative Council toyed with the idea
of assisting the churches to attach colleges to the proposed university.
Broughton bemoaned, even in the best of colonial men, a temperament
which found dogma narrowing and liberalism congenial to the expansive
mood of an era of snap prosperity.[81] Only the grammar schools prospered,
and in planning a third for St Philips parish Broughton realized he
must rely increasingly on them to instil in the youth some notion of
dogma as they passed from national primary schools to a secular university. As for continuing the fight for denominational schools the Roman
Catholic press was doing that as ably as Broughton in his prime.[82]

Broughton did not sail as planned on 10 May. His ship the *Zetland*
lost its original crew to the diggings and sailed at twenty-four hours
notice two weeks ahead of schedule the instant it had another. No other
vessel departing in May suited the bishop. He refused to risk the Torres
Straits in ships short-crewed or padded with raw hands. He feared the
turmoil of the Horn at his age, and though the idea of sailing to the Red
Sea and going overland past the 'celebrated' sights of the east attracted
him he found it too expensive. He had asked the SPG for £200 towards
his expenses but would sail before knowing if he had it. The route he
favoured was across the Pacific to Peru and then on to pick up the West

Indies packet for London. For months after May nothing happened, and when three gold-field chaplains arrived Broughton undertook a thorough reorganization of the placement of chaplains.[83]

Then on 11 August without prior announcement Broughton created Allwood, Grylls, and Walsh (who had just returned) canons of St Andrews cathedral, and two days later surrendered them and Archdeacon Cowper the management of the diocese. Next day, a Saturday, he celebrated a valedictory Eucharist for any who cared to come; and he afterwards explained to them that the simultaneous movement for synods from all quarters of the empire, and the adoption of the same idea by some English statesmen, marked it as a providential arrangement of God that he and those similarly inspired must meet and settle. He would have wished it done more easily. He was too old to go around the globe. He then shook hands with all present and prayed forgiveness of any he had harmed. The next day he preached at noon in St Andrews, and the day after went from his wife's grave to the wharf and sailed for Lima. The bishop who as an archdeacon twenty-three years earlier had sailed for the colony in the most comfortable quarters with silver and servants and none of the fire of a Paul or a Xavier, now left Sydney a lone bishop with little luggage for a rough journey through strange places to fulfil the self-conceived destiny of preaching the reformed faith in the capital of the Incas. But he would return to New South Wales. 'To this country I am attached by long connection, by the strongest sense of duty, and by all domestic ties and remembrances', he told those who came to farewell him. 'To England, on the contrary, absence has rendered me comparatively a stranger.'[84]

The voyage to Lima would take a month of fine weather. Caged at sea Broughton mulled over his case. His first task was to upset the much rehearsed claim in parliament that any provision for colonial synods had to await parliament's decision on whether or not to allow a more active convocation in England. Broughton thought the colonial issue distinct from the English. In England synods or convocations had existed for centuries and were regulated by 25 Henry VIII cap. 19, and any restoration of convocation's powers hinged on parliament's willingness to amend that statute. Broughton doubted, however, whether 25 Henry VIII cap. 19 had ever been extended to New South Wales. The statute 9 Geo. IV cap. 83 of 1828 transferred to the colony only those laws then in force in England which could be meaningfully applied within the colony. Since New South Wales in 1828 was a mere archdeaconry without the shadow of a synod, Broughton argued that 25 Henry VIII cap. 19 could not have been applied meaningfully and was therefore not among the laws transferred to the colony. Thus there was no statutory prohibition on colonial synods, and no reason why their establishment should await the outcome of a debate in parliament on 25 Henry VIII cap. 19.[85]

Whether or not that argument prevailed Broughton was certain a constitution would result from his visit. For all its turmoil the first half of 1852 had seen the laity consolidate a determined claim to share in ecclesiastical government. 'His Grace owes us no thanks for having raised that question', Broughton admitted, 'but would far rather it

should be allowed to sleep. He will however find that this *cannot* be.'[86]
That alone would ensure action. What else followed was in the grey area
of politics. The archbishop was unlikely to claim the right to veto colonial
canons which some of the laity urged on him. The Society for the Reform
of Colonial Government had already rejected such a suggestion as popish
in principle and unBritish.[87] Broughton on the other hand could reasonably hope to see the diocesan bishop confirmed as a separate estate, and
therefore with a separate vote, in the synod. Selwyn insisted on it, and
clergy conferences in South Africa and Canada had taken it for granted.[88]
The real debate would be whether appellate jurisdiction should remain
with the Archbishop of Canterbury and the superior English ecclesiastical
courts or be transferred to provincial synods. The former had the formidable support of the archbishop himself, of Perry, and of what seemed
to be the bulk of the clergy of Port Phillip, Tasmania, and South Australia, as well as a sizeable portion of the laity of every colony.[89] But
Broughton was determined to fight for the autonomy of the bishops
gathered in provincial synod. He argued that justice was uncertain in
'any distant court or tribunal to which we can convey no accurate notice
of the facts and merits of any disputed case'. Too many of the clergy and
laity who clamoured for Canterbury's supremacy based their thinking
on the facile premise that the colonial bishops were Tractarians who
would exact a tyrannical servitude unless some evangelical authority
abroad interposed a saving hand. In history Broughton saw the opposite
lesson: Rome had climbed to power on an exclusive appellate jurisdiction
exercised at an all-defeating distance, and no one could guarantee Canterbury would never do the same. But Broughton feared the colonial clergy
and laity too glib of mind to catch the point: 'In the Irish mind especially
there seems to be something which disqualifies it from grasping a subject
and reasoning upon causes and effects', he said.[90]

Broughton's one misgiving was of Gladstone having already introduced
the bill for colonial church self-government that he had foreshadowed
during debate on the Australian Colonies bill in 1850. Broughton had
then approved Gladstone's proposals except for the appellate jurisdiction
reserved to Canterbury, and he wrote correcting that.[91] But in 1852 he
was obsessed by the notion of a 'federal union' of colonial dioceses, or
of an even grander union of all episcopal churches in America, Scotland,
Britain and the colonies. Broughton believed, if only they had the will
to act the bishops alive in 1852 could do much to restore the sacrament
of unity enjoyed in the early church; and he told the Archbishop of
Canterbury it would be unworthy of them to strive after less. But a
world-wide union of dioceses could live in harmony only if they had a
common constitution on fundamental points, and to attract the American
dioceses into a union Canterbury must accept a primacy without power.
Moreover, Gladstone's principle of leaving the colonies 'to the uncon-
trolled management of their own local affairs, whether it be for ecclesiastical or for civil purposes' had once attracted Broughton but now repelled
him. The result, Broughton said, would be 'incurable differences . . .
which instead of binding us into one will separate us into many . . . and

the church of the future will . . . have reason to deplore the error'. So before leaving Sydney Broughton had written asking the SPG to delay any bill presented to parliament before his arrival.[92]

Ten days after Broughton had sailed news reached Sydney that in April Gladstone had presented a bill of the very character Broughton feared.[93] In the colony the *Empire*, which prayed failure on Broughton's mission, considered the bill would hinder the bishop's cause. It excited Sadleir. He had dared to see in Gladstone's movement a breakthrough for the Sydney laity believing it would throw back into the colony the making of the constitution, and was eager to launch an evangelical newspaper to advocate his ideas.[94] Ironically Gladstone commended his bill to the Commons as being in accordance with Broughton's principles and then found himself under pressure to withdraw it 'on the ground of the negotiations that are now going on between the Archbishop of Canterbury and the Metropolitan of Sydney'. Suspecting a ruse Gladstone asked for the correspondence to be tabled. He had been briefed only a week before by Coleridge who knew nothing of such negotiations.[95]

It was a ruse. Sumner tried to wriggle out of meeting Gladstone's request but had finally to table a letter Broughton wrote him in the midst of a bush visitation in December 1851. In it Broughton spoke of his intended consultation with the clergy and laity, and reaffirmed that the Bishops' Minutes were a sufficient basis for proceeding with reform. 'I had hoped', he told Sumner, 'that the minutes of the meeting of the bishops of the province last year, of which your Grace has received a copy, might possibly have been regarded as embodying a sufficiently definite expression of our wants and wishes.' Broughton scarcely appeared to be negotiating and Sumner had not bothered to acknowledge the letter. When Gladstone read the tabled letter he must have realized that Broughton's letter sent him in August 1851, reviewing his book on the royal supremacy and commenting on the bishops' meeting, left him as well informed as Sumner. Neither man in April 1852 had yet heard of Broughton's hopes for a federal union of colonial dioceses. The only possible pretext Sumner had for claiming Broughton was negotiating with him was a concluding comment in the letter of December 1851 that Broughton would write again when he returned to a more ordered life in Sydney.[96]

Sumner probably clutched at that because he wanted Gladstone's bill delayed for other reasons. In February 1852 he had received a chilling prediction from Perry that with colonial ecclesiastical autonomy 'a system of doctrines and ritual observances might be enforced in a Colonial Diocese which was totally repugnant to the decisions of the courts at home'. This convinced Sumner that the Australian bishops were unfit to exercise the independence they sought. He had already condemned their one attempt at exercising an independent judgement in dissenting from the Gorham Judgment on infant baptism. Sumner believed that resolution of dissent had plunged the colonial dioceses into near schism; and he had received so many complaints from Adelaide and Hobart that, for fear of agitating the colony further, had refused to take any initiative in setting up an enquiry into colonial church needs when

Wilberforce had parliament approve one in 1850.[97] Moreover, the CMS had threatened to terminate its £10 000 annual subsidy to the New Zealand mission if its missionaries submitted to a constitution modelled on the Bishops' Minutes. Sumner saw his choice as between a few dissatisfied bishops or a number of torn dioceses with an abandoned mission, and chose the former.[98] There was, too, a domestic consideration. In February 1852 enthusiasts for a more active English convocation had threatened to extend a meeting of convocation beyond it formal one-day sitting and Sumner pleaded with them 'to forbear pressing the subject at the moment'. But as Tyrrell had forecast, the archbishop could scarcely expect restraint in England while he encouraged colonial synods, especially as the more extreme of the English enthusiasts hailed the episcopal synod in Sydney 1850 as precedent.[99] For many different reasons then Sumner wanted a quick end to the debate on Gladstone's colonial church bill in April and May 1852, and if he rather falsely insinuated that he and Broughton were consulting on synods his aim in terminating the debate without resolution advantaged Broughton's plans.

Though Sumner quietened parliament in May 1852 the Secretary of State for Colonies, Sir John Pakington, believed the archbishop to be genuinely negotiating with Broughton, and he promised the colonial churches their synods if he remained in office until May 1853. This set the SPG publishing monthly reports on the world-wide movement of the churches towards 'free agency and self-government'. It had received documents from Toronto, Quebec, Antigua, the Cape, New Zealand and again and again from the Australian dioceses, and the Bishop of Maryland capped all by calling for a conference of all the bishops of all the English churches.[1] 'It is hard to assign limits to possibility', commented an SPG editor. 'Necessity often accomplishes schemes which at first sight seem little better than the dreams of enthusiasts or visionaries.'[2]

On 7 October 1852 Broughton fulfilled his vision and preached in the capital of the Incas. He then went across the isthmus of Panama by mule, canoe, and along thirty miles of newly laid railway destined soon to carry colonial gold by a quick, safe route to London. 'Unquestionably the most indescribable of all terrestrial operations', he commented. Finally he crossed the Carribean to St Thomas in the Virgin Islands and boarded the West Indian royal mail steamer *La Plata*, captained by Mr Allan, a friend of Coleridge, and sailing for Southampton with a cargo of cochineal and sarsparilla. The *La Plata* sailed on 4 November, and as the roar of its 1000 horsepower mingled with 'Home Sweet Home' Broughton retired to the ship's saloon: 'I thought to myself, where is that home of mine, from which death and absence have removed those who once rendered it so truly sweet'. A nightmare followed. A malignant yellow fever broke out amongst the crew on the third day and on the fourth bronchitis confined Broughton to his cabin. When the first sailor died Broughton staggered into a steaming 130° on deck for a funeral, opened his mouth but had no voice, handed the captain his prayer-book and gazing at the corpse thought he must soon follow it. Four days later he buried the captain, then an engineer, the purser, and three more sailors before the ship anchored off Southampton early on Thursday 18 November 1852. 'A most calamitous passage', he called it.[3]

The Southampton health officer Mr Walbin boarded with newspapers and forecast a ten day quarantine. Broughton chafed. The newspapers described a London buzzing with action he longed to be part of. That very day the Duke of Wellington was to be buried in a spectacle equalled only by the Great Exhibition. The nation indulged its hero, relived his victories, and dubbed him England's Fabius, Marcellus, Themistocles and 'the highest incarnation of English character' before burying him in the crypt of St Pauls. Broughton thought the comment just to the Duke but ungracious to the Duchess. 'It seems as if by common consent she has been put out of notice and remembrance', he observed. 'The motive of this is obvious. This is the *one* part of the history in which all is unsatisfactory.' Broughton resolved to redress the injustice, and, when the occasion came, to speak six sentences in praise of the Duchess whose gentleness, goodness, faith, meekness and temperance would have satisfied and fixed the affections of any reasonable man. Broughton later asked if Coleridge thought it sounded mischievous. Coleridge did, and the bishop put aside his chivalry. 'I feel indeed the injustice of such "suppressio veri"', he confessed, 'but nature, I believe, ordains that the woman *must*, when occasion requires, be a sacrifice even to the reputation of the man.' Broughton decided instead to enhance the reputation of the man and to show the Duke in a fresh light as the patron of the colonial church. When the Duke might have used the £2000 archdeaconry of New South Wales to fob off some claimant on his patronage he gave it to a mere curate, Broughton said, because he had the interest of the church at heart.[4]

There was, however, another and a better spectacle in London. When the new parliament opened early in November 1852 Convocation scheduled its formal one-day sitting for 12 November, and the Home Secretary reassured an anxious parliament that the 135 year-old tradition of its being merely a formal one-day sitting would prevail. It didn't. Convocation stole a third day's sitting the Thursday the *La Plata* anchored, and when it dodged the effect of prorogation by electing committees to continue its work the *Times* warned that the church might again become an empire within the empire of a most formidable kind. 'In point of fact, it is the Archbishop of Canterbury who has opened the door to these proceedings', Broughton read among the *Times* delivered to the ship on 19 November. The prospected excited him: had Sumner converted to synods? Broughton desperately wanted to contact someone who might tell him of these developments, but quarantine regulations forbade him to send even a note ashore. When he enquired on the 19 November how long the quarantine might last he learned that Sir William Pym the superintendent-general of quarantines was coming from London to take charge of the case, the worst for years. Broughton faced an indefinite delay. He visited the sailors still ill, reread the newspapers, wrote letters he could not post, and distracted himself pacing the deck trying to fix the direction of Hartley Wespall. Then late on Friday afternoon the passengers were suddenly permitted to disembark

by ferry, but when two sick sailors were refused hospitalization on land
Broughton stayed on board. Both sailors died over night, and at noon
on Saturday the *La Plata* steamed eight miles out to sea where Broughton
buried them and preached to the surviving crew. The *La Plata* was
cleared to dock at 4 p.m. Broughton landed, and discovering himself
too feeble to move on booked into the Dolphin Hotel.[5]

On Tuesday 23 November Broughton left Southampton for Birming-
ham to visit his ninety-three-year old mother. He caught a chill before
reaching London and spent the next two weeks convalescing in Surrey
from a mild relapse of bronchitis. His voice disappeared and the physician
forbade him to preach for three months. That made havoc of his plans.
By Wednesday 8 December Broughton felt fit for business and was
again in London. His nonappearance over the past few weeks had baffled
the SPG, and its secretary Hawkins had finally to track him down through
Lady Gipps who then arranged a dinner where the two could discuss
their tactics.[6]

Broughton told Hawkins that despite the exciting progress towards
a more active English convocation he wanted the case for colonial synods
separated from the English movement. He had already declined to
associate himself with the Society for the Revival of Convocation though
he sympathized with its aims. 'I must guard myself against every imputation of coming into these questions as a partizan', he said. He had read,
too, in Southampton of the Bishop of Cape Town's attempt to edge
himself into a seat on convocation as a suffragan of Canterbury, and
thought he might ape the move. The prospect of colonial bishops swamp-
ing convocation might compel the archbishop to attend more quickly
to the colonies' case. Broughton certainly intended taking a legal opinion
on the matter. Broughton, however, confessed that his original strategy
was to bypass the archbishop and ask the queen to appoint a commission
of enquiry to 'define certain *principles* which must be admitted and
acted upon in proposing the framework of a constitution for the entire
Colonial Church'. The queen should also appoint colonial subcommittees
to write local variations into the commission's recommendations, and
then 'in the exercise of Her Supremacy' the queen should ratify a final
report and direct colonial legislatures to pass any necessary enabling
legislation. Broughton wanted the Bishop of London or Winchester and
not the Archbishop of Canterbury to preside over the commission, and
listed the other possible commissioners as the Bishops of Lichfield,
Salisbury and St Asaph, Archdeacon Harrison and Hawkins himself,
Gladstone and Sir Robert Inglis from the parliament, Sir John Patterson
the jurist, and Mr Dickenson who had so ably presented the colonies'
case in the *Colonial Church Chronicle*.[7]

Hawkins pointed to the errors in Broughton's strategy. The Bishop
of Winchester despised synods more than his brother at Canterbury,
and Sir Robert Inglis had spoken curiously against Gladstone's bill as
designedly fragmenting the Church of England. Broughton would only
slowly discover his true supporters.[8] The SPG thought it a better tactic
for the colonial bishops to appear to act alone in the early stages, and the
Society on its own initiative had invited a Canadian and a West Indian

bishop to join Broughton and the Bishops of Cape Town and Newfoundland in forming a convention of colonial bishops.[9] Broughton should preside. English churchmen considered him father of the movement and author of the Minutes of the Sydney Bishops' Conference which, since the Canadian bishops had adopted them, were a natural agenda for a conference.[10] The SPG journals would publicize the bishops' case but the bishops must appear to take the lead.

Hawkins's strategy required an initiative Broughton scarcely had the strength to meet. Fortunately Allwood had offered to join him and Broughton wrote for him to come speedily.[11] Nevertheless Broughton spent the day after dining with Hawkins lobbying three prelates and the Chancellor of the Exchequer. 'A good day's work for a convalescent', he congratulated himself. The Bishop of Oxford, who spearheaded the revival of the English convocations, invited him to Cuddesdon for three days in January; the Bishop of London invited him for another three days at Fulham; and Gladstone arranged for him to meet Sir John Graham and Mr Sidney Herbert, two other members of the cabinet who might assist his cause in parliament. Broughton also visited Archbishop Sumner who complained that he and Lord Grey might have done more for the colonial church had Broughton given them clear and precise details of its wants! After that Broughton set off on his much delayed visit to his mother, spent three days with her, and then returned in leisurely fashion, dining his way to London with such old friends as Joshua Watson, Archdeacon Harrison and Norris's widow.[12]

Back in London, Broughton was amazed at the invitations he received. Dr Wordsworth, his combatant over the *EIKON BASILIKA*, wanted him to call; Keble asked him to Hursley; Sir John Pakington, though no longer Secretary of State for Colonies, wanted to be briefed to be helpful; Mowbray the publisher and Baron Alderson, to whom he could only have been a remote name before arriving in England, invited him to dine; invitations to preach came from the mighty St Pauls and obscure villages but he could accept none; over 106 letters arrived in three weeks and every day new callers left their cards. 'Every leisure moment I spend riding in a Fly; and yet with all my assiduity have not gone through more than a third of my list', he wrote revelling in the new company. But Coleridge eluded him. Both men were in London without meeting in mid-December, then the headmastership of Eton fell vacant and Coleridge was busy promoting his candidature. The two finally met at Brighton over the New Year. It was another three weeks before he met his brother Mr Justice Coleridge whose legal opinion was Broughton's lone comfort in the days when he faced total bankruptcy. Theirs was a meeting of spirits and Broughton decided to find accommodation near the judge in Crescent Park when negotiations began on the constitution. The judge offered Broughton a seat by him in court on 31 January when Newman was to be sentenced for libelling the ex-papist priest Dr Achilli. 'I had a curiosity to witness the proceedings', Broughton confessed, 'but *perhaps* upon second thoughts it is as well that I should not appear.' He left the invitation open.[13]

Meanwhile on 21 January 1853 the SPG officially welcomed Broughton

and praised him for planting episcopacy in the remoteness of the empire
and for opposing Rome's encroachment on it, and for striving after
self-sufficiency. Broughton in return asked the SPG to help end transportation, provide emigration chaplains, and not to assume that gold
in the colony meant gold for the churches. He also told the meeting
that the Bishops' Conference of 1850 was the great event of his episcopate,
and it proved that bishops could consult, agree, and depart indubitably
stronger for the experience. The London *Guardian* seized upon those
words: 'He bears his testimony that he rejoiced in such meetings between
himself and his suffragans', its editor commented in a chiding allusion
to the many recent remarks by English bishops that synods could bring
only dissension and weakness. 'The testimony of a man so distinguished
by sober judgment and moderation of sentiment cannot fail to have its
due weight.'[14]

Then on Tuesday 25 January 1853 Broughton began the business
that he came for. The colonial bishops met for a Eucharist at the Curzon
St Chapel where Broughton broke rule and preached, and the following
Friday at 11 a.m. he presided over the inaugural session of a convention
of colonial bishops. He gave each bishop a copy of a letter in which he
had set before the Archbishop of Canterbury his hope of a world-wide
union of Protestant episcopal dioceses and asked them each to submit
their ideas on the fundamental principles of such a union.[15] The convention adjourned to February and this signalled the SPG into action:

> The Church is entitled in common fairness to occupy one or other of
> two positions: —
>   I. That of favour and privilege derived from her connexion with
>   the State; or,
> II. That of freedom and independence, accorded to other tolerated
>   but non-established communions.
> At present, however, she is in the unhappy condition of possessing
> neither the substantial advantages of an established, nor the compen-
> sating freedom of a voluntary, Church.
>   Now on one or other of these alternative conditions we must per-
> emptorily insist. The former we know to be absolutely hopeless in
> the Colonies; and we claim, therefore, in the full confidence of right,
> as well as with an unhesitating preference, the latter. Plainly, and in
> set terms, we demand that the particular religious communion,
> attached to the doctrine, and using the service book of the Church of
> England, be left at liberty in the several Colonial Dioceses to regulate
> its own internal order and discipline, and to manage the affairs of its
> own parishes and schools, in such manner as it shall deem most con-
> ducive to God's honour and service.[16]

The SPG instanced the hazardous journey to England of the two aged
bishops Broughton and George Mountain of Quebec, neither of whom
had left their dioceses since consecration, as a measure of the desperation
of the colonial churches. It admonished parliament against fogging the
issue again with nonsensical declamation about the colonies being
ecclesiastical despotisms. It warned that parliament could either assist
in the orderly introduction of colonial synods or watch them grow piece-

meal, for the colonies were set upon having synods and the attorney-general appeared to be in agreement with the Bishop of Sydney's opinion that 25 Henry VIII cap. 19 did not extend to the colonies to prohibit them.[17]

On the Sunday after the convention, 30 January 1853, Broughton preached at the Lambeth parish church in honour of Howley (a prelate who would have cleared rather than obscured the path to colonial synods) and asked the congregation to repair the church. 'You are called to provide a stronghold in this church for the perpetual maintenance of the true doctrines of the Church of England', he said warning his hearers against the Cains of this world who dared God to accept what they chose to offer him; the Balaams who preached what doctrines were lucrative; and the Korahs who were laymen parading as ministers. He had confronted all three errors in the colony, seen them in England, and prayed that the parishioners of Lambeth would share Howley's vision and resist them. By Monday Broughton was exhausted. He woke up with a dry throat and no voice, and decided against hearing Newman sentenced. Instead he sat an hour for Richmond the portraitist. Next day, however, he was out telling the assembly at his old Barnet Grammar School of his Ulyssian wanderings: 'Imagine . . . having one church at St Albans, another in Denmark, another at Constantinople', he said. It made a good tale for boys. But the tales were better at dinner that evening as Judge Coleridge told of the Irish crowd in the court that cheered when he fined Newman £100 and of how he gave the convert a 'most horrible jobation' for deteriorating from a gentle Protestant apologist into a bitter Catholic controversialist. Broughton thought the deterioration inevitable. Judge Coleridge hoped otherwise: his son had just converted.[18]

A few days later Broughton visited Farnham and stayed in the mighty castle gazing down on the curate's cottage where Mr Briscall had once come knocking with the Duke's offer. It was a cold February, and when Broughton returned to London his dry throats worsened and the first symptoms of a bronchial relapse appeared. Lady Gipps insisted on nursing him at her Chester Road home, and for a week he lay unwell but not seriously ill. Then around 12 February he sank rapidly. Lady Gipps telegraphed Eton on 15 February for Coleridge to come immediately, and on his entering the bedroom Broughton sat up and spoke: 'God bless my soul, my dear Coleridge how glad I am to see you; Now let us sail at four today'. For two days more he lingered in a sanctified delirium preaching to imagined congregations, advising on synodal matters, and taking ship for Sydney, then he rallied. Dr Latham his physician declared him past the crisis, and on Friday pronounced him substantially better. An apothecary called at 10 p.m. on Saturday to administer drugs and found him even better. Three hours later the bishop turned to Lady Gipps and said: 'The earth is full of the glory: full of the glory of the Lord, as the waters cover the sea'. He died within minutes at 1.15 a.m. on Sunday 20 February. When Richmond came to view the corpse for the half-completed portrait he found no sign of pain or of a struggle on the bishop's countenance. 'He must have died very easily', sighed Coleridge.[19]

The *Guardian* announced the bishop's death and claimed for him an exceptional burial: 'Would it be impossible to bury him at Canterbury, amongst the English Metropolitans of that ancient and vast province?' It was a novel request. Canterbury's interior had not been disturbed for a prelate's body since Cardinal Pole's. What claim did the dead bishop have on Canterbury? Was he anything more than a worthy bishop with a marvellous gravity? 'Bishop Broughton may be regarded as the founder of the Church in Australia', stated the SPG. Others thought him a colonial missionary and metropolitan like Augustine, and death had taken him in office while abroad on an ecclesiastical mission for his province. Obscurity should not cover him. As metropolitan he belonged to Sydney, but as a diocesan bishop he still belonged to Canterbury for the colonial and mother provinces were 'even yet, not entirely separated'. Since Sydney could not honour him Canterbury must, and if St Pauls was the cathedral of the nation and the spot for the Duke of Wellington, St Augustines was the cathedral of the English church and the place for such missionary heroes as the Metropolitan of Sydney.[20]

A telegraphic message to Canterbury on Thursday evening 24 February decided the matter: Broughton was to be buried in the cathedral nave on Saturday. The Dean engaged workmen immediately, had torches lit, and a hole begun. The pavement gave way readily but the flint and mortar foundations beneath it shattered eight pickaxes in a row and sent sparks flying half way to the roof. By Saturday morning the grave was a shallow three feet. Meanwhile on Friday Broughton's body was placed in the chapter house across from the cloister graveyard where Gipps lay, and two mutes with staves were posted by the door to keep the night vigil.[21]

At 11 a.m. on the Saturday when the patter of feet by the door of the chapter house announced the arrival of fifty King's Scholars the Dean nodded and Dr Croft's burial setting filled the vaulted heights that had heard a half millennium of song. The headmaster of the King's School led his boys along the ancient cloisters to the north-west door followed by choristers, clerks, vergers and canons. Then came the velvet and silk draped coffin surmounted with plumes and bearing the bishop's cap under a black veil. Old friends attended him: George Mountain who had knelt with him for consecration and must now steer the convention's business; Edward Coleridge who vowed at the consecration never to see him want; Ernest Hawkins who fostered every ambition he had for his diocese; the younger George Gipps who knew him as family pastor; Henry Bailey the Warden of St Augustines Missionary College who must send his successor more men; and the retired Bishop Carr of Bombay stood in for Gladstone, detained by an emergency in London. Mourners, students of St Augustines, and robed clergy followed and found the nave packed with every class of citizen. Benjamin Harrison read the service and the body went into its grave to Reading's anthem 'I Heard a Voice'. 'The effect of the voices in the magnificent nave of the Cathedral can scarcely be imagined', reported the local *Kentish Gazette*.[22]

When the nave cleared the bishop's close friends were by the grave discussing its completion. They decided the bishop must match his companion heroes and have a stone tomb complete with recumbent figure. Eight friends promised £100 each on the spot, and calculated there would be £1500 without an appeal and more with one. Later over lunch at the Harrison's the idea of endowing scholarships at the King's School and St Augustines was also discussed. Joshua Watson proposed a bolder memorial: roof St Andrews cathedral and finish it. 'I really should think the Australians with all their immense gold fields might accomplish that without our help', Mrs Harrison remarked.[23]

In Australia Cowper announced Broughton's death to the clergy on 25 May 1853, and caught the colonial Catholics in a fit of indignation over the bishop's Protestant mission to Peru. 'Old and infirm at present, see the journeys he undertakes and the voyages he makes', expostulated a Catholic commentator who feared the bishop's other stunts. Such men relaxed and reverently forgot him after May 1853.[24] But some of his own clergy were soon heard 'to speak light of the dead', and James Norton the diocesan registrar noted wryly they were the first to seek Broughton's advice and would be the first to complain that the church was no longer directed by the vigorous hand of a master.[25] Colonists generally, irrespective of faith and politics, paid tribute to Broughton's profound knowledge, untiring benevolence and fervent piety; and the colonial secretary Deas Thomson spoke of the bishop's 'zeal, wisdom, and fidelity' as a member of the colony's councils. But Robert Campbell voiced a stronger sentiment: 'His efforts on behalf of the anti-transportation cause were enough to cover his memory with glory in the hearts of the colonists'. After that the Legislative Council adjourned out of respect for its former colleague.[26] Churchmen remembered him for other things: his struggle for schools; his voluntary cut in salary to found other bishoprics; his patience with those in error and gentleness towards those in trouble; and above all his self-effacing generosity towards those in distress.[27] 'His charity was never of a levitical cast that begins and ends with a gentle expression of sympathy', the diocesan registrar recalled.[28] But a neighbour on Lyons' Terrace during the bishop's last months of colonial life saw deeper. 'I knew him well', the chief justice Sir Alfred Stephen told a memorial gathering on 30 May:

> There was not one great object for the promotion of civilisation and special advancement in the colony with which he was not connected; there was not one effort to raise its name in the estimation of the world with which his name was not identified .... Out of his Church, indeed, he knew no sect, no party, and his whole efforts were for the common good; and if ever there was a patriot, in the best and highest sense of the word, that patriot, in the colony of New South Wales, was Bishop Broughton.[29]

Abbreviations

ANL	National Library of Australia, Canberra
AP	Arthur Papers, ML
A & P	*Acts and Proceedings of Bishop of Australia* (later *Sydney*), Diocesan Registry, Sydney
Aust. Chron.	*Australasian Chronicle*
Bk. P	Bourke Papers, ML
BM	British Museum, London
BP	Broughton Papers on microfilm at ANL and ML
CCC	*Colonial Church Chronicle*
CMS	Church Missionary Society
CO	Colonial Office, London
Col. Obs.	*Colonial Observer*
CSIL	Colonial Secretary's Office, Inward Letters
CSOL	Colonial Secretary's Office, Outward Letters
EC	The Reverend Edward Coleridge, Eton College
Gazette	*Sydney Gazette*
GP	Grey Papers, Durham University, England
HRA	*Historical Records of Australia*, Series I
LMS	London Missionary Society
MC	Moase Collection, University of Tasmania
ML	Mitchell Library, Sydney
Monitor	*Sydney Monitor*
Morn. Chron.	*Morning Chronicle*
NSWA	State Archives of New South Wales, Sydney
OBF	Overseas Bishopric Fund, Westminster, England
PLB	Perry Letter-book, Diocesan Archives, Melbourne
PD	*Parliamentary Debates*, British
PP	*Parliamentary Papers*, British
PRO	Public Records Office. London
Proc. Ex. C.	*Proceedings of the Executive Council of New South Wales*
SH	*Sydney Herald*
SMH	*Sydney Morning Herald*
SPCK	Society for Promoting Christian Knowledge
SPG	Society for the Propagation of the Gospel in Foreign Parts
Syd. Chron.	*Sydney Chronicle*
TKS	Archives of the King's School, Parramatta
V & P	*Votes and Proceedings of the Legislative Council of New South Wales*
WGB	William Grant Broughton

References

The citation WGB to EC refers to correspondence between Broughton and Edward Coleridge in the Broughton Papers (BP) on microfilm at the ANL and ML.

The citation WGB to SPG refers to Broughton's letters to the Organizing Secretary of the SPG in the SPG Papers on microfilm at the ANL. These letters are to be found filed chronologically as C. MSS. Australian Papers, Box 12, Bishop Broughton's Letters 1834–49, and, Letters Received Original, Sydney—Melbourne; Adelaide; Newcastle; Tasmania—1850–9.

In the interests of brevity multiple references within the same paragraph from the same source have been grouped together.

1   Before New South Wales

[1] On the King's School in the eighteenth century see J. S. Sidebotham, *Memorials of the King's School Canterbury*, London, 1865; J. Shirley (ed.), *Reminiscence of the Reverend George Gilbert 1796–1874*, Canterbury, 1938; D. L. Edwards, *History of the King's School Canterbury*, London, 1957; Walter Pater, 'Emerald Uthwart', in *Miscellaneous Studies*, London, 1920.

[2] Early memoirs of Broughton appeared in *Gentleman's Magazine*, vol. 39, 1853, pp. 431–6; *Annual Register*, 1853, pp. 214–17; Broughton, *Sermons on the Church of England*. The Rev. George Gilbert, who knew Broughton from 1813, wrote the memoir in the *Gentleman's Magazine* in consultation with James Broughton the bishop's brother and Benjamin Harrison, who, as Archbishop Howley's chaplain, knew Broughton from 1843; see correspondence between Gilbert and James Broughton during 1853 in items 2b, 2d, BP. The memoir in the *Annual Register* is possibly Harrison's for it reads like a precis of his acknowledged memoir.

[3] Shirley, *Reminiscences*, p. 21.

[4] WGB to EC, 16 June 1842; James Broughton to Sarah Broughton, 26 June 1849, ML. 913; H. Bailey, *Mission Heroes*, London, no date, p. 2.

[5] *SMH* 26 Apr. 1851; WGB to EC, 28 Dec. 1844.

[6] WGB to EC, 21 Jan. 1845, 15 Jan. 1849; Sidebotham, *Memorials*, pp. 101–2.

[7] WGB to EC, 16 June 1842; Gilbert to James Broughton, 31 Mar. 1853, item 2a BP.

[8] Shirley, *Reminiscences*, p. 22. On the French Revolution, Broughton, *The Present Position and Duties of the Church of England*, p. 14.

[9] Based on Broughton, *Speech of the Bishop of Australia to Mr Justice Burton*, p. 5; WGB to EC, 1 July 1845, 24 Apr. 1846; WGB to Sarah Broughton, 5 Mar. 1829, ML. B1612.

[10] WGB to EC, 16 June 1842.

[11] *Gentleman's Magazine*, vol. 83, 1813, pp. 40, 189.

[12] WGB to EC, 5 Jan. 1848; Shirley, *Reminiscences*, p. 21.

[13] *Admission Book 1797–1891*, pp. 36–7, MS. Pembroke College, Cambridge.

[14] WGB to EC, 4 May 1844.

[15] H. Marsh, 'Enquiry into the Consequences of Neglecting to Give the Prayer Book with the Bible', in, *Pamphleteer*, 2nd ed., London, 1813, vol. 1, p. 125.

[16] Broughton, *Charge to the Clergy ... 1844*, p. 44; also Broughton, *Charge ... at the Primary Visitation*, p. 8. On desirable clerical qualities, WGB to EC, 19 Oct. 1837, 14 Feb. 1842. On national histories, W. G. Broughton, *The Counsel and Pleasure of God ...*, passim. On Broughton's study habits, WGB to EC, 1 Feb. 1851; Bailey, *Mission Heroes*, p. 24.

[17] WGB to EC, 12 June 1846. Almost all of Broughton's arguments against Bourke's education proposals (see chapters 6, 7) appeared in H. Marsh, *Vindication of Dr Bell's System ...*, London, 1811, and, H. Marsh, 'National Religion the Foundation of National Education', in *Pamphleteer*, op. cit.

[18] Compare the views of H. Marsh, 'Address to the Senate of the University of Cambridge, Occasioned by the Proposal to Introduce in that Place an Auxiliary Bible Society', in *Pamphleteer*, op. cit. with Broughton's removal of Alexander McLeay as chairman of the local SPG branch when McLeay simultaneously accepted the presidency of the local auxiliary of the British and Foreign Bible Society, *Atlas*, 23 Oct. 1847.

[19] *Cambridge University Calendar 1818*, Cambridge, 1818, p. 134.

[20] *Register 1773–1884*, pp. 112–19, 122, MS. Pembroke College, Cambridge.

[21] *Gentleman's Magazine*, vol. 39, 1853, p. 431; Gilbert to James Broughton, 17 Mar. 1853, item 2d BP.

[22] WGB to Keate, 13 Feb. 1826, ML. 913; WGB to Wagner, 6 Feb. 1825, ML. Ab29/5c.

[23] WGB to Keate, 13 Mar. 1826, ML. 913.

[24] WGB to EC, 9 Jan. 1847, 3 July 1846, 1 Feb. 1851.

[25] WGB to Keate, 13 Feb., 6 Dec. 1826, ML. 913.

[26] Broughton, *Sermon Preached at Monthly Clerical Lecture ... Reading*, pp. 11–15.

[27] WGB to Wagner, 6 Feb. 1825, ML. Ab29/5c.

[28] Broughton, *An Examination of the Hypothesis, Advanced in a Recent Publication, Entitled 'Palaeoromacia'*; Tomline to WGB, 1 Mar. 1824, MS. TKS.

[29] *Edinburgh Review*, vol. 36, 1821, pp. 17–19; *Quarterly Review*, vol. 32, 1825, pp. 468–70.

[30] C. Wordsworth, *Who Wrote EIKON BASILIKA ... ?*, 2 vols. London, 1824; E. Churton (ed.), *Memoir of Joshua Watson*, London, 1861, vol. 1, p. 248.

[31] Broughton, *Letter to a Friend Touching the Question, Who was the Author of EIKON BASILIKA?*, pp. 3, 33; Broughton, *Additional Reasons in Confirmation of the Opinion that Dr. Gauden and NOT King Charles the First was the Author of EIKON BASILIKA*.

[32] Broughton, *Letter to Friend*, pp. 88–91.

[33] Tomline to WGB, 14 Mar. 1826, MS. TKS. Details of Broughton's licences at Farnham supplied by Hampshire Records Office.

[34] WGB to EC, 14 Jan. 1846.

[35] *Gentleman's Magazine*, vol. 39, 1853, p. 431.

[36] Broughton, *Sermons on the Church of England*, p. xii; WGB to Duchess of Wellington, 20 June 1827, 25 May 1829. Letters of W. G. Broughton 1826–9, Duke of Wellington Collection, m/f, ML. (Hereafter cited as Wellington Collection); Duchess of Wellington to WGB, 17 Feb. 1828, 1 Apr. 1829, ML. 913.

[37] WGB to Duchess of Wellington, 4 Mar. 1826. Wellington Collection.

[38] Duchess of Wellington to WGB, 24 Apr. 1828, ML. 913; WGB to Sarah Broughton, 26 Jan. 1829, MS. TKS.

[39] WGB to Grey, 24 Dec. 1835, CO 201/250. Broughton produced this figure when disputing his reduction to half salary in England in 1834–6. He probably included such items as house rent and travel which he was personally responsible for in NSW. The sum suggested is nevertheless an impressive income.

[40] Wellington to Murray, 29 Oct. 1828, PRO, WO 80/2. On Scott's troubles, Darling to Horton, 26 Mar. 1827, *HRA*, xiii, pp. 189–94; Scott to Hamilton, 18 Aug. 1828, Scott Letter-book II, ML.

[41] Broughton, *Sermon at Reading*, p. 12; WGB to mother, 27 Oct. 1828, item 2a BP.

[42] James Broughton to Sarah Broughton, 26 June 1849, ML. 913.

[43] *Quarterly Review*, vol. 37, 1828, pp. 1–31.

[44] WGB to Sarah Broughton, 24 Jan. 1829, ML. B1612.

[45] WGB to mother, 27 Oct. 1828, item 2a BP.

[46] WGB to Sarah Broughton, 24 Jan. 1829, op. cit.

[47] Wellington to Murray, 1 Nov. 1829, Nat. Lib. of Scotland, MS. 46/3/3.

[48] WGB to mother, 4 Nov. 1828, item 2a BP.

[49] Scott to Hamilton, 21 May 1827, C. MS. SPG.

[50] Broughton's Address to SPG, 21 Jan. 1852, *CCC*, vol. 6, p. 313; WGB to mother, nd, item 2a BP.

[51] WGB to Wellington, 5 Nov. 1828, PRO, WO 80/2; WGB to Duchess of Wellington, 25 May 1829, Wellington Collection.

[52] WGB to Norris, n.d., quoted in Whitington, *William Grant Broughton*, p. 24; Wellington to Murray, 6 Nov. 1829, PRO, WO 80/2.

[53] W. G. Broughton, *The Resurrection of the Dead and Life Everlasting*, p. 12. Copy at Pembroke College, Cambridge.

[54] WGB to Sarah Broughton, 24 Jan., 5 Mar. 1829, ML. B1612; WGB to Sarah Broughton, 26 Jan. 1829, MS. TKS.

[55] Twiss to WGB, 14 Apr. 1829, CO 202/24.

[56] WGB to Duchess of Wellington, 23 Mar., 25 May 1829. Wellington Collection.

[57] Duchess of Wellington to WGB, 1 Apr. 1829, ML. 913; WGB to EC, 9 Mar. 1844.

[58] Twiss to WGB, 14 Apr., 1 May 1829; Twiss to Commissioner of Navy, 23 Apr. 1829, CO 202/24.

[59] WGB to EC, 8 May 1850.

[60] Twiss to WGB, 28 Mar. 1829, CO 202/24; Hay to Barnard, 21 Jan. 1829, Hay to WGB, 3 Feb. 1829, CO 202/23.

[61] Hay to WGB, 10 Feb. 1829, Hay to Barnard, 11 Feb. 1829, CO 202/23; Twiss to WGB, 22 Apr. 1829, CO 202/24.

[62] WGB to Duchess of Wellington, 25 May 1829, Wellington Collection.

[63] Entry for 26 May 1829 in a manuscript diary in Broughton's handwriting kept on board the ship *John*, item 1 BP. Hereafter cited as *John* Diary.

[64] S. T. Coleridge, *Biographia Literaria*, Everyman ed., London, 1965, p. 130.

[65] *John* Diary, 26 May 1829.

[66] Ibid., 29 May, 15 June 1829.

[67] Ibid., 27 May 1829.

[68] Ibid., 12 June 1829.

[69] Ibid., 16 June 1829.

[70] Ibid., 17 June 1829.

[71] Ibid., 13, 16 June 1829.

[72] Ibid., 1 June 1829.

[73] Ibid., 31 May, 14 June 1829.

[74] Ibid., 5 July 1829.

[75] Ibid., 30 May 1829.

[76] See WGB to Bourke, 14 Jan. 1833, 33/518, Box 4/2169, CSIL.

[77] *John* Diary, 6 June, 6 July 1829.

[78] R. Heber, *Narrative of a Journey through the Upper Provinces of India* ..., 2nd. ed., 3 vols., London, 1828; *Quarterly Review*, vol. 43, 1830, p. 366.

[79] *John* Diary, 26 June 1829.

[80] Ibid., 3 July 1829.

[81] Ibid., 25 June 1829; cf Broughton, *Letter to a Friend*, pp. 88–92.

[82] *John* Diary, 5 June 1829; W. Harris, *History and Critical Account of the Life and Writing of Charles I* ..., London, 1753.

[83] *John* Diary, 18, 21, 22 June and 7–11, 12 July 1829.

[84] Ibid., 27, 28 July, 2, 3, 4, 5, 9, 10 Aug. 1829; 'A Daily Record of Position and Weather', ML. 913.

[85] *John* Diary, 7–10, 12 Sept. 1829.

[86] Ibid., 13 Sept. 1829.

2   *The Reception*

[1] Whitington, *Broughton*, p. 32; Scott to Arthur, 23 Apr., 19 Sep. 1829, AP, vol. 13, ML; Scott to Darling, 19 Aug. 1828, 1 Sep. 1829, Scott Letter-book II, ML.

2 'Lines Written in the Cove of Sydney', *Australian Almanack*, Sydney, 1832, p. xix; R. Burford, *Description of a View of the Town of Sydney, New South Wales*, London, 1829. On Scott's personality, Darling to Bathurst, 6 Mar., 1 May 1826, *HRA*, xii, pp. 210–11, 256.

3 Darling to Murray, 24, 29 Nov. 1828, 22 Apr. 1829, *HRA*, xiv, pp. 475–7, 501–6, 716–19; *Australian*, 27 Dec. 1826.

4 *Gazette*, 17, 20 Oct. 1829; J. D. Lang, *Historical and Statistical Account of New South Wales*, London, 1834, vol. I, p. 215.

5 *Gazette*, 17 Sep. 1829; *Australian*, 18 Sep. 1829; *Monitor*, 19 Sep. 1829; also Whitington, *Broughton*, pp. 32–3.

6 *Gazette*, 19 Sep. 1829.

7 Whitington, *Broughton*, p. 32. Broughton later shifted to Bunker's Hill, 'Street Directory' in *Australian Almanack*, Sydney, 1834. On Rocks area see *Gazette*, 24 Oct. 1829.

8 Hall's ecclesiastical views are in *Monitor*, 26 Oct. 1831, 18 Feb., 1 Apr. 1835, and his protest in ibid., 5 July 1828, 25 Apr. 1829.

9 23 Sep. 1829.

10 *Gazette*, 29 Sep. 1829; *Monitor*, 3 Oct. 1829.

11 *Monitor*, 3 Oct. 1829; *Gazette*, 24, 27 Oct. 1829; *Australian*, 3 Feb. 1830.

12 18 Sep. 1829.

13 *Australian*, 4 Nov. 1829; *Gazette*, 5, 19, Jan. 1830.

14 *Australian*, 20 Jan. 1830.

15 *Gazette*, 15, 20 Oct., 14 Nov. 1829; *Australian*, 6 Nov. 1829.

16 Broughton, *The Counsel and Pleasure of God*, p. 10.

17 Ibid., p. 12.

18 Ibid., p. 17.

19 Darling to Twiss, 7 July 1829 and encls., *HRA*, xv, pp. 70–5. For campaign against Darling see C.M.H. Clark, *A History of Australia*, Melbourne, 1968, vol. II, chapters, 4, 5. On Darling's absence, *Gazette*, 17 Nov. 1829.

20 Darling to Murray, 26 Jan. 1830, *HRA*, xv, p. 345. Official patronage of publication indicated on title-page of printed sermon.

21 J. D. Lang, *Narrative of the Settlement of the Scots Church, Sydney*, Sydney, 1828, p. 1.

22 WGB to mother, quoted in Whitington, *Broughton*, p. 33.

23 Title-page of *Australian*.

24 Broughton, *Charge . . . Primary Visitation*, pp. 9–10, 17, 34; *Gazette*, 5 Dec. 1829.

25 Broughton, *Charge . . . Primary Visitation*, p. 23. Broughton's first official report on the archdeaconry praised Scott's achievements. *Despatches from Governor of New South Wales. Enclosures etc. 1830–1*, p. 732, ML.

26 Broughton, *Charge . . . Primary Visitation*, p. 27.

27 Ibid., p. 29.

28 See *Gazette*, 23 June, 15 Sep. 1825.

29 Ibid., 2 Feb. 1830.

30 *Australian*, 5 Dec. 1829; *Gazette*, 14 Jan. 1830.

31 'Plan for the Permanent Provision of the Church Establishment' (dated Whitfield, England, 30 Mar. 1824) in *Despatches of Governor of New South Wales 1823–4*, vol. 5, pp. 742–3, ML.

32 Marsden to Coates, 12 Sep. 1826, Bonwick Transcripts, Box 53, vol. 5, pp. 1694–6, ML; 'Copy of Minute of the Ven. Archdeacon Scott submitting . . . the Establishment of a Grammar School at Windsor etc.', 4 Jan. 1828, copy in BP; Scott to Arthur, 5 Sep. 1828, AP, vol. 13.

33 Scott to Darling, 12 July 1828, Scott Letter-book II.

34 *Gazette*, 24 Feb., 5, 24 Mar. 1829.

35 Ibid., 1 Dec. 1829; Lang, *New South Wales*, vol. II, pp. 340–2.

36 *Gazette*, 12 Dec. 1829.

37 Ibid., 12, 19 Dec. 1829.

38 Ibid., 19 Dec. 1829, 21 Jan. 1830.

39 Lang, *New South Wales*, vol. II, pp. 341–2.

40 Based on *Gazette*, 7 May, 22 Sep. 1829, 5 Feb., 30 Aug. 1831, 15, 20 Mar. 1832. Broughton used the *Gazette* to leak information on the King's School before a

prospectus was ready and to reveal Lang's early association with the project. *Gazette*, 21 Jan. 1830, 31 Dec. 1831.

[41] *Prospectus of the Sydney College*, Sydney, 1830, passim; *Australian*, 2, 27 Jan. 1830; *Monitor*, 27 Jan. 1830; R. S. Watsford, *Sydney Grammar School from its Earliest Days*, Sydney, 1924, pp. 8–9.

[42] Darling called the Executive Council to meet at noon rather than the normal 2 pm and dealt with routine business only. This made a fifth meeting that month, two above average. See Minute, 26 Jan. 1830, *Proc. Ex. C.*, CO 204/3.

[43] WGB to Lang, 16 Jan. 1830, ML. A2236.

[44] Ibid., also *Gazette*, 16, 19, 23, 26 Jan. 1830, *Australian*, 2, 22 Jan. 1830.

[45] Darling to Murray, 10 Feb. 1830 and encls., *HRA*, xv, pp. 356–67.

[46] Ibid., p. 356.

[47] Based on *Church and Schools Corporation Minute Book, No. 3, 1829–30*, pp. 216–8. MS. 7/2704, NSWA. Scott to Darling, 1 Sep. 1829 and WGB to Darling, 26 Jan. 1830, *HRA*, xv, pp. 220–1, 363. The six trustees sitting on the Legislative Council were Broughton, A. McLeay, M. C. Cotton, W. Lithgow, R. Campbell, R. Jones.

[48] WGB to Darling, 26 Jan. 1830, *HRA*, xv, pp. 362–6.

[49] *Prospectus, Sydney College*, p. 10.

[50] WGB to Darling, 26 Jan. 1830, op. cit., p. 363.

[51] Ibid.

[52] 'Plan Prepared by the Venerable Archdeacon Broughton, upon which to form Grammar Schools and eventually a College in New South Wales', and, WGB to Darling, 4 Feb. 1830, *HRA*, vol. xv, pp. 358–60, 366–7.

[53] WGB to Darling, 26 Jan. 1830, op. cit., p. 362. Compare R. Ward, *Australian Legend*, Melbourne, 1962, chapter 2 and especially the story of 'poor Kelly' and Tom Petrie. On Broughton's country tour, *Gazette*, 16 Jan. 1830.

[54] WGB to Darling, 26 Jan. 1830, op. cit., pp. 362–6. For Scott's proposals on boarding schools, Scott to Darling, 1 Sept. 1829, *HRA*, xv, p. 220.

[55] 'Plan Prepared by the Venerable Archdeacon Broughton . . .', op. cit., p. 358.

[56] For details of proposed syllabus, sub-encls. 1, 2, 3, Darling to Murray, 10 Feb. 1830, *HRA*, xv, pp. 358–62.

[57] WGB to Darling, 26 Jan. 1830, op. cit., p. 364.

[58] *Edinburgh Review*, vol. 34, 1820, p. 250.

[59] 'Plan Prepared by the Venerable Archdeacon Broughton . . .', op. cit., p. 358.

[60] 'Plan for the regulation of the "King's Schools" . . .', *HRA*, xv, p. 361.

[61] *Gazette*, 21 Jan. 1830. On Scott's fees, 'Plan for a General Boarding School . . .', *HRA*, xii, pp. 319–20. On other boarding school fees, Scott to Hamilton, 27 Aug. 1828, Scott Letter-book, II. The Sydney College announced fees of £5 but charged £12, *Prospectus, Sydney College*, pp. 11–12, and *Eighth Annual Report of the Sydney College*, Sydney, 1838, p. 16. On wages see *Gazette*, 22 May 1830.

[62] WGB to Darling, 26 Jan. 1830, op. cit., pp. 365–6.

[63] Darling to Murray, 10 Feb. 1830, *HRA*, xv, p. 356.

[64] *Edinburgh Review*, vol. 34, 1820, pp. 214–54, vol. 35, 1821, p. 224; *PD*, June 1820, col. 74ff; *Gazette*, 14 Jan. 1830.

[65] *Gazette*, 21 Jan. 1830; *Monitor*, 13 Mar. 1830; 'Shareholder' to editor in *Gazette*, 23 Jan. 1830.

[66] Argus to editor in *Monitor*, 13 Mar. 1830. As E. S. Hall's dislike for the Church of England increased his respect for Broughton personally remained, ibid., 7 Apr. 1832, 24, 31 July 1833.

[67] WGB to Lang, 16 Jan. 1830, ML. A2236; Lang, *New South Wales*, vol. II, p. 344.

[68] Based on Lang, *New South Wales*, vol. I, pp. 148–79, vol. II, pp. 341–5, 346–7; *Australian*, 2, 27 Jan. 1830; Watsford, *Sydney Grammar School*, p. 9.

[69] *Hobart Town Courier*, 27 Feb., 6 Mar. 1830; *Australian*, 2 Apr. 1830.

[70] *Colonial Times*, 16 Apr. 1830; *Hobart Town Courier*, 24 Apr. 1830; *Charge Delivered to the Clergy of Van Diemen's Land at the Primary Visitation*. See also *Australian*, 1 May 1830.

[71] Minute, 12 May 1830, *Proc. Ex. C.*, CO 204/3.

[72] WGB to Arthur, 6 Aug., 16 Nov. 1830, AP, vol. 12.

[73] Based on *Tasmanian*, 23 Apr. 1830; *Hobart Town Courier*, 24 Apr. 1830; Minutes,

16, 17 Apr. 1830, *Proc. Ex. C. (VDL)*, CO 282/2; Minute, 17 Dec. 1829, *Proc. Ex. C.*, CO 204/3.
[74] WGB to Arthur, 6 Aug. 1830, AP, vol. 12.
[75] WGB to Arthur, 3 June 1830, ibid.

3   The Darling Years

[1] *John* Diary, 5 June 1829; Bourke to Glenelg, 28 Nov. 1836, 'Copies or Extracts of Despatches Relative to the Establishment of Episcopal Sees in Australia, Etc.', *PP*, 1850, vol. 37, p. 571. Broughton did sit with the Executive Council to review capital cases on three occasions between Darling's departure and Bourke's arrival, and all sentences were commuted, see Minutes, 12, 22 Nov. 1831, *Proc. Ex. C.*, CO 204/4.
[2] Minute, 1 Feb. 1830, *Proc. Ex. C.*, CO 204/3.
[3] Darling to Hay, 10 Oct. 1826, *HRA*, xii, p. 645; Darling to Hay, 17 Feb. 1831, *HRA*, xvi, p. 88; Darling to Murray, 26 Jan. 1830, *HRA*, xv, p. 345; Minute, 16 June 1830, *Proc. Ex. C.*, CO 204/3.
[4] Based on Minutes, 20 Feb., 16 Mar., 2 Aug., 9 Oct. 1832, 28 Aug. 1833, *V & P*; Lang, *New South Wales*, vol. II, p. 367.
[5] Darling to Twiss, 22 Dec. 1829 and Darling to Hay, 13 Jan. 1830, *HRA*, xv, pp. 300, 333–5; *Gazette*, 5 Jan. 1830; Minute, 29 Jan. 1830, *V & P*; Darling to Horton, 15 Dec. 1826, *HRA*, xii, pp. 761–3; Minute, 4 June 1831, *Proc. Ex. C.*, CO 204/4.
[6] *PD*, 18 Apr. 1828, cols. 1565–6, 20 June 1828, cols. 1456–63; Murray to Darling, 31 July 1828, *HRA*, xiv, p. 261–3.
[7] Forbes to Darling, 19 Jan. 1828, *HRA*, xiii, pp. 738–9; Minutes, 2, 15, 16 Sept. 1829, *V & P*. The respective parts played by Scott and Broughton were confused in C. H. Currey, *Sir Francis Forbes*, Sydney, 1968, p. 363.
[8] From an annotation in Scott's handwriting in a copy of (James Macarthur), *New South Wales. Its Present State and Future Prospects*, London, 1837, p. 127. Copy at ANL; Minute, 16 Sept. 1829, *V & P*; *Gazette*, 26 Sept. 1829.
[9] Minutes, 15, 24 Sept. 1829, *V & P*; *Gazette*, 26 Sept. 1829; *John* Diary, 6 June, 5 July 1829.
[10] Minute, 29 Jan. 1830, *V & P*; WGB to Darling, 14 Sept. 1830, *HRA*, xv, p. 775.
[11] WGB to Darling, 14 Sept. 1830, op. cit. p. 776. Whether England could furnish reliable juries after Peterloo was an issue, see *Annual Register*, 1819, pp. 103–15, 1820, pp. 29–39, 849–98.
[12] WGB to Darling, 14 Sept. 1830 and Forbes to Darling, 5 Oct. 1830, *HRA*, xv, pp. 773–7; (Macarthur), *New South Wales, Prospects*, appendix no. 16.
[13] *PD*, 20 June 1828, col. 1458; WGB to Darling, 14 Sept. 1830, *HRA*, xv, p. 777.
[14] See encls. no. 3, 7, 10 in Darling to Murray, 7 Oct. 1830, *HRA*, xv, pp. 777–9, 782, 786–7; WGB to Darling, 19 June 1830, *HRA*, xv, pp. 725–8.
[15] Lang, *New South Wales*, vol. II, pp. 244–5.
[16] WGB to Darling, 19 June 1830, *HRA*, xv, p. 726.
[17] WGB to Darling, 19 June 1830, op. cit., pp. 725–8; WGB to Arthur, 3 June 1830, AP, vol. 12; 'Report ... Clergy and School Lands ... 1 March to 31 December 1830', in *Despatches from Governor of New South Wales 1830–1*, p. 811. ML.
[18] Darling to Murray, 20 Sept. 1830, *HRA*, xv, p. 725; WGB to Darling, 12 Aug. 1830, 30/6217, Box 4/2080, CSIL; Colonial Secretary to WGB, 19, 23 Aug., 1 Sept. 1830, 30/95, 96, 101, CSOL (Letters to Clergy).
[19] Scott to Arthur, 16 Aug. 1827, AP, vol. 13; Scott to Hamilton, 10 Nov. 1827, Scott Letter-book II, ML; 'Proceedings of the General Court No. 1 of the Trustees of the Clergy and Schools Lands', p. 293, MS. 4/291, NSWA. For Corporation lands see Darling to Murray, 12 Dec., 1828, 11, 19 Feb. 1829, *HRA*, xiv, pp. 518, 638–41, 659–60.
[20] 'Report From Select Committee on the Civil Government of Canada', *PP*, 1828, vol. 7, pp. 9–10, 224; Murray to Darling, 25 May 1829, *HRA*, xiv, p. 789; WGB to Colonial Secretary, 11 Dec. 1829, 29/9752, Box 4/2056, CSIL.
[21] 'Schedule of Lands granted to Trustees of Clergy and School Lands showing

whether sold or leased, etc.', and, 'Receipts and Disbursements for the Year
1828 and 1829', encls. in Darling to Murray, 17 Aug. 1830. CO 201/213; 'Report
... Church and School Lands ... 1 March 1828 to 28 February 1830', and,
'Report ... 1 March to 31 December 1830', in *Despatches from Governor of
New South Wales. 1830–1*, pp. 737–8, 808.

22 Broughton, *Charge ... Primary Visitation*, pp. 27–8; *Gazette*, 9 Jan. 1830.
For a picture of native life around Sydney as Broughton would have encountered
it, see G. Bennett, *Wanderings in New South Wales*, London, 1834, vol. I, p. 338.

23 Captain Irvine to CMS, 8 Aug. 1821, CN/012, CMS; Minutes of Committee
of Native Institution, 12 Dec. 1821, CN/013, CMS; Marsden to Coates, 4 Jan.
1833, Bonwick Transcripts, Box 54, vol. 6, pp. 1858–62, ML; Scott to Hill,
18 Dec. 1826, CN/05a, CMS; Scott to Darling, 9 Dec. 1826, *HRA*, xii, pp. 796–7;
Scott to Darling, 1 Aug. 1827, *HRA*, xiv, pp. 55–63; Hill to Scott, 18 Sept.
1827, CN/05a, CMS.

24 L. E. Threlkeld, *Specimens of a Dialect of the Aborigines of New South Wales,
Being the First Attempt to Form their Speech in a Written Language*, Sydney,
1827; L. E. Threlkeld, *A Statement Chiefly Relating to the Formation of a Mission
to the Aborigines of New South Wales*, Sydney, 1828, pp. 11–15, 31–2.

25 C. P. Wilton (ed.), *The Australian Quarterly Journal of Theology, Literature
and Society*, vol. I, 1828, pp. 54–5; Threlkeld, *Statement*, p. 61; Hankey to
Darling, 18 Aug. 1829, *HRA*, xv, pp. 672–4; 'Abstract of Revenue for New
South Wales and its Appropriation for 1832', *V & P 1833*.

26 Marsden to London Missionary Society, 5 Dec. 1829, and, WGB to Threlkeld,
7 Nov. 1829, in Gunson (ed.), Reminiscences and Australian Papers of the Rev.
Lancelot Threlkeld, Missionary to the Aborigines of New South Wales, pp. 86,
332–3; Broughton, *Charge ... at Primary Visitation*, p. 29; Colonial Secretary
to WGB, 13 Jan. 1830, 30/7, CSOL (Letters to Clergy).

27 Threlkeld to WGB, 17 Nov. 1829, 9 Jan. 1832, and, Harrington to Threlkeld,
13 May 1830, in Gunson, op. cit., pp. 334–7, 358, 685–6; WGB to Darling,
3 June 1830, *HRA*, xv, p. 675–6; Colonial Secretary to WGB, 1 Oct. 1831,
31/108, CSOL (Letters to Clergy).

28 Marsden to London Missionary Society, 22 Jan. 1830, in Gunson, op. cit., p. 86;
Threlkeld's 'Journal', 9 July 1831, ibid., p. 356; 'Journal of James Backhouse
and G. W. Walker', ibid., p. 398. For Broughton's debt, see Colonial Secretary
to WGB, 8 Jan. 1830, 30/4, CSOL (Letters to Clergy).

29 Goderich to Darling, 6 July 1827, *HRA*, xiii, pp. 433–4; Twiss to Coates, 18
Feb. 1830 and Stephen to Coates, 1 Dec. 1829, CH/050, CMS; Minute, 24
Nov. 1829, MC Committee Minutes, vol. 10, CMS; Coates to Twiss, 1 Jan. 1830,
CH/LI, CMS.

30 Minutes, 30 Mar., 6 Apr., 18 May, 8 June 1830, MC, Committee Minutes,
vol. 11, CMS; Howick to Coates, 11 Dec. 1830, CO 202/26; Coates to Howick,
9, 17 Feb. 1831, CO 201/222; Howick to Coates, 18 Feb. 1831, CH/053, CMS.

31 Minute Book entries for 16 Oct. 1829, 26, 27 Jan., 2 Feb. 1830, CN/01, CMS;
Marsden to Coates, 14 Oct. 1829. Bonwick Transcripts, Box 53, vol. 5,
pp. 1805–6; Hill to Coates, 31 May 1830, CN/02, CMS.

32 Hill to Coates, 9 Feb., 21 July 1831, CN/02, CMS; Handt to Coates, 30 Sep.
1831, CN/051, CMS.

33 Hill to Coates (private), 3 Oct., 9 Nov. 1831, CN/02, CMS; Handt's instructions
are not available but those issued to his companion W. Watson are among Colonial
Office correspondence dated 7 Oct. 1831, CO 201/222.

34 See Captain Irvine to CMS, 8 Aug. 1821, CN/012, CMS; also James Stephen
to Coates, 1 Dec. 1829, CH/050, CMS.

35 Minute Book entry, 11 Aug. 1831, CN/01, CMS; Hill to Coates (private), 9 Nov.
1831, CN/02, CMS.

36 WGB to Hill, 22 May, 7 Nov. 1831, 4 June 1832, and Hill to WGB, 23 Aug.,
7 Nov. 1832, CN/05a, CMS; Hill to Coates, 2 June, 18 Sep. 1832, CN/02, CMS;
Watson to Coates, 4 June 1832, CN/093, CMS; Minute Book entry, 7 Nov.
1832, CN/01, CMS; Minute, 4 Dec. 1832, MC, Committee Minutes, vol. 12,
CMS.

37 Lang, *New South Wales*, vol. II, pp. 328, 345–6.

38 'Outline of a Prospectus etc.', encl. Lang to Goderich, 28 Dec. 1830, CO 201/215; J. D. Lang, *Account of Steps Taken in England etc.*, Sydney, 1831, pp. 4, 17–18, 24–5; Hay to Lang, 15 Oct. 1830, Howick to Lang, 13, 19 Jan. 1831, CO 202/26; Goderich to Darling, 12 Jan. 1831, Lang to Goderich, 15 Mar. 1831, Goderich to Bourke, 13 June 1832, *HRA*, xvi, pp. 22–3, 224–5, 658–62.

39 Goderich to Darling, 24, 29 March 1831, *HRA*, xvi, pp. 116–17, 223–4. Both despatches arrived on the ship *Georgina*. The facility with which the grant was obtained also puzzled later officials, see Minute attached to Lang to Secretary of State, 6 Nov. 1833, CO 201/235.

40 *Gazette*, 15 Oct. 1831; *First Report of the Council of Australian College*, Sydney, 1832, pp. 6–7; Lang, *New South Wales*, vol. II, p. 353; WGB to Darling, 19 Oct. 1831, encl. Darling to Goderich, 13 Nov. 1831 (at sea), CO 202/221.

41 *Gazette*, 10 Dec. 1831; WGB to Darling, 19 Oct. 1831, op. cit.

42 Minute, 8 Nov. 1831, *V & P.*

43 Colonial Secretary to WGB, 19 Dec. 1831, CSOL (Letters to Clergy); Goderich to Darling, 22 Mar. 1831, *HRA*, xvi, pp. 112–14; Howich to Bishop of London, 9 Apr. 1831, CO 202/26; Minute, 8 Nov. 1831, *V & P*; *Australian*, 25 Nov. 1831; *Gazette*, 10 (advertisement), 17, 23, 27, 31 Dec. 1831.

44 *Sydney Almanack, 1832*, Sydney, 1832, p. xvi.

45 *Second Annual Report of Sydney College*, Sydney, 1832, pp. 6–7; *Australian*, 16 Dec. 1831, also 20 Jan. 1832; *Monitor*, 21 Jan., 21 Mar. (Carthusian to editor) 1832; *Gazette*, 16, 26, 28 Jan. 1832. The dispute revived in *Gazette*, 29 Sep., 2 Oct. 1832. Lang, despite denials, hoped to collapse the Sydney College, see Lang to John Macarthur, 14 Nov. 1831, Macarthur Papers, vol. 4, ML.

46 *Monitor*, 28 Jan. 1832.

47 Murray to Darling, 25 May 1829, *HRA*, xiv, pp. 789–90; Murray to Darling, 28 Dec. 1829, 19 June 1830, *HRA*, xv, pp. 307–8, 560–1; *Gazette*, 7 Dec. 1830; 'Instructions to Commission for Managing the Affairs of the Church and School Estates', encl. no. 2, Darling to Goderich, 27 Apr. 1831, CO 201/219.

48 WGB, Lithgow, and McQuoid to Darling, 17 Mar. 1831, encl. no. 6, Darling to Goderich, 27 Apr. 1831, 201/219; Goderich to Darling, 9 Jan., 14 Feb. 1831, *HRA*, xvi, pp. 19–22, 80–3; Darling to Murray, 1 Feb. 1831, Darling to Goderich, 27 Apr. 1831, ibid, pp. 59–60, 254–5; Minute, 1 June, 8 July 1831, *Proc. Ex. C.*, CO 204/4.

49 *PD*, 4 Apr. 1829, col. 431; R. Southey, *Sir Thomas More: or Colloquies on the Progress and Prospects of Society*, 2 vols., London, 1829, vol. I, pp. 30–1; 'Report of ... Church and Schools Establishment in N.S.W., 29 September 1831', in *Despatches from Governor of New South Wales. Enclosures etc. 1832–5*, p. 1136, ML.

50 Minute, 1 Aug. 1831, *Proc. Ex. C.*, 204/4; 'Observation of the Venerable the Archdeacon', 1 Aug. 1831, and, 'Letter from Judges of Supreme Court to Governor', 8 Aug. 1831, encls. in *Despatches from Governor of New South Wales. Enclosures etc. 1830–1*, pp. 1014–19, ML; Darling to Goderich, 28 Sep. 1831, *HRA*, xvi, p. 381.

51 William Cowper to Macquarie Cowper, 3 July 1831, ML.A 3315; Darling to Goderich, 28 Sep. 1831, *HRA*, xvi, p. 381; 'Report of ... Church and Schools Establishment in N.S.W., 29 September 1831', op. cit., pp. 1132–8.

52 Goderich to Darling, 14 Feb. 1831, Goderich to Bourke, 25 Dec. 1832, *HRA*, xvi, pp. 80–1, 830.

53 'Report of ... Church and Schools Establishment in N.S.W., 29 September 1831', op. cit., pp. 1133–5; 'Third Report on Revenues in the Colonies', *PP*, 1830–1, vol. 4, pp. 71, 74–5, 85. On Corporation's poverty in 1828, see 'Proceedings of General Court No. 1 of the Trustees of the Clergy and School Lands,' pp. 169–78, MS. 4/291, NSWA.

54 *Monitor*, 5 Dec. 1829; *Australian*, 12 Dec. 1829, 22 Oct. 1830, 29 Apr., 27 May 1831; 'Report of ... Church and Schools Establishment in N.S.W., 29 September 1831', op. cit., p. 1134.

55 Lang, *Account of Steps Taken in England*, pp. 25–6; Lang, *New South Wales*, vol. II, pp. 359–62.

56 'Commissioners for Managing Affairs of Church Corporation to Acting Governor',

18 November 1831, encl. Lindesay to Goderich, 18 Nov. 1831, *HRA*, xvi, p. 459.
[57] *Gazette*, 17 Dec. 1831, 26 Jan. 1832.
[58] Ibid., 22 Dec. 1831.
[59] WGB to Goderich, 19 Nov. 1831, *HRA*, xvi, pp. 451–2.
[60] 'Report of Archdeacon Broughton on his first visitation of Van Dieman's Land', pp. 33–8, encl. Arthur to Murray, 19 Aug. 1830, CO 325/28.
[61] 'Commissioners for Managing Affairs of Church Corporation to Acting Governor', 18 November 1831, op. cit., pp. 453–9.
[62] Darling to Arthur, 4 June 1831, AP, vol. 7; Minute, 18 Oct. 1831, *Proc. Ex. C.*, CO 204/4.
[63] Darling to WGB, 25 Aug. 1830, *Correspondence between Governor and Officials*, MS. 4/1664, NSWA; Colonial Secretary to WGB, 19, 23 Aug, 1 Sep. 1830, 30/95, 96, 101, CSOL (Letters to Clergy).
[64] WGB to Colonial Secretary, 18 Dec. 1829, 14 Jan. 1830, 29/9981, 30/327, Box 4/2064, CSIL; Colonial Secretary to WGB, 28 Jan. 1830, 30/19, CSOL (Letters to Clergy).
[65] WGB to Colonial Secretary, 23 Dec. 1830, 23 Mar. 1831, 30/9776, 31/2151, Box 4/2101, CSIL.
[66] 'Motion proposed for discussion' signed Francis Forbes, encl. no. 3, Darling to Hay, 4 Sep. 1828, *HRA*, xiv, pp. 390–1.
[67] Darling to Hay, 4 Sep. 1828, op. cit., pp. 386–8.
[68] Colonial Secretary to WGB, 26 May, 28 June, 12 Aug. 1831 (permission to repair fence, buy forage, repair a leaking roof), 31/48, 66, 85, CSOL (Letters to Clergy).
[69] Broughton commented sharply on Darling in later years, see WGB to EC, 19 Oct. 1837.
[70] WGB to Darling, 17 Feb. 1831, Goderich to Bourke, 18 Sep. 1831, *HRA*, xvi, pp. 90–1, 356–7; Darling to WGB, 16 Aug. 1830, *Correspondence between Governor and Officials*, MS. 4/1664, NSWA; WGB to Colonial Secretary, 8 Nov., 6 Dec. 1831, 31/9144,9856, Box 4/2122, CSIL; Colonial Secretary to WGB, 26 Nov. 1831, 31/134, CSOL (Letter to Clergy).
[71] On Vincent, WGB to Darling, 6 Oct. 1829, 29/7896, Box 4/2047; WGB to Vincent, 23 Nov. 1829, 29/9256, Box 4/2058; WGB to.Bourke, 4 Nov. 1833, 33/7334, Box 4/2169, CSIL. On Wilkinson, Wilkinson to Colonial Secretary, 27 Nov. 1830, WGB to Colonial Secretary, 6 Dec. 1830, 30/9101,9178, Box 4/2090, CSIL. On Wilton, Colonial Secretary to WGB, 6 Oct. 1831, 31/84, CSOL (Letters to Clergy); WGB to Wilton, 10 Aug. 1831, WGB to Colonial Secretary, 3 Oct. 1831, 31/7946, Box 4/2118, CSIL; WGB to Colonial Secretary, 17 Aug. 1832, 32/6162, Box 4/2153, CSIL.
[72] 'Report of Archdeacon Broughton on the State of the Church and Schools Established in N.S.W.', *Despatches from Governor of New South Wales. Enclosures etc. 1832–5*, p. 1129, ML; *Australian*, 24 Apr. 1829; WGB to Arthur, 25 Feb. 1832, AP, vol. 12.
[73] WGB to Darling, 13 June 1831, 31/4721, Box 4/2019, CSIL.
[74] 'Report of Archdeacon Broughton on the State of the Church and Schools Established in N.S.W.', op. cit., p. 1138.
[75] Ibid., p. 1147, also pp. 1141–2,6.
[76] Ibid., p. 1131.

4 *Bourke and the Year 1832*

[1] WGB to Arthur, 16 Nov. 1830, AP, vol. 12; *Gazette*, 20 Sep. 1831.
[2] *Monitor*, 19, 22 Oct. 1831.
[3] Attorney-General (John Kinchela) to McLeay (private), 31 Oct. 1831, ML. Ak42; *Monitor*, 15, 19, 26 Oct. 1831; *Australian*, 14 Oct., 9 Dec. 1831.
[4] *Gazette*, 22 Oct. 1831.
[5] *Monitor*, 3 Dec. 1831.
[6] *Gazette*, 10 Dec. 1831.
[7] Goderich to Darling (private and confidential), 15 Mar. 1831, CO 202/25. On Arthur's disappointment, Arthur to WGB, 12 May 1834; Stephen to Arthur, 8 July 1835, AP, vols. 39, 4.

[8] *Monitor*, 16 Jan. 1833.
[9] Based on Minute, 3 Dec. 1831, *Proc. Ex. C.*, CO 204/4; Hill to Coates, 21 July 1831, CN/02, CMS; 'To the Right Honourable Thomas Spring Rice ... the Memorial of the ... Archdeacon of New South Wales', 1 Sep. 1834, CO 201/244; *Royal Instructions to Sir Richard Bourke etc.*, p. 3, MS. 394, ANL.
[10] WGB to Bourke, 22 Dec. 1831, *HRA*, xvi, pp. 500–1.
[11] Bourke to Goderich, 22, 28 Feb. 1832, ibid., pp. 527, 542; Currey, *Forbes*, p. 399; Minute by Bourke, 29 Dec. 1831 in Minute, 3 Jan. 1832, *Proc. Ex. C.*, CO 204/5.
[12] Encls. A and B to Minute no. 1, 1832, in Appendix, *Proc. Ex. C.*, CO 204/5; Riddell to Bourke, 24 Feb. 1832 in Minute, 5 Mar. 1832, ibid.; Bourke to Howick, 10, 28 Feb. 1832, CO 201/225.
[13] Bourke to Riddell, 2 Mar. 1832 in Minute, 5 Mar. 1832, *Proc. Ex. C.*, CO 204/5.
[14] Minute, 10 Jan. 1832, *Proc. Ex. C.*, CO 204/5. The other voice was probably that of the judges, see Forbes, Stephen, Dowling to Bourke, 17 Feb. 1832, encl. Bourke to Goderich, 22 Feb. 1832, CO 201/225. When pressed for evidence of his sweeping powers Bourke could produce none and hastily had to forward to England for approval a copy of notes he had made after a conversation with Goderich before departing England and in which he insisted such powers were granted him; see 'Copy of Minutes of Instruction to Governor Bourke', June 1831, encl. Bourke to Goderich, 11 Jan. 1832, CO 201/225.
[15] Based on Mrs Percival to Bourke, undated fragment, letter no. 47, Bk. P, vol. 10, ML; Bourke to Secretary of Commission of Enquiry, 12 Dec. 1824, 'First-Report of Commissioners of Irish Education Enquiry', *PP*, 1825, vol. 7, p. 640; Broughton, *Sermons on Church of England*, p. 59; *John* Diary, 25 June 1829.
[16] Bourke's evidence to 'Select Committee of House of Lords Appointed to Enquire into the State of Ireland', *PP*, 1825, vol. 9, pp. 172, 180.
[17] Minute, 19 Jan. 1832, *V & P*; *Australian*, 17 Feb. 1832. The bill became 2 William IV, No. 4.
[18] WGB to Bourke, 4 Feb. 1832, *HRA*, xvi, pp. 514–15.
[19] 'Report of Archdeacon Broughton ...', *Despatches from Governor of New South Wales. Enclosures etc. 1832–5*, p. 1136, ML.
[20] Ibid., pp. 1137–8.
[21] WGB to Arthur, 17 July 1832, AP, vol. 12.
[22] 'Report of Archdeacon Broughton ...', op. cit., p. 1137.
[23] *Monitor*, 7 Jan. 1832.
[24] Goderich to Bourke, 4 July 1832, *HRA*, xvi, pp. 672–3; Goderich to Colborne, 5 Apr. 1832, 'Copies ... Correspondence Respecting the Clergy Reserves in Canada ...', *PP*, 1840, vol. 32, pp. 95–6.
[25] *Gazette*, 10 Aug. 1830; *Australian*, 20 Jan. 1830; Mansfield to J. J. Therry, 19 Jan. 1830, Therry Papers, ML.
[26] WGB to Duchess of Wellington, 20 June 1827, Wellington Collection, ML; *Gazette*, 7 Nov. 1829, 16 Feb. 1832.
[27] E. Woolestonecroft to J. J. Therry, 5 Feb. 1830, Therry Papers; *Gazette*, 7, 21 Jan., 9 Mar. 1830.
[28] *Gazette*, 9 Mar. 1830; *PD*, 5 Mar. 1829, cols 778–9.
[29] Bourke's evidence to 'Select Committee of House of Lords Appointed to Enquire into the State of Ireland', op. cit., p. 183; Minute of Bourke's on Ullathorne to Colonial Secretary, 29 Apr. 1833, 33/3059, Box 4/2175.2, CSIL.
[30] 'Report of Archdeacon Broughton ...', op. cit., pp. 1141–2; Bourke to Goderich, 28 Feb. 1832, *HRA*, xvi, p. 542.
[31] Minute, 9, 15 Mar. 1832, *V & P*; *Gazette*, 31 Mar. 1832.
[32] Based on Edward Parry, *Journal 1829–1832*, 10, 17 Jan., 2, 25 Apr., 25 July 1830, 3 June, 3 Oct. 1832, Parry Papers, ANL; Parry to Therry, 5 May 1832 in *Gazette*, 4 Aug. 1832.
[33] Based on Parry, *Journal*, 28 Apr. to 1 May, 6 May 1832; Ann Parry, *Parry of the Antarctic*, London, 1963, pp. 11–12; E. Parry, *Memoirs of Rear-Admiral Sir W. Edward Parry*, fourth ed., London, 1858, pp. 12, 236–8; Parry to Therry, 5 May 1832, op. cit.
[34] *Gazette*, 4, 7, 21 Aug. 1832; *Monitor*, 8 Aug. 1832.
[35] *Gazette*, 18 Aug. 1832; H. Fulton, *Reasons Why Protestants Think the Worship*

of the Church of Rome an Idolatrous Worship, Sydney, 1833, pp. 3, 22, 32; R. Therry, *An Appeal on Behalf of the Roman Catholics of New South Wales*, Sydney, 1833, p. 7.

36 Broughton, *A Letter in Vindication of the Principles of the Reformation*, pp. 5–11, 23–5.

37 See H. Fulton, *Strictures Upon a Letter Lately Written by Roger Therry*, Sydney, 1833, p. 5; Busby to J. J. Therry, 11 Nov. 1833, James Macarthur to J. J. Therry, 10 Nov. 1834, Therry Papers.

38 Therry, *Appeal on Behalf of Catholics*, pp. 34–5.

39 *Monitor*, 29 Sep., 3 Oct. 1832.

40 William Cowper to Macquarie Cowper, 28 Oct. 1832, ML. A3315.

41 Broughton, *Letter in Vindication*, p. 26.

42 WGB to J. J. Therry, 11 Oct. 1830, J. J. Therry to McGarvie, 17 Nov. 1832, Therry Papers; WGB to Bourke, 21 Nov. 1832, Bk. P, vol. 11.

43 Broughton, *Letter in Vindication*, pp. 4, 24, 27.

44 Ibid., p. 26.

45 Minutes, 20 July, 8, 12 Aug., 12 Sep. 1831, *Proc. Ex. C.*, CO 204/4; *Gazette*, 8 Oct. 1831. Broughton claimed Darling relied exclusively on him in the drafting of the regulations, see concluding paragraph 'To the Right Honourable Thomas Spring Rice . . .' 1 Sep. 1834, CO 201/244.

46 Bourke to Howick (private), 28 Feb. 1832, CO 201/225.

47 *Gazette*, 1 Dec. 1831.

48 Details of debtors to Crown and Corporation are in Encl. PPP to Minute no. 40, 1831, Appendix, *Proc. Ex. C.* CO 204/4; 'Schedule of Lands Granted to the Trustees of Clergy and School Lands Showing Whether Sold or Leased etc. . . .', encl. Darling to Murray, 17 Aug. 1830, CO 201/213. The Colonial Office originally supported Broughton's recommendations, see Goderich to Bourke, 1 May 1832, *HRA*, xvi, pp. 626–7.

49 *Gazette*, 3 Dec. 1831; Minute, 3 Jan. 1832, *Proc. Ex. C.*, CO 204/5; Bourke to Howick, 28 Feb. 1832, CO 201/225.

50 Minutes, 31 Oct. 1831, 25 Feb. 1832, *Proc. Ex. C.*, CO 202/4,5; Minutes, 13, 15 Mar. 1832, *V & P.* The two despatches involved were Goderich to Darling, 12 Jan. and 29 Mar. 1831, *HRA*, xvi, pp. 22–6, 223–5.

51 *Gazette*, 1 Dec. 1831; *Australian*, 6 Jan. 1832; *Monitor*, 7 Jan, 1832.

52 *Gazette*, 26, 28 Jan. 1832; *Second Annual Report of the Sydney College*, Sydney, 1832, pp. 7–8.

53 Bourke to Goderich, 1 May 1832 and encl. no. 1, *HRA*, xvi, pp. 627–8.

54 WGB to Bourke, 5 June 1832, *HRA*, xvi, pp. 703–5; WGB to Darling, 19 Oct. 1831, CO 202/221.

55 Bourke to Goderich, 17 Aug. 1832, *HRA*, xvi, p. 703.

56 Based on WGB to Bishop of Calcutta and Minute attached, (no date) encl. Bishop of Calcutta to Secretary of State, 23 Apr. 1833, CO 201/235; WGB to Bourke, 17 Oct. 1832 and Minute of Bourke, 25 Dec. 1832, 32/9507, Box 4/2169, CSIL. The next Bishop of Calcutta recommended that Broughton be given full authority in such matters; see Bishop of Calcutta's letter above.

57 *Australian*, 14 Sep. 1832; William Cowper to Macquarie Cowper, 1 Jan., 17 Sep. 1832, ML. A3315; Hill to Coates, 18 Sep. 1832, CN/02, CMS.

58 WGB to Bourke, 21 Nov. 1832, Bk. P, vol. 11.

59 Bourke to Goderich, 7 Aug., 23 Nov. 1832, *HRA*, xvi, pp. 695–6, 806–7; Minutes, 27 Sep., 2, 8, 12, 13 Oct. 1832, *V & P.*

60 WGB to Bourke, 5 June 1832, *HRA*, xvi, pp. 703–5.

61 *Australian*, 2 Feb. 1832; *Monitor*, 14 Aug., 3 Nov. 1832; *Gazette*, 8 Sep., 11 Oct., 8 Nov. 1832.

62 WGB to Bourke, 24 Sep. 1832, encl. Bourke to Goderich, 3 Nov. 1832, CO 201/227.

63 Bourke to Goderich, 3 Nov. 1832, *HRA*, xvi, p. 790–1.

64 Goderich to Bourke, 3 Apr., 13 May, 13 June 1832, *HRA*, xvi, pp. 590–1, 646, 658–62.

65 Based on WGB to Bourke, 29 Dec. 1831, 31/10476, Box 4/2125.5, CSIL; Colonial Secretary to WGB, 31 Dec. 1831, 31/153, CSOL (Letters to Clergy). WGB to

Arthur, 25 Feb., 19 Mar. 1832, AP, vol. 12; WGB to Bourke, 14 Jan. 1833, 33/518, Box 4/2169, CSIL.
[66] WGB to Bourke, 24 Sep. 1832, op. cit.

5 1833. The Assault

[1] Broughton, *Religion Essential to the Security and Happiness of Nations*, p. 5.
[2] Kinchela to Hay, 23 Sep. 1832, ML. A2146; 'Copy of Minutes of Instruction to Governor Bourke, June 1831,' encl. Bourke to Goderich, 11 Jan. 1832, CO 201/225; Forbes to Bourke, 25 Feb. 1837, Bk. P, vol. 11, ML.
[3] *Monitor*, 7 Apr. 1832.
[4] Ibid., 4 July, 6 Oct., 17 Nov. 1832.
[5] Ibid., 6, 20 Oct., 12 Dec. 1832; *Gazette*, 20 Oct. 1832; *Australian*, 21 Dec. 1832. Mansfield ceased editing the *Gazette* in Sep. 1832 and until mid-1833 remained under the direction of an editor unfriendly to Broughton.
[6] *Monitor*, 24 July 1833.
[7] *Australian*, 16 Nov. 1832, 1 Feb. 1833; also *Monitor*, 20 Oct., 3 Nov. 1832.
[8] SH, 31 Jan. 1833. For Goderich's disapproval, 'Copy of Minutes of Instruction to Governor Bourke, June 1831', op. cit. On the Irish precedent, *Monitor*, 10 Feb. 1830.
[9] *Gazette*, 29 Jan. 1833.
[10] Ibid. For an adverse comment of Wentworth's behaviour from those who agreed with his case see Lang, *New South Wales*, vol. 1, pp. 332–5; SH, 28 Jan. 1833.
[11] *Monitor*, 30 Jan. 1833.
[12] *Gazette*, 29 Jan. 1833.
[13] See WGB to Hay, 24 Dec. 1834, CO 201/244.
[14] *Tasmanian*, 1, 8 Mar. 1833.
[15] On Aborigines Committee, N.J.B. Plomley (ed.), *Friendly Mission. The Tasmanian Journals and Papers of George Augustus Robinson*, Tas. Hist. Research Assn., 1966, pp. 98–100. On Aboriginal mission, ibid., pp. 823, 919 (note 116); Minute, 4 Apr. 1833, *Proc. Ex. C. (VDL)*, CO 282/5. On Wesleyan subsidy, Minute, 4 Apr. 1833, op. cit.; Arthur to WGB, 12 May 1834, AP, vol. 39. On college, *Hobart Town Courier*, 17, 31 May, 14 June 1833; *Tasmanian*, 1 Feb., 21 June 1833.
[16] *Tasmanian*, 24 Apr. 1833; W. G. Broughton, *A Sermon Preached on Whit Sunday, 1833 . . . for the Relief of the Surviving Passengers and Crew of the Ship 'Hibernia'*, pp. 5, 12.
[17] Ibid., p. 15.
[18] *Colonist*, 11 June 1833; *Colonial Times*, 25 June 1833 quoted in *Monitor*, 20 July 1833.
[19] Goderich to Bourke, 13 June 1832, HRA, xvi, pp. 658–62. On CMS manoeuvres to be free of Broughton, Coates to Stanley, 5 July 1833, CH/L2, CMS.
[20] Goderich to Bourke, 5 Aug. 1832, HRA, xvi, pp. 690–1. James Stephen supplied Goderich with an explanation of Broughton's demotion which Goderich did not care to repeat. By the original warrants setting up the councils the chief justice, archdeacon, and the senior military officer next after the governor, were to take precedence according to their length of service in the colony. Lindesay should therefore have taken precedence over Broughton in 1829 but Broughton would have regained that precedence after Lindesay's departure in 1832, see Minute of James Stephen attached to Bourke to Goderich, 2 Jan. 1832, CO 201/225.
[21] Goderich to Bourke, 4 July 1832, HRA, xvi, pp. 672–3.
[22] WGB to Bishop of London, 30 Sep. 1833, encl. Bishop of London to Secretary of State for Colonies, 3 May 1833 (sic), CO 201/235. For Stiles's patrons see Lady Kennedy to Bourke, 27 Jan. 1833 and James Stephen to Bourke, 2 Mar. 1833, Bk. P, vol. 10.
[23] Goderich to Bourke, 25 Dec. 1832, HRA, xvi, pp. 829–33; 'Table A. Proposed numbers, stations, and services of the Clergy in New South Wales', encl. in Bourke to Goderich, 28 Feb. 1832, CO 201/225.
[24] See Goderich to Bourke, 4 July 1832, HRA, xvi, pp. 672–3. On Goderich's

career, W. D. Jones, *Prosperity Robinson. The Life of Viscount Goderich 1782–1859*, New York, 1967, p. 20 and passim.
25 Minute, 9 Oct. 1832, 28 June 1833, *V & P*; Bourke to Stanley, 1 Sep. 1834, *HRA*, xvii, p. 495.
26 *Gazette*, 12, 26 Mar., 11 May, 11, 13 July 1833; *SH*, 22 Apr., 15 July (supplement) 1833; *Monitor*, 24 July 1833.
27 *SH*, 1, 25 July 1833; *Gazette*, 13 July 1833; Minute, 10 June 1833, *Proc. Ex. C. (VDL)*, CO 282/5.
28 *Gazette*, 16 July 1833; Fulton, *Strictures*, p. 35.
29 See letters to editor in *Gazette*, 23, 27 July, 3 Aug. 1833. Petition published in ibid., 16 July 1833.
30 Bourke to Hay, 17 Aug. 1833, Bourke to Stanley, 12 Sep. 1833, *HRA*, xvii, pp. 190–1, 213–6; 'Communication of Roger Therry ... as to the Extension of Trial by Jury', encl. B to Minute No. 1, 1832, Appendix, *Proc. Ex. C.*, CO 204/5.
31 *Gazette*, 21 Jan. 1832 (pro-jury reform), 4 June (quoting *Monitor*), 9 July, 17 Aug. 1833 (anti-jury reform). For Bourke's views on punishment Bourke to Goderich, 30 Oct. 1832, *HRA*, xvi, pp. 780–2; Bourke to Stanley, 15 Jan. 1834, *HRA*, xvii, pp. 321–6.
32 WGB to Arthur, 27 July 1833, AP, vol. 12; Arthur to Bourke (private), 23 Aug. 1833, ML. A1962; Broughton, *Religion Essential to Security and Happiness of Nations*, pp. 2–3. Broughton's friend Judge Burton was attacking the prevalence of perjury in the colony's courts at this time, *Gazette*, 26 Sep. 1833.
33 Bourke to Stanley, 12 Sep., 2 Oct. 1833, *HRA*, xvii, pp. 213–6, 236–8; WGB to Arthur, 27 July 1833, AP, vol. 12; Robert Campbell to Bourke, 11 Sep. 1833, Bk. P, vol. 2.
34 William Ullathorne, *Autobiography of Archbishop Ullathorne with Selections from his Letters*, London, 1891, pp. 66, 71; W. B. Ullathorne, *A Few Words to the Reverend Henry Fulton, and His Readers; With a Glance at the Archdeacon*, Sydney, 1833, pp. 37–8, 55–6; Ullathorne to McLeay, 29 Apr. 1833, Bourke to Stanley, 2 Oct. 1833, *HRA*, xvii, pp. 204–6, 233–5.
35 Goderich to Bourke, 26 Mar. 1833, Bourke to Goderich, 29 June 1833, *HRA*, xvii, pp. 60, 157; 'Minute ... of Expenditure as Estimated for the Year 1834', *V & P 1833*; WGB to Arthur, 27 July 1835, AP, vol. 12.
36 Based on section IV of 'Estimates of the Probable Expense of the Various Departments ...', *V & P 1832–4*; Goderich to Darling, 22 Mar. 1831, Bourke to Goderich, 22 Sep. 1832, *HRA*, xvi, pp. 112–4, 750; WGB to Bishop of London, 30 Sep. 1833, encl. Bishop of London to Secretary of State, 3 May 1833 (sic), CO 201/235. Docker's predicament is discussed later in this chapter.
37 Minute of James Stephen to Hay, attached to Darling to Goderich, 28 Sep. 1831, *Despatches from Governor of New South Wales. Enclosures etc. 1830–31*, pp. 1008–9, ML; Goderich to Bourke, 10 Mar. 1833, *HRA*, xvii, p. 34.
38 WGB to Colonial Secretary, 12 Aug. 1833, 33/5219, *Index to Register of Letters Received*, CSIL; Broughton, *Charge ... at the Visitation ... 1834*, p. 16; Minute 15 Oct. 1833, *Proc. Ex. C.* CO 204/6; Broughton, *Religion Essential to Security and Happiness of Nations*, p. 7
39 WGB to Bishop of London, 30 Sep. 1833, op. cit.
40 Copy of memorandum in *Despatches from Governor of New South Wales Enclosures etc. 1832–5*, pp. 1215–23, ML. Hereafter referred to as Memorandum.
41 Memorandum, pp. 1219–20.
42 Bourke's marginal comments on Memorandum, pp. 1215–16, 1220–3.
43 Based on Colonial Secretary to WGB, 31 Aug. 1833, 7 Mar. 1834, 33/119, 34/60, CSOL (Letters to Clergy); Colonial Secretary to Stiles, 16 Sep. 1833, Stiles Papers, ML; Bourke to Stanley, 4 Oct. 1833, *HRA*, xvii, p. 240.
44 WGB to Bishop of London, 30 Sep. 1833, op. cit. For Forbes's opinion see encl. no. 11 in Darling to Bathurst, 7 May 1826, *HRA*, xii, pp. 287–9; Forbes to Wilmot-Horton, 22 Mar. 1827, ML. A1819.
45 Bourke to Stanley, 30 Sep. 1833, *HRA*, xvii, pp. 224–33; Memo of Bourke attached to Ullathorne to Colonial Secretary, 29 Apr. 1833, 33/3059, Box 4/2175.2, CSIL.

[46] Bourke to Goderich, 8 July 1833, *HRA*, xvii, pp. 165–6.
[47] Bourke to Stanley, 30 Sep. 1833, op. cit., pp. 231–2; see also Bourke to Arthur, 12 Mar. 1835, AP, vol. 8, and, Bourke to R. Bourke Jnr., 26 July 1836, Bk. P, vol. 6.
[48] Bourke to Stanley, 30 Sep. 1833, op. cit., pp. 227, 231–2.
[49] WGB to Arthur, 24 Jan. 1834, AP, vol. 12.
[50] Broughton, *Religion Essential to the Security and Happiness of Nations*, pp. 3–5 and passim. On lawlessness, Bourke to Stanley, 2 Oct. 1833, 15, 19. Sep. 1834, *HRA*, xvii, pp. 233–5, 520–3, 539–41. On Hitchcock and Poole, *SH*, 30 Dec. 1833; *Monitor*, 10 Jan. 1834.
[51] On Docker, Colonial Secretary to WGB, 13 Aug. 1833, 33/106, CSOL (Letters to Clergy); WGB to Stiles, 24 Sep. 1833, Stiles Papers; WGB to Bourke, 12 Sep. 1833, 33/6111, Box 4/2169, CSIL. On Wilton, WGB to Bourke, 8 Jan. 1833 (sic), 16 Jan. 1834, 34/229, 466, Box 4/2220, CSIL; Colonial Secretary to WGB, 13 Jan. 1834, 34/7, CSOL (Letters to Clergy); *Monitor*, 10 Jan. 1834. On the John Stephen case, *Monitor*, 10 Jan. 1834; Minute, 29 Oct. 1833, *Proc. Ex. C.*, CO 204/6; Goderich to Bourke, 24 Dec. 1832, *HRA*, xvi, p. 824. On St James, *Monitor*, 3 Aug. 1833.
[52] *SH*, 9 Dec. 1833; *Gazette*, 27, 29 Sep. 1832; WGB to Hay, 28 Jan. 1835, CO 323/174; also Clark, *History of Australia II*, p. 193.
[53] WGB to Colonial Secretary, 26 Sep., 18, 23 Dec. 1833, 33/6451, 8347, 8403, Box 4/2169, CSIL.
[54] Colonial Secretary to WGB, 19 Nov. 1833, 33/185, CSOL (Letters to Clergy); WGB to Colonial Secretary, 18 Feb. 1834, 34/1475, Box 4/2220, CSIL.
[55] Colonial Secretary to WGB, 22, 28 Oct. 1833, 33/163, 171, CSOL (Letters to Clergy); Memo to Bourke attached to WGB to Colonial Secretary, 17 Feb. 1834, 34/1150, Box 4/2220, CSIL. When Marsden administered the archdeaconry in Broughton's absence, 1834–6, Bourke gave him an ever freer hand, see Marsden to Bourke, 17 Nov. 1835, 35/9209, Box 4/2266.1, CSIL.
[56] Stanley to Bishop of London, 17 June 1833, CO 202/29. Colonial Secretary to WGB, 8 Nov. 1833, 33/178, CSOL (Letters to Clergy).
[57] *Australian*, 25 Jan. 1833; WGB to Arthur, 24 Jan. 1834, AP, vol. 12.
[58] Broughton, *Visitation Charge 1834*, pp. 5–15, 20; *Gazette*, 15, 17, 18 Feb. 1834; *Australian*, 14 Feb. 1834.
[59] *SH*, 24 Feb. 1834 (advertisement); Colonial Secretary to WGB, 8 Nov. 1833, 33/178, CSOL (Letters to Clergy).
[60] *SH*, 24 Feb. 1834. Broughton's luxury accommodation is referred to in Grey to WGB, 22 Dec. 1835, CO 202/23.

6 Waiting in Corridors

[1] Parry, *Journal*, 4 June 1832; *SH*, 9, 10, 17, 27 (advertisement) Feb. 1834.
[2] Bourke to Spring Rice, 12 Mar. 1834, Bk. P, vol. 9.
[3] Based on Barrington to Bourke, 26 Jan. 1833, Percival to Bourke, 1 Mar., 1 May 1833, James Stephen to Bourke, 2 Mar. 1833, Mrs Percival to Bourke, 2 Oct. 1834, Bk. P, vol. 10. On Percival replacing McLeay, see Arthur to Bourke, 4 Aug. 1833, ML. 1962. For Bourke's attack on Broughton, see Bourke to Spring Rice, 12 Mar. 1834, Bk. P, vol. 9.
[4] Sarah Broughton, *Diary*, 16, 18, 20 Aug. 1834, m/f, ANL; WGB to Arthur, 13 Oct. 1834, AP, vol. 12.
[5] WGB to Hay, 6 Sep. 1834, CO 323/172; *Times*, 25 Sep. 1834. The guest list at a Tory rally celebrating Melbourne's dismissal bore a striking resemblance to that of the King's School Feast Society, see *Times* 21 Nov. 1834.
[6] WGB to Spring Rice, 29 Aug. 1834 (and minute by Grey), and, 'Memorial of the Reverend William Grant Broughton etc.', encl. WGB to Spring Rice, 1 Sep. 1834, CO 201/244.
[7] WGB to Spring Rice (and minutes attached), 3, 30 Sep. 1834, WGB to Grey, 13 Sep. 1834, WGB to Hay, 4 Oct. 1834, CO 201/244; WGB to Hay, 6 Sep. 1834, CO 323/172.
[8] WGB to Arthur, 13 Oct. 1834, AP, vol. 12.

⁹ WGB to Campbell, 9 Dec. 1834, Bonwick Transcripts, Box 54, vol. 6, p. 1927.
¹⁰ See items 123, 124 in Box 10, C. MS. SPG; Minutes of Nov. 1834, *Journal of SPG*, vol. 41, p. 428, and, WGB to SPG, 17 Nov. 1834, SPG.
¹¹ Minute of SPG meeting, 16 Mar. 1821, Bonwick Transcripts, Box 57, vol. 3, p. 788; Hamilton to Goderich, 13 Aug. 1831, CO 201/222; Howick to Hamilton, 30 Sep. 1831, CO 202/28.
¹² Copy of Howick to Hamilton, 21 Aug. 1832, and Minutes of Dec. 1832, Apr. 1833, Jan., Feb. 1834, *Journal of SPG*, vol. 41, pp. 173, 217, 322, 340, 370–1, 391, SPG.
¹³ WGB to SPG, 17 Nov. 1834; WGB to Campbell, 9 Dec. 1834, Bonwick Transcripts, Box 54, vol. 6, pp. 1927–39.
¹⁴ Minutes of Jan. 1835, *Journal of SPG*, vol. 41, pp. 437–8, SPG; *Report ... SPG, 1834–5*, London, 1835, pp. 46–7; Darling to Arthur, 14 Feb. 1835, AP, vol. 7.
¹⁵ For the change in Broughton's stand on the Corporation Lands compare 'Heads of Subjects for Conference with Archdeacon Broughton; comments prepared by Mr Hay', CO 201/250 (out of sequence at f 155), and 'Memorandum to Sir George Grey on the Ecclesiastical Establishment in New South Wales', encl. WGB to Grey, 23 Sep. 1834, CO 201/244. The timing of the change, the probable influence of James Stephen, and the Canadian precedent is based on a reading of documents set out in G. P. Shaw, William Grant Broughton and His Early Years in New South Wales (Ph. D. thesis, ANU), pp. 324–6.
¹⁶ Based on *British Critic*, vol. 15, 1833–4, pp. 229–30, 495, vol 16, 1834–5, pp. 178, 487–9; *PD*, 12 Feb. 1833, col. 576 and 21 June 1833, col. 1095; *Times*, 17, 18, 21 Nov. 1834.
¹⁷ See documents in note 15 above, and, 'Being a Draft of a Reply to the Memorial of the SPCK such as Archdeacon Broughton would like to Receive from the Colonial Office', encl. WGB to Hay, 2 Dec. 1835, CO 201/250.
¹⁸ WGB to Grey, 23 Sep. 1834 and encl. CO 201/244. For Broughton's earlier insistence on higher salaries, see 'Report ... Church and Schools Establishment, 29 Sep. 1831', in *Despatches from Governor of New South Wales. Enclosure etc. 1832–5*, p. 1129, ML.
¹⁹ WGB to Arthur, 13 Oct. 1834, AP vol. 12.
²⁰ WGB to Hay, 5 Feb. 1835, CO 201/250; Hay to WGB, 9 Feb. 1835, CO 202/33.
²¹ See Goderich to Colborne, 5 Apr. 1832 in 'Copies or Extracts of Correspondence Respecting the Clergy Reserves in Canada 1819–1840', *PP*, 1840, vol. 32, pp. 95–6.
²² Stanley to Bourke, 25 June 1833, 26 Mar. 1834, *HRA*, xvii, pp. 152, 405. Bourke's despatch on national schools arrived at the Colonial Office in Feb. 1834 and remained out of circulation until 22 July 1834, see Minute, 22 July 1834 on Bourke to Stanley, 30 Sep. 1833, CO 201/233.
²³ Bishop of London to Secretary of State for Colonies, 3 May 1833 (sic. 1834), CO 201/235.
²⁴ Based on *Times* 11, 12 Nov. 1834; Spring Rice to Russell, 29 Jan. 1835 in Rollo Russell (ed.) *Early Correspondence of Lord John Russell*, London, 1913, vol. I, pp. 80–1; *PD*, 20 Mar. 1826, col 9, 7 Apr. 1835, col. 968; *Annual Register*, 1835, pp. 199–206.
²⁵ See Minute, 22 July 1834 on Bourke to Stanley, 30 Sep. 1833, CO 201/233.
²⁶ R. Bourke jnr. to Bourke, 30Sep. 1834, Bk. P, vol. 12.
²⁷ *Times* 18, 21, 24, 28 Nov., 4 Dec. 1834.
²⁸ Aberdeen to Bourke, 13 Feb. 1835, *HRA*, xvii, pp. 656–7; WGB to Marsden, 14 Mar. 1835, Marsden Papers, vol. 1, ML; WGB to Hay, 26 Jan. 1835, CO 201/250. Aberdeen's liberal views on education also shocked Gladstone, M.R.D. Foote (ed.), *Gladstone Diaries, Vol. 11 1833–1839*, Oxford, 1968, pp. 156–7.
²⁹ Howley to Abberdeen, 4 Nov. 1811, 1 June 1817, BM. Add. MS. 43195.
³⁰ See WGB to Glenelg, 22 May 1835, CO 201/250.
³¹ WGB to Hay, 26 Jan. 1835, CO 201/250.
³² WGB to Archbishop of Canterbury, 2 Apr. 1835, CO 201/250.
³³ WGB to Arthur, 21 Jan. 1834, AP, vol. 12; Bourke to Arthur, 17 Aug. 1835, AP, vol. 8; Bourke to R. Bourke jnr., 13 Oct. 1835, Bk. P, vol. 6.

34 Section 3 'Heads of Subjects for Conference with Archdeacon Broughton: comments prepared by Mr Hay', CO 201/250 (out of sequence, folio 155).
35 This is implied by considering together, WGB to Archbishop of Canterbury, 2 Apr. 1835, op. cit., with Minute of Glenleg attached to WGB to Glenelg, 22 May 1835, CO 201/250.
36 WGB to Glenelg, 22 May 1835, op. cit.; R. Bourke jnr. to Bourke, 15 Apr. 1835, Bk. P, vol. 12.
37 WGB to Glenelg, 22 May 1835, op. cit.
38 WGB to Sarah Broughton, 24 Jan. 1829, ML. B1612; *Times*, 15, 16 Sep. 1834; *British Critic*, vol. 15, 1833–4, pp. 444–9.
39 WGB to Glenelg, 22 May 1835, op. cit; 'Memorial Addressed to His Majesty's Government by the Society for Promoting Christian Knowledge', and, Archbishop of Canterbury to Melbourne, 8 May 1835, encls. Melbourne to Glenelg, 9 May 1835, CO 201/251 (out of sequence on folios 211–14, 219–24).
40 Glenelg to WGB, 22 June 1835, CO 202/33; R. Bourke jnr. to Bourke, 24 June 1835, Bk. P, vol. 12; 'Instructions ... to the Inspector to Visit the Schools of the West Indies, etc.', *PP*, 1837, vol. 43, p. 311.
41 WGB to Arthur, 27 July 1835, AP, vol. 12.
42 WGB to Hay, 19, 22 June 1835, CO 201/250; Glenelg to WGB, 22 June 1835, CO 202/33.
43 Keate to WGB, 10 July 1835, ANL. 1731; Sarah Broughton *Diary*, 12 May, 4 June, 26, 28 July, 3, 6, 9, 10, 18, 20 Aug. 1835, ANL.
44 Sarah Broughton, *Diary*, 12, 14, 15, 20, 29 Jan., 17 Feb., 28 Mar., 2 Apr., 20, 26 May, 3 June, 31 Oct., 25 Dec. 1835.
45 WGB to Hay, 27 Nov. 1834, CO 201/244; WGB to Grey, 24 Dec. 1835, CO 201/250.
46 Based on 'Notes. Drought's Case', encl. Pedder to Arthur, no date, AP, vol. 10; Arthur to WGB, 12 May 1834, AP, vol. 39; WGB to Arthur, 20 Nov. 1835, AP, vol. 12; and on Arthur 'the Just', James Stephen to Arthur, 8 July 1835, AP, vol. 4.
47 WGB to Arthur, 27 July 1835, also 13 Oct. 1834, 13 June 1836, AP, vol. 12.
48 WGB to Arthur, 13 Oct. 1834, op. cit.; Bedford to Palmer and Palmer to Bedford, 25 Oct. 1834, AP, vol. 39; WGB to Arthur, 6 Aug. 1830, 27 July 1833, Arthur to WGB, 4 Feb. 1834, AP, vol. 12; WGB to Bishop of London, 30 Sep. 1830, encl. Bishop of London to Secretary of State for Colonies, 3 May 1833 (sic. 1834), CO 201/235.
49 WGB to Glenelg, 7 Sep. 1835, CO 201/250; WGB to Grey, 4 Feb. 1836, CO 201/257; WGB to Arthur, 13 June 1836, AP, vol. 12.
50 WGB to Arthur, 13 Oct. 1834, AP, vol. 12; Arthur to Hay, 30 Sep. 1835, AP, vol. 1; sheet 11 of a draft despatch to Secretary of State, undated (filed at 31 Dec. 1835), and, Arthur to WGB, 12 May 1834, AP vol. 39.
51 WGB to Arthur, 13 Aug. 1834, 27 July 1835, AP, vol. 12; WGB to Bedford, 14 Oct. 1834, WGB to Palmer, 25 Nov. 1835, AP, vol. 39.
52 Arthur to WGB, 14 Feb. 1835, AP, vol. 39; Arthur to Spring Rice, 25 Apr. 1835, Arthur to Hay (private), 30 Sep. 1835, AP, vol. 1; Arthur to James Stephen, 23 Apr. 1835, AP, vol. 4.
53 James Norman to Arthur, 16 Apr. 1835, AP, vol. 39; Arthur to Bourke (private), 2 Feb. 1836, ML. A1962.
54 Based on *Broughton and Parry Correspondence*, pp. 21–32, 39–40, 44–5, 47–9, ML.B377.
55 Ibid., pp. 2–3, 49–55.
56 Bourke to Stanley, 18 Feb. 1833 and encl., *HRA*, xvii, pp. 374–5; W. M. Cowper, *Autobiography and Reminiscences of William Macquarie Cowper, Dean of Sydney*, Sydney 1902, pp. 84, 105–6; WGB to M. Cowper, 22 May 1835, ML.Ab29/4.
57 Sarah Broughton, *Diary*, 3, 4 Aug. 1835; 'Report from Select Committee on Aborigines etc.', *PP*, 1836, vol. 7, pp. 20–4.
58 Sarah Broughton, *Diary*, 5 Sep. 1835; WGB to Glenelg, 7 Sep. 1835, CO 201/250; WGB to Marsden, 25 Sep. 1835, Marsden Papers, vol. 1; Marsden to Coates, 25 June, 26 Nov. 1835, 22 Jan., 23 Feb. 1836, Bonwick Transcripts, Box 54, vol. 6, pp. 1872–8. On resignation, WGB to Arthur, 20 Nov. 1835, AP, vol. 12.

⁵⁹ Norris to WGB, 26 Sep. 1835, ML. 913.
⁶⁰ Broughton, *The Present Position and Duties of the Church of England*, pp. 5, 7–11.
⁶¹ Broughton, *Sermons on Church of England*, p. xviii; WGB to Marsden, 25 Sep. 1835, Marsden Papers, vol. 1; *British Critic*, vol. 22, 1837, p. 14.
⁶² Hay to WGB, 26 Nov. 1834, CO 202/30; WGB to Hay, 28 Nov. 1834, CO 201/244; Minutes, 7, 24 Sep. 1830 (and encl. HH in Appendix), *Proc. Ex. C.*, CO 204/3.
⁶³ Glenelg's prosposals can be deduced from Broughton's comments in his 'Memo left at Colonial Office, 4 Nov. 1835', CO 201/250. Glenelg probably hoped for a compromise as in the West Indies, see WGB to Grey, 13 Nov. 1835, ibid.
⁶⁴ Bourke to Arthur, 17 Aug. 1835, AP, vol. 8; Bourke to R. Bourke jnr., 26 Dec. 1835, Bk. P, vol. 6; Broughton, 'Memo . . . 4 Nov. 1835', op. cit.
⁶⁵ WGB to Glenelg, 19 Nov. 1835, CO 201/250; Broughton, 'Memo . . . 4 Nov. 1835', op. cit.
⁶⁶ WGB to Hay, 24 Nov. 1835, CO 201/250.
⁶⁷ See Minute AA (Glenelg's handwriting) attached to draft of Despatch on Education, folios 172–84, CO 325/28.
⁶⁸ Glenelg to Bourke, 30 Nov. 1835, *HRA*, xviii, pp. 201–7.
⁶⁹ Glenelg to WGB, 1 Dec. 1835, CO 325/28.
⁷⁰ WGB to Glenelg, 3 Dec. 1835, CO 201/250.
⁷¹ Glenelg to WGB, 17 Dec. 1835, CO 202/33.
⁷² WGB to Glenelg, 10 Dec. 1835, CO 201/250.
⁷³ WGB to Grey, 17 Dec. 1835, ibid. On financial arrangements see 'Schedule of Expenses', encl. WGB to Grey, 21 Dec. 1835, ibid., and, Grey to WGB, 15, 16 Dec. 1835, CO 202/33.
⁷⁴ Grey to WGB, 18, 22 Dec. 1835, CO 202/33; WGB to Grey, 21 Dec. 1835, CO 201/250.
⁷⁵ WGB to Arthur, 20 Nov. 1835, 21 Sep. 1836, AP, vol. 12.
⁷⁶ WGB to Grey, 24 Dec. 1835, CO 201/250.
⁷⁷ WGB to Grey, 28 Dec. 1835, ibid; Grey to WGB, 5 Jan. 1836, Grey to Tyner, 15, 18 Mar. 1836, CO 202/33.
⁷⁸ Minute A (James Stephen's handwriting) attached to draft of Despatch on Education, folio 123, CO 325/28.
⁷⁹ See document 'Being a draft of a reply etc . . .', encl. WGB to Hay, 2 Dec. 1835, CO 201/250. No drafts of the letters patent were forwarded to Broughton, see WGB to Grey, 21 Jan. 1836, CO 201/257.
⁸⁰ Bishop of Australia to Glenelg, 20 Feb. 1836, Grey to Bishop of Australia, 12 May 1836, *HRA*, xviii, pp. 419–22.
⁸¹ WGB to Arthur, 27 July 1835, AP, vol. 12.
⁸² WGB to Marsden, 30 Dec. 1835, ML. A5412/1; Bourke to Stanley, 10 Mar. 1834, *HRA*, xvii, pp. 390–4; Forrest to Bishop of London, 11 Mar. 1834, unattached document being folios 188–91, CO 201/251.
⁸³ WGB to Marsden, 30 Dec. 1835, op. cit.
⁸⁴ Hay to WGB, 18 Apr., 20 May 1835, Grey to WGB, 7 Mar. 1836, CO 202/33; WGB to Hay, 21 May, 18 Dec. 1835, CO 201/250; WGB to Grey, 28 Jan. 1836, CO 201/257.
⁸⁵ See 'Report . . . Church and Schools Establishment . . . 29 September 1831', in *Despatches from Governor of New South Wales. Enclosures etc. 1832–5*, p. 1143. ML.
⁸⁶ Grey to WGB, 23 Jan. 1836, CO 202/33; WGB to Grey, 28 Jan. 1836, WGB to Glenelg, 20 Feb. 1836, CO 201/257.
⁸⁷ J. E. N. Molesworth, *Foundations of Episcopacy. A Sermon Preached on the Consecration of the Right. Rev. William Grant Broughton etc.*, London, 1836, pp. 43–5. Hampden was appointed against Howley's wishes on 7 Feb. 1836. Broughton knew of the appointment though the affair became public only after his departure, see WGB to Keate, 26 July 1836, ANL. 1731, and O. Chadwick, *The Victorian Church. Part I*, London, 1966, pp. 112–18.
⁸⁸ WGB to Arthur, 13 June 1836, AP, vol. 12; WGB to Keate, 26 July 1836, ANL. 1731.
⁸⁹ WGB to Arthur, 21 Sep. 1836, AP, vol. 12.

7   Founding the Citadel. 1836

1 'Abstract from Ship Camden's Log', ML. 913; WGB to EC, 26 July 1836, ANL. 1731; *Gazette*, 7 June 1836.
2 *Gazette*, and *SH*, 2 June 1836.
3 Darling to Arthur, 14 Feb. 1835, AP, vol. 7; Bourke to Spring Rice, 7 June 1835, Bk. P, vol. 9; *Gazette*, 31 May, 2 June 1836.
4 Bourke to Glenelg, 3 Oct. 1835 and encls., 18 Dec. 1835, 10 June 1836, *HRA*, xviii, pp. 110–30, 228–32, 436–38; R. Bourke jnr to Spring Rice, May 1835, Bk. P, vol. 11. On the politics of the appointment, see Bourke to R. Bourke jnr., 26 Dec. 1835, 15 June 1836, Bk. P, vol. 6. On Burton's need for money see Burton to Edmund Burton, 4 Oct. 1832, 29 Nov. 1833, ML. 834.
5 On Riddell, see Bourke to Glenelg, 2 Dec. 1835 and encls., *HRA*, xviii, pp. 216–23; H. King, *Richard Bourke*, Melbourne, 1971, pp. 237–9. For Bourke's attack on the local aristocracy, see 'List of Persons ... any 12 of whom may be selected by the Governor', encl. in Bourke to Glenelg, 26 Dec. 1835, *HRA*, xviii, p. 252. The list omitted the names of R. Jones and E.C. Close, two existing members of the Council and critics of Bourke, and was contrived to allow for the exclusion of Hannibal and James Macarthur, Robert Campbell and McLeay.
6 Bourke to R. Bourke jnr., 30 Nov. 1835, 17 Jan. 1836, Bk. P, vol. 6.
7 Bourke to R. Bourke jnr., 15 Apr. 1836, Bk. P, vol. 6; *Gazette*, 12, 14, 21, 23, Apr., 12 May, 11 June 1836.
8 Bourke to R. Bourke jnr., 4 Feb., 7 Nov. 1835, Bk. P, vol. 6.
9 Bourke to R. Bourke Jnr., 15 June 1836, ibid. On loss of contact at the Colonial Office, R. Bourke jnr. to Bourke, 10 Feb. 1836, Bk. P, vol. 12.
10 Bourke scarcely referred to educational change in his opening address to the Legislative Council, see *Gazette*, 4 June 1836.
11 R. Bourke jnr. to Bourke, 10 Feb. 1836, Bk. P, vol. 12; Bourke to Glenelg, 18 June 1836, *HRA*, xviii, pp. 445–6.
12 WGB to Bourke, 2, 3 June 1836, ML. Ab29/6a; *Australian*, 7 June 1836.
13 *SH*, 9, 13 June 1836; *Gazette*, 11 June 1836, on McLeay's rumoured retirement *Australian*, 10 June 1836; W. G. Broughton, *The Righteousness of Faith*; *Australian*, 7 June 1836.
14 Bourke to Glenelg, 11 June 1836 and encl., 18 June and 25 July 1836, *HRA*, xviii, pp. 439–40, 445–6, 457; Glenelg to Bourke, 21 Dec. 1835, ibid., pp. 233–4; Bourke to R. Bourke jnr., 28 July 1836, Bk. P, vol. 6.
15 *SH*, 7 July 1836, (WGB to editor); WGB to Glenelg, 16 June 1836, CO 201/257.
16 Glenelg to Bourke, 1 Dec. 1836, *HRA*, xviii, pp. 606–8; W. W. Burton, *State of Religion and Education in New South Wales*, London, 1840, p. 95; WGB to Keate, 26 July 1836, ANL. 1731.
17 *Monitor*, 18 June, 23 July 1836; *Gazette*, 7, 11 June, 26 July 1836; *Colonial Times*, 5 July 1836; *Australian*, 10 June 1837; on the state of the Church of England, Bourke to Arthur, 13 May 1836, AP, vol. 8; *Colonist*, 9 June 1836.
18 On the clergy, WGB to EC, 19 Oct. 1836; Burton, *Religion and Education*, p. 64. Fulton, aged 75; Marsden, 70; Cartwright, 65; Cowper, 58; Raddall, 56; Cross, 55; Broughton, 48; and J. J. Therry, 46. Marsden and Reddall died 1838, Fulton in 1840. On churches, *Diary of Reverend Richard Taylor*, 20 Dec. 1836, 24 June 1837, ML. A3816. On Polding's and Broughton's appointments, *SH*, 14 July 1836 (letter from Polding to Bourke), WGB to Marsden, 30 Dec. 1835, ML. A5412/1. On the vitality of the younger Roman Catholic clergy, Bourke to Arthur, 13 May 1836, AP, vol. 8; Bourke to R. Bourke jnr., 21 Aug. 1836, Bk. P, vol. 6.
19 *Monitor*, 22 June 1836; *SH*, 23 June 1836. On contributors, *Statement of the Objects of the Committee of the Societies for the Propagation of the Gospel etc.*, Sydney, 1836, pp. 28–31; on Macarthur's plans for Camden, WGB to Keate, 26 July 1836, ANL. 1731; on Bourke's parsimony, *Gazette*, 20 June 1837 (letter Protestant to editor). Gipps and Franklin both contributed to church funds, *Report of Diocesan Committee, 1839*, List of Donors, and, *Hobart Town Courier*, 1 June 1838.
20 'Circular from Diocesan Committee', dated 22 June and 9 July 1836, copy in

ML. A.106; *Statement of Objects of ... SPG*, pp. 18–19; *Report of Diocesan Committee, 1837*, Sydney, 1837, p. 69; *Taylor Diary*, 14 July 1836, 21 July, 18 Sep. 1837.

21 *Report of Diocesan Committee 1837*, pp. 25–6, 34, 36–52; *Statement of Objects of ... SPG*, p. 31. Broughton's energy in this period acknowledged in *Colonist*, 14 Dec. 1837.

22 Grey to WGB, 23 Jan. 1836, Stephen to Spearman (treasury), 8 Mar. 1836, CO 202/33; WGB to Grey, 22 Feb. 1836, CO 201/257; Colonial Secretary to WGB, 16 June 1836, 36/119, CSOL (Letter to Clergy); Grey to Stephen, 17 May 1837, attached to Campbell to Grey, 15 May 1837, CO 201/265.

23 7 William IV, No 3 clauses iii-v, *Acts and Ordinances of Governor and Council of New South Wales*, vol. 2, part 2, pp. 720–1; *Colonist*, 16 June 1836; *SH*, 4 July 1836. The Church Acts are discussed in J. Barrett, *That Better Country*, Melbourne, 1966, pp. 32–7.

24 *Monitor*, 30 Aug. 1836.

25 *Gazette*, 30 Sep. 1830, 14 Jan. 1832; *Monitor*, 3 Aug. 1833.

26 8 William IV, No 5, clause xi, *Acts and Ordinances*, pp. 808–9; Bourke to Glenelg, 4 Nov. 1837, *HRA*, xix, pp. 148–9; WGB to Colonial Secretary, 27 Dec. 1836 and minute of Bourke's attached, 36/10987, Box 4/2266.1, CSIL.

27 *SH*, 4 July 1836.

28 See WGB to Bourke, 13 July 1836 and a letter following it dated Wednesday, ML. Ab29/6a.

29 *Colonist*, and *Gazette*, 16 June 1836; *Australian*, 10 June 1836; *SH*, 4, 21 July 1836.

30 See document titled 'Being a draft of a reply to the Memorial of the SPCK etc.' encl. WGB to Hay, 2 Dec. 1835, CO 201/250; also WGB to EC, 25 Feb. 1839.

31 J. H. Newman, *Apologia pro Vita Sua* (ed. M. J. Svaglic), Oxford, 1967, p. 54; Bourke to Glenelg, 8 Aug. 1836, *HRA*, xviii, p. 476.

32 Bourke to Glenelg, 8 Aug. 1836, *HRA*, xviii, p. 476.

33 Bourke to R. Bourke jnr., 30 July 1837, Bk. P, vol. 6.

34 'Estimates ... of the Church Establishment ... 1837', *V & P 1836*.

35 WGB to Keate, 1 May 1837, ANL. 1731.

36 WGB to Arthur, 21 Sep. 1836, AP vol. 12.

37 Broughton, *Sermons on Church of England*, p. 47.

38 Based on *Colonist*, 22, 29 Jan., 5 Feb., 12 Mar., 30 Apr. 1835; Ullathorne, *Autobiography*, p. 109. J. D. Lang, *Historical and Statistical Account of New South Wales*, third edition, London, 1852, vol. II, pp. 512–14.

39 *Colonist*, 5 May 1836.

40 WGB to Keats, 26 July 1836, 1 May 1837, ANL. 1731. For Broughton's opinion on dissenters in England, WGB to Arthur, 27 July 1835, AP, vol. 12.

41 'Resolution at a Meeting of Protestants ... June 24, 1836' encl. Bourke to Glenelg, 8 Aug. 1836, *HRA*, xviii, pp. 472–3.

42 *Colonist*, 30 June 1836; 'Petition of the Undersigned Protestants', *V & P 1836*, pp. 534–5.

43 *Gazette*, 19, 28 July 1836 (advertisement).

44 Compare 'Petition of the Undersigned Protestants', op. cit. with WGB to Glenelg, 22 May 1835, CO 201/250.

45 *Gazette*, 19 July 1836; Bourke to R. Bourke jnr., 21 July 1836, Bk. P, vol. 6.

46 *SH*, 1 Sep. 1836; 'Circular to Police Magistrates', 23 July 1836, and, 'Sub-Committee of Protestant Association', *HRA*, xviii, pp. 471–4.

47 Blaxland to Bourke, 5 Dec. 1835, Bk. P, vol. 11.

48 Bourke to Glenelg, 8 Aug. 1836, *HRA*, xviii, pp. 466–70; Bourke to R. Bourke jnr., 21 July 1836, Bk P, vol. 6.

49 Petitions from WGB to Legislative Council, 22, 25 July 1836, *V & P 1836*, pp. 527, 531–4.

50 Broughton, *Speech Delivered to Committee of Protestants on Wednesday, August 3, 1836*, pp. 5, 21–2.

51 Compare instructions in Glenelg to Bourke, 30 Nov. 1835 and Grey to Bourke, 31 Dec. 1835, *HRA*, xviii, pp. 205–6, 253, with 'Minute Explanatory of the System of the Proposed National Schools', *V & P 1836*, p. 531.

52 Based on *SH*, 18 Aug. 1836; Bourke to Glenelg, 8 Aug. 1836, *HRA*, xviii, pp. 460–70; Broughton, *Speech to Committee of Protestants*, pp. 13–4; *Gazette*, 28 July 1836. A committee of enquiry was requested by R. Campbell and others, see Protest of 11 Aug. 1836, *V & P 1836*.
53 Bourke to R. Bourke jnr., 7 Nov. 1835, Bk. P, vol. 6.
54 Broughton, *Speech to Committee of Protestants*, pp. 3, 22–3. Evidence of non-Anglican acceptance of Church of England schools mentioned earlier in, Cowper and Hill to WGB, 19 Jan. 1835, published in Broughton, *Speech of the Lord Bishop of Australia in The Legislative Council Upon The Resolution for Establishing a System of General Education*, pp. 41–2.
55 *Colonist*, 25 Aug. 1836.
56 Evidence of Mansfield 1 July 1844 in 'Report from Select Committee on Education', *V & P 1844*, vol. 2, pp. 9–18.
57 *Colonist*, 11 Aug. 1836.
58 Bourke to Glenelg, 8 Aug. 1836, *HRA*, xviii, pp. 468–9. Bourke to R. Bourke jnr., 21 Aug. 1836, Bk. P, vol. 6; *Gazette*, 11, 16 Aug. 1836; *Australian*, 9 Aug. 1836.
59 WGB to Keate, 1 May 1837, ANL. 1731; *Gazette*, 2 Aug. 1836; *Monitor*, 17, 21, 28 Sep. 1836; Bourke to Glenelg, 7 Oct. 1836, *HRA*, xviii, pp. 565–6. For Church of England domination of subcommittees see list of subcommittees in *HRA*, xviii, pp. 473–4, and *Colonist*, 22 Sep. 1836.
60 Compare *SH*, 1, 25 July 1833 with ibid., 1 Aug. 1836.
61 *SH*, 13 Oct. 1836, also 4 July, 1 Aug. 1836.
62 The *Gazette* went volte-face around Sep. 1836. For changes in editors and proprietors see *Gazette*, 1 Sep. 1836, 23 Feb. 1837.
63 Based on *SH*, 25 Aug., 12, 22, Sep., 3, 6, 10, 20 Oct., 7 Nov. (supplement), 26 Dec. (supplement) 1836; *Colonist*, 11 Aug. 1836; *Gazette*, 31 Jan. 1837. From 25 Aug. 1836 to the end of the year the *SH* serialized W. D. Killen, *The Bible versus the Board-the Priest-and the Court of Chancery; or, the Workings of the New System of National Education as exemplified in the History of Ballyholey School, in the Parish of Raphoe, County of Donegal*, Belfast, 1835. On Woollongong and Yass, *SH*, 11, 15 Aug. 1836; *Colonist*, 18 Aug. 1836; *Gazette*, 29 Sep. 1836.
64 WGB to Keate, 1 May 1837, ANL. 1731.
65 Glenelg to Bourke, 29 Aug. 1836, *HRA*, xviii, pp. 507–8.
66 Bourke to Glenelg, 8 Aug. 1836, *HRA*, xviii, p. 476; Bourke to R. Bourke jnr., 28 July 1836, Bk. P, vol. 6.
67 *Monitor*, 20 July, 17 Sep. 1836.
68 *SH*, 6, 20 Oct. 1836.
69 WGB to Keate, 1 May 1837, ANL. 1731.
70 Based on WGB to EC, 26 July 1836, ANL. 1731; WGB to EC, 19 Oct. 1837; Whitington, *Broughton*, p. 82; A. B. Sparke, *Diary*, 17 Aug. 1836, ML. A4869; T. L. Suttor, *Hierarchy and Democracy in Australia 1788–1870*, Melbourne, 1965, p. 30.

8   Building the Citadel

1 WGB to SPG, 21 July 1837; Broughton's priority for churches rather than schools WGB to SPG, 17 June, 25 July 1836, 22 Feb., 1 Aug. 1837; WGB to EC, 19 Oct. 1837; *Report of Diocesan Committee 1837*, pp. 36–52.
2 WGB to Grey, 18 June 1836, CO 201/257; WGB to Bourke, 1 June 1837, ML. Ab29/6a; WGB to SPG, 17 June 1836.
3 WGB to EC, 8 Sep., 19 Oct. 1837; WGB to SPG, 17, 18 June, 1 Aug. 1837; Simeon to Marsden, 10 Nov. 1835, ML. A1992.
4 WGB to EC, 26 July 1836, ANL. 1731; WGB to EC, 19 Oct. 1837; 'An Appeal to the Friends of the Church of England on Behalf of their Brethren in Australia', in *Report of Diocesan Committee 1837*, pp. 80–93.
5 WGB to SPG, 1 Aug. 1837; WGB to EC, 8 Sep., 19 Oct. 1837, 25 Feb. 1839.
6 WGB to EC, 25 Feb. 1839.
7 WGB to EC, 26 July 1836, 19 Oct. 1837; WGB to SPG, 2 June 1835; *SH*, 18

May 1837; WGB to Bourke, 13 Feb. 1837, ML. Ab29/6a; S. M. Johnstone, *The Book of St Andrew's Cathedral*, Sydney, 1937, pp. 20–1.

8 WGB to Norton, 12 May 1837; WGB to Bourke, dated Sunday, ML. Ab29/9; *SH* and *Gazette*, 18 May 1837.

9 Based on Appendix to Broughton, *Present Position and Duties of Church of England*, pp. 23–4, 27–30; WGB to EC, 26 July 1836, 25 Feb. 1839.

10 Gipps to Normanby, 29 July 1839 and encl. Polding to Gipps, 2 July 1839, *HRA*, xx, pp. 265–70.

11 *Gazette*, 29 Apr. 1837; *SH*, 1 June 1837; WGB to Bourke, 30 May 1837, *HRA*, xx, pp. 266–7; WGB to Bourke, 1 June 1837, Bourke to WGB, 3 June 1837, ML. Ab29/6a,b.

12 WGB to EC, 25 Feb., 13 Sep. 1839; WGB to Bourke, 5 June 1837, ML. Ab29/6a.

13 Bourke to WGB, 3 June 1837, ML. Ab29/6b; Polding to Gipps, 2 July 1839, op. cit., p. 268.

14 WGB to Bourke, 5 June 1837, op. cit.

15 On the King's School, see WGB to EC, 26 July 1836, ANL. 1731; on the church episode, see *Monitor*, 21 Sep. 1836; on the Jamison affair, see WGB to Bourke, 29 Apr. 1837, ML. Ab29/6a. Others found Jamison's presence at government house socially objectionable, see Bourke to Jamison, 19 July 1834, Jamison to Bourke, 19, 20 July 1834, Bk. P, vol. 11.

16 WGB to Keate, 1 May 1837, ANL. 1731. Bourke also appeared to wage a vendetta against Mansfield for his role as organizing secretary of the Protestant Association, see *Colonist*, 13 Oct. 1836, Bourke to Glenelg, 8 Aug. 1836, *HRA*, xviii, p. 475.

17 A. B. Sparke, *Diary*, 16 May, 20 June 1837, ML. A4869; *Monitor*, 26 July 1837.

18 Bishop of London to Grey (and minute attached), 12 Dec. 1836 CO 201/258; WGB to SPG, 1 Aug. 1837.

19 Pedder to Arthur, 5 Aug. 1833, AP, vol. 10; WGB to Barnard, 7 July 1835 CO 201/249; Arthur to Bourke, 2 Feb. 1836, ML. A1962; Bourke to Arthur, 12 Mar. 1835, 15 Mar. 1836, AP, vol. 8.

20 Pedder to Arthur, 3 Aug. 1836, AP, vol. 10; WGB to Arthur, 21 Sep. 1836, AP, vol. 12.

21 Minutes, 28, 29 July 1836, together with Bedford to WGB, 21, 27 July 1836, *Proc. Ex. C. (VDL)*, CO 282/10; Bedford to Glenelg, 29 Oct. 1836 and encl. Bedford to Arthur, 9 Sep. 1836 CO 280/71; Glenelg to Franklin, 17 June 1837, 'Papers relating to Cases in which the Bishop of any Diocese in the Australian Colonies has attempted to exercise Ecclesiastical Jurisdiction over any of his Clergy', *PP*, 1850, vol. 37, p. 687.

22 WGB to Glenelg, 12 Dec. 1837, 'Papers relating to Cases . . .', op. cit., pp. 687–91.

23 Minute, 25 Aug. 1836, *Proc. Ex. C. (VDL)*, CO 282/10.

24 WGB to Marsden, 15 Aug. 1836, ML. A1994; Taylor, *Diary*, 12 July, 13 Dec. 1836, ML. A3816.

25 WGB to Bourke, 7, 17 Oct. 1836, Colonial Secretary to WGB, 11, 25 Oct. 1836, Memo of Attorney General to Bourke, 20 Oct. 1836, in 'Correspondence between Broughton and Bourke over the erection of Consistorial Courts', MC.

26 See *SH*, 7 Nov. 1836; *Gazette*, 17 Dec. 1836; *Colonist*, 29 July 1837, 7 Apr. 1838.

27 See correspondence (16 letters) between Bowen and Stiles, Bowen and WGB, Stiles and WGB, Hassall and Stiles during 1836–9, and, Bowen to Stiles, 13 July 1835, 6 Oct, 1857 in Stiles Papers, ML. A1323. C. M. G. Bowen, *The Language of Theology Interpreted*, Sydney, 1836. *SH*, 12 Dec. 1836; *Colonist*, 25 May 1837.

28 Broughton's problem is best approached through 'Correspondence between Broughton and Bourke over the erection of Consistorial Courts', in MC, which were the documents Broughton took to England in 1852 in negotiations on synodical government. The documents in 'Papers relating to Cases in which the Bishop of any Diocese in the Australian Colonies has attempted to exercise Ecclesiastical Jurisdiction over any of his Clergy . . .', Part I, II, *PP*, vol. 37, 1850 are relevant, and the issue is appraised in R. Border, *Church and State in Australia*, London, 1962, chs. 12, 13.

29 WGB to EC, 6 Feb. 1838; *Colonist*, 7, 14 Dec. 1837, also in Religious Intelligence column in *Colonist*, 1836–7.

30 *SH*, 11 Jan. 1838; *Colonist*, 26 Oct. 1837; WGB to Glenelg, 12 Dec. 1837, 'Papers relating to Cases ...', op. cit., pp. 687–91.
31 *Colonist*, 12 Oct., 21 Dec. 1837, 31 Jan. 1838; *Gazette*, 27 Jan. 1838; *SH* 18 Jan. 1838.
32 *Colonist*, 28 Dec. 1837; WGB to EC, 6 Feb. 1838. Gipps gave £7 to Coleridge's appeal, see *Report of Diocesan Committee 1837*, p. 90.
33 WGB to SPG, 22 May 1838.
34 *Hobart Town Courier*, 27 Apr. 1838; Jane Franklin to John Griffin (her father), 8 Dec. 1837, Jane Franklin to Mary Simpkinson, 9 Dec. 1837, Jane Franklin, Journal, Jan. 1839, Franklin Papers, m/f, ANL; Jane Franklin to WGB, 12 Jan. 1844, ML. B1612. On Thomas Arnold, see Arnold to Franklin, 20 July 1836 in James Aitken (ed.), *English Letters of XIX Century*, Middlesex, 1946, pp. 162–3; Franklin to Glenelg, 26 June 1838, CO 280/95; Jane Franklin to Mary Simpkinson, 6 Jan. 1841, Jane Franklin to Captain Ross, 16 Sep. 1841, Franklin Papers.
35 WGB to SPG, 22 May 1838; *Hobart Town Courier*, 15 June 1838; WGB to Franklin, 5 June 1838, CO 280/95 (edited and reprinted in *PP*, 1850, vol. 37, pp. 693–4).
36 Minute, 26 June, 3 July 1838, *V & P*; *Colonist*, 10 Mar. 1838. A draft of Gipps's Commission shows the reversal of precedence as having been detected but the correction was not incorporated in the final document, see 'Draft of Commission etc.', CO 380/104, folio 65, 112.
37 Gipps to Glenelg, 1 May 1838, *HRA*, xix, p. 402. The nature of the proposal put forward by Gipps can be deduced by reading together note 84, *HRA*, vol. xix, p. 807, and A.C.V. Melbourne, *Early Constitutional Development in Australia*, 2nd ed, St Lucia, 1963, pp. 235–6.
38 *Gazette*, 14, 21 July 1838; Minute, 17 July 1838, *V & P*.
39 Minute, 7 Aug. 1838, *V & P*; 'Petition ... adopted at a Public Meeting ... 25 May', *V & P 1838*, pp. 583–6; *Colonist*, 26, 30 May 1838.
40 *Gazette*, 14 July 1838; 'Report from Committee on Emigration', *V & P 1838*, pp. 758–62. On female emigration, WGB to Hay, 28 Jan. 1835, CO 323/174. On the imbalance of sexes, 'Report ... of the Church and Schools Establishment, 29 September 1831', *Despatches from Governor ... 1832–5*, p. 1147, ML.
41 *Gazette*, 20 Sep., 20 Nov. 1838; 'Report From Committee on Aboriginal Question with Minutes of Evidence', *V & P 1838*, pp. 1055–8, 1070–4, 1078–9.
42 Glenelg to Gipps, 31 Jan. 1838, *HRA*, xix, pp. 252–5; 'Report from Select Committee on Aborigines etc ...', *PP*, 1836, vol. 7, pp. 25, 688–90.
43 Cowper to Coates, 4 Aug. 1838, CN/02, CMS; 'Report of Committee on Aboriginal Question ...', op. cit., pp. 1047–8. Broughton never respected Robinson's methods, see 'Report from Select Committee on Aborigines etc ...', op. cit., p. 30.
44 *Gazette*, 20, 22 Nov., 11, 20 Dec. 1838.
45 *Colonist*, 7 Apr., 30 June, 15 Aug., 29 Sep. 1838.
46 *Colonist*, 9, 30 June, 8 Aug. 1838.
47 'Extract from Minute ... 28 May 1838, Executive Council of New South Wales', encl. Gipps to Glenelg, 12 June 1838, CO 201/273; *Gazette*, 4 Aug., 13 Sep. 1838; *Colonist*, 15 Aug. 1838.
48 *Gazette*, 21 July 1838; *Report of Diocesan Committee 1838*, pp. 21–32; Norris to WGB, 21 Mar. 1838, ML. 913; WGB to Dr Warneford, 12 Nov. 1838, C.MS. SPG.
49 *Colonist*, 25 July 1838.
50 *Gazette*, 31 July, 2, 7 Aug. 1838.
51 W. McIntyre, *Is the Service of the Mass Idolatrous? Being a Candid Inquiry into the Doctrine Maintained on the Subject by Bishop Polding in His Pastoral Address*, Sydney, 1838.
52 WGB to EC, 13 Sep. 1839; H. L. Clark, *Constitutional Church Government*, London, 1924, p. 36.
53 Cowper to Coates, 11 Oct. 1838, CN/02, CMS; WGB to (Norris), Mar. 1841, ML. 913; WGB to Jowett, 11 Aug. 1837, CN/03, CMS.
54 Minute of 28 Nov. 1838, CN/01, CMS; Cowper to Coates, 7 Oct. 1837, 29 Sep.

1838, CN/02, CMS; WGB to Jowett, 29 Nov. 1838, CN/03, CMS.
[55] WGB to Jowett, 28 Mar. 1839, 'Address of the Missionaries to Bishop of Australia', 5 Jan. 1839, 'The Bishop's Address to the Missionaries', 5 Jan. 1839, CN/03, CMS.
[56] WGB to Jowett, 28 Mar. 1839, op. cit.; *Gazette*, 31 Jan. 1839.
[57] WGB to SPG, 22 May 1838.

9　*A Season of Black and White*

[1] WGB to EC, 14 Oct. 1839; WGB to Jowett, 27 Mar. 1840, CN/03, CMS.
[2] WGB to SPG, 13 Sep. 1839 (private); WGB to EC, 25 Feb., 3 Apr. 1840.
[3] *Gazette*, 30 Aug. 1838.
[4] Jane Franklin to Sir John Franklin, 20 June 1839 in G. Mackaness, *Some Private Correspondence of Sir John and Lady Jane Franklin, Part I*, Sydney, 1947, p. 92; Gipps to Normanby, 9 Dec. 1839, *HRA*, xx, pp. 426–30; [Macarthur], *New South Wales, Prospects*, pp. 230–7; *SH*, 30 June 1836, 1 Mar. 1838; *Colonist*, 16 May 1838.
[5] *Report of Diocesan Committee ... 1839*, pp. 23–8.
[6] 'Address of Governor to Legislative Council', 11 June 1839, *V & P 1839*, and, 'Minute ... explanatory of a System of Education ...', ibid., pp. 451–6; *SH*, 2 Sep. 1839 (supplement).
[7] WGB to EC, 13 Sep. 1839; *SH*, 2 Sep. 1839 (supplement).
[8] Minutes, 20, 21, 22, 27 Aug. 1839, *V & P*, and documents pp. 521–48; *SH*, 26 Aug. 1839 (supplement).
[9] *SH*, 28 Aug. 1839.
[10] *Gazette*, 27 Aug. 1839; *SH*, 2 Sep. 1839 (supplement).
[11] Broughton, *Speech of the Lord Bishop of Australia in the Legislative Council*, etc., pp. 5, 16–23.
[12] Ibid., pp. 9, 15, 26–8, 31–2.
[13] Based on *SH*, 2 Sep. 1839 (supplement); Jane Franklin to Mary Simpkinson, 6 Jan. 1841, Franklin Papers, ANL; Russell to Gipps, 25 June 1840, *HRA*, xx, pp. 685–7; Gipps to Franklin, 8 Sep. 1839 in Jane Franklin's Journal, vol. 3, Franklin Papers; Gipps to Normanby, 9 Dec. 1839, *HRA*, xx, p. 428.
[14] WGB to EC, 14 Oct. 1839.
[15] Gipps to Franklin, 7 Aug. 1839 in Jane Franklin's Journal, vol. 2, Franklin Papers; Gipps to Franklin, 8 Sep. 1839, op. cit.; *SH*, 2 Sep. 1839 (supplement).
[16] WGB to SPG, 13 Sep., 30 Oct. 1839; WGB to EC, 13 Sep. 1839.
[17] Minute of Gipps dated 2 Nov. 1839 on WGB to Gipps, 29 Oct. 1839 in Box 4/2434.4, and Colonial Secretary to Secretary of Diocesan Committee, 6 Aug. 1839, 11 Jan. 1840 in Box 4/3543, and, Minute of Gipps 4 Dec. 1839, on Secretary of Diocesan Committee, 11 Oct. 1839, 39/11107, Box 4/2434.4, CSIL; Colonial Secretary to WGB, 21 May 1840, 40/136, CSOL (Letters to Clergy).
[18] Gipps to Normanby, 9 Dec. 1839, *HRA*, xx, pp. 426–30.
[19] See Campbell to Under Secretary Vernon Smith, 8 July 1840, *HRA*, xx, p. 709.
[20] Broughton, *Speech in Legislative Council 1839*, p. 27.
[21] Colonial Secretary to WGB, 9 Mar. 1840 in Box 4/3619, CSOL (Letters to Clergy); WGB to SPG, 24 Oct. 1840; SPG to Hutchins, 28 Aug. 1839, F.MS., SPG.
[22] Gipps to Glenelg, 9 Nov. 1838, *HRA*, xix, pp. 656–7; Russell to Gipps, 6 July 1841, *HRA*, xxi, p. 420.
[23] Bishop of Australia to Russell, 5 Apr. 1840, *HRA*, xx, pp. 813–5; WGB to SPG, 25 Apr. 1840 (and two attached letters, Gipps to WGB, 30 Apr. 1840 and WGB to Gipps, 4 May 1840), C.MS., SPG.
[24] *SH*, 7 June 1839.
[25] WGB to SPG, 3 Sep. 1840, 24 Oct. 1841; SPG to WGB, 2 Aug. 1841, F.MS., SPG. On passage money see Colonial Secretary to WGB, 19 July 1841, 41/207, CSOL (Letters to Clergy).
[26] *SH*, 25 Nov. 1841. On the Presbyterian signatures see WGB to Gipps, 29 Nov., 22 Dec. 1841 (attached to WGB to SPG, 6 Nov. 1841).

27 Colonial Secretary to WGB, 25 Nov., 11 Dec. 1841, 41/329, 338, CSOL (Letters to Clergy).

28 *Aust. Chron.*, 29 May 1841.

29 Based on Colonial Secretary to WGB, 3, 18 June, 25 July 1839, 27 Feb., 1 May, 3 June, 28 Aug. 1840, in Box 4/3619, CSOL (Letters to Clergy).

30 Colonial Secretary to WGB, 19 July 1841, 41/207, CSOL (Letters to Clergy).

31 On colonial popery, WGB to EC, 6 Feb. 1838, 13 Sep. 1839, 3 Apr. 1840. On Broughton's alleged schemes, *Aust. Chron.*, 6, 9, 13, 16 Aug. 1839. On levée, WGB to Gipps, 25 May 1839, *HRA*, xx, pp. 265–6; WGB to EC, 13 Sep. 1839.

32 *Aust. Chron.*, 2 Aug. 1839; Minutes, 24 Jan., 19 Mar., 10 Dec. 1838, 1, 2, 26 Feb., 28 May 1839, *Proc. Ex. C.*, 4/1520, NSWA.

33 WGB to EC, 13 Sep. 1839; *SH* and *Aust. Chron.*, 29 May 1841; Broughton, *Speech of the Bishop of Australia to Mr Justice Burton.*

34 *Aust. Chron.*, 7 Sep. 1841, also 6 Apr. 1841.

35 'Report from Committee on Immigration, 1841', p. 7, *V & P*; *Aust. Chron.*, 21 Aug., 16 Sep. 1841.

36 *Aust. Chron.*, 16, 30 Sep. 1841; *SH*, 16 Sep. 1841.

37 'Report of Committee on Immigation, 1839', pp. 12–4, *V & P*; *SH*, 25, 29 May, 3 June 1840.

38 Gipps to Russell, 26 Aug. 1840, *HRA*, xx, pp. 777–8; *SH*, 1 (supplement), 3 June 1840, 4 May 1841.

39 *SH*, 17 July 1840.

40 *SH*, 3 June, 5, 8 Oct. 1840. For Broughton's complaint in 1834 see WGB to SPG, 17 Nov. 1834.

41 *SH*, 8 Oct. 1840.

42 *SH*, 8 Jan. 1840; on CMS lands see *ibid.* 26 Jan. 1841.

43 *SH*, 6, 8, 13 July 1840.

44 *SH*, 15 Dec. 1840; Russell to Gipps, 31 May 1840, *HRA*, xx, pp. 641–8.

45 *SH*, 7, 10 Dec. 1840; *Aust. Chron.*, 12 Dec. 1840.

46 *SH*, 12 Dec. 1840.

47 Minute, 10, 11 Dec. 1840, *V & P*; *SH*, 14 Dec. 1840.

48 *Gazette*, 22, 24 June 1841; *SH*, 17 Oct. 1840, 17, 19, 24 June 1841; 'Minutes of Evidence . . . on the Shooting on Sunday Prevention Bill', *V & P 1841.*

49 *SH*, 19 May 1842; WGB to EC, 14 Oct. 1839.

50 *SH*, 17 Oct. 1840, 19, 28 June 1841.

51 WGB to EC, 25 Feb. 1839; WGB to Vincent, 23 Nov. 1829 encl. WGB to Darling, 23 Nov. 1829, 29/2956, Box 4/2058, CSIL.

52 Based on WGB to EC, 15 Feb. 1841; WGB to SPG, 15 Feb., 16 Aug., 18 Sep., 30 Nov. 1841; SPG to WGB, 21 Mar. 1840, F. MS., SPG; Colonial Secretary to WGB, 10 May 1839, 39/177, Box 4/3619, CSOL (Letters to Clergy).

53 Broughton, *Speech to Burton*, p. 12; *Report of Diocesan Committee*, 1840, p. 42; WGB to SPG, 30 Oct. 1839.

54 *Report of Diocesan Committee, 1839*, pp. 21–2, 25; WGB to SPG, 24 Oct. 1840, 22 Mar. 1841, 6 Jan. 1842; Broughton, *Speech to Burton*, p. 14; WGB to EC, 1 Apr. 1845.

55 On diocesan library and clergy, WGB to EC, 19 Mar. 1841, ANL. 1731; WGB to EC, 27 Dec. 1841, 14 Feb., 14 Apr. 1842; WGB to SPG, 15 Feb. *1841*. On lay and council libraries, *Report of Church of England Book Society 1841*, pp. 5, 13–14, and, *SH*, 22 July 1840.

56 Broughton, *Charge to Clergy of New South Wales, 1841*, p. 33; WGB to SPG, 30 Oct. 1839 (two letters), 22 Mar. 1841 (private); WGB to EC, 15 Feb. 1841.

57 *SH*, 26 June 1840; WGB to EC, 14 Feb. 1842; WGB to William Boydell, 20 Nov. 1841, MS. TKS.

58 *SH*, 7, 9 Feb. 1842; Minutes, 8 to 24 Dec. 1841, *Proc. Ex. C.*, 4/1520, NSWA.

59 WGB to EC, 4, 27 Dec. 1841; WGB to SPG, 18 June 1842.

60 WGB to SPG, 26 June, 16 Aug. 1841 and encl. WGB to Bishop of London, 23 June 1841, C. MS. SPG.

61 WGB to EC, 15 Feb. 1841, 14 Feb. 1842.

10 How far to Retire?

[1] *SH*, 9 Oct. 1841; WGB to EC, 17 Feb. 1842.

[2] *SH*, 11, 15–18, 25 Feb. 1842; *Aust. Chron.*, 10, 15, 17, 19, 22 Feb., 3 Mar. 1842; WGB to EC, 17 Feb. 1842. On Royal Hotel clientele see Joseph Fowles, *Sydney in 1848*, Sydney, 1973, p. 50.

[3] WGB to EC, 17 Feb. 1842.

[4] Ibid.

[5] Ibid.

[6] EC to Peel, 20 Sep. 1841, B M Add. MS. 40489; WGB to EC, 14 Jan. 1843.

[7] Lang's campaign based on *Col. Obs.*, 2 Mar. 1842; *SH*, 27 Apr., 20 May 1842; *Australian*, 30 Apr. 1842.

[8] W. B. Clarke to EC, 2 Feb. 1843, B P; SPG to WGB, 30 July 1842, F. MS., SPG. See also WGB to EC, 3 Jan. 1844.

[9] *Australian*, 18, 29 Jan., 22 Mar., 19, 26 Apr., 3 May, 13 July, 1 Aug. 1842; *SH*, 20 Jan., 19 May 1842.

[10] *Australian*, 9 June 1842 (WGB's speech); 'Report from Committee on Immigration, 1840', pp. 1, 3, and ibid. for 1841, p1, *V & P*; George Arthur, *Observations upon Secondary Punishments to which is added a Letter upon the same Subject by the Archdeacon of New South Wales*, p. 95.

[11] *SH*, 18 May 1842 (WGB's speech).

[12] *SH*, 19 May 1842.

[13] *Australian*, 31 May 1842; *SH*, 1 June 1842. For later debate see *SMH*, 18 (Anti-Transportation Meeting), 19, 27 Sep., 4 Oct. 1850.

[14] Based on Gipps to Russell, 31 Jan. and encls., 17 July, 2 Nov., 24 Dec. 1841, *HRA*, xxi, pp. 196–8, 433, 574–7, 607–10; Russell to Gipps, 16 July 1841 and Stanley to Gipps, 14 Oct. 1841 and encl. no. 3, ibid., pp. 429–32, 543–52.

[15] *Aust. Chron.*, 22 Jan. 1842.

[16] *SH*, 18, 20 May 1842.

[17] WGB to EC, 14 Feb., 14 Apr., 16 June 1842, 14 Jan. 1843.

[18] See WGB to EC, 14 Feb. 1842.

[19] Based on WGB to EC, 27 Dec. 1841, 14 Apr., 16 June 1842, 14 Jan. 1843, 4 Jan. 1845, 15 Aug. 1850; *SH*, 7 May 1842.

[20] *SH*, 21 May 1842; WGB to EC, 16 June 1842; WGB to SPG, 20 May 1842.

[21] *SH*, 21 May 1842.

[22] *SH*, 21 May 1842; W. B. Clarke to EC, 2 Feb. 1843, BP. On Clarke's career see *SH*, 26 June 1840; WGB to SPG, 15 Feb., 16 June 1842; WGB to Clarke, 17 Sep., 29 Oct. 1840, 16 June, 27 Aug. 1841, ML. 490/1.

[23] Based on *Australian*, 10, 17 May, 21, 25 June, 13 July, 28 Sep. 1842; *SH*, 21 Mar., 11, 26 May 1842; *SMH*, 18 Aug. 1842; Russell to Gipps, 16 July 1841, Stanley to Gipps, 14 Oct. 1841 and encl. no. 2, 8 Feb. 1842, *HRA*, xxi, pp. 429–32, 543–50, 677.

[24] Based on *SH*, 18 May 1842; Legislative Council debates in *SH*, 8 June 1842, *Australian*, 9 June 1842, *SMH*, 8 Sep. 1842; 'Report of Committee on Immigration, 1839', pp. 17–8, and ibid. for 1841, p. 4, *V & P*; WGB to EC, 14 Feb. 1842.

[25] *SH*, 8 June 1842.

[26] *SH*, 11 May 1842; *Australian*, 1 Aug. 1842; *SMH*, 2, 4 Aug. 1842; Gipps to Russell, 1 Feb. 1841, *HRA*, xxi, pp. 198–200.

[27] See Broughton's remark in Legislative Council on being outvoted in committee 6 to 1 on the high upset price of land, *SMH*, 8 Sep. 1842, and *Australian*, 7 Sep. 1842; *SH*, 26 May 1842; *Aust. Chron.*, 28 May, 6 Sep. 1842.

[28] *Australian*, 18 June 1842.

[29] *SH*, 2 July 1842.

[30] *Australian*, 21, 25 June 1842.

[31] Based on Broughton's speeches in Legislative Council in *SH*, 8 June 1842, *Australian*, 9 June 1842, *SMH*, 8 Sep. 1842; *Australian*, 18 June, 3 Aug., 19 Sep. 1842; 'Report from Committee on Immigration, 1842', pp. 5–6, *V & P*.

[32] *SMH*, 8 Sep. 1842.

[33] *Australian*, 1, 10, 17, 31 Aug., 16, 19 Sep. 1842; *SH*, 21 July 1842; *SMH*, 20 Aug. 1842; *Aust. Chron.*, 24, 29 Sep. 1842.

[34] *SMH*, 8, 9, 10 Sep. 1842; Gipps to Stanley, 20 Sep. 1842, *HRA*, xxii, pp. 290–1; Stanley to Gipps, 17 Sep. 1843, *HRA*, xxiii, pp. 136–7.

[35] *Australian*, 21 June 1842.

[36] *Australian*, 21 June, 28 Sep. 1842; 'Report from Committee on Immigration, 1842', p. 5, *V & P*; *SMH*, 8 Sep. 1842.

[37] *SMH*, 4 Sep. 1842, 3 Mar. 1843.

[38] Based on Russell to Gipps, 7 Oct. 1840 and encls., *HRA*, xxi, pp. 14–31; Gipps to Russell, 2 Nov. 1841, ibid., pp. 574–7; *SMH*, 10 Sep. 1842 (Gipps's speech in Legislative Council).

[39] 'Report of Committee on Immigration, 1839', p. 9, *V & P*; Colonial Secretary to WGB, 4 June 1840, 40/150, Box 4/3617, CSOL.

[40] Based on 'Report of Committee on Immigration, 1842', p. 4 and Appendix A, *V & P*; Gipps to Stanley, 14, 23 May 1842, *HRA*, xxii, pp. 42–52, 67; *SMH*, 8, 10 Sep. 1842 (especially Deas Thomson's speech).

[41] *Australian*, 10 May 1842; *SH*, 19 June (supplement), 20 July 1840, 18 June 1842; *Aust. Chron.*, 23 July 1840.

[42] *SH*, 26 Aug. 1841.

[43] *SH*, 14 Sep. 1841; 'Report from Committee on Immigration, 1841', pp. 2, 7, *V & P*.

[44] Figures quoted by Broughton in 'Report from Committee on Immigration, 1842', pp. 6–7, *V & P*.

[45] *Australian*, 21 May, 1 Aug. 1842.

[46] *SMH*, 8 Sep. 1842. On costs, frauds, and immorality see 'Report from Committee on Immigration, 1842', pp. 1–3, *V & P*; *SH*, 18 June 1842.

[47] *SMH*, 8 Sep. 1842 (Deas Thomson's speech in Legislative Council); 'Report on Immigration for the year 1841, by Francis L.S. Merewether Esq. Agent for Immigration', pp. 1–5, *V & P 1842*.

[48] *SMH*, 8 Sep. 1842 (WGB's speech in Legislative Council); WGB to Gipps, 20 Sep. 1841, 41/8648, Box 4/2521.3, CSIL. On selection of immigrants see 'Report of Committee on Immigration, 1839', p. 7, *V & P*.

[49] *SMH*, 8, 9 Sep. 1842 (WGB's and Therry's speeches in Legislative Council); *Australian*, 16 Sep. 1842. The passage expunged from Immigration Report is quoted by Therry in *SMH*, 9 Sep. 1842.

[50] *SMH*, 9 Sep. 1842 (WGB's speech).

[51] *Col. Obs.*, 1 Mar. 1843.

[52] *SMH*, 9 Sep. 1842 (WGB's speech).

[53] *SMH*, 8 Sep. 1842 (WGB's speech); see also *SH*, 26 Oct. 1840, 'Report from Committee on Immigration, 1841', p. 2, *V & P*.

[54] Stanley to Gipps, 17 Sep. 1843 and encls., *HRA*, xxiii, pp. 136–47.

[55] Gipps to Stanley, 2 Apr. 1842, Stanley to Gipps, 29 July, 5 Aug. and encls. 1842, *HRA*, xxii, pp. 2–3, 166–8, 192–4; *SH*, 8 June 1842 (speeches of James and Hannibal Macarthur); *Australian*, 17 Aug. 1842.

[56] *Australian*, 9 June 1842.

[57] *SMH*, 3 Mar. 1843.

[58] WGB to EC, 16 June 1842; Colonial Secretary to WGB, 16 May 1842 and encls., 42/112, Box 4/3620, CSOL; *Aust. Chron.*, 3 Mar. 1842; *SH*, 12 Apr. 1842.

[59] *SH*, 15 Apr. 1842; *Col. Obs.*, 20 Apr. 1842; WGB to SPG (private), 3 Feb. 1846, 14 July 1848.

[60] *SH*, 15 Apr. 1842; *Col. Obs.*, 25 May 1842; WGB to SPG (private), 3 Feb. 1846.

[61] WGB to EC, 15 Aug. 1844.

[62] W. B. Clarke to EC, 2 Feb. 1843, and WGB to EC, 14 Jan. 1843, BP.

[63] WGB to EC, 17 Feb. 1842.

[64] Stanley to Gipps, 5 Sep. 1842 (private), *HRA*, xxii, pp. 244–5; WGB to Gipps, 20 Sep. 1843 published in *SMH*, 24 Feb. 1843; see also WGB to EC, 17 Feb. 1842.

[65] *SMH*, 3 Mar. 1843; also *Australian*, 8 Mar. 1843.

[66] *SMH*, 24 Feb. 1843.

[67] *SMH*, 2, 7, 11 Feb. 1843 (letters to editor); WGB to Mayor, 8 Mar. 1843 published in *SMH*, 9 Mar. 1843; WGB to EC, 17 Feb. 1842.
[68] *SMH*, 24 Feb. 1843.
[69] *Col. Obs.*, 1 Mar. 1843.
[70] *Australian*, 6 Feb. 1843; *Aust. Chron.*, 9 Feb. 1843; *SMH*, 11 Feb. 1843; *Col. Obs.*, 8 Feb., 1 Mar. 1843.
[71] Based on *SMH*, 21, 27, 28 Dec. 1842, 5, 20, 27 Jan., 3, 8, 11, 15 Feb., 31 Mar., 9, 22, 25–27 May, 2 June 1843; *Australian*, 6 Feb., 19 June 1843; *Aust. Chron.*, 9 Feb. 1843.
[72] *SMH*, 28 Dec. 1842 (Wentworth's speech), 26, 31 May 1843; *Aust. Chron.*, 30 May 1843; *Australian*, 19 June 1843.
[73] *SMH*, 19 Jan. 1843.
[74] *Aust. Chron.*, 14, 21, 28 Jan. 1843.
[75] *Col. Obs.*, 22 Oct. 1842, 25 Jan., 8 Feb. 1843; *Australian*, 6 Feb. 1843.
[76] *SMH*, 9 Feb. 1843.
[77] *Aust. Chron.*, 28 Feb. 1843.
[78] *SMH*, 24 Feb. 1843.
[79] WGB to EC, 14 Jan. 1843.
[80] *Aust. Chron.*, 17 Jan. 1843.
[81] *Australian*, 8 Feb., 19 June 1843; *SMH*, 28, 31 Jan., 3, 8, 9 Feb., 31 May 1843; *Aust. Chron.*, 30 May 1843; William Macarthur to James Macarthur, 28 Dec. 1842, ML. A2934; R. Forrest to James Macarthur, 5 July 1843, ML. A2922.
[82] WGB to EC, 14 Jan. 1843, WGB to Walsh, 3 Jan. 1843, BP.
[83] Robert Campbell resigned from O'Connell's committee, see committee lists *Aust. Chron.*, 27, 31 Dec. 1842, 5 Jan., 21 Mar. 1843.
[84] *SMH*, 26 Apr. 1843.
[85] E. Hamilton to James Macarthur, 8 July 1843, ML. A2922; *SMH*, 26 Apr. 1843, and Macarthur's and Therry's speeches in *SMH*, 8 Feb., 1 July 1843.
[86] *SMH*, 28 June 1843.
[87] *SMH*, 8, 9 Feb., 6 June (letter to editor), 1 July 1843.
[88] Rev. R. Forrest to James Macarthur, 5 July 1843, ML. A2922; *Aust. Chron.*, 30 May 1843.
[89] Based on *Aust. Chron.*, 27 June 1843; *SMH*, 28 June, 7 July, 10 July (letter to editor) 1843; *Australian*, 30 June, 10 July 1843.
[90] *SMH*, 3, 4 July 1843; R. Forrest to James Macarthur, 5 July 1843, op. cit.; *Australian*, 28, 30 June, 3 July 1843.
[91] *SMH*, 4, 10, 11–13 (letters to editor) July 1843; *Australian*, 5, 10, 21 July 1843; *Col. Obs.*, 14 Jan. 1843; *Aust. Chron.*, 28 Jan., 8 July 1843; R. Forrest to James Macarthur, 5 July 1843, op. cit.
[92] *SMH*, 3, 26 July 1843.
[93] *Aust. Chron.*, 14, 27 Jan., 23 Mar. 1843.
[94] *Australian*, 26 June, 3, 5 July 1843.
[95] *SMH*, 7 July 1843 (Cowper's speech).
[96] WGB to EC, 16 Feb. 1843.
[97] Stanley to Russell, 10 Sep. 1841, PRO. 30/22/43, f. 565; 'Gladstone Misc. Journal Notes', 26 Apr. 1844, BM. Add. MS. 44777.
[98] WGB to SPG, 27 Feb. 1843; WGB to EC, 14 Jan., 16, 17 Feb. 1843; On colonies as a pretext for change elsewhere see 'Gladstone Misc. Journal Notes', 12 Mar. 1844, op. cit.
[99] WGB to EC, 16, Feb., 27 Mar. 1843; WGB to Clergy, 25 Mar. 1843 in *SMH*, 27 Mar. 1843.
[1] WGB to EC, 3, 16 Feb. 1843.
[2] WGB to SPG, 27 Feb. 1843.
[3] WGB to EC, 16 Feb. 1843; WGB to SPG, 27 Feb. 1843.
[4] *Col. Obs.*, 18 Mar., 5 Apr. 1843.
[5] *Aust. Chron.*, 11 Mar. 1843.
[6] WGB to Stiles, 11, 23 Mar. 1843, ML. A269; WGB to EC, 9 Mar. 1844.
[7] WGB to EC, 27 Mar. 1843.
[8] [W. G. Broughton], 'Sydney—the Festival of the Annunciation', in *Despatches from Governor of New South Wales 1843*, vol. 42, pp. 555–7, ML; W. G. Brough-

ton, *Letter to Right Rev. Nicholas Wiseman D.D.*, p. 8.
[9] W. A. Duncan, *Letter to the Lord Bishop of Australia*, Sydney, 1843, p. 6.
[10] *Col. Obs.*, 28 Mar., 19 Apr. 1843.
[11] *Aust. Chron.*, 18, 21, 28, 30 Mar. 1843.
[12] Duncan, *Letter*, pp. 7–11; R. Allwood, *Lectures on the Papal Claim of Jurisdiction*, Sydney, 1843, serialized during May and June 1843 in *SMH* and *Col. Obs.*; W. G. Broughton, *A True Account of the Anglican Ordinations in the Reign of Elizabeth. Part I*; R. K. Sconce, *Answers to the Question, Why do I Submit to the Teaching of the Church?*, Sydney, 1843.
[13] Duncan, *Letter*, p. 5.
[14] Minute by Gipps on Norton to Colonial Secretary, 17 Apr. 1843, 43/2910, Box 4/2598.1, CSIL.
[15] Bishop of Australia to Stanley, 27 Mar. 1843, *HRA*, xxii, p. 597; Stanley to Gipps, 12 Sep. 1843, *HRA*, xxiii, p. 125.
[16] Archbishop of Canterbury to EC, 25 Aug. 1843, and WGB to EC, 3 Feb. 1843, 3 Jan. 1844, BP; EC to Pusey, 11 Nov. 1842 (sic.), Pusey Papers, Box Rev. E. Coleridge to Pusey 1839–76, Pusey House, Oxford.
[17] WGB to EC, 9 Mar. 1844; SPG to WGB, 3 Aug. 1843, F. MS., SPG; *Report of the Society for the Propagation of the Gospel*, London, 1843, pp. 60–4.
[18] WGB to SPG, 5, 17 May 1843.
[19] *Australian*, 31 Mar. 1843; *Aust. Chron.*, 4 May 1843.
[20] *SH*, 26 June 1840 (Diocesan Committee meeting); WGB to SPG, 16 Aug. 1841, 3 Jan. 1842.
[21] WGB to SPG, 3 Feb., 5 May 1843.
[22] Close and Rusden to WGB, 13 Feb. 1842, and, Rogers to WGB, 28 Feb. 1842, and, WGB to SPG, 3 July 1843, C. MS., SPG.
[23] WGB to SPG, 3 Apr. 1844.
[24] WGB to SPG, 5, 17 May 1843, 24 Feb. 1844.
[25] WGB to SPG, 5 May 1843; also WGB to EC, 16 Feb. 1843.
[26] Edward Hamilton to James Macarthur, 8 July 1843, ML. A2922; Broughton, *The Church in Australia. Two Journals of Visitation to the Northern and Southern Portions of His Diocese*, passim.
[27] Broughton, *Church in Australia*, p. 6; Phoebe Broughton to William Boydell, 10 Apr. 1843, BP.
[28] Broughton, *Church in Australia*, pp. 8–9; WGB to SPG, 3 July 1843.
[29] Broughton, *Church in Australia*, pp. 21–2; Cowper to CMS, 11 Jan. 1841, series CN/02, CMS.
[30] WGB to SPG, 3 July 1843.
[31] 'Report from the Committee on the Aborigines Question, with Minutes of Evidence, 1838', *V & P*; WGB to SPG, 16 Aug. 1841.
[32] 'Report from Committee on Immigration', 1841 with appendix, pp. 5, 36, *V & P*.
[33] WGB to SPG, 5 May, 14 Sep. 1843, 3 Apr. 1844; on general progress of diocese see *SMH*, 13, 14 Apr., 22 May, 6, 13 June 1843.
[34] WGB to EC, 20 Sep. 1843.
[35] Based on Broughton, *Church in Australia*, pp. 27–42; WGB to SPG, 3 Sep. 1840, 3 Feb. 1843, 2 Mar. 1844, 3 Feb. 1846; WGB to EC, 11, 22 Dec. 1843.
[36] WGB to SPG, 3 Feb. 1843; *Col. Obs.*, 21 Sep. 1842; *SMH*, 11 Feb. 1843; *Report S.P.G.*, 1843, London, 1843, p. 59; Broughton, *Church in Australia*, p. 42.
[37] WGB to SPG 22 June 1844.
[38] *Report S.P.G., 1843*, p. 56; *SMH*, 13 June 1843.
[39] WGB to EC, 2 Apr., 4 May 1844, and WGB to Cowper and Allwood, 6 May 1844 encl. in WGB to EC, 18 May 1844, BP; WGB to SPG, 22 June 1844.
[40] WGB to EC, 14 Jan. 1843.
[41] Based on Sarah Broughton to Mrs Coleridge, 6 Oct. 1843 (filed as 6 Oct. 1845), WGB to EC, 22 Dec. 1843, 2 Apr. 1844, BP; WGB to Keate, 10 July 1844, ANL. 1731.
[42] WGB to EC, 4 May 1844; see also WGB to EC, 27 Dec. 1841, 16 June 1842, 18 May 1844; Lady Franklin to Sir John Franklin, 20 June 1839 in Mackaness, *Correspondence Part I*, p. 92.
[43] WGB to EC, 14 Jan., 3 Feb. 1843.

11   *Gris Eminence*

[1] Based on *SMH*, 18 May, 2, 13 June, 10, 12 Oct., 17 Nov., 1843, 26 July 1844; *Australian*, 10 Oct. 1843; *Col. Obs.*, 1 Mar. 1843.

[2] WGB to Colonial Secretary, 22 Feb. (with encls.), 31 Mar. (with governor's minute of 11 Apr.) 1841, 41/2556, 2536, Box 4/2521.3, CSIL; Colonial Secretary to WGB, 7 Apr. 1841, 41/101, CSOL (Letters to Clergy).

[3] Colonial Secretary to WGB, 17 Dec. 1840, 27 May 1841, 40/291, 41/151, CSOL (Letters to Clergy); Gipps to Stanley, 8 Feb. 1842 and encls., *HRA*, xxi, pp. 681–5; Minute of Gipps to Colonial Secretary, 9 Feb. 1843, 43/749, Box 4/2598.1 CSIL. On the exchange of concessions Colonial Secretary to WGB, 28 Feb., 28 Sep. 1843, 43/50, 188, CSOL (Letters to Clergy); Colonial Secretary to James (WGB's secretary), 22 Apr. 1843 (with minute attached), and Rev. E. Rogers to Colonial Secretary, 29 Nov. 1843, 43/3094, 10418, Box 4/2598.1, CSIL.

[4] WGB to SPG, 3 Apr. 1844; *SMH*, 29 Sep. 1843.

[5] On Port Phillip *SMH*, 29 Sep., 12 Oct. 1843; Stanley to Gipps, 29 July 1843 and encls., *HRA*, xxiii, pp. 62–70. On Parramatta education levy *Australian*, 9, 14 Nov. 1843; *SMH*, 17 Nov. 1843.

[6] *SMH*, 10 Oct. 1843. Lowe's pledge inferred from Gipps to Stanley, 10 Nov. 1843, 27 July 1844, *HRA*, xxiii, pp. 216, 708–9. On Hamilton, *Australian*, 2 Aug. 1843.

[7] WGB to EC, 2 Apr. 1844; Colonial Secretary to WGB, 11 July 1844, 44/93, CSOL (Letters to Clergy).

[8] Based on 'Minutes of Evidence … Select Committee on Education', *V & P 1844*, vol. II, pp. 80–95. Polding's arguments were similar, *Australian*, 10 Sep. 1844.

[9] WGB to EC, 15 Aug. 1844, William Jones to EC, 26 Oct. 1844, BP; 'Minutes of Evidence … Select Committee on Education', op. cit., pp. 87–8; *SMH*, 7 Oct. 1844 (Lang's speech), 11 Oct. 1844 (Cowper's speech).

[10] 'Report … Select Committee on Education', *V & P 1844*, vol. II, pp. 1–4; *SMH*, 7 Sep., 11 Oct. 1844; *Australian*, 14 Sep. 1844.

[11] WGB to EC, 7 Oct. 1844.

[12] *SMH*, 3, 4 Sep. 1844. Broughton's accusations are substantially upheld in D. H. Akenson, *The Irish Education Experiment*, London, 1970, ch. 5.

[13] WGB to EC, 11 Sep, 4 Oct. 1844; *SMH*, 7, 11, 28 Oct., 12 Dec. 1844.

[14] Gipps to Stanley, 1 Feb. 1845, *HRA*, xxiv, p. 232–3; *SMH*, 7, 11 Oct. 1844.

[15] WGB to EC, 15, 17 Aug. 1844; *SMH*, 28 Oct., 12 Dec. 1844; *Australian*, 2 Sep. 1844.

[16] WGB to EC, 21 Oct., 5 Nov. 1844.

[17] Bishop of Australia to …, 17 Feb. 1846, *HRA*, xxiv, p. 781; WGB to EC, 18 May 1844. On squatting, Gipps to Stanley, 3 Apr. 1844, and 'Memorandum' enclosed with Gipps to Stanley, 17 May 1844, *HRA*, xxiii, pp. 507–18, 604.

[18] *SH*, 8 June 1842; *SMH*, 9 Apr. 1844.

[19] 'Report of the Committee on Immigration, 1840', pp. 4–5, and, ibid, 1842, p. 6, *V & P*; *Aust. Chron.*, 12 Dec. 1840, 8 Sep. 1842; *Australian*, 3 Aug. 1842; *SMH*, 8, 10 Sep. 1842.

[20] Bishop of Australia to …, 17 Feb. 1846, op. cit., pp. 780–6; Gipps to Stanley, 16 Apr. 1844, *HRA*, xxiii, 545–9; WGB to EC, 18 May 1844.

[21] *Australian*, 3 May 1844; WGB to EC, 18 May, 15 Aug. 1844.

[22] Based on Gipps to Stanley, 1 May 1844, and, 'Paper delivered to Executive Council by Lord Bishop of Australia on the Squatting Question', *HRA*, xxiii, pp. 558–9, 831–41; Archbishop of Canterbury to Stanley, 2 June 1845, and, Gipps to Stanley, 23 Feb. 1846 and encls., *HRA*, xxiv, pp. 494–6, 780–7; WGB to SPG, 4 Apr. 1844.

[23] WGB to SPG, 3 Apr. 1844; WGB to EC, 4 May 1844.

[24] *Australian*, 22, 23 Oct., 30 Dec. 1844; WGB to EC, 15 Aug., 11 Sep. 1844.

[25] *Australian*, 2 Jan., 26 Dec. 1844; Minute, 25 May 1844, *Proc. Ex. C.*, Box 4/1521, NSWA; WGB to EC, 15 Aug., 4, 7 Oct. 1844.

[26] Broughton, '*Take Heed*'. *A Sermon* …, second edition, pp. 3–7; WGB to SPG, 17 May 1843 (copy in BP).

27 Broughton, *Take Heed*, pp. 2, 10–11; *Morn. Chron.*, 18, 21 Sep. 1844.
28 WGB to EC, 3 Jan. 1844; *Morn. Chron.*, 21 Sep. 1844; *Report of Church of England Lay Association for the Year 1844–5*, p. 7; *Southern Queen*, 1, 23 Jan., 27 Feb., 6 Mar. 1845; *Col. Obs.*, 12 Sep. 1844.
29 WGB to Keate, 10 July 1844, ANL 1731; *Morn. Chron.* 19 June, 6 July 1844; *SMH*, 20 June 1844; *Australian*, 6 July 1844; WGB to EC, 4, 21 Oct. 1844.
30 WGB to EC, 4, 7 Oct. 1844.
31 WGB to EC, 21 Oct. 1844.
32 Gipps to Stanley, 6 Oct. 1844, *HRA*, xxiv, pp. 6–8; WGB to EC, 29 July, 4, 21 Oct. 1844; J. N. Molony, John Hubert Plunkett in New South Wales 1832–1869, Ph. D. Thesis, ANU, pp. 161–8.
33 *Atlas*, 7 Dec. 1844, 10, 17 May 1845.
34 Ibid.; *Southern Queen*, 31 May 1845.
35 *Atlas*, 12 Apr., 17 May 1845; *Southern Queen*, 31 May 1845.
36 WGB to SPG (private), 3 Feb. 1846.
37 WGB to EC, 15 Aug. 1844.
38 *Report, Lay Association*, pp. 1, 8, 9–10, 37–42; *Southern Queen*, 27 Feb., 27 Mar., 9, 23 Apr., 14, 18, 28 June 1845.
39 WGB to Committee of Lay Association, 4 Dec. 1844 in *Report—Lay Association*, pp. 44–6; *Atlas*, 12 Apr., 17 May 1845.
40 *Atlas*, 24 May 1845; *Southern Queen*, 6 Mar. 1845; *Sentinel*, 12, 26 Mar. 1845.
41 *Atlas*, 17, 24 May, 6 Dec. 1845.
42 *Sentinel*, 1 Jan., 12, 26 Mar. 1845, 1 Jan., 19, 26 Feb., 19 Mar., 2 Apr., 14 May 1846.
43 *Southern Queen*, 6 Mar. 1845.
44 *Atlas*, 6 Dec. 1845, 18, 25 Apr. 1846; *Sentinel*, 23 Apr. 1846.
45 *Report, Lay Association*, p. 12.
46 *Aust. Chron.*, 5 Feb. 1842; WGB to EC, 14 Jan. 1843.
47 Based on *Southern Queen*, 7 June 1845; *SMH*, 28 Apr. 1843, 29 May 1845; *Australian*, 24 Oct. 1843; *Sentinel*, 1 Oct. 1845; Broughton, *Charge to Clergy of New South Wales ... 1841*, pp. 14–15, 22–5, 31; Broughton, *Charge to Clergy of the Diocese of Australia, 1844*, p. 51; WGB to EC, 20 Oct. 1843.
48 WGB to SPG, 24 Feb. 1844.
49 Broughton, *Charge 1841*, pp. 28–32; W. G. Broughton, *Charge 1844*, pp. 40–1, 54–8; WGB to EC, 14 Feb. 1842, 21 Oct. 1844.
50 Broughton, *Charge 1841*, pp. 12–13, 24–5; Broughton, *Charge 1844*, pp. 31–3 and passim.
51 WGB to EC, 20 Sep. 1843, 5 Nov. 1844.
52 WGB to EC, 11 July 1842, 31 Jan. 1844; Broughton, *Charge 1844*, pp. 36–41, 49–51.
53 WGB to EC, 20 Sep. 1843, 10 July 1844.
54 WGB to EC, 9 Mar., 10 July 1844.
55 WGB to EC, 31 Jan., 9 Mar., 10 July 1844.
56 WGB to EC, 20 Sep. 1843.
57 *Col. Obs.*, 5 Apr. 1843, 11 Apr. 1844.
58 WGB to SPG, 3 Feb. 1843; *Col. Obs.*, 19 Apr. 1843.
59 *Aust. Chron.*, 3 Feb. 1842; WGB to EC, 22 Dec. 1843, 4 May 1844.
60 WGB to EC, 4 May, 24 June, 28 Dec. 1844, 4, 21 Jan., 1 Apr. 1845; WGB to Phoebe [Boydell], 6 May 1844, MS. TKS.
61 WGB to EC, 15 Feb. 1841, 2 Apr., 18 May 1844; WGB to Keate, 10 July 1844, ANL. 1731. Family life at Tusculum is detailed in a cache of family letters held at the Archives of The King's School, Parramatta.
62 WGB to EC, 10 July, 15 Aug., 28 Dec. 1844.
63 WGB to EC, 4 May, 4 Oct. 1844, and, WGB to Sir John Coleridge, 16 Aug. 1845 BP.
64 WGB to EC, 22 Dec. 1843, 21 Jan., 1 Apr. 1845; [Broughton], *Church in Australia Part III. A Journal of Visitation by the Lord Bishop of Australia in 1845*.

12   The Season for Exertion

[1] WGB to EC, 2 Apr. 1844.
[2] WGB to EC, 31 Jan., 2 Apr., 10 July 1844; WGB to SPG, 2 Mar. 1844; *Documents Relative to the Erection and Endowment of Additional Bishoprics*, pp. 47–9; Broughton, *Charge 1844*, p. 10.
[3] *Morn. Chron.*, 21 Aug., 14 Sep. 1844; WGB to EC, 15 Oct. 1844.
[4] *Documents Relative to ... Additional Bishoprics*, pp. 42, 61, 93; Gladstone to Hawkins, 2 Mar. 1842, Letter Book, OBF; Stanley to Archbishop of Canterbury, 18 Mar. 1842, Journal, OBF; Stanley to Gipps, 29 Aug. 1845 and encl., *HRA*, xxiv, pp. 491–2.
[5] WGB to EC, 15 Oct. 1844.
[6] WGB to EC, 10 July 1844, 21 Jan., 1 Apr. 1845; WGB to Judge Coleridge, 27 Jan. 1845, OBF.
[7] WGB to SPG, 16 Aug. 1845; Hawkins to Stanley, 21 July 1845, OBF; Gladstone to Hawkins, 14 July 1845, Letters re foundation see of Melbourne 1845–6, OBF; Gladstone to Howley, 14 Jan., 26 Mar. 1846, BM. Add. MS. 44363.
[8] Based on Hawkins to Gladstone, 10 Mar. 1846, Australia. Letters re division of diocese 1845–6, OBF; Gladstone to Hope, 8 Jan. 1846, and, Stephen to Gladstone, 13 Jan. 1846, BM. Add. MS. 44213; WGB to EC, 1 July 1845; Gladstone to Fitzroy, 30 Mar. 1846, *HRA*, xxiv, pp. 836–8; WGB to Fitzroy, 25 Aug. 1846, CO 201/368.
[9] WGB to EC, 1 July 1845. On Broughton's net income see WGB to EC, 21 Jan. 1845.
[10] WGB to EC, 21 May, 1 July 1845; WGB to Judge Coleridge, 19 June 1845, OBF.
[11] WGB to EC, 12 Oct. 1846.
[12] WGB to EC, 21 Jan. 1845; Gladstone to Fitzroy, 30 Mar. 1846, *HRA*, xxiv, p.836.
[13] WGB to EC, 1 July, 10 Dec. 1845; WGB to Judge Coleridge, 19 June 1845, OBF.
[14] WGB to Gladstone, 7 Nov. 1846, 18 Aug. 1851, BM. Add. MS. 44365, 44370.
[15] *Australian*, 7 Oct. 1843 (Therry's speech in Legislative Council); *Morn. Chron.*, 3 Jan 1844; Polding to Gipps, 11 Jan. 1844, *HRA*, xxiii, pp. 350–1.
[16] WGB to EC, 3 Jan. 1844; WGB to Gipps, 18 Jan. 1844, *HRA*, xxiii, pp. 351–2; WGB to Gipps, 10 Jan. 1846, CO 201/365.
[17] WGB to Gipps, 18 Jan. 1844, and, Stanley to Gipps, 24 Aug. 1844 (2 letters with encls), *HRA*, xxiii, pp. 351–2, 732–8;
[18] WGB to Judge Coleridge, 19 June 1845, OBF; Gipps to Stanley, 7 Aug. 1845 and encls. WGB to Gipps, 4 Aug. 1845 and Minute of Executive Council, 4 Aug. 1845, CO 201/358.
[19] James Stephen to Gladstone, 13 Jan. 1846, BM. Add. MS. 44213; Gladstone to Gipps, 17 Jan. 1846, *HRA*, xxiv, pp. 712–5.
[20] *SMH*, 25 Oct. 1845.
[21] Bishop of London to WGB, 6 June 1844, Fulham Papers, MS. 375, Lambeth; WGB to EC, 31 Jan., 5 Nov. 1844.
[22] WGB to SPG, 22 Mar. 1841; WGB to EC, 11 July 1842.
[23] WGB to EC, 25 Feb. 1839, 15 Feb. 1841, 14 Feb., 11 July 1842.
[24] WGB to EC, 16 June, 11 July 1842.
[25] WGB to EC, 4 May 1840; EC to Pusey, 11 Nov. 1842 and Pusey to EC, 17 Nov. [1842], Pusey Papers, Pusey House, Oxford.
[26] EC to Pusey, 11, 16 Nov. 1842, 26 May, 10 Aug. 1843, 3 Apr. 1844, Pusey Papers.
[27] WGB to EC, 16 June 1842, 28 Dec. 1844.
[28] WGB to SPG, 27 Feb. 1843; WGB to EC, 4 Jan., 1 Apr. 1845.
[29] *Report of Diocesan Committee of the SPG and SPCK 1845 and 1846*, p. 8; WGB to EC, 4 May 1844, 8, 14, 30 Jan. 1846.
[30] *Report of Diocesan Committee ... 1845 and 1846*, p. 9; WGB to EC, 30 Jan., 12 June, 18 Aug., 3, 12 Oct. 1846; WGB to SPG, 16 Mar. 1846.
[31] WGB to EC, 3 July, 18 Aug., 12 Oct. 1846; WGB to Burdett-Coutts, 10 Oct. 1846, MS. 1384, Lambeth.
[32] WGB to EC, 18 Aug., 4 Sep., 3, 12, 15 Oct. 1846; *Report of Diocesan Committee ... 1845 and 1846*, p. 25.

33 WGB to EC, 3, 12 Oct. 1846.
34 Howley to Grey, 21 Dec. 1846, GP80/5; WGB to Judge Coleridge, 19 June 1845, OBF; WGB to EC, 1 July 1845.
35 WGB to EC, 1 Apr. 1845, 12 June, 3 July 1846.
36 WGB to EC, 3 July, 12 Oct. 1846; C. Kemp, *Diary*, 30 July 1847, ML. A2063.
37 WGB to EC, 8, 14 Jan. 1846. On Broughton's stamina, WGB to EC, 10 Dec. 1845, 14 Jan. 1846.
38 EC to Pusey, 8 Jan. 1845, Pusey Papers; WGB to EC, 28 Dec. 1844.
39 EC to Pusey, 27 Jan. 1845 Pusey Papers; EC to Peel, 19 Jan. 1845, BM. Add. MS. 40558; WGB to EC, 14, 30 Jan. 1846.
40 WGB to EC, 14 Jan., 12 June, 18 Aug. 1846; *SMH*, 12 Aug. 1845; *Atlas*, 12 Apr. 1845.
41 *Southern Queen*, 15 Jan. 1845.
42 Bishop of London to WGB, 6 June 1844, Fulham Papers, MS. 375, Lambeth; SPG to WGB, 30 Dec. 1844, 31 Mar., 30 Sep. 1845, F. MS., SPG.
43 WGB to SPG, 15 July 1847, 6 Jan., 19 June 1848.
44 William Jones to EC, 22 April 1845, BP.
45 WGB to SPG, 11 July 1846 and encl. 'Minute to the Standing Committee', p. 1, C. MS., SPG; WGB to EC, 3 Oct. 1846. The *Minute* raised £58 12s, *Report of Diocesan Committee . . . 1845 and 1846*, p. 40.
46 Based on William Jones to EC, 22 April 1845, BP; *Atlas*, 5, 19, 26 July 1845, 25 Apr., 18 July 1846. Broughton, *Charge 1844*, pp. 11–14. On the shift into the countryside for financial recovery, *Sydney Guardian*, 2 Apr. 1849.
47 WGB to EC, 30 Jan. 1846, and, William Jones to EC, 26 Oct. 1844, BP; *Report of Diocesan Committee . . . 1845 and 1846*, p. 22.
48 Broughton, *Charge 1841*, pp. 6, 10; *Southern Queen*, 19 Apr., 14 June 1845; *SH*, 13 May 1842; WGB to EC, 15 Aug. 1844; *Sentinel*, 1 Oct. 1845.
49 WGB to EC, 4 Jan. 1845; WGB to SPG, 3 Apr. 1844; *Southern Queen*, 8 Jan. 1845; W. G. Broughton, *Letter to Henry Osborne*, Sydney, 1848, pp. 5–8.
50 Based on WGB to EC, 4 Jan. 1845, 18 Aug., 3 Oct. 1846; *Report of Diocesan Committee . . . 1845 and 1846*, pp. 25–6; *SH*, 28 May 1842; WGB to SPG, 6 Jan. 1842, 3 Apr., 22 June 1844; *Australian*, 23 Mar. 1844.
51 Emily Broughton to Phoebe Boydell, 2 Aug. 1844, MS., TKS.
52 Based on *SMH*, May and July 1846; *Report of Diocesan Committee . . . 1845 and 1846*, p. 40. On Sydney's bowel epidemic *SMH*, 22 May 1846.
53 *SMH*, 13 July, 3, 4 Aug. 1846; *Sentinel*, 9 Apr. 1846.
54 Gipps to Stanley, 7 Aug. 1845, 28 Mar. 1846, *HRA*, xxiv, pp. 444, 829–31.
55 Gipps to Stanley and WGB to Gipps, 10 Jan. 1846, CO 201/365; WGB to EC, 14 Jan., 4 Sep. 1846.
56 *SMH*, 8 Aug. 1846; *Report of Diocesan Committee . . . 1845 and 1846*, pp. 23, 36–7; WGB to SPG, 9 Jan. 1847; WGB to Gladstone, 7 Nov. 1846, BM. Add. MS. 44365; Charles Kemp, *Diary*, 16 Dec. 1846, ML. 2063.
57 Fitzroy to Gladstone, 19 Aug., 1 Oct., 6 Nov. 1846, *HRA*, xxv, pp. 169–71, 202, 249–50; WGB to EC, 3 Oct. 1846.
58 Grey to Fitzroy, 29 May, 30 June 1847, *HRA*, xxv, pp. 606–8, 640–3.
59 *SMH*, 4 Aug. 1846; *Atlas*, 8 Aug. 1846.
60 Gipps to Stanley, 28 Mar. 1846, *HRA*, xxiv, p. 829–31; *Times*, 3 Nov. 1845; WGB to Gipps, 9 Mar. 1846, CO 201/366.
61 *Atlas*, 5 Apr., 24 May, 6 Dec. 1845, 31 Jan., 21, 28 Feb., 14 Mar., 4, 25 Apr., 6 June, 12 Sep. 1846.
62 *SMH*, 11, 17, 23 Sep. 1846; *Atlas*, 6 June 1846; WGB to EC, 3 Oct. 1846.
63 *SMH*, 23 Sep. 1846; WGB to EC, 3 Oct. 1846.
64 WGB to EC, 3 Oct. 1846; *Atlas*, 26 Sep., 3 Oct. 1846.
65 *SMH*, 11, 17, 23 Sep. 1846. On Lowe's frustrated ordination, *Australian*, 11 July 1846; *SMH*, 18, 20 July 1846.
66 *SMH*, 17 July 1846; WGB to SPG, 24 Feb. 1844, 3 Feb., 9 Apr., 20 Aug., 26 Nov. 1846; WGB to Clarke, 18 May 1844, ML. 490/1.
67 WGB to EC, 2 Apr. 1844.
68 WGB to SPG, 3 Feb. (two letters), 26 Nov. 1846; SPG to Grylls, 30 Nov. 1844, F. MS., SPG.

⁶⁹ *SMH*, 23 Sep. 1846; *Sentinel* 8 Jan. 1845; *Report of Diocesan Committee of the SPG and SPCK. 1851*, p. 55.
⁷⁰ WGB to SPG, 9 Apr. 1846.
⁷¹ WGB to SPG, 3 Feb. 1846.
⁷² WGB to EC, 9 Mar. 1844; WGB to SPG, 22 Mar. 1841, 3 Feb. 1846.
⁷³ Based on WGB to SPG, 20 Feb., 16 Mar. 1846, 3 Jan., 19 June, 14 July 1848, and, Edmondston to SPG, 31 Mar. 1846, 15 May, 9 June 1848, and, Edmondston to WGB, 20 Feb. 1846, C. MS., SPG; SPG to WGB, 21 July 1846, F. MS., SPG; Bishop of London to Edmonston, 1 May 1849, Fulham Papers MS., 382, Lambeth.
⁷⁴ WGB to Clarke, 18 May 1844, ML. 490/1. Clarke's career based on correspondence in ML. 490/1, and, SPG to Clarke and W.G.B., 31 Dec. 1844, F. MS., SPG, and, WGB to SPG, 3 Feb. 1846 (private), C. MS., SPG.
⁷⁵ *SMH*, 23 Sep. 1846.
⁷⁶ *SMH*, 15 June 1843.
⁷⁷ Based on Broughton, *Charge 1841*, pp. 14–15, 26–32; Broughton, *Charge 1844*, p. 41; *Southern Queen*, 6 Mar. 1845; WGB to EC, 14 Feb. 1842, 4 May 1844, 7 Sep. 1845; *Report Church of England Book Society 1841*, p. 13; Broughton, *A True Account of the Anglican Ordination in the Reign of Queen Elizabeth*; Broughton, *Baptismal Regeneration. Two Sermons*.
⁷⁸ WGB to EC, 20 Sep. 1843, 10 July, 15 Aug. 1844; Broughton, *Charge 1841*, pp. 14–22; Broughton, *Charge 1844*, pp. 51, 55–6.
⁷⁹ WGB to EC, 4 May, 5 Nov. 1844.
⁸⁰ WGB to EC, 4 Jan. 1845.
⁸¹ On Allwood, WGB to EC, 14 Feb., 14 Apr. 1842; on Walsh, WGB to SPG, 10 Dec. 1840, WGB to EC, 14 Apr. 1842; on Sconce, WGB to SPG, 6 Jan. 1842, WGB to EC, 14 Apr. 1842, 9 Mar. 1844; on Cowper, Kemp, *Diary*, 3 Jan. 1848, ML. 2063, WGB to EC, 14 Feb. 1842; on Russell, WGB to SPG, 2 Oct. 1847.
⁸² WGB to SPG, 30 Mar. 1841, 15 July 1847; WGB to EC, 18 Aug., 12 Oct. 1846.
⁸³ *SMH*, 23 Sep. 1846.
⁸⁴ WGB to EC, 3 Oct. 1846; *Atlas*, 5 Dec. 1846, 2, 9 Jan., 6 Feb. 1847.
⁸⁵ *Atlas*, 31 Oct. 1846, 16 Jan., 27 Feb., 6 Mar. 1847.
⁸⁶ *Atlas*, 4 July, 15, 28 Aug. 1846; 16 Jan., 30 Oct. 1847; *SMH*, 6 Aug. 1847 (Lay Association meeting).

13   End of an Era

¹ Howley to Gladstone, 29 June 1846, BM. Add. MS. 44364; WGB to EC, 6 Mar. 1847; Gladstone to Howley, 2 June 1846, BM. Add. MS. 44528.
² Howley to Grey, 21, 23 Dec. 1846, 10 Apr. 1847, GP80/5; Grey to Sumner, 20 Dec. 1848, GP80/7.
³ Howley to Grey, 7 Sep. 1846, and, Grey to Howley, 15 Sep., 18 Dec. 1846, GP80/5; Bishop of Bath and Wells to Grey, 14 Dec. 1846, GP77/10.
⁴ Howley to Grey, 22, 23 Dec. 1846, 1 Jan., 10 Apr. 1847, GP80/5. On troubles with CMS missionaries see EC to Gladstone, 28 Apr. 1845, BM. Add. MS. 44137; Bishop of London to Selwyn, 26 Aug. 1845, Fulham Papers, MS. 377, Lambeth.
⁵ Howley to Grey, 14, 27 Jan. (and a letter simply dated January), 4 Feb., 12 Mar. 1847, and, Grey to Howley, 2, 5, Feb. 1847, GP80/5; WGB to SPG, 15 July 1847.
⁶ Bishop of Bath and Wells to Grey, 24, 29, 30 Dec. 1846, GP77/10.
⁷ Howley to Grey, 12 Mar. 1847, GP80/5; A. P. Elkins, *Diocese of Newcastle*, Newcastle, 1955, pp. 135–7; Bishop of Bath and Wells to Grey, 16, 18 Mar. 1847, GP87/4.
⁸ Judge Coleridge to SPG, 14 Mar. 1846, Aust. letters re division of diocese, OBF; WGB to EC, 12 Oct. 1846; SPG to WGB, 1 Feb. 1847, F. MS., SPG.
⁹ Gladstone to Howley, 14 Jan. 1846, and, Howley to Gladstone, 16 Jan. 1846, BM. Add. MS. 44363.
¹⁰ Howley to Russell (undated), PRO 30/22/3D, ff. 1562–3; Bishop of London to Pusey, 7 Nov. 1840, Pusey Papers; Gladstone to Rogers, 27 Mar. 1846, BM.

Add. MS. 44107; Gladstone to Howley, 15 May 1846, BM. Add. MS. 44528; Howley to Grey, 21 Dec. 1846, GP80/5.

[11] WGB to SPG, 26 Nov. 1846; WGB to EC, 12 June 1846; Howley to Harrison, 20 Jan. 1847, and, Grey to Howley, 22 Jan. 1847, GP80/5.

[12] Stephen to Grey, 8 July 1847, GP126/11–3; Harrison to Nixon, 26 Jan. 1847, BM. Add. MS. 44377.

[13] Fitzroy to Gladstone, 29 Sep. 1846 (together with minutes by James Stephen, extract from Executive Council minutes, 12 Aug. 1846, and Colonial Office Minutes on Ecclesiastical Affairs in NSW) CO 201/368; Gladstone to SPG, 28 Feb. 1846, BM. Add. MS. 44528.

[14] Under-Secretary to Perry and Tyrrell, 6 May 1847, and, WGB to Fitzroy, CO 201/368.

[15] Grey to Sumner, 20 Dec. 1848, GP80/7; *CCC*, vol. 1, pp. 41–6.

[16] WGB to EC, 26 Oct. 1847; *Atlas*, 18 Sep., 23 Oct. 1847.

[17] Howley to Gladstone, 29 June 1846, BM. Add. MS. 44364; WGB to SPG, 26 Nov. 1846; Kemp, *Diary*, 30 July 1847, ML. A2063; William Jones to EC, 8 May 1847, BP.

[18] Howley to Grey, 21, 23 Dec. 1846, GP80/5; WGB to SPG, 30 June 1847; SPG to WGB, 31 Dec. 1846, F. MS., SPG.

[19] Kemp, *Diary*, 30 July 1847; WGB to EC, 26 Oct. 1847.

[20] WGB to EC, 5 Jan. 1848; *Atlas*, 2, 9 Jan. 1847; T. Hassall to J. Hassall, 20 June 1847, ML. A1677/4.

[21] Judge Coleridge to Hawkins, 29 Mar. 1846, Aust. letters re division of diocese, OBF; Minute of James Stephen, 24 Mar. 1846, on draft despatch, Gladstone to Fitzroy, 30 Mar. 1846, BM. Add. MS. 44363; WGB to EC, 18 Aug. 1846.

[22] WGB to EC, 18 Aug. 1846. On the need for uniformity and a conference, WGB to EC, 24 Feb., 4 May 1844, 7 Sep. 1845.

[23] Churton, *Joshua Watson*, I, pp. 34–5; WGB to EC, 1 July 1845, 24 Apr., 12 June, 3 July 1846.

[24] WGB to SPG, 15 July 1847.

[25] WGB to EC, 18 Aug. 1846.

[26] WGB to SPG, 26 Nov. 1846; 'Return of Churches 1840–6', Box 4/7239–41, NSWA; *A & P*, 1 Jan., 10, 18 June 1846.

[27] Based on *A & P*, 17 Aug., 13 Sep., 9, 16 Oct., 8, 9 Nov. 1847; WGB to SPG, 6 Jan., 28 Feb. (and encls.) 1848.

[28] 'Bishop Broughton's Argument in Defence of Ecclesiastical Discipline of New South Wales', in WGB to SPG, 28 Feb. 1848. On Lowe's argument, *SMH*, 23 Sep. 1846.

[29] 'Bishop Broughton's Argument etc.' op. cit.

[30] Kemp, *Diary*, 9 Nov. 1847; *SMH*, 18 Nov. 1847; *Atlas*, 13, 20 Nov. 1847.

[31] WGB to SPG, 20 Mar. 1846; *Atlas*, 23 Oct. 1847 (Woodward's letter); Woodward to Colonial Secretary, 31 Dec. 1846 in 'Return of Churches etc.', Box 4/7240, NSWA; Colonial Secretary to WGB, 27, 29 Apr. 1847, 44/87, Box 4/3621, CSOL.

[32] *Atlas*, 16, 23, 30 Oct. 1847; C. Woodward, *Oration . . . at Consecration of a Provincial Grand Lodge*, Sydney, 1849. On Broughton's views of Freemasonry, WGB to Stiles, 29 June 1839, ML. A1323.

[33] *A & P*, 31 Dec. 1847, 24, 26, 31 Jan., 13 Feb. 1848; *SMH*, 27 Jan. 1848.

[34] WGB to SPG, 6 Jan. 1848; Elkin, *Diocese of Newcastle*, pp. 149–52; WGB to EC, 26 Oct., 13 Nov. 1847, 5 Jan. 1848.

[35] Based on WGB to EC, 5 Jan. 1848; WGB to SPG, 30 June, 13 Nov. 1847; Tyrrell to WGB, 29 Feb. 1848, ML. 913.

[36] See WGB to SPG, 3 Feb. 1846; WGB to EC, 6 Mar. 1847.

[37] WGB to EC, 26 Oct. 1847; *SMH*, 27 Jan. 1848 (Diocesan Committee meeting). On Mrs Chisholm, WGB to Stiles, 21 Oct., 17 Nov. 1841, ML. 1323. On Dr Gregory, Tyrrell to WGB, 29 Feb. 1848, ML. 913, and WGB to—(private), ML. B1612. On O'Connell, WGB to EC, 14 Jan. 1843. On McLeay, *Atlas*, 23 Oct. 1847.

[38] *Sydney Guardian*, 1 June 1848; WGB to SPG, 15 July 1847.

[39] 'Circular', WGB to clergy, 17 Apr. 1847, copy in ML. A1672/2, pp. 1051–3;

WGB to EC, 26 Oct. 1847. On the questionable loyalty of priests paid from French funds, WGB to Gipps, 10 Jan. 1846, CO 201/365. On Nixon and Roman Catholics, William Jones to EC, 22 Apr. 1845, BP.

[40] Tyrrell to WGB, 2 (?) Feb. 1848, ML. 913.

[41] Based on Sconce to Stiles, 3, 18 Jan. 1848, and, Walsh to Stiles, 16, 17 Feb. 1848, and, WGB to Stiles, 21 Feb. 1848, ML. A269; WGB to EC, 4 July 1848; *SMH*, 24 Feb. 1848 (Broughton's Address to Clergy); Tyrrell to WGB, 2? Feb. 1848, ML. 913; WGB to Tyrrell, 22 Feb. 1848, MC; WGB to Archdeacon Cowper, 27 Apr. 1848, ML. A1677/2; WGB to SPG, 26 Apr. 1848; *A & P*, 21 Feb. 1848. On Sconce's shaky powers of deduction, WGB to EC, 9 Mar. 1844. On Coleridge's faltering after Newman's defection, WGB to EC, 7 Sep. 1845, 12 Oct. 1846.

[42] WGB to EC, 4 July 1848; *SMH* 24 Feb. 4 Mar. 1848 (Address to Clergy and Lay Association).

[43] WGB to Tyrrell, 22 Feb. 1848, MC; Walsh to Stiles, 17 Feb. 1848, ML. A269.

[44] WGB to EC, 14 Jan., 12 June 1846, 4 July 1848; *Atlas*, 26 Feb. 1848; Short to WGB, 6 Mar. 1848, ML. B1612.

[45] WGB to EC, 10 Dec. 1845, 4 July 1848; Walsh to Stiles, 17 Feb. 1848, and, Mrs Sconce to Stiles, 18 Jan. 1848, ML. A269. For Broughton's repudiation of post-1839 Tractarians see Broughton, *Charge 1841*, p. 23; Broughton, *Charge 1844*, pp. 41–4; WGB to EC, 20 Sep. 1843, 4 May 1844, 12 Oct. 1846; WGB to SPG, 15 July 1847.

[46] *Sentinel*, 24 Feb. 1848; *Atlas*, 4, 11 Mar. 1848; Stiles to Sconce, no date, ML. A269, pp, 155–8.

[47] WGB to SPG, 26 Apr. 1848; WGB to Stiles, 15 Apr. 1848, and, Sconce to Stiles, 26 Apr. 1848, ML. A269; WGB to EC, 15 Jan. 1849. On Ambrose and popery WGB to EC, 7 Sep., 10 Dec. 1845.

[48] *Atlas*, 4, 25 Mar., 22 Apr., 6, 27 May 1848.

[49] WGB to Selwyn, 2 Mar. 1848, MC; *SMH*, 24, 28 Feb., 4 Mar. 1848; Colonial Secretary to Gregory, 27 Mar., 10 Apr. 1848, 48/62, Box 4/3622 CSOL; *Sydney Guardian*, 1 June 1848.

[50] *A & P*, 26 Feb., 6 May 1848; WGB to Tyrrell, 22 Feb. 1848, MC; WGB to EC, 4 July 1848, 15 Jan. 1849; WGB to SPG, 26 Apr. 1848.

[51] Sconce to Stiles, 29 July 1849, ML. A269; R. K. Sconce, *Reasons for Submitting to the Catholic Church*, Sydney, 1848; WGB to EC, 4 July 1848.

[52] Sconce, *Reasons for Submitting*, pp. 32–4; R. K. Sconce, *Letter to the Lord Bishop of Sydney*, Sydney, 1848, pp. 8–9, 15–6.

[53] *Sentinel*, 8, 22, 29 June 1848. The third pamphlet was R. K. Sconce, *Second Letter to Lord Bishop of Sydney*, Sydney, 1848. On Jesuits, WGB to Stiles, 15 Apr. 1848, ML. A269.

[54] Sconce to Stiles, 12, 26 Apr. 1848, 29 July 1849, ML. A269.

[55] Sconce to Stiles, 12 Apr. 1848, and, WGB to Stiles, 15 Apr. 1848, ML. A269; Stiles to Sconce, no date, ML. A269, pp. 155–8; WGB to SPG, 26 Apr. 1848.

[56] WGB to EC, 15 Jan. 1849; Sconce to Stiles, 26 Apr. 1848, ML. A269.

[57] On Walsh, *A & P*, 11 July 1850. On Stiles, Stiles to WGB, 31 July 1848, and, WGB to Stiles, 2 Aug. 1848, 21 May 1849, ML. A269. On Beamish, Tyrrell to WGB, 14 Apr. 1848, ML. 913; WGB to EC, 15 Jan. 1849.

[58] WGB to EC, 4 July 1848; *SMH*, 4 Mar. 1848 (Address to Lay Association); 'Return of Churches', Box 4/7240–1, NSWA.

[59] WGB to Selwyn, 2 Mar. 1848, MC; Short to WGB, 6 Mar. 1848, ML. B1612; WGB to EC, 4 July 1848.

[60] Colonial Secretary to WGB, 31 May 1848, 38/117, Box 4/3622, CSOL.

[61] WGB to Joshua Watson, 11 Mar. 1843, MC.

[62] WGB to Gipps, 25 Mar. 1846, *HRA*, xxiv, pp. 832–3; Minutes of James Stephens and Mr Hawes on Gipps to Stanley, 28 Mar. 1843, CO 201/366; Grey to Fitzroy, 28 Aug. 1846, and, WGB to Fitzroy, 11 Jan. 1847, *HRA*, xxv, pp. 175–6, 451.

[63] Fitzroy to Grey, 15 July 1848 with encls. and minutes, CO 201/398; Gladstone to Howley, 15 May 1846, and, Howley to Gladstone, 21 May 1846, BM. Add. MS. 44528, 44364; WGB to EC, 15 July 1848.

[64] WGB to EC, 15 Jan. 1849. See also WGB to Joshua Watson, 14 Sep. 1839, MC.

⁶⁵ WGB to EC, 15 July 1848; WGB to Fitzroy, 23 June 1848, CO 201/398.
⁶⁶ WGB to Fitzroy, 3 May 1847, 47/4785, Box 2/1717, CSIL; WGB to Stiles, 17 Apr. 1847, ML. B269; *SMH*, 20 Aug. 1847.
⁶⁷ WGB to EC, 9 Jan. 1847; WGB to Stiles, 17 Apr. 1847, ML. A269.
⁶⁸ WGB to Fitzroy (and minute attached), 3 May 1847, 47/3785, Box 2/1717, CSIL; Colonial Secretary to Riddell, 4 Jan. 1848, Denominational Schools Board Letters Received 1848, MS. 1/310, NSWA; *Atlas*, 1 Jan. 1848; *SMH*, 23 Mar. 1848. For another view of this event see K. Grose, '1847: The Educational Compromise of the Lord Bishop of Australia', *Journal of Religious History*, vol. 1, no. 4, Dec. 1961, pp. 233–48.
⁶⁹ *SMH*, 27 Jan. 1848; *Atlas*, 19 Aug. 1848; WGB to Riddell, 30 May, 26 Sep., 21, 23 Dec. 1848, Denominational Schools Board Letters Received 1848, op. cit.
⁷⁰ Compare Broughton's speech in *SMH*, 27 July 1848 with Broughton, *Speech in Legislative Council 1839*, pp. 18–19.
⁷¹ *Syd. Chron.*, 13 May 1848; *SMH*, 12, 15 May, 6 June 1848; *Atlas*, 13 May 1848.
⁷² *Atlas*, 15 Jan. 1848; Minute, 3 Feb. 1846, *Proc. Ex. C.*, 4/1522, NSWA.
⁷³ *SMH*, 16 Feb. 1848. On Oath of Supremacy, WGB to EC, 3 Jan. 1844.

14 A Consultation

¹ *CCC*, vol. 3, pp. 346–53, vol. 4, pp. 477–8; Lord Lyttelton, *The Colonial Experience of Great Britain, Especially in Its Religious Aspect*, London, 1849; Lord John Manners, *The Church of England in the Colonies. A Lecture*, London, 1851.
² WGB to SPG, 14 Feb. 1849.
³ On diocesan finance, *SMH*, 23 Feb. 1849; *Sydney Guardian*, 2 Apr. 1849. On King and Naylor, WGB to SPG, 4 June, 9 July 1849. On immigration, *SMH*, 23 Feb. 1849; WGB to SPG, 4, 28 June 1849. On Cowper *SMH*, 2 May 1849.
⁴ Based on WGB to SPG, 14 Feb. 1849, and, Jones to Bishop of Sydney, 4 June 1849, C. MS., SPG; WGB to EC, 15 Jan. 1849; *SMH*, 22 Mar. 1849.
⁵ WGB to EC, 15 Jan. 1849; Perry to Archbishop of Canterbury, 20 July 1848 in *CCC*, vol. 2, pp. 336–53.
⁶ WGB to SPG, 27 Mar. 1849.
⁷ WGB to EC, 26 Mar., 2 Apr., 21 May 1849.
⁸ WGB to EC, 2 Apr., 1, 21 May 1849. On providing for his family, WGB to Joshua Watson, 9 Sep. 1839, MC.
⁹ WGB to EC, 1, 21 May 1849.
¹⁰ SPG to WGB, 1 Feb. 1847, F. MS., SPG; [W. G. Broughton], *Correspondence Between ... Bishop of Sydney and ... E. T. C. Russell and P. T. Beamish*, pp. 10–15, 28–36, (referred to hereafter as *Corresp. Bp. Sydney & Russell*).
¹¹ *Corresp. Bp. Sydney & Russell*, p. 14–15, 21.
¹² Ibid., pp. 43–7.
¹³ Ibid., pp. 15–16, 48–53.
¹⁴ Ibid., pp. 24–6.
¹⁵ W. G. Broughton, *Report of Proceedings in Case of F. T. C. Russell*, pp. 3–4, 20–1 (referred to hereafter as *Report. Case of Russell*); *Corresp. Bp. Sydney & Russell*, pp. 22–4.
¹⁶ F. T. C. Russell, *Statement of Rev. F. T. C. Russell to His Parishioners and Congregation*, pp. 44–5, 51 (referred to hereafter as *Statement. Russell to Parishioners*); *SMH*, 5 June 1849.
¹⁷ *Corresp. Bp. Sydney & Russell*, pp. 8–9, 22–4.
¹⁸ Ibid., pp. 19–21; *Report. Case of Russell*, p. 3.
¹⁹ *SMH*, 5 June 1849; *Corresp. Bp. Sydney & Russell*, p. 7.
²⁰ *Report. Case of Russell*, 27–9, 33–6; *Statement. Russell to Parishioners*, pp. 12–19, 25, 36, 46.
²¹ *Report. Case of Russell*, p. 14; *Corresp. Bp. Sydney & Russell*, pp. 9, 17. On party divisions, see Broughton, *Charge 1841*, p. 33; WGB to Joshua Watson, fragment dated Nov. 1848, MC.
²² *Report. Case of Russell*, pp. 1–19.
²³ *Statement. Russell to Parishioners*, pp. 3–7; R. Lowe, *Speech of Robert Lowe ... 7th*

of August 1849, Sydney [no date, but 1849], pp. 6, 9, 12–15, 19, 28–9. On Nicholson's role see *Report. Case of Russell,* pp. 21–3, 27–8.

24 *SMH,* 8 Aug. 1849; Lowe, op. cit., p. 12.

25 *SMH,* 8 Aug. 1849.

26 Based on *SMH,* 5 June, 26 July 1849; Lowe, op. cit., p. 3; *Report. Case of Russell,* pp. 33–5; WGB to EC, 21 May 1849.

27 Lowe, op. cit., p. 16; *Statement. Russell to Parishioners,* pp. 19–20; *A & P,* 25 July 1849.

28 *Statement. Russell to Parishioners,* pp. 6, 24, 50; *Report. Case of Russell,* pp. 11; *SMH,* 9 Aug. 1849.

29 WGB to EC, 21 May 1848; *A & P,* 14 May, 14, 17 Aug. 1849, 1 May 1850.

30 WGB to EC, 13 July 1850, and, WGB to Walsh, 30 Mar., 1 Apr. 1850, BP; WGB to Stiles, 26 Aug. 1846, 6 Oct. 1857, ML. A1323; *A & P,* 11 July 1850.

31 See 'Wreck of Governor Phillip', an open letter signed H. Elliott, 10 Aug. 1849, ML. A3071.

32 Based on WGB to EC, 21 May 1849: WGB to Tyrrell, 1 Oct. 1849, ML. 913; P. Hill to J. Hassall, 2 Oct. 1849, ML. A1677/1. For Broughton's recollection of his first meeting Sarah Francis, WGB to EC, 21 Jan. 1845.

33 WGB to EC, 2 Apr. 1850; *Sydney Guardian,* 1 Dec. 1849.

34 *Report of Diocesan Committee of the SPG and SPCK 1849,* pp. 10–11.

35 WGB to EC, 2 Apr., 8 May 1850; WGB to Tyrrell, 1 Oct. 1849, ML. 913.

36 WGB to Tyrrell, 1 Oct. 1849, ML. 913.

37 Perry to WGB, 3 June 1850, PLB. II; Perry to WGB, June 1850, PLB. I; Perry to Grey, 27 Nov. 1849, GP115/3; *Argus,* 3 Aug. 1850.

38 Perry to WGB, 3 June, 4 July 1850, PLB. II; *Argus,* 25 July 1850.

39 *SMH,* 18 July 1850; *Argus,* 6 to 12 Aug. 1850. Perry attacked Broughton's despotism in Perry to WGB, 4 July 1850, op. cit., and had to defend himself against a similar charge in Perry to Editor, 25 July 1850 in *Argus,* 27 July 1850. On Perry's withdrawal, *Melbourne Church of England Messenger,* vol. I, pp. 221–4.

40 Perry to Russell, 20 Dec. 1849, PLB. I; Perry to WGB, 29 Apr., 3 June 1850, and Perry to Russell, 4 June 1850, PLB. II; *A & P,* 2, 17 Apr., 16 May 1850.

41 WGB to EC, 2 Apr. 1850; Joshua Watson to SPG, 15 Aug. 1849; Deeds of Assignment, 7 Aug. 1850, in ML. A5328/9.

42 WGB to EC, 15 Aug. 1850, 10 Dec. 1852.

43 *SMH,* 24, 25 May 1850.

44 *Sydney Guardian,* 1 June 1849; WGB to Fitzroy, 19 May 1849, and, Clergy to Colonial Secretary, 30 June 1849, Box 4/2839.1, CSIL.

45 Minutes of Merivale and Grey on WGB to Fitzroy, 23 June 1848, encl. in Fitzroy to Grey, 15 July 1848, CO 201/398; Colonial Secretary to WGB, 29 June 1849, 49/118, Box 4/3622, CSOL.

46 WGB to Fitzroy, 22 May 1850, encl. in Fitzroy to Grey, 30 July 1850, CO 201/430; Perry to WGB, 3 June 1850, PLB. II; WGB to EC, 15 Jan. 1849. For Broughton's threats to cease administering the Act of Supremacy, WGB to Joshua Watson, 9 Sep. 1839, MC; Broughton, *Charge 1844,* p. 30; WGB to Archbishop of Canterbury, 17 Mar. 1851, Sydney Letters 1850–9, SPG.

47 Minutes by Grey, Merivale, Hawes on Fitzroy to Grey, 30 July 1850, CO 201/430. The matter was settled by Grey's successor Sir John Pakington following Merivale's advice, see draft despatch, Pakington to Fitzroy, [13] Nov. 1852, CO 201/430.

48 WGB to Emily and Phoebe, 19 Jan. 1850, ML. 913; Abrahams to Gladstone, 13 Mar. 1850, BM. Add. MS. 44369.

49 WGB to EC, 13 July, 15 Aug. 1850.

50 WGB to Gladstone, 13 July 1850, BM. Add. MS. 44369.

51 *Melbourne Church of England Messenger,* vol. I, pp. 225–31.

52 Emily [Crawley] to Phoebe [Boydell], 22 Sep. 1850, MS. TKS; R. Boodle, *Life and Labours of Rt. Rev. William Tyrrell,* London, no date, p. 7; J. E. Evans, *Churchman Militant,* London, 1964, p. 36; WGB to EC, 15 Aug. 1850.

53 C. Perry, *Diary Kept by Perry in Sydney at the Bishops' Meeting 1850,* p. 6, manuscript held in Melbourne Diocesan Registry (referred to hereafter as Perry,

Diary 1850); *A & P*, 1 Oct. 1850; T. Hassall to J. Hassall, 4 Oct. 1850, ML. A1677/1.

[54] WGB to Tyrrell, 1 Oct. 1849, 10 Sep. 1850, ML. 913; WGB to Gladstone, 13 July, 19 Nov. 1850, BM. Add. MS. 44369.

[55] Perry, *Diary 1850*, pp. 1–2; WGB to Tyrrell, 10 Sep. 1850, ML. 913.

[56] WGB to EC, 1 Feb. 1851; Perry, *Diary 1850*, pp. 2–4; C. Perry, *Report of Bishops' Conference*, p. 1, a manuscript in the Melbourne Diocesan Registry of an early draft of the resolutions and amendments agreed to at the Bishops' meeting (referred to hereafter as Perry, *Conference Report*).

[57] Perry, *Diary 1850*, pp. 3–4.

[58] Perry, *Diary 1850*, pp. 6–7; Perry to Grey, 27 Nov. 1849, GP115/3.

[59] Perry, *Diary 1850*, pp. 7–8.

[60] On the Huntingford affair, WGB to SPG, 15 July 1847. On Broughton's and Howley's view of Metropolitical jurisdiction, 'Points of importance to be determined in reference to the proposed division of the present Diocese of Australia', (no date but probably 1844), manuscript in Broughton's handwriting, MC; and, Howley to Gladstone, 16 Jan. 1846, BM. Add. MS. 44363. On Grey and Sumner's reaction, Grey to Sumner, 20 Dec. 1848, Sumner, to Grey, 28 Dec. 1848, GP80/7.

[61] Perry, *Diary 1850*, p. 8.

[62] Perry, *Diary 1850*, pp. 8–13,20; WGB to Tyrrell, 28 Jan. 1852, MC; *Minutes of Proceedings at a Meeting of the Metropolitan and Suffragan Bishops of the Province of Australasia ... 1850*, pp. 7–8.

[63] Perry, *Diary 1850*, pp. 16–21. On Broughton's earlier concession to the laity, *SMH*, 4 Mar. 1848. On subsequent lay agitation, *Atlas*, 6 May 1848; the pamphlet 'Australian Church Society', in *Church of England. Constitution Minutes and Correspondence 1852*, ML. A2110; Russell, *Statement. Russell to Parishioners*, pp. 1–2.

[64] *Minutes of Proc. Prov. of Aust. 1850*, pp. 7–8. Perry's *Diary 1850*, shows the matter as being discussed on 8 Oct. 1850, but Perry's *Conference Report* shows that no resolution on lay participation was adopted until 24 Oct. 1850 whilst most others were adopted by 16 Oct. 1850.

[65] Perry, *Diary 1850*, pp. 26–31. A copy of Broughton's translation of Cyprian's *Epistle to Rogatian* is in ML. 913.

[66] *Minutes of Proc. Prov. of Aust. 1850*, pp. 14–16.

[67] Perry, *Diary 1850*, pp. 21–6; *Minutes of Proc. Prov. of Aust. 1850*, pp. 15–16.

[68] *Minutes of Proc. Prov. of Aust. 1850*, pp. 17–21.

[69] WGB to Gladstone, 19 Nov. 1850, BM. Add. MS. 44369.

[70] Perry to Nixon, 7 July, 9 Aug. 1852, PLB. I.

[71] WGB to Tyrrell, 10 Sep. 1850, ML. 913; WGB to EC, 1 Feb. 1851.

[72] Emily [Crawley] to Phoebe [Boydell], 10 Oct. 1850, MS. TKS; M. Hassall to J. Hassall, 10 Oct. 1850, ML. A1677/1; *SMH*, 18 Oct. 1850.

[73] For the original agenda see WGB to Gladstone, 13 July 1850, BM. Add. MS. 44369.

[74] WGB to EC, 9 May 1851. On Tahiti and Hong Kong, WGB to Selwyn, 29 Aug. 1842, and, WGB to EC, 11 Dec. 1843, 4 May 1844, BP.

[75] Selwyn to Broughton, 22 Sep. 1849, ML. 913; *Minutes-Proc. Prov. of Aust. 1850*, p. 23; *SMH*, 18 Oct. 1850

[76] *SMH*, 2 Nov. 1850.

[77] M. Hassall to J. Hassall, 11 Nov. 1850, ML. A1677/1; *SMH*, 2 Nov. 1850.

[78] T. Hassall to J. Hassall, 30 Oct. 1850, ML. A1677/1; *A & P*, 1 Nov. 1850.

[79] Tyrrell to Joshua Watson, 26 May 1852, MS. 1562 Lambeth; *SMH*, 2 Nov. 1850.

[80] Tyrrell to Joshua Watson, 26 May 1852, op. cit.; *SMH*, 2 Nov. 1850; *A & P*, 2, 9 Nov. 1850.

[81] WGB to Gladstone, 19 Nov. 1850, BM. Add. MS. 44369. Broughton's intended procedure after the conference based on a reading of the above letter to Gladstone, and, WGB to EC, 1 Feb. 1851; also EC to Gladstone, 26 Mar. 1852, BM. Add. MS. 44137, and, Tyrrell to Joshua Watson, 26 May 1852, op. cit.

[82] Perry, *Diary 1850*, pp. 6–7.

[83] WGB to EC, Easter Tuesday, 1851.

[84] Perry to WGB, 26 June 1851, PLB. I.
[85] Grey to Sumner, 11 Feb 1850 (sic. 1851), 9 June 1851, GP80/7.
[86] Tyrrell to WGB, 28 Oct. 1851, MC; Tyrrell to Joshua Watson, op. cit.
[87] *A & P*, 11 July 1850, 25 Aug. 1851; *CCC*, vol. 5, p. 320. ·
[88] WGB to EC, 13 July 1850, 1 Feb., 9 May 1851; Broughton, *Baptismal Regeneration. Two Sermons*; WGB to Gladstone, 19 Nov. 1850, BM. Add. MS. 44369. For a taunting press, *Freeman's Journal*, 4 July, 1 Aug., 5, 12 Dec. 1850.

15 Uncompleted Mission

[1] WGB to EC, Easter Sunday and 9 May 1851; WGB to EC, 7 Aug. 1851, ML. 913.
[2] WGB to EC, 1 Feb. 1851.
[3] On funds, *Report of Diocesan Committee of the SPG and SPCK 1850*, p. 45. On Broughton's self-doubts, WGB to EC, 15 Feb. 1841, 14 Jan. 1843, 14 Jan., 18 Aug. 1846, 13 Nov. 1847, 1 Feb. 1851.
[4] *Freeman's Journal*, 5 Dec. 1850. For Broughton's pseudonym 'Churchman' see document ML. Ak43/8.
[5] WGB to EC, 4 May 1844; WGB to SPG, 15 July 1847; *Report of Diocesan Committee ... 1850*, p. 18. On Cowper, see Stiles to WGB, 31 July 1848, ML. A269; *A & P*, 24 Jan. 1848.
[6] WGB to EC, 1 Feb. 1851.
[7] *SMH*, 16 May, 8, 13 Aug., 16 Sep. 1851; *Freeman's Journal*, 5 June 1851; James Macarthur to Deas Thomson, 29 May 1851, and Thomson's reply, 30 May 1851, ML. A2920.
[8] WGB to SPG, 24 May 1851; WGB to EC, 8 May, 10 July 1850.
[9] *CCC*, vol. 5, pp. 432–4.
[10] WGB to William Boydell, 5 Feb. 1852, MS. TKS.
[11] *SMH*, 14 June 1851.
[12] Based on *SMH*, 31 Dec. 1850, 5, 8 Apr., 7 July 1851; WGB to SPG, 14 Mar. 1851 (encl. WGB's circular).
[13] *SMH*, 7, 21, 28 Sep., 5, 11, 12 Oct. 1849.
[14] Minute, 20 Aug. 1850, *V & P*; *SMH*, 12 Sep. 1850; *Freeman's Journal*, 14 Nov. 1850.
[15] WGB to EC, 1 Feb., 9 May 1851.
[16] *Sydney Guardian*, 1 Dec. 1849; WGB to SPG, 3 Mar. 1852; WGB to EC, 9 May 1851.
[17] WGB to EC, 9 May 1851.
[18] WGB to SPG, 14 Mar. 1851 and encl. WGB to Archbishop of Canterbury, 17 Mar. 1851; *Freeman's Journal*, 21, 28 Nov. 1850.
[19] W. G. Broughton, *Letter to Right Rev. Nicholas Wiseman D.D.*, pp. 18, 27–9; *Freeman's Journal*, 9 Jan. 1851.
[20] *SMH*, 13, 15 Mar. 1851; WGB to SPG, 14 Mar. 1851. For Broughton's warning of Rome's tactic, WGB to Joshua Watson, 14 Sep. 1839, MC.
[21] *Freeman's Journal*, 13 Mar. 1851 (supplement).
[22] WGB to Archbishop of Canterbury, 17 Mar. 1851, op. cit.; WGB to Tyrrell, 1 Feb. 1852, MC. On a global Protestantism, WGB to EC, 9 May 1851, 9 Mar. 1852.
[23] WGB to SPG, 16 Sep. 1851, 8 Mar. 1852; *Report of the SPG, 1852*, London, 1852, p. lxvi.
[24] *Freeman's Journal*, 13 Feb. 1851.
[25] Gregory to Colonial Secretary, 25 May 1850 and Fitzroy to Grey, 20 July 1850, CO 201/430; WGB to SPG, 14 Mar. 1851.
[26] *SMH*, 15, 16, 17 Sep. 1851.
[27] WGB to EC, 7 Aug. 1851, ML. 913.
[28] *PD*, 6 May 1850, cols. 1196–8, 1208–9, 1230.
[29] Gladstone to Venn, 20 May 1850, BM. Add. MS. 44369; *PD*, op. cit., col. 1197.
[30] WGB to Gladstone, 19 Nov. 1850, BM. Add. MS. 44369.
[31] *PD*, 10 June 1850, col. 974; Fitzgerald to Gladstone, 8 Jan. 1850, BM. Add. MS. 44369
[32] *PD*, 6 May 1850, cols. 1226–8, 1230, 10–11 June 1850, cols. 975, 1067.

[33] *CCC*, vol. 4, p. 2.

[34] *Freeman's Journal*, 2 June 1850.

[35] Tyrrell to Joshua Watson, 26 May 1852, MS. 1562, Lambeth.

[36] WGB to EC, 9 May 1851.

[37] *Melbourne Church of England Messenger*, vol. 2, pp. 218, 233, vol. 3, pp. 172–3.

[38] Perry to WGB, 26 June 1851, PLB. I, and, Perry to Conference, 24 June 1851, *Melbourne Church of England Messenger*, vol. 2, p. 220; Tyrrell's support for Perry's freedom to act as he did implied in Tyrrell to Joshua Watson, op. cit.

[39] Perry to Grey, 15 Aug. 1851, GP115/3.

[40] Broughton, *Letter to Wiseman*, pp. 7, 10, 15.

[41] WGB to Gladstone, 18 Aug. 1851, BM. Add. MS. 44370.

[42] Ibid.

[43] Sumner to WGB, 4 July 1851 in *Melbourne Church of England Messenger*, vol. 3, pp. 87–8. Tyrrell's reaction in Tyrrell to Joshua Watson, op. cit.

[44] WGB to Tyrrell, 24 Nov. 1851, 9 Feb. 1852, MC. On Hilderbrand, WGB to EC, 2 Apr. 1844.

[45] Based on Tyrrell to Joshua Watson, op. cit.; WGB to Tyrrell, 28 Jan., 9 Feb. 1852, MC.

[46] WGB to Tyrrell, 9 Feb. 1852, MC; *SMH*, 20 Mar., 17 Apr. *1852*,

[47] *Church of England. Constitution Minutes and Correspondence 1852*, p. 217, ML. A2110; *SMH*, 27, 31 Mar. 1852; *Empire*, 31 Mar. 1852.

[48] *SMH*, 8 Mar., 1 Apr. 1852.

[49] *SMH*, 6 Apr. 1852.

[50] *SMH*, 1, 3, 10, 12–15 Apr. 1852.

[51] WGB to Tyrrell, 13 May 1852, MC.

[52] *SMH*, 15 Apr. 1852. For the debate on temporal and spiritual authority see *Empire*, 2, 6 Apr. 1852; *SMH*, 5 Apr. 1852 (Blackett's letter).

[53] *SMH*, 1, 5 Apr. 1852.

[54] WGB to EC, 19 Apr. 1852, ML. 913.

[55] Ibid.; *SMH*, 15 Apr. 1852.

[56] *Empire*, 15 Apr. 1852. For the debate on biblical exegesis, *SMH*, 1, 15 Apr. 1852.

[57] Based on *SMH*, 16, 19 Apr. 1852; *Freeman's Journal*, 9 Jan., 1 May 1851, 11 Mar. 1852.

[58] WGB to EC, 19 Apr. 1852, ML. 913.

[59] Ibid.; *SMH*, 27 Mar. 1852.

[60] *SMH*, 16 Apr. 1852.

[61] *SMH*, 15 Apr. 1852; Broughton, *Sermons on Church of England*, pp. 351–2.

[62] *SMH*, 16 Apr. 1852; WGB to EC, 19 Apr. 1852, ML. 913.

[63] *SMH*, 6, 16, 17, 19 Apr., 12 May 1852; *Empire*, 19, 20, 22, 24 Apr., 20 May 1852; Tyrrell to Joshua Watson, op. cit.

[64] *SMH*, 6 May 1852; *Empire* 6 May 1852; Sadleir to King, 17 July 1852, ML. A2110.

[65] Based on [R. Sadleir] Autobiographical Fragment, p. 3, ML. A1631; Sadleir to Bishop of Melbourne, no date, ML. AsB4; *SMH*, 2 June 1862.

[66] *Empire*, 6 May 1852.

[67] Tyrrell to Joshua Watson, *op. cit.*

[68] *Empire*, 6, 28 Apr. 1852.

[69] See *Empire*, 18, 19 May 1852.

[70] *SMH*, 6 May 1852.

[71] *SMH*, 1 Apr. 1852; *Empire*, 6 May 1852; King to Lowe, 28 Aug. 1852, ML. A2110.

[72] Sadleir to King, 15, 31 May 1852, C. Campbell to King, 17 May 1852, J. Macarthur to Sadleir, 17 May 1852, Dumaresq to King, 14 May 1852, ML. A2110.

[73] Sadleir to King, 8 May 1852, ML. A2110; *Empire*, 20 May 1852.

[74] *SMH*, 19 May 1852; *Empire*, 20, 22 Apr., 6, 20 May 1852; King to Lowe, 31 Aug. 1852, ML. A2110.

[75] WGB to King, 12 May 1852, ML. A2110; *SMH*, 30 Mar., 6, 12, 19, 20, 21 May 1852.

[76] WGB to EC, 19 Apr 1852, ML. 913 (undecided), WGB to SPG, 23 Apr. 1852 (decided).

77 WGB to EC, 9 Mar. 1852.
78 Based on Colonial Secretary to WGB, 5 May 1852, 52/117, Box 4/3623, CSOL; WGB to Tyrrell, 15 Feb., 14 June 1852, MC; WGB to SPG, 10 Aug. 1852; Indenture of 7 Aug. 1850 assigning policies in ML. A5328/9.
79 Based on *Report ... SPG, 1852*, p. cxil; *Report of the SPG, 1853*, London, 1853, p. lxxii; Colonial Secretary to WGB, 13 Feb., 27 July 1852, 52/204, Box 4/3623, CSOL; WGB to EC, 7 Aug. 1851, ML. 913; *SMH*, 28 Feb. 1852; WGB to SPG, no date [but July 1852].
80 Tyrrell to WGB, 14 Jan. 1852, MC. On Cape, *SMH*, 11, 14 Jan. 1851, 28 Feb. 1852. On Unitarian chapel, WGB to Sharpe, 19 July 1852, ML. A1502; Circular, in Hassall Papers, vol. 2, pp. 1073–5, ML. A1677/2.
81 WGB to SPG, 3 Mar. 1852.
82 *Freeman's Journal*, 15, 18 July 1850, 1 Jan. 1852; also petitions of Roman Catholics against Sydney University, *V & P 1850*, vol. 2.
83 WGB to SPG, 28 Apr., [July 1852]; WGB to Tyrrell, 13, 20 May 1852, MC.
84 *A & P*, 11, 13 Aug. 1852; *Empire*, 14 Aug. 1852; *SMH*, 16 Aug. 1852; WGB to SPG, 23 Apr. 1852.
85 *SMH*, 15 Apr. 1852 (reprinted in *CCC*, vol. 6, p. 140).
86 WGB to EC, 9 Mar. 1852. For lay determination see, *SMH*, 13 Apr. 1852.
87 Fitzgerald to Gladstone, 22 Jan. 1852, BM. Add. MS. 44369.
88 WGB to Tyrrell 13 May 1852, MC; *CCC*, vol. 5, pp. 411, 416–17.
89 Sumner to Gladstone, 29 Mar. [1852] BM. Add. MS. 44371 (Archbishop's opinion); Perry to Archbishop of Canterbury, 15 Aug. 1851, GP115/3 (Perry's opinion); *PD*, 19 May 1852, cols. 737–91 (Inglis's opinion); *Empire*, 13 Apr., 18 Aug. 1852 (clergy opinion at Port Phillip, Adelaide, Tasmania).
90 WGB to SPG, 23 Apr. 1852; *SMH*, 15 Apr. 1852; WGB to Tyrrell, 13 May 1852, MC.
91 WGB to SPG, 10 Aug. 1852; WGB to Gladstone, 18 Aug. 1851, BM. Add. MS. 44370.
92 WGB to Archbishop of Canterbury, 22 Mar. 1852, MC; WGB to SPG, 10 Aug. 1852. For Gladstone on colonial self-management, *PD*, 28 Apr. 1852, col. 1265.
93 *PD*, 28 Apr. 1852 cols. 1263–78.
94 *Empire*, 27 Aug. 1852; Sadleir to King, 21 May, 17 July 1852, ML. A2110.
95 *PD*, 28 Apr. 1852, col. 1273–4, 19 Mar. 1852, col. 761, 790–1; EC to Gladstone, 26 Mar. 1852, BM. Add. MS. 44137.
96 Sumner to Gladstone, 21 May 1852, Gladstone to Pakington, 27, 28 May 1852, BM. Add. MS. 44372; WGB to Archbishop of Canterbury, 1 Dec. 1851 in 'Correspondence between Archbishop of Canterbury and Bishop of Sydney ... communicated to the Secretary of State for the Colonies', *PP*, 1852, vol. 37, pp. 3–6; WGB to Gladstone, 18 Aug. 1851, op. cit.
97 Perry to Archbishop of Canterbury, 15 Aug. 1851, GP115/3; Sumner to Gladstone, 29 Mar. [1852], BM. Add. MS. 44371; Grey to Sumner, 28 Jan. 1851, GP80/7.
98 Tyrrell to WGB, 28 Oct. 1851, MC; Gladstone to Venn, 20 May 1850, BM. Add. MS. 44369.
99 E. Carpenter, *Cantuar*, London, 1971, p. 308; O. Chadwick, *The Victorian Church, Part I*, London, 1966, p. 314. Tyrrell to WGB, 28 Oct. 1851, MC.
1 *PD*, 19 May 1851, col. 761. Reports from colonies, *CCC*, vol. 4, pp. 1, 445, vol. 5, pp. 161, 287, 342, 410, 416.
2 *CCC*, vol. 6, pp. 47–8.
3 WGB to EC, 19, 22 Nov. 1852; WGB to SPG, 19 Nov. 1852.
4 *Times* 16, 17, 18 Nov. 1852; WGB to EC, 4 Dec. 1852; *CCC*, vol. 6, pp. 312–3.
5 *Times* 17–22 Nov. 1852; WGB to EC, 19 Nov., 4 Dec. 1852; WGB to SPG, 19 Nov. 1852.
6 WGB to EC, 22 Nov., 4, 10 Dec. 1852.
7 WGB to EC, 4 Dec. 1852. On colonial bishop in Convocation, *Times* 18 Nov. 1852; WGB to EC, 27 Jan. 1853. Broughton's tactic outlined in WGB to Tyrrell, 13 May 1852, MC.
8 *Times* 17 Nov. 1852; *PD*, 28 Apr. 1852, col. 1266, 19 May 1852, cols. 769–71.

9 A. Mountain, *A Memoir of George Jehoshaphat Mountain*, Montreal, 1866, chapter 20; *CCC*, vol. 6, p. 283.
10 See Grey to Sumner, 28 Jan. 1851, GP80/7; *CCC*, vol. 4, p. 445; R. Border, *Church and State in Australia*, London, 1962, p. 184.
11 *SMH*, 7 Feb. 1853.
12 WGB to EC, 10, 12 Dec. 1852; Gladstone to Fitzroy, 21 Feb. 1853, BM. Add. MS. 44528; WGB to Gladstone, 20 Dec. 1852, BM. Add. MS. 44373.
13 WGB to EC, 4, 10, 22 Dec. 1852, 25 Jan. 1853; *Times* 21 Jan. 1853. On Judge Coleridge and Newman, WGB to EC, 2 Apr. 1850, 27 Jan. 1853.
14 *CCC*, vol. 6, pp. 309–15; *Guardian*, 26 Jan. 1853 reprinted in *Tasmanian Church Chronicle*, 2 May 1853.
15 Whitington, *Broughton*, p. 269; WGB to EC, 27 Jan. 1853; WGB to Archbishop of Canterbury, 22 Mar. 1852, MC.
16 *CCC*, vol. 6, p. 282.
17 *CCC*, vol. 6, pp. 281–3; *PD*, 6 May 1850, col. 1230.
18 Based on Broughton, *Sermons on Church of England*, pp. 346–60; WGB to EC, 27 Jan. 1853; *CCC*, vol. 6, p. 393; C. Dessain and V. Blehl, *Letters and Diaries of John Henry Newman*, London, 1964, vol. 15, pp. 89, 278–9.
19 Based on M. Lord to WGB, 27 Jan. 1853, ML. B1612; [Diocese of Sydney], *Farewell Address of William Grant Broughton*, p. 14; EC to Selwyn, no date, quoted in, Whitington, *Broughton*, pp. 270–1; *Guardian*, no date, newspaper cutting in ML. 913.
20 *Guardian*, no date, op. cit.; E. Churton to Hawkins (SPG), 14 Nov. 1859, ML. 913; *Report ... SPG, 1853*, p. xxvii.
21 Mrs Harrison to Mrs Howley, 8 Mar. 1853, MS. 2203, Lambeth.
22 [Diocese of Sydney], *Farewell Address*, pp. 13–16.
23 *CCC*, vol. 6, pp. 471–2; *Journal of SPG*, 17 Mar. 1853, m/f, SPG Papers, ANL; Mrs Harrison to Mrs Howley, op. cit.
24 *Freeman's Journal*, 7, 14, 21, 28 May 1853.
25 J. Norton, *Australian Essays on Subjects Political, Moral and Religious*, London, 1857, essay iv.
26 *Freeman's Journal*, 14, 28 May 1853; *SMH*, 26 May 1853.
27 W. Simpson, *A Sermon on the Death of the Lord Bishop of Sydney*, Sydney, 1853, passim; *CCC*, vol. 7, pp. 255–9; *SMH*, 31 May 1853.
28 [J. Norton], *The Late Bishop Broughton*, no date, pamphlet vol. 396, ANL.
29 *Report ... SPG, 1853*, p. lxxi.

Bibliography

of Principal Manuscript Holdings and Published Correspondence, and the Writings of William Grant Broughton

I AUSTRALIA MANUSCRIPT

(i) *Commonwealth of Australia*

Historical Records of Australia, series I reproduces much of Broughton's official correspondence. Many of the letters marked 'missing', and those set aside for publication in the disbanded series VIII, can be read on microfilm in the Colonial Office 201 series. See entry further on under Public Records Office.

(ii) *New South Wales*

Diocesan Registry (Church of England), Sydney, houses the Acts and Proceedings of Bishop of Australia (later Sydney) which records Broughton's official episcopal administration.

King's School, Parramatta, has a unique collection of personal family letters of the 1840s.

Mitchell Library, Sydney, holds five major collections of Broughton manuscripts.

1 Two reels of microfilm containing Broughton's correspondence with the Reverend Edward Coleridge, Eton College; the diary kept on the ship *John*, 1829; miscellaneous correspondence with mother, Reverend George Gilbert, Bishop of Melbourne, and correspondence of Gilbert with James Broughton (brother) and Mrs Crawley (daughter).

2 MS. 913 being papers deposited by F. T. Whitington after completing his study *William Grant Broughton*, published Sydney, 1936.

3 MS. Ab29/1–9 miscellaneous letters including twenty-two with Bourke, 1836–7.

4 MS. B1612 correspondence with wife and Bishop Short.

5 Letters of W. G. Broughton 1826–9, Duke of Wellington Collection, microfilm, mainly correspondence with Duchess of Wellington.

Other important manuscript sources.

Arthur, G. Papers.

Bonwick Transcripts (Missionary).

Bourke, R. Papers.

Broughton, Phoebe. Diary, MS. 756.

Church of England. Constitution Minutes and Correspondence 1852, MS. A2110.

Clarke, W. B. Papers.
Eyre, E. J. Papers.
Hassall, T. Papers.
Kemp, C. Diary, MS. A2063.
Lang, J. D. Papers.
Macarthur Family, Papers.
Marsden, S. Papers.
Norton Smith and Co. Clients' Papers, MS. A5412/1.
Parry, W. Papers, MS. B337.
Riley, A. Papers.
Sadleir, R. Papers.
Scott, T. H. Letter-books.
Sharpe, T. Papers.
Sparke, A. B. Diary, MS. A4869.
Stiles, H. Papers.
Taylor, R. Diary, MS. A3816.
Therry, J. J. Papers.
Threlkeld, L. Papers.
Public Library of New South Wales Dixson Collection has an uncollated assortment of official and personal letters.
State Archives, Sydney, houses the correspondence generated by Broughton's office on the colony's councils as well as his official ecclesiastical appointment. They are located in four main areas.
1 Colonial Secretary's Office, Inward Correspondence (CSIL) 1829–52, location 4/2012–3179. The letters are widely scattered and best located by referring first to *Guide to State Archives. Colonial Secretary. Part II*, Sydney, 1972, then by tracing entries through *Index to Letters Received*, location 2344–2451. The index often indicates briefly the substance of the letter.
2 Correspondence between governors and officials, 4/1639.
3 Colonial Secretary's Office, Outward Correspondence (CSIL) Letters to Clergy, 4/3615–24.
4 Executive Council Minute Books 1829–47, location 4/1516–22, and Appendices to Minutes 1829–47, location 4/1440–51, contain letters and opinions Broughton submitted to the council.

Special bundles of interest.
Clergy and School Lands Corporation Records, 4/291–2, 7/2704.
Denominational Schools Board Records, 1/305, 310–13.
Immigration, 4/1160.1.
King's School, 4/7169.
Letters from Bishop of Australia re Churches and Education, 2/1717.
(iii) *A. C. T. Canberra*
National Library of Australia holds the two reels of Broughton correspondence on microfilm listed as item 1 under Mitchell Library.

Other important sources.
Broughton, Sarah. Diary, microfilm.
Franklin Papers, especially Lady Franklin's Journal and her correspondence with John Griffin and Mary Simpkinson, microfilm.
Parry, (Sir) Edward. Journal, microfilm.
MS. 1731, Correspondence with Dr Keate and E. Coleridge.

Australian National University, Research School of Pacific Studies. In possession of Dr N. Gunson a typescript of the Reminiscences and Australian Papers of the Rev. Lancelot Threlkeld.

(iv) *Victoria*

Diocesan Registry (Church of England), Melbourne, holds Bishop Perry's Letter-books and the diary he kept at the Bishops' Conference, 1850. There is also Perry's manuscript of the draft resolutions of the conference which differs slightly from those published as *Minutes of Proceedings at the Meeting of the Metropolitan and Suffragan Bishops of the Province of Australasia 1850*, Sydney, 1850.

(v) *Tasmania*

University of Tasmania has microfilmed the collection of Mr G Moase which includes Broughton's correspondence with Archbishop of Canterbury, Bishops Selwyn, Nixon, Tyrrell, Short, and R. Alwood, Joshua Watson, E. Coleridge.

II ENGLAND MANUSCRIPT

(i) *London*

British Museum
  Gladstone Papers contain letters from Broughton or about Broughton's affairs, especially vols. 128, 252, 278, 283–7, 292, 443, 502, 533.
  Peel Papers, vols. 209, 343, 367, 398, 428.
Church Missionary Society series CN/01, 02, 03, 05a, 012, 013, 051, 093, CH/050–9, L1–3, and MC Committee Minutes vols. 10–13. These series are held on microfilm at the National Library of Australia.
Lambeth Palace Library
  Burdett Coutts Papers, MS. 1384.
  Fulham Papers, MS. 334–86.
  Howley Papers, MS. 2203.
  Joshua Watson Papers, MS. 1562.
Overseas Bishopric Fund, Dean's Yard, Westminster, houses four collections containing correspondence between Broughton and Mr Justice Coleridge, Archbishop of Canterbury, Rev. E. Hawkins, Gladstone and E. Coleridge.
  1 Australia. Letters re division of diocese.
  2 Additional Colonial Bishoprics Journal.
  3 Letter-book, vol. I.
  4 Colonial Bishoprics. Melbourne. Letters re foundation and boundaries of see, 1845–6.
Public Records Office. Since the status of the colonial Church of England was in a state of flux for most of Broughton's administration much of his official correspondence was forwarded to England for comment. These letters are found in four major series.
  1 CO 201, Despatches from governors. Most of Broughton's letters cited in *Historical Records of Australia*, series I as missing or deferred for publication in series VIII, are to be found attached to their original despatch. Some detached for forwarding outside the Colonial Office were often filed, on return, in the Miscellaneous bundles alphabetically under C (Archbishop of Canterbury), L (Bishop of London), S (SPG).
  2 CO 202, correspondence from the Colonial Office to Broughton.

3 CO 323, correspondence from Broughton to permanent under-secretary at Colonial Office.

4 CO 324, correspondence from permanent under-secretary to Broughton.

Of particular interest is Broughton's correspondence with the Colonial Office while in England 1834–6. This is in CO 201/224, 249–51, 257–8, 265; CO 202/31–3, 38; CO 325/28. There are also important reports on ecclesiastical and Aboriginal matters in CO 280/24, CO 282/2, 5, 10, CO 325/28.

Society for the Propagation of the Gospel.

1 C. MSS. Australian Papers, Box 12, Bishop Broughton's Letters, 1834–49.

2 C. MSS. Australian Papers, Box 14, enclosures extracted from Broughton's letters.

3 Letters rec'd Original Sydney, Melbourne, Adelaide, Newcastle, Tasmania 1850–9.

4 F. MSS. Copies of Letters sent Australia, 2 vols.

5 Minute Books, Journals, and Annual Reports (printed). Copies of these papers are held on microfilm at the National Library of Australia.

(ii) *Durham*

University of Durham, Department of Palaeography and Diplomatic. The Earl Grey (3rd. Earl) Papers contain information on Broughton or his ecclesiastical administration 1846–52. These are provisionally catalogued as Box 77/10 (Grey to Bishop of Bath and Wells), Box 80/5 (Grey to Archbishop Howley), Box 80/7 (Grey to Archbishop Sumner), Box 82/12 (Grey to Earl Stanley), Box 115/2 (Grey to Bishop Perry), Box 127/10 (Grey to Bishop Nixon).

There are also comments on Broughton's administration by James Stephen in the special collection cited as Correspondence with James Stephen.

(iii) *Oxford*

Pusey House. The Pusey Papers include letters passing between E. Coleridge and Pusey on Broughton's needs, on the founding of St Augustine's College, and on the procedures involved in subdividing the diocese of Australia. Pusey also corresponded with the Bishop of London on the same topics.

III   COLLECTIONS OF PRINTED LETTERS

Broughton, W. G. *Correspondence Between . . . Bishop of Sydney and . . . F. T. C. Russell and P. T. Beamish.* Sydney, 1849.

Report of Proceedings in Case of F. T. C. Russell. Sydney, 1849.

Edmondston, J. *Proceedings in London in Connection with An Appeal to His Grace The Lord Archbishop of Canterbury, against the Conduct of the Lord Bishop of Australia.* London, 1848.

Russell, F. T. C. *Statement by the Rev. F. T. C. Russell . . . with the Documents in Confirmation, furnished to his Parishioners and Congregation, as requested by them in an address to that gentleman presented 2nd August.* Sydney, 1849.

IV BROUGHTON'S PUBLICATIONS

Sermon Preached at Monthly Clerical Lecture . . . Reading. London, 1822.
An Examination of the Hypothesis, Advanced in a Recent Publication, Entitled 'Palaeoromaica'. London, 1823.
A Reply to the Second Postscript in the Supplement to Palaeoromaica. London, 1825.
Letter to a Friend Touching the Question, Who was the Author of EIKON BASILIKA? London, 1826.
Additional Reasons in Confirmation of the Opinion that Dr Gauden and NOT King Charles the First was the Author of EIKON BASILIKA. London, 1829.
The Resurrection of the Dead and Life Everlasting. Farnham, 1828.
The Counsel and Pleasure of God in the Vicissitudes of States and Communities. Sydney, 1829.
Charge to the Clergy of the Archdeaconry of New South Wales, at the Primary Visitation. Sydney, 1830.
Charge Delivered to the Clergy of Van Diemen's Land at the Primary Visitation. Hobart, 1830.
A Letter in Vindication of the Principles of the Reformation. Sydney, 1832.
A Sermon Preached on Whit Sunday, 1833 . . . for the Relief of the Surviving Passengers and Crew of the Ship 'Hibernia'. Hobart, 1833.
On the True Nature of the Holy Catholic Church. Sydney, 1833.
Religion Essential to the Security and Happiness of Nations. Sydney, 1834.
Charge Delivered to the Clergy of New South Wales, at the Visitation . . . 1834. Sydney, 1834.
The Present Position and Duties of the Church of England. London, 1835.
The Righteousness of Faith. A Sermon. Sydney, 1836.
Speech Delivered to Committee of Protestants on Wednesday August 3, 1836. Sydney, 1836.
Two Sermons Preached in the Church of St James, at Sydney. Sydney, 1837.
Speech of the Lord Bishop of Australia in the Legislative Council upon the Resolution for Establishing a System of General Education. Sydney, 1839.
The Knowledge of the Glory of God in the Face of Jesus Christ. A Sermon. Sydney, 1839.
The Nature and Intention of Holy Communion Explained. A Sermon. Sydney, 1841.
Speech of the Bishop of Australia to Mr Justice Burton. Sydney, 1841.
Charge to the Clergy of New South Wales . . . 1841. Sydney, 1841.
The Perpetuity of the Church. A Sermon. Sydney, 1842.
A True Account of the Anglican Ordinations in the Reign of Queen Elizabeth. Part I. Sydney, 1843.
'Take Heed'. A Sermon, preached in the Female Factory at Parramatta. Sydney, 1844.
Charge to the Clergy of the Diocese of Australia . . . 1844. Sydney, 1844.
Address Delivered on the Occasion of Laying the Foundation Stone of a Church. Sydney, 1845.
Church in Australia. Two journals of Visitation to the northern and southern portions of his diocese by the Lord Bishop of Australia. London, 1846.
Church in Australia Part III. A Journal of Visitation by the the Lord Bishop of Australia in 1845. London, 1846.
The Lord's Message Unto the People. A Sermon. Sydney, 1847.

Letter to Henry Osborne ... on the Propriety and Necessity of Collections at the Offertory. Sydney, 1848.
The Value and Authority of Holy Scripture. A Sermon. Sydney, 1848.
Two Sermons Preached in the Church of St Andrew, Sydney, at the Ordination of Priests and Deacons ... 1847. Sydney, 1849.
Letter to Right Rev. Nicholas Wiseman D.D. Sydney, 1850.
Baptismal Regeneration. Two Sermons. Sydney, 1851.
Farewell Address of William Grant Broughton. Sydney, 1853.
Sermons on the Church of England. Its Constitution, Mission, and Trials (edited with memoir by Benjamin Harrison). London, 1857.

V MISCELLANEOUS SOURCES OF BROUGHTON'S LETTERS, SERMONS AND STATEMENTS

Arthur, G, *Observations Upon Secondary Punishment, to which is added a Letter upon the same Subject by the Archdeacon of New South Wales.* Hobart, 1833.
Broughton, (Mrs) W. G., *Selections from the Prayers and Private Devotions of the late Mrs Broughton; for circulation among her surviving relatives and friends.* Sydney, 1849.
[Church Missionary Society], New Zealand Mission. *Visit of Bishop of Australia to the Church Missionary Society Mission in New Zealand.* London, 1840.
Documents Relative to the Erection and Endowment of Additional Bishoprics. Second edition. London, 1846.
Elkins, A. P., *Diocese of Newcastle.* Newcastle, 1955.
First Annual Report of the Church of England Book Society. Sydney, 1842.
Gunson, N. (ed.), Reminiscences and Australian Papers of the Rev. Lancelot Threlkeld, Missionary to the Aborigines of New South Wales. (Typescript copy in possession of N. Gunson, ANU). Much of this material is now available in N. Gunson (ed.), *Australian Reminiscences and Papers of L. E. Threlkeld, Missionary to the Aborigines 1824–1859.* 2 vols. Australian Aboriginal Studies no. 40. Canberra, 1974.
Memorial of Bishop and Clergy Concerning Transportation. [Sydney, 1849].
Minutes of Proceedings at a Meeting of the Metropolitan and Suffragan Bishops of the Province of Australasia, held at Sydney from October 1st. to November 1st, A. D. 1850. Sydney, 1850.
Mackaness, G. (ed.), *Some Private Correspondence of Sir John and Lady Jane Franklin. Part I.* Sydney, 1947.

Parliamentary Papers, British
   Report from Select Committee on Aborigines (British Settlements) with Minutes of Evidence. 1836, vol. 7.
   Correspondence Relative to Religious Instruction in New South Wales. 1837, vol. 19.
   Correspondence between Bishop of Sydney and the Governor of New South Wales, and between the Governor and the Colonial Office, relative to the Titles and Rank of Roman Catholic Prelates in the Colonies. 1849, vol. 34.
   Copies or Extracts of Despatches Relative to the Establishment of Episcopal Sees in Australia. 1850, vol. 37.
   Papers relating to Cases in which the Bishop of any Diocese in the Aus-

tralian Colonies has attempted to exercise Ecclesiastical Jurisdiction over any of his Clergy. 1850, vol. 37.

Letters Patent constituting Episcopal Sees in Australia, and appointing the Right Rev. William G. Broughton Bishop of Sydney; Despatch as to his place and precedency in the Executive Council. 1850, vol. 37.

Letter from the Bishop of Sydney to Sir Charles Fitzroy, Governor-General of the Australian Colonies, in relation to the Rank and Precedence of Bishops appointed by the Pope within Her Majesty's Dominions. 1851, vol. 35.

Correspondence between the Archbishop of Canterbury and Bishop of Sydney . . . communicated to the Secretary of State for the Colonies. 1852, vol. 32.

Correspondence respecting the Division of the Diocese of Australia into Three Sees, and on various matters relating to the Affairs of the Church in the Colony of New South Wales. 1852, vol. 32.

Copies of any Petitions to the Queen, of any Representation to Her Majesty's Principal Secretary of State in the Colonial Department, on Colonial Church Legislation, or on any Points affecting the Management of the Affairs of the Church of England in the Colonies since 1845. 1852, vol. 32.

Pastoral Letter (with declaratory protest in resistance to certain acts of the See of Rome). Sydney [1843]

Pastoral Letter (requesting a special collection on Whit Sunday 1849 for Colonial Bishoprics' Fund). Sydney [1849]

Pastoral Letter, Ascension Day, 1851 (on dangers likely to follow the establishment of a Unitarian Association). Sydney, [1851].

Report of Church of England Book Society 1841. Sydney, 1841.

Report of Church of England Lay Association for the Year 1844–5. Sydney, 1846.

Rules for the Church of England Schools of the Middle District. Sydney, 1850.

Society for the Propagation of the Gospel.

Church in Australia. Two journals of Visitation to the northern and southern portions of his diocese by the Lord Bishop of Australia. London, 1846.

Church in Australia, Part II. Two Jorunals of Missionary Tours in the Districts of Manero and Moreton Bay. London, 1846.

Church in Australia, Part III. A Journal of Visitation by the Lord Bishop of Australia in 1845. London, 1846.

The Church in the Colonies. Dioceses of Australia and New Zealand, 1843, 1844. London, 1846.

Report of the Diocesan Committee of the Societies for the Propagation of the Gospel in Foreign Parts and for Promoting Christian Knowledge. Sydney, 1837, 1838, 1839, 1840, 1842, 1845–6, 1847, 1849, 1850, 1851.

Proceedings of the Parramatta District Committee of Society for Promoting Christian Knowledge. Sydney, 1839, 1840.

Statement of the Objects of the Committee of the Society for the Propagation of the Gospel in Foreign Parts . . . Established in Australia, June 20, 1836. Sydney, 1836.

Sydney. *Festival of the Annunciation.* Sydney, 1843. (Circular concerning popery).

To the Reverend the Clergy of the United Church of England and Ireland within the Diocese of Australia. Sydney, 1847. (Circular concerning popery).

To the Queen's Most Excellent Majesty. The Memorial of the Bishop of Australia. Sydney, 1847 (Circular concerning transportation).

The Late Bishop Broughton. Sydney, 1853 (Circular announcing Broughton's death).

Votes and Proceedings of Legislative Council of New South Wales.
    Report from Committee on Aboriginal Question with Minutes of Evidence. 1838.
    Report from Committee on Immigration. 1838, 1839, 1840, 1841, 1842.
    Minutes of Evidence . . . Select Committee on Education, vol. 2. 1844.

Whitington, F. T., *William Grant Broughton, Bishop of Australia.* Sydney, 1936.

Index

Aberdeen, Lord, 88, 146

Aboriginals: Broughton's attitude to in NSW, 23, 33, 41-2, 93, 167, 229; in Van Diemen's Land, 32-3, 71; in L.C., 123-4; in House of Commons, 93; at Parramatta, 41; and Colonial Office, 43; mission to, 41, 43, 44-5, 56, 66-7, 69-70, 72, 133-4, 167, 239-40; and Threlkeld, 41-2; at Myall Creek, 123-4; and Docker, 167; and Polding, 167; and Perry, 219; *see also* Church Missionary Society; Wellington Valley

Abrahams, Rev. C. J., 233

Achilli, Dr, 270

Adelaide, *see* South Australia

Albury, 230, 231

Alderson, Baron, 270

Allan, Rev. J., 168, 181

Allwood, Rev. R., 165, 210, 214, 226, 229, 264, 270; Broughton's opinion of, 199, 204; and St James Theological College, 141, 188-9, 204; bishopric for, 189, 204; health, 188, 241, 244; clergy conference, 256-9, 260, 262

Ambrose, St, 211; *see also* Fathers of the Church

American Church, *see* Protestant Episcopal Church of America

American Institutions, 145; *see also* Republicanism

Andrewes, Bishop, 5, 163, 188

Anglican Communion, 247, 262, 265, 271; *see also* constitution of colonial churches

Anglo-Catholic Library, 163

Antigua, 267

antinomianism, 38, 55, 75, 157; *see also* perjury

anti-transportation, 147-8, 151-2, 199–200, 217, 245, 271, 274; *see also* transportation; convicts

apostolic authority: Broughton's view of, 44, 125-7, 149, 163-4, 180, 184, 189, 198, 202, 257; attacks on, 58, 104, 164, 178, 180, 194-5, 262; and citadel, 99; and Oxford principles, 115-16, 180-1; and letters patent, 125; and unity of church, 149-50, 177, 202; and converts, 168; and clergy, 177; and synods, 234-5, 241; *see also* Hadfield, O.; episcopal authority

appellate courts, 195, 202, 226, 231, 241, 249, 261, 265

Appin, 179

Archdeaconry of NSW: Broughton's appointment to, 10, 11, 18; powers of, 22, 78; and Darling, 35, 51; and Broughton's status, 56, 59, 72, 84; Bourke weakens, 66-7, 78, 221; attack on, 70, 71; and visit to England, 90-2; Broughton threatens resignation, 94; *see also* Walker versus Scott

aristocracy, 146

Armytage, G., 205, 206

Arnold, Thomas, 97, 122

Arthur, Col. George, 32-3, 55-6, 88, 91, 121; relationship with Broughton, 33-4, 92, 98, 108, 118, 119; as liberal churchman, 71, 108, 118; on trial by jury, 75; interference in clergy discipline, 90-2, 119; *see also* Bedford, W.; Drought, Rev. Dr

Ashfield, 196

Atlas: attack on Broughton, 176-9, 193, 194-6, 199-200, 204, 207-8, 211; political policies of, 176-7, 199, 200; interference with Church of England, 177, 178-9, 194, 207-8, 211; and Puseyism, 178, 199, 211; and Church Acts, 178, 186; assessment of, 199-200, 218, 260

Australasian Chronicle: attacks Broughton, 134, 135, 148, 164; and poll (1843), 159, 161, 162; and working class, 144-5, 152; and *Tracts*, 181

Australia, Diocese of: named, 97-8; objections to, 103-4; endowed by Moore, 116; and letters patent, 126,

93-4, 95, 98, 103-4, 126, 149
Marsh, Bishop, 6, 9
Martyns, Conrad, 191, 192
Maryland, Bishop of, 267
masonic lodge, 208; *see also* Odd Fellows; Woodward, C.
materialism, 52, 79, 81, 133, 146, 147, 219
Maynooth, 136, 145, 162, 186
Melbourne, Bishopric of, 168, 201-4, 230-1, 262; *see also* Perry, Bishop
Mereweather, Mr, 154
Merivale, H., 232
Metropolitan of Australaisa: creation of, 199, 203, 205, 208; Broughton's reaction to, 205; and Perry, 231; status of rival Roman Catholic, 232; and church government, 235-6, 249; and Broughton's burial, 273
Michie, Archibald, 220-1
middle classes: and church support, 191, 208
Minutes of Bishops' Conference of 1850, *see* Bishops' Conference of 1850
missionary college, *see* St Augustines College
mission to Aboriginals, 41, 43-5, 69-70, 93, 239-40; *see also* Aboriginals
Mitchell, Dr, 229
mobs, 4, 22, 36-8, 49, 54-6, 58, 75, 172, 192, 216; *see also* French Revolution
Moberly, Rev. G., 202
Molesworth, W., 249
monarchy: relation with colonial church, 31, 77, 78, 117, 205, 208, 234-5, 236, 241; and episcopal authority, 126; and Act of Supremacy, 134; ideal role in church, 135, 146; and colonial loyalty, 144-5, 217; and Wiseman, 247; and synods, 234-5, 259; *see also* Privy Council; royal supremacy; Supremacy, Act of
Monitor, 19, 54, 74-5; and Broughton, 18-9, 63, 80, 106, 113, 118; and voluntaryism, 74
Monk, Bishop, 99
Montagu, J, 119
Moor (Registrar, Diocese of Melbourne), 230-1
Moore, Thomas, 116, 188, 220-1
morality: Broughton's ideas on, 9, 14, 27, 79-80, 91, 195; standards of in NSW, 20-1, 24, 29, 52, 102, 158, 238, 245; endangered by Church and Schools Corporation, 49; and sexual imbalance, 52, 123; and orphanage, 69; and trial by jury, 38-9, 75; case of John Stephen, 80; and sabbath, 81, 139; British government ignores, 85;

and clergy, 90-1, 120, 141, 156-7, 168, 187, 194-5, 205-6, 208, 228, 237; case of J. Ready and J. J. Therry, 95; Broughton defends colony against House of Commons, 123; and anti-transportation, 147-8, 151; *see also* antinomianism; perjury
Moreton Bay, 52, 167-8, 179, 245, 248
Morpeth, 184, 185, 201-4; *see also* Allwood, R.; Newcastle, Bishopric of; Tyrrell, Bishop
Mort, T. S., 223, 260
Mountain, Bishop, 99, 271, 273
Mozart, Wolfgang, 248
Mozley, Rev. T., 233
Mulgoa, 229
Murphy, Rev. Dr, 136, 183-4
Murray, Sir George, 40-1, 43, 45, 79
Muswell Brook, 167
Myall Creek, 123-4

national destiny: Broughton's theory of, 21, 31, 79-80
national schools: idea approved, 95-6, 110; for poor, 98; attempts at setting up, 108-12, 128-31, 171-3, 177, 215-6, 263; at Parramatta, 171; and university, 246; and deism, 263; *see also* education; Irish Schools System
National Schools Board, 215-16
native born, *see* colonial born
Naylor, Rev. C. (King's School, Canterbury), 1
Naylor, Rev. T. B., 196, 218-19, 223-4
New England, 182
Newcastle, Bishopric of, 201-4, 208-9, 213, 221, 237, 250, 253; *see also* Tyrrell, Bishop
Newfoundland, Bishop of, 270
Newman, Rev. J. H., 107, 115, 180-1, 190, 194, 210-11, 270, 272
Newspaper Restriction Bill, 36
newspapers: welcome to Broughton, 18-9; and crime reports, 39; attacks on Broughton, 69, 81, 103-4, 113, 120-1, 218, 259; Broughton uses against Gipps, 133; and Roman Catholics, 134, 218; and Irish immigration, 154-5; on Broughton's retirement, 157; elections 1843, 159, 161-2; on *Tracts*, 181; and *Atlas*, 200; Broughton ignores, 209; and Sconce, 211-3; used by Russell against Broughton, 223, 224, 227; and Gorham Judgment, 241; and democracy, 248
Newtown, 210
New Zealand, Bishop of, *see* Selwyn, Bishop